The Montagnard People in the Indochina Wars, 1945-1991

Michael A. Eggleston

Cover shows 1ˢᵗ Air Cavalry Division Long Range Reconnaissance Patrol Montagnard scanning for enemy troops, March 1968
Courtesy of Creative Commons

Other Books

by

Michael A. Eggleston

10th Minnesota Volunteers, McFarland & Company Publishers, 2012.

The White Man's Fight, Author House, 2012.

President Lincoln's Recruiter, General Lorenzo Thomas and the United States Colored Troops in the Civil War, McFarland & Company Publishers, 2013.

Exiting Vietnam, The Era of Vietnamization and American Withdrawal Revealed in First-Person Accounts, McFarland & Company Publishers, 2014.

The 5th Marine Devil Dogs in World War I McFarland & Company Publishers 2016.

Dak To and the Border Battles of Vietnam, McFarland & Company Publishers 2017.

One Man's Traitor is Another's Patriot, George Washington and Robert Rogers, CreateSpace, 2017.

Operation Hannibal, The World War II Evacuation of East Prussia and the Disaster at Sea, CreateSpace, 2018.

Table of Contents

Acknowledgments

I would like to express my gratitude to my wife Margaret, for her endless patience and efforts to comment on and edit this book. I would also like to thank Dennis Kaltreider, Michael D. Benge and Frances O. Rogers for their assistance. I would also like to recognize Steve Sherman for his help in providing reference material and comments. This book is far from perfect but it is much better than when I started this effort thanks to Steve Sherman.

Preface

This history tells the story of the Montagnards, the mountain people of Indochina from the end of World War II into the 21st Century. They are ethnic minorities that live in the Central Highlands of Vietnam. The Montagnards remain a oppressed and exploited minority. Today, the conflict between the Montagnards and the government of Vietnam continues.

This book covers the military history of the Indochina Wars from 1945 to 1991 and the Montagnard participation in these wars. The details of what was occurring in Hanoi, Saigon[1], and the United States are included in order to provide a complete picture of events to the reader. Also, some events that had a major impact on the war are described even though no Montagnards were involved in them. While this history does not focus on the ethnicity of the Montagnard people, a summary of the Montagnard tribes involved in the conflict is included as an appendix. More important, the works of Gerald C. Hickey, the famous anthropologist, are quoted throughout this history. Dr. Hickey spent 18 years in Indochina working with the Montagnards and supporting their cause.

The Montagnards were loyal fighters alongside U.S. forces and fought against the North Vietnamese, the Viet Cong, and sometimes against the Saigon government because it exploited them. The history of the Montagnards and the U. S. Army Special Forces is closely linked since they fought together during U. S. involvement in the war. For this reason attention is also focused on the Special Forces in this history. The Highlanders (another name for the Montagnards) sought autonomy for the Montagnard tribes through their FULRO (Front Unifie de Lutte des Races Opprimees, or United Struggle Front for the Oppressed Races), movement. FULRO started on 1 August 1964 continued long after the fall of South Vietnam and Cambodia in 1975.

Many of the Montagnards fled Vietnam when they were

abandoned by the U. S. in 1975. Thanks to U. S. Army Special Forces veterans and many others, hundreds of Montagnards were evacuated to the United States following the war where they live and thrive today. In order to place their history into perspective, the entire conflict is summarized including key battles that involved Montagnard troops including their uprisings against the South Vietnamese government. This book compiles the histories of many Vietnam historians and the recollections of others who interacted with the Montagnard people during the war in Vietnam. This author's participation in the second 1965 FULRO uprising in 1965 is included. This book is in chronological order providing an overall summary of the war followed by the Montagnard and Special Forces involvement in it, year by year until the fall of the Saigon government to the North Vietnamese Army in 1975. From then forward it describes the continuing conflict between the mountain people and the Communist government of Vietnam.

Over the last forty years the U. S. government has occasionally addressed the plight of the Montagnard people in Vietnam including Congressional hearings which produced very little effect.

Michael A. Eggleston
Nokesville, Virginia, 2019

Dramatis Personae

Listing of key people identified in this history is provided, below. Information about their lives after their involvement in the war in Vietnam is found in Biographical Sketches.

Creighton Williams Abrams Jr., was born in Springfield, Massachusetts, on 15 September 1914. Abrams graduated from the U.S. Military Academy with the class of 1936. He was commissioned in the armor branch and served during World War II. He was an aggressive and successful armored commander, receiving two Distinguished Service Crosses for bravery. He served in the Korean War and was promoted to general in 1964. He was assigned as General Westmoreland's deputy in Vietnam and succeeded him on 10 June 1968.

Bao Dai was the last emperor of Vietnam. He was born in Hue, Vietnam, on 22 October 1913. His reign as emperor was from 8 January 1926 to 25 August 1945. He collaborated with the Japanese during World War II, but was retained by Ho Chi Minh as his "supreme advisor" to add legitimacy to Ho's regime. From 13 June 1949 to 25 August 1955, he was chief of state.

Charles Alvin Beckwith was born in Atlanta, Georgia on 22 January 1929. He joined the Special Forces in 1958. Beckwith commanded the Special Forces Camp at Plei Me during the NVA attack in 1965.

William Laws Calley dropped out of college due to failing grades and then held jobs such as bellhop and dishwasher before entering the army, where he graduated from OCS and was commissioned a second lieutenant in the infantry in 1967. He was deployed to South Vietnam as a platoon leader.

Christian de Castries was the French commander at the Battle of Dien Bien Phu in 1954. De Castries was born in Paris on 11 August 1902. He served in World War II and was assigned as the French commander at Dien Bien Phu in December 1953.

William Egan Colby was a U. S. intelligence officer born on 4 January 1920. During World War II he served with the Office of Strategic Services. During the Vietnam War he served as CIA chief of the Far East Division, and head of the Civil Operations and Rural Development effort, as well as overseeing the Phoenix Program.

Phillip Buford Davidson, Jr. was born on 26 November 1915 in Hachita, New Mexico. He graduated with the United States Military Academy Class of 1939 and served as an intelligence office in the 96th Infantry Division during World War II. During the Vietnam War Davidson was Chief of Intelligence under General Westmoreland and General Abrams.

Ngo Dinh Diem was born on 3 January 1901 in Quang Binh, Vietnam. Following the 1954 Geneva Accords and the departure of the French from Vietnam, Diem became president of the Republic of Vietnam (South Vietnam).

Pham Van Dong was born on 1 March 1906. He was a Vietnamese politician who served as Prime Minister of North Vietnam from 1955 to 1976.

Roger H. Donlon was born Saugerties, New York on 30 January 1934. He joined the United States Air Force in 1953 and was admitted to West Point in 1955, but resigned for personal reasons. He re-enlisted, this time in the United States Army. He went to Officer Candidate School, was commissioned and in August 1963, he joined the Special Forces. In May 1964, Donlon led the Special Forces team that established an outpost at Nam Dong, about 15 miles from the Laotian border. On 6 July 6 1964, the base was attacked by a large force of Vietcong and the attack was repelled.

George Edward Dooley was born in Chicago, Illinois on 10 January 1941. He served two tours in Vietnam with the U. S. Army Special Forces. Dooley commanded a Special Forces A-Team in the Central Highlands and trained the Montagnard soldiers to fight the VC and NVA.

Le Duan was born on 7 April 1907. He was a Vietnamese

Communist politician. He rose in the party hierarchy in the late 1950s and became General Secretary of the Central Committee of the Communist Party of Vietnam (VCP) at the 3rd National Congress in 1960.

Van Nguyen Duong was born on 8 January 1934 in the Camau District of South Vietnam. In May of 1954 he was drafted into South Vietnam's Army and was subsequently commissioned. Over the years that followed he advanced in rank becoming a senior officer in the field of intelligence.

Y Bham Enuol was born in 1923. He was a Rhade civil servant who established the Bajaraka autonomy movement in 1958. He was selected a president of the FULRO and was arrested following the failed uprising. He was subsequently released and fled to Cambodia.

Bernard B. Fall was a war correspondent and historian who covered the Vietnam War from its earliest days. Fall was born in Austria on 19 November 1926. He moved to France, and after the fall of France during World War II, he fought with the Resistance against the Nazis. After the war, he moved to the U.S. and studied at Syracuse and Johns Hopkins University. Fall visited Vietnam several times, writing several books, including *The Street Without Joy*, which may have been his best.

Vo Nguyen Giap was born in Quang Binh Province, Vietnam, on 25 August 1911. He commanded NVA forces during the French war and the Vietnam War that ended in 1975. Giap graduated from the University of Hanoi with bachelor's degree in politics, economics, and law. He fought with the resistance against the Japanese during World War II. During the French war, he defeated the French in the battle of Dien Bien Phu in 1954.

Alexander Meigs Haig, Jr., was born in Philadelphia, Pennsylvania, on 2 December 1924. He studied for two years at the University of Notre Dame before entering the U.S. Military Academy, where he graduated in 1947. He served in the Korean War and commanded a battalion in Vietnam before returning to the U.S., where he was assigned to the U.S. Military Academy in 1967. In 1969 he was appointed an assistant to national security advisor Henry Kissinger.

Paul D. Harkins was born in Boston, Massachusetts, on 15 May 1904. He graduated from the U.S. Military Academy with the class of 1929. He advanced in rank to command U.S. forces in Vietnam (1962–1964).

Colonel Oran Henderson was born in Indianapolis, Indiana, on 25 August 1920. Henderson had twenty-five years of service, including World War II and the Korean War, and commanded a brigade in the Americal Division during the Vietnam War.

Gerald Canon Hickey was born on 17 December 1925. As anthropologist, he first went to Vietnam in 1956 with the Michigan State University Group. His first significant ethnographic research project (in 1958-1959) was a study of Khanh Hau, a Mekong River delta village in Vietnam. His research effort focused on the Montagnards and continued for years.

Harold K. Johnson was born in Bowesmont, North Dakota, on 22 February 1912. He attended the U.S. Military Academy, graduating with the class of 1933. He was commissioned in the infantry, and his assignments included the 57th Infantry (Philippine Scouts). With the fall of Bataan, Johnson became a prisoner of war of the Japanese. After World War II, he served in the Korean War and in Vietnam.

Francis John Kelly was born on 18 February 1919. A native of the Bronx, Kelly first enlisted in the Army in 1941. He received a commission in the Armored Corps the following year and went ashore in the early waves at Omaha Beach in the D-Day invasion of Normandy. Colonel Kelly, who devised Army plans for unconventional warfare in the early 1960's, commanded the Special Forces in Vietnam from June 1966 to June 1967.

Henry Alfred Kissinger was born in Furth, Germany, on 27 May 1923. He and his family fled Germany in 1938 to escape persecution by the Nazis. They settled in New York City, where Kissinger attended high school and started community college. He was drafted into the army in 1943 and served in the 84th Division in Europe. Following the war, he earned his bachelor's degree, followed by his master's and Ph.D. at Harvard in 1954. He advanced in the academic community and was the director of the Harvard Defense Studies Program between 1958 and 1971. Nixon chose Kissinger to be his national security advisor in 1968.

Samuel W. Koster was born in West Liberty, Iowa, on 29 December 1919 and graduated from the U.S. Military Academy with the class of 1942. He was the commander of the U.S. Army Americal Division in 1968.

Nguyen Cao Ky was born in Hanoi, Vietnam, on 8 September 1930. Ky started as an infantry officer but was sent for pilot training by the French before Vietnam was partitioned. Ky moved to South Vietnam and joined the air force. He rose through the ranks and eventually became the commander of South Vietnam's air force. In November 1963, Ky participated in the coup that resulted in the assassination of Ngo Dinh Diem. In the succession of generals who followed Diem, Ky eventually sided with Nguyen Van Thieu, and the two ran for office in 1967.

Melvin R. Laird was born in Omaha, Nebraska, on 1 September 1922. Laird graduated from Carleton College in Minnesota and served in the navy during World War II. After the war, he succeeded his deceased father in the Wisconsin State Senate and became Secretary of Defense under President Nixon in 1969.

Henry Cabot Lodge, Jr. was born on 5 July 1902. He served as United States Senator from Massachusetts and a United States ambassador to South Vietnam where he supported the 1963 coup that resulted in the death of South Vietnam President Diem.

John C. Loving graduated from the University of Richmond in 1967 and was commissioned a lieutenant in the U. S. Army under the R.O.T.C program. He served in Vietnam as an advisor to Regional Forces in the Army of the Republic of Vietnam from April 1969 to January 1970. His assignment was in Tay Ninh Province.

Nay Luett was born in May 1935 in Bon Me Hing south of Cheo Reo. He was a member of the Jarai Montagnard tribe. He became Minister for the Development of Ethnic Minorities (MDEM) in the South Vietnamese government.

Theodore C. Mataxis was born on 17 August 1917. He enlisted in the Washington National Guard in the fall of 1939. His service in World War II was as a battalion commander of the 2nd Battalion 276th Infantry Division during the last German offensive in the winter of 1944. His service in the U. S. Army continued and in 1964, he volunteered for Vietnam, where he served as Senior Adviser, II ARVN Corps, for 16 months.

Robert S. McNamara was born on 9 June 1916. He was selected by President John F. Kennedy to be his Secretary of Defense shortly after Kennedy took office. He remained in office, serving Lyndon B. Johnson, after Kennedy was assassinated.

Doung Van Minh "Big Minh" was born in My Tho province, Vietnam, on 16 February 1916. Minh joined the French army at the start of World War II. He became a South Vietnamese general and politician who helped Ngo Dinh Diem consolidate power after Vietnam was partitioned in 1955.

Ho Chi Minh was born Nguyen Sinh Cung in Nghe An Province, Vietnam, on 19 May 1890. He used a number of aliases throughout his life in order to avoid arrest but is known today as Ho Chi Minh. Ho Chi Minh was educated in Hue and traveled extensively, visiting France, the U.S., Russia, China, and the United Kingdom. In 1941, he returned to Vietnam to lead the Viet Minh independence movement. He led the Viet Minh against the French and the Japanese, receiving support from the U.S. At the end of World War II, Ho declared the independence of Vietnam under the title of the Democratic Republic of Vietnam.

Thomas Hinman Moorer was born in Mount Willing, Alabama, on 9 February 1912. He graduated from the U.S. Naval Academy with the class of 1933 and served as a pilot during World War II. Moorer served as Chief of Naval Operations between 1967 and 1970.

Madame Nhu was born of a wealthy family in Hanoi, Vietnam, on

22 August 1924. She married Ngo Dinh Nhu in 1943. He was the brother of Ngo Dinh Diem, who would become the president of South Vietnam.

Ngo Dinh Nhu was born in Phu Cam, Vietnam, on 7 October 1910. Nhu received his bachelor's degree in literature in Paris. He pursued academic interests until the end of World War II, when he became politically active and helped in mobilizing support for his brother Diem.

Marshal Lon Nol was born in Prey Veng, Cambodia, on 13 November 1913. He served as prime minister and defense minister of Cambodia.

Bruce Palmer, Jr., was born in Austin, Texas, on 13 April 1913. He graduated from the U.S. Military Academy with the class of 1936. He served in World War II and commanded the XVIII Airborne Corps, 1965–1967.

Pol Pot was born in Kampong Thom Province, Cambodia, on 19 May 1925. He joined a Communist cell in 1951. He gained control of the Khmer Rouge movement in Cambodia.

H. Norman Schwarzkopf, Jr. was born on 22 August 1934. He graduated with the U. S. Military Academy Class of 1956. He served as an advisor to a Vietnamese battalion and later commanded a U. S. battalion in Vietnam.

Prince Norodom Sihanouk was born in Phnom Penh, Cambodia, on 31 October 1922. He attended cavalry school in France and was selected as King of Cambodia in 1941. During World War II, the Japanese took control of Cambodia. At the end of the war, Sihanouk proclaimed Cambodia's independence and held a series of appointments as prime minister until 1960, when he was elected head of state.

Prince Souphanouvong was born in Laos on 13 July 1909. He along with his half-brother Prince Souvanna Phouma and Prince Boun Oum of Champasak, was one of the "Three Princes" who represented respectively the Communist (pro-Vietnam), neutralist and royalist political factions in Laos.

Nguyen Van Thieu was born in Phan Rang, Vietnam, on 5 April

1923. Initially, Thieu joined the Viet Minh Communists but quit after a year and joined the South Vietnamese army, rising in rank to command a division by 1960. Thieu participated in the coup against Diem in November 1963 and became a member of the military junta after Diem's death.

John Paul Vann was born in Norfolk, Virginia, on 2 July 1924. Vann enlisted during World War II and remained in the service after the war. He also served in the Korean War and Vietnam.

Cao Van Vien was born on 21 December 1921. He was one of only two ARVN generals who achieved four-star rank. He was appointed Chief of Staff of the Joint General Staff (JGS) on September 11, 1964.

Nguyen Phuoc Vinh Loc was a cousin of emperor Bao Dai. Vinh Loc commanded the ARVN II Corps from 23 June 1965 to 28 February 1968.

William Childs Westmoreland was born in Saxon, South Carolina, on 26 March 1914. He attended the U.S. Military Academy, graduating with the class of 1936. He served in World War II, the Korean War, and commanded U.S. Forces in Vietnam.

Introduction

This history focuses on the Montagnard People (called the Children of the Mountains) in the Central Highlands of Vietnam during the wars that occurred in Southeast Asia from the end of World War II to 1991, the end of the Third Indochina War. It starts with the First Indochina War called the French War from 1947-1954 and continues with the Second Indochina War called the American War (1954-1975). The Third Indochina War followed the fall of the Saigon government and Cambodia in 1975. It involved China, the USSR, Cambodia, Laos and Vietnam. In all of these conflicts the Montagnard tribes participated and sometimes played a key role.

This book is not simply a record of battles fought, but also tells the story of the governments and key leaders involved in the struggle including anti-war movements, government corruption, and many other factors that produced the outcomes. Most important, it tells the story and history of the people involved including their eyewitness accounts of events.

This history provides an account of the Montagnard people who escaped Vietnam following the fall of Saigon. Many of these people now reside in the United States. U. S. Army retired Special Forces personnel and other veterans were instrumental in gaining escape for these Montagnards to the United States. Persecution by the government of Vietnam continues for those Montagnards who remained in Vietnam.

This book includes appendices to assist the reader. These are individual biographies, chronology of events and definition of terms less familiar to us today.

The history starts with the background of the Montagnard tribes.

1. The Montagnard

Montagnards have in common an ingrained hostility toward the
Vietnamese and a desire to be independent.[2]

Francis J. Kelly

Colonel Francis J. Kelly, U. S. Army, Retired developed army plans for unconventional warfare in the early 1960's and he also commanded U. S. Army Special Forces in Vietnam from June 1966 to June 1967. Colonel Kelly provided this background and description of the Montagnards. Appendix D, Montagnard Tribes provides further details.

The Montagnards constitute one of the largest minority groups in Vietnam. The term Montagnard, loosely used, like the word Indian, applies to more than a hundred tribes of primitive mountain people . . . spread over all of Indochina [a French term that included Vietnam, Laos, and Cambodia].[3] Even within the same tribe, cultural patterns and linguistic characteristics can vary considerably from village to village. In spite of their dissimilarities, however, the Montagnards have many common features that distinguish them from the Vietnamese who inhabit the lowlands. The Montagnard tribal society is centered on the village and the people depend largely on slash-and-burn agriculture for their livelihood. Montagnards have in common an ingrained hostility toward the Vietnamese and a desire to be independent.

Throughout the course of the French Indochina War, the Viet Minh worked to win the Montagnards to their side. Living in the highlands, these mountain people had been long isolated by both geographic and economic conditions from the developed areas of Vietnam, and they occupied territory of strategic value to an insurgent movement. The French also enlisted and trained Montagnards as soldiers, and many fought on their side.

. . . The Rhade were the first to be approached and to participate in the CIDG [Civilian Irregular Defense Group] program. For many years, the Rhade have been considered the most influential and strategically located of the Montagnard tribes in the highlands of Vietnam. . . .

The Rhade have lived on the high plateau for centuries, and their way of life has changed little in that time; whatever changes came were mainly the result of their contact with the "civilized" world through the French. They settle in places where their livelihood can be easily secured, locating their houses and rice fields near rivers and springs. Because they have no written history, not much was known about them until their contact with the French in the early nineteenth century. . . .

In order of descending importance, the social units of the Rhade are the family, the household, the kinsmen, and the village. The Rhade have a matrilineal system; the man is the breadwinner, but all property is owned by the wife. The oldest female owns the house and animals. The married man lives with his wife's family and is required to show great respect for his mother-in-law. If a man is rich enough he may have more than one wife, but women may have only one husband. Marriage is proposed by the woman, and the eldest daughter inherits her parents' property.

Building a house is a family enterprise. All members of families who wish to live together pitch in and build the longhouse in accordance with the size of the families. The house is made largely of woven bamboo and is long and narrow, sometimes 400 feet long, with entrances at each end. Both family and guests may use the front entrance, but only the resident families may use the rear. The house is built on posts with the main floor usually about four feet above the ground and is almost always constructed with a north-south orientation, following the axis of the valleys.

Montagnard Dwelling (Olen C. Phipps, Jr.).

The tasks of the man and woman of the family are the traditional ones. The man cuts trees, clears land, weaves bamboo, fishes, hunts, builds houses, carries heavy objects, conducts business, makes coffins, buries the dead, stores rice, makes hand tools and weapons, strikes the ceremonial gongs, an important duty, and is responsible for preparing the rice wine. Authority in the Rhade family is maintained by the man, the father or the grandfather. It is he who makes the decisions, consulting with his wife in most cases, and he who is responsible for seeing that his decisions are carried out. The average Rhade man is between sixty-four and sixty-six inches tall, brown in complexion, and usually broadshouldered and very sturdy. The men have a great deal of endurance and manual dexterity and have the reputation of being excellent runners.

The woman draws water, collects firewood, cooks the food, cleans the house, mends and washes the clothes, weaves, makes the traditional red, black, yellow, and blue cotton cloth of the Rhade, and cares for the children. . . .

The life of the Rhade is governed by many taboos and customs. Outsiders are expected to honor these, and therefore delicacy was required of Special Forces troops who dealt with the Rhade and other tribes. Healing is the responsibility of the village shaman, or witch doctor, and the general state of health among the Rhade is poor. Religion is animistic — natural objects are thought to be inhabited by spirits — but the tribe also has a god (Ae Die) and a devil (Tang Lie).

. . . . At the beginning of the rainy season the people plant corn, squash, potatoes, cucumbers, eggplant, and bananas. Once these crops are in the ground, the rice is planted.

The Rhade proved to be enthusiastic participants in the CIDG [Civilian Irregular Defense Group] program . . . . The Montagnards were not, of course, the only minority group involved in the CIDC program; other groups were Cambodians, Nung tribesmen from the highlands of North Vietnam, and ethnic Vietnamese from the Cao Dai and Hoa Hao religious sects.[4]

Francis J. Kelly

2. First Indochina War (French War)

"You can kill ten of my men for everyone I kill of yours, but even at those odds, I will win."[5]

Ho Chi Minh

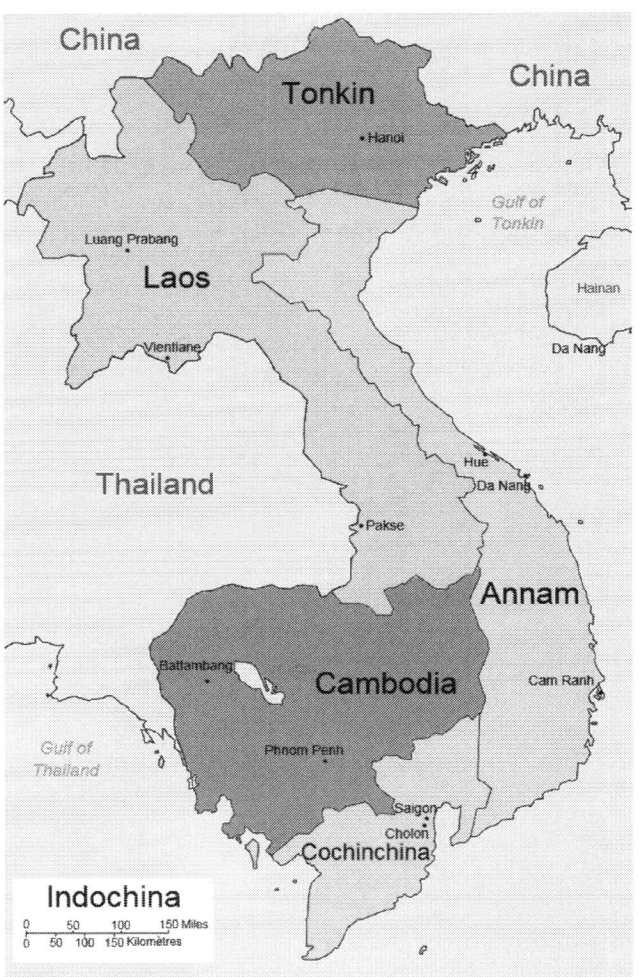

French Indochina in 1945 (Wikipedia).

French involvement in Vietnam started in August 1883, when a French fleet arrived at the mouth of the Perfume River near the imperial capital of Vietnam, Hue, and demanded the surrender of the government. Before the Vietnamese could respond, the fleet opened fire, killing thousands of unarmed Vietnamese.[6] The French seized Vietnam and turned it into a colony of France. There were many riches that France wanted to exploit, as most colonial powers do. Rubber, tea, and rice were not the least of these. Vietnam had been invaded and occupied several times in the past, but the French occupation was the most recent. As a result of the slaughter in Hue in 1883, the Vietnamese capitulated. The French took over and declared that Vietnam was now their protectorate. They sent in troops. What followed was over seventy years of French exploitation of Vietnam that ended in 1954.

Along the way, there were some strange occurrences. At the World War I peace conference at Versailles in 1919, a very young man attempted to see U.S. President Woodrow Wilson. The young man wanted to argue for self-rule in Vietnam. His name was Ho Chi Minh,[7] but Wilson refused to see him.[8] Had he done so, the history of Vietnam might have been different, but that is very unlikely. Most say that Ho was a Communist, while others argue that he was a nationalist. It appears that he was a nationalist when he sought to see Wilson, but his political leanings changed to communism after he visited Moscow in 1925. Dean Acheson, secretary of state, put it another way in 1949: "Question whether Ho [Chi Minh] as much Nationalist as Commie is irrelevant. All Stalinists in colonial areas are nationalists."[9] Today, it does not really matter, given the outcome of the war, but his political leanings did change over time. A very strange situation emerged in Vietnam during World War II. The Japanese left the French bureaucratic colonial administration intact to rule Vietnam while they directed its activities.[10] During World War II, while the Japanese exported their plunder from Vietnam, nearly twenty percent of the population in the North died from starvation.[11] The reasons for the starvation were crop failures and the inability of the North to buy rice from the south. The North was not self-sustaining and suffered the most since it was relying on crops from the South. Years later, the mayor of Hanoi described the scene:

> Peasants came in from the nearby provinces on foot, leaning on each other, carrying their children in baskets. They dug in garbage piles, looking for anything at all, banana skins, orange peels, discarded greens. They even ate rats. But they couldn't get enough to keep alive. They tried to beg, but everyone else was hungry, and they would drop dead in the streets. Every morning, when I opened my door, I found five or six corpses on the step. We organized teams of youths to load the bodies on oxcarts and take them to mass graves outside the city. It was terrifying—and yet it helped our cause because we were able to rally the nation.[12]
>
> ***Tran Duy Hung, Mayor of Hanoi***

At the close of World War II in 1945, the Japanese, who had occupied Indochina during the war were on their way home. The French sought to reclaim their colonial empire and this was not what the Vietnamese had in mind. After fighting the Japanese through a long war, the Vietnamese wanted independence.

Ho Chi Minh in 1946 (Library of Congress).

Ho Chi Minh, the Vietnamese leader, summarized: "If they [the French] force us into war, we will fight. The struggle will be atrocious, but the Vietnamese people will suffer anything rather than renounce their freedom."[13] Hɔ's words were prophetic, as would be proven thirty years later when North Vietnamese tanks rumbled through the gates of the South Vietnamese palace in Saigon, ending the American war.

As attractive as it was for budding highlander nationalists and strongmen, French protectorate rule placed the people of the massifs [another name for the Central Highlands] in a very dangerous position in 1945, when the Japanese overturned the French colonial state before capitulating to the Allies a few months later. Stepping into the vacuum, Vietnamese nationalists seized power. On 2 September 1945, Ho Chi Minh declared the birth of the Democratic Republic of Vietnam [DRV]. This government immediately decreed laws unifying Tonkin, Annam, and Cochinchina into one sovereign territory and turning the great majority of those born or residing within 'Vietnam's' borders into 'Vietnamese citizens'. This included the two million non-Viet people who were living in the highlands. Ho did not recognize French rule there or any other special colonial arrangements. It was, he insisted, simply 'Vietnamese'.[14]

Christopher Goscha

In August 1945, after the U.S. Army Air Corps incinerated the Japanese towns of Hiroshima and Nagasaki with nuclear weapons, the Japanese decided to surrender unconditionally.[15] This left a vacuum in Indochina where the French and Vietnamese Viet Minh, sought to claim the country.

Bao Dai (1913–1997) (Wikipedia).

Bao Dai was the titular leader of Vietnam throughout the First Indochina War. He resided in Hue, the traditional capital of Vietnam, and also spent time at his hunting lodge at Ban Me

Thuot. When World War II ended, he moved to Hanoi and became the pawn of the Vietnamese under Ho Chi Minh. He was a play-boy who did nothing, but the Viet Minh led by Ho Chi Minh, used him to their advantage. They appointed him "Supreme Advisor" and manipulated him for their own purpose.[16]

By the fall of 1945, it was clear that a war between the French occupiers and the Viet Minh was imminent. As the French general Etienne Valluy summarized, "If those gooks want a fight, they'll get it."[17]

The French got their fight. At the same time, Ho appealed to the United States to recognize his cause. At this time, the U.S. president, Harry Truman, was not inclined to support an avowed Communist such as Ho against a very weak ally: France.

In the postwar period, the French strengthened their control of Vietnam without regard to the Vietnamese people. Atrocities were committed by both sides, including the massacre of about one hundred and fifty French civilians in Saigon.[18] The war with the French would drag on for nine years. At one point, General Leclerc, the French commander, declared victory and would learn otherwise, as General Westmoreland would learn twenty years later. The French historian Philippe Devillers summarized:

> If we departed, believing a region pacified, the Viet Minh would arrive on our heels…There was only one possible defense, to multiply our posts, fortify them, arm and train the villagers, coordinate intelligence and police. What was required was not Leclerc's thirty-five thousand troops but a hundred thousand—and Cochinchina was not the only problem.[19]
>
> ***Philippe Devillers***

A key part of the French strategy was to establish French control over the Central Highlands. Historian Christopher Goscha explained.

Until 1954, the French continued to support a separate territorial administration, highlander education, language training, and military service. In so doing, the French brought isolated highlanders together like never before. Hundreds of young men coming from across the central massif [Central Highlands] met each other in the classrooms of the newly opened College Sabatier. Many accepted administrative positions outside their native lands, and in so doing developed long-lasting and often unprecedented relationships extending across the hills. Similar things happened in highlander combat units. Marriage across clan lines increased. French and, increasingly, Rhade began to serve as a common language. Protestant missionaries, mainly American started attracting thousands of converts in the highlands. Their schools and missions circulated highlander youth across tribal lines. And from 1950 onward, the French and Americans promoted special agricultural and infrastructure programs for this area.[20]

Christopher Goscha

Bao Dai was lured back by the French and served as chief of state until after the final French defeat in 1954 and their withdrawal in 1956.

Although Leon Pignon, the French high commissioner between 1948 and 1950, had allowed for the unification of this Vietnam, his team intentionally attached the operation of the highlands to Bao Dai, convinced that they could control their emperor and, through him, the central massif, as they had done in the past. This is how and why the Crown Domain of the Southern Highlander Country (Domaine de la couronne du pays Montagnards du Sud) came to life in 1950. By winning over Bao Dai's collaboration, the French had devised a method to continue to maintain a separate hold over this militarily important part of Indochina. Although the French nominally recognized Vietnamese sovereignty over the highlands, they maintained a 'special status' for the highlands because of 'special French obligations'. In 1950, immaculately dressed in white suits, Leon Pignon and Bao Dai stepped before two thousand highland chiefs in Ban Me Thuot to participate in the oath ceremony. But everyone knew that France's longtime Indochina hand, Jean Cousseau, ran the highlands as the 'special delegate', not the Vietnamese monarch. The Crown Domain of the Southern

Highlander Country thus serves as a case study in Bao Dai's failure to force the French to decolonize completely, when he could have done so. The Crown Domain was nothing more than a new term for the continuation of the de facto French protectorate over the `sixieme pays' of colonial Indochina.[21]

Christopher Goscha

Ngo Dinh Diem (1901–1963) (Department of Defense).

Bao Dai was the last emperor of Vietnam. Among the people in Bao Dai's cabinet before the war was a bureaucrat named Ngo Dinh Diem. Diem would play a key role in the history of Vietnam.

There was much bad news for the West in the 1949–1950 time-frame, all of which influenced Vietnam. Chairman Mao defeated the Nationalist government in China and stationed his troops along the border of Vietnam. They were ready to provide support to the Viet Minh. Soul-searching in the U.S. revolved around who lost China. With Senator Joseph McCarthy initiating a red witch hunt in the United States, there was no sympathy for anyone such as Ho who could be viewed as a Communist. Although Ho Chi Minh wrote at least eight letters to President Truman, Truman had no interest in initiating any contact with or negotiating with Ho. This was also a Cold War issue. The U.S. would support the French in Vietnam, and in return, the French would support the U.S. doctrine in Europe for containment.

The Soviet Union had constructed and detonated its first nuclear weapon, thanks to input from traitors in the U.S. and the U. K. The U.S. had lost its sole possession of nuclear technology, and with that went enormous leverage. This could have been used to negotiate a settlement in Vietnam if Truman had wished to do so, but it was now too late.

The French continued to drain their military resources fighting a losing war in Vietnam. By 1950, French losses exceeded 50,000, and the Viet Minh were killing French officers at a rate faster than they could be graduated from officer schools in France.[22] This reduced France's ability to meet its NATO requirements in Europe. By late 1952, French casualties (dead, wounded, captured, and missing) were up to more than 90,000.[23] By this time, the U.S. was funding forty percent of the cost of the French war, but France did not ask for the commitment of U.S. ground forces.[24]

In the meantime, the war in Korea had an effect on Vietnam. When the North Koreans invaded South Korea in June 1950, the U.S. responded by moving thousands of troops to defend its ally, South Korea, and this was one of the most curious wars in recent history. It was called a "Police Action" by the U.S. Some background is relevant. In 1950, Dean Acheson, the U.S. secretary of state, announced that Korea was outside the U.S. "Defense Perimeter." This occurred during his Press Club speech on 12 January 1950. The North Koreans believed what Acheson said and viewed his statement as a green light for them to invade the South. They should not have believed Acheson's statement. The U.S., as it turned out, would fight to defend its ally. Acheson would later deny his statement and indicated that his Press Club speech was "grossly distorted."[25] This was symptomatic of the U.S. view of Asia during the 1950s. Korea and Vietnam were sideshows that did not deserve much thought or time until major conflicts there erupted. The focus was on the Soviet Union and Senator Joseph McCarthy.[26] These two were the major threats to our democracy. U.S. troops were tied up in Korea, and the U.S. had a reduced capability to assist France in Vietnam, except for funding and some air support missions. The French sought a "set piece battle" with the Viet Minh. This meant a conventional fight in which both sides faced off and fought it out in a battle, one side winning and the other side losing. The Viet Minh did not fight that way. It came down to guerrilla warfare, with ambushes on the French, and the Viet Minh would then fade away. Ho made it clear to the French: "You can kill ten of my men for everyone I kill of yours, but even at those odds, I will win."[27]

Dien Bien Phu

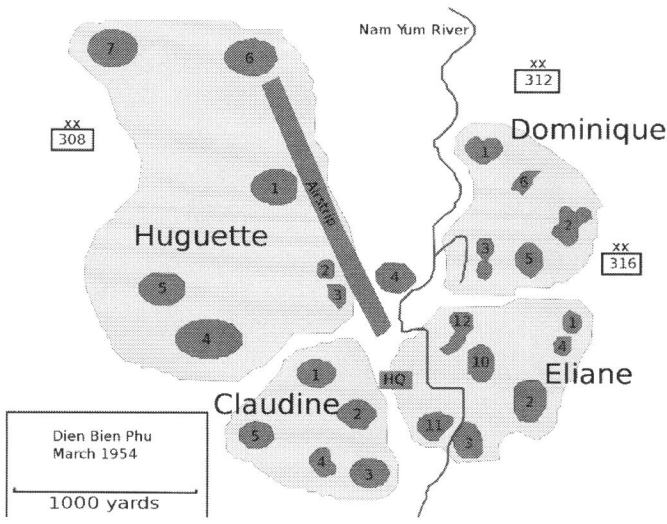

Dien Bien Phu in Spring 1954 (Wikipedia).

The French would get their "Set-Piece Battle" at a place called Dien Bien Phu. The French decided that they would establish a base camp west of Hanoi in a valley called Dien Bien Phu. *Operation Castor* was an airborne operation to establish an airhead at Dien Bien Phu. This was accomplished on 20-23 November 1953. It was intended to block the return of Viet Minh General Vo Nguyen Giap into Laos, which he had easily accomplished in 1953, but withdrew because of the rains.[28] A French base at Dien Bien Phu would block Giap's invasion of Laos and he would have to either fight the French or abandon his invasion of Laos. Author Douglas Porch offers another reason for *Operation Castor*. It could assist the hill tribes of the North who were supporting the French. It seems that the Viet Minh were seizing opium crops from the hill tribes and selling the opium in Hong Kong, Hanoi and other capitals in Asia. Funds generated by the sales were used to support the war effort. The Montagnards were upset by the continuing thefts and were siding with the French. In effect the

French wanted to maintain control of the opium harvest by supporting their Montagnard allies residing near the Dien Bien Phu valley.[29]

> The Democratic Republic of Vietnam's shift to conventional warfare from 1950 onward led both the belligerents to rely ever more heavily on Tai, Hmong, and Nung peoples to supply highland battlefields with recruits, porters, intelligence, and food. The political autonomy the people there enjoyed up to this point began to disappear as the Communists mobilized for war in the massifs. And the intensification of the war also brought more Americans into the highlands (although American Protestants had been in Vietnam since the 1920s). The Americans pushed the French hard to build up their special forces in the highlands where they jutted into China's underbelly, convinced of the threat of a wider Communist thrust into Southeast Asia and now also themselves at war with the Chinese in Korea.[30]
>
> ***Christopher Goscha***

For these reasons, the French hoped to force the Viet Minh to attack them and they would then be able to destroy the Viet Minh with air and artillery fire.

The French got their wish. Giap marshaled his forces around the French garrison. By 13 March 1954, Giap was prepared to attack. He had assembled 50,000 troops at Dien Bien Phu. The French had 13,000, and about half of these were fighters.[31] One of Giap's soldiers recalled:

> We had to cross mountains and jungles, marching at night and sleeping by day to avoid enemy bombing. We sometimes slept in foxholes, or just by the trail. We each carried a rifle, ammunition, and hand grenades, and our packs contained a blanket, a mosquito net, and a change of clothes. We each had a week's supply of rice, which we refilled at depots along the way. We ate greens and bamboo shoots that we picked in the jungle, and occasionally villagers would give us a bit of meat. I'd been in the Viet Minh for nine years by then, and I was accustomed to it.[32]

The French battle plan was a soldier's nightmare. The French established their camp in a valley, which meant that any force on the surrounding hills could destroy the French. If the Viet Minh closed in, the French would have to rely on air resupply and had limited assets, although the U.S. agreed to provide some airlift capability. The French thought that this would be a perfect "set piece battle." The Viet Minh would be cut to pieces by air support and artillery as they attacked. This would defeat the Viet Minh and end the war. This was similar to the situation experienced by the ARVN/U.S. and NVA in other later battles such as Khe Sanh and Lam Son 719.

The French commander, Colonel Christian de Castries, had established strong points on the hills surrounding Dien Bien Phu. He named these for his French mistresses (Huguette, Claudine, Dominique, and Eliane). Perhaps like his mistresses, it was a French fantasy: the outposts could easily be overcome by the Viet Minh, and they were. The greatest miscalculation was artillery. The French concluded that since the Viet Minh had no artillery at Dien Bien Phu and the French had air support, Dien Bien Phu could survive an attack by the Viet Minh.[33] Giap solved the problem for the Viet Minh. The troops dismantled their artillery pieces and humped them up the mountains to overlook Dien Bien Phu. Some 50,000 Chinese coolies assisted the Viet Minh in doing the seemingly impossible task of moving the artillery pieces and anti-aircraft guns up over the steep mountains and digging caves to conceal these weapons. Chinese artillery officers advised on positing these weapons to allow firing on French support aircraft and on the fortified positions below with optimum effect. This positioning in caves made them nearly impervious to French counter-battery fire. To fill the Viet Minh's bellies during the siege, these coolies also, bicycled in relays down the narrow mountain footpaths, each straining under a load of 600 lbs. of sacked rice.[34]

Viet Minh artillery overlooking Dien Bien Phu fired at will. It was a "turkey shoot." Giap's battle plan was simple:

> By launching a big offensive with fresh troops, we could have foreshortened the duration of the campaign, and avoided the wear and tear of a long operation…. [But] we saw that these tactics had a very great, basic disadvantage. Our troops lacked experience in attacking fortified entrenched camps. If we wanted to win swiftly, success could not be assured…. Consequently, we resolutely chose to strike and advance surely … strike to win, strike only when success is certain. If it is not, then do not strike.[35]
>
> ***Stanley Karnow***

Initially, Giap lost heavily and changed his battle plan. A veteran of the battle recalled:

> General Giap changed the entire plan. He stopped the attack and pulled back our artillery. Now the shovel became our most important weapon. Everyone dug tunnels and trenches under fire, sometimes hitting hard soil and only advancing five or six yards a day. But we gradually surrounded Dien Bien Phu with an underground network several hundred miles long, and we could tighten the noose around the French.[36]
>
> ***Stanley Karnow***

It was a hard fight. Giap's infantry moved through the tunnels and trenches to the French line while his artillery pounded the French position. Bad weather limited air support for the French. Two U.S. CIA/CAT pilots were killed at Dien Bien Phu: Captain James McGovern and his copilot, Wallace Buford, died when their supply aircraft was shot down by the Viet Minh. These were among the earliest U.S. casualties in the Vietnam War. Over 58,000 U.S. dead would follow after the French war.[37]

The French artillery commander, faced with defeat, committed suicide. The French defenses were easily overcome. On 7 May 1954, the French surrendered at Dien Bien Phu, and thousands of the surviving French soldiers became what was known as "pearls." This meant that they were hostages until France paid a ransom for their release.

The Last French Defeat

The best example of the Viet Minh "hit and run" tactics was the destruction of the French Groupement Mobile 100 (G.M. 100) that Doctor Bernard Fall described in his book *Street Without Joy*. G.M. 100 was one of the best units of its type. Its troops had fought in Korea as a part of the U.S. 2nd Infantry Division, and the French troops were seasoned fighters. It was an elite force. In December 1953, G.M. 100 moved into Vietnam's Central Highlands, in an area that would later be called II Corps Tactical Zone (II CTZ) and still later Military Region 2 (MR 2), not far from Ban Me Thuot. When the Viet Minh attacked the French at Kontum near Dak To and further south at Cheo Reo, G.M. 100 was ordered to reinforce Cheo Reo on New Year's Day, 1954. The G.M. 100 assembled at Cheo Reo and performed road clearance of Route 7 to the coast. By 1 February 1954, the threat to Kontum had become clear, and G.M. 100 was ordered north to Kontum, where the civilians were in panic over Viet Minh activities. The Viet Minh were transitioning from guerrilla warfare to a full-scale conventional war. Thirteen years later, this same transition occurred at the same place—Dak To—during the Border Battles. It was perfect for this purpose due to terrain and proximity to nearby border safe havens. Dr. Fall described the action.

> To the north and northeast of the town [Kontum], the mountain tribesmen partisans had either withdrawn into the jungle or, undermined by Communist propaganda, had murdered their French NCOs and this time, the enemy did not avoid contact. A strong patrol from the 2d Korea [these were French veterans of the Korean War] to Kon Brai, led by

Lieutenant de Bellefont, fell into a well-laid ambush, in which the whole platoon was nearly wiped out, leaving seven dead (including the lieutenant) and thirteen wounded, while the Viet Minh lost five dead.

At 1300, on February 2, all the posts to the northwest of Kontum, including the important post of Dak-To, were simply submerged by enemy troops in battalion strength attacking in several waves. Air support, called in from the fighter-bomber airfields in NhaTrang and Seno, continued strafing missions around Dak To until nightfall, but only a handful of survivors succeeded in reaching the outposts of Kontum. The 2d Korean continued its patrol activities in the direction of Kon Brai and suffered casualties from mines and booby traps.

Slowly, the 803d Viet Minh Regiment continued to narrow its stranglehold around the G.M. In a wide sweep beyond the city it attacked the post of Dak Doa, 28 kilometers to the southeast of Kontum, which suffered 16 casualties but continued to hold. On February 5, the enemy blew up several bridges to the north of Kontum, thus prohibiting any jeep-borne patrolling north on highway 14. It was only a matter of hours before the G.M. would be totally encircled in Kontum, but the High Command decided not to defend Kontum; the evacuation of the town by all troops, The evacuation of European civilians and Vietnamese civil servants was completed without major incident by February 7, and the G.M. now grimly dug in around Pleiku for a last-ditch defense of the central region of the Southern Mountain Plateau.[38]

Bernard B. Fall

This had become a conventional war rather than a guerrilla conflict. As the Viet Minh activity continued around Pleiku, rain, mud, and mosquitoes plagued the French.   Next, G.M. 100 was ordered east to An Khe, the town that would later become the home of the 1st Air Cavalry Division in 1965. After spending weeks at An Khe, on 24 June 1954, G.M. 100 received orders to abandon its defensive positions at An Khe and withdraw to Pleiku, moving west on Route 19. At road marker "Kilometer 15," Sergeant Li-Som's unit was in the lead and stopped.

Within a few moments, the whole column fell completely silent. Nothing could be heard now save the slight rustling of the wind in the top of the grass blades—and a slight knacking: knackknack- kna-a-ack. This was what Li-Som had been listening for: the slight knacking sound which high jungle grass makes a few minutes after the passage of a large body through it, as the long, resilient strands return to their normal position; the knacking continues even a few minutes after the strands have returned to their normal position, making the ear (as often in the jungle) a more precious auxiliary than the eye. To Li-Som, the message was clear. The Viets were here. The big, the final ambush to engulf all of Mobile Group 100, was ready to be sprung...The main Communist striking force was already in place, its weapons poised, while the French were strung out along a road where their heavier firepower could hardly come into play. Two Communist machine guns opened up at a range of about 30 yards, but Li-Som had not stopped; as soon as he had realized what was happening, he had stormed forward—as much as one can "storm" in tall grass which has the consistency and stopping power of as many feet of water.[39]

Bernard Fall

It was a massacre. The column was ambushed by the Viet Minh and suffered heavy losses. The survivors of G.M. 100 managed to break through the ambush and finally reached Pleiku on 29 June, after days of fighting on Route 19. The destruction of G.M. 100 was the last battle of the French War.

While Giap and the French were fighting at Dien Bien Phu, a peace conference was scheduled in Geneva, Switzerland. The peace conference started on 7 May 1954, the same day that the French surrendered at Dien Bien Phu.

The French would soon be out of Vietnam, and the forces left behind would be Ho in Hanoi and Bao Dai enjoying the life of a playboy in Paris. Bao Dai appointed Ngo Dinh Diem, the nationalist, as his prime minister for South Vietnam. Diem would reside in Saigon. Diem had an inflexible personality and was a Catholic in a predominantly Buddhist country: two items that would haunt the U.S. years later.

The peace conference was short as most conferences go and was concluded on 21 July 1954. One observer at the peace conference had stated: "You cannot expect to negotiate at the conference table what you have lost on the battlefield." This was proved wrong. The French had been beaten, but Vietnam would be partitioned at the 17th parallel (North of Khe Sanh) with the Viet Minh controlling the North and Bao Dai in the South. The 17th parallel became the Demilitarized Zone (DMZ), separating North and South Vietnam. Neither The United States nor South Vietnam signed the agreement. Author Shelby L. Stanton described South Vietnam.

> Vietnam's southern half was officially the Republic of Vietnam, a thin 1,500-mile crescent-shaped country more commonly known as South Vietnam. Its long outer coasts are washed by the Pacific Ocean, and its interior mosaic of mountains, jungles, plains, and swamps are hedged in by the spine of the Chaine Annamitique, a western mountain range, which fades south into a vast alluvial plain created by the delta of the Mekong River.
>
> Palm-lined white sand beaches fringe coves and bays where coral reefs can be clearly seen through the glassy sea. A vibrant green mantle of rice paddies extends inland. These stretch almost endlessly across the flat delta, crisscrossed by ribbons of canals. At the time of the war, many areas of South Vietnam remained a wild and exotic wilderness. Mountain slopes dropped deep into luxurious growths of tropical flora, bracken, tuft-twisted bamboos, and majestic jungle trees. Silver rivers and waterfalls laced the deep rain forests. These were steeped in a wonderful variety of folklore and legend. Large rubber and coconut plantations stretched across rolling plains, and tigers stalked pine-forested plateaus.
>
> Tropical monsoons allowed only two seasons; hot and dry and hot and rainy and the alternation of the monsoons and dry seasons determined the pattern of life. The majority of the eighteen million inhabitants lived in the open lowland plains and rice-bearing deltas. Their hamlets and villages were generally self-governing. An old proverb states that the Emperor's law stops at the village gate. The people had existed through the centuries by cultivating rice on lands irrigated by

primal pumps and sluices. The rugged uplands region was left to the ethnically alien and primitive mountain tribes.[40]

Shelby L. Stanton

The plan was for free elections to be conducted two years after the treaty to reunify Vietnam. The Soviet Union and China had dominated the discussions. The Viet Minh would leave the South, and the French would leave the North. Few participants were happy with the outcome. The Viet Minh were outraged. After winning Vietnam on the battlefield, the Viet Minh now had to settle for a divided country. Pham Van Dong, the Viet Minh representative, speaking about China's representative, Zhou Enlai, simply said, "He has double-crossed us."[41] Zhou supported the partitioning of Vietnam. The migration of people between the North and the South had started. Added into the mix were Vietnamese nationalists and Catholics who fled south rather than live in Ho's Communist regime. Diem consolidated his power in the South, while Ho did the same in the north. The planned elections to reunify the country in 1956 never occurred. In April 1956, the last French soldiers left South Vietnam. The U.S. inherited Diem's anti-Communist regime in the South. At the same time, Cambodia and Laos achieved independence as the French departed.

3. Second Indochina War (American War)

"Americans had underwritten Diem because we knew of no one better."[42]
John Foster Dulles

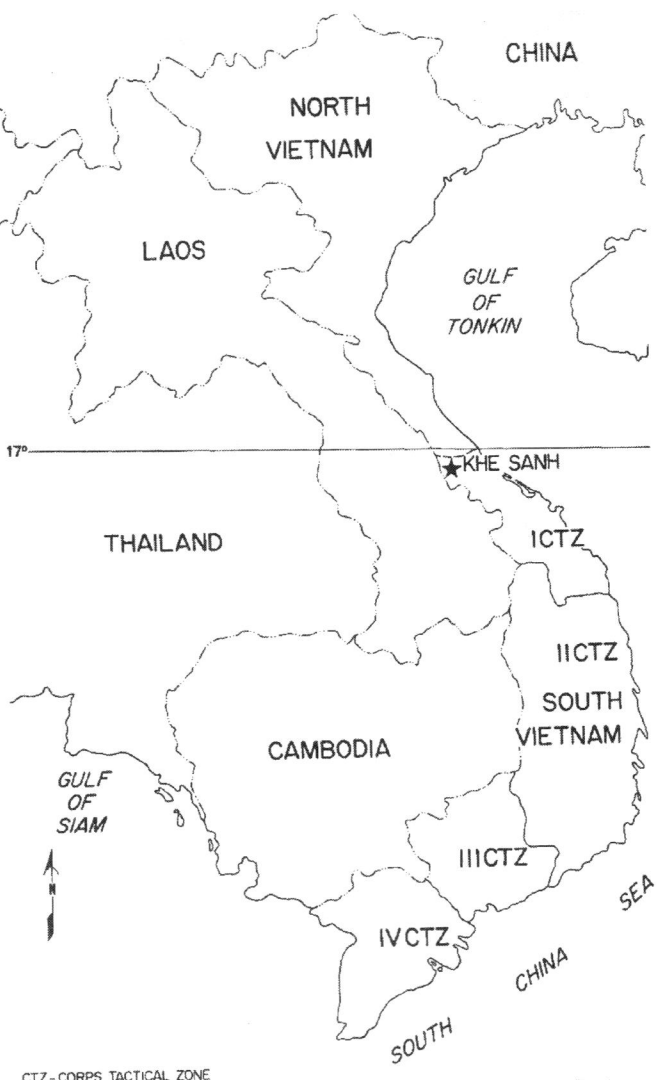

Vietnam Divided—1954 (Moyer S. Shore).

Until the French defeat, the U.S. had provided funds and hardware, including aircraft to help the French fight their war against the Viet Minh. Ngo Dinh Diem took control of the government in the South. Diem inherited a nightmare. He was faced with an almost nonexistent government apparatus and a farce for an army and police force. He was an unpopular leader hated by the Buddhists in the South but respected by Ho since Diem was a nationalist. Ho expected the government in the South to fall of its own weight.[43] As Secretary of State John Foster Dulles put it: "Americans had underwritten Diem because we knew of no one better."[44] The Joint Chiefs opposed any support of Diem until he proved that he had a stable government, something that never occurred.

It now became the task of the United States to prop-up the Diem regime. In the years that followed the Geneva Accords, the U.S. increased aid to Ngo Dinh Diem while Ho infiltrated more troops into South Vietnam. In December 1960, Hanoi established a new organization in the South: the National Liberation Front (NLF). Its purpose was to unify the various groups opposing Diem.[45] At that time, the U.S. was involved in a major effort to train the South Vietnamese Army.

President Eisenhower embraced the regional domino theory and explained it with this metaphor: "You have a row of dominoes set up, you knock over the first one, and what will happen to the very last one is that it will go over very quickly."[46] In other words, if South Vietnam fell to the Communists, so would Southeast Asia. This would lead to a global bandwagon effect, with countries appeasing and joining the Soviet Union, since the U.S. could not be trusted.

Each president following Eisenhower embraced the domino theory, which was flawed. It assumed that all nations had the same culture, background, and aspirations, which they did not.

The Vietnam, Laos, and Cambodia dominoes would later fall, but others such as Thailand would not. With the defeat of the French, the conclusion was that the U.S. would need to shore up the Diem regime to prevent the South Vietnam domino from falling to the North.

The strategic and political importance of the Vietnamese highlands has always been recognized by the various parties in the conflicts in Vietnam. After the disastrous defeats of the French in the central highlands and at Dien Bien Phu, the Vietnamese politicians and generals both in the North and the South, as well as some Americans, began to realize that strategically, whoever controls the *Tây Nguyen* mountains holds the key to all of South Vietnam.

Though but 10% of the population of Vietnam, the Highlanders control of the key terrain of MR 1, 2 and part of MR 3 was untenable to the GVN. General Vo Nguyen Giap, the victor of Dien Bien Phu and one of the architects of the Communist strategy, declared, "To seize and control the highlands is to solve the whole problem of South Vietnam."

The Communist Party's Central Committee authorized a move to open armed struggle in the South during 1959. In most parts of the country Communist forces began this armed struggle—that is, serious guerrilla warfare as opposed to occasional assassinations—early in 1960. The results were dramatic. In some provinces there was a sudden and obvious collapse of government control over large areas of the countryside. Police, Civil Guard, and Self-Defense Force units became ineffective. Many of their arms fell into Communist hands. In some areas Communist leaders were rapidly establishing themselves as the real government. Vietnam was at war again, and the initiative seemed to be firmly in Communist hands.[47]

When the Republic of Vietnam was first established, the Diem government instituted a policy of assimilation, forcing the Montagnards to take Vietnamese names, took away their court systems and banned traditional dress, as well as other customs and traditions that had been respected by the French. The Montagnards, who had considerable autonomy under the French who inhabited the once-Crown Domain lands in the Central Highlands. After 1954, a large number of North Vietnamese refugees, as well as impoverished Vietnamese from coastal provinces in South Vietnam were resettled in Land Development Centers (LDCs) that were located on ancestral agricultural lands of the Montagnards without their permission or compensation. Likewise, Vietnamese migrants and planters also took the Montagnards' ancestral lands without permission or compensation, and loggers were indiscriminately logging and destroying the forests that they depended on for sustenance. Both the planters and the loggers paid taxes to the Viet Cong, and the Vietnamese in several of the LDCs, especially those from the coast, collaborated with or joined the Viet Cong.[48]

Michael D. Benge

The Bajaraka Autonomy Movement, 1957-1958

Early in 1957 Highlander students attending a lycee in Dalat established a committee to investigate the possibility of organizing a Highlander autonomy movement. Eventually, Y-Bham Enoul, a member of a prestigious Rhade family born in 1913 and educated at the Ecole Nationale d'Agriculture at Tuyen Quang in northern Vietnam, became this movement's leader. According to reports that reached the ears of CIA officers, he called a meeting of representatives of all the Highland tribes in May 1957. The same reports indicated that leaders representing most of the tribes attended a conference at the village of Buon Trap in Darlac Province to air their grievances, but a later CIA study was skeptical, positing that this may have been a meeting of Rhade representatives only.

By 1958, however, the autonomy movement was developing real momentum. Its leaders were largely missionary-educated Rhade, but other tribes were becoming involved. "The organizers went amongst the villages soliciting support for their movement." They established an organization claiming to have the backing of some 200,000 people and with the aim of defending the rights of Highlanders and establishing autonomy for them. In 1958 this movement started to call itself the Bajaraka autonomy movement—the name being an amalgamation and compression of the names of the tribes involved: Bahnar, Jarai, Rhade, and Koho [Kaho was the original tribe name changed to Koho, possibly by missionaries].[49]

J. P. Harris

While Diem followed a policy of assimilation in the south, Ho used a different approach in North Vietnam. Thousands of members of the hill tribes immigrated to South

Vietnam after the division of the country in 1954. To govern those who remained, North Vietnam set up the North Vietnam Autonomous Zone. This covered the highlands and included nearly a million multiethnic people. Local languages, administration, religions and cultures were respected. Autonomous rule was permitted, but the real power was wielded by a parallel party administration. Hanoi promoted ethnic Vietnamese emigration into the highlands as Diem had done.

Hanoi trained Vietnamese in the languages, customs, and cultures of the Montagnards and sent them south to help assure the security of the Ho Chi Minh Trail by infiltrating the Central Highlands. These North Vietnamese administrators often spoke flawless Montagnard languages and worked to win over popular support. In 1969, the North Vietnamese working in the south were astonished to find one of their own who had gone native.

> At first we thought he was ethnic minority. He was thin, and his skin was dark. He wore his gray hair twisted into a bun like an onion atop his head. His teeth were filed, and he had a large hole pierced through his earlobe. He wore no shirt but only a loincloth; he carried a small bag on his back and a machete in his hand. I was surprised that he spoke fluent Vietnamese; I soon learned that he was originally from Thai Binh and had joined the march to the south in 1946. He had worked as a cadre organizing the masses during the resistance war against France. When peace was restored in 1954, he received orders to stay in the south and continue his activities undercover. . . He filed his teeth and pierced his ears, so he could look like the ethnic minority people, thereby avoiding enemy suspicion and also facilitating his organizational work.[50]
>
> *Christopher Goscha*

Communist Aims and Activities, 1954-1960

At the end of the First Indochina War ethnic minority peoples migrated in both directions—north and south of the seventeenth parallel. According to CIA figures, about 10,000 Muongs (members of a northern hill tribe) went south at the time of the Geneva Accords. The same was true of 55,000 Nungs; these were not primitive tribesmen but members of a group that originated in

China and migrated to Vietnam in the seventeenth century. At the same time, the CIA estimated that approximately 10,000 indigenous people from the Central Highlands had regrouped in the north. . . .the Rhade, generally considered the most educated and politically sophisticated of the Highland tribes; these migrants included four of the five qualified Rhade doctors.[51]

The Communists proceeded to conduct propaganda meetings in each village they were trying to control. Cadres who spoke the tribal language of the area led these meetings, and they explained why the Communists sought to help the tribesmen against the Diem government—depicting the latter as oppressing virtually all its people, Vietnamese as well as Highlanders. . . .The Communists agreed to adhere to certain standards themselves. They would treat all those who abided by their rules fairly and justly. They would levy taxes but would not steal. They would not rape women or force their attentions on them. In general, they would observe strict discipline and not allow individual self-interest to get in the way of the common cause.[52]

J. P. Harris

Diem's Government, 1954-1958

From July 1954 onward, new Vietnamese regimes North and South were confronted with the problem of dealing with Highland ethnic minorities. It seems fair to say that the Communist regime in Hanoi had the easier task. Its Highland minorities were smaller in relation to the total population of North Vietnam, and the areas they inhabited would be less crucial strategically in the Second Indochina War than the Central Highlands. Although some of the Thai groups of northern Vietnam had sided with the French against the Viet Minh in the First Indochina War, in general, as a CIA analysis of Highland politics noted, "the Highland minorities of the north were more used to central authority and less likely to express their discontent through armed resistance than their counter-parts in the south."

As more than one CIA study noted, a policy of benevolent assimilation of Highlanders was not really practiced on the ground by Vietnamese government officials, soldiers, and settlers in 1954-1958:

There were numerous instances where government administrators and military forces treated the Highlanders with contempt and even with great brutality. The Highlanders were exploited by the military and by merchants [and] land was grabbed by settlers. There developed a deep sense of frustration among the Highlanders at not being able to do anything about the situation. Towns such as Ban Me Thuot and Pleiku doubled in size and the areas surrounding them were dotted with new [Vietnamese] villages and fields.[53]

J. P. Harris

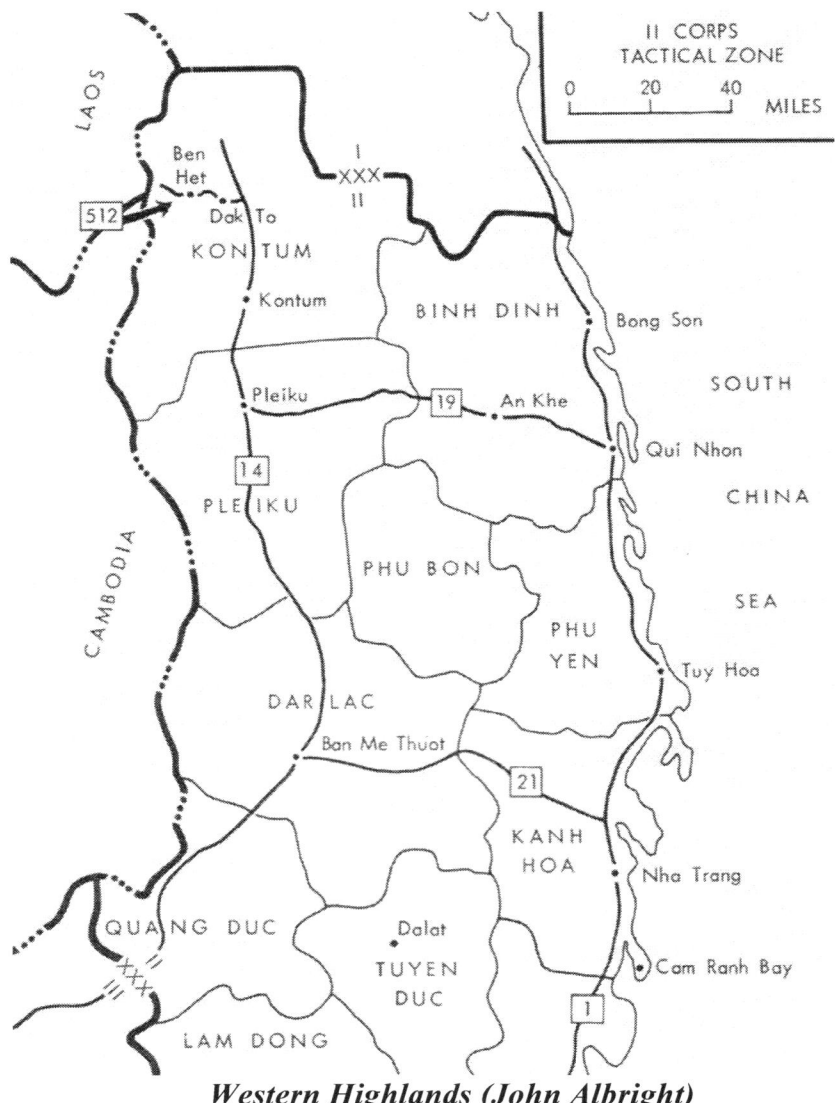

Western Highlands (John Albright)

The consequence of Diem's mismanagement in the Highlands was again demonstrated by his Highlander Resettlement Program.

Highlander Resettlement Program, 1958-1960

Starting in 1957, the Diem government policy was to resettle Montagnards in permanent villages near roads. This facilitated government control. By 1959 the program was close to collapse. There were several reasons for the failure of the program. Hanoi launched a campaign of antigovernment propaganda and assassination in the Highlands years earlier that was now effecting the resettlement program. The villagers were sullen and unhappy because the resettlement was involuntary and tribal traditions and religious beliefs had been ignored. As an example Montagnards were ordered to build their houses on the ground in the Vietnamese style, rather than on stilts, which was their custom.[54]

1960–The Year of the Rat

After our exhausting labor we'd go back to our camps and sing songs or perform plays. We sang all the time to keep our spirits up. We used to joke that you couldn't hear the bombs over our singing.[55]

Vu Thi Vinh on the Ho Chi Minh Trail

Heavy fighting occurred in October as ARVN units moved north to counter the VC offensive. As many as 1,000 VC troops became involved. The VC were defeated in a series of meeting engagements by elements of the 22nd ARVN Division.

Ho Chi Minh Trail

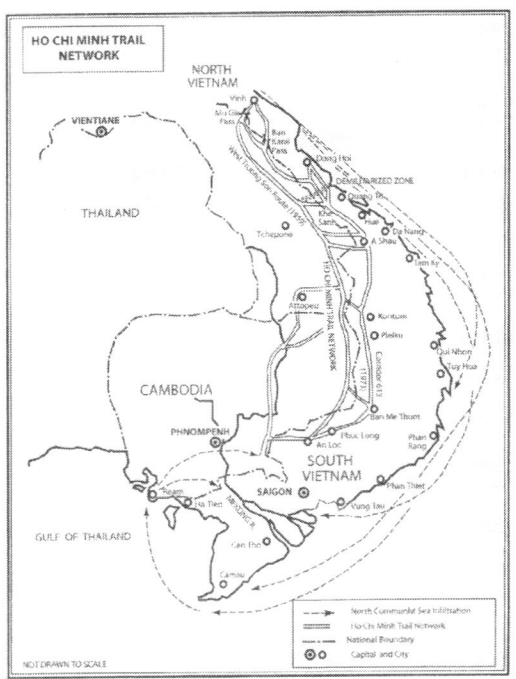

Ho Chi Minh Trail Network (Van Nguyen Duong).

During the Second Indochina War, North Vietnam relied upon the Ho Chi Minh Trail to move people, supplies, and equipment from North Vietnam to the South, The trail followed paths from the north along Vietnam's border with Laos and Cambodia. The North Vietnamese called it the Strategic Supply Route (Duong Truong Son) while the Americans named it Ho Chi Minh Trail after the North's leader. Parts of it had existed for centuries as primitive footpaths to facilitate trade. At the start of the war it was little more than a dirt path but it had been expanded to a paved highway including a fuel pipeline by the end of the war.

Vu Thi Vinh was a young girl who volunteered to work on the Ho Chi Minh Trail.

Most of the time we worked only at night because that's when the trucks and soldiers came and we needed to be ready to help if they got stuck. Usually we slept from about seven-thirty to eleven in the morning. Then we had lunch and took classes to continue our education. After that we slept again until four- thirty. Supper was at five o'clock and then we were off to work again. Of course, in emergency situations we worked day and night. If the trail blocked for just one hour there'd be a terrible traffic jam and that was an invitation to American bombers. Anytime bombs hit the trail, we had to rush and fill in the craters immediately.

After one bombing strike we discovered a big bomb lying unexploded in small stream next to a bridge. There was a danger that a truck passing over bridge might set it off so our leader selected a "dare to die" team to defuse the bomb. Everyone wanted to be on the team so we had to write a short essay to apply. The only safe way to defuse the bomb was to explode it, even though that meant destroying part of the bridge we'd built. But we managed to explode the bomb and repair the bridge before the trucks came that night.

Needless to say, life in the jungle was extremely hard. When we weren't supplied with rice we ate whatever we could find. We searched for crabs under rocks in the streams and occasionally we were lucky enough to come up with some cassava. Sometimes we had to scrape fungus and moss off rocks. "Aircraft `vegetables" we called them because they were the only edible things left after all the bombing. We were so hungry everything tasted good. The mountains were filled with red ginseng trees. We'd boil the leaves and stems and then throw them away and drink the broth. It was very sweet and nutritious. The Truong Son jungle gave us life.

After our exhausting labor we'd go back to our camps and sing songs or perform plays. We sang all the time to keep our spirits up. We used to joke that you couldn't hear the bombs over our singing.[56]

Vu Thi Vinh

1961–The Year of the Buffalo

"Any Rhade who had co-operated with the VC in any way was to be identified, re-educated to the government cause, and carefully observed. Amnesty would not be granted immediately."[57]

J. P. Harris

After Ngo Dinh Diem took over as president of South Vietnam in 1954, there were a few years of relative peace while Ho rearmed in the north and Diem cleaned out stay-behind enemies of his regime. Although he was from a Mandarin family, Diem saw himself as a revolutionary.[58] His regime had many problems, such as lack of popular support and his repression of the Buddhist majority, which did not trust him because he was a Catholic.

By the time President John F. Kennedy took office in January 1961, the Viet Cong in South Vietnam had already rebounded from a decimated, apparently moribund handful in the late 1950s to some 14,000 fighters. They waged a combination guerrilla war and campaign of terror and assassination, successfully targeting thousands of civil officials, government workers, and police officers. The new president commissioned a study in the spring of 1961, which concluded that South Vietnam had entered "the decisive phase in its battle for survival." Accordingly, on April 29, 1961, President Kennedy authorized an additional 100 MAAG [Military Assistance Advisory Group] advisors as well as the creation of a combat development and test center in South Vietnam. He also asked for increased economic aid. Less than two weeks later, on May 11, the president committed 400 U.S. Special Forces troops to raise and train a force of South Vietnamese "irregulars" in areas controlled by the Viet Cong, particularly along the border.

The Special Forces, an elite army organization trained in small unit tactics—guerrilla warfare— had been in existence since the U.S. Army created the Rangers in 1942. President Kennedy would give the soldiers a higher profile, new status, and a new item of uniform: the Green Beret. For their part, these "Green Berets" soon came to respect the skill, courage, and determination of the Viet Cong.[59]

Alan Axelrod

The U. S. Army Special Forces

President John F. Kennedy announced on 21 September 1961 a program to provide additional military and economic aid to Vietnam. The government of the United States was by this time deeply concerned over the insurgency in South Vietnam and the necessary steps were being taken to help the republic to deal with it.

On 21 September 1961 the 5th Special Forces Group, 1st Special Forces, which would eventually be charged with the conduct of all Special Forces operations in Vietnam, was activated at Fort Bragg. It was at this point, in the fall of 1961, that President Kennedy began to display particular interest in the Special Forces. His enthusiasm, based on his conviction that the Special Forces had great potential as a counterinsurgency force, led him to become a very powerful advocate for the development of the Special Forces program within the Army. President Kennedy himself made a visit to the Special Warfare Center in the fall of 1961 to review the program, and it was by his authorization that Special Forces troops were allowed to wear the distinctive headgear that became the symbol of the Special Forces, the Green Beret.

Up to 1961 the government of South Vietnam and the U.S. Mission in Saigon in dealing with the insurgency had placed primary emphasis on developing the regular military forces, which for the most part excluded the ethnic and religious minority groups. Under the sponsorship of the U.S. Mission in Saigon, however, several programs were initiated in late 1961 to broaden the counterinsurgency effort by developing the military potential of certain of these minority groups. Special Forces detachments were assigned to the U.S. Mission in Saigon to provide training and advisory assistance in the conduct of these programs, which eventually came to be known collectively as the Civilian Irregular Defense Group (CIDG) The development of paramilitary forces among the minority groups became the primary mission of the Special Forces in Vietnam.

Originally attention was concentrated on the Montagnards, who lived in the strategic Central Highlands. The first step was taken in October 1961 with the beginning of a project designed to prevent the Rhade tribesmen in Darlac Province from succumbing to Viet Cong control. Exploratory talks were held with Rhade leaders in Darlac to seek their participation in a village self-defense program. One Special Forces medical noncommissioned officer participated in that first effort.

Early in 1962 the government of the United States under President Kennedy began to set up the actual interdepartmental machinery for aiding South Vietnam. The Executive Branch, the Department of State, the Department of Defense, the Joint Chiefs of Staff, the United States Information Agency, the Agency for International Development, and the Central Intelligence Agency were all involved. Because of the nature of the growing conflict in Vietnam and because the Special Forces was designed for unconventional warfare, it was inevitable that the Special Forces would play a conspicuous role. It was also plain that the actions and suggestions of the various government agencies would heavily influence that role.

In 1961 a serious examination of the responsibility of the U.S. Army in the cold war had been instituted at the Command and General Staff College, Fort Leavenworth, Kansas. The strategy of "wars of liberation" as practiced by the Communists was analyzed in detail, lessons learned were reviewed, and a comprehensive assessment of U.S. Army capabilities was prepared to show the resources available to the United States for resisting insurgency. Doctrinal gaps were identified, mission statements amended, and training requirements defined.

The initial efforts of the United States to counter subversive insurgency in Vietnam quickly became a coordinated departmental endeavor at the highest national level. In addition to mustering the talent, technical ability, and equipment of the military, the government called on each department to nominate certain units and numbers of forces which it considered best prepared to deal with the peculiarities of countering insurgencies. The U.S. Army chose as its vanguard unit the Special Forces, whose highly trained group of combat specialists numbered at the time approximately 2,000 men.

An assessment of insurgent strategy, particularly as it was being practiced at the time in the Republic of Vietnam, indicated that good use could be made there of the U.S. Army Special Forces. The requirement for a unit that was combat-oriented, capable of performing with relative independence in the field, ruggedly trained for guerrilla operations, and geared for cooperation with the Vietnamese, was admirably met in the organization, training, equipment, and operational procedures of the U.S. Army Special Forces.

In November 1961 the first medical specialist troops of the Special Forces were employed in Vietnam in a project originally designed to provide assistance to the Montagnard tribes in the high-plateau country around Pleiku. Out of this modest beginning grew one of the most successful programs for using civilian forces ever devised by a military force, the Civilian Irregular Defense Group. Eventually the organization, development, and operation of the CIDG proved to be the chief work of the U.S. Special Forces in the Vietnam War.[60]

Francis J. Kelly

Initially the U. S. Army Special Forces Vietnam (Provisional) group was organized and was followed by the establishment of the 5th Special Group (Airborne) on 1 October 1964. The 5th Group headquarters was split with the Tactical Operations Center (TOC) in Saigon and the administrative and logistical support at Nha Trang until the headquarters was consolidated in Nha Trang on 10 September 1965.[61] The basic unit that ran camps was the A Team while these were grouped under B Teams and finally, each CTZ had a C Team controlling Special Forces units within it. For example the II CTZ had detachment C-2 located at Pleiku. By March 1965 when the first U. S. combat troops arrived, the total Special Forces strength in Vietnam was 1,465 people and these controlled 19,842 tribal riflemen.[62] In June 1965 the Special Forces mission statement was approved by MACV.

United States Army Special Forces Vietnam resources will be employed in missions which (1) exert constant, versatile, offensive pressure against the Viet Cong in areas where the ARVN is not present in strength, (2) will interdict Viet Cong movement across international boundaries, (3) will, by quick response, prevent VC takeover of a critical area, and (4) will assist in extending GVN control.[63]

Shelby L. Stanton

The mission statement makes no mention of intelligence collection a function commonly performed especially along the border. Also, it pits the Montagnards who had limited equipment and training against the VC who frequently outnumbered and out-gunned them. No mention is made of the NVA who at that time had started moving regular units into South Vietnam. Presumably the NVA would be dealt with by the ARVN and U. S. troops units that had just started to arrive at that time. The organizational structure of Special Forces in Vietnam evolved over time. At the top of the structure was the Special Forces Group located in Nha Trang with "C" teams below it.

> So C's finally emerged above B's, and consisted of a beret commander and some twenty-four officers and senior noncoms each. C's appeared in or near certain Vietnamese cities or towns, where it was harder for big Communist forces to get at them without taking heavy losses. Three to eight B teams eventually came to be under each C, and a good many B's developed.

> The workhorse B teams were scattered everywhere below as command and control units, and each was "over" its own batch of A's. The B's were also out there in the action, although some were in towns like Pleiku. B's lived the action of their A teams, and their commanders and men rode circuit to their A's. Majors commanded many of those B's. and the B team's style with its A's often reflected the kind of man commanding the B and the way his dozen or so berets operated.

> Four to twelve A teams were under each B commander, who thus held the reins differently. Some B commanders rode circuit constantly, and huddled with A's on everything. B's "controlled" all the little irregular armies out with each A. B's were in on how A's used those fighters on operations, and knew A team intelligence, logistics, how VC prisoners were handled, and more. Some B commanders flew in and stuck around while their A's fought off VC attacks.

> So some B team commanders held tight reins on their A teams, and others let them freewheel. One freewheeling B team

major, down near the Cambodian border in VC land, "covered" for his A's and let them do what they could. His area was a hot strip of jungle-covered border country, where his veteran A's had their hands full trying to survive. Other B's hovered over most moves made by A teams they had "out there."[64]

Gordon M. Patric

CIA Involvement with Counterinsurgency, 1961
The Genesis of the Rhade Project

The counterinsurgency effort in South Vietnam was influenced by factors outside the theater. Soon after John F. Kennedy took office in 1961 he encountered the Bay of Pigs fiasco, the failed attempt to invade Cuba. The CIA had the lead in organizing the abortive attempt and Kennedy wanted to make sure that it did not occur again. At the same time, he was concerned over the possibility of a Communist takeover of Indochina. The result was his National Security Action Memorandum 52, dated 11 May 1961. In it he authorized a "program for covert action to be carried out by the Central Intelligence Agency which would precede and remain in force." At the same time controls would be put in place that would assure that the Defense Department would take over if the program escalated to a military conflict.

In the fall of 1961 the CIA decided to introduce a counterinsurgency effort in South Vietnam and started casting about looking for initiatives. A young International Voluntary Service worker based in Darlac Province, David A. Nuttle, was concerned about the possibility that the Rhade might fall under Communist domination. He persuaded Colonel Gilbert Layton, commander of the CIA's Military Operations Section to launch a program and the Buon Enao Experiment was born.[65]

The Buon Enao Experiment

The village defense experiment started by David A. Nuttle was conducted in late 1961 in Darlac province of the

Central Highlands. The Montagnard village of Buon Enao northeast of Ban Me Thuot was selected for this experiment that was devised by the CIA. It was designed to counter expanding VC influence in villages by training the villagers to defend their homes. The Buon Enao Experiment became the most successful counterinsurgency program carried out by the U. S. in Vietnam.

The villagers would be armed and trained while a local reaction force would be established to come to the aid of the village if it were attacked. This would become known as the CIDG. The majority of the villages were inhabited by Montagnards and the Special Forces was enlisted to execute the program. The South Vietnamese Special Forces (LLDB - Lac Luong Dac Biet) provided the camp leadership while the SF was the LLDB advisors.[66] Once the CIDG Program was successfully established in a village, it served as a training base for surrounding villages. This "ink blot" approach assured expanding government control in the region. It was similar to the Strategic Hamlet Program but differed in several ways. Villagers were not forced from their homes to a central hamlet and since the program was funded by the CIA and executed by the U. S. Army, Saigon corruption was eliminated or at least minimized.[67]

A major problem needed to be resolved before any defense program could be established. The village elders knew that the VC would retaliate if they were seen cooperating with the government. In effect they would be seen as taking sides and could expect VC attack.

The village elders were tough negotiators when the CIA started setting up the program. They would resist the Communists, but only on certain conditions. First, all attacks on Rhade and Jarai villages by South Vietnamese forces must cease. Second, any Rhade "who had been forced to train with or support the VC would be given an amnesty upon declaring allegiance" to the government. Third, Rhade medical, educational, and agricultural assistance would be provided. Colonel Trong, commander of the ARVN 23d Division accepted these terms for the South Vietnamese government with a caveat "Any Rhade who had co-operated with the VC in any way was to be identified, re-educated to the government cause, and carefully observed. Amnesty would not be granted immediately." This was agreed by all and a water buffalo was killed in preparation for a celebration in the traditional Rhade manner with drums, a feast, and plenty of rice wine.[68]

Preparing for a Feast (Olen C. Phipps, Jr.).

The villagers agreed to take certain steps to show their support for the government and their willingness to cooperate. They would build a fence to enclose Buon Enao as a protection and as a visible sign to others that they had chosen to participate in the new program. They would also dig shelters within the village where women and children could take refuge in case of an attack; construct housing for a training center and for a dispensary to handle the promised medical aid; and establish an intelligence system to control movement into the village and provide early warning of attack.

In the second week of December when these tasks had been completed, the Buon Enao villagers, armed with crossbows and spears, publicly pledged that no Viet Cong would enter their village or receive assistance of any kind. At the same time fifty volunteers from a nearby village were brought in and began training as a local security or strike force to protect Buon Enao and the immediate area. With the security of Buon Enao established, permission was obtained from the Darlac Province chief to extend the program to forty other Rhade villages within a radius of ten to fifteen kilometers of Buon Enao. The chiefs and subchiefs of these villages went to Buon Enao for training in village defense. They too were told that they must build fences around their respective villages and declare their willingness to support the government of the Republic of Vietnam.[69]

Francis J. Kelly

The Advisors

They [ARVN] fought because they had to, while their enemies, the VC and the North Vietnamese regulars, fought with a burning desire, fueled by nationalism, to unite their country and rid it of foreign influence.[70]

John C. Loving, Advisor

Military Assistance Command, Vietnam Crest (Author's Collection).

While the Special Forces effort was expanding, U. S. advisors were also increasing support to the RVNAF. The advisors' mission statement was broad:

> To represent the United States of America in South Vietnam; to perform assigned and implied duties in such a way as to further the best interest of the United States of America; to advise and assist officials of the Government and/or members of the Armed Forces of South Vietnam in performance of their duties and in the defense of this Country against communism; and to conduct one's self personally in such a way as to bring respect for and credit to the Armed Forces of the United States of America.[71]
>
> ***Martin J. Dockery***

The Military Assistance Command, Vietnam (MACV)

advisor structure paralleled that of the South Vietnam armed forces. Advisors were assigned to MACV Headquarters in Saigon and field Advisory Teams were at all levels down to the South Vietnamese district level.

The command and staff advisers at MACV headquarters and the U.S. Embassy in Saigon were among the most important and the most prominent. They included the MACV commander, the U.S. ambassador, and at least a portion of the senior officers and executives in their subordinate staff sections and offices. In general, the counterparts of these command and staff advisers were the corresponding national-level Vietnamese leaders. More numerous but less prominent were the military field advisers that permeated almost every echelon of the South Vietnamese Army, Navy, Marine Corps, and Air Force. They constituted the heart of the military advisory system and included the U.S. Army advisory teams assigned to the South Vietnamese corps, divisions, regiments, and battalions; those teams assigned to provinces and districts; those to combat support organizations, schools, and training centers; the separate U.S. Naval and Air Force Advisory Groups; and the bulk of the U.S. Army Special Forces teams. Supplementing the work of these advisory elements were special U.S. military training teams that visited South Vietnam on a temporary basis and a smaller civilian field advisory network that had quasi-military responsibilities.

The MACV staff had a variety of advisory-related duties. Advisory cells within each of the major staff sections closely monitored the activities of their Joint General Staff counterparts, and several MACV offices were devoted entirely to the advisory mission. . . . The network included the U.S. Army and Marine Corps tactical teams, those assigned to Vietnamese province and district commands, and those assigned to logistical support units and training camps. The number of U.S. military personnel concerned with advisory duties in the field totaled almost 8,250 by the end of 1965.

Battalion and district detachments consisted of 5 men each, and province teams were 20 strong (not counting representatives from nonmilitary U.S. agencies); regimental teams were small, a mere 3; and division and corps teams averaged 52 and 143, respectively, with most members providing administrative support to a smaller number of key staff advisers. Although personnel shortages sometimes reduced the actual strength of the advisory teams by as much as 50 percent, their authorized strength remained fixed.

Far more important than the structure of the advisory system was its basic philosophy, which emphasized technical proficiency and personal relationships. Originally, the United States had stationed military advisers in Vietnam to ensure that equipment provided to France was maintained properly and used for the purpose intended. With the departure of the French, the advisers extended their work throughout the South Vietnamese armed forces—first to the staffs, training centers, and schools, and then to the tactical units and military area commands. During this transition the advisory system began to take on its unique characteristics. Its most distinguishing trait was its extreme decentralization. Assistance and guidance from MACV itself was minimal. The advisory chain of command became primarily administrative, an apparatus for placing and maintaining the individual adviser within the South Vietnamese military structure. Once installed, the field adviser—relying on his American military experience and know-how—faced the challenge of not only recommending solutions to his counterpart's tactical, operational, and administrative problems but also persuading him to implement those solutions. . . .

The role of the American tactical advisers had expanded far beyond that of military advice to their counterparts. They served as combat air support coordinators, directing American fixed- and rotary-wing support in the field. This responsibility had given them greater control over battlefield firepower and transport, and, as a by-product, more influence over Vietnamese plans and operations. The growth of this influence, however, was concomitant with the advisers receiving tactical radios (AN/PRC-10s) that enabled them to communicate directly with supporting aircraft (equipped with complementary AN/ARC-44 sets). The continued expansion of combat operations and the growing number of American support units available severely overextended the advisory communications system, and it was barely able to support the tempo of combat activity. Nevertheless, the provision of air support was one of the chief responsibilities of the tactical advisers.

The field advisers also had a task, of gauging the performance of the South Vietnamese armed forces and thereby providing MACV with a rough idea of how the war was progressing. Because of the small size of the field detachments, their internal staff and administrative capabilities were weak. But face-to-face talks with superiors became less frequent and written reporting requirements of the advisory teams more demanding. As the war grew in size and complexity, so did the paper work demands on individual advisers, and some were preparing as many as forty reports every month. Two became major bellwethers of the war effort: the senior adviser monthly evaluation (SAME) report, which forced advisers to rate each South Vietnamese unit being advised; and the province monthly evaluation report, prepared jointly by the MACV sector senior adviser and the USAID [U.S. Agency for International Development] province representatives. Higher military commands all the way up to Washington scrutinized both, and an adviser's career often seemed to depend on the content and acceptability of these reports.

The American troop buildup in 1965 forced other changes in the lives of the field advisers. Almost overnight, the corps, division, and province advisory teams began furnishing liaison officers to U.S. units operating in the territorial jurisdiction of the Vietnamese commands that they advised. In addition, they found it necessary to establish 24-hour operations centers similar to those in U.S. troop units so that tactical information could be exchanged on a moment's notice. Advisers at all levels also found themselves forced to spend more time addressing such matters as law enforcement, morale and recreation, post exchanges, living facilities, and press and community relations in response to policies and procedures established by American commanders. As the size of the U.S. ground commitment increased, these requirements increased proportionately, and, without additional personnel, the field detachments had to perform these tasks at the expense of their normal advisory duties. . . .

The task of the ground-level adviser was extraordinarily difficult. He had to be a jack-of-all-trades, not only advising but also solving his own supply and administrative problems, often living on the local economy and training his own subordinates as best he could. Most were unfamiliar with their strange Asian allies and the type of war they were supposed to be fighting. Their morale was high but their work frustrating. With only sporadic contact with the echelons above them, they often had only their own individual resources to guide them in their unusual mission.[72]

Jeffrey J. Clarke

The Americans created ARVN in their own image as much as possible. The organizational structure, equipment, ranks, supply system, and personnel system were almost exact copies of those in the US Army. Starting with the smallest element, ARVN had infantry platoons of about 30-40 men and infantry companies of 150-200 men in four platoons and a headquarters element. There were three or four companies in a battalion, and three or four battalions in a regiment. The configuration varied by division, and the 23rd ARVN Division had three companies per battalion and four battalions per regiment.

The ARVN artillery batteries, armor companies, and armored cavalry troops had fewer men than similar infantry units, but they were also organized in battalions—or squadrons for the cavalry. An ARVN infantry division also had an artillery regiment consisting of three artillery battalions with 105-mm howitzers. Each infantry regiment had two 81-mm mortars, and each infantry company had two 60-mm mortars. ARVN was plagued by desertions, so most units had fewer men present for duty than was authorized.

The South Vietnamese also had the Airborne Division and Ranger battalions in Ranger groups. They were moved around the country like chess pieces to block enemy threats or to plug holes in the defenses. In addition, Border Ranger battalions were manning static bases along the border. Most of the troops in Border Ranger battalions were from local ethnic groups, like the Montagnards, but most of their officers were Vietnamese. The Border Rangers did not receive the same training as the regular Ranger battalions, and they were not moved around the country to deal with military emergencies.

Regional Forces (RFs), or "Ruffs," were recruited in each province. The RFs were organized like ARVN units and were under the command of the province chiefs, most of whom were ARVN officers. They could be deployed anywhere in their home province but were seldom sent to other provinces. They were as well armed—including their own artillery—and almost as well trained as the ARVN units. Popular Forces (PFs), or "Puffs," were also recruited in each village. These forces had the same small arms as ARVN or the RF, but they stayed near their homes and guarded local bridges, government buildings, and their own villages.[73]

Thomas P. McKenna

At the grass-roots level RF/PF defense units grew toward the end of the war to over 250,000 troops.

Lieutenant John Loving was assigned as an advisor to Regional Forces in MR 3. He summarized the environment and his duties.

Ben Cau was located in an area of Vietnam called the "Angel's Wing" because it stuck out into Cambodia, looking like the wing of an angel on the map. The village was very close to the Cambodian border in an area that was notorious as a VC stronghold. The infamous Ho Chi Minh Trail, which originated in North Vietnam and ran south through Laos and Cambodia, actually terminated in this area of Tay Ninh Province. Most of the men, material, and supplies that fueled the Vietcong insurgency came down this trail from the north to the south.

Ben Cau was actually made up of three small villages, or hamlets, with the seat of control, group headquarters, in the middle hamlet next to the bridge. The headquarters building was a crude, wooden structure with a tin roof, which, I noted from the air, was full of holes caused by mortar rounds or rockets. The other two villages also had a South Vietnamese company assigned to each for security. This was an effective method of securing the rural areas against the activities of the VC in the countryside, working very well as a defense against small VC forces and occasional attacks from North Vietnamese Army units passing through the area. The government troops were called Regional Forces but were manned with soldiers from all over, especially Saigon. Mobile Advisory Team 66 was assigned with the Regional Forces to provide support and advice. The support, I would discover, amounted mostly to calling in firepower from artillery and helicopter gunships, as well as bringing in medical helicopters called "dust-offs" or "medevacs" to evacuate the wounded. Another, unofficial support activity was helping the Vietnamese troops obtain certain supplies and munitions. At first, the advisory function seemed a bit presumptuous to me since our counterpart Vietnamese officers had generally been fighting for years and had more experience with war than I would ever have. However, I would soon learn that the thing that we could never give our counterparts was the will to fight. They fought because they had to, while their enemies, the VC and the North Vietnamese regulars, fought with a burning desire, fueled by nationalism, to unite their country and rid it of foreign influence.[74]

John C. Loving

The Year of the Buffalo Ends

In 1960 and 1961, over large parts of South Vietnam, the initiative was in Communist hands. By the end of 1961, the Diem regime faced an intense crisis. By November 1961, the US embassy reckoned there were 20,000 "hard-core" Communist troops in Vietnam south of the seventeenth parallel, roughly double the Communist strength at the same time the previous year.[75]

Of the major Highland provinces, Darlac was making the greatest economic progress, and of all the Highland tribes, the Rhade had the greatest number of well-educated people, some of them holding "positions of some importance in [its] administration."[76]

J. P. Harris

1962–The Year of the Tiger

"Why should I die to protect a government rifle?"
Strategic Hamlet Villager

The Strategic Hamlet Program like its predecessor, the Rural Community Development Program, sought to move rural peasants into protected villages where they would be provided with protection, economic support and aid by the government. In this way, their ties to the RVN government would be strengthened and exploitation by the VC would be denied.

By 1962 the Diem regime was losing the war to the VC and the U. S. suggested that a program was needed to deny access of the rural population to the VC. Diem endorsed the concept in April 1962. Fortified villages would be established including a self-defense force of 75-100 people, an identity card system for the villagers, curfews, free fire zones outside of the hamlet and the identification of villagers who were VC. ARVN reaction forces would be available on-call to aid a hamlet if it were attacked.

Diem's implementation of the Strategic Hamlet Program assured its failure. He started in area west of Saigon that was infested with VC rather than a more pacified area where lessens could be learned and the program improved. Villagers were rounded up at gunpoint and moved to the hamlet. After they left, some villages were burned so that inhabitants could not return. Since they had close ties to these villages where their ancestors were buried, they were outraged by the forced move. Poor screening of the villagers before they were issued identity cards allowed VC to receive cards and slip away with cards that would give them access elsewhere. In some cases, weapons were issued to the villagers, but this proved to be a weapons cache for the VC who could walk in and seize the weapons, unopposed. The ARVN reaction force could seldom relieve a hamlet under attack. The speed of implementation of the program was astonishing. The Pentagon Papers revealed that by September 1962, 4.3 million people were housed in 3,225 completed hamlets with 2,000 more under construction.[77] Establishing protection for this number of hamlets in that short amount of time would be impossible. Part of the reason for the rush may have been Saigon corruption. The U. S. provided $21 per family for people relocated. This money often lined the pockets of members of Diem's regime and the peasants received no benefit. The failure of the program was insured since Diem's brother, Nhu, put Colonel Pham Ngoc Thao in charge of the program. Thao was, in fact, a Communist double agent. He placed the hamlets in VC strongholds which insured that many of the peasants who occupied the hamlets were VC. The Strategic Hamlet Program ended when Diem and Nhu were killed in the RVN coup of November 1963.[78]

At the same time as the Strategic Hamlet Program was failing, the Buon Enao Experiment had succeeded. The difference was that the Strategic Hamlet Program forced the relocation of the inhabitants from their homes to fortified villages while the Buon Enao Experiment and the CIDG Program that followed simply helped the Highlanders defend their villages.[79]

Civilian Irregular Defense Group Program

Twenty-six Special Forces A Teams were in Vietnam by November 1962. In addition to the CIDG mission, they also accomplished border surveillance and scouting roles. The effectiveness of the program was limited by the six-month rotation of individuals in and out of South Vietnam with no guarantee that a soldier would return to the same area on return tours. The role of Special Forces was gradually shifting from protection of the population to finding and killing the enemy. Winning the allegiance of the population became secondary. Between 1 November 1962 and 1 July 1963 a total of 40 CIDG camps were opened and eight were closed. This rapid expansion did not allow time to prepare the people and establish security. The emphasis was on speed. Perhaps the most important failure was the focus on working through province and district chiefs rather than tribal leaders.[80]

In 1962 as the CIDG was expanding the first SF deaths occurred near Da Nang when the VC attacked and overran a Republican Youth group that was escorted by four SF trainers. Two of the SF soldiers were wounded and later executed by the VC because they could not keep up during the VC withdrawal.[81]

Operation Switchback

In spite of problems, by 1962 the CIDG Program was widely successful and it was time for the CIA to get on with their primary intelligence mission and hand over the program to the U. S. Army Special Forces. A part of the rational for the hand-over was CIA involvement in the Bay of Pigs fiasco. NASM #57 that followed the Bay of Pigs provided that "whenever a secret paramilitary operation becomes so large and overt that the military contribution, in terms of manpower and equipment, exceeded the resources contributed by the CIA, the operation should be turned over to the Department of Defense." CIA lacked manpower resources to accomplish the program and needed additional Special Forces teams. A transfer of the CIDG program from the CIA to MACV and the Special Forces would help achieve success of the CIDG Program. *Operation Switchback* accomplished that transfer.[82]

The Year of the Tiger Ends

While the U.S. was sending more advisors, the Viet Cong was also expanding. By the end of 1962, the U.S. had 11,300 people in South Vietnam.[83] They were advisors to the South Vietnamese.

Although the Communists were clearly experiencing difficulties throughout the Republic of Vietnam's 2d Tactical Zone, and especially in the Central Highlands, no one suggested that they were anywhere near final defeat. Indeed, "1962 was characterized by a steady increase in Viet Cong activity during the early part of the year and into the rainy season." "Whereas II Corps' G-2 (intelligence) staff had estimated 10,824 armed Communist insurgents in the area on 1 January 1962, its estimate for the same zone at the end of the year was 18,113. The larger year-end figure may have been as attributable to an increased volume of intelligence reports as to an actual increase in Communist military manpower, but it was hardly indicative of an enemy on the ropes.[84]

J. P. Harris

1963–The Year of the Cat

The way many Jarai corpses lay in their tents made the berets think they had been killed the instant they awoke. It looked like a typical Communist lesson to Jarai or any other tribesmen "foolish enough" to lash up with berets.[85]

Gordon Patric

It appeared that the year 1963 would show the turning point in the war in defeating Communist forces, thanks at least in part to increasing U. S. support of the war. Any optimism was easily overturned by early South Vietnamese defeats and assassinations that would occur late in the year.

Ap Bac

The officers of the Seventh Infantry Division who performed so ignominiously at Ap Bac—[and] were later decorated by Diem, for they seized the Viet Cong radio transmitter that afternoon—had been chosen by Diem for their loyalty to him, for coup insurance, not courage or proficiency in war.[86]

Deborah Shapley

David Halberstam was a journalist in Saigon during the early years of the Vietnam War. His book, The *Making of a Quagmire*, was published in 1964, before many of the significant events of the war had occurred. Halberstam covered the battle of Ap Bac, January 2, 1963. Lieutenant Colonel John Paul Vann was advisor to the South Vietnamese 7th Division. A force of 2,500 members of Republic of Vietnam Armed Forces (RVNAF), supported by U.S. helicopters, ARVN armored personnel carriers (APCs), and advisors were defeated by three hundred Viet Cong. As the ARVN force moved in on the VC, the VC opened fire. One VC leaped up and tossed a grenade at the advancing APCs, which did no harm but encouraged other VC to do the same.[87] This stopped the ARVN advance. Nothing could persuade the ARVN officers to move forward. The

ARVN under Ngo Dinh Diem, the South Vietnamese president, were accustomed to avoiding combat and faking operations. The battle was a disastrous defeat, and it demonstrated that the war was rapidly being lost, something that few in the Kennedy administration wanted to hear. After briefings and efforts to get official recognition of the problem without success, John Paul Vann went public about the situation in discussions with David Halberstam and reporter Neil Sheehan. It made news in the States. Halberstam received the Pulitzer Prize for reporting after he returned to the U.S. in December 1963.

Ap Bac was a turning point in the war. Until then, it had been a war on the cheap for the Kennedy administration. U.S. aid and advisors were sent, but the war was well down on Kennedy's list of priorities and received little press coverage. Earlier, Kennedy had decided to let Robert McNamara, the secretary of defense, "handle the war." This was not working. McNamara knew nothing about Ap Bac until he read about it in the New York Times (Halberstam's article). Now, people, Vann and others, were publicly stating the war was being lost. "New York Times … headline noted that five helicopters had been downed and another nine hit. The subhead was uncompromising: 'Defeat Worst Since Buildup Began—Three Americans are Killed in Vietnam.'"[88]

At first the U.S. military shrugged off the results of Ap Bac. General Paul D. Harkins, MACV commander, called the Viet Cong "those raggedy-ass little bastards."[89] In a comment worthy of Diem, Admiral Felt, CINCPAC, stated: "The Viet Cong left the battlefield, didn't they?" It was apparent to Kennedy that the military (and perhaps McNamara as well) had become detached from reality: General Harkins was still claiming victory. "Yes, I consider it a victory. We took the objective. We've got 'em on the run." What Harkins did not say was that the ARVN occupied Ap Bac two days after the victorious Viet Cong had conducted an orderly withdrawal.[90]

Kennedy had always liked and trusted journalists. He told

his friend in the press corps, Charles Bartlett: "We don't have a prayer of staying in Vietnam. Those people hate us. They are going to throw our asses out of there at almost any point. But I can't give up a piece of territory like that to the Communists and then get the people to reelect me [in 1964]." To his aide, Kenny O'Donnell: "If I tried to pull out completely now from Vietnam we would have another Joe McCarthy red scare on our hands, but I can do it after I'm reelected. So we better make damn sure that I am reelected."[91] Kennedy was getting input from many sources after Ap Bac. While the military argued for more advisors, helicopters, weapons, and generals, the Harriman group argued against a purely military solution. Nation-building and civic action programs were the answer: "What was needed was a consuming motive to lead South Vietnamese to fight for Saigon. Why, for example, should peasants die for a government which, when it recovered territory from the Viet Cong, helped the landowners collect back rent?" In the end, Kennedy settled for a modest increase in the number of advisors while he waited for his second term, which would never arrive.[92]

The era of charm and easy deceit by the U.S. government was coming to an end. In the long term this may have been one of the most significant outcomes of Ap Bac. It started a trend in the press and later in the entire nation that government could not be trusted to tell the truth: a fact that subsequent events would prove correct. Newspapers were now pressing for answers and MACV continued to blame correspondents for bad press. If there was a time for the U.S. to abandon Diem and leave Vietnam it was now. Diem's actions after Ap Bac further condemned him and his regime. Journalist Deborah Shapley explained what had happened.

> The officers of the Seventh Infantry Division who performed so ignominiously at Ap Bac—[and] were later decorated by Diem, for they seized the Viet Cong radio transmitter that afternoon—had been chosen by Diem for their loyalty to him,

for coup insurance, not courage or proficiency in war. Neil Sheehan, the young UPI reporter in Saigon at that time [Sheehan would later write a history of the Vietnam War and John Paul Vann], would later learn that Diem had promulgated a secret order to his trusted officers the previous fall: they were not to take casualties on their own side. Casualties would make army service unpopular, and Diem needed a loyal army so that his family could stay in power.[93]

Deborah Shapley

Stanley Karnow's history of the war was published in 1983. It won the Pulitzer Prize and was the basis for the public television series Vietnam: A Television History. Karnow served as chief correspondent for the series. He claimed that he had no cause to plead in writing this book,[94] but he had biases that become apparent in reading his history. He demonstrated that the U.S. made every mistake possible in fighting this war; he said that Ho Chi Minh was a nationalist who should be admired and the Nixon administration was self-serving (this last may be due to the fact that Nixon had Karnow on his "enemies" list).[95] In 1959 Karnow wrote the dispatches on the first U.S. deaths in Vietnam.[96] "The outcome at Ap Bac aggravated the friction then growing between the American government and the news media. Neither Kennedy nor his successors would impose censorship, which would have required them to acknowledge that a real war was being waged. Instead, they wanted journalists to cooperate by accentuating the positive."[97]

That did not happen. Correspondents simply told the truth, with their own twist, which is their privilege. Just after the Ap Bac battle, when Peter Arnett of the Associated Press asked him a tough question, Admiral Felt shot back: "Get on the team."[98] Sheehan's coverage of the battle of Ap Bac is quite lengthy, possibly because of Vann's involvement. Vann was in and out of Vietnam a number of times before he was killed in a helicopter crash in 1972. Sheehan's thesis is that Vietnam was a wrongful war, and he uses military reports to prove his point. Sheehan quotes a story that made the rounds after Ap Bac. "A Viet Cong porter spends two and one half months toting three mortar shells down the mountain and rain forest tracks of the Ho Chi Minh Trail. He finally reaches a battle and hands them to a mortar man, who fires them off faster than the porter can count and says: 'Now go back and get three more.'"[99] Sheehan always captured humor, and this makes his history very readable. Francois Sully (a correspondent for Newsweek) clashed with U.S. Ambassador Nolting over the Hamlet program. The Strategic Hamlet Program was designed to concentrate rural populations into camps, where they could be isolated from the Viet Cong. The problems were that it uprooted the rural populations from their traditional lands where their ancestors were buried, and there was no way of knowing how many of the people in the camps were VC.[100] Nolting asked, "Why, Monsieur Sully, do you always see the hole in the doughnut?" Sully replied "Because, Monsieur l'Ambassadeur, there is a hole in the doughnut."[101] To the relief of Nolting, Diem expelled Sully.[102]

The result of the Ap Bac disaster was changes by Kennedy, including the removal[103] of General Harkins and his subsequent retirement. It appears that Harkins and Admiral Felt were the only U.S. persons of any rank who believed that the South Vietnamese had won a victory at Ap Bac. Harkins was the subject of ridicule in the army. He was called "General Blimp" because of his efforts to inflate ARVN successes. After Harkins returned to the U.S., a common phrase in the army upon screwing up was "I just pulled a Harkins."[104] Harkins was not without defenders. Author Mark Moyar described Harkin's as a good "technical coach."[105] Unfortunately what was needed was honesty and leadership, not technical coaching.

Author Mark Moyar disagrees with the consensus of the Ap Bac battle. His thesis concludes that John Paul Vann misled the media and the ARVN loss was caused by bad terrain.

The government's attack on Ap Bac constituted a tactical failure, for government forces did not annihilate the Viet Cong and they suffered heavy losses despite having many more troops and far better weaponry. On the other hand, Ap Bac was a defeat for the Viet Cong in a strategic sense. At the beginning of 1963, the government's regular forces outnumbered the Viet Cong's regulars by approximately ten to one, yet the ratio of government to Viet Cong casualties at Ap Bac was no higher than two to one, so the Viet Cong lost a much higher portion of their total armed strength. The government's casualties at Ap Bac amounted to only a few hundredths of one percent of total strength.

Soon after the battle ended, Colonel Vann gave Sheehan, Halberstam, and other reporters a highly distorted version of the events, in which all of the day's failures were the fault of the South Vietnamese. "It was a miserable damn performance," Vann told the reporters, "just like it always is. These people won't listen. They make the same goddamn mistakes over and over again in the same way." Vann sought to expose South Vietnamese flaws as a means of pressuring the South Vietnamese into accepting the changes he favored. He was also trying to escape responsibility for the day's unpleasant results by putting all of the blame on his South Vietnamese counterparts, whom he especially resented for failing to overcome the difficulties created by his mistakes. The journalists gobbled it up. Sheehan, for example, wrote that American advisers faulted the South Vietnamese commanders for a "lack of aggressiveness," and the Americans were "disappointed — and angered — that the South Vietnamese troops should fail one of their biggest tests after more than a year of training." The South Vietnamese inaction at Ap Bac, Vann went on to tell the reporters, was the result of serious defects in the Diem government. "The advisers feel that there is still too much political interference in the Vietnamese army and that promotion too often depends on political loyalty rather than military ability," wrote Halberstam in the *New York Times.* "Some commanders are said to feel that they will not be promoted and may lose command if they suffer too many casualties."

Vann neglected to tell the young journalists the many details of the battle that reflected positively on South Vietnamese forces or reflected negatively on him and other Americans. The newsmen's stories did not state that the American advisers had expected the enemy to field a much smaller force, or that they had assumed the enemy would flee once attacked as in the past. Nowhere was it written that the Americans had landed the 7th Division's reserve company much too close to the tree line based on Vann's faulty assessments, or that Vann had concentrated the government's forces at a landing zone that was a most inauspicious point for launching attacks, or that design defects had consigned the machine gunners on the M-113 s to death. The correspondents largely overlooked the Communists' enormous defensive advantages and the numerous and costly government attacks that did take place. They did not write that the Vietnamese armored unit had been following procedures learned from the Americans when it attacked piecemeal and when it refused to drive into the middle of the enemy position, and in fact they wrote the opposite. Nor did they mention that a reputedly hard-charging American adviser, Scanlon, had called off an infantry attack across the rice paddies because he considered it to be suicidal, or that the 8th Airborne Battalion had been ordered to spearhead a concerted attack before nightfall but had been prevented from accomplishing this mission because one person's inability to adjust the drop location properly had landed them in the wrong place. . . The Battle of Ap Bac was, like its most famous participant, not what it first appeared to the outside world. Far from being the "golden opportunity" for the South Vietnamese forces that Halberstam was to call it in *The Making of a Quagmire,* the battle was a golden opportunity for the Viet Cong, as they entered the battle with tremendous advantages, thanks to the terrain. The South Vietnamese forces did not perform well at Ap Bac, but neither did they display gross ineptitude or cowardice. Most of their troubles could be traced to the terrain, to the prowess of crack Viet Cong troops, or to Clausewitzian friction —the inevitable mishaps that make easy tasks difficult in war. Colonel John Paul Vann committed the most grievous error of the battle by landing the reserve company too close to the western edge of the Viet Cong's defensive positions, which he mistakenly believed to be free of enemy forces. Vann succeeded in misleading the American press corps, and hence the world, about the events at Ap Bac by exaggerating the faults of the South Vietnamese and hiding his own. The mischaracterization of Ap Bac as the epitome of the Diem government's incompetence would not take root so quickly, since contrary evidence abounded at the time. The rise of that misinterpretation, like that of many other denigrations of the Diem regime, would have to await the overthrow of the Diem government.[106]

Mark Moyar

The battle of Ap Bac was a decisive event. The defeat was so bad that the ARVN left their dead and wounded behind and fled in panic. General Robert York, R&D Field Unit, Vietnam, later visited Ap Bac and found that the ARVN dead still littered the battlefield. U.S. advisors loaded about twenty ARVN dead on a vehicle and departed. General York was the only U.S. general who visited Ap Bac after the battle.[107] It got worse. When Harkins and Diem trumpeted victory, the Viet Cong commander challenged the ARVN to a rematch and returned to Ap Bac with his battalion. The ARVN took no action on the VC challenge.[108]

ARVN Pressure, January—June 1963

In the first half of 1963 ARVN forces were involved in offensive operations that failed to produce any significant gains but did keep the VC and NVA off-balance through destruction of supply bases and disruption of enemy planning. Hanoi's history of the war noted.

> As 1963 began, the enemy strove to finish the network of strategic hamlets in the areas they controlled while at the same time they massed their forces to launch a large number of operations striking deep into our base areas to force us to defend against them in order to give them time to carry out their plan to move people into strategic hamlets. The enemy doubled both the number and the size of his operations as compared with those he conducted during 1962. During the first six months of 1963 the enemy conducted 109 sweep operations ranging in size from three to ten battalions each.[109]

The Turnover of Buon Enao, Spring 1963

Two concepts were established for the transfer of camps to the South Vietnamese. Turnover meant that authority and responsibility for the camp were transferred to the ARVN. The CIDG forces retained their CIDG status. Turnover to the province control was accomplished when the area was considered to be secure. Conversion meant the same as transfer, but additionally, the CIDG forces were converted to regular ARVN soldiers. The troops lost their CIDG status and this was not popular among the Montagnards but most eventually converted. Whether it was conversion or turnover the result was the same: Special Forces control and support (e.g., funding and health care) were replaced by South Vietnamese. The Province chief accomplished several actions that doomed the turn over. First troops were moved from Buon Enao complex that now included 214 villages to a new camp at Bu Prang. Another 604 troops were moved to Ban Me Thuot for indoctrination. These were assigned elsewhere and were not returned to Buon Enao. Dependants started to leave. Sadly, the turnover of Buon Enao was considered a failure. Francis J. Kelly summarized.

> The reasons for the failure of the Buon Enao turnover can be summarized as follows: mutual suspicion and hostility between the Rhade and Vietnamese province and district officials; overly generous distribution by U.S. agencies of weapons and ammunition to tribesmen whose reaction to government enforced repossession of some of the weapons was understandably hostile; apparent disregard on the part of the Vietnam government for the interests, desires, and sensitivities of the Montagnards; inadequate Vietnamese government administrative and logistical support; and, finally, failure of U.S. authorities to anticipate these difficulties and avoid them.[110]
>
> *Francis J. Kelly*

The Resurgence of Bajaraka

Continuing settlement of ethnic Vietnamese in the highlands and rough treatment of Montagnards by government troops caused a resurgence of the Bajaraka. The dissolution of Buon Enao also played a role since it had become a symbol of Montagnard hopes for the future. Mistrust of the Vietnamese reached the point that the Montagnards believed that there was a Vietnamese plot to exterminate them. Some members of the Rhade community in Ban Me Thuot contacted the Americans asking them to intercede on their behalf. Meetings were scheduled with the Vietnamese and the outlook was promising. It appeared that the Bajaraka might change their goal from autonomy to racial equality within South Vietnam. Y-Bih, a Rhade leader who sided with the Communists indicated that he might be interested in changing sides. This would be a major blow to the Communists in Darlac province. Y-Bham, the chairman of the Bajaraka Central Committee, was still imprisoned in Ban Me Thuot. He was enlisted to entice Y-Bih to negotiate. Y-Bih responded that he would negotiate on the condition that Y-Bham would be permanently set free and Y-Bham was released from prison. Negotiations quickly collapsed when the ARVN, using information supplied during the negotiations, mounted an operation to capture Y-Bih which failed. Y-Bham was returned to prison. This ended negotiations with Bajaraka.[111] The government turned its back on efforts to enlist the Montagnards in the war against the Communists.

Some senior officials of the Diem government were sympathetic to the native cultures of the Central Highlands and were open to a certain degree of Highlander self-determination within an essentially Vietnamese state. Politically aware Highlanders recognized Major Hoang Van Dinh, province chief in Kontum, and Major Ngo Nhu Bich, who became province chief in Tuyen Duc in April 1963, as belonging to this category. Most officials in the region, however, were unwilling or unable to relate to most of the people they governed. The arrival of increasing numbers of ethnic Vietnamese, Highlanders' consequent fear of losing their traditional lands, and their rough treatment by government troops remained contentious issues. By late 1962, there was another sharp deterioration in the relationship between Highlanders and the Saigon government. This became a serious security issue in 1963 and a critical one in 1964. The dissolution of the Buon Enao complex, an important symbol to Highlanders and an embodiment of their hopes for the future, played a crucial part in these developments.

It may be no coincidence that October 1962, the same month Dave Nuttle left Vietnam, was pivotal in the resurgence of the Bajaraka autonomy movement. In the middle of that month four Rhade, some of them apparently junior officials in Darlac's provincial administration, contacted a Rhade-speaking American in Ban Me Thuot and asked for US help. Claiming the existence of a Vietnamese plot to exterminate Highlanders, they referred to an ancient legend: The Rhade had first arrived in Darlac after an underground migration from a cave near Dalat. They had emerged through a small aperture known as the Hole of Drung (a real geological feature located about halfway between the city of Ban Me Thuot and Lac Thien). According to the legend, when the Hole of Drung closed, the Rhade people would face extinction. The Rhade spokesmen told the American that their people feared this was happening now. They wanted the Americans to intercede with the Diem government to have their grievances addressed.

A second meeting was scheduled for later that month, but Y-Thinh Eban was the only Rhade to show up. The others, believing they were already under government surveillance, had taken flight. Y-Thinh had been arrested for his part in the Bajaraka autonomy movement in 1958 and imprisoned until May 1962, after which he was employed as a translator at Buon Enao.[112] He now declared himself to be the general secretary of the Bajaraka Central Committee, based at Ban Me Thuot. The tone of this meeting was far less apocalyptic than the previous one. Y-Thinh's remarks were rational and constructive, leading the Americans to believe that a useful dialogue was possible.

The experience of the Buon Enao project, Y-Thinh indicated, had made some Highland leaders rethink the necessity of striving for autonomy. Bajaraka was now contemplating limiting its demands to racial equality within the southern Vietnamese state. A proposal of particular interest to both the Americans and the Saigon government was that Y-Bih, a Rhade leader actively involved in the Communist insurgency, be approached. Convincing Y-Bih to "rally" to the government side, it was generally agreed, would be a major blow to the Communists in Darlac. Some in the Bajaraka movement thought his involvement in negotiations with the government offered the best hope of a successful and lasting settlement of Highlanders' grievances.

On 29 October 1962 the CIA informed Ngo Dinh Nhu and Colonel Le Quang Tung about these meetings. Colonel Tung told the CIA on 13 December 1962 that he had the authority (presumably from his immediate superior, President Diem) to approach Y-Bih and offer him amnesty. Tung's only caveat was that a member of the PSO should be present at any meetings between CIA officers and Y-Bih. The CIA made a concerted effort to contact Y-Bih and recruited Y-Bham, chairman of the Bajaraka Central Committee and still imprisoned in Ban Me Thuot, to help with the negotiations. Y-Bham wrote several letters to Y-Bih, encouraging him to surrender. Such efforts assumed a particular urgency by a development in mid-January. Y-Preh, a Rhade associated with the Ban Me Thuot Bajaraka committee, informed the CIA that the Kontum and Pleiku committees had sent an oral message to their comrades in Darlac proposing a general Highlander revolt against the government. The authenticity of this message was suspect; some Bajaraka members and some CIA officers believed it might have been a Communist plot. If so, it failed. The Americans told the Ban Me Thuot committee that neither they nor Y-Bham would support such a revolt.

On 18 January 1963 Layton addressed a letter to the Pleiku Bajaraka committee suggesting that its members meet with General Nguyen Khanh, commander of II Corps. In a separate development, on 1 February a message was received from Y-Bih, who stated that he was willing to meet representatives of the Saigon government provided Y-Bham was released from prison. Given the CIA's judgment that Y-Bham's influence was needed to head off a revolt in Pleiku, it used its influence to secure his temporary release.

Preliminary discussions involving Layton's people, some Highlanders, and General Khanh occurred on 6 February. A more formal meeting involving Khanh, representatives of the Pleiku Bajaraka committee, and Y-Bham (flown to Pleiku from Ban Me Thuot for this purpose) took place eight days later. The CIA personnel present deemed this meeting a success, later claiming: "The prospective revolt was thwarted." Reading between the lines, however, it seems that the CIA had only a vague idea of what was going on among politically active Highlanders in Kontum and Pleiku. Whether an armed uprising there was ever a real possibility is not certain.

Events that spring gave Highlanders further cause to doubt the benevolence and trustworthiness of the Saigon government. Y-Bham, who had never been promised a permanent release, was returned to prison by the end of February. The effort to bring Y-Bih into talks collapsed when, on 15 March, elements of the ARVN 23rd Division, possibly taking advantage of information supplied by Bajaraka to assist negotiations, mounted an operation to capture him. Apparently, division commander Colonel Le Quang Trong intended to have Y-Bih summarily executed, but the operation failed. Y-Bih then broke off all communication with the CIA and the South Vietnamese government. Having already played a substantial role in wrecking the Buon Enao project, Trong had now severely damaged the prospect of addressing Highlanders' grievances more broadly. Whether he was motivated purely by racial prejudice, perceived some personal advantage in exacerbating tensions between Highlanders and ethnic Vietnamese, or was following secret orders from Saigon remains unclear.

As early as February 1963, it seems the Diem government was having second thoughts about working with Bajaraka, fearing that its Central Committee wanted to use American support and money to rebuild its organization. On 13 April the Minister of Defense, Nguyen Thuan, informed the embassy that his government wanted the Americans immediately to cease all involvement in matters connected with the autonomy of Highlanders. On 17 April Layton met with government ministers and Colonel Tung of the PSO and agreed, probably with extreme reluctance, to break off all contact with Bajaraka and to cease all efforts to mediate between Highland leaders and the Vietnamese government.[113]

Michael D. Benge

During May, members of the Bajaraka committee in Ban Me Thuot, no longer protected by the Americans and fearing arrest, dispersed to their villages. That same month, the CIA heard rumors of a revolt by CIDG Strike Force personnel in the Highlands. Although no such insurrection took place at this time, some of the camps rumored to be involved participated in a real rebellion the following year.[114]

Francis J. Kelly

Communist Gains, 1963

Support for the Communist war effort was triggered by a

very unlikely source. Buddhists had long protested the Diem regime human rights violations. Antigovernment demonstrations started in May 1963. Marches and self-immolations by monks captured world attention. The world press saw the self-immolation of Buddhists in the streets as a means of protest. Madam Nhu, the wife of Diem's brother, in her best style offered that if they needed more gasoline to kill themselves, she would be happy to provide it. "Let them burn!" she exalted. "And we shall clap our hands."[115] On 21 August the government declared a state of siege and a crackdown started on the militants. The Communists took advantage of the chaos and mounted a counter-offensive. While no towns were captured a weapons count revealed their progress.

> "The ratio of weapons losses which favored the government earlier this year has turned dramatically in favor of the Viet Cong. . . . The 1,800 weapons lost by government forces since June would be enough to arm either six [Communist] 'main force' battalions, 22 district companies, or 70 village platoons."[116]
>
> *J. P. Harris*

The Fall of Diem (1963)

Faking operations and promotions of ARVN generals based upon loyalty to Diem and not military competence took their toll. For Diem, it was a family enterprise. His brother Nhu was a good organizer and expert at intrigue, which helped the regime remain in power.[117] Some ARVN generals, perhaps motivated by hope of promotion or a realization that the war could not be won by Diem, planned a coup. The U.S. cooperated. Henry Cabot Lodge, the U.S. ambassador in Saigon, summarized. "We are launched on a course which there is no respectable turning back: the overthrow of the Diem government…There is no possibility, in my view, that the war can be won under a Diem administration."[118]

Kennedy had hoped for a sort of "bloodless coup" in

which Diem would be deposed and given an airplane ticket to live elsewhere and a military junta would replace him. The ARVN military was not that stupid: if you depose someone, you want to make sure they do not return later and depose you. Their concern was well founded. In a previous coup, Diem had regained power and punished those who had ousted him. The coup was executed on 2 November 1963. Diem and Nhu fled to a Catholic church in Saigon and hoped to escape from there, but they were trapped and surrendered to the insurgents, who offered them some sort of safe-conduct. Diem and Nhu were loaded into the back of an armored vehicle and were murdered there. Photos of their riddled corpses circulated around the world.

Kennedy was horrified.[119] He had not expected this. Less than three weeks later, Kennedy was killed in Dallas, and Vice President Lyndon B. Johnson (LBJ) assumed the presidency. In less than a month, two heads of state had been murdered. The war in Vietnam was now under new management. What followed was a succession of ARVN generals who took over the government and were in turn replaced by other ARVN generals. The first to lead the military junta was General Duong Van Minh, called "Big Minh." He lasted only a few months before he was replaced. This was not helpful to the war effort.

Le Lieu Browne worked for Diem's Ministry of Information and had good insight into Diem and what followed. She was the wife of Malcom Browne, an anti-Diem American journalist.

> As for Diem, he was once a good man. But he was considered too traditional and too aloof. I was often told that people were so afraid of him that after a meeting they avoided turning their back to him on the way out for fear of being accused of disrespect to our "royalty." I met him on many occasions, either during diplomatic functions or during trips to strategic hamlets, which were regarded at that time as Diem and Nhu's proud achievements. He was

always reserved and courteous. He spoke very little and smoked a lot. He was often accused of behaving as a mandarin toward his subjects. That was certainly visible as he traveled in rural areas and peasants lined up to greet him. I found him distasteful.

After the coup against Diem, the military generals competed with one another to take power and there was one coup after another. These Vietnamese generals had no experience in administration. They were even more corrupt than Diem and Nhu. It wasn't good to have generals as presidents. They gave me no hope. But the American buildup also left me skeptical. If the French who colonized our country for a century could not win our support, how could the Americans, the newcomers with a different culture and language, hope to win the war against the Communists? We seemed to return to the situation in the fifties in which the government controlled the cities and the Viet Cong controlled the countryside. Corruption and police harassment made people distrust the government and sympathize more with the Viet Cong. But still I didn't think the Viet Cong would win. I just thought the war would go on forever.[120]

Le Lieu Browne

The Year of the Cat Ends

The year ended with great optimism in Hanoi. Government paralysis in the south meant that the war could enter a new phase. While there was continuing concern over U. S. increasing involvement, it was thought that a protracted war could be avoided. Hanoi replaced the protracted war strategy with one of offensive action, a strategy of "going for broke" in 1964.[121]

1964–The Year of the Dragon

...the South Vietnamese seemed more intent on barracks politics than battlefield peril. Westmoreland spent many valuable hours trying to find out who was in charge, and more hours pleading with malcontents not to kill the current incumbent.[122]

Robert Pisor

Following the death of President Kennedy, Vietnam appeared to be the last priority of the new president. Lyndon B. Johnson was more concerned about civil rights and economic issues. He was determined that his Great Society program would be his greatest accomplishment. LBJ continued Kennedy's policies in Vietnam. It soon became apparent that the situation in South Vietnam had been degenerating since the death of Diem. The Strategic Hamlet Program was in shambles, started by Diem and hated by the peasants who were forced to live in the camps. Many of the ARVN in the field were pulled back to Saigon to participate in coups attempts and other activities that made it more difficult to prosecute the war. By December, 1963, in one area, three quarters of the hamlets had been destroyed by the VC or the inhabitants themselves.[123] Word finally reached Washington that all was not well in South Vietnam. LBJ sent Secretary of Defense McNamara to South Vietnam for an assessment. He blamed poor U.S. leadership (no surprise: Harkins) and also indicated that the situation should be monitored. If no improvement, stronger measures should be taken. The Joint Chiefs of Staff (JCS) argued for stronger measures. General Curtis "Bombs Away" LeMay, the air force chief, argued for bombing North Vietnam, as one might expect. He said: "We are swatting flies when we should be going after the manure pile."[124] By early 1964, the JCS proposed a plan to LBJ. The most extreme measure was the introduction of U.S. troops to take over the war. The U.S. would guide the direction of the war. The war would become

"Americanized." LBJ did not approve the plan at that time. It was before the election. LBJ thought that "wars are too serious to be entrusted to generals." He also knew that the armed forces "need battles and bombs and bullets in order to be heroic."[125] This is not far from President Eisenhower's warning when he left office about the threat of the military-industrial complex.

Several things happened that forced LBJ's hand. The effectiveness of the South Vietnamese regime continued to plummet, and it was clear that South Vietnam would soon lose the war. In August 1964, Hanoi handed the U.S. a gift that provided the U.S. with an excuse to intervene in a major way in the war in Vietnam. Many of the details have been contested ever since. North Vietnam torpedo boats attacked a U.S. destroyer in international waters in the Gulf of Tonkin. U.S. warships returned fire. There were claims that a second attack followed, but these were false. Also, a separate, unrelated RVNAF operation was ongoing at that time, and it is possible that the North mistook U.S. ships for a part of that operation.[126] McNamara lied to the U.S. Congress on this point, maintaining that both attacks were genuine. Both the U.S. and North Vietnam contested the events, but this was an election year for LBJ, so he needed to appear as a firm leader. The U.S. retaliated with air strikes, which blew up some boats and did other damage, but further actions by the U.S. were more serious. LBJ presented to Congress what has been called the Gulf of Tonkin Resolution. It was approved by Congress on 7 August 1964 and gave LBJ the authority to deploy troops without a formal declaration of war by Congress. LBJ ordered the deployment of U.S. troops to rescue the South Vietnamese regime in Saigon.

After the fall of Diem, General William C. Westmorelend replaced General Paul D. Harkins as Commander of USMACV in June 1964. Correspondent Robert Pisor summarized.

Coups and counter-coups paralyzed the government and the armed forces of Vietnam. The primitive people of the mountains, the Montagnards who were abused and exploited by the Vietnamese even in the midst of war, declared themselves "neutral." U.S. Army Green Berets, who relied on these people for soldiers and reports on enemy movements, struggled to win them back. Enemy mortars blasted a huge airfield near Saigon, destroying American planes. University students and Buddhist monks and nuns clogged the streets with demonstrators to protest South Vietnamese war policies and growing American influence. On Christmas Eve, the Viet Cong exploded a bomb at the front door of the Army's Brink Hotel in downtown Saigon, killing two Americans and wounding fifty-eight. Tile-roofed, tree-lined Saigon was changing, and Kitsy [Westmoreland's wife] and the kids joined the exodus of American dependents.

In the last week of 1964 the Viet Cong 9th Division captured a town east of Saigon, then ambushed and all but annihilated two separate relief columns. The government's control slipped to a dwindling third of the population, and the first intelligence reports came in with word that North Vietnamese troops might enter the war to hasten its end.

Still, the South Vietnamese seemed more intent on barracks politics than battlefield peril. Westmoreland spent many valuable hours trying to find out who was in charge, and more hours pleading with malcontents not to kill the current incumbent. A teetotaler, he repressed disgust while applauding the imaginative American junior officers who helped preserve a semblance of order by drinking putative coup leaders under the table.[127]

Robert Pisor

While Hanoi had made bold pronouncements of a major change in tactics to "General Offensive, General Uprising," (GO-GU), activity in early 1964 was mild. Kidnappings and minor acts of violence continued as usual and VC harassment spread across the highlands to the most vulnerable government population centers: the Strategic Hamlets.

The problem was that there was no effective defense

by the villagers to the attacks. In some cases fences were destroyed and in others hamlet officials were kidnapped. Rice supplies were seized and hamlet offices, houses and watchtowers were destroyed. In Darlac Province a hamlet defended by Combat Youth, the VC killed a hamlet official, seized weapons, and kidnapped Combat Youth and [other] hamlet officials. The other inhabitants were dispersed.[128]

The Hanoi ambiguous goals of forcing a major battle and expanding "liberated zones" had not been achieved by mid-1964. The problem was that they had neither the numbers nor the manpower to seriously challenge the South Vietnamese government. While the ARVN lacked the will to fight and seldom challenged Communists, Hanoi's forces also were reluctant to fight. This would change.[129]

Battle of Nam Dong (5-6 July 1964)

The battle of Nam Dong occurred when the VC attempted to overrun the CIDG camp. A force of 381 Montagnards, 50 Nungs, seven LLDB, one Australian advisor and 12 Special Forces troops defended the camp led by Captain Roger Donlon. The camp was laid out with an outer and inner perimeter; a design feature that saved the camp and would later become the standard for other camps.[130] Nam Dong was located in I CTZ 32 miles west of Da Nang in a valley near the Laotian border. The VC force of about 1,000 men attacked the camp at 0230 hours on 6 July 1964. The VC achieved surprise and reached the perimeter but did not break through. Roger Donlon described the action.

> The blast of the first mortar round jolted Dan out of bed. He flicked on the radio. While it warmed up, he slipped into his shoes, scooped up the ammunition he had laid out on the shelf and put it into the big pockets of his jungle-suit trousers. He strapped on his holster. The explosions boomed, louder as they got closer. A southpaw, he held his .45 in his

left hand and cocked it, watching the door, waiting for a tone on the radio transmitter. The field telephone rang. It was Alamo.

"Call for a flare ship and an air strike!" he heard. "We're under attack!"

"I'm doing it," he said.

He threw down the phone. The set was already beamed to the B Detachment in Da Nang. He called in the clear—that is, in plain English and not in code.

"Hello Da Nang . . . Nam. Dong calling . . . I have an `operation immediate' message. .        . `operation immediate'

"Roger. Roger. Go ahead, Nam Dong."

"Request flare ship and an air strike . . . we are under heavy mortar fire . . . repeat, we are under heavy mortar fire . . . request flare ship and air. strike . . ."

"Roger. . . . Stand by for reply. . . ."

Dan waited. The crashing, rending blasts of the mortars walked closer. A direct hit exploded on the Supply Room next door. Dan reckoned the Communications Room was next. He holstered his .45, picked up his AR-15, threw on the suspenders of his AR-15 ammunition belt, and raced for the door. Like a diver going off the low board, he took three quick steps, and belly-flopped as far as he could stretch. The rocks and earth of the hard ground bit into his bare shoulders and chest.

Behind him, the Communications Room blew up. The concussion from the mortar shell's blast slapped the soles of his jump boots. The whole long house was burning, flames crackling in the dry thatch and rattan.

Dazed, Dan stumbled across the road and toward the dispensary at the back of the camp. There he helped Gregg and Terry carry a big steel medical chest from the dispensary, which also had begun to burn. They dropped it for safety in a communications trench. The M-5A kit, as big as a foot locker, was fully packed, ready for village sick call. They brought out another and stowed it. Both would be needed.

When the first mortar round hit, Gregg rolled out of bed and picked up his shotgun. It was a Winchester pump with a five-round magazine. He went through the back door of the dispensary to the protective wall where it formed an L. He looked around, ran back inside and got out an old pair of

Army fatigues, ragged and with the sleeves cut off. He put them on over his swimsuit and stepped out the front door.

The shells were falling faster. The small arms fire was a steady stutter. The mess hall was burning. It cast an eerie, dancing light over the camp, spectacular now with swirling smoke and flashes of shells exploding on its zeroed-in center.

"Damn the strike force!" Gregg muttered. "Here we go again!"

He moved over to an old shower room, now used to store medical supplies.

It was to the right of Brown's mortar pit, backed up against the inner perimeter wire. Outside the barrier, in the glare of the fire and the pale moonlight, he saw crouched figures moving forward, not over twenty yards away. Bullets cracked and fluttered past him as he closed on them. He could see flashes of gunfire from behind the men . . . six shapes floating in the half-light, coming on at a trot.

Gregg stopped, raised his shotgun and fired. He pumped and fired again. He pumped and fired a third time. The blasts caught the VC almost point-blank. One second they were trotting forward, the next they were propelled backward like leaves caught in a gust of wind. Gregg rushed back to the burning dispensary, to evacuate as much of his precious equipment as he could before it disintegrated.[131]

Roger Donlon

Anthropologist Gerald C. Hickey was at Nam Dong at the time of the attack. Hickey was there to do a survey of advisors. He recalled the conclusion of the battle.[132]

The aftermath brought a mixture of relief, hope, pain, anger, and wonderment. All survivors of A-Team 726 had been wounded, their faces and bodies blackened from explosions and thick smoke. Still, they exuded resolve, the resolve that had brought victory. Sitting amidst the cinder blocks, badly wounded Donlon, Disser, Olejniczak, and Terrin needed medical evacuation to Danang. But they grasped their weapons. Despite his wounds, Donlon talked of reorganizing for a possible new VC assault. Brown and Daniels left with a party of Nungs to start an ammunition check and they found by the ammunition bunker piles of dead VC. Gregg continued to tend the wounded.

I walked over to Disser's mortar pit where the bodies of Conway and Alamo lay and then to the swimming pool where Houston was sprawled. How can those who survived ever express their deep feelings of mourning and gratitude for those who fell saving the camp and everyone in it?

Once over the shock of the post-attack scene, my sense of organization emerged and I asked Gregg what I could do to help. He shook his head as he said that most of the medical supplies were exhausted. We were very short of bandages or material to make bandages. Gregg had a little morphine that he gave Olejniczak who was in dire pain. Gregg noted that the jungle shower was miraculously still standing so we had a small supply of water. We could only carry the wounded CIDG to the parade ground and put bits of wet cloth in their mouths to alleviate the dehydration that battle inflicts. The Vietnamese nurses emerged from their trench near the dispensary and set about treating the wounded as best they could. Co Cuc crawled under the fence to remove needed medical kits from dead VC.

Soon the parade ground was filled with dead and wounded CIDG. Many of Strike Force Company 122 men had their throats slit or had had their necks broken with gun butts. Moving these victims out to the parade ground proved extremely difficult because they had to be kept level. Some of the wounded writhed, moaned, or shouted hysterically while others lay deadly still. I went around and tried to reassure them that planes would come to take them to Danang.[133]

Gerald C. Hickey

Australian Warrant Officer Kevin Conway supported the defense with mortar fire until he was killed. A 93 man relief force was brought in by air and this ended the attack. Those killed at Nam Dong were 58 CIDG, 2 Special Forces and the Australian advisor. Enemy losses were estimated at 55.[134] Conway was recommended for the award of the Victoria Cross his nation's highest valor award and Donlon received the first Medal of Honor awarded of the Vietnam War.

FULRO
(United Front for the Liberation of Oppressed People)

The Vietnamese regarded the Montagnards as "Moi" (savages). The Montagnards were treated as second class citizens similar to Native Americans in the 19th century United States. The similarity between the treatment of these minorities is quite striking. The outcome of uprisings in the Central Highlands and in 19th Century America had a predictable outcome as seen by Little Crow, Chief of the Lakota as he tried in vain to stop what would become the greatest Indian uprising in U. S. history in 1862.

> You are like dogs in the Hot Moon when they run mad and snap at their own shadows. We are only little herds of buffaloes left scattered ... [but] the white men are like the locusts when they fly so thick that the whole sky is a snow-storm. You may kill one — two — ten; yes, as many as the leaves in the forest yonder, and their brothers will not miss them. . .You are fools. You cannot see the face of your chief; your eyes are full of smoke. You cannot hear his voice. Your ears are full of roaring waters. . .You are fools. You will die like rabbits when the wolves hunt them in the hard moon. Taoyateduta [Little Crow] is not a coward. He will die with you! [135]

Little Crow

The end of the French war in 1954 caused great migrations of Vietnamese between North and South Vietnam. This caused the movement of many Vietnamese in the lowland cities to the highlands where the vast majority of the population was Montagnard. Friction between the two cultures was on the rise and by 1964 Montagnard unrest reached the breaking point. Since they had been armed by the CIA and the U. S. Army Special Forces to fight the VC and NVA, the Montagnard now had the tools needed to rebel. It started in Darlac Province in the area around Ban Me Thuot. The FULRO uprising started on

19 September 1964 in the Special Forces camps. Not all of the camps rebelled. Captain Vernon Gillespie at Buen Brieng persuaded the Montagnard to stay out of the uprising.[136] As a prelude to the uprising, political games continued in Saigon

> The week of 12-19 September saw both an attempted coup against General Khanh's regime and the year's highest rate of Communist military activity up to that point across South Vietnam as a whole. But again, there was relatively little fighting in the Central Highlands, and the following week the Communist effort slackened markedly throughout the country.
>
> Political maneuvers continued in Saigon. Mere rumors of a coup brought ARVN troops into the streets in late September. Next Khanh convened the generals and representatives of Buddhists, Catholics, students, and traditional political parties in a High National Council to agree on a provisional government and draft a constitution while he kept control. General Tran Thien Khiem, a junta member, was sent on an open-ended diplomatic mission, effectively into exile. Khanh resigned as prime minister, but the civilian who replaced him soon faced fresh charges of discrimination against Buddhists and old ones of complicity with Diem and even Emperor Bao Dai. Students facing conscription added to the unrest, which rose to the level of scandal when the Surete announced it had broken up a ring of Khanh's officers who had been selling draft exemptions. There were more demonstrations. On November 26 the government declared martial law. Some saw that as Khanh retaliating against the Surete, since the decree permitted the army to control the police.[137]
>
> *John Prados*

In September 1964, General Nguyen Huu Co, the ARVN II Corps commander met with FULRO leaders to end the Montagnard revolt.

> General Co conducted an excellent discussion, which lasted three hours. He gave the rebel leaders every opportunity to present their demands. Despite the belligerent manner of some of them, the general did not allow anything to upset him.
> Among other things the Montagnard wanted:
>
> - A Montagnard elected representative in the National

Assembly.
  - Montagnard to be commissioned as officers and to command Montagnard troops.
  - District chiefs and perhaps province chiefs to be Montagnard appointees in the central highlands.
  - Their own Montagnard flag.
  - Montagnard children in schools to learn their own tribal dialect before Vietnamese.
  - The right to own the land they actually cultivated. Higher academic and tertiary education opportunities for Montagnard school children.
  - American aid, destined for the Montagnard, to be given direct to the Montagnard, and not administered by the Vietnamese.

General Co said that some of the requests were quite reasonable, and that he would implement those within his power almost immediately. `Others,' he said, 'will require consideration at national level.'[138]

Barry Peterson

The rebel leaders agreed to return to their bases and discuss the terms. In return for concessions they would fight the Viet Cong, not the South Vietnamese. After some confusion it became evident to the revolt organizers that progress toward Montagnard autonomy would not occur and they packed up heading to Cambodia with Y-Bham Enuol, chairman of the FULRO.[139] They took with them ammunition and all the other supplies that they could carry. Those Montagnards who remained officially surrendered to the South Vietnamese. The entire affair accomplished nothing but left in its wake a dissident mood among the Montagnard.[140] At the national level the political chaos continued as the military situation deteriorated.

General Mataxis [the II Corps US Advisor] said, "I arrived in the middle of a Montagnard revolt. I found General Co, the II Corps commander, furious at the CIA for writing a letter to the leaders of the Montagnard FULRO movement for suggesting while independence was not feasible, however, other steps could be taken. This was viewed by the Vietnamese as usurping their authority over the Montagnard tribesman. This caused a major crisis between the US Embassy in Saigon and the Vietnamese government. And in the Highlands it resulted in a very initial frosty reception and strained relationship with the Corps Commander...it raised my first critical advisory problem. The Vietnamese were threatening to execute the FULRO leaders they had captured and General Westmoreland told me to warn General Co that such action would seriously impact on US support to the Vietnamese government. Not the sort of advice that would develop a close relationship. After many cups of green tea and long hours of discussion over the next few days and innumerable calls from Saigon on 'How are you doing?' General Co agreed to form the FULRO leaders into an Eagle Flight (heliborne strike force) advised and commanded by a SF Captain and several NCOs. This Strike Force was to be available to the Corps Commander to respond to emergency ambushes and surprise attacks throughout II Corps to which ARVN was unable to respond. This Strike Force was commanded by a Special Forces team, something which Saigon conveniently ignored. The advantage for the Corps Commander was the immediate availability of a helicopter Strike Force supported by US helicopters and Vietnamese A-1 Skyraider aircraft based at Pleiku to respond to emergencies throughout II Corps. The advantage to our MACV Team and the SF Headquarters was now, for the first time, we had a Strike Force available to respond immediately to any crisis faced by our unit advisors." Additionally, this provided the Special Forces camps a tactical capability they did not have previously and greatly expanded their area of influence. The Eagle Flight concept was adopted and used effectively throughout the war."[141]

Ted Mataxis, Jr.

As 1964 closed, U.S. forces in Vietnam had increased to 23,300 advisors. The total of U.S. dead stood at 140 as 1965 opened.[142]

1965 – The Year of the Snake

"No, no," the general said. "Please get the microphones out of here. I want to talk to this man."[143]

Norm Schwartzkopf

VC activity remained high in early 1965 with guerilla attacks while main force NVA units were in the midst of moving south, regrouping and planning for major attacks consistent with the GO-GU goals.[144]

Ambush at the Mang Yang Pass, February 1965

Mang Yang Pass lies between Pleiku and Qui Nhon on Highway 19 in II CTZ. It is a place with steep highway grades and high mountains on either side of the road. During the First Indochina War the French Mobile Group 100 was destroyed there by the Viet Minh but some survivors reached Pleiku after the massacre.

Following the September 1964 FULRO uprising some of the Montagnards involved in the uprising were forcibly relocated from the closed camps to new camps near Mang Yang Pass. The move created the same problems seen in the demise of the Strategic Hamlet Program: dissatisfaction among the Montagnards and loss of combat effectiveness. The move was caused by the increasing VC threat in the II CTZ. General Westmoreland's concern was that the enemy would attempt to cut South Vietnam in half along the route of Highway 19 from the Cambodian Border to the coast. This was a serious threat because the NVA was in process of moving major combat forces into South Vietnam while U. S. combat troops were just starting to arrive. The 1st Cavalry Division would not arrive until September 1965 and it would set up at a base camp near An Khe that would be called Camp Radcliff (named for Major Donald R. Radcliff who was KIA) as the division arrived in

Vietnam. ARVN was not capable of countering the NVA/VC threat.

It was against this backdrop that several hundred CIDG of the Rhade tribe and their families were moved from Darlac Province to two new camps, one to the west of Mang Yang Pass and one at nearby An Khe Pass. The Montagnards protested because they knew that they were being used as cannon fodder against a far better equipped and more numerous enemy force. Charles M. Simpson explained the impact.

In 1965, the situation in II Corps was badly deteriorated. The highway from coastal Qui Nhon to Pleiku was cut, Pleiku was near starvation, and there was a critical shortage of troops throughout the corps.

The top brass in II Corps ordered SF to move several companies of Rhade Montagnard CIDG from Darlac Province to An Khe to open the highway. Special Forces officers protested the order on the grounds that road-clearing against VC and NVA regulars was no mission for CIDG, that the troops had been recruited to defend their own tribal areas and families, and worst of all that you just couldn't move Rhade into the middle of Bahnar country. SF was told in no uncertain terms to stop clouding the issue with a "bunch of anthropological crap," that there was a war on, and to "get on the team." The Rhade were moved, taking heavy casualties. Many deserted and returned to Darlac, reinforcing Vietnamese arguments about the "worthless savages (moi)," and fueling the MACV complaint about never being able to count on "that undisciplined Special Forces rabble." Back in Darlac, the SF recruited the Rhade remnants back into the CIDG.

To many officers in the air-conditioned headquarters of Saigon, the entire CIDG concept was wrong. Its very name "civilian irregular" was unmilitary, and the whole operation, including that loose CIA money, badly needed discipline and regularizing. Fiascos, such as the Montagnard revolts of 1964 and 1965, only reinforced that belief. Overlooking the centuries-old sociological problem, the military "solution" was to "put all those damned people in the Army where they can be controlled."

Col. Jasper "Jap" Wilson, senior advisor of II, I, and finally III Corps, hated all airborne and the SF worst of all. He made no bones that he would rather have none in his area, and then went back to the States and blasted his anti-SF message from the podiums of the Army's service colleges.[145]

Charles M. Simpson

On 15 February 1965 a large RVN convoy was destroyed in Mang Yang Pass. Two days later the Special Forces established two FOBs nearby along Highway 19. This was followed by VC attacks and ambushes on the CIDG. One CIDG convoy to reinforce the FOBs was ambushed and relief forces were unable to break through the VC roadblocks. In one ambush the VC attacked from both sides of the road. When the Montagnards ran out of ammunition and tried to surrender they were executed by the VC. CIDG reinforcements sent in by helicopter were unsuccessful in rescuing survivors. ARVN reinforcements sent from Pleiku were repulsed with heavy losses and withdrew. All forces in II CTZ had been committed to the fight without success and further efforts to save surviving CIDG troops were abandoned on 24 February. Some CIDG stragglers made it back to camps on their own. The Montagnards were close to mutiny and some refused to participate in any combat operations. Some were discharged and one camp was closed. This was a rerun of the destruction of French Mobile Group 100 ten years earlier on a much smaller scale. A small group of Montagnards had been sacrificed to hold II CTZ pending the arrival of U. S. combat troops.[146] This economy of force approach using Montagnards would be seen again in 1975.

Mobile Strike (Mike) Forces

The daddy of what was to become known as the "Mike Forces" was a battalion of Nungs formed in Danang in 1965. The Nungs are a tribal group originally from the area near the North Vietnamese— Chinese border. During the French and early Diem regimes, there had been an entire Nung Division which earned a top reputation for professionalism and fighting quality. That division was later

106

demobilized, and the Nungs settled in several enclaves in South Vietnam. They were not active again until the CIA and Special Forces recruited them to serve as personal bodyguards for the SF teams in the new CIDG program. Hired at a high pay scale, the Nungs proved their worth on numerous occasions, winning the respect of the Special Forces. The successful defense of Nam Dong, described above, was only possible because of the loyal defense of the inner perimeter by Nungs and Special Forces. In the early days, it was often the Nungs who provided the backbone of training, the defensive capability, and the element of stability on patrol that made the difference between success and failure. They posed some problems, too, because they attached their loyalty to the Americans rather than the Vietnamese, and because their pay scale exceeded that of even the Vietnamese regular army.[147]

Charles M. Simpson

Mobile Strike Force (Jeffrey J. Clarke)

The 184-man Mike Force companies became the reserves of Special Forces, each containing a thirty-four-man eagle flight

107

reconnaissance platoon. The Mike Forces differed from the camp strike forces in many respects. Mike Forces were specifically designed for employment under short reaction time conditions and were not restricted by camp defense responsibilities. The Mike Forces were conventionally organized with crew-served weapons, such as medium mortars and a range of recoilless rifles, which allowed them to deliver much of their own supporting fire. Because of the higher wages and more strenuous training, the Mike Force troops were better-than-average CIDG soldiers. They were also theoretically airborne-qualified, although personnel turbulence and continual combat requirements kept many companies from achieving that status (as late as 1970, for example, only two of the twelve companies in the 4th Mobile Strike Force Command were actually airborne.)[148]

Shelby L. Stanton

LBJ at War

I have asked the commanding general, General Westmoreland, what more he needs to meet this mounting aggression. He has told me. And we will meet his needs. We cannot be defeated by force of arms. We will stand in Vietnam[149]

Lyndon Johnson

Lyndon Johnson had won the Presidency in a landslide over Barry Goldwater in November 1964. LBJ now had a mandate to pursue his policies, the first of which was his Great Society, a program to eliminate poverty and racial injustice in the United States. At the same time he was concerned about his legacy and did not want to go down in history as the first president to lose a war. Accordingly, he was determined to provide General Westmoreland with all of the support and resources that he needed, but the resources needed were beyond what LBJ could provide. General Westmoreland explained.

Noting the relatively small size of South Vietnam, some might have considered it practicable to seal the land frontiers against North Vietnamese infiltration, thus facilitating the task of rooting out the Viet Cong. Yet small though the country is, its land frontiers extend for more than 900 miles. In World War I close to 6 million Allied troops were needed to man the 455 miles of the Western Front. In World War II, 4.5 million Allied troops were needed to man a 570-mile Western Front. In Korea close to a million United Nations troops were needed to man a 123-mile front across the waist of the Korean Peninsula. To have defended the land frontiers of South Vietnam in similar density would have required many millions of troops, plus others to carry on the fight against the insurgency, numbers that it would have been absurd to contemplate. At peak strength in South Vietnam, achieved in early 1969, American troops numbered 543,400, Allied troops 62,400, and ARVN troops, including militia, approximately a million, for a total well under 2 million.

To provide at least some check, however inadequate, on enemy infiltration, I had to depend primarily on mobility. Employing only about 45,000 troops, the CIDG-Special Forces camps along the frontier provided bases for patrols that might detect major infiltration, to which units arriving by helicopter might react. The SOG teams [Studies and Operations Group conducted covert unconventional warfare operations] operating in Laos harassed infiltrators and collected intelligence on enemy movements, as did both American and South Vietnamese long-range reconnaissance patrols operating within South Vietnam. When those patrols located enemy formations, I could react either with troops or with artillery and air strikes, including strikes by B-52s, although Washington's restrictions on operations in Laos and Cambodia for a long time limited the response there.[150]

William C. Westmoreland

The first U.S. combat forces sent to Vietnam were U. S. Marines who waded ashore at Da Nang to protect the U. S. Air Base located there. The arrival of the marines was quickly followed by the 173rd Airborne Brigade. The VC and NVA would soon learn of the tremendous firepower that the U. S. infantry brought to the battlefield. The heavily burdened U. S. troops were called "Elephant Soldiers" by the Montagnards.

Gary Walls, 173rd at Dak To in 1967 (Gary Walls).

Siege of Duc Co (30 June – 17 August 1965)

Duc Co Special Forces Camp (Olen C. Phipps, Jr.).

Duc Co was a Special Forces CIDG camp that was designed to stem the flow of infiltration into South Vietnam from Cambodia. By 1967, seven SF/CIDG surveillance camps from north to south were Ben Het, Plei Djereng, Duc Co, Tieu Atar, Ban Don, Duc Lap, and Bu Prang.

> Camp Duc Co, a border surveillance camp situated west of Pleiku almost to the Cambodian border, was besieged from 30 June until mid-August 1965. During the forty-eight-day siege, Capt. Richard B. Johnson's Detachment A-215 suffered heavy losses. When eight ARVN infantry, ranger, and paratrooper battalions fought their way through the surrounding Viet Cong into the camp on 17 August, they had the potential backup of two battalions of the crack 173d Airborne Brigade. This marked the first time that a large American reaction force had been earmarked to help a CIDG camp.[151]

Shelby L. Stanton

111

Major Norm Schwartzkopf was the U. S. Senior Advisor to the ARVN 2nd Airborne Task Force. His unit was tasked to relieve Duc Co in July 1965. Schwarzkopf relates what happened.

During the last week of July, we were ordered to carry out a mission for Major General Vinh Loc, the commander of II Corps of the South Vietnamese army, headquartered in Pleiku. Vinh Loc wanted us to drive the Vietcong away from a South Vietnamese special forces camp, Duc Co (which we pronounced "due koh"), that sat in the so-called 24th tactical zone at the western end of Route 19, where the road crossed into Cambodia. Due Co had been established to prevent guerrillas from coming across the border, but the camp had been more or less under siege all summer and the guerrillas had gained the upper hand. Nobody knew how many enemy were in the camp's vicinity, but the estimate was two VC battalions—about seven hundred men.

. . .Peter Arnett, at the time an AP reporter, was in Duc Co for the first three days of the siege. After shooting lots of film, he told me he wanted to leave to file his story. One of the South Vietnamese battalion commanders had been seriously wounded and I persuaded Pleiku to try a medevac flight at night. "You can come in with your lights off and the VC won't see you," I said.

To guide the helicopter in, Pleiku instructed me to position four men with flashlights at the corners of the landing pad. Holding one of those flashlights took nerve: a sniper might shoot you. I told Arnett, "Okay, if you want a ride, you have to hold one of these." We brought the wounded man out to the landing zone and listened as the helicopter began its descent. Over the radio the pilot told us, "I can't see your lights. How about shaking them so I can pick them up?" I called out that instruction to the others around the pad. A voice in the dark replied, "I don't know about you guys, but my flashlight's been shaking ever since we got out here." That was Arnett. The helicopter landed safely and he was able to leave.

As the days went by, conditions in the camp became grim. Early on, the mortars destroyed the water tank. Although there was a watering hole outside camp, the enemy knew about it; so when we needed water, we had to send a platoon to fight its way down and back. Food ran low, but when the airborne tried dropping fresh supplies, the planes stayed so high that the wind blew the parachutes outside the perimeter. We asked them to stop, because all they were doing was feeding the enemy. We were soon down to rice and salt. Sometimes Sergeant Hung would crawl out through the wire and come back with a certain kind of root he'd dig up in the jungle. It looked like a big turnip, and could be eaten raw, so we'd sit with our rice and pass the root back and forth, taking bites.

Finally, after about ten days, a task force of South Vietnamese marines arrived from the east to relieve us. The enemy, which had by now been identified as two full regiments of North Vietnamese regulars—several times as numerous and much better trained and equipped than the two Vietcong battalions we'd expected to fight—turned to ambush the marines before they reached the camp. A battle erupted and the marines forced the Communists back to their sanctuary across the Cambodian border. Our daylight patrols stopped getting shot at, and planes were able to fly low enough to air-drop supplies.

A radio call came from a staff officer in Pleiku, and I was asked for an enemy body count. "I haven't the slightest idea," I told him. "We didn't stop to count, for crissakes. We were fighting through them trying to get back to the camp."

"Well, give us your best estimate, because we're required to report a number." I called the battalion advisors, who said things like, "I don't have any idea. But my Vietnamese counterpart says maybe fifty." I compiled those guesses and called Pleiku. "Look, I have an estimate. It's one hundred and fifty. But I want you to understand that I have no confidence in that number. We pulled it out of a hat." When the official report went in, it said, "Body Count: 150." I felt like I'd been party to a bureaucratic sham. . .

Soon the sky filled with helicopters. Only one of them contained the general and his staff—the rest were full of reporters and cameramen, who walked into the camp and ignored us standing there dog-tired and filthy from two weeks of combat. They looked at us, through us, and away from us all at the same time. Then they went inside for their briefing.

Eventually the general and the colonel emerged. The colonel said to him, "Sir, this is Major Schwarzkopf, who was the senior advisor on the ground." The general came over and recoiled a little because I hadn't had a change of clothes in a week and had been handling bodies and stank. Meanwhile, the cameramen had followed and several reporters came up with microphones. "No, no," the general said. "Please get the microphones out of here. I want to talk to this man."

I'm not sure what I expected him to say. Maybe something like, "Are your men all right? How many people did you lose?" or "Good job—we're proud of you." Instead there was an awkward silence, and then he asked, "How's the chow been?"

The chow? For chrissakes, I'd been eating rice and salt and raw jungle turnips that Sergeant Hung had risked his life to get! I was so stunned that all I could say was, "Uh, fine, sir." "Have you been getting your mail regularly?"

All my mail had been going to my headquarters in Saigon and I assumed it was okay. So I said, "Oh, yes, sir." "Good, good. Fine job, lad." Lad? And with that he walked off. It was an obvious PR stunt. He'd waved off the microphones, but the cameras were still whirring away. At that moment I lost any respect I'd ever had for that general. The next night, back in New Jersey, the local TV station called my mother and told her that her son was going to be on the evening news. She watched the report, and until the day she died, she always spoke glowingly of the wonderful general she'd seen talking to her son in Vietnam and bucking up his morale.[152]

Norm Schwarzkopf

Schwarzkopf had been exposed to General Westmoreland's strategy of attrition even though Ho Chi Minh promised, "You can kill ten of us to one of you and still we will win." The measure of success of the Allied effort that was used was the body count, which led to false reporting and even the deaths of innocent civilians.

Other programs, such as pacification, offered a better chance of success. The U.S. Marines from the commandant down supported pacification and opposed General Westmoreland's strategy of attrition. Furthermore, bad tactics were used. General Westmoreand's reaction to an enemy force was to attack with massive U.S. forces. This produced massive U.S. casualties. Colonel William J. Livsey, (the 4th Infantry Division operations officer during the Dak To fight), promoted a different approach: use small patrols to locate the enemy and massive air strikes and artillery to destroy it[153] or in the words of Napoleon: "Artillery kills and infantry occupies."

The battle was considered a major defeat for the NVA which was no surprise since they had suffered heavy losses from air strikes, disparity between their firepower and that of ARVN, and malaria. Malaria remained a catastrophe for the NVA throughout the war. Four out of five NVA doctors had malaria and 4-5 soldiers died of it each day. In contrast the Montagnards enjoyed total or at least partial immunity to the disease.[154]

Siege of Plei Me (19 – 25 October 1965)

Plei Me was a CIDG camp located 25 miles southwest of Pleiku and about 20 miles from the Cambodian border. It was located there in order to gather intelligence on the NVA infiltration of troops into South Vietnam. About 450 CIDG troops of the Jarai tribe were located there with 12 Special Forces troops commanded by Captain Charles Beckwith.[155] About 4,500 ARVN troops were located at Pleiku with the recently arrived U. S. Army 1st Cavalry Division now set up at Camp Radcliff, An Khe 54 miles east of Pleiku. NVA General Man commanding the NVA B-3 Front had about 4,200 men moving south near Plei Me. On 19 October a CIDG patrol near Plei Me was struck by an NVA company. Early on 20 October the NVA attacked Plei Me. The NVA plan was to lure ARVN forces out from Pleiku and destroy them. General Man moved up his attack on Plei Me since he wanted to strike before the 1st Cavalry Division was ready. ARVN forces took the bait and moved to support Plei Me on 21 October. The ARVN armored column was ambushed on 23 October and suffered heavy casualties but U. S. air strikes forced the NVA to withdraw. On 25 October the ARVN reached Plei Me lifting the siege as U. S. air power inflicted heavy casualties on the withdrawing NVA. The U. S. Air Cavalry Division was now ordered in to pursue the NVA. Charles Beckwith recalled the battle.

The nights were worse, far worse, than the days. Ropes of green and orange tracers flew into and out of the camp. Overhead, circling C-46 Flareships kept the area illuminated. Multicolored parachutes, which had been used to resupply us, were strewn here and there and gave the camp a raffish appearance. The pounding intensified. Mortars and recoilless rifles fired relentlessly. Amazingly, during these terrible nighttime hours the camp rats, oblivious to the havoc they were a part of, continued to come out and run over the ruins just as if everyone was asleep.

Bombers came over again on October 24th and began to eat up the NVA. I'd say our side flew seventy-five to one hundred sorties a day. We just walked these air strikes all around the outside of the camp. We used a lot of air, and we broke the enemy's back with it. Many of the strikes were so close to the wire we took shrapnel in the camp. One particular string of bombs hit very close. Major Thompson, who was calling in the strikes, kept hollering, "I like it! I like it!" Captain Moore had wanted to take a photograph of one of these strikes. I tried to warn him to keep his head down. A piece of shrapnel from one of the hard bombs ripped half his shoulder off.

During the daytime, between the air strikes, I tried to sleep. Besides the newspaper photographer who was killed during our run for the camp, I had two other unauthorized newspaper people with me in the camp. We taught them how to shoot a .30-caliber machine gun and gave them one to man in the south corner of the perimeter. They did a first-class job for us.

The situation on the third day: We were putting in a lot of air strikes and I wasn't sure what was going to happen next. We learned by radio that a South Vietnamese armored column trying to reach us had been pinned down and stopped cold by an enemy ambush.

Sometime, I'm not sure when, Khoi, the Vietnamese helicopter pilot I thought so much of, flew into the camp. I told him he was crazy, and he should fly his ass out of there. "You know, Boss," he spoke perfect English, "your problem is you worry too much." He loaded up a lot of dead. We had problems keeping the Montagnards off. They wanted to get out, too. Khoi made two flights in and out. He took fire the first time but not the second. His luck held that day. Sometime later, though, he was killed in Military Region I when his chopper crashed into a mountain in bad weather.

With the napalm and bombs doing their work, the NVA began to relax their hold on us. The mortar barrages fell off, so did the small arms and machine-gun fire. It got so that even a couple of Huey slicks (small troop-carrying helicopters) flew in. We were then able to get a lot of the kids and women out. We also began flying out our dead. Some of the dead had been lying in the jungle heat for six days. They were ripe. I know that John Pioletti, while loading one of the choppers, was throwing up over the body bags.

There was another problem that worried me. The first day in Plei Me, Captain Pusser had been killed with the Ranger companies outside the wire; in the melee that followed, they hadn't brought his body back. I knew I had to recover his body. We mounted an operation. It was on either day four or five. I asked for volunteers. "The Vietnamese," Major Tut told me, "will get his body for you. We want to do this." Some Vietnamese went out and brought Captain Pusser's body back. He could only be identified by his dog tag. The heat had distorted his body terribly. It was a damn shame.

We received word by radio on Monday, the 25th, that the relief force of tanks, armored personnel carriers, and troops was on the move again. A slick arrived and left a forward observer in the camp who would help direct artillery fire down the road, walking it just in front of the slow, chugging armored column. As the sun went down the first tanks finally clanked into view and took up a defensive positions around the camp's perimeter.

The following morning the 2nd Battalion, 1st Brigade, from the 1st Cavalry Division (Airmobile) was helicoptered into Plei Me. I was asked by their liaison officer where I would recommend he put his unit. I selected an appropriate area for the Cav to land in. Around and beyond the north slope there were a lot of dead enemy soldiers and the stench was terrible. Landing there would be an instructive introduction for the 1st Cav, which had only arrived in country a short time before. No better way to let them know war is hell. After the battalion landed, because his people were throwing up all over themselves, their CO asked if they could move somewhere else.

Before I left I walked around the outside perimeter of Plei Me. The ground was pitted by bomb craters and blackened as far as I could see by napalm. There were also a lot of dead out there. In one case I noticed two enemy soldiers who were actually chained to their machine guns. It was later estimated there were 800 or 900 dead North Vietnamese regulars in front of the camp. I don't know the exact number and I didn't run around counting them. Eventually a bulldozer came in and just covered everything up.[156]

Charles Beckwith

Plei Me represented the opening shot of what Hanoi would call its "Winter-Spring Campaign" *(dong xuan)* of 1965-1966. This was no casual sally but a calculated flexing of the military muscle Hanoi was pushing down The Trail. New regiments made the offensive possible; new staffs, which the Vietnam Peoples' Army (VPA) called "field fronts," directed them. The Tay Nguyen Front, with its strength in the Chu Pong massif, was to fight in the Central Highlands. Major General Chu Huy Man led this front.

Hanoi's selection of Chu Huy Man to command in the Central Highlands was another sign of the political sophistication it applied to this war. Man was Hanoi's Montagnard, born in 1914. He became one of the earliest Viet Minh, joining a peasant rebellion in 1930. Imprisoned by the French at Kontum, Man learned the Central Highlands the hard way. Joining the People's Army in August 1945, Man soon became a regiment commander, and thereafter the party and the VPA constantly used Man in posts where his minority knowledge paid off. General Man had been at Dien Bien Phu as political commissar for the VPA 316th Division, a unit composed primarily of Montagnards. Under the DRV he served as both political and military leader of the Tay Bac, an upland minority region. Chu Huy Man had been a member of the party's central committee since 1951, and from 1960 he sat on the government's national defense council. During 1962-1964 General Man headed the section of the VPA General Political Department responsible for Montagnard policy in the South. Chu Huy Man trekked South himself in 1964, passing through his native Vinh, where he had risen from a landless peasant family. Man's first assignment was as deputy commander of the 5th Interzone. Soon after, the People's Army set up the Tay Nguyen Front under Man's charge.[157]

John Prados

Ia Drang Valley Campaign (14 – 19 November 1965)

My commanders and soldiers reported there was very vicious fighting. I tell you frankly, your soldiers fought valiantly. They had no choice. You are dead or not. It was hand-to-hand fighting. Afterward, when we policed the battlefield, when we picked up our wounded, the bodies of your men and our men were neck to neck, lying alongside each other. It was most fierce.[158]

Nguyen Huu An, NVA

Following the Plei Me attack, search and destroy operations were conducted north and west of the camp. Many contacts occurred in October and early November 1965. Finally on 14 November 1/7th Air Cavalry air assaulted into the Ia Drang Valley 14 miles northwest of Plei Me at a place called LZ X-Ray. The Ia Drang Valley Campaign was fought for four days, 14-18 November 1965.

A separate related battle was fought by the 2/7 Cavalry and a company from the 1/5th near LZ Albany on 17-19 November 1965. The U. S. units were moving toward the LZ Albany to be withdrawn back to base camp. The units were in a long stretched out column when the commander, LTC Robert McDade ordered a halt in place so he could move to the front of the column to interrogate prisoners just captured. He ordered company commanders to move forward to join him which left the troops on the trail without their commanders, a bad situation in the jungle, The NVA had been planning an ambush and this was a perfect opportunity. They hit the column from all sides. In the ensuing battle about 70% of the 400 U. S. troops involved were killed or wounded. It was a crushing defeat for the U. S. and the first major victory for the NVA against the U. S. The commander of the 1/7th Cavalry, LTC Hal Moore left no man behind but LTC McDade of the 2/7th ended his fight with 155 killed, 125 wounded and at least four men missing in action.

The Ia Drang Valley Campaign apparently convinced General Westmoreland that the use of "Body Count" as a metric was the best measure of progress toward victory because of the high number of NVA killed in the battle. The enthusiasm for body count was not shared by parents back home as coffins arrived back in the states. Helicopter pilots Bruce Crandall and Ed Freeman were awarded the Medal of Honor for their actions during this battle.

LTC Harold G. Moore, Jr., commander of 1/7th Cavalry described the end of his fight.

> Now came the body count. From the beginning of the fight I had known that higher headquarters would eventually want to know what damage we had done to the enemy. So after each major action in this battle, hating it, I asked my company commanders for their best estimates of enemy killed. With the battle raging back and forth over three days and two nights, it was anything but orderly. There was no referee to call time out for a body count. We did the best we could to keep a realistic count of enemy dead. In the end it added up to 834 dead by body count, with an additional 1,215 estimated killed and wounded by artillery, air attacks, and aerial rocket attacks. On my own I cut the 834 figure back to 634, a personal allowance for the confusion and fog of war, and let the 1,215 estimated stand. We captured and evacuated six enemy prisoners.
>
> On our side, we had lost 79 Americans killed in action, 121 wounded, and none missing [count is of Moore's troops, ony].
>
> But the body count on both sides, tragic as it was, did not go to the heart of the matter. What had happened here in these three days was a sea change in the Vietnam War. For the first time since Dien Bien Phu in 1954, the North Vietnamese Army had taken the field in division strength. Peoples Army soldiers were pouring down the Ho Chi Minh Trail in unprecedented numbers, and now they had intervened directly and powerfully on the battlefield in South Vietnam. Seventy-nine Americans had been killed in just three days in X-Ray. The cost of America's involvement in this obscure police action had just risen dramatically. Vietnam was now a whole new ball game militarily, politically, and diplomatically. Decisions would have to be made in Washington and in Hanoi, and they would have to be made soon.
>
> For now, however, my first priority was getting my troopers out of LZ X-Ray safely and quickly and turning responsibility for this battered, blood-soaked piece of earth over to Lieutenant Colonel Bob Tully.[159]
>
> *Harold G. Moore, Jr.*

Dennis Deal was with the 1/7th Cavalry and recalled the

end of the battle.

The next morning—the 15th of November—at six o'clock, an outpost from Charlie Company saw some North Vietnamese and ran back and said "They're coming." Charlie Company was decimated— one platoon KIA in action. It was horrendous. I was less than a hundred yards away.

There wasn't good visibility so no airplanes could come in for support. After that platoon got wiped out, I got my platoon shoulder to shoulder on northern side of the perimeter in a military assault formation and prepared for the worst. I thought I was gonna die. Every time we encountered an ant hill I threw a hand grenade behind it. It was to give us confidence as much as it to kill them, cause we were scared to death this whole thing was gonna be up on us again. But this time, finally, there was no resistance.

All of a sudden we got to Henry Herrick's platoon. There was Serge Ernie Savage. He looked like he was a piece of the earth. These guys, along with air strikes and artillery, had held off countless attacks for thirty hours. There were dead enemy bodies all over the place, somewhere between one and three hundred North Vietnamese.

None of the people who were in the lost platoon were standing, not a one of 'em. They were laying down and looking at us like we had totally taken leave of our senses. They were still in a state of shock. They didn't want to get up. Even the men who *could* stand up were so traumatized by what had happened to them they preferred to lay down and be as safe as possible. And we didn't push 'em. We let 'em lay for a while but then finally we had to say "Look, we gotta get outta here. We don't know what's coming next." Then one of the guys who was still laying down said, "Sir, there's something over there that's red and it's bothering me. Will you go get it?" So I went over and picked it up. It was a diary next to a dead Vietnamese soldier. I looked through it and it was a bunch of beautiful script writing in different colored pencils. We had it translated later. It had a note to his wife that said: "Oh, my dear. When the troops come home after the victory and you do not see me, please look at the proud colors. You will see me there and you will feel warm under the shadow of the bamboo tree." So I took it over to the guy and said, "Look, there's nothing to worry about, this is just a diary. It isn't going to hurt you. Why don't you get up and walk with me. I'll be your security guard."

As we prepared to leave, I noticed one of the North Vietnamese bodies had literally had his buttocks shot off and his insides were leaking out a large hole—a very ugly sight. But what this guy did is an amazing story of human endurance. As he was lying there, wounded about as bad as you can be, he had taken a hand grenade, armed it, and wrapped it around the upper hand guard of his rifle stock. He had booby-trapped himself. I thought, "Man, if we're up against this, it's gonna be a long-ass year."[160]

Dennis Deal

17 – 21 December 1965 FULRO Uprising

Promises made by the Vietnamese after the 1964 FULRO uprising were not met and Montagnard resentment continued to simmer in 1965. The events of the 1965 FULRO uprising are described by the people that were there at that time. Anthropologist Gerald C. Hickey was in Vietnam in late 1965 and recalled the FULRO uprising.

While in Ban Me Thuot on 15 December 1965 I accidentally met FULRO delegation leaders Y Dhe Adrong and Y Preh Buon Krong. They invited me to the delegation house, a large frame building with a wide balcony, a style reminiscent of the old American West. Sipping coffee, the two highlanders were discouraged and angry. They pointed out that the intensification of the war had made life difficult for their people. Villages were being bombed by the Americans and Vietnamese or were getting caught in the increasing number of military operations. Communists entered villages to exact their "taxes" and force young men to go with them and the South Vietnamese military came into villages to steal. The government made many promises but did little for the highlanders. Then they informed me that talks between them and the government had broken off. The Vietnamese government representatives, Col. Thanh and Gen. Vinh Loc (an imperious portly man) claimed that they were "too busy" to see the FULRO representatives. Vinh Loc, they said, did not want the negotiations to continue. He was more interested in stamping out the FULRO than fighting Communists, and when South Vietnamese troops entered highland villages they busied themselves trying to locate FULRO sympathizers. Y Dhe warned that the present situation could lead to serious trouble.

I returned to Saigon the following day, 16 December, to notify some members of the Montagnard Committee that there was a chance that trouble might erupt in the highlands. On the morning of 17 December the second FULRO revolt began.

The first indication that another uprising was in the offing came on 16 December when a group of FULRO cadremen who were arrested at Pleiku revealed that on 17 December there would be attacks against the town and Special Forces camps. Acccrding to my friend, Y Thih Eban, it was the result of anger and frustration over what the FULRO leaders considered Vietnamese duplicity in not keeping promises made at Pleiku in 1964. They felt the Vietnamese government was indifferent to the highlanders' needs. The order to revolt came from Y Bham who had sent word to his followers in the Vietnamese armed forces and the CIDG, explicitly instructing them to avoid bloodshed. There were minor incidents at three Special Forces camps, but north of Cheo Reo FULRO forces attacked Phu Thien district, killing thirty-five Vietnamese.[161]

Gerald C. Hickey

FULRO accounts from Special Forces camps arrived.

At Camp Lac Thien, newly opened by Detachment A-236 on 8 November, Capt. John McKinney prevented his camp's overthrow in tense 18 December negotiations with internal FULRO leaders, during which three LLDB hostages were released. Capt. Jackie Schmidt's Detachment A-213 at Camp Plei Djereng used a Nung reaction force and radio jamming to prevent his camp from being seized on 20 December. One day earlier eighty-two Montagnard rebels from the 269th and 503d Regional Forces companies sought asylum in Capt. Charles Gregor's Mai Linh Camp (A-112) after killing thirty Vietnamese soldiers at Plei Kanong. They were disarmed and turned over to government authorities.[162]

Shelby L. Stanton

I recall that when I arrived in Vietnam on a commercial aircraft in November 1965 I was acclimated to winter temperatures in the States and heat from the tarmac hit me in the face like a brick and I was staggered by the high temperature. One of my classmates met me at the airport and drove me to MACV where I checked in. He told me that a big fight was going on up north in the Ia Drang valley and I could get a flight to Pleiku my final destination the next morning. I spent a sleepless night looking up at the ceiling watching a salamander climbing around with those marvelous paws that allowed it to hang upside down. I thought that if he fell, he and I would exchange places. I was 28 years old at the time and a recently promoted captain in the U. S. Army Signal Corps with three years experience in the army. I had been assigned to Germany in the 3rd Infantry Division before I had returned to the states where I spent a short time before flying out to Vietnam. My assignment in Vietnam was as an advisor to a Vietnamese Signal Battalion, the 620th that was based at Pleiku with detachments scattered around the Central Highlands. I spoke no Vietnamese and was to advise a Vietnamese major twice my age who had spent many years fighting the Viet Cong. This would be a challenging assignment.

I was on a small twin engine cargo aircraft called a Caribou[163] with one stop at An Khe before heading to Pleiku. It was a quick stop and I sweated in the aircraft watching some of the 1st Air Cavalry Division troops hanging a huge Cav patch on the signal hill that overlooked their new base camp. Most of the troops were out fighting in the Ia Drang Valley. When the aircraft landed at Pleiku I was met by Sergeant Trung, a South Vietnamese interpreter assigned to Advisory Team 21, my new unit. Trung was a very smart guy and spoke nearly perfect English. My new boss told me that I was to fly to Duc Co Special Forces camp on the border to help with supply. The Ia Drang Valley campaign was being fought nearby.

Shortly after I returned to Pleiku the ARVN II Corps Signal Officer came to me and was quite excited. It appeared that ARVN thought that a FULRO uprising would be launched very soon. The ARVN thought that the Montagnards would send a message via a clandestine radio station to announce the uprising. They wanted me to get U. S. radio equipment to jam the FULRO transmitter. This did not appear to be a good solution since the Montagnard could easily seize a government radio station as they had done to announce the September 1964 uprising.[164] A powerful government radio station would be difficult if not impossible to jam. Nevertheless I scrambled around and achieved very little. Finally I told the Signal Officer to use his own ARVN radios to jam the signal because U. S. had none available at that time. I can find only one instance of radio being used to signal the uprising and that was at Plei Djereng.

The first FULRO uprising started months before I arrived in Vietnam. Now the Montagnards were angry at the failure of the South Vietnamese to implement the promises General Co (the ARVN II Corps Commander at that time) made to them in 1964. The FULRO leadership developed a plan for a general uprising in the Central Highlands. The goal was the creation of a "Federal State of the Montagnard-Cham people" administered by a French/US/United Nations trusteeship for the Vietnamese highlands. CIDG camps with strike forces would defect and join other FULRO units in attacks on the provincial capitals of Pleiku, Kontum, Ban Me Thuot, Gia Nghia and Cheo Reo. The CIDG camps at Lac Thien, Plei Djereng, and Mai Linh were affected.

While the uprising achieved some initial success, it was quickly suppressed.[165] The uprising in December 1965 led to the killing of 35 South Vietnamese at the Phu Thien District headquarters in Darlac Province northwest of Ban Me Thuot as well as others in Pleiku Province. After the uprising failed, General Vinh Loc ordered the execution of four FULRO leaders.[166] This was accomplished in Pleiku City just before Christmas in 1965. Our interpreter, Sergeant Trung, witnessed the executions and described them to me just after they occurred.[167]

Mike Eggleston

Author Gordon M. Patric related his recollections.

Then—in mid-December 1965—a huge revolt engulfed the high-lands but lighting-fast Vietnamese moved in as berets lost a string of camps. This time it was large scale fighting, which swirled across some seven up country provinces including Dar Lac. Five or more beret camps fell—temporarily. For a brief instant it looked like Montagnard rebels had won.

Buon Brieng fell and was blacked out for several days, as determined Rhade took over. As those rebels rose the beret captain there then got off a last message to the outside, warning people away from his camp while he tried putting the lid on things. Days later contact was restored, but the captain had failed. Later on a weakened Buon Brieng reappeared, but the heart of its army and many guns were gone. Hostile, veteran irregulars had shouldered bundles of weapons and padded off into the bush along with some 200 green recruits.

Other camps fell about the same way. Plei Mroung went down, and its radio blacked out for several days. Plei Djereng fell, and other camps collapsed and barely recovered. Out of five or so of them poured confident, well-armed rebels but they had no idea what was up ahead.[168]

Whereas berets may have seen sluggish Vietnamese troops in 1964, they ran into only sharp, fast-moving ones in December 1965. As the first shot sounded Ky's troops had moved secretly and caught everyone by surprise, including the Americans. There had been no leaks, and only moments before had Vietnamese generals observed custom and told Westmoreland's officers what was up.

This time it was the Vietnamese who captured berets, and they seemed eager to do that just to make sure. Almost before the shooting had started Ky's troops were on top of one beret-irregular force. They surrounded it, disarmed it, and stripped the Americans of all further advisory duty.

So Ky's highly mobile forces moved all over the seven province battlefields as they wound up the December revolt. Revolt reeled back everywhere, and beret camps and city and district headquarters were taken without much trouble. Some battles, mopping up, and punishment followed. At Pleiku there were trials, convictions and executions. And then came more futile talks at Ban Me Thuot.[169]

Gordon M. Patric

General Westmoreland recalled the uprising in his memoir.

For all the best efforts of American Special Forces advisers, foment among the Montagnards also continued. In August 1965 FULRO supporters surprised a CIDG-Special Forces camp near Ban Me Thuot and carried off a store of arms, but swift ARVN reaction prompted the rebels to surrender. In December 1965 Montagnards seized a district capital, but again quick ARVN reaction squelched the revolt. Soon after the Honolulu conference of February 1966, Thieu and Ky moved to bring a Montagnard leader into the Cabinet as Special Commissioner for Montagnard Affairs. That appeared to diminish Montagnard unrest.[170]

William C. Westmoreland

Build-Up

As U.S. Forces were deployed to South Vietnam, a logistical expansion of enormous proportions was needed to support the war. Author Shelby Stanton described the problems.

President Lyndon B. Johnson announced on July 28, 1965, that United States forces in Vietnam would be expanded immediately to 125,000 men. The administration made it clear that it intended to meet these growing overseas requirements without mobilization. New soldiers would be gained through more drafting and increased enlistments. This political decision engaged the military in a major war without any of its anticipated National Guard or Reserve component assistance. The peacetime standing Army had a very thin crust of engineers, signalmen, logistics supervisors, and service units. Soon a crisis developed in supply and support of the combat formations going to Vietnam. The adverse consequences were legion, but this basic governmental policy never really changed. The ammunition situation was so chaotic that the 173d Airborne Brigade arrived in Vietnam with only fifteen days' worth of bullets. Daily cargo flights from Okinawa were instituted just to keep rifle magazines full. Ammunition for other deploying units was being sent on ahead and off-loaded, a good practice which was undone whenever the units were diverted from their original destinations. As a result, ammunition crates and stacks of shells were piled up all over the beaches at Cam Ranh Bay and aboard leased sampans and barges floating on the Saigon River. The lack of transportation truck companies, another type of basic logistical unit, prevented ready transfer of such stockpiles to where they were needed.

A number of mad scrambles typified early logistical experiences in Vietnam. One of the worst happened during the summer deployment of the 2d Brigade, 1st Infantry Division, from Fort Riley, Kansas, to Vietnam. The unit was directed to secure the coastal town of Qui Nhon, where a natural harbor promised an ideal enclave site. Supplies were loaded by truck and aircraft at Saigon and hauled 250 miles north. Two days before arrival in Vietnam, the ships were diverted so that the brigade could secure the Saigon area. A battalion was offloaded to defend Cam Ranh Bay until the programmed American garrison (the 1st Brigade of the 101st Airborne Division) could get there, and the rest of the brigade then proceeded to Bien Hoa. A frantic last-minute relocation of supplies was made in an effort to get the tons of materials back south. The 1st Infantry Division's 2d Brigade arrived at Bien Hoa, located on the banks of the Dong Nai River outside Saigon, on July 16, 1965, minus large quantities of its supplies. The only port worth its name in Vietnam was the bustling commercial dock fifty miles inland at Saigon…Viet Cong sappers were having a field day destroying massive quantities of supplies, but no one could measure the losses. Without inventory control no one knew what was where.[171]

Shelby L. Stanton

Final Assessment of the Pleiku Campaign

1965 ended on a mixed note.

Initially, at least, the determination and ferocity of PAVN troops made them, as many Americans would testify, extremely formidable. It was possible that in the future, in more carefully planned operations in which they enjoyed the initiative and were able to make fuller use of the "grabbing the belt" technique or were able to hit and run more cleanly, they might inflict more casualties than the Americans could endure. . . . On the one hand, PAVN battle casualties in this campaign, though certainly lower than US estimates, were probably much more severe than Vietnamese Communist writers such as Hiep were prepared to admit.[172]

J. P. Harris

As 1965 closed, U.S. forces in Vietnam had increased to 184,000. The total of U.S. dead since the start of our involvement stood at 2,344 as 1966 opened.[173]

1966–The Year of the Horse

"Let go, dumb-shit. I'm in charge now."[174]

Charles M. Simpson

America Takes Over the War – 1966

As 1965 ended, the U.S. build-up was in full swing, and U.S. units were taking the war to the enemy in what became known as "search-and-destroy" operations. The ARVN was relegated to the secondary role of defense. The measure of success used was the number of enemy killed, wounded, or captured. The term "body count" entered reports, indicating the number of enemy dead bodies found on the battlefield. By the end of 1965, the number of U.S. troops in Vietnam had increased to 184,300, up from 23,000 at the end of 1964. As 1966 opened, the air war continued. *Operation Rolling Thunder* (1965–1968) included the heavy bombing of targets in North Vietnam, but there was no indication that it was reducing Hanoi's support for the war in the south.[175] Infiltration of NVA troops to the south increased from 1,500 per month in 1965 to 4,500 in 1966.[176] That year also saw an endless stream of U.S. combat operations in South Vietnam. These search-and-destroy operations were not designed to clear and hold ground, but only to attack the enemy, roll up an impressive body count, and move on. Very often, the enemy moved back in as the U.S. departed, as described in the account of the French war. It had become a war of attrition. General Westmoreland had a point to what seemed like a pointless exercise in blood. He called it the "cross-over point," or the point at which the rate of enemy losses exceeded the rate at which the enemy could replace its losses. To LBJ's frustration, there was no way of telling when the cross-over point would be reached, and as the rate of coffins sent back home increased, opposition to the war also increased. There was no end in sight.

As the U. S. buildup continued in 1966, the Special Forces stepped up its operations against the VC and NVA. A methodology was in place at that time to increase security within South Vietnam. Special Forces camps were set up in untamed areas and as an area was secured, the South Vietnamese government would take over the camp. In most cases the CIDG at the camp would be converted to Regional Forces or discharged and the Special Forces would move on to set up in a new area and start over. This was not without problems. The CIDG Montagnards were attached and loyal to their Special Forces comrades and transfer to the LLDB (Vietnamese Special Forces) or ARVN was detested due to the incompetence of the South Vietnamese. Worse, the Montagnards were treated as Moi by the Vietnamese. Movement to another area was avoided since the Montagnards had roots in the area of their camp where their ancestors were buried.[177]

Mobile Guerilla Forces (Blackjack)

Mobile guerrilla forces were created by the 5th Special Forces Group in late 1966 to harass and interdict the enemy in his own backyard in South Vietnam. They were to do so using the enemy's own guerrilla tactics, principally stealth and surprise. The guerrilla forces were to infiltrate by stealth, interdict enemy lines of communications, conduct surveillance of enemy base camps and way stations, and gather intelligence. When possible, they would destroy food and ammunition caches, leave booby traps and delayed-action explosives, and generally spread chaos and despair. As it was envisioned that the operations would continue for weeks at a time, and as it would not be possible to live off the land entirely, a method of resupply was devised. At first or last light an A-1E fighter-bomber would proceed to the resupply point, not necessarily a DZ or LZ. The guerrilla band would signal the desired impact area, and the A-1E would "bomb" napalm containers filled with food, uniforms, and ammo. It would then go to another point safely away from the guerrillas and drop high-explosive bombs. In the jungle, uniforms last about a week and are a necessary resupply item. The guerrillas can carry food enough for five days on their persons, so resupply took place about every five days, weather permitting. The pilots that flew those resupply missions were from the 1st Air Commando Squadron in Pleiku, and among the best in the Air Force.

The mobile guerrilla forces differed from the mobile strike forces in several ways. Organizationally, they had a full U.S. Special Forces A Team in command. The force consisted of a Mike Force company of 150 men, less the weapons platoon, and had an organic reconnaissance platoon, bringing the overall strength to about 184 indigenous and 12 U.S. As an unconventional warfare unit, they followed UW procedures. Each mission was preceded by a detailed area assessment and highly detailed planning. . .Dozens of Black Jack mobile guerrilla operations were carried out in all four corps, and all were successful, due to the detailed analysis and planning. In almost every case, each Black Jack operation attracted so much enemy reaction that they had to be extracted before they reached their planned exit point. In no case did a Black Jack operation take heavy casualties or fail to interdict and harass the enemy's lines of communication as planned. The success of those missions definitively proved that mobile guerrilla forces can and should be used against a guerrilla enemy in counterinsurgency operations.[178]

Charles M. Simpson

During the second half of 1966 action focused on joint CIDG/U.S./ARVN unit operations and movement into VC war zones. In the approaches to Saigon, three companies of Chinese Nungs moved into War Zone C and pinpointed the location of the 272nd VC Regiment. This enabled U. S. units to attack the VC as a part of the first search-and-destroy operation of the war, *Operation Attleboro.*[179]

Successes were offset by losses, some severe. The A Shau Valley is located in I CTZ near the Laotian border. It was primeval area with mountain peaks rising to 5,000 feet. A Special Forces camp of the same name was located in the valley 30 miles southwest of Hue and about a mile from the border. The camp was strategically located near the Ho Chi Minh Trail where NVA troops were funneled through the valley and into populated areas. Detachment A-102 was commanded by Captain John D. Blair and he had 17 Green Berets and 410 CIDG.

In early March 1966 two NVA defectors turned up at the camp reporting that the camp would be attacked by four battalions of the NVA 325th Division. Recce aircraft observed NVA troops on the move and airstrikes were called in. The camp was reinforced by more Special Forces personnel and a MIKE Force Company. On the night of 8 March the NVA attacked the camp but were beaten back. On 9 March the NVA attack was preceded by a heavy mortar attack that destroyed many of the defensive positions as close air support aircraft circled the camp inflicting heavy casualties on the NVA attackers. By 10 March the NVA broke through the camp perimeter forcing defenders back to the north wall. One company of CIDG defected to the NVA. Heavy NVA antiaircraft fire hampered close air support and resupply. The fight continued throughout the day forcing the withdrawal of the defenders as ammunition ran out. Captain Blair ordered the camp abandoned. Helicopters were sent in to evacuate survivors, but these were overwhelmed by many of the CIDG who panicked and mobbed the evacuation aircraft. Troops on the aircraft were forced to fire on the mob in order to allow the aircraft to take-off. Some of the evacuation aircraft were shot down by the NVA adding to the chaos and casualties of the fight. Casualty numbers varied. A total of 5 Special Forces and 288 CIDG were killed or missing, but many of those missing later turned up. The NVA lost about 800 troops. The camp was abandoned and the A Shau valley remained under the control of the NVA throughout the rest of the war.[180]

Author Charles Simpson described the friction that existed between the regular army officers and the Special Forces.

> Other problems with the Americans came from their tendency to equate the light little CIDG companies with their own heavy infantry.

They also mistakenly thought of them as subordinates rather than allies, and frequently took command of situations that were well in hand of the SF leaders. In early 1967, the company commander of A Company in III Corps, Lt. Col. John Hayes, had two Mike Force companies patrolling in War Zone C. They bumped into a VC hospital which the VC defended fiercely until it could be evacuated, and the lead Mike Force company was badly mauled. John joined the operation after they blasted a one-chopper LZ in the jungle and called for a replacement Mike Force company to fly in and evacuate the combat-ineffective company. Twenty HU-1D helicopters from a helicopter unit that usually supported the Big Red One Division, one by one deposited the replacements, loaded casualties and evacuees, and took off. John was on the ground guiding each chopper in with hand signals, and everything was going about as well as it could. The chopper movement attracted an assistant division commander of the 1st Division, known for his macho and profanity, who radioed to John on the ground, "Let go, dumb-shit. I'm in charge now." Under the guidance of the airborne general, the last two choppers, numbers nineteen and twenty, crashed upon landing and created a major evacuation problem themselves.[181]

Charles M. Simpson

As 1966 closed, U.S. forces in Vietnam had increased to 385,300. The total of U.S. dead stood at 8,694 as 1967 opened.[182]

1967–The Year of the Goat

"They're all dead," Flynt gasped.[183]

John Leppelman

North Vietnam Invades the Central Highlands – 1967

In 1967, controversy reigned in Hanoi. Should the NVA continue guerrilla warfare, or should a conventional military attack be launched? The decision was to launch a conventional military offense in the South, with the goal of causing a South Vietnamese uprising to reject their government. In the early spring of 1967, the Vietnamese Communists were losing the war due to the massive influx of U.S. troop units. A plenum was convened to consider a new strategy to win the war. Clearly, the anti-war movement in the U.S. and the friction the war caused with our European allies[184] were very encouraging to Hanoi, but a brilliant stroke was needed to win the war. The new strategy that emerged from the 13th Plenum was "to cause a spontaneous uprising in order to win a decisive victory in the shortest possible time."[185] This meant the abandonment of guerrilla warfare, with a general offensive to win in a single stroke. Work started to develop a plan that would become known as Tong Cong Kich, Tong Khai Nghia, "General Offensive, General Uprising,"(GO-GU) shortened to TCK-TKN.[186] The concept appeared very promising.

Hanoi's Phase I (September–December 1967) would include an NVA invasion in South Vietnam's border areas with Cambodia and Laos. This would draw U.S. units out of the populated areas. The infiltration into South Vietnam had already been increasing from two battalions per month in 1964 to fifteen battalions per month in 1966.[187] The VC would then attack in the cities, hoping to cause a popular uprising (Phase II). The plan was well known and even appeared in the U.S. press. Nevertheless, General Westmoreland moved elements of

134

the 173rd Airborne Brigade, 1st Air Cavalry Division, the 1st Infantry Division, the 4th Infantry Division, and other U.S. and ARVN units to the western border areas. The marines would defend the DMZ in MR 1. As always, North Vietnam wanted to isolate and annihilate entire U.S. units in order to have an impact on the American public. Hanoi's dogma of little regard for their own casualties remained unchanged. North Vietnam would always counter its heavy losses with a flow of replacements sent south. North Vietnam would also test its concept of mass attacks and command and control of large formations.[188] A high rate of U.S. casualties was expected, and this would enhance the flow of U.S. coffins back home in order to fuel the anti-war movement. General Giap, North Vietnam's commander, knew that he would pay a high price in blood for this campaign, but it could end the war. The decision-makers in Hanoi had in mind Dien Bien Phu, the great victory over the French in 1954. In that battle, the loss of the equivalent of a single French division had caused the collapse of the French in Vietnam. Hanoi's plan was based upon four assumptions.

1. The ARVN would collapse and desert in large numbers.
2. The people would rally to support the VC.
3. The ARVN and the people would turn on the Americans.
4. The tactical situation at Khe Sanh would parallel that at Dien Bien Phu in 1954.[189]

Phillip B. Davidson

The assumptions appeared to be unrealistic, and events that followed would prove them to be invalid. The problem was that the clique in Hanoi that had managed the war were the same people since 1954. They were not in touch with reality. For example, their belief that a war-weary South Vietnamese population would suddenly switch sides was clearly unrealistic. Hanoi's entire plan hinged upon success in the cities (Phase II). With success in the cities, Phase III, the general offensive to end the war, could proceed. It was a soft plan that assumed that the allies would do nothing, especially at Khe Sanh. U.S. air power and the ability to move forces quickly over long distances seemed omitted from consideration. The planning did not mention the impact on the American home front, e.g., causing the American public to lose heart and trigger the withdrawal of U.S. forces. It did not need to. The impact on the U.S. home front was built into the dogma of the Vietnamese Communists. From switching dog tags on dead U.S. troops[190] to confuse the identification of the dead to wiping out entire units, the propaganda value of actions was always considered.

The U.S. had ample forces to counter the NVA. At the start of 1967, the U.S. strength was 385,300 in Vietnam. This was approaching the all-time high for U.S. forces during the Vietnam War (536,300 in 1968). Elements of four U.S. divisions would ultimately be deployed to the border regions during these battles. Additionally, local ARVN battalions were committed as well as the ARVN strategic reserve (airborne and rangers) and local forces such as the CIDG. The fact that there would be a major attack by Hanoi in the Central Highlands and in the cities was widely known. The problem was that the exact time, location, and strength of the enemy attacks were not known. The Hanoi timeline of Phase I was to start with attacks in the border regions in September 1967 by four NVA regiments. This would surprise the U.S. infantry, since they were accustomed to fighting poorly equipped and poorly trained VC units. Instead, mainline well-disciplined NVA regiments with brand-new equipment were committed to the fight. More importantly, they would attack in force, sometimes in waves—a far cry from the hit-and-run guerrilla tactics of the past.

On the Allied side, U. S. continued to build up forces as the CIDG expanded.

By 1967 the 5th Special Forces Group had become committed primarily to fielding its 285 CIDG companies in the rugged and remote areas of South Vietnam that were not suitable for sustained allied presence. The group had eighty-two A-Detachments, twelve B-Detachments, four companies, and six special project detachments scattered in over 100 different locations. The total number of border camps that year (twenty-eight) had doubled over the fourteen border surveillance camps of 1966. The geographical pattern of Special Forces camps in Vietnam was being patterned in consonance with allied campaign plans, in contrast to the scattered, disjointed placement of earlier years.[191]

Shelby L. Stanton

Highland villagers, already suffering because of fighting and bombing, were at this time subjected to another source of disruption—forced relocation. In a war without front lines, American and Vietnamese military commanders sought to create them with "free strike zones" for shelling and bombing.

When in January 1966, the 3d Brigade of the U.S. 25th Division arrived in Pleiku, its commander and Gen. Vinh Loc envisaged a scheme for resettling almost all of the Jarai villages (with an estimated population of ten thousand) west of Pleiku city in order to provide a "free strike zone." The program was discussed through 1966, and early in 1967 the U.S. 4th Infantry Division, commanded by Gen. William Peers, began implementation in conjunction with Gen. Vinh Loc and the South Vietnamese army. This marked the first organized large-scale relocation of highlanders since the 1957 scheme of the Diem government. The plan called for relocating some eight thousand highlanders from forty-eight villages to a large settlement called Edap Enang (which in Rhade means "peace and prosperity" but planners thought it was a Jarai term). . . .Viet Cong propaganda teams were active in and around Edap Enang playing on Jarai villagers' discontents.[192]

Gerald C. Hickey

Dak To

The increase in border surveillance camps helped counter Hanoi's Phase I (September–December 1967) plan for the NVA invasion in South Vietnam's border areas with

Cambodia and Laos. Border surveillance paid off especially in II CTZ where the bloodiest battle of the war would be fought at Dak To located on the Cambodian border northwest of Pleiku. It started with what became known as the Battle of the Slopes, Hill 1338.

On 17 June, the 173rd battalions, 1/503rd and 2/503rd were ordered to move from Catecka to Dak To. The objective was Hill 1338, about five kilometers south of Dak To. The bodies of two Americans were discovered, mutilated. They were cut from groin to head, with internal organs exposed. One person who saw the bodies said that they looked like a page from an anatomy book.

> A particularly grisly aspect of this fighting involved the constant discovery of human skeletons from past battles. On June 20th, the 173rd Airborne Brigade paratroopers found the osseous remains of two Special Forces, eight of their indigenous CIDG strikers, and one NVA soldier. Three days later, the bones of a missing radioman from one of their own patrols was found. Still more skeletal corpses of Army Special Forces and their CIDG soldiers were discovered throughout the period. Ghosts seemed to haunt every tropical mist-shrouded sepulcher, and the unnerved parachutists freely admitted the whole area "spooked them out."[193]
>
> ***Shelby L. Stanton***

Sa Won Chang, A/1/503rd, reported the discovery of remains.

> In mid–June 1967, I was a point man on that steaming hot day. Moving up a ridgeline, I smelled rotting human flesh and notified our platoon leader, Lieutenant Gerald Quinn. I found a CIDG body lying in middle of trail. The body wore the regular OD green uniform, not tiger fatigues. The remains were skull and bones, except for the very end of the fingers that had flesh left. Then our squad leader, Sergeant Eugene Porter, moved while I was still on point and moving westerly on the ridgeline. I caught something in the corner of my right eye, like a white

balloon by a big tree. I immediately turned to my right side and readied my weapon to fire. I then moved toward what appeared to be the white balloon. Instead I found the body of a U.S. Special Forces soldier. The body had puffed up while under the shade of that big tree. The body didn't have a shirt or boots. The head was gone and there was a big hole in the chest, but it had OD green pants on. The next day, we brought in body bags, and Sergeant Porter and I put his body into a body bag. We also found four or five other CIDG bodies and put them in plastic body bags to be flown out. When we found them, they were all scattered in every direction as they tried to run from a large NVA force. We also found many hand grenade explosion sites.[194]

Sa Won Chang

On 20 June, the 2/503d started its move up Hill 1338. Alpha Company, led by Captain David H. Milton, was in the lead. His orders were to cut an LZ for resupply helicopters and sew CS (tear gas) crystals around it to prevent the enemy from encircling the LZ. This was a bad decision, as seen by the account of one survivor.

On the morning of 6/22, my squad had the unenviable "gas" detail. Our early-morning task was to saturate our laager site with CS crystals. If Charlie had notions of a rear assault, he was in for a stinging surprise. None of us were aware that CS came in a solid compound, and [we] were unfamiliar with its protocol. We hadn't checked our gas masks since who knows when, and at stand down, all who needed to were ordered to shave before saddling up for the airstrip. I remember vividly the immediate, unrelenting excruciating pain when the gas contacted our open pores, not only on our faces, but under arms, and sweaty crotch areas as well.[195]

Sky Soldier Magazine

Charlie Company, commanded by Captain Ronald R. Leonard, moved through Alpha Company on its way farther up Hill 1338. At about 1700 hours, Milton was ordered to return to Dak To the next day to take over security at the battalion CP, relieving Bravo Company. As night fell, the 2/503d had two companies on Hill 1338, with Charlie Company about fifteen hundred meters farther up the hill than Alpha. The troops dug into their night firing position. The next morning, Charlie Company continued its move up Hill 1338, while Alpha Company started its return to Dak To. To this point, not a shot had been fired, but elements of the 24th NVA Regiment had had ample time to prepare a welcome for the 2/503rd, Charlie Company had a platoon of CIDG with it to act as guides. By mid-afternoon, 21 June, Captain Leonard halted Charlie Company and started looking for a night laager position (a fortified campsite). As the troops settled, a night listening post (LP) moved out beyond the perimeter of the camp. A CIDG soldier with them stopped dead. "Beacoup [many] VC, no go!" He was forced forward as troops moved out. The stillness was shattered by an exchange of gunfire. The point man had run into an NVA soldier, and the two exchanged fire. Both missed, but a nearby CIDG soldier was killed as the NVA soldier escaped. The dead CIDG was placed in the center of the perimeter to be airlifted out the next day.

The rest of the night was uneventful, and dawn, 22 June, found both companies in thick fog and low clouds. People were jumpy after waiting all night for an NVA attack that did not happen. At Charlie Company, a new guy, PFC Jimmy Lee Cook, made a new-guy mistake. He left the camp to urinate and forgot to tell his buddies. As he returned in the poor light, his buddies thought he was NVA, and he was shot dead. Captain Leonard now had two dead bodies to be evacuated. Farther downhill, Alpha Company prepared for its return to Dak To, and Lieutenant Judd, second platoon leader, started downhill in the lead at 0625. Rifle fire broke the morning calm as Judd's point squad collided with the NVA, and a firefight followed. Milton called the battalion tactical operations center (TOC) at Dak To to report the encounter, but the TOC seemed unconcerned. Judd pulled back up the hill a bit as Milton sent him another platoon, led by

Lieutenant Hood, to help. The NVA was closing in on the platoons, which were starting to lose people very quickly. Milton called in his position to the TOC, requesting artillery support, which followed. Because of the high trees and fog, the artillery fire was ineffective. The heavy volume of fire could now be heard all the way to the TOC, and everyone realized that something big was happening. The NVA had launched a series of frontal attacks to overwhelm and destroy the two platoons. So far the platoons were holding, but they would not last long. Close air support was called in, but when the troops threw smoke to mark their position, the trees and bamboo dissipated the smoke and the aircraft could not determine where the friendly troops were located. Much worse, on the ground, the smoke marked friendly positions for the NVA, and they converged on the smoke.

Farther up the hill, Captain Leonard heard the firing and was ready to move his Charlie Company down to support Alpha Company. The TOC for some reason told Leonard to hold his position, and it was not until 0900 hours that the TOC ordered Leonard downhill. Critical time had been lost in supporting Alpha Company. Charlie Company moved very slowly, fearing an NVA ambush. As time passed, the TOC became agitated by the slow progress. "Charlie Six, [Leonard], you've got to move faster. Get down that hill!" Meanwhile, Milton held his position as he sent a third platoon under Lieutenant Sexton to reinforce the other two. Milton had no further help that he could send. The situation had become desperate. An M-60 machine gunner changed the red-hot barrel with his bare hands as their position was being overrun. The three platoon leaders were now dead, and most of their troops were dead or wounded. The platoons were being surrounded. It was the end of the line, and a move back up to Milton's command post (CP) seemed prudent, but this presented a horrifying dilemma. It would mean leaving most of the wounded behind, and most knew the fate of the two

Special Forces advisors killed with their CIDG troops. In the end it was every man for himself, and everyone who could crawled out in an effort to reach Milton's CP. As they fled, they heard the screams of the wounded being executed by the NVA. Milton sent men down to help the wounded crawling up, but only a few reached the CP. Milton called in artillery support at about 1130 hours, as Leonard continued his slow movement down to Alpha Company. John Leppelman was in C/2/503rd and recalled his sliding effort to reach Alpha Company.

> Frenchy slowly slid over the edge and then slid about ten feet, where he stopped by digging his heels into the thick mud. The rest of us quickly followed. We moved almost silently as we slipped and slid down the dark side of the mountain. It took us about fifteen minutes to get about midway down the steep slope to where we could look into the valley. I peered over the edge and could see part of the valley floor below us. Several bodies were scattered around. None were moving. The valley floor was quiet; then Flynt pointed, and we saw several NVA moving through some bamboo. Before we had a chance to do anything, bullets started splattering in the ground around us. In the panic mode, we ran zigging and zagging back up where men were offering us hands to pull us over the top. The LT and K were demanding to know what we had seen. "They're all dead," Flynt gasped.[196]
> **John Leppelman**

The fog had cleared, making the artillery support more effective. Bravo Company was airlifted into a position below Alpha but was too late to do any good. Close Air Support (CAS) arrived at 1335 hours to support Bravo Company's move. Five-hundred-pound bombs and napalm added to the din of the battle. One survivor stated nearly half a century later that the noise of all of the exploding ordnance and small-arms fire was so intense that he could not hear commands shouted next to him or even think.

As Captain Leonard's Charlie Company approached

Alpha, the folly of spreading CS crystals become apparent. As his troops approached the old LZ, the protective masks of the troops were found to be ineffective due to the moisture. Soon half of the company was on the ground, temporarily disabled by the CS. At 1420 hours, Leonard arrived at Milton's CP, and the two briefly conferred before sending a team down to check on the fate of the three platoons. The team was driven back by NVA fire, and at that point it was too late in the day to launch a rescue mission, so Charlie Company dug in to spend the night. Helicopters were brought in to evacuate the wounded and the Alpha Company survivors. Captain Milton, who was wounded, was among the first out. Later he explained that he had been ordered out by the TOC. Through the night, artillery ringed the friendly positions as the troops waited for dawn. The battle was over, and the NVA had abandoned the field. Paul Donahue was nearby as the battle ended.

> I had pulled a 12P.M. to 6A.M. switchboard shift, went to bed and awoke about 4 hours later, too hot to sleep long. Upon awakening, I stepped outside my tent to see an F-100 diving out of the sky and thought to myself, "What the hell is this?" When he dropped a bomb, I watched the bomb fall through the fog hanging on to the hill behind us; it exploded with a dull thud. Upon looking up, I saw a group of my friends gathered around a radio on the back of a Jeep. I went over and asked "what's up," and they told me a company of infantry had been ambushed up on the hill. This was June 22nd; the day A Co. 2/503 was ambushed, suffering 75 KIA and 35 WIA. We listened to the battle on the radios and knew they were in a world of shit, as every time a mike was keyed, all you could hear was automatic weapons and screams. They started to bring in the dead and wounded, and we walked over to the B-Med area and saw about fifty bodies wrapped in ponchos laying all over the ground with doctors and medics attending them. It was hard to believe that just a few months ago I was in Jump School with a lot of these men.[197]

> ***Paul Donahue***

At 0700 hours, 23 June, Bravo Company, which had

taken no part in the battle, started up the hill, while Charlie Company moved, down looking for Alpha Company survivors. They found a clearing where the three platoons had attempted to hold the NVA. It was a scene from hell, with dead bodies stacked everywhere. Only three survivors were found. Most of the dead had been executed with a single gunshot to the back of the head. John Leppelman, C/2/503rd described what he saw.

In the early dawn, as the first light started to seep through the canopy, the brush started moving directly in front of my position. Several of us took aim on the foliage as a man staggered out, yelling at us in English not to shoot him. He was a survivor from the disaster below. As he made his way through our line, we saw that a large chunk of his skull was missing, and we could actually see his brain. He told us that after the NVA had overrun Alpha's position, they started executing all the survivors by shooting them in the head. Many men had begged for mercy but were executed. He had lain in a pile of American bodies while a gook had placed a rifle barrel against his head and pulled the trigger. By some miracle the bullet had glanced off his head, taking a big chunk of skull, hair, and flesh. He had been stunned but recovered and, once it was dark, escaped back up the mountain. We were furious, and the word quickly was passed around among the enlisted men that we would take no prisoners. The gooks had executed Americans who were wounded and out of ammunition. When we reached the valley floor, we spread out on line and moved forward slowly. When we stepped from the bamboo cover, we saw about ten American bodies stacked like cordwood in front of us. They were dead, with bullet holes in their heads. They had been stripped of weapons and gear. Welch and I moved around the bodies and moved down the trail slowly to where another eight of our men were scattered in various positions of death. Suddenly one of the bodies moved and stood up. He had multiple wounds but, to our amazement, was still alive. I called the CO and told them we had found a survivor and needed a medic at our location.

American bodies were scattered all through the bullet-scarred jungle. Welch and I came to another group. Welch whispered, "Look, his hand's moving." I looked at the pile of bodies and saw a man clenching and unclenching his fist. I got back on the horn, described what we had, and told the company to hurry. We needed medics fast. My God, I thought, these men lay here, out of ammo, waiting to die. They didn't have a prayer. As I moved, I found several men with weapons jammed, and a couple had died with their M-16s broken down, trying to fix the malfunction. As I moved among the men, I got madder and madder until I wanted to turn around and go back and shoot Alpha Company's CO [Milton]. He had definitely fucked up by not being with his men. He had stayed top and sent one platoon after another to their death as the battle had raged on below him; he had called artillery in on top of the besieged troops, as well as runs from gunships. This had almost no impact on the situation because of the triple canopy overhead.[198]

John Leppelman

The Battle of the Slopes was over, but the major battles of Dak To would soon follow. Over the summer of 1967 a series of hill fights would be fought along the border as the NVA moved into South Vietnam. These culminated in the battle of Hill 875.

In late spring, 1967, the NVA prepared an elaborate defense system on Hill 875. On the crest, a series of interconnecting bunkers were dug in with up to eight feet of dirt and teak logs. These could only be penetrated by the heaviest of bombs. The battle for Hill 875 lasted five days and would be the costliest fight of the Vietnam War. The weather and terrain were typical of that experienced in the earlier battles around Dak To. By mid–November the monsoon had passed and the mornings were clear and bright. Earlier on 3 November 1967, Sergeant Vu Hong, an artillery specialist assigned to the 66th NVA Regiment, surrendered to South Vietnamese Popular Forces near Dak To. He explained that the mission of his division was to annihilate a major U.S. unit in order to force the Allies to send additional units to the border region from the populated areas. General Peers, Commander of the 4th ID, later wrote, "The Enemy had prepared the battlefield well. Nearly every key terrain feature was heavily fortified with elaborate bunker and trench complexes. He had moved quantities of supplies and ammunition into the area. He was prepared to stay." Sergeant Lawrence Okendo of the 4th Battalion, 503rd, explained the background.

> On 17 November, 1967, units of the 2nd battalion, 503rd Airborne Infantry, 173rd Airborne Brigade (Sep.) located an abandoned enemy encampment that was used as a hospital area by the NVAs. The treatment area was large, with bed-like clusters and extensive land lines in place. CHICOM field medical dressing and other medical paraphernalia littered the area, indicating the area was used very recently. This area was proof that the NVA suffered heavy casualties in prior battles with the Sky Soldiers in the nearby hills of 830, 815, 823, and 882.[199]

Lawrence Okendo

On 18 November a small Special Forces group collided with the NVA 174th Regiment in bunkers on the slopes of Hill 875. The Special Forces and Montagnards pulled back. The 2/503rd got the mission to clear Hill 875. Lieutenant Colonel Steverson, commander of 2/503rd, assigned the mission of planning and executing the attack to his senior company commander, Captain Harold J. Kaufman of Charlie Company. Colonel Steverson would be airborne, circling above. Kaufman laagered near the base of Hill 875 and started his assent the next morning, 19 November. The NVA were waiting and had set a trap for Kaufman. While Kaufman moved up the hill with C and D Companies, A Company remained behind to cut a landing zone. A and C were within 300 meters from the crest of Hill 875 when the NVA opened fire from concealed positions forcing the 173rd troops to ground. Meanwhile, A Company at the foot of the hill was attacked and moved up the hill to join the other two companies. The three companies were surrounded when one of the worst friendly fire incidents of the war occurred. A ground support aircraft dropped two 500-pound bombs into the 503rd perimeter instantly killing 42 people and wounding another 45. The bombs destroyed the command group. As night fell the survivors dug in and waited for reinforcements.

The following morning another battalion, the 4/503rd started its accent of Hill 875 but was slow due to enemy mortar and sniper fire. The 4/503rd reached the 2/503rd at nightfall. On the afternoon of 21 November both battalions moved forward to take the crest of the hill and reached the trench line after fierce fighting but then pulled back because it was dark. The following day was spent on airstrikes and artillery placed on the top of the hill. On Thanksgiving Day, 23 November the attack was renewed and the two battalions occupied the top of the hill. The NVA had withdrawn during the night.

During the battle of Hill 875 (19-23 November 1967) the 173rd Airborne Brigade, alone, suffered 115 KIA, 253 WIA and seven MIA. NVA losses were estimated at 1,700 KIA and 1,000-2,000 WIA. Three Medals of Honor were awarded to members of the 173rd Airborne Brigade for valor during the fight and the 173rd was awarded the Presidential Unit Citation.[200]

> The belt of border camps in II CTZ was given renewed emphasis after MACV's difficult November campaign in the highlands, which had consumed the 4th Infantry Division and 173d Airborne Brigade. Previously, many camps of II CTZ were scheduled for closure and their assets projected for northward insertion into I CTZ. The chain of surveillance camps included launch sites for long-range MACV-SOG teams in the rugged tri-border region. Ben Het was already being built for such purposes in the northern Plei Trap Valley. Complementing this Plei Trap—Bu Prang highland border camp line was Tieu Atar, opened on 20 December 1967. Opened two months ahead of schedule and constructed by the 299th Engineer Battalion, it was the last fighting camp constructed during the year.[201]
>
> ***Shelby L. Stanton***

Loc Ninh (29 October – 7 November 1967)

On 10 December 1966, the Loc Ninh camp was set up as a border surveillance camp in Bing Long Province near the Cambodian border west of Saigon.[202]

Nearly a year later while the Border Battles continued in MR 1 and MR 2, enemy activity increased farther south along the Cambodian border. On 27 October 1967, a NVA regiment, the 88th, attacked an ARVN battalion at Song Be, the capital of Phuoc Long Province, near the Cambodian border in MR 3. The outnumbered ARVN repulsed the attack and pursued the retreating NVA. The NVA lost 134 men killed, while ARVN losses were thirteen KIA.[203]

Two days later, the VC attacked nearby Loc Ninh in the adjacent province of Binh Long. Loc Ninh district town was located in MR 3, eight miles from the Cambodian border   in a VC-controlled area. Several battles were fought at Loc Ninh before and after this October 1967 fight, which was the most significant.

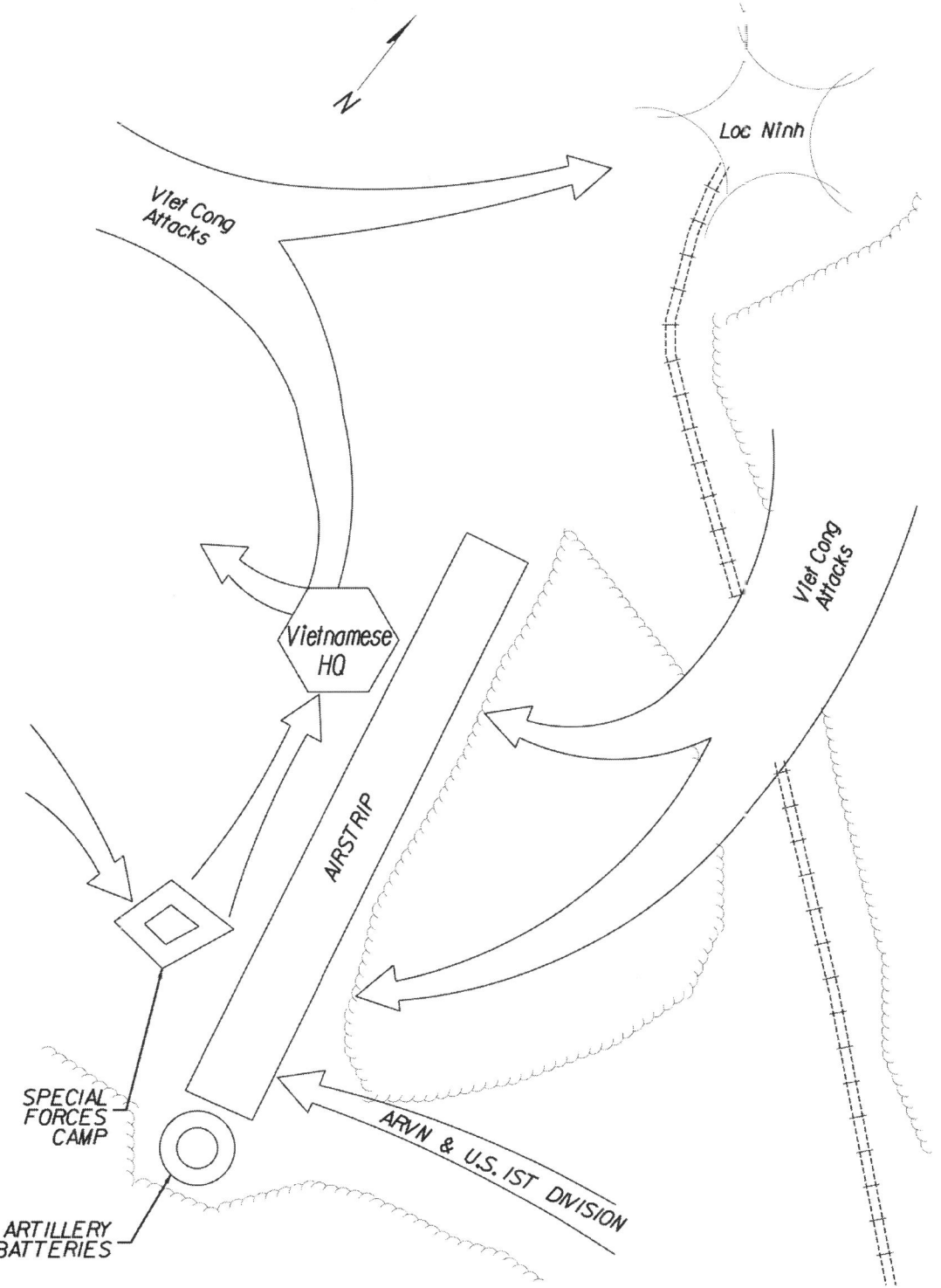

N

Loc Ninh

Viet Cong
Attacks

Viet Cong
Attacks

Vietnamese
HQ

AIRSTRIP

SPECIAL
FORCES
CAMP

ARTILLERY
BATTERIES

ARVN & U.S. IST DIVISION

The Battle of Loc Ninh (Connor Eggleston).

Nestled in a gently rolling plain in rubber country—many of the 10,000 or so Vietnamese who lived in the district worked for the plantations—Loc Ninh had been little affected by the war. Some plantations had been abandoned, but the largest, the Societe des Caoutchoucs d'Extreme-Orient, fully met its schedules. The managers had their compound on a hill overlooking the town, complete with tile-roofed villas, flower beds, manicured lawns, a red-clay tennis court, and a nice-size swimming pool. Loc Ninh also featured a U.S. Special Forces camp, established the previous December to watch the border, held by Detachment A-331 of the 5th Special Forces, with three companies of Vietnamese, Nung, and Montagnard irregulars. The camp lay southwest of the plantation, at the edge of Loc Ninh's airstrip. At the other end stood the ARVN district headquarters, encompassing some old French buildings plus more recent bunkers, crowned by an observation tower and surrounded by concertina wire. The district chief, Captain Tran Minh Cong, held sway there, backed by two under strength companies of ARVN Regional Forces, barely 100 men in all.[204]

John Prados

The VC were less trained and poorly equipped compared to the NVA fighting in MR 1 and MR 2. In early October, the VC began preparation for an assault on Loc Ninh. Both the town and the camp would be seized. The VC at Loc Ninh had a major underground headquarters nearby and did not want to draw attention to it by an attack but they did attack. One of the motives for the attack was the inauguration of South Vietnam President Nguyen Van Thieu, which would occur at the end of October. The attack would occur at that time in an effort to embarrass the new president by seizing a district capital.

Author Gordon Rottman described the camp.

The camp was unusually, but efficiently shaped. It was an elongated diamond shape oriented from southwest to northeast, but its four sides were indented with shallow "Vs," in effect giving it eight walls. The perimeter was a high berm topped with a zigzag trench and two-man fighting positions. These were constructed of sandbags with a speed pallet roof topped by one or two layers of sandbags. A firing port was provided in the front. The trench was unrevetted with a one-layer-thick sandbag parapet. Several coils of razor concertina wire fronted the berm. At the inner point of the indented "Vs" was a machine gun bunker with others on the corners. The southwest end was blunt and had two machine gun bunkers several yards apart.

The entrance road ran from the airfield, which ran from southeast to northwest just outside the wire, curving through the wire barriers to enter the camp at the southeast wall's "V." Any attacker attempting to use the road would be exposed to short-range flanking fire from their right for the entire length of the wall. Above-ground Striker barracks were spotted at irregular intervals around the perimeter. A total of 530 Cambodians, Vietnamese, Montagnards, and Nungs manned four companies. One company was assigned to each of the four walls.[205]

Gordon Rottman

The VC 272nd and 273rd Regiments of the 9th VC Division attacked Loc Ninh beginning at 0115 hours on 29 October. VC mortar rounds announced the start of the attack, and sappers penetrated the CIDG defenses at the camp but were driven off. The VC attack on the town was successful, but at dawn, two CIDG companies from the camp counterattacked and cleared the town. The U.S. advisor and the district chief, Captain Cong, who were holed up in the Tactical Operations Center (TOC), were rescued. Meanwhile, part of the 2nd Battalion, 28th Infantry of the 1st Infantry Division and two artillery batteries were brought into the airfield. John McCoy described events at the airfield.

> It was a LARGE python. I mean a really huge python. It took about eight or more men to pick it up. It was at least 12 feet long, maybe a lot longer. I have never seen a longer or bigger python before or since. We were out on patrol, headed back in to the NDP [Night Defensive Position] at the south end of the Loc Ninh airstrip, when Lt. Fortenberry walked up, holding the front of the snake, followed by several men from his platoon trying to hold the rest of this enormous constrictor. He informed me that we had all just walked over the snake. That

didn't make me feel too comfortable. The snake apparently had eaten recently, as it had a bulge about the size of a small pig about three or four feet back from its head. We all speculated on what it had eaten. Lt. Fortenberry managed to find a large cardboard box, about the size of a refrigerator, and put the snake in that. They named the snake "Lurch." Either that night, or the next night, we came under attack again. I remember Fred Hill and I were heading for our bunker when the first mortar rounds started dropping in on the runway. Fred looked over at the box that had held Lurch, and realized the box had been tipped over somehow and Lurch was loose. When Fred brought this to my attention, I hesitated to jump in the bunker, as I figured Lurch just might be in there. The mortar rounds were moving down the runway, falling closer to our bunkers, so I opted to take my chances with the snake and jumped in the bunker. I may have let Fred go first. Lurch wasn't there, and we never saw him again. I hope he crawled out to the rubber trees and scared a few VC to death.[206]

John McCoy

Sporadic contact with the VC continued that day until 0055 hours on 31 October, when two battalions of the 272nd VC Regiment resumed the attack on the camp and the town. Devastating firepower met the attack from air, artillery, and direct ground fire by the defenders.

After the last air strike, the VC was seen dropping their weapons and fleeing the scene completely disorganized.[207] The major reason for the success of the defense was the close coordination and cooperation between U.S. Special Forces, LLDB (*Lac Luong Dac Biet)* (Vietnamese Special Forces), Vietnamese subsector, and U.S. Army units.

Everyone got a little of what they wanted out of Loc Ninh. COSVN [NVA] had succeeded in coordinating attacks from two different divisions. According to Hanoi's war history, the campaign— which it considered active until December (including two division- and five regiment-size engagements, sixty in all)—"consolidated our offensive springboard north of Saigon and marked a new step forward in the capacity of COSVN's main force soldiers to fight a concentrated battle."

MACV could claim a victory too, even though the 1st Division had given up a planned sweep of the Long Nguyen Secret Zone to fight at Loc Ninh. And Lyndon Johnson, who wanted publicity for the new, improved ARVN, could get Walt Rostow's Vietnam Information Group to give out details and induce MACV's public relations people to secure favorable press coverage.[208]

John Prados

At Loc Ninh, the NVA attacked an artillery position in waves. The artillerymen lowered their howitzer tubes to the horizontal and fired "beehive" rounds that were similar to firing a mass of ball bearings. The result was devastating. The VC soldiers fell in heaps. A total of 852 lay dead.[209] General Westmoreland got his coveted body count.

Massacre at Dak Son

Shortly after the battle of Loc Ninh the Communists attacked the Montagnard village of Dak Son 75 miles northeast of Saigon on 6 December 1967. The village of 2,000 Montagnards had acted as a safe haven for 800 Montagnard refugees who had escaped Communist control. It is possible that the Communists also feared that other Montagnards in Phuoc Long Province might also flee their control. It was for this reason that the Communists were bent on revenge against the village. The local village militia was pushed back, but was then ignored. Military victory seemed of no interest. The Communists were only interested in killing as they moved through the village murdering unarmed men women and children inhabitants using flamethrowers and grenades. Those who were able to get to burrows under their houses were asphyxiated. When the flamethrowers ran out of fuel the Communists finished off most of the survivors with gunfire. As many as 252 of the inhabitants died in the attack with many of the survivors taken hostage.[210]

Michael D. Benge identified the unit responsible as the 88th Regiment of the 1st NVA Division. War crimes and atrocities by the VC and NVA were common throughout the war, many other incidents were reported.

> Just before Tet in 1971 I read the daily intel briefing that indicated that the VC in the Highlands had banned peoples' travel before Tet. This would be difficult to enforce because most people traveled to be with their families during the Tet holidays. Apparently, this was a move by the VC to demonstrate their authority over the population. The next day I had to travel from Pleiku to An Khe on Route 19 and needed to be in An Khe as early as possible so my driver and I pulled in immediately behind the morning road clearing vehicles that were first on the road in the early AM. It was a fast trip until we reached Mang Yang pass when the MP's stopped. We dismounted from our vehicle and cautiously moved forward to the MP's who were at the edge of a small clearing. I saw what I can only describe as a "field of blood." A bus with door open stood before a mass of dead bodies, men, women, and children. All had been executed during the night when the bus was stopped and everyone was forced to dismount. There was nothing we could do. The VC had made sure that everyone was dead. We figured that the VC wanted to prove their point by senseless murder of anyone who violated their travel ban.[211]
>
> *Mike Eggleston*

Hanoi's Phase I started with assaults on Con Thien and Dak To, followed by others, with the final attack at Khe Sanh in January 1968. As 1967 closed, U.S. forces in Vietnam had increased to 480,000. The total of U.S. dead stood at 20,057 as 1968 opened.[212]

1968-The Year of the Monkey

Tet (30 January-28 March 1968)

It will be straight, if slow, ploughing ahead with the
light at the end of the tunnel growing brighter all the time.[213]
Henry Cabot Lodge, U.S. Ambassador

Throughout 1967, U.S. combat operations continued to spiral at an upward rate as did the casualties. At this time Hanoi was planning a major operation intended to win the war. Final Hanoi approval for what has become known as the Tet offensive was given in October [1967]. Part of the scheme's genius lay in the realization that the groundwork could not be laid without Washington and Saigon becoming aware of it. The plan therefore included a deception, an alternative set of expectations the Americans could believe in. In each major war zone Hanoi would battle near the South Vietnamese border, giving the impression it intended to carry out a more conventional operation [away from the population centers].[214]
John Prados

Tet, or the Vietnamese Lunar New Year, is the most important celebration in Vietnamese culture. The date usually falls in late January or early February, with celebrations lasting for three days. Vietnamese people usually return to their families during Tet to visit graves of their ancestors in their homeland or to worship at the family altar. In 1968, Tet was scheduled to start on 31 January. It was called in Vietnamese "Tet Mau Than": The Year of the Monkey.

General Westmoreland and his intelligence chief, General Davidson, thought that the enemy offensive would begin either before or after Tet, since all sides respected the Tet holiday. Hanoi intended the attack to coincide with Tet, starting on the first day of the holiday, but fate intervened to confuse the timing, to the advantage of the Allies. In Hanoi and the South's Central Highlands, the Lunar New Year started on 30

January, while in the remainder of South Vietnam it started on the 31st. When the error was discovered, there was a massive rush by the VC to move up their attacks in the South to 30 January. The mistimed VC moves and some early assaults alerted U.S. commanders that the attack would start at the beginning of Tet. General Weyand was II Force Commander responsible for MR 3. At his headquarters, staff officers had established a betting pool on the start time, with fifteen-minute time blocks starting at dusk on the 30th. Most favored midnight to 0500 hours on 31 January.[215] The winner held the time of 0300 hours, when the VC attacked Saigon.

At Saigon, the VC penetrated Tan Son Nhut airbase and did damage there while attacks at Bien Hoa airbase at 0300 hours consisted of 122mm rockets and mortar attacks.[216] Other attacks included nearby Long Binh. Heavy fighting in the streets of Saigon proved that the VC had infiltrated thousands of troops into the capital for this offensive without being detected. General Davidson, Westmoreland's chief intelligence officer, concluded years later that Hanoi had lost strategic surprise, but achieved tactical surprise at some locations[217]

In South Vietnam, debates between the CIA and MACV continued over the strength of Communist forces in the South. The CIA estimated a total of 430,000 in the South, while MACV estimated no more than 300,000 were available. MACV realized that the higher number would indicate that Hanoi had the military strength to pursue a protracted war, something not acknowledged by General Westmoreland at this point in time.

U.S. public support for the war had declined. For this reason, the CIA estimate was suppressed. The numbers of troops available during Tet '68 were 325,000 to 595,000 Communists and nearly a million available to fight for the South.

It was a strange situation. All in the South realized that

there would be a major offensive during Tet, but exactly when and where were unknown.[218] In spite of the threat, business went on as usual. For example, South Vietnamese President Thieu insisted on sending many of his soldiers home on leave for Tet.[219]

General Westmoreland expected that the attack would consist of an NVA invasion of South Vietnam at Khe Sanh. He appears to be one of the few fooled by Hanoi's deception, but he made no major move of troops to the DMZ other than 15,000 that he sent to reinforce the marines.[220] He did not need to. The U.S. strategic mobility capability allowed the quick movement of troops to Khe Sanh if an invasion materialized. Similarly, the troops could be quickly moved back to the population centers, if needed.[221] General Westmoreland was prepared to use all means available to stop the invasion at Khe Sanh and recommended the use of nuclear weapons against what he perceived as a lucrative target of massed NVA troops. His request was denied. Most intelligence indicated an attack on Saigon. There were indicators in advance of the attack. For weeks, an unusually large number of funerals were seen in Saigon. Later it was realized that many of the coffins contained weapons smuggled into Saigon for the uprising. At Weyand's headquarters, a young intelligence officer noticed that the VC had realigned their zones of responsibility to converge on Saigon. This would facilitate an attack on the capital. In Hanoi, they likened it to a grapefruit with Saigon at the center.[222] Weyand responded quickly by doubling the number of U.S. battalions in Saigon between 11 January and Tet.[223] Weyand's actions may well have saved Saigon in the battle that followed.

As Saigon was attacked, thirty-five of South Vietnam's forty-four provincial capitals were also attacked as well as other government locations. The total number of VC targets was 166.[224] As the province capitals were attacked, Steve Vorthmann in the 173rd Airborne Brigade was at Tuy Hoa in MR 2. C Company was involved in the defense of Tuy Hoa during the 31 January 1968 Tet Offensive.

> There were several KIAs from Charlie Company, including machine gunner Jack McKee, who was ten to twenty meters to my right and was killed as a result of a friendly air strike on the village. One night, six kilometers west of Tuy Hoa, our side of the company harbor site was attacked with grenades and small arms fire. All of my squad was wounded except for two of us. Our squad was disbanded, and we were assigned to another. I still have my grenade shrapnel imbedded canteen cup. C Company was also involved in a firefight at Ban Me Thuot, where the attached ARVNs hid behind a little mound. The last month or two, I was in the rear at Tuy Hoa, where I was responsible for delivering supplies to the company in the field. Our company was in the field humping for twenty to thirty-five days at a time, getting resupplied every five days.[225]
>
> ***Steve Vorthmann***

General Phillip B. Davidson, MACV J-2, considered the broad conventional offensive spread across the country to be Hanoi's greatest blunder at Tet. The amount of coordination and synchronization needed to accomplish this seemed to be beyond Hanoi's capability, but, in fact, this had been practiced successfully during the Border Battles. Davidson believed that the offensive should have been centered on a few targets, but Hanoi's approach was entirely consistent with their plan to cause an uprising against the Saigon regime. By attacking across the entire country, they had the best chance for a general uprising. In Saigon, a diligent effort was made to seize the government radio station in order to announce the uprising, but it could not be held and was retaken by the government.[226] That did not matter, since the people were in no mood to listen to a broadcast to join an uprising against their government, and this was true throughout South Vietnam. Hanoi had failed. Throughout South Vietnam, at government locations, VC attacks were repulsed or towns were quickly retaken. It was only at Saigon and the Vietnamese traditional capital of Hue that fighting persisted. In Saigon, the fighting lasted two weeks before the VC were eliminated. In Hue, the VC took and held the city for twenty-five days. They entered the city with lists of names of government officials and others loyal to Saigon. Thousands of these were rounded up, executed, and buried in mass graves. In a twist of fate, one government official escaped with a list of names of local VC agents. When the South Vietnamese government returned, the suspects were rounded up and dealt with.[227]

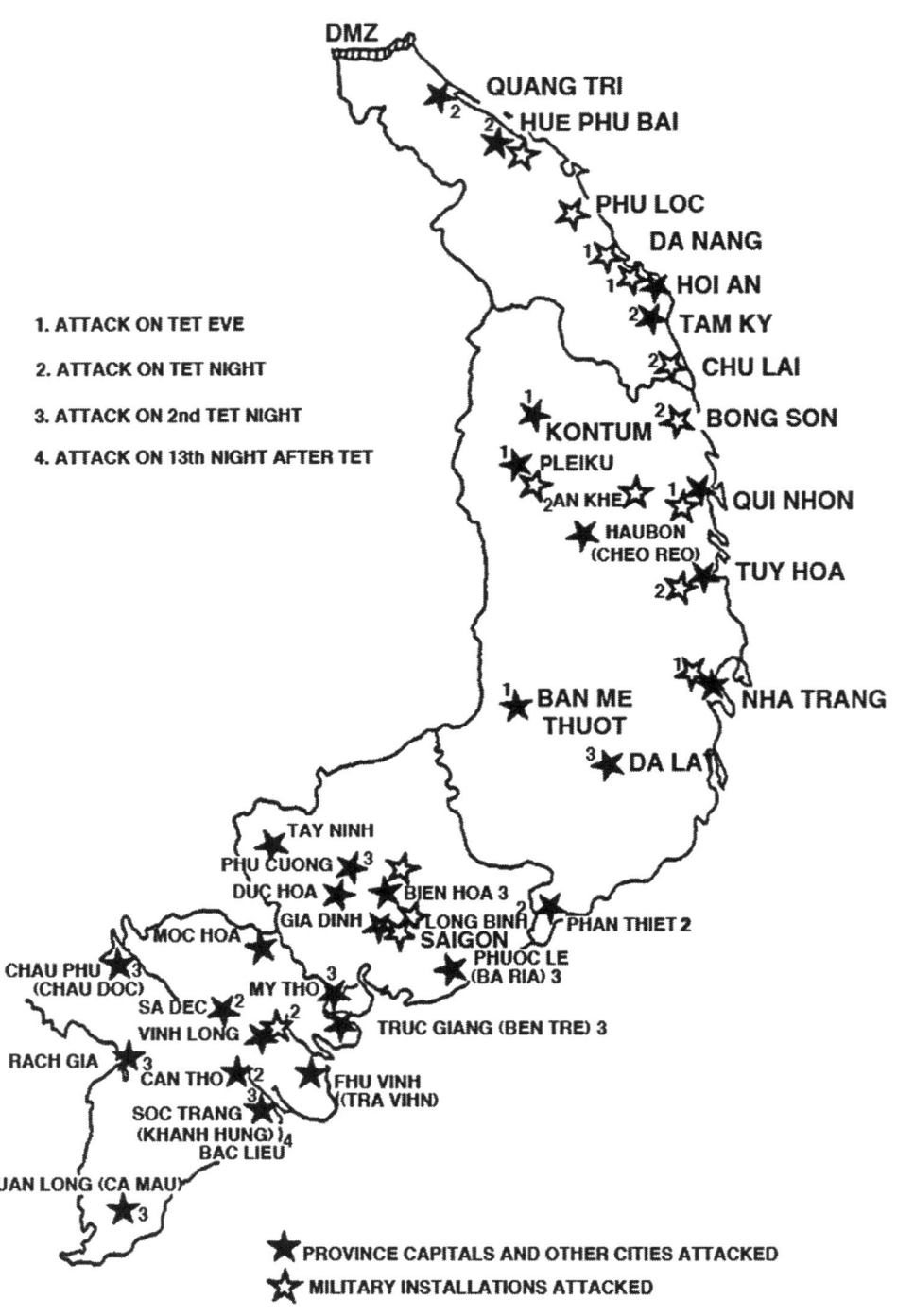

1. ATTACK ON TET EVE

2. ATTACK ON TET NIGHT

3. ATTACK ON 2nd TET NIGHT

4. ATTACK ON 13th NIGHT AFTER TET

DMZ

QUANG TRI

HUE PHU BAI

PHU LOC

DA NANG

HOI AN

TAM KY

CHU LAI

BONG SON

KONTUM

PLEIKU

AN KHE

QUI NHON

HAUBON
(CHEO REO)

TUY HOA

NHA TRANG

BAN ME
THUOT

DA LAT

TAY NINH

PHU CUONG

DUC HOA

BIEN HOA 3

GIA DINH

LONG BINH

PHAN THIET 2

MOC HOA

SAIGON

PHUOC LE
(BA RIA) 3

CHAU PHU
(CHAU DOC)

MY THO

SA DEC

TRUC GIANG (BEN TRE) 3

VINH LONG

RACH GIA

CAN THO

FHU VINH
(TRA VIHN)

SOC TRANG
(KHANH HUNG)

BAC LIEU

QUAN LONG (CA MAU)

★ PROVINCE CAPITALS AND OTHER CITIES ATTACKED

☆ MILITARY INSTALLATIONS ATTACKED

Tet Offensive of 1968 (Ngoc Lung Hoang).

The Montagnards During Tet '68

Ample intelligence was available to the U. S. before Hanoi's attack in January 1968. At Ban Me Thuot, FULRO connections warned missionaries of the Communist build-up around the town. Y Bham Enuol even sent a warning from Cambodia of the impending attack. Reverend Robert Ziemer who was killed during the attack informed U. S. intelligence at Ban Me Thuot, but was not believed. He was told by his army contacts that missionaries did not understand intelligence. This was in line with Westmoreland's 1965 directive that messages from FULRO should not be accepted.[228]

CIDG and Tet

In the course of the Tet offensive, CIDG troops were employed in the defense of certain urban centers, a combat role new to them but one in which they proved to be very effective. Further, after Tet, the CIDG came to be regarded as an economy of force element which could be used to release conventional units for deployment in response to new enemy buildups. These tactical and strategic changes in the employment of civilian irregulars reflected once again the flexibility and responsiveness of the U.S. Special Forces CIDG effort and were further evidence of the Special Forces' wide-ranging counterinsurgency capabilities.

With the large-scale introduction of conventional North Vietnamese Army forces and sophisticated enemy weapons into South Vietnam, the CIDG program was re-evaluated to analyze its effectiveness in the light of the transition from an insurgency situation to one of insurgency coupled with "hot" war. During the twelve months major changes in enemy armament occurred. Introduced in quantity were tube artillery, large rockets, large mortars, modern small arms of the AK47 type, antiaircraft artillery up to 37-mm., and heavy machine guns. Tanks were employed on one occasion against the CIDG camp at Lang Vei, and others were sighted in Laos and Cambodia near the border and in South Vietnam. In central and southern South Vietnam, North Vietnamese Army replacements were used to bolster main force Viet Cong units that had lost many men.

The enemy launched his Tet offensive on 29 January 1968. This was followed by a massive buildup at Khe Sanh and the armor-supported attack that overran the camp at Lang Vei in I Corps. Pressure on CIDG camps, except for the attack on Lang Vei, was unusually light during the entire Tet offensive and for approximately sixty days thereafter. As the enemy withdrew from the vicinity of the urban areas, pressure on the CIDG camps increased, principally in the form of frequent attacks by mortar and rocket fire on camps near known enemy infiltration routes and base areas. CIDG forces responded in an exemplary manner in all corps tactical zones during Tet and were responsible for the successful defense of several urban areas, as well as the rapid relief of others. Among the urban centers successfully defended by the CIDG were Nha Trang, Qui Nhon, Kontum, Pleiku, Chau Doc, Ban Me Thuot, Phan Thiet, and Dalat. The street-fighting ability demonstrated by the CIDG troops in the defense of these towns was somewhat surprising in view of the fact that their training had not been geared for that kind of combat, but their superior performance demonstrated conclusively that the CIDG soldier was the combat equal of any soldier in Vietnam. Immediately following Tet, a major tactical redeployment of conventional troop units was necessary in order to provide forces to counter the increased enemy threat in northern I Corps. It was at this point that CIDG troops were used as economy of force elements in order to make this redeployment of conventional units possible.

The effects of the Tet offensive were also felt in the effort to turn over the CIDG program to the Vietnamese. In many cases the schedule for the turnover or conversion of certain camps was brought to a virtual standstill by the Tet offensive. Areas thought to be secure and ready for conversion or turnover proved not to be in the light of Tet, and the schedules had to be revised.[229]

Francis J. Kelly

Charles Hartley and Bruno Rizzato were at Kontum and described the battle.

Early in the evening of 29 January, 1968 we received word in the B24 TOC that a LLDB (VNSF) camp located between Kontum and Pleiku had been subjected to an attack by a VC force of unknown size. LTC Cole, the B Detachment commander, assembled the primary staff personnel in the TOC and told us he didn't think the cease fire for the TET Lunar New Year would hold and we should immediately prepare for an attack on the compound. Shortly after midnight, the Kontum airfield and U.S. forces located in that vicinity came under a very heavy ground force and mortar attack. About the same time, the CIDG manning the security posts at the main gate came under heavy small arms fire. The guards, which were augmented by B-24 staff members, returned fire resulting in 5 VC personnel becoming KIA as they were running toward the main gate. Thus began the battle at the B-24 compound. . . .

I [Bruno Rizzato, who had been traveling to Nha Trang] arrived at the B-24 compound about a half hour prior to sunset on January 31st on an ammunition resupply helicopter destined for B-24 in Kontum. I was informed that the attack on the compound (only the B-24 portion) commenced the previous evening with NVA utilizing RPG, mortars, machine guns, and AK fire. The enemy was able to get partially through the barbed wire and almost made it into the compound; however, two helicopter gunships arrived at dawn and repelled the enemy; luckily, because our personnel were very low on ammunition.

I took back command of my bunker position which was the center concrete bunker on the south side, which was also forward of the other two bunkers located to the east and west. My bunker not only defended the most forward position of our compound, but also had the visibility and fire lanes forward and covering the front of the other two bunkers. This bunker was the crux of the defense because of its fire lanes and forward location of the compound, the NVA directed a great deal of their attacks, probing, and fire at this location. I initially had two M-60 machine guns and was assisted by an NCO (SFC?), one Vietnamese SF soldier, and one Montagnard soldier. The Vietnamese soldier cowered in a corner most of the time. I and the SFC each manned a machine gun, and the Montagnard fired an M-16 from our bunker's three slits.

Occasionally, the SFC and I alternated placing our machine guns to the opposite side slit in order to lay down fire in front of our other bunker to the west — the NVA troops and fire was more pronounced from the south and southeast. Directly to the south was a church and steeple [The Language Institute] which the NVA was using to direct fire and assemble troops. To the southeast there were a cluster of other low buildings which the NVA were using for cover and command and control. We were also getting fire from some homes to the southwest. Sporadically, I also used an M-79 launcher from the trench by the bunker to hit some of the closest buildings and the church. We were fired upon and attacked all night long and exchanged fire continuously with two of their machine guns. ARVN artillery did provide us with some fire support that helped considerably. Next morning, the NVA pulled back, hid, and regrouped for another night of attacks.

On the evening of February 1, we received two tanks into the compound from the 4th Inf Div which we positioned on the perimeter. Early that night, my NCO was firing from the bunker east side slit, trading fire with an enemy machine gun, when he was hit in the eyes by cement chips and dust, as enemy fire went through the east slit and out the west slit which was not manned. I had thrown out the Vietnamese SF soldier because he was useless and cowering in a corner and the Montagnard was providing us with ammunition. I sent the NCO to the C&C Center for treatment. We exchanged fire with the NVA until about 3 or 4am when the enemy went silent. Except for occasional recon fire, we also paused. While still dark, I heard the tanks firing their anti-personnel fleshette rounds through the wire. LTC Cole, our commander, was worried that NVA were trying to infiltrate. I was particularly worried about flame throwers, because a small recon element our command sent out during the day had spotted an NVA body with flame thrower apparatus just beyond our perimeter wire.

Next morning, all was quiet as usual; however, we detected little activity to our front. The commander sent out a small scout element which found numerous NVA bodies within 200 meters of our barbed wire perimeter and a small enemy element still entrenched in and around small buildings. By late morning, a 4th Inf armored cavalry element swept the area to our front (south) going west to east. It was like watching a 3D movie from the top of our bunkers. The small NVA delaying force was retreating and exchanging fire with the US troops. NVA were foolishly trying to fire AK 47s at US Armored Personnel Carriers which were returning fire with 50 caliber machine guns (literally cutting NVA soldiers in half). Helicopter gunships were also firing and unfortunately hit some US soldiers with friendly fire. The sweep went by in approximately 20 minutes. Our recon element went out later and reported that they saw approximately 300 NVA bodies to the south and southeast of our perimeter. The next day, I personally took a group of SF and Montagnard to view the battle field and the NVA positions. I also estimated approximately 300 NVA dead just prior to a US Engineer unit digging a mass grave, pouring lye, and burying the dead. Some bodies, dead for several days, were very bloated and the stench was nauseating; as a result many of our guys were vomiting and gagging. . . .

In Ban Me Thuot, the VC had heavy casualties (919 KIA in

BMT) while the friendly casualties were very light (1 USASF and 1 CIDG WIA in BMT, plus about 10 other American advisors KIA in other units as well as an unknown number of ARVN) About a third of BMT was destroyed by enemy mortar attacks. Civilians and VC did not fare so well. Y Pioc Knul, now living in Greensboro NC, was an eight-year old boy in BMT. He says he could cross the street without touching it, stepping from body to body.

In other cities in II CTZ, the story was the same. In Phan Thiet, Tuy Hoa, Ninh Hoa, Tan Canh, Bao Loc, CIDG, RF/PF and, in Dalat, even OCS students took on the Viet Cong and trounced them.

"Aint no Danger -- Never was" was a common sign that popped up at various locations, usually in the rubble of a mortar barrage.[230]

Charles Hartley and Bruno Rizzato

Khe Sanh (21 January – 9 July 1968)

Dead and dying North Vietnamese soldiers now littered the slopes of 861 and nearby terrain. The NVA attack had been broken.[231]

Greg Jones

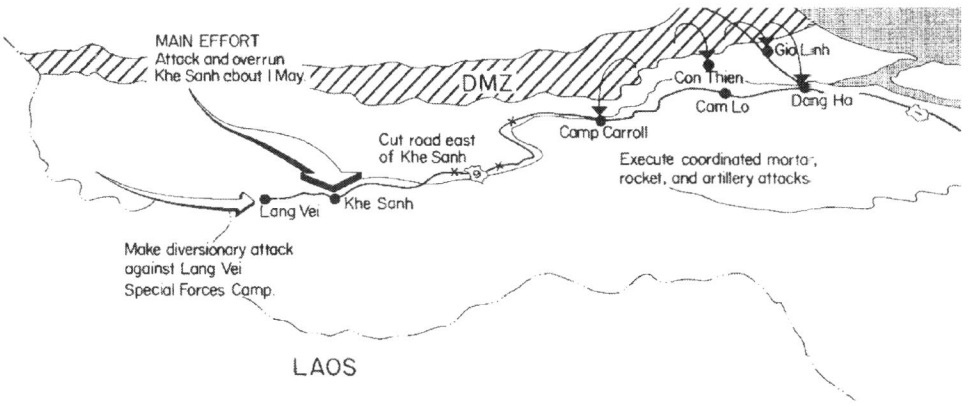

The NVA Plan (Moyers S. Shore, II).

The battle of Khe Sanh and its neighbor Lang Vei did not start with Tet, but ended with it. The battle started a year earlier in January 1967. The Montagnards played a key role in the battle and their story starts with a description of the Bru who inhabited the region.

The people of the mountains probably numbered two million or more in the years before the war. They were scattered in tribal clusters throughout the Annamite Mountains, from the border with China in the north to the low foothills in the far south. Dark-skinned, primitive, they had developed distinct tribal identities in the thousand years of their mountain isolation. The Bru, a Montagnard tribe of more than thirty thousand, had never known national boundaries. Now they found their lands divided among Laos, North Vietnam, and South Vietnam—and well-armed soldiers telling them where they could and could not live.

More than 13,000 Bru lived in the immediate vicinity— "reachable by road" was the South Vietnamese rule—of Khe Sanh village by 1960. Many had been forced to leave rich mountain hamlets that had small orchards, tobacco plots, and gardens.

The Bru practiced slash and burn agriculture, clearing small patches of jungle to grow rice, sweet potatoes, manioc, and corn. Every adult Bru worked in the rice fields, which had to be moved every two or three years when the soil was exhausted. Fish and game were abundant.

Even after the resettlement, no Bru lived in Khe Sanh. The Vietnamese lived there, and their contempt for the mountain people was blatant. The Vietnamese traders and small farmers routinely cheated the Bru out of the rice they earned on the coffee plantations. The Montagnards *were* naive, unskilled in business matters, and utterly without guile—but they were not stupid. They knew they were being cheated, and they searched for an understanding of behavior alien to their own culture. The conclusion was unanimous, and it could be heard in every household: "The Vietnamese have two gall bladders."

Not until 1966, when American combat troops began to arrive in larger numbers, was General Westmoreland able to turn his attention to the small outpost at Khe Sanh. He was, in fact, growing concerned about the entire northern region.

Quang Tri Province was only thirty-five miles wide in some places. It was the first barrier to Communist invasion across the De-Militarized Zone. Apart from the Bru in the western mountains, a few vegetable farmers on the broad piedmont, and scattered fishing villages at the river mouths, *all* of Quang Tri's 280,000 people lived in a narrow band of rich paddy land between Route 1 and the coast. Slogging French soldiers in the First Indochinese War knew this last area, which stretched south into Thua Thien Province to the former imperial capital at Hue, as "la rue sans joie"—an endless series of fortified villages and ambushes, literally "a street without joy."

In the first months of 1966, the northern part of South Vietnam was wracked by anti-government protests. ARVN units ignored orders from Saigon, and actually drew guns on several American units. Soldiers joined Buddhists and students in street marches in Hue and DaNang. The USIS library in Hue was torched. At the height of turmoil, U.S. intelligence learned that Vo Nguyen Giap had decided to place the two northernmost provinces under his jurisdiction; henceforth, the North Vietnamese Army would work this battleground—not the Viet Cong.

"If I were General Giap," Westmoreland said in February, "I would strike into Quang Tri and Thua Thien Provinces for a quick victory."

The general ordered the Marines to "familiarize" themselves with the region—and to take a particularly close look at the western mountains near Khe Sanh.

Marines came to Khe Sanh in April 1966 when the First Battalion, First Marines moved in to conduct *Operation Virginia*. The Marine command for I CTZ, III Marine Amphibious Force (III MAF) subsequently decided to garrison Khe Sanh on its own, after *Operation Prairie* that September, and the Special Forces camp was moved a few miles west to the vicinity of Lang Vei, where navy seabees constructed reinforced concrete bunkers for the Montagnards. Special Forces Detachment A-101 moved to the camp with its Bru tribesmen toward the end of the year. Lang Vei was declared operational on December 21, 1966. It was the only hardened Special Forces camp in I CTZ.[232]

John Prados

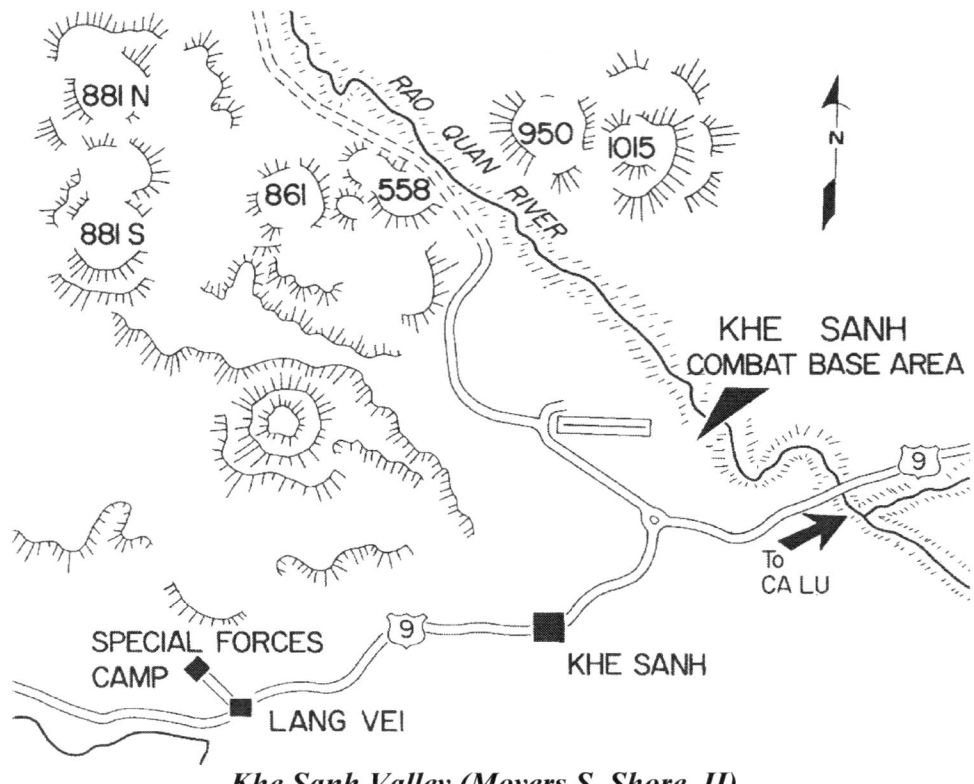

Khe Sanh Valley (Moyers S. Shore, II).

"Attention to Colors." The order having been given, Captain William H. Dabney, a product of the Virginia Military Institute, snapped to attention, faced the jerry-rigged flag-pole, and saluted, as did every other man in Company I, 3d Battalion, 26th Marines. The ceremony might well have been at any one of a hundred military installations around the world except for a few glaring irregularities. The parade ground was a battle-scarred hilltop to the west of Khe Sanh and the men in the formation stood half submerged in trenches or foxholes. Instead of crisply starched uniforms, razor sharp creases, and gleaming brass, these Marines sported scraggly beards, ragged trousers, and rotted helmet liner straps. The only man in the company who could play a bugle, Second Lieutenant Owen S. Matthews, lifted the pock-marked instrument to his lips and spat out a choppy version of "To the Colors" while two enlisted men raced to the RC-292 radio antenna which served as the flag-pole and gingerly attached the Stars and Stripes. As the mast with its shredded banner came upright, the Marines could hear the ominous "thunk," "thunk," "thunk," to the southwest of their position which meant that North Vietnamese 120mm mortar rounds had left their tubes. They also knew that in 21 seconds those "thunks" would be replaced by much louder, closer sounds, but no one budged until Old Glory waved high over the hill.

When Lieutenant Matthews sharply cut off the last note of his piece, Company I disappeared; men dropped into trenches, dived headlong into foxholes, or scrambled into bunkers. The area which moments before had been bristling with humanity was suddenly a ghost town. Seconds later explosions walked across the hilltop spewing black smoke, dirt, and debris into the air. Rocks, splinters, and spent shell fragments rained on the flattened Marines but, as usual, no one was hurt. As quickly as the attack came, it was over. While the smoke lazily drifted away, a much smaller banner rose from the Marines' positions. A pole adorned with a pair of red silk panties—Maggie's Drawers—was waved back and forth above one trench line to inform the enemy that he had missed again. A few men stood up and jeered or cursed at the distant gunners; others simply saluted with an appropriate obscene gesture. The daily flag raising ceremony was over.[233]

Moyers S. Shore

The village of Khe Sanh is west of Con Thien and about ten kilometers from the Laotian border. It is the seat of the Huong Hoa district government, in an area of coffee plantations and Montagnard villages. It was near a deteriorated road, Route 9, which ran east to west from the coast area and across the Laotian border. It was first occupied by the U.S. Special Forces in 1962. A runway was constructed at an old French fort near the village. The purpose was to monitor NVA infiltration along the border. U.S. Marines took over the plateau camp in 1966 and rebuilt the camp, extending the runway to twelve hundred meters.[234] Strength of the marines at Khe Sanh fluctuated to as low as a company by late January 1967. LTC Peter A. Wickwire was the commanding officer of the 1st Battalion, 3rd Marines. In January Wickwire received welcome news. His battalion would rotate back to Okinawa. He was stunned when he learned that his battalion would be replaced by a company. "When I found out we were being replaced by a single rifle company I thought that was absurd. There was no way one company could patrol all that ground. And, if the enemy hit, they wouldn't last a day."[235] If Giap's purpose was to draw the Allies away from the populated coastal regions, his plan was not working. Phase I of Hanoi's plan had included the positioning of two NVA divisions near Khe Sanh.[236] One U.S. Marine company tying up two divisions was a losing plan for the NVA. Before the siege of Khe Sanh Combat Base (KSCB) ended over a year later, NVA attacks would cause the marines to reinforce KSCB.[237] General Westmoreland summarized the situation.

> As the New Year, 1967, began, evidence mounted of continued enemy build-up within the DMZ, including an influx of artillery pieces, which finally prompted the State Department to relax its restriction on firing into the DMZ. The upsurge of North Vietnamese activity in Quang Tri province apparently presaged an enemy attempt to overrun the province, then to close on Hue. Although the effort began with heavy shelling of Con Thien, Gio Linh, and the backup positions, the first attack by enemy ground troops was to be at Khe Sanh. Relative quiet having long prevailed at Khe Sanh, Lew Walt by April 1967 had substituted a company for the battalion that previously manned the combat base. From the base, located on a high plateau, the men of the company patrolled through elephant grass, bamboo thickets, and dense jungle covering nearby hills and mountains. On the morning of April 24, a platoon-size Marine patrol brushed against a seemingly small enemy force on one of the plateau slopes, but when another Marine patrol came to relieve the first, at least a company of North Vietnamese attacked. Outnumbered, the marines lost thirteen men killed, but the bulk of the two patrols got away. They had made contact, it turned out, with a regiment of the North Vietnamese 325 C Division that had occupied several of the heights in the vicinity and was bringing in artillery for an assault to take the Khe Sanh Combat Base. The patrol action triggered what became known as the "hill fights." Two

battalions of the 3d Marine Regiment, flown in by helicopter and C- 130 planes to the upgraded air strip, prepared to occupy three nearby peaks held by the enemy, Hills 861, 881S, and 881N.[238]

William C. Westmoreland

General Westmoreland did not believe the NVA's intention in attacking KSCB was to draw his troops away from the populated regions in preparation for Tet '68. He even planned the use of nuclear weapons rather than lose KSCB.[239] The marines thought that Khe Sanh was a waste of time. North Vietnam's General Giap believed that the KSCB was held as the first step of a U.S. invasion of North Vietnam. He kept pressure on KSCB to draw the Allies away from the populated areas. The highest concentration of bombing during the war was accomplished around KSCB, and in the end KSCB was abandoned. The history of KSCB has been the subject of many books and articles. Following is what happened during the Border Battles, which is a short version of the long history of Khe Sanh.

In September 1966, Lieutenant General Lewis W. Walt commanded the III Marine Amphibious Force (MAF) that included the marines in Vietnam. He had a major disagreement with his boss, General Westmoreland. Walt fully supported the philosophy of the Commandant of the Marine Corps, General Wallace M. Greene, Jr.: "The real targets in Vietnam are not the Viet Cong or the North Vietnamese, but the Vietnamese people."[240] Author Edward Murphy summarized.

> So strongly did Walt believe in this strategy that he approved a number of innovative programs to rid the native villages of their insurgent infrastructure and make the South Vietnamese people feel safe in their homes. But this emphasis on pacification programs did not mean that Walt possessed an unwillingness to engage the enemy in full combat. Indeed, quite the contrary was true.... If anyone in the Marine Corps knew how to battle with an enemy, it was fifty-three-year-old Lewis

William Walt. But he recognized that the civil war in South Vietnam would not be won by the Marines' historic method of wresting terrain objectives from the enemy's armies. In his view, if the Viet Cong and the North Vietnamese Army were to be vanquished, it would happen only if the people want it to happen. And the only way to get them to want that was to allow them to feel safe in their villages. General Westmoreland, however, had different plans for fighting this war. Although he acknowledged the benefits of pacification...Westmoreland knew he could not protect the people and battle the enemy's main-force units. He had to make a choice. His 1966 battle plan revealed that choice. According to his master plan for conducting the war, American troops, better trained and with greater firepower than the Army of the Republic of Vietnam (ARVN), would conduct major "search-and-destroy" operations in the rural, unpopulated areas. Here the combat units could "find, fix and destroy" the enemy and his base areas. The ARVN would follow up with "clearing operations" designed to ferret out any surviving guerrilla forces. Then the local militia units, or Popular Forces, would move in to provide a permanent defense for area villages. As far as Westmoreland was concerned, the Marines' preferred strategy for winning the war had been seriously downgraded.[241]

Edward F. Murphy

By April 1967, it became apparent that the NVA had moved major forces to attack KSCB, but the Marines also had other problems. The combat rifle, the M-16, had been issued to replace the M-14.

The M-16 used a smaller cartridge—5.56mm—than the standard NATO 7.62mm round fired by both the M-14 and the M-60 machine gun. Thus, each Marine could carry more rounds. And they would need them. The M-16 fired at a higher rate than the M-14, meaning it would burn up rounds much faster. But that was the way it was supposed to be. The designers made the M-16 a weapon that sprayed out rounds in a wide pattern rather than the more selective, pinpoint accuracy of the M-14. The situation at Khe Sanh meant Marines had only a limited time to practice with the new rifle. All they could do was sight their individual weapons on a makeshift twenty-five-meter range and fire off three or four magazines. Almost immediately the rifle displayed its tendency to jam. Often, after just a few rounds, a spent cartridge stuck in the breech. To remove it, a cleaning rod had to be shoved down the weapon's barrel, but only one cleaning rod was issued for every four men. So a Marine with a jammed rifle could either borrow the pieces of a cleaning rod or try to pry the jammed cartridge loose with the tip of a knife or bayonet. That took time and rarely worked.[242]

Edward F. Murphy

While few knew it, this was precisely the same situation that Custer faced at the Little Big Horn battle. His troops pried spent cartridges from their jammed Springfield rifles with knives as they were overrun by the Sioux. Not good then, nor was it any better a hundred years later. The M-16 problem would be solved, but not until months later.

On 20 April 1967, operational control of KSCB was passed to the 3rd Marine Regiment. On 24 April 1967, a Marine patrol engaged the NVA near Hill 861. This prematurely triggered the NVA plan to overrun Khe Sanh and was the start of a twelve-day battle. This became known as the First Battle of Khe Sanh and is also called the Hill Fights.[243]

That portion of the enemy plan which pertained to Khe Sanh involved the isolation of the base by artillery attacks on the Marine fire support bases in the eastern DZ area (e.g., Camp Carroll, Con Thien, Gio Linh, etc.). These were closely coordinated with attacks by fire on the logistical and helicopter installations at Dong Ha and Phu Bai. Demolition teams cut Route 9 between Khe Sanh and Cam Lo to prevent overland reinforcement, and later, a secondary attack was launched against the camp at Lang Vei, which was manned by Vietnamese CIDG personnel and U.S. Army Special Forces advisors. Under cover of heavy fog and low overcast which shrouded Khe Sanh for several weeks, the North Vietnamese moved a regiment into the Hill 881/861 complex and constructed a maze of heavily reinforced bunkers and gun positions from which they intended to provide direct fire against the KSCB in support of their assault troops. All of these efforts were ancillary to the main thrust—a regimental-sized ground attack—from the 325C NVA Division which would sweep in from the west and seize the airfield.[244]

Moyers S. Shore

On the morning of 25 April, the K/3/3 Marines unit was brought in and immediately moved towards Hill 861 to support Company B, 1st and 3rd Platoons. Company K moved up Hill 861 on different approaches, and 1st Platoon was hit by fire from well-entrenched NVA 300 meters from the summit. Second Platoon was sent to reinforce 1st Platoon, and the fighting continued until nightfall, when the marines dug in. At 1800 hours, K Company, 9th Marines, was flown into KSCB to support the attack.

At 0500, 26 April, the 3rd Battalion command post and KSCB were hit by mortar and recoilless rifle fire. Company K continued its assault on Hill 861 and was joined by Company K, 9th Marines, around midday. The assault made little progress, and the marines withdrew, protected by fire from helicopter gunships. Company B was also heavily engaged throughout the morning, eventually breaking contact at 1200 and establishing a defensive perimeter on a knoll. Medevac helicopters were called in, but as they approached, they brought NVA mortar fire, and by 1445, the company commander reported that he was unable to move. Artillery hit around the company's position, forcing the NVA to fall back. A marine platoon was then sent to assist Company B as it fell back to the battalion command post.

On 27 April, the 3/3 Marines returned to KSCB. Marine artillery and aircraft were used to pound Hill 861 throughout the 27th and 28th, dropping 518,700 pounds of bombs and 1800 artillery rounds on the hill. Due to the dense foliage and overhead cover protecting many of the bunkers, aircraft dropped Snake Eye bombs to remove the foliage and expose the bunkers. Larger bombs (up to two thousand pounds) were used to destroy them. The marines' plan was for 2/3 Marines to take Hill 861, then 3/3 Marines would move west, securing the ground between Hill 861 and Hill 881S. The 2/3 Marines would then provide flank security for 3/3 Marines and take Hill 881N.[245]

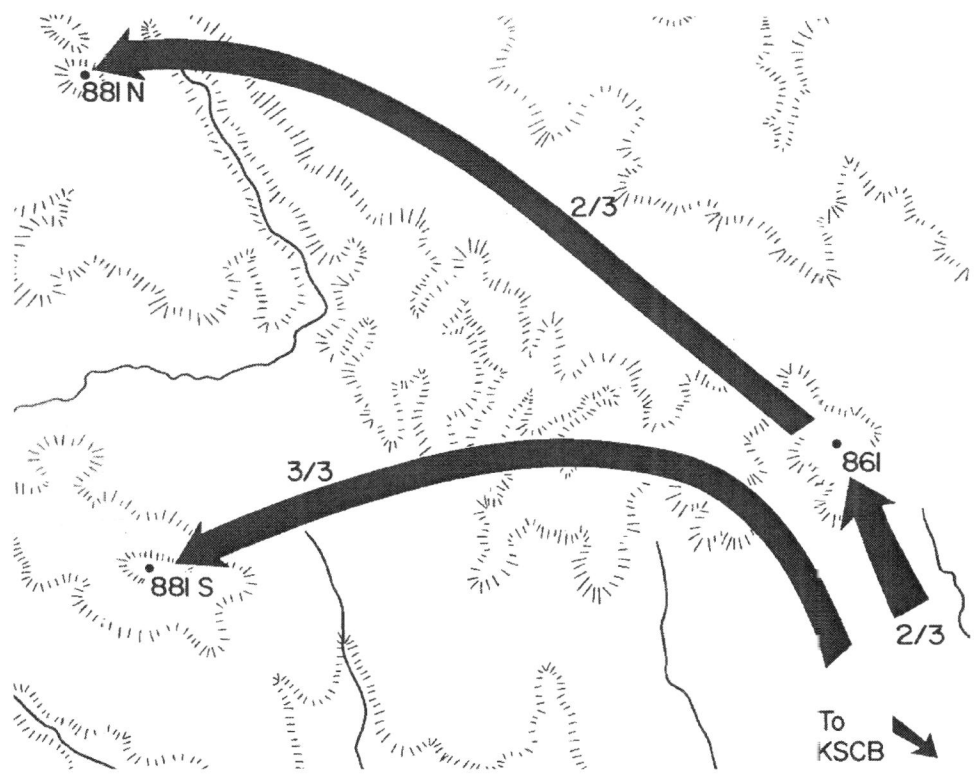

The Marine Plan for 28 April 1967 (Moyers S. Shore, II).

On the afternoon of 28 April, 2/3 Marines moved up Hill 861 with little contact. The NVA had withdrawn from the hill. The marines found twenty-five bunkers and numerous fighting positions. They also reported an odor of dead bodies across the hilltop. On 29 April, the 2/3 Marines secured Hill 861, while the 3/3 Marines advanced from KSCB towards a hill 750m northeast of Hill 881S. This was to be used as an intermediate position for the attack on Hill 881N. Company M, 9th Marines, engaged an NVA platoon, while Company M, 3rd Marines, secured the intermediate position and dug in. On 30 April, 2/3 Marines moved from Hill 861 to support 3/3 Marines and walked into a NVA bunker complex, suffering nine killed and forty-three wounded. The marines backed off to let artillery and air support hit the bunkers and then overran them. Company M, 3rd Marines, and Company K, 9th Marines, began their assault on Hill 881S. Minimal resistance was encountered until 1025, when they were hit by mortar fire and then heavy fire from numerous NVA bunkers. The marines were pinned down and only able to disengage after several hours with gunship and air support. The marines suffered forty-three killed and 109 wounded in the engagement. NVA losses were 163 killed. As a result, Company M, 3rd Marines, was rendered combat-ineffective and was replaced by Company F, 2/3 Marines. Company E, 9th Marines, was also deployed to KSCB on the afternoon of 1 May. On that day, the marines withdrew from Hill 881S to allow for an intense air bombardment. One hundred sixty-six sorties were flown against Hills 881N and South and over 650,000 lbs. of bombs were dropped on them, resulting in over 140 NVA killed.

On 2 May, Companies K and M, 9th Marines, assaulted Hill 881S, capturing it with minimal resistance by 1420 hours. The marines discovered over 250 bunkers protected by two to eight layers of logs and then four to five feet of earth; only fifty bunkers remained intact after the bombing. At 1015 on 2 May, Companies E and G, 2/3 Marines, assaulted Hill 881N. Company G encountered an NVA position and pulled back to allow for artillery support. Company E almost reached the summit of the hill when it was hit by an intense rainstorm and the battalion was pulled back into night defensive positions.

At 0415 on 3 May, an NVA force attacked Company E's night defensive position. The attack broke through the east of the position and reoccupied some bunkers. A marine squad sent to drive out the NVA was hit by machine-gun fire. Air and artillery strikes were called in on the NVA. A flare ship arrived overhead, and the marines on Hill 881S could see approximately two hundred NVA forming up to attack Company E from the west. The marines fired over one hundred rounds of recoilless rifle fire to break up this fresh assault. At dawn, reinforcements were flown in to support Company E, while Company H, 2/3 Marines, attacked the NVA from the rear. The last bunker was cleared at 1500. Twenty-seven marines were killed and eighty-four wounded in the attack. The NVA lost 137 killed and three captured. Prisoner interrogations revealed plans for another attack on the marine positions that night, but this did not occur.

At 0850, 5 May, Companies E and F, 2/3 Marines, began their assault on Hill 881N. NVA fire increased as they neared the summit, and both companies pulled back to allow for air and artillery strikes. The assault resumed at 1300, and by 1445 the hilltop had been captured. After securing Hill 881N, the marines thoroughly searched the area around Hills 881N and 881S, and air and artillery strikes were called in on suspected NVA positions, but it appeared that the NVA had withdrawn north across the DMZ or west into Laos.

On 9 May, Company F, 2/3 Marines, encountered an NVA force three km northwest of Hill 881N. Artillery fire was called in, and Company E was deployed in support. The engagement resulted in twenty-four marines killed and nineteen wounded, while NVA losses were thirty-one killed. A total of 203 recent NVA graves were discovered in the area. At midnight on 9/10 May, the NVA attacked Reconnaissance Team Breaker of the 3rd Reconnaissance Battalion. The NVA easily could have overrun the marines, but instead targeted the marine helicopters attempting to extract them, severely damaging several. Marine losses were four Reconnaissance Team members and one helicopter pilot dead, while NVA losses were seven dead.

The Hill Fights ended on 10 May. Marine losses were 155 dead and 425 wounded, while NVA losses were 940 confirmed dead. Intelligence gathered after the battle found that the NVA plan was to build up stores and positions north of KSCB, isolate the base from resupply by attacks on marine bases in northern I Corps, and launch a diversionary attack on Lang Vei Special Forces Camp (which occurred as scheduled on 4 May), and then several regiments of the 325C Division would overrun KSCB. The encounter on 24 April had frustrated the NVA plan.

As a result, the marines occupied Hills 861, 881N, and 881S. This was necessary in order to prevent the NVA from having KSCB airfield and base under direct observation from these higher hills. The marines would hold these hills for the remainder of their stay at KSCB.

Steven Johnson arrived after the Hill Fights and described the scene.

> The hills, numbered for their elevation in meters above sea level, were Hill 861 and Hill 881S. There was another 881, slightly to the north, so to avoid confusion; the two were always referred to as 881N and 881S. These hills overlooked the airstrip and provided excellent observation to their west. The only thing west of Khe Sanh was a tiny outpost of Army Green Berets at Lang Vei, and then there was Laos and the Ho Chi Minh trail. Small as the Khe Sanh area was, it was a very strategic location and a lot of marines died taking those hills from the NVA. That battle was to become known as the Hill Fights. The Marines now owned this real estate. A company of infantry was placed on 861 and 881S, and they began working like beavers to fortify them. Oddly, the NVA had barely threatened the main base, even though it was the source of supplies supporting the marines on the hills. Since most of the battalion that took the hills was now in residence on them, there were relatively few troops on the base. The brass must have felt that the location was going to become even more important, so the 26th Marines, currently in the Phu Bai tactical area of responsibility (TAOR), were being moved to Khe Sanh to reinforce. Since Bravo was the Recon company OpConned to 26th Marines, that meant we were moving with them. This move was supposed to take place in about a week, so there was

much activity packing up the company office, supply, armory, and so on in preparation. Patrols were also suspended in order to allow teams already out in the bush to finish their patrols and get the company all back on base at the same time.[246]

Steven Johnson

For the balance of May and into June, the 1st Battalion, 26th Marine Regiment, continued to find traces of the NVA 325C Division near KSCB. On 6 June 1967, the NVA hit the marines on Hill 950. Six marines were killed and nine wounded. The next day, a marine patrol from B/1/26 was hit near Hill 881S. In the ensuing fight, eighteen marines were killed and twenty-eight wounded. The NVA lost sixty-two dead. As a result, the 3/26th Marines were ordered to KSCB and arrived on 13 June. More contacts followed in June and July, but activity subsided as summer faded. Continuing patrols failed to locate any trace of the NVA.[247]

In August 1967, a supply convoy to Khe Sanh was ambushed on Route 9. This ended resupply by land. KSCB would be exclusively resupplied by air during the siege. As fall arrived, so did the monsoon and marine opposition to remaining at KSCB. As the assistant division commander of the 3rd Marine Division, General Lowell English, said, "When you're at Khe Sanh, you're not really anywhere. You could lose it and you really haven't lost a damn thing."[248] General Westmoreland disagreed, since he wanted a base to oppose an NVA invasion and to cut the Ho Chi Minh Trail. The marines would stay. While it was quiet at Khe Sanh in September 1967, the NVA had shifted its attention to Con Thien, a few kilometers northeast of Khe Sanh.

In November, intelligence reported that two NVA divisions were now located near KSCB, so the 3/26th was ordered back to reinforce KSCB. *Operation Scotland* kicked off on 14 December, but there were no major contacts. As 1968 arrived, so did more reinforcements to KSCB, since a major attack was expected.

As Tet approached in January 1968, Allied forces in and around KSCB included five infantry battalions, the 37th ARVN Ranger Battalion, and supporting artillery units.[249] On 19 January 1968, marine patrols from Hill 881S made heavy contact with the NVA on Hill 881N. For three weeks it had been quiet, but in the past few days, enemy presence was increasing. During the skirmish, the marines had lost a radio and code sheets. They needed to go back and search the area for these items. A platoon left for Hill 881N when an ambush struck and the platoon got pinned down. Air support and artillery were called in. The company commander, Captain Bill Dabney, ordered the platoon to break contact and fall back. The marines returned after losing one man, PFC Leonard Lee Newton, KIA.[250]

On Saturday morning, 20 January 1968, fog enshrouded Hill 881S. Captain Dabney led his men down Hill 881S to Hill 881N, less than 500 meters away. On the way down, they ran into the NVA and exchanged fire with the enemy. Medevac choppers were needed for a mounting number of wounded as the fight continued into the afternoon. As the wounded were evacuated, friendly artillery pounded Hill 881N. Captain Dabney had lost forty-two people, including seven dead or mortally wounded.[251] As the fight continued, Captain Dabney got a call on the radio from KSCB ordering him to return to his position on Hill 881S. The reason soon became apparent. On 20 January 1968, an NVA defector slipped into KSCB and warned the marines of an impending NVA attack. He provided the NVA attack plans against KSCB, including an attack that night against Hill 861.[252]

Author John Prados tells the story of John Corbett.

A recent arrival [21 January 1968] sent to Khe Sanh, Private Corbett was a gunner with the 81-millimeter mortar section that was a key fire support for the First Battalion, Twenty-sixth Marines on the eastern face of the combat base. John Corbett had just a few weeks in country when the siege began, with an early-morning bombardment by North Vietnamese mortars and rockets. By the standards of Con Thien, this shelling—a hundred mortars of roughly the same caliber (82 millimeter) as Corbett's own (81 millimeter), plus sixty rockets—was about a day's ration. But Khe Sanh Combat Base had not previously been targeted like this, and some facilities were not well protected against bombardment. This was true of the main ammunition dump, just a few dozen yards from Corbett's position, which sustained a direct hit. The first explosion started fires and destroyed some of the shells, while the heat and successive explosions ignited even more rounds. Private Corbett writes in the present tense.

Even with our base's main dump exploding, with fires burning all around us, with our mortar's barrel still glowing and overheating, with an unexploded enemy mortar round sticking out of the dirt several feet away, the men in my squad are singing. Though I am undoubtedly the most scared Marine in Khe Sanh at that moment, I am also the proudest because of the song we are singing: the "Marine Corps Hymn." "From the halls of Montezuma to the shores of Tripoli, we will fight our country's battles on land or on the sea." I join in. This singing together, under these circumstances, keeps our courage up. I am very proud to be here with these Marines. [The ammo dump fire was a huge disaster at the very outset of the siege. The previous night Marine medium artillery (105 millimeter) had expended almost a third of its shells firing in support of a nearby position, Hill 861, which was under attack. Fortuitously, a few days earlier, some of the ammunition had been moved to another dump. Brave Marines rushed into the maelstrom of exploding shells to move—and save— the munitions. But the combination of expenditure and the fires deprived Khe Sanh of 80 percent   of its 105-millimeter ammunition.] I am sure the explosions can be seen by the Marines on the hill-top(s). From our mortar emplacements we have the most spectacular view because Khe Sanh's ammunition dump is our neighbor. [The People's Army shifted target to Khe Sanh village, about three miles away, where VPA troops opened a ground assault. Marine commander Colonel Lownds, thinking it too dangerous to send reinforcements, restricted help to fire support. Corbett describes shelling on behalf of the defenders—one of those Marine combined action companies.] We fire for the Marines at Khe Sanh village with our mortar. We drop the bombs where they tell us. We use our remaining ammo in an attempt to help them. . . .When we are out of mortar rounds, an order is given from our fire direction center, via our radio headset: "Stand down. Take cover!" It's about time. Our mortars have been returning fire since the attack first started. I believe we are the last to leave our guns.[253]

John Corbett.

When the siege started on 21 January with an NVA attack on Hill 861, the marines were ready. Four hundred members of the NVA 325C Division closed in on Hill 861 and were opposed by 150 marines of Kilo Company, 3/26. Enemy sappers (combat engineers) slipped up to the defenses in the darkness. The night was alive with sounds of the sappers as they closed in on the defenses of Hill 861. Clearly these were not the experienced, stealthy sappers seen in VC units. They were laughing and chatting as they approached the barbed wire in front of the marine trenches. At about 2100 hours, artillery was called in and pounded the hill in front of Kilo Company's positions, but the sappers were getting too close, less than thirty meters away, so the artillery did little good. By midnight, the wire was breached and the NVA reached the trench line. The marine outpost on Hill 881S was monitoring the fight. Most of the battalion staff had stayed on the hill after the previous day's engagement, and the following exchange occurred when a call came in from a rattled lieutenant on Hill 861.

A frantic voice transmitting from 861 cut through the static. "We're being overrun! Command group is all down!" Major Matthew Caulfield, the battalion operations officer, took the handset. "A Marine unit doesn't get overrun," Caulfield coolly replied. "Now calm down and tell me what is really happening." The frantic voice belonged to Jasper's executive officer, First Lieutenant Jerry N. Saulsberry. The fear in

Saulsberry's voice was palpable as he laid out the grim situation. "Get your gunny," Caulfield said. "Make sure you rely on him." "The gunny is dead," Saulsberry replied.

"Get your first sergeant," Caulfield said, mindful of Ben Goddard's stellar reputation. "He's dying," came the response. (Goddard, in fact, would live.) Caulfield, a charming Irishman, summoned all his powers of inspiration to steel the overwhelmed lieutenant. "Now Jerry, I know you can do this," Caulfield exhorted. "I want you to take that ball and run with it!" There was silence on the other end. Finally, Saulsberry responded in a weak voice. "Run? Did you say run, sir?" "No, no, Jerry!" Caulfield shouted back into the handset. "You gotta stay right there!"[254]

Greg Jones

Although the NVA broke through the perimeter, the attack was beaten off after hand-to-hand fighting.[255]

The first hint of dawn found the men of Kilo Company shaken and bloodied, but still in control of the hill. During the night, the North Vietnamese assault commander had been overheard in a radio transmission, screaming for his reserves to join the attack. But the American response had been swift and decisive, from the riflemen and machine gunners on 861 to the artillery crews at 881S, Khe Sanh, and Camp Carroll, farther east along Route 9. Dead and dying North Vietnamese soldiers now littered the slopes of 861 and nearby terrain. The NVA attack had been broken.[256]

Greg Jones

Meanwhile, the main base was being shelled with hundreds of rounds. The incoming ignited stored CS gas that blanketed KSCB, and a round touched off a large quantity of C-4 explosives. Two NVA divisions were now poised to attack KSCB, the 325th and 304th, a total of 20,000 men.[257] The base was reinforced by the 1/9 Marines and the 37th ARVN Ranger Battalion. In spite of the chaos caused by the shelling, it was not followed by an NVA ground attack on KSCB; however, the nearby village of Khe Sanh was attacked in the early hours of

21 January. The village was the home of one of Saigon's district headquarters and was defended by 175 Americans, South Vietnamese, and Montagnard Bru tribesmen. The NVA attack got under way at 0530 hours and was answered by artillery support from KSCB. After hours of fighting, the initial NVA attack failed and they withdrew. Jubilation at the district headquarters ended when the marine commander at KSCB, Colonel Lownds, called in and indicated that Khe Sanh village could no longer be provided with artillery support from KSCB. That made the village indefensible, and all troops would need to be withdrawn. As they withdrew to KSCB, a scene of shocking horror was observed by the troops from Khe Sanh village. Hundreds of NVA lay dead, the result of artillery support from KSCB. The fight at Khe Sanh village had cost the NVA 640 dead and wounded, while the Allies lost twelve ARVN and seven Bru killed and twenty-five wounded. No Americans had been killed. As night fell on 22 January, the NVA entered Khe Sanh village and claimed the district headquarters without firing a   shot.[258]

As NVA reinforcements were rushed forward, U.S. air support was called in to hit suspected routes of advance and specific targets. At this point, General Westmoreland had decided that U.S. artillery and air would save Khe Sanh against a vastly superior force.[259] The massive air campaign was dubbed *Operation Niagara.* It was a wise move. General Giap had 20,000 troops surrounding Khe Sanh, with another 20,000 nearby. These presented many lucrative targets. The air campaign kicked off on 22 January, while a total of 6,000 marines defended Khe Sanh.[260]

Early on 22 January, the NVA probed the defenses of KSCB and pounded them with artillery. Something strange unfolded that morning.

> A frightened crowd of about 1,500 Vietnamese and ethnic Bru—young and old; men, women, and children—still huddled at the main gate. Hurried discussions between American and

South Vietnamese officials produced an agreement to evacuate the Vietnamese, but not the Bru. The South Vietnamese I Corps commander, General Hoang Xuan Lam, insisted there was no place for the minority refugees, so they were told to return to their homes, now a no-man's-land between the combat base and the converging North Vietnamese troops. The virtual abandonment of the Bru people at Khe Sanh stands as a sordid chapter for the Americans and South Vietnamese, ultimately leading to the deaths of as many as several thousand men, women, and children caught in the escalating battle.[261]

Greg Jones

The runway at KSCB was busy on 22 January. Incoming flights brought in ammunition and 1/9 Marine reinforcements, and shuttle flights lifted 1,100 noncombatants to safety during a 24-hour period. That night at 2200 hours, enemy probes were illuminated by flares and NVA scrambled back over their dead comrades after heavy fire cut down many. That morning, more supplies arrived, including a shipment of 4,000 body bags. It was large enough to be noticed and was not a morale builder. The NVA massed their artillery and presented their answer to *Operation Niagara*. Guns of all calibers as well as rockets and artillery rained down on KSCB and its outposts.

As at Dien Bien Phu, the North Vietnamese forces set about weakening Khe Sanh and its outposts with artillery, mortar, and sniper fire. The bulk of the damage was inflicted by two NVA artillery regiments, the 45th and 675th, now scattered through the rugged countryside west of Khe Sanh. The North Vietnamese had targeted Khe Sanh with 212 heavy weapons, including eight 152-millimeter guns, sixteen 130-millimeter guns, thirty-six 122-millimeter guns, more than one hundred 122-millimeter rocket launchers, and a supporting cast of assorted smaller guns and howitzers. To protect the artillery from American air strikes, the North Vietnamese had forty-two 37-millimeter anti-aircraft guns, twelve 57-millimeter guns, and 130 anti-aircraft machine guns. Highly mobile mortar teams had completely surrounded the American outposts, and they unleashed deadly fire that was targeted and adjusted by artillery forward observers, who had established camouflaged positions around the combat base and forward posts.[262]

Greg Jones

On 24 January, NVA howitzers pounded Hill 881S, Hill 861, and the main base. The troops hoped for a Tet truce scheduled from 29–31 January 1968, but on 30 January, KSCB was notified that the truce had been cancelled. People in Saigon and Washington were scurrying around considering General Westmoreland's warning that nuclear and chemical weapons would be needed if the situation deteriorated at KSCB, but use of these weapons was denied. What began then was considered by many to be "the most concentrated application of aerial firepower in the history of warfare."[263] The aerial firepower saved KSCB.

In March 1968 a relief expedition called *Operation Pegasus* was launched to relief KSCB. The combined Army/Marine/ARVN task force eventually broke through and relieved the base.

> On the morning of June 17, just six days after Westmoreland left Vietnam, the Marines began slashing sandbags, blowing up bunkers with plastic explosive, filling in trenchlines with bulldozers, and peeling up the pierced steel plates of the airstrip. All supplies, equipment, ammunition, vehicles, building beams, and airfield matting were to be trucked out, the order read, "[and] everything else buried by bulldozer, burned, or blown up."
>
> It was imperative that no identifiable landmark remain that could become the centerpiece for a North Vietnamese propaganda film.[264]

John Morocco

On 9 July 1968, the NVA hoisted their liberation flag at KSCB long after the siege was over. Ho Chi Minh sent his congratulations to the troops. In the previous two years, many actions had occurred, and there was a great deal of controversy. President Johnson had ordered the KSCB held at all costs.

General Westmoreland had held it for a time, believing that an attack on the KSCB would be part of an NVA invasion of South Vietnam. He also planned to use it as a base of operations to cross the Laotian border and cut the Ho Chi Minh Trail if he could get approval to do that. The marines wanted no part of it. In the end, the U.S. abandoned KSCB because it was no longer needed.

Battle of Lang Vei (6-7 February 1968)

The most excruciating part of the whole time in the TOC was the hours I spent with my back to the wall where they were digging. Tap, tap, tap, for several hours. When they finally blew in the wall, the hole was only about two feet from where I'd been sitting.[265]

Paul Longgrear

Lang Vei was astride Route 9 a mile and a half from the Laotian border. Lang Vei was attacked during 1967 long before Tet.

While the battles of Tet in the cities were at their height, another North Vietnamese attack occurred at Lang Vei. When Khe Sanh was encircled by NVA divisions in January 1968, Lang Vei was in a precarious position since it was further west and threatened by NVA tank units moving in from Laos.

At that time, the Long Vei camp was manned by about 300 South Vietnamese and Bru CIDG Montagnards; a MIKE Force of nearly 200 Hre Montagnards; three combat reconnaissance platoons; 13 Vietnamese Special Forces, and 24 U. S. Special Forces.[266] Additionally, there were 2,300-2,800 Bru in a nearby village.[267] Earlier, the camp had been overrun and in June 1967 it was decided that a new camp would be constructed with better observation and fields of fire. The mission would be to secure and pacify the surrounding area and conduct border-surveillance operations.[268] There were now both a new and an old camp with both occupied.

The Special Forces camp was commanded by Captain Frank C. Willoughby and Lieutenant Paul R. Longgrear commanded the MIKE Force. The senior NCO was SFC William T. Craig.

> The MIKE Forces were distinct from the CIDG, which normally served in their own living area and had their own tribesmen as officers. Led by Green Berets, the MIKE Forces received more thorough training and became airborne qualified. They were mercenaries, to be sent wherever needed. In addition to their regular pay, they received bonuses according to the number of captured enemy weapons they returned after each battle. With four of his Green Berets as platoon commanders—Specialist Fourth Class Moreland was the medic and not in a command billet—Lieutenant Longgrear was intensely training his company of Hre. Under prior company and platoon commanders, they had acquired a reputation for breaking under fire. Longgrear had been executive officer for just a week before being sent to this northwest corner of Quang Tri province. During his brief time with the MIKE Force company, Longgrear had seen much improvement in the Hre troops.[269]
>
> **_William R. Phillips_**

The situation was complicated by the 33rd Laotian Elephant Battalion with dependents (500 soldiers and about 2,200 civilians) who streamed into the camp from Laos fleeing NVA tank units. The Laotians would be quartered at the old Lang Vei camp.[270] The Laotian battalion commander refused to accept the authority of the U. S. Army officer on site since he was junior in rank. Lieutenant Colonel Daniel F. Schungel flew in to remedy that and the 12th Mobile Strike Company arrived to reinforce the camp.[271]

Shortly after Schungel's arrival the NVA attacked with infantry led by tanks at midnight, 7 February. It was the first successful use of tanks in the war. By 0230 hours the NVA had broken through the perimeter of the camp. The defenders fought back with recoiless rifles and LAWs. SFC James Holt knocked out three tanks and went to the ammo bunker for more ammunition. He was not seen again and was presumed KIA. The command bunker was partially destroyed and the LLDB people that came out to surrender were executed by the NVA.[272] A few Special Forces troops remained behind in the rubble.

Paul Longgrear was trapped in the TOC when word came that the Marines were not coming.

> When Schungel called Willoughby, he told him that the marines were not coming, but if we could hold out till dawn, reinforcements would come. When Willoughby told us, I went ballistic! I said, "You guys can stay here and die like a worm, but I'm going up on top and die like a man, and I'm taking my two men with me." I grabbed Moreland and he grabbed my rifle with both hands. I kept yelling at him, "Moreland! Moreland! It's me, Longgrear! Let go of my rifle!" We were immediately in what was almost a death battle. He had no idea of who I was. His eyes were glazed over. He was looking right through me! We rolled around on the floor. He was my size, and I had a real struggle even when I finally got on top. I had to press my rifle across his neck to keep him down, but he was strong enough to keep me from getting loose. Fragos came over to give me a hand. "What do you want me to do?" he asked. "Pop him with morphine!" I answered. "But he's got a bad head wound and it could be fatal!" "Son, if you've got a better idea, let me know right now! He's got to let go of me!"[273]
>
> ***Paul Longgrear***

Paul Longgrear also gives this account of hell in the TOC:

> The most excruciating part of the whole time in the TOC was the hours I spent with my back to the wall where they were digging. Tap, tap, tap, for several hours. When they finally blew in the wall, the hole was only about two feet from where I'd been sitting. The only reason I moved was to get a better shot against them coming down the escape hatch in the tower. One of the frag grenades they dropped got me in the ankle, but I never loosened my boot, and that helped. We sat there in pure darkness. It was tough to keep the indige [indigenous troops] from talking or moving. In the dark, I worried that one of them might be trying to kill me, reaching to find my throat with a knife. I knew that if we made it to daylight, we'd be okay.[274]
>
> ***Paul Longgrear***

The Laotian commander refused to fight but SFC Eugene Ashley, Jr. managed to assemble 100 Laotians volunteers in an unsuccessful effort to retake the camp. After several attempts Ashley was killed and the Laotians fled. Khe Sanh was asked to send troops to Lang Vei and refused. Colonel David Lownds, the commander at Khe Sanh, explained.

> I knew that at some point that place [Lang Vei] was going to come under attack. So I took a battalion and ran them down there, not on the road, because I realized that when the time came, I probably couldn't go down the road. And it took the battalion, 1/26 [First Battalion, 26th Marine Regiment], under [Lt. Col.] Jim Wilkinson, moving as fast as they could, not going down the road, as I remember, roughly twelve hours. So that ruled out that possibility. The second possibility was to go down the road. The next possibility probably was to go by helicopter. Landing zones there were covered by tanks—tanks on my landing zone. So I couldn't go in by helicopter. Going down the road, where the tanks were, they would have pretty well controlled that road and so I really had no possibility of getting those people out, when he [Willoughby] had nothing to fight with.
>
> In other words, he just had his army people, and so there was nothing I could do but try to get the air wing to see if they were willing to go in. My helicopters were not suitable for that mission. As I remember it, the army wouldn't send anybody in. And as I remember it, finally the Marine Corps sent in some Hueys, which was probably correct and the only thing that could have gotten in there to get them.[275]

David Lownds

The decision was made to break out and that was successfully accomplished. Air strikes finally forced the NVA to withdraw the next morning. Lang Vei was evacuated and the Special Forces survivors were removed by air. Most of the Bru and Laotians walked to Khe Sanh.[276] SFC Ashley was posthumously awarded the Medal of Honor.

Of the 24 Americans at Lang Vei seven were killed, 11 were wounded and three were captured and released in 1973. The CIDG lost 309 killed, 64 wounded and 122 captured. The

NVA claimed losses of 90 killed and 220 wounded.[277]

An estimated 6,000 civilians and soldiers from the camp made their way to Khe Sanh. These included CIDG soldiers, their families and the Laotians. Upon arrival the commander at Khe Sanh refused to admit them since he feared that NVA and VC were included in their midst. For days they were kept under guard in bomb craters outside of the wire as the NVA continued to rain artillery on Khe Sanh. The civilians finally walked back to Laos and the Laotian military were flown back on 15 February.[278]

And how dearly did the 33rd Laotian Elephant Battalion pay for its brief appearance on the stage at Khe Sanh? Overrun by tanks, panicked into flight to Vietnam, caught in the battle for Lang Vei, disarmed at the gates of the combat base, and trapped on the most heavily bombed battlefield of the war, the Laotian battalion surely lost hundreds from its long columns of disheartened soldiers, and women, and children.

Three thousand Bru tried to walk out on Route 9 in late January, when the road was considered impassable, but only 1,643 made it to Cam Lo, including a sixty-year-old man who had carried his crippled wife the whole way. In March, the Marines airlifted 1,432 Bru to safety.

Most of the Montagnards had to seek shelter on a plateau where there was no shelter.

"The amount of firepower put on that piece of real estate," Westmoreland had boasted, "exceeded anything that has ever been seen before in history." The general sternly preached "the sanctity and sacredness of the civilian who was on the Vietnam battlefield through no fault of his own," but Niagara's deluge could hardly be selective.

On one occasion, U.S. fighter bombers attacked a column of Bru civilians who were being forced by North Vietnamese soldiers to carry boxes and equipment along Route 9. The pilots regretted killing the Bru, but "the immediate situation dictated an attack to prevent the movement of supplies."

Chaplain Stubbe estimated that 5,000 Bru were killed during the battle at Khe Sanh.[279]

Robert Pisor

End of Tet, Phase 1

"If I've lost Cronkite, I've lost middle America."
Lyndon B. Johnson

By the end of March, Tet was over, and assessments were coming in. Eventually, it was concluded that Hanoi had suffered a total defeat on the battlefield, but the U.S. had sustained a political defeat at home from which it would not recover. Those in government blamed the media for turning a battlefield victory into a defeat, but it appears that the government did this with little help from the media.

General Bruce Palmer, the army Vice Chief of Staff, said the Allies were surprised and likened the attack to Pearl Harbor.[280] As seen above, this was an unduly harsh judgment, given the planning to counter the enemy's attacks. One cannot conclude that it was a total surprise if staff officers had a betting pool for the hour of the attack. Yet many of the Allies behaved as if no attack were expected. Sending ARVN troops on leave on the eve of the attack is an example. General Westmoreland and his deputy, Creighton Abrams, were in their quarters when they were awakened by their aides and the gunfire.[281] The South Vietnamese president was enjoying the Tet holiday with his family in My Tho.[282]

> As for eyewitnesses, Ambassador Robert Komer would later reflect, "I knew in one day that whatever had happened out there, Tet had changed absolutely everything in Washington." Komer came to that insight instantly, before the media reporting had appeared. Ambassador Bui Diem comments, "The general feeling was consternation, and I was there during those days in Washington."[283]
>
> ***John Prados***

The attacks provided two iconic images of the war: a VC officer executed in the street by a shot to the head and

VC dead bodies strewn on the U.S. embassy grounds. Both had a negative impact on the U.S. public's support for the war. The casualty numbers told the story. Hanoi had lost 40,000–72,000, mostly VC.[284] Enemy casualty numbers were always debatable, but this range of numbers seems correct. It was a devastating defeat for the enemy. Allied losses were much less: 11,500.[285] Senator Aiken of Vermont opined, "If this is a failure, I hope the Viet Cong never have a major success."[286]

Stanley Karnow reported a meeting in Ho Chi Minh City in 1981 with a prominent Communist figure, Dr. Duong Quynh Hoa:

> "We lost our best people," she said mournfully, recalling that Viet Cong units composed mostly of indigenous southerners had borne the brunt of the fighting and had suffered the heaviest casualties. Over the next year, she went on; the southern Communist political organization was to be badly battered by the CIA's Phoenix program, a covert campaign to uproot the Viet Cong's rural structure.[287]
>
> *Duong Quynh Hoa*

Although the real numbers of enemy dead were staggering, MACV and the Pentagon inflated the numbers, as they usually did, with interesting results. When General Westmoreland requested an increase in troop strength of 206,756, LBJ was stunned. This would require U.S. mobilization that he had always resisted, and in the current political climate, it was impossible.[288] When briefing at the State Department, General Depuy, from the Pentagon, claimed 80,000 enemy dead. When asked about enemy wounded, Depuy stated there were three wounded for every one dead, for a grand total of 320,000 enemy casualties. He should have seen where this was headed, but didn't. The next question was how many enemies faced the Allies during Tet. Depuy answered: 230,000. Arthur Goldberg, one of the

President's Wise Men[289] replied "Who the Hell is there left for us to fight?" General Westmoreland's request for more troops was denied. The next day, the Wise Men recommended to President Johnson that it was time to "disengage,"[290] a polite term meaning get the hell out of Vietnam. After years of promising reports by General Westmoreland and others, it became obvious to the American public that we were not winning the war. A "credibility gap" was widening between the government and its citizens. As the fighting concluded, Westmoreland stated, "We've got 'em on the run."[291] This was the same remark made by General Harkins years earlier, after the battle of Ap Bac.[292]

> Broadcaster Walter Cronkite made a hurried tour of Vietnam in late February 1968 and shortly there after on national television dolorously called Tet an American defeat, saying on 27 February that "the only rational way out will be to negotiate, not as victors but as an honorable people." President Johnson, watching this program, lamented to his press secretary, George Christian, "If I've lost Cronkite, I've lost middle America."[293]
>
> ***Phillip B. Davidson***

For the U.S., some good came from Tet. McNamara was sacked, and Westmoreland would go home. McNamara would leave government to take over the World Bank, while Westmoreland took over the army as Chief of Staff. At Tet '68 and earlier, from the middle of 1967, Hanoi was losing the shooting war in Vietnam, but the U.S. was losing public support for the war among its own people.[294] Although there was support for the war during and immediately after Tet: "the rally around the flag and support our troops effect" had dwindled.[295] The Gallup Poll counted 53 percent support for the war in October 1967. In September 1968 it had dropped to 46 percent.

One of the most important results of Tet '68 was LBJ's decision to hand over the war to the South Vietnamese.

Vietnamization was born.[296] The push for peace talks was also a key event. On 31 March 1968, President Johnson announced that he would not run for reelection and ordered a bombing halt in North Vietnam.[297] Since the 1950s, pundits in Washington had said that the last domino to fall would be the U.S. president, and it happened. The light at the end of the tunnel disappeared.

McNamara's War

Aren't you a damn liar, sir?[298]

David Boies

Robert S. McNamara was Secretary of Defense from 1961 to 1968. He is best known for bringing systems analysis to the Pentagon, which helped balance resources against needs. While he was in office, army staff officers had a saying that if McNamara had it figured out correctly, the last rifle bullet in the inventory would be fired as the peace treaty was being signed. The fact is that war is the most wasteful enterprise on the face of the earth. The best one can do is control it a bit, and McNamara did that.

If any single person can be blamed for precipitating our full involvement in the war in Vietnam, it was Robert McNamara. Based upon McNamara's comments to Congress, the Tonkin Gulf Resolution was approved and gave LBJ broad powers to wage war on North Vietnam. At the start, this involvement was based upon deceit. Much of McNamara's involvement in the war was revealed when he testified in court in General Westmoreland's 1984 libel suit against CBS.[299] He was very clever in avoiding responsibility for his decisions and actions throughout his long career. During his testimony at the Westmoreland trial, McNamara gave the CBS attorneys an opportunity to question him on broader issues. The testimony below is a remarkable example of the use of semantics to deceive. David Boies (CBS) believed he had a historic opportunity to show the world that McNamara had deceived the public. In evidence was McNamara's pessimistic memo to the president of May 19, 1967, which was declassified for the trial and of which the Pentagon Papers had quoted only excerpts. Boies's grilling aimed to show, as Judge Leval correctly interpreted the line of questioning, that "the witness is not a truth-teller."

> The listing figure in the witness box [McNamara] said he did not believe in 1967 that they had reached the "cross-over point" and were winning, as Westmoreland claimed. He said the tables attached to his May 19 memo showed this. Boies protested: But you say in the memo's text that "we reached the cross-over point." "No," McNamara shot back, "the sentence you have quoted…quotes General Westmoreland." He said he had put the statement in quotation marks in the memorandum to show it was Westmoreland's, not his own. McNamara had pulled up the blind on his semantic game, the key to the riddle.
>
> Boies showed him an article from Newsweek from September 1967. In it McNamara was asked if "the war" was "stalemated"; he had said, "Heavens, no." To Boies and the jury McNamara now claimed he had been talking about the two tracks, not just the shooting war, he said. The courtroom was hushed; he was coming to life, assuming some of his old authority.
>
> I did say it's a no-win militarily…I said it cannot be won by military action. We had a two-track approach, one political and the other military, and the military was designed to move us along the political track.
>
> His subtext was: Therefore, I was being ethical. I was working for a resolution with probes to Hanoi as the carrot and military punishment as the stick. So the fighting was not in vain. Yet it was hard to grasp, between his own digressions and the lawyer's verbal pounding. "I admit these seem like hairline distinctions," he said at one point, as Boies hung over him with body language that said, *Aren't you a damn liar, sir?*[300]
>
> ***Deborah Shapley***

Author Deborah Shapley summarized: "Most of the lessons drawn from McNamara's life have been negative: that management by numbers ruined America's manufacturing know-how; that the [World] Bank's lending left the poorest countries with crippling debt; that the deceits and subterfuges of Vietnam disillusioned a generation with government. David Halberstam has called McNamara a 'dangerous figure' because of his 'special skill to fool people,' to 'seem better than his official acts,' whereas 'the real McNamara' is 'someone who says one thing in public and always follows the mandate of his superiors in private.'"[301]

Deborah Shapley

As an autopsy of Tet and the demise of Robert McNamara's career, author Deborah Shapley described McNamara's final performance in government.

> The shock of the Tet offensive rippled instantly through the United States. Millions were appalled as television relayed images of spectacular defeat, contradicting official reports that the enemy was being defeated. McNamara was less shocked than many in the upper reaches of government. His mathematical mind had long since reckoned that the enemy was not being killed off at anything like the rates Westmoreland had claimed. "You couldn't reconcile the number" of enemy, "the level of infiltration, the body count and the resultant figures. It just didn't add up. I never did get the answer," McNamara said years later in a deposition for the Westmoreland-CBS lawsuit. In his posture statement released that January, he warned of a future enemy buildup in the South. McNamara had been struggling to stave off needless additional U.S. deaths for more than a year. But his power was running out daily, almost by the hour. McNamara's successor, Washington lawyer and superhawk Clark Clifford, would determine the choice with the president, not McNamara.[302]

Deborah Shapley

Tet Phase 2 (29 April – 30 May 1968)

The VC up there are too tough and our CIDG are too sorry.[303]

The Phase 2 of the Tet Offensive also called the May Offensive was conducted from 29 April – 30 May 1968. Hanoi's purpose was to improve its position at the Paris Peace Talks; attack the enemy in their "Own Lairs" shifting the fighting from the country-side into the cities; and continue the offense of January Tet before the arrival of the southern monsoon in mid-May. This offensive would be against a far more limited number of cities attacked than those in January because of the severe VC losses that had occurred at that time.

The summer of 1968 was a decisive period for the war in Vietnam. As a consequence of the Tet offensive popular support for the war at home had fallen to 46%. Negotiations continued in Paris to find a solution to end the war and plans were forming to withdraw U. S. troops from Vietnam. These would be formalized in 1969 under the program called Vietnamization. Perhaps most significant was the appointment of a new U. S. commander in Vietnam, General Creighton Abrams. Abrams succeeded Westmoreland as commander on June 10, 1968. Westmoreland had used search-and-destroy tactics and these were replaced by the clear-and-hold strategies that Abrams implemented. Under his authority, American forces were broken up into small units that would live with and train the South Vietnamese civilians to defend their villages. More time would be spent on training and equipping the ARVN.[304] The shift in strategy had a major impact on the Montagnards and the U. S. Army Special Forces.

> Under General Abrams's new campaign plans, Colonel Aaron's 5th Special Forces Group was charged with (1) exercising command of subordinate Special Forces detachments; (2) advising and assisting the LLDB; (3) subsector advisory roles in I and IV CTZs; (4) providing intelligence to the MACV commander; (5) conducting

special operations; (6) running the MACV Recondo School, which trained long-range patrol personnel for major combat units; (7) providing logistical support to the CIDG program; and (8) organizing, training, equipping, and commanding the Mobile Strike Force (MSF) commands.

In actuality General Abrams was moving to feld Special Forces down in harmony with his "One War" campaign plans[305]. By mid-November 1968 it was evident that a phasedown of the CIDG force levels would be forthcoming. Along with it General Abrams was planning a sizable reduction in Special Forces personnel, with the ultimate objective of dispensing with the group. The peak 5th Special Forces Group strength of 3,542 was reached on 30 September 1968. Thereafter it was continually trimmed by a series of cutbacks that followed hasty CIDG camp conversions.

Since U.S. policy now dictated that the South Vietnamese would defend themselves, General Abrams ordered the CIDG camps converted to Regional Force status or turned over to the exclusive control of the LLDB as soon as possible. The remaining years of formal Special Forces presence in Vietnam were marked by the headlong rush to rapidly turn over Special Forces installations to the Vietnamese government, regardless of their readiness or the consequences.

The premature conversion of Camp Ben Soi (A-321) to complete LLDB control on 2 July 1968 was an early example of Vietnamese inability to take over full CIDG responsibility. Apparently, a large factor in making the turnover was the excellent English proficiency and assurances of the local LLDB camp commander. Once the transition was made, padded CIDG strengths became rampant, intelligence and operational reliability dwindled, and camp defenses deteriorated. Finally, the II Field Force Vietnam commander was forced to reestablish the Special Forces A-Detachment in the camp.[306]

Shelby L. Stanton

During the U. S. drawdown period that followed, the CIDG became an economy of force asset for the Allied effort. The numbers are startling. The total CIDG and mobile strike forces had 52,000 people to cover over 13,000 square miles of terrain.[307] This amounted to 20% of South Vietnam.

Further, the CIDG were not professional soldiers. Nevertheless, the CIDG soldiers were exempt from the draft, a status that was highly prized in South Vietnam. This gave the Special Forces leverage to bring the CIDG companies under control.[308] They were civilians hired as soldiers often lacking in training and equipment. Glaring examples such as bring blaring transistor radios on patrol assured an ambush or no contact with the enemy.[309] The dubious leadership of the LLDB often resulted in operational disasters as seen, above.

While the May Offensive targeted the cities, some Special Forces camps were targets since the NVA wanted to clear their infiltration routes.

Tet Phase 3 (9 August – 23 September 1968)

Hanoi had already defined their strategy for the Tet offensive.

> Kham Duc proved the high point for Hanoi of the second wave of Tet [Tet Phase 2] in the northern provinces of South Vietnam. Except for Saigon, where again there would be major fighting, mortar bombardments and rocket attacks dominated the action. Back when Hanoi planned Tet, at the headquarters cave of the Tri-Thien-Hue military region, General Tran Van Quang kept telling his aides they should think of Tet as a process, not a battle. The waves of Tet—and there would be a third one, in August 1968—show this was indeed Hanoi's intent. In August rocket and mortar attacks were again the highlights.[310]
>
> **John Prados**

Following the VC failure of the Tet Offensive (January-March 1968) and the offensive of May, Hanoi decided to launch what was called Phase 3 of the Tet Offensive of 1968. This offensive would be against military targets, not cities and was designed to demonstrate that a military victory by the U. S. was not possible, another move designed to influence the peace talks. Attacks would be accomplished against camps in MR 2 and MR 3 as well as the U. S. Marines in MR 1. Since the CIDG border camps in MR 1 had been eliminated, the VC could now attack camps within the interior of MR 1.

Tay Ninh Province in MR 3 was selected as a target because of its proximity to the Cambodian border and the ability of the NVA to threaten Saigon after success in Tay Ninh.

Battle of Duc Lap (24-27 August 1968)

"Welcome to Duc Lap" said the sign at the entrance of the camp.[311] Duc Lap was a CIDG camp in on the Cambodian border southwest of Ban Me Thuot. Duc Lap was established in November 1966 near the site of the Bon Sar Pa camp that was closed after the FULRO revolt. It covered the approaches to Ban Me Thuot.

On the night of 23 August NVA forces assembled near the Duc Lap camp in preparation for the attack. A separate force moved nearby to block Highway 14 preventing any relief force from reaching the camp. At midnight on the 24th sappers cut through perimeter wire and entered the subsector headquarters four miles from the camp throwing satchel charges in buildings and fighting positions. A satchel charge thrown into the advisory team headquarters wounded five Americans. The advisors radioed the Duc Lap camp requesting assistance but were told that the camp was also under attack.

U. S. units from the 4th Infantry Division and 173rd Airborne Brigade were lifted to Duc Lap while the ARVN reinforced Ban Me Thuot and sent units on the ground toward Duc Lap. Action on the 24th was not decisive with a number of helicopters shot down and losses among both the

U. S. and ARVN. An Australian Warrant Officer, Lawrence Jackson was with the MIKE force as it reached the camp gate. Jackson recalled seeing the welcome sign and the mangled sapper bodies scattered all around thinking "Some welcome."

On the 25th of August the NVA renewed attacks on the camp and subsector headquarters but the defenders held out. Close air support aircraft dropped napalm on captured bunkers. This terrified the Montagnards and they streamed away from the scene with their families toward the Special Forces inner compound. Sergeant Alward recalled.

> We threatened, and pushed them. I grabbed this one guy, he had been in the second 81 [mm mortar position]. He could get along in broken English. I said, "You get those damn people back into those trenches or we're dead." I pushed him toward them. Then I walked toward clusters of CIDG, threw out my arms, and said, "Get back, get back, into those positions." It seemed we were being overrun by the CIDG. They brought all their families with them. There's nothing you can do when a Montagnard's with his family. That's his one concern. So we decided to let them get their families into the bunkers and pits. Then we hustled their asses out. All of us Americans were out there, physically pushing them, grabbing them, shaking our rifles in their noses, making them go back to their positions. They finally did, not as well as before, but at least we had a real tight perimeter at the top of the hill. At that time this was the only position that the friendlies had. We just sat tight then. That's all we could do. We went back to our mortar pits and constantly watched that these people didn't break again.[312]
>
> *James Alward*

At the camp the NVA forced the CIDG back into the southern end of the camp when two MIKE companies arrived and hit the NVA flank forcing them to withdraw as air support inflicted heavy casualties. On the 26th the ARVN pursued the NVA and the battle ended on 27 August. Allied casualties were 114 KIA including seven U. S. advisors. Over 700 NVA were killed.

The battle of Ha Thanh occurred on 23-28 August 1968. Ha Thanh (A-104) guarded the western approach to Quang Ngai City in MR 1. On 23 August the NVA attacked one of Ha Thanh's outposts. The next day Ha Thanh was reinforced by units of the Americal Division and the 1st Mobile Strike Force from Da Nang. On the night of 25 August the NVA attacked and was repulsed. The arrival of reinforcements the next day allowed the Special Forces to sweep the area. Firefights and rocket attacks of the camp and nearby villages continued until 28 September when the NVA withdrew.[313]

On 28 September the camp at Thuong Duc (A-109) was attacked by the NVA. Thuong Duc was located in MR 1 on the western approach to Da Nang. Villages around the camp were attacked over the next few days. An NVA resupply unit was caught in nearby open fields and suffered heavy casualties. NVA attacks continued into early October when ARVN and U. S. Marine units reinforced Thuong Duc and the enemy withdrew.[314]

On 18 August the Special Forces camp of Dak Seang (A-245) in MR 2 was attacked by the NVA. Dak Seang protected the northern approach to Kontum City. The enemy attack occurred in bad weather which limited friendly air support. Nevertheless, artillery support and a determined defense from well-fortified positions caused the enemy defeat.[315]

Although the Tet offensive was a clear military victory for Allied forces, it was also developing into a political defeat in the U. S. As 1968 closed, U.S. forces in Vietnam had increased to 530,000, an all time high. The Year of the Rooster would see the decline of support at home for the war and a reduction in our involvement. The total of U.S. dead stood at 36,956 as 1969 opened.[316]

1969–The Year of the Rooster

We took them out of loincloths and put them into uniforms, and now they are elite forces.[317]

Michael D. Healy

The Project GAMMA Affair

Colonel Robert B. Rheault assumed command of the 5th Special Forces Group on 29 May 1969. He came from his assignment as commander of the 1st Special Forces Group on Okinawa. One of the Special Forces missions was to provide intelligence and Project GAMMA, a secret intelligence collection operation, targeting enemy base areas in Cambodia. GAMMA was extremely successful and provided up to 75% of the intelligence information on Cambodia available to MACV.

By early 1969 it became apparent that Major David Crew's Detachment B-57 GAMMA had been compromised: its agents were disappearing. Counterintelligence started the search for the leak. In the spring of 1969 during an operation a roll of film was discovered. One of the photos showed agent Thai Khac Chuyen meeting with NVA intelligence agents. He was arrested and subsequently failed a polygraph test. Crew and his executive officer visited the CIA headquarters in Saigon. A CIA official concluded that the "elimination" of Chuyen "might be the best course of action." On 20 June 1969 Chuyen was taken in a motorboat into Nha Trang Bay where he was shot and the body was dumped. A cover-story was developed that said that Chuyen had been sent on a mission and did not return. Colonel Rheault endorsed the story but it unraveled when one of the participants fearing for his own safety confessed the plot to the CIA. An investigation was launched which confirmed the story.

General Abrams was enraged because Rheault had given him the cover story instead of the truth. All involved were charged with murder. Publicity about the incident followed and a great deal of interest was generated in the U. S. Since the CIA refused to allow any of their witnesses to testify, all charges were dropped. Colonel Rheault was allowed to retire. Special Forces morale sagged as a result of the media attention but on 31 August 1969 Colonel Michael "Iron Mike" Daniel Healy, assumed command of the 5th Special Forces Group. Colonel Healy did much to restore the spirit of the Special Forces troops.[318]

Vietnamization was our ticket out of Vietnam. The myth of Vietnamization started in March 1969. It was a fig leaf used to cover the U. S. bug-out from Vietnam. The nation was unable to cope with the war, and the majority did not continue to support it. There were many other problems that forced withdrawal as early as possible. The U.S., of course, did not have an unlimited budget, and paying for the war was at the expense of other things. Vietnam had already cost LBJ his program called the "Great Society."[319]

Vietnamization was a foreign policy disaster. As Henry Kissinger was trying to negotiate a peace treaty for Vietnam, the U. S. gave away his biggest bargaining chip: U.S. withdrawal from Vietnam. Why would North Vietnam want to negotiate a treaty when the U.S. was leaving Vietnam and the South Vietnam regime appeared incapable of defending itself? The Vietnamization concept was simple: turn the war over to the South Vietnamese. It started in 1969.

> Laird [the Secretary of Defense] coined the term Vietnamization as an improvement on de-Americanization, the more straightforward word for unilateral withdrawal then in use. Recognizing Laird's invention as a stroke of public-relations genius. Nixon immediately adopted the euphemism as official terminology…Everyone present understood that Vietnamization was designed to mollify American critics of the war, not a policy for the effective defense of South Vietnam.[320]
>
> *Alexander M. Haig*

The withdrawal would be conducted in three phases. First, the ground war would be turned over to the South Vietnamese. Second, the South Vietnamese would develop their own combat support capability, and finally, the U.S. presence would revert to an advisory role, where it had started over ten years earlier.

The heart of Vietnamization was a "buddy-up" concept that allowed U.S. units to work with their Vietnamese counterpart units to help equip, train, and hand over responsibility to the RVNAF. Numbers defeated the concept. In July 1969, the United States started its withdrawal and had about 544,000 troops in South Vietnam. This number was down to about 27,000 by November 1972. This meant that over half a million U.S. troops left, but the RVNAF only increased strength by about 300,000 and this number is suspect. Meanwhile, Hanoi was increasing troop strength in South Vietnam. As an example, sapper battalions were increased from thirty-nine in 1969 to sixty-five a year later.

Hanoi had a strategy to counter Vietnamization, but it appeared to more political jargon than actual strategy:

> To attack U.S. forces vigorously and cause them losses and difficulties as to deny them the chances to "clear and hold" and to implement the step-by-step de-escalation in strength. The goal to be achieved through these attacks was to force the U.S. to withdraw completely.
>
> To attack the RVNAF vigorously so that they would be unable to replace U.S. forces and unable to consolidate, and therefore would have to crumble.
>
> To build up forces and to wrest back the right to become master of large rural areas strategic bases in jungles and mountains, and strategic lines of communication.[321]
>
> *Nguyen Duy Hinh*

Vietnamization was to be done in about two years. It was an impossible schedule, and it would take longer. Some things were doable, such as training ARVN infantry troops and artillerymen that already had the weapons of their trade and had been using them for years. Training ARVN combat support troops was far more difficult. Combat support was the Achilles heel of the Vietnamization concept. It takes years to develop a training structure to produce troops capable of maintaining complex equipment such as a helicopter and establishing inventory control over weapons and spare parts.

ARVN Takes Over the CIDG

By far the biggest increase in ARVN infantry forces during the period of Vietnamization came when the number of Ranger battalions more than doubled. . . . But this was not really a South Vietnamese force increase. Rather, the RVNAF took over the CIDGs the Americans had created and transformed them into Rangers. These units were composed of Montagnards, who had been treated shabbily by the Saigon government for decades. In fact, Montagnard groups (such as FULRO) that were opposed to the South Vietnamese government fled to Cambodia and became guerrillas just as the ARVN started up these Ranger battalions. This shows Saigon's error in not resolving the Montagnard political imbroglio much sooner. Instead, in late 1971, Saigon's II Corps commander began uprooting Montagnards from their villages and resettling them in camps.[322]

John Prados

The major task of the Special Forces during the last two and a half years of the 5th Group's stay in South Vietnam was to complete the turnover of the Civilian Irregular Defense Group program to the Vietnamese. The concept of Vietnamization, which became the focal point for all U.S. strategy in the period 1968-1969, was not new to the 5th Special Forces Group (Airborne). The Vietnamese Special Forces, however, had been slow to develop soldiers of high professional skill, partly because the introduction of large U.S. regular military forces had made the war in Vietnam a more conventional conflict. Nevertheless, command emphasis from the 5th Special Forces Group continued to be placed strongly on the importance of delegating responsibility to the Vietnamese. The goal of conventional forces was the conventional one of winning the war. For Special Forces, however, the goal was to help the South Vietnamese win what was really their war, and that goal was never forgotten. A victory or defeat was a victory or defeat for the people of Vietnam, represented by the indigenous Civilian Irregular Defense Group troops.

The U.S. Special Forces troops were in combat right up until the day they left. New camps continued to be built and old ones were fortified and strengthened in preparation for the Vietnamese take-over.[323]

Francis J. Kelly

As 1969 closed, U.S. forces in Vietnam declined to 475,000. The total of U.S. dead stood at 48,736 as 1970 opened.[324]

1970 –The Year of the Dog

It was clear to the packing team from Saigon that they better hurry up because if the VC attacked they were outside our perimeter and would be the first to die.[325]

Mike Eggleston

The year 1970 saw continuing increase in NVA forces in South Vietnam and its attacks while the U. S. Forces continued to withdraw and Vietnamization continued.

The North Vietnamese Army and the Viet Cong continued to be active in I Corps during the year. Company C, 5th Special Forces Group, was charged with Special Forces operations in I Corps. The camp at Tien Phuoc achieved one of the highest kill ratios of any camp in the zone in 1970. For a period of two to three months, the camp averaged 50 to 60 of the enemy killed each month and itself suffered few casualties. The camp at Mai Loc received an early morning sapper attack in which most of the camp structures were destroyed before the CIDG troops succeeded in driving the Viet Cong out. Shortly after the attack on Mai Loc, the camp at Thuong Duc was taken under siege by the enemy, who used mortar and rocket barrages. The siege lasted sixty days, but the camp held out. Again, in October, Thuong Duc came under attack, but the camp defenders seized the initiative and in a three day period killed 74 of the enemy by small arms alone. Over a seven-day period, three heavy battles resulted in a final total of 150 of the enemy killed.[326]

Francis. J. Kelly

The Special Forces Stand-Down

By 1 June 1970, the number of Civilian Irregular Defense Group camps in Vietnam had been reduced to thirty-eight, either by conversion to Regional Forces status or by closure. The Vietnamese Joint General Staff and the Military Assistance Command, Vietnam, staff then decided to convert the remaining camps to Vietnamese Army Ranger camps, with a target date of 31 December 1970…The participation of the 5th Special Forces Group in the Civilian

209

Irregular Defense Group program, like the program itself, ended on 31 December 1970. The program was in many ways a chronicle of the larger war. Developed in response to the needs of the Vietnamese Army, the government, and the Free World Military Assistance Forces, the program and the 5th Special Forces Group displayed an organizational flexibility and competence in the field that is rare in the annals of modern warfare. The U.S. Army Special Forces came home from Vietnam confident that the men they had advised, trained, and led would be able to carry on the struggle bravely and well.[327]

Francis. J. Kelly

Dr. Hickey assessed the impact of Vietnamization on the Montagnards.

One result of Vietnamization I had not anticipated was new, harsh forced relocations in the highlands by the Vietnamese military. With the American troops withdrawing and the Vietnamese assuming greater responsibility for conduct of the war, in mid 1970 Gen. Ngo Dzu, the new commander of II Corps, issued an order stating that by 31 October 1970 there would be no more "D or C hamlets" (in the Hamlet Evaluation System, D and C hamlets were not under government control) in the region. His method of attaining this goal was to launch a massive resettlement of highland villages in areas that were supposed to be "insecure." The first phase of this effort took place in the northwestern portion of Buon Ho district, north of Ban Me Thuot, where, General Dzu claimed, the Jarai Krung population was lending support to the Communists by supplying them with rice and recruits. The 23d Division made a "sweep" of the area, and Regional and Popular Forces were sent in to move the villagers. By early 1971 large numbers of Jarai Krung were being relocated.[328]

Gerald C. Hickey

I returned to Vietnam for my second tour in March, 1970 I was assigned as Executive Officer of the 43rd Signal Battalion at Pleiku. I also had served my first tour in Pleiku. It had been nearly four years since I had left. The situation seemed less secure in 1970 than it was in 1966. There were more ambushes on Route 19 and rocket attacks on the U. S. bases that surrounded Pleiku. The VC were now using 122mm rockets. These could be quickly set up and fired. The VC could leave their launch site before the first rocket landed within a defensive perimeter.

When I arrived my battalion was already involved in Vietnamization and we were training ARVN signal soldiers in the equipment that we were operating and would hand over to them. I recall receiving a telephone call from John Paul Vann late one night. He was in Cheo Reo and was very direct. It seems that the ARVN troops who took over our switchboards went to sleep on the job when the sun went down and communications stopped. He wanted me to send U.S. soldiers back to take over. I told John Paul Vann that we couldn't do that because we were already deactivating some of our companies and the troops involved were either reassigned in Vietnam or had returned to the states.[329]

Mike Eggleston

The Cambodian Incursion

Cambodia served as a safe haven for FULRO members who escaped there after failed uprisings. These included Y-Bham Enoul who arrived in Cambodia along with other FULRO members after the 1964 uprising. Cambodia was also a safe haven for the NVA and VC who frequently drifted across the border when things were not going well for them in South Vietnam.

In April 1970 the Executive Officer of the 124th Signal Battalion of the 4ID stopped by our bunker at Camp Radcliff, An Khe, to announce that the 4ID along with others was invading Cambodia. This became known as the Cambodian Incursion (29 April-22 July 1970), a move ordered by President Nixon into Cambodia to destroy NVA/VC HQ and supplies. It would also eliminate the cross-border threat to South Vietnam. This was occasioned by a change of government in Cambodia when Prince Norodom Sihanouk was deposed by General Lon Nol. The 4ID representative asked that my battalion provide support for the 4ID stay behinds not going into Cambodia. I agreed and set to work to make that happen.

At that time US forces were mostly in stand-down mode since Vietnamization and the Paris peace talks were in progress. The U.S. was leaving Vietnam. After the 4ID crossed the border, I grabbed a chopper ride into Cambodia. Anything to escape base camp boredom during stand down. Six photographers from a detachment attached to our battalion also got a chopper ride into Cambodia, but unlike me, they had a job to do: provide photo coverage of operations. My chopper made it, theirs did not. On the way in, an NVA surface-to-air missile was launched that exploded their chopper. All were killed instantly along with the crew. Cameras were recovered and it appears that one of the photographers had snapped photos of the missile as it lifted off and flew toward the chopper. I have no idea what was in his mind, but one can imagine. The intel people immediately grabbed the cameras and took off. They figured that there might be something of intel value in the photos. They later told us what they saw but could not identify the missile.

General Rienzi, Commander of the 1st Signal Brigade flew in from Saigon to talk to the troops. This was the biggest single day loss that the battalion had ever had and we, including Rienzi, were deeply saddened.

The operation into Cambodia destroyed a lot of enemy supplies, but not much else. The reaction in the States was swift. Congress produced the Cooper-Church Amendment that was signed into law on 22 December 1970. Among other things, it rescinded the Gulf of Tonkin Resolution under which Presidents Johnson and Nixon had conducted military operations for seven years without a declaration of war. It also barred U. S. Advisors and ground troops from military actions in Laos and Cambodia.[330]

Mike Eggleston

Equipment Buildup & Maintenance

The U.S. was flooding the ARVN with large quantities of all sorts of equipment. Author Neil Sheehan identified hundreds of tanks, squadrons of jetfighter-bombers, and over 500 Hueys and Chinook helicopters.[331] How the South Vietnamese were expected to operate and maintain this extravagant flood of equipment is anyone's guess. Transferring signal equipment and aircraft was more complicated than other items that the ARVN already had in large quantities, such as rifles and artillery.

Horror stories started to appear. During the so-called

Cambodian Incursion in May 1970, ARVN Major General Nguyen Viet Thanh was killed in an aircraft collision. Was it because the ARVN pilots had not had adequate training? No one can say. Lieutenant General Do Cao Tri was considered by many to be the best fighting general that the South Vietnamese had. He was killed when his helicopter crashed shortly after takeoff. The crash was attributed to mechanical failure. Since a Newsweek correspondent, François Sully, had also been killed in the crash, Ed Behr of Newsweek was sent to investigate the airworthiness of the now South Vietnamese helicopter fleet. Here is part of his report.

> At Bien Hoa, SFC John Keith had been a helicopter maintenance man for eight of his eighteen years in the U.S. Army. Keith showed him row after row of Hueys with serious maintenance deficiencies— oil and fuel leaks, engine filters and compressor blades caked with dirt, and missing rivets. Over U.S. objections, many of the helicopters had nevertheless been rated fit to fly by the Vietnamese maintenance men. One chopper, with a torque so low that the advisors called it a "potential crash just waiting to happen," had been rated unfit to fly early one day, but a Vietnamese technician later blithely gave the chopper a "positive checkout" and certified it as ready to fly. Taking the machine up, Sergeant Keith said, would be "tantamount to suicide."[332]
>
> **Ed Behr**

Training

For signal units, equipment training was extremely important because the ARVN had no experience with some of the items that would be transferred to them.   The job was made more difficult because there were no operator or maintenance manuals written in Vietnamese. To provide for this need, a signal school was established to train South Vietnamese soldiers on complex equipment on 1 July 1970.[333] It was a bit late for that, given the U.S. withdrawal schedule. Nevertheless, most of the ARVN officers spoke some English, so the turnover was made to work.

There were exceptions. Some of the signal equipment was so huge and complex that there was no way training could be accomplished in the withdrawal schedule that we had. For these sites, such as the communications complex at Pleiku, the U. S. Army turned to the U.S. private sector to run these, and Federal Electric Corporation was hired.[334] The contractors were Americans for the most part, but Federal Electric tried to hire Vietnamese and would train the South Vietnamese to take over the Pleiku complex. Federal Electric was still in place after the U.S. Army departed.[335]

Some fixed signal equipment was deinstalled and shipped back to the States. It got interesting at Camp Radcliff near An Khe. The 4ID was the occupant of Camp Radcliff and was being redeployed elsewhere with no unit scheduled to replace it. That left a 21KM perimeter at Camp Radcliff with no one to defend it. We expected that our supporting 43rd Signal Battalion troops would leave with the 4ID. Our troops would withdraw to Pleiku and join the rest of the battalion, but that was not going to happen as planned. Instead, the staff in Saigon decided that some of the fixed signal equipment would be packed up and shipped back to the States where it could be reused. We were to stay until a specialized packing team from Saigon arrived and packed up the gear. This would take a couple of weeks so it was our problem to defend Camp Radcliff until the team finished.

After I got that word things seemed to get a bit out of hand. We pulled back all of our signal troops to high ground near the fixed signal gear and dug in with all the weapons and ammunition we could lay our hands on. It was clear to the packing team from Saigon that they better hurry up because if the VC attacked they were outside our perimeter and would be the first to die. That seemed to speed up their work. At night we could hear explosions as the VC slipped into Camp Radcliff and blew up some of the vacant buildings, but not near our perimeter. We were never attacked while we were there. It appears that the VC had more important things to do.

Next I got a call from Saigon telling me that it had occurred to the brass in Saigon that there must be a lot of water pipe at Camp Radcliff and the golf course at Fort Huachuca, Arizona could use that. My reply was not very enthusiastic. I simply said no. A two-star general appeared a bit later in a chopper. While the chopper blades were still turning he jumped out, said "Hi, How are things going? Hang in there." and was back in the chopper on his way. It occurred to me that Camp Radcliff was not a good place to be at that time.

Finally Saigon called stating that an inventory of Camp Radcliff was needed and I should do that and get ARVN to sign for Camp Radcliff. I said okay because I had a plan in mind. I traveled back to Pleiku where I met with an ARVN officer at one of the bars. He would sign for anything if he had enough drinks and he did: It read: "The undersigned has received and accepts responsibility for one each base camp called Camp Radcliff.

The packing team finished their job and left for Qui Nhon with the gear.[336] We were free to leave and headed back to Pleiku. The important point is that during this entire fiasco no U. S. troops got hurt which is all that we cared about. We were very lucky.

A few weeks after we left Camp Radcliff, Montagnards were selling beautiful colorful woven baskets by the roadside on Route 19. It was made from U.S. Army multicolor communications wires left behind at Camp Radcliff. I thought at the time that at least someone got something out of this wretched war.[337]

Mike Eggleston

There were some training disasters. Toward the end of the war, most South Vietnamese aircraft were grounded due to the inability to locate needed parts. There were warehouses full of parts, but apparently no one trained the South Vietnamese on how to locate them in the warehouses. There was very little inventory control. Although the U.S. attempted to train some Vietnamese civilians, the ARVN officers had no interest in that.[338]

At the end of 1970, U.S. force levels had been reduced by 200,000 and more major reductions were scheduled for 1971.[339] Both President Richard M. Nixon and South Vietnamese President Thieu had elections coming up soon, and a military victory would fit nicely into their reelection plans.

As 1970 closed, U.S. forces in country numbered 350,000. The total of U.S. dead stood at 54,909 as 1971 opened.[340]

1971–The Year of the Pig

Can you imagine, eight hundred RVNAFs being attacked by six thousand NVA? You can understand why they are getting their asses kicked. It's just plain and simple: It's the United States advisors and the Vietnamese higher-ups who don't know what in the hell they are doing. They're just dicking around with people's lives.[341]

Tom Marshall, Helicopter Pilot, Lam Son 719

Lam Son 719

The Lam Son 719 operation into Laos in early 1971 was intended to demonstrate the success of Vietnamization, but it did not quite work out that way.

Henry Kissinger, President Nixon's national security advisor, summarized. "The operation, conceived in ambivalence and assailed by skepticism, proceeded in confusion. It soon became apparent that the plans on which we had been so eloquently and frequently briefed reflected staff exercises, not military reality."[342]

The name Lam Son was the place of an ancient Vietnamese victory over the Chinese. The number 719 was derived from the year, 1971, and the major axis of advance: Highway 9 ran along the south edge of the DMZ, past Khe Sanh and through Con Thien before reaching the Laotian border.

Early in the war, the Ho Chi Minh Trail was established to move men and material from North Vietnam to South Vietnam through Laos and Cambodia. Initially, it was footpaths used by porters and bicycles, but by 1971, it had expanded to a two-lane road. Fleets of trucks moved the material south in massive quantities. While there were efforts made to interdict the trail, they were largely ineffective. It was not just a single trail but a web that moved the material south. The total length of the web was 3,500 miles.[343] Incredibly, it included a fuel pipeline that ran south from North Vietnam to the A Shau

Valley in the South that was added later.

On 31 January 1971, Hanoi's Van Tien Dung, deputy chairman of the Politburo's Central Military Party Committee and the chief of the general staff, visited the front to address the troops. He made Hanoi's objectives clear to the troops.

> The coming engagement will be a strategically decisive battle. We will fight not only to retain control of the strategic transportation corridor, but also to annihilate a number of units of the enemy's strategic reserve forces, to deal a significant defeat to a portion of the "Vietnamization plot," to advance our resistance effort to liberate South Vietnam and defend North Vietnam, to gloriously fulfill our international duty, and to hone our main force troops in the fires of combat. Our Army must certainly win this battle.[344]
>
> *Van Tien Dung*

To summarize Lam Son 719: Hanoi was committed to win with whatever resources were required. The U.S. would be on the sidelines watching the fight, since the Cooper-Church Amendment prohibited U.S. servicemen from entering Laos, but U.S. air support was not prohibited by the amendment. The problem was that the ARVN troops that would call in U. S. air support did not have a good command of the English language.[345] President Nixon was hopeful that Lam Son 719 would prove that Vietnamization was working and that this would help him secure his 1972 reelection. President Thieu wanted a victory and wanted to minimize casualties in order to secure his reelection.

Weather was a key factor in all of this. The dry season, from November to March, was prime time for the NVA to move supplies, stockpile, and prepare for an invasion of South Vietnam after the monsoons (rainy season) passed. The goal of the penetration into Laos was the town of Tchepone, forty-two kilometers inside the Laotian border. Tchepone was a valuable target since it was a crossroad for the Ho Chi Minh Trail but slightly west of it. Thieu, in a rare moment of candor, ordered Lieutenant General Lam, the MR 1 commander and operation commander: "You go in there just long enough to take a piss and then leave quickly." Major General Nguyen Duy Hinh, an infantry division commander, put it more politely. "It was apparent that President Thieu had decided at the outset that once Tchepone had been entered by ARVN, the withdrawal should begin without delay."[346]

Lam Son 719 was planned as a six-week operation in February–March 1971 and was designed to disrupt the Ho Chi Minh Trail in Laos. With the monsoon approaching, it was thought that Hanoi would have great difficulty rebuilding supplies in the bad weather, and this would delay their invasion of South Vietnam scheduled for 1972.[347] Lam Son 719 would follow an unprecedented bombing campaign against the trail, ordered by Secretary of Defense Laird that started in mid-October 1970.[348] The air force claimed that twenty-five thousand trucks were destroyed on the Ho Chi Minh Trail between October 1970 and May 1971, but Laird thought that the extensive bombing raid would not be enough to stop the NVA offensive in 1972.[349] Private First Class Clyde Baker wrote to Nixon. "In my opinion the Cambodian operation and this operation [Lam Son 719] are the two most intelligent moves we made since we have been in S. Vietnam. This operation may end the war and may save hundreds of lives in the long run, and everyone here is putting out 100%. I'm sorry for the lousy handwriting, but I'm writing this letter down inside a tank."[350]

On the first day, 8 February 1971, as the ARVN armored columns prepared to enter Laos, the airlift was meeting unexpected resistance. "We are fighting a conventional war out there,"[351] said a U.S. helicopter pilot who came under heavy anti-aircraft fire. The NVA had carefully planned its air defenses, which consisted of various flak guns, surface-to-air missiles (probably the Soviet-made Strela), and the deadly 12.7mm machine guns. Some of the guns were radar-controlled. They were set up with interlocking fire, so that if a helicopter received fire and turned to avoid it, another anti-aircraft gun would engage. From the NVA point of view, it would be a "turkey shoot." This was a new phase of the war. Rather than fade away, the NVA would stand and fight, as it did during the Border Battles.

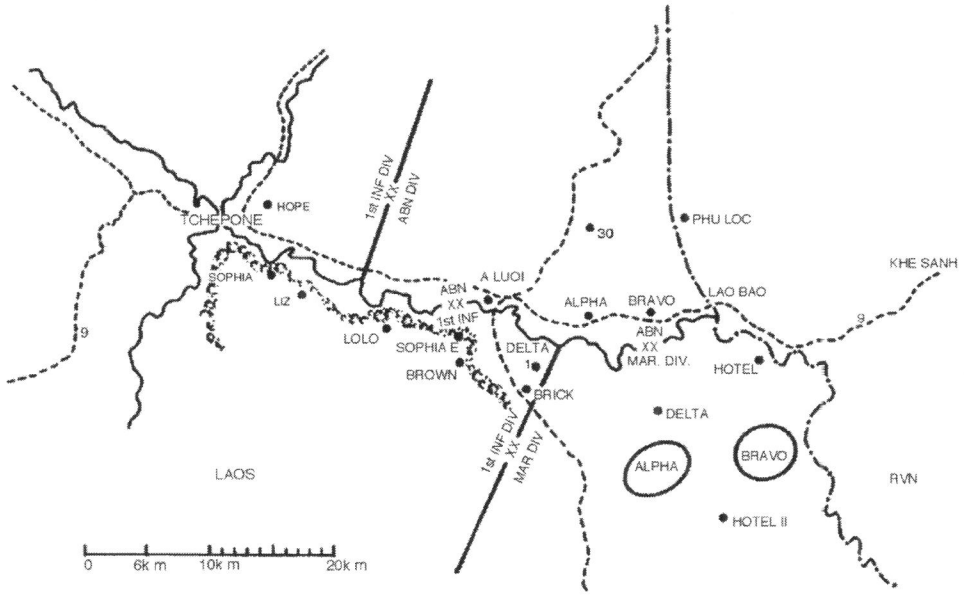

The Move on Tchepone (Ngoc Lung Hoang).

A correspondent riding in the armored column reasoned the NVA patrols must surely be following and watching. But "with Cobra gunships firing rockets all around us," he wrote, "we advanced the next day 25 klicks into Laos. There was no return fire and I felt it was an NVA tactic to draw us in deeper."[352]

David Fulghum

Inside Laos, progress slowed. On the first day in Laos, only nine kilometers were made by the ARVN troops. This was caused by bad roads and slow-down due to fear of ambush: nine kilometers; only thirty-three to go to get to Tchepone. On the second day, things got worse. The rains came, and everything bogged down. Route 9 turned into a quagmire.[353] On the third day, The ARVN had reached the half way point to Tchepone. As the campaign progressed, the NVA increased efforts to ambush convoys and attack rear bases.

By this time, the press smelled a disaster, and Laird held a news conference on 24 February. Lt. Gen Vogt, the director of the joint staff, explained the objectives of Lam Son 719 and showed a piece of pipe explaining that this was a part of the pipeline that carried fuel south to NVA forces. Vogt left the impression that this piece of pipe was fresh from the battlefield, which it was not. It had been collected months earlier during a Special Forces raid. Abrams called Laird, reminding him that bad information had been given to the press, and Laird held another press conference to correct the record. The press had a field day. Humorist Art Buchwald wrote an imaginative story that had Laird showing rifles from Custer's Last Stand, chickens from World War I, sandbags from Iwo Jima, etc.[354] The point of all of this was that the credibility of the U.S. government was never high and continued to decline. Laird was concerned that the press would turn a military victory into a defeat, as had been done after Tet in 1968, but at this point; no one knew the outcome of Lam Son 719. For weeks the ARVN move against Tchepone stagnated as casualties mounted.

Author David Fulghum described the "taking" of Tchepone.

> On March 6 an armada of 120 Huey helicopters, protected on all sides by Cobra gunships and fighter planes, lifted the 2d and 3d Battalions of the 2d Regiment from Khe Sanh to Tchepone—the largest, longest helicopter assault of the war. The NVA response to the assault on Tchepone was to increase fire against ARVN firebases, notably Lolo and A Luoi. On March 9 the battalions and the 2d Regiment command post set out on foot to climb the ridge to Firebase Sophia. Cautious about ambushes, the troops maintained radio silence so as not to

disclose their location and moved their positions every two hours during the night. They arrived safely at the firebase the following day, and the ARVN "occupation" of Tchepone, a principal terrain objective of Operation Lam Son 719, was complete.[355]

David Fulghum

ARVN General Hinh summarized best. "By this time, Tchepone was a worthless objective. It was a ruined town and [NVA] caches were stored in the forests and mountain tops."[356] On 9 March, Thieu ordered the ARVN out of Laos, and the ARVN withdrawal from Laos started while the NVA intensified its buildup. The NVA ability to reinforce, its use of tanks and anti-air to destroy ARVN troops and support, led to a rout. The NVA had every advantage: leadership, troop morale, firepower, terrain, weather, and numbers. It was a slaughter of the ARVN, which would be seen again in the fall of Vietnam in 1975. Some ARVN units were simply surrounded and annihilated. While U.S. helicopters tried to evacuate the ARVN from Laos, there were not enough, due to many helicopter losses earlier in the campaign. As the NVA overran ARVN bases in Laos, there were many accounts of ARVN valor. One ARVN survivor recalled what happened as ammunition ran out.

> Ammunition began to run out, however, and the next day the NVA overran the base. They launched the assault from positions inside the marine perimeter, supported by ten flame throwing tanks. NVA infantrymen rushed over the bodies of their slain comrades to charge into the base. The marines knocked out four tanks, then fell back. Trying to break out, the three battalions ran into NVA ambushes. The troops scattered. One survivor recounted: The last attack came at about 8:00 P.M. They shelled us first and then came the tanks moving up into our positions. The whole brigade ran down the hill like ants. We jumped on each other to get out of that place. After each firing, there were fewer and fewer of us. A marine who escaped Delta described the agony of the Vietnamese leaving their wounded comrades. They lay there crying, knowing the B-52 bombs would fall on

them. They asked buddies to shoot them, but none of us could bring himself to do that. So the wounded cried out for grenades, first one man, then another, then more. I could not bear it. We ran out at 8:00 P.M. and about midnight we heard the bombs explode behind us. No more bodies! They all became dust.[357]

David Fulghum

U.S. helicopters suffered heavy losses getting the ARVN in, and after the failure of the operation, more helicopters were lost removing the South Vietnamese from Laos. By late March, panic had set in among the ARVN in Laos. President Nixon provided his view of the battle.

On February 8, the operation began. South Vietnamese troops fought bravely and effectively, but some problems soon developed. Communist forces put up stronger resistance than we had anticipated, and American military commanders in Saigon failed to respond with a corresponding increase in air cover. When South Vietnamese forces sustained large casualties about ten miles into Laos, they made the mistake of temporarily digging in, which gave the North Vietnamese a sitting target to hit. Thieu became overly cautious and ordered his commanders to stop their offensive as soon as casualties reached 3,000. By the middle of March, soon after the South Vietnamese reached Tchepone, their casualties hit Thieu's arbitrary ceiling and they began to retreat to the southeast along Route 914. American news media reports presented a distorted picture of the operation by focusing almost exclusively on the failings of the South Vietnamese troops. Because of inadequate air support during the withdrawal, a few units took such a severe pounding from enemy artillery that they panicked. It took only a few televised films of soldiers clinging to the skids of our evacuation helicopters to reinforce the widespread misconception that South Vietnam's armed forces were incompetent and cowardly.[358]

Richard M. Nixon

The disaster would not be repeated. Nixon noted that Lam Son 719 would be the last American-directed ground operation in Indochina.[359] Correspondents had their own opinions of Lam Son 719.

> According to Life magazine "the NVA drove the invading forces out of Laos with their tails between their legs." New York Times reporter Gloria Emerson interviewed ARVN survivors at Khe Sanh and concluded that their morale was "shattered": Through an interpreter they spoke of how the North Vietnamese outnumbered them and advanced in wave after wave, running over the bodies of comrades and never stopping...It was a test, and now most South Vietnamese forces admit frankly that their forces failed....What has dramatically demoralized many of the South Vietnamese troops is the large number of their own wounded who were left behind, begging for their friends to shoot them or to leave hand grenades so they could commit suicide before the North Vietnamese or the B-52s killed them....Some soldiers who had been in the drive into Cambodia said they had never dreamed that the Laos operation would not be as simple. Since there was no significant fighting in Cambodia, these South Vietnamese felt that the enemy was no longer a threat. They learned differently in Laos and they will not soon forget it. In American helicopters they came out of Laos this week without their combat packs, their rations or their steel helmets—and sometimes without their weapons. Nothing mattered, they said, except getting out."[360]
>
> *Life Magazine*

The lesson learned by Hanoi was that the ARVN could be easily defeated once the U.S. departed. For Hanoi, it became a waiting game: wait for the U.S. to depart and then invade South Vietnam, which is exactly what happened in 1972 and later in 1975. President Thieu realized the incompetence of his commander in the North, General Lam, and ordered that he be replaced.

Thieu, Abrams, and Nixon were publically proclaiming that it was an ARVN victory and a proof that Vietnamization was working. The battle was supposed to set back the Hanoi plan to invade South Vietnam in 1972 but did not do that. Kissinger stated that it was hoped that the operation would delay the NVA invasion of 1972,[361] but the NVA moved forward into Vietnam on 30 March 1972.

In South Vietnam, the citizens wanted to know the truth. Thousands of ARVN soldiers had been killed. On 1 April 1971, Thieu announced in his press conference that Lam Son 719 was still under way.[362] This was a lie, matched by Nixon, who said that Lam Son 719 proved that Vietnamization was a success.

Kissinger was inclined to be lenient with the South Vietnamese for this failed operation. He blamed the lack of South Vietnamese planning and using only two divisions when four were needed. "On the whole, the South Vietnamese extracted themselves in tolerable fashion, except for unedifying and untypical television pictures of a few panicky soldiers clinging to the skids of helicopters."[363]

Historian Lewis Sorley, who transcribed tapes made by Abrams during this period, found that Abrams viewed the operation as a success. "I'm beginning to have a conviction about Lam Son 719 that it was really a death blow."[364] The question remains: Whose death blow? General Philip Davidson summarized.

> On 7 April, shortly after ARVN's forced withdrawal from Laos, President Nixon, in a television broadcast to the nation, proclaimed, "Tonight I can report that Vietnamization has succeeded"—an Orwellian untruth of boggling proportions. Lam Son 719 had demonstrated exactly the opposite, that Vietnamization had not succeeded.[365]
>
> ***Philip B. Davidson***

Author Jeffrey Kimball also quoted Davidson.

> Military analysts such as General Philip Davidson in his postwar history of the war not only agreed there were deficiencies but also viewed them as incurable. ARVN military leadership was politicized; Thieu was wanting in judgment and

nerve; several commanders were inept [such as Lam], many officers, without American advisory support, lacked the professional skills necessary to coordinate ground, tank, artillery, and air operations; ARVN lacked offensive initiative and mobile fighting capability; and, like the Americans, the South Vietnamese relied too much on maneuver by helicopter when walking would have been swifter. American blunders— hasty planning, poor judgment, inadequate coordination with the ARVN, and inter-service rivalry—had compounded the ARVN short-comings.[366]

Jeffrey Kimball

Press reporting of the disaster caused a national outrage. "In March 1971, a poll reported that public confidence in Nixon had dropped to 50 percent, the lowest rating since he had entered office. Support for his conduct of the war slid to 34 percent, another survey stated 51 percent of Americans were persuaded that the conflict was 'morally wrong.'"[367] Street protests resumed, followed by a 200,000-strong march on Washington.[368] Laird agreed to deliver a speech at the University of Wisconsin, which was clearly one of the most unfriendly environments and a hotbed of student unrest. Laird cancelled at the last minute and sent General "Chappie" James to give the address. James received a rather violent welcome, as would be expected at the University of Wisconsin during that period. Laird's biographer Dale Van Atta tells the story.

> General "Chappie" James went in his [Laird's] place and received an antiwar reprimand from the chancellor and a thirty-name petition protesting the war from the students serving the luncheon. Out in the cold were about two thousand antiwar protesters led by Rennie Davis, who had been convicted in the "Chicago Seven" trial of crossing state lines to incite a riot at the 1968 Democratic National Convention. He shouted to the demonstrators in Wisconsin, "If the government doesn't stop the war, we are going to stop the government." And he chided Laird for not showing up: "Laird is not all fool. If he would have come here today, we would have really kicked some ass!"

On February 10, several hundred students at the University of Illinois in Champaign burned Laird in effigy.[369]

Dale Van Atta

Bui Diem, South Vietnam's ambassador in Washington at this time, reported to Thieu.

> The view is of thousands of students carrying the VC flag in the streets of Washington, and of ten thousand troops. All these images coalesce on the TV screen every night. These things undoubtedly provoke reflections from the American people who ask the question, more than ever—when will the war end? These reflections will perhaps push the ordinary man into a situation where he thinks it is better to give up than continue. And this situation is like a mirror staring back at Richard Nixon when he looks at the future of the war…. In the meantime, the antiwar elements have tried their best to put forward the idea that it is past—time to think about such things as a schedule for withdrawing troops. Now it is simply—when will this war be ended? That is to say, the attitude is—we don't care about the consequences.[370]

Bui Diem

The NVA needed to restock its massive losses that occurred during Lam Son 719 due to air strikes, but this would not take long.

For the ARVN, any confidence in their fighting ability that had been built up over the past year was undermined by Lam Son 719. While small units fought bravely against overwhelming odds, the senior ARVN leadership continued to be viewed as incompetent and corrupt.

The conclusion is that Lam Son 719 disrupted NVA operations in early 1971, but the NVA planned to invade South Vietnam in 1972, not 1971. The 1972 invasion went ahead as planned during the dry season in early 1972. Furthermore, it was a conventional attack across the DMZ, and supplies followed the NVA advance, as would be expected. Stockpiled supplies from the Ho Chi Minh Trail were therefore less important, but the supply losses during Lam Son 719 may have affected the invasion. The worst impact was on the ARVN, whose morale had been building since the Cambodian Incursion the previous year. The NVA sustained devastating casualties during Lam Son 719, but these were quickly replaced.

Lam Son 719 was a disastrous defeat for the ARVN and the U.S. Both realized that South Vietnam was unlikely to survive long after the last U.S. combat troops were withdrawn.

As 1971 closed, U.S. forces in numbered 158,000. The total of U.S. dead stood at 57,323 as the Year of the Rat opened.

1972–The Year of the Rat

Grunt logic argues that since the U.S. has decided not to go out and win the war, there's no sense in being the last one to die.[371]
Keith William Nolan

Because of Vietnamization, the U.S. could withdraw its forces. The very first U.S. troop withdrawal occurred as eight hundred men from the 9th Infantry Division were sent home. The phased troop withdrawal occurred in fourteen stages, starting in August 1969, through June 1972.[372] By the time the U.S. Army started its withdrawal in late 1969, it was obvious to everyone in the field that our army was disintegrating. A senior brigade officer spoke to the point when he said, behind the cloak of anonymity, "Nobody in the brigade gives a damn about this war any more, including me. We will be happy to get home, and when we do, the enemy will march down out of the hills and take over." That senior officer's bitter statement was widely shared among the departing American soldiers. The Vietnam experience had carried U.S. armed forces to the point of defeat. Said army Captain Steve Adolph, a veteran of three tours, "When I came home, I didn't think the U.S. Army could whip the North Vietnamese Boy Scouts, and I wasn't sure about the Girl Scouts either." Brigadier General Theodore C. Mataxis, who had served as a MR 2 advisor, brigade commander, and acting division commander, summed up the army's tortuous journey this way: It's been the opposite of Korea. There we went in with a bad army and came out with a good one. In Vietnam we went in with a good army and came out with a bad one."[373]

General Bruce Palmer, who commanded II Field Force Vietnam (IIFFV) and later became the acting U.S. Army Chief of Staff, summarized:

American direction and conduct of the war and the

operational performance of our armed forces, particularly during the 1962–69 period, generally were professional and commendable. Performance continued to be of a high quality until the 1969–70 period, when dissent at home began to be reflected in troop attitudes and conduct in Vietnam. From 1969 until the last U.S. combat troops left in August [1972], a decline in performance set in; the discovery of widespread drug use in Vietnam in the spring of 1970 signaled that more morale and disciplinary troubles lay ahead. The so-called "fraggings" of leaders that began in 1969–70 were literally murderous indicators of poor morale and became a matter of deep concern. Extremely adverse environmental conditions and very trying circumstances contributed to this decline in performance. Particularly galling to our forces in the field were the widely publicized statements of highly placed U.S. officials, including senators, against American involvement. Such statements were perceived to support the enemy and badly damaged the morale of our troops. The deteriorating climate at home also affected the conduct of American prisoners of war (mostly airmen) held in North Vietnamese POW camps; this was reflected in the increasing number of men who were accused of collaborating with the enemy in the 1969–71 period, as compared to the very few during the earlier years of the war.[374]

Bruce Palmer

There are many other factors not mentioned by General Palmer in detail that also had an effect on the fighting ability of the U.S. Army in Vietnam. Historian Keith William Nolan summarized:

Virtually no draftee wants to be fighting in Vietnam anyway, and in return for his reluctant participation he demands, and gets, personal freedoms that would have driven a MacArthur or a Patton apoplectic. It is an Army in which all questions— including "Why?"—are permissible. Alpha Company seethes with problems, and it has now fallen into chaos … the company commander's continuing problem is to find an effective compromise between his own professional dedication and his draftees' frank disinterest in anything that might cost an American life…. Grunt logic argues that since the U.S. has decided not to go out and win the war, there's no sense in being the last one to die.[375]

Keith William Nolan

Battles Lost and Search & Avoid

The Mary Ann affair[376] demonstrated that the U.S. Army had lost its fighting ability. Fire Support Base (FSB) Mary Ann was located in the westernmost part of the Americal Division's area of responsibility in Quang Tin Province, in the north of South Vietnam. It w a s scheduled to be handed over to the ARVN. At Mary Ann, security was lax, and the VC had been watching it for weeks. A carefully planned attack was launched against it by about one hundred sappers on the night of 28 March 1971. They cut the wire and swarmed over Mary Ann. The result was very heavy losses for the U.S. battalion there. Thirty were killed and eighty-two wounded. One medevac pilot described the scene. "It was the worst carnage I have ever seen…Some [bodies were] burned to charcoal…There were nine body bags full of bits and pieces of flesh.[377] An investigation followed, and the report concluded:

> The reduced level of combat activity and the increasing publicity by the news media focused upon ending of the war tend to create a great complacency among both the troops and their commanders. Coupled with this is the effect of anti– Vietnam and anti-military attitudes [in the United States] and the growth of permissiveness within the military establishment. All of these factors confront a commander in Vietnam today with a formidable task (challenge) of maintaining a high state of discipline and alertness among his troops.[378]

David Fulghum

A part of the problem was the new Army Chief of Staff Westmoreland's policy to send people home who had served the longest in Vietnam rather than send units home.[379] Westmoreland overrode the objections of General Abrams, the commander in Vietnam, and others. It is difficult to understand what Westmoreland was thinking. If you send home your most experienced people and replace them with new people, it is disruptive to the effectiveness and discipline of the unit before the unit, itself, goes home.

As a result, as the war progressed, the U.S. forces in Vietnam were faced with multiple problems. The demonstrations at home against the war generated disrespect for authority, and this influenced the attitude of the troops. The system of rotation, especially the rotation of the officers within Vietnam to get their tickets punched, produced a less than competent force. Author Neil Sheehan summarized the problem.

> The American military system of the 1960s provided for the unlearning rather than the learning of lessons. The one-year tour that Westmoreland had decided to carry over from the advisory era because he thought it would help morale meant that all ranks from colonel to private first class left the country by the time they were beginning to acquire some experience and perspective. The turnover was twice as fast, every six months, at the operating levels of battalion and brigade (regiment was the equivalent of brigade in the Marine Corps), where experienced leadership was needed most. The officer spent the other six months of his tour in a staff job or as an executive officer at a higher level. There were few exceptions, and only rarely could a man hold a command longer than six months by volunteering to extend his tour. (Often the turnover was faster than six months because the officer became a casualty or got sick.)
>
> The Army personnel bureaucracy tended to view Vietnam as an educational exercise and rationalized the six-month rule as a way of seasoning more officers for the "big war" yet to come with the Soviets in Europe and for more of these "brushfire wars." The real reason, which held true for the Marine Corps

too and which explained why the practice was derisively called "ticket-punching," was a mechanistic promotion process and the bureaucratic impetus this created. To win eagles, a lieutenant colonel had to punch a battalion command on his record. To gain a star, a colonel had to punch a command of a brigade or a regiment. To keep an officer in a battalion or brigade or regimental command longer than six months was regarded as unfair to his contemporaries. Much the same system of ticket-punching held true for the general officers, although they were on eighteen-month tours. A general was seldom permitted to hold a division or corps command for more than a year, because so many other generals were waiting in line to qualify for another star…. The Vietnamese could thus count on their American opponents to behave according to pattern.[380]

Neil Sheehan

Ron Beckett, a veteran of three tours in Vietnam, echoed Neil Sheehan's assessment.

The decision for a twelve-month tour was disastrous in U.S. units, and doubly so in the advisory effort. Although defended in terms of preventing "burn out," all it really did was cycle officers through command and other key combat assignments to punch their tickets and enhance their careers. About the time that an officer was starting to learn his job, he was moved to another position or his tour was over. We were constantly being led by the inexperienced, and the men serving under these officers paid the price. This practice led John Paul Vann to observe, "We didn't fight a ten-year war, we fought a one-year war ten times."

For a district- or province-level advisor to be most effective, a minimum of a two-year tour would have been necessary to absorb all the knowledge that was essential, to establish rapport, and to build trust and confidence. Eighteen months should have been the minimum for those assigned as advisors to tactical units. The standard twelve month tour was simply an insufficient length of time.

Compounding this problem was the army's decision, in the face of mounting criticism over repeated tours, to fill many advisory positions with officers below the required grade: lieutenants in captain positions, captains in major positions, and majors in lieutenant colonel positions. The net result was inexperienced junior officers frequently being assigned to advise experienced officers senior to them. The implicit message was that a young, inexperienced American officer was somehow more capable than an older, experienced, and more senior Vietnamese officer, and could therefore effectively advise him—hardly the basis for the trust, respect, and rapport required. The enhancements in advisor training and the extension of the advisory tour to eighteen months in the latter part of the war were recognitions of this fact. While these were important improvements, they were too little, too late.[381]

Ron Beckett

Drugs, pills, and alcohol were plentiful and cheap. The unfairness of the draft system that sent young blacks to war while wealthy whites got student deferments was a national disgrace. Racial unrest in the United States caused by such events as the murder of Martin Luther King influenced the attitude of many black Americans toward authority. Senseless Westmoreland policies such as "body count" killed many innocent civilians by mistake did nothing but infuriate the Vietnamese and add to the ranks of the VC. All of these factors produced atrocities by those with no moral compass such as William Calley, and that led to the massacre at My Lai.

> Actually, the My Lai massacre itself reflected the stark terror of a war of attrition, in which military success, for lack of terrain objectives, was measured statistically by counting corpses. While casualty counts are valid measurements of war, in Vietnam they unfortunately became more than yardsticks used to gauge the battlefield. Rather than means of determination, they became objectives in themselves. The process became so ghoulish that individual canteens were accepted as authorized substitutes if bodies were too dismembered to estimate properly.[382] Guidelines were even issued by MACV on factoring additional dead based on standard percentages by type of encounter and terrain. This appalling practice produced body counts that went largely unquestioned, and were readily rewarded by promotions,

medals, and time off from field duty. For example, General Westmoreland had issued a special commendation to the 11th Infantry Brigade based on its claim of 128 enemy killed at My Lai.[383]

Shelby L. Stanton

War crimes by U.S. forces added to war protests at home and provided the enemy with propaganda that was used very effectively. In a strange twist of fate, General Westmoreland, while commanding forces in Vietnam, commended Calley's unit for the high body count at My Lai. Later as Army Chief of Staff, he moved to court-martial Calley and others for the murders at My Lai when it was discovered that the body count consisted of murdered civilians, not enemy bodies.[384]

The result was that by 1970, all realized that the total effort should be in getting the troops home safely. For the infantry, it became an exercise of "search and avoid" rather than engaging the enemy.[385] All realized that this war was a lost cause. The corrupt regime in Saigon under President Thieu could never hope to win without U.S. forces, and the U.S. Army was disintegrating due to lack of discipline, drugs, racial problems, and opposition to the war on the home front. While there are many examples of valor by South Vietnamese units and their leaders, they were operating in a sea of incompetence that started in Saigon.

Napoleon is said to have remarked that a strategy of defense is deferred suicide, and this strategy was used during unit stand-downs. Firebase Ripcord is a good example. The 101st Airborne Division established the firebase in April 1970. The purpose of Ripcord is not clear, but the NVA moved in to attack the firebase in July 1970 and bombarded the fire-base to the point that the army decided to withdraw the troops. Over a three-week period, while the 101st defended, it lost 61 killed and 345 wounded.[386] Another incident: Firebase Charlie 2 near the DMZ was attacked during meal time. The troops scattered to a nearby bunker, and a delayed-fuse round penetrated six feet of bunker protection, killing twenty-nine soldiers.[387]

The Easter Invasion

Nixon practiced the "Madman Theory" of foreign policy while in office. He explained it best during a discussion with his White House Chief of Staff, H.R. Haldeman, quoted below.

> I call it the Madman Theory, Bob. I want the North Vietnamese to believe I've reached the point where I might do anything to stop the war. We'll just slip the word to them that "For God's sake, you know Nixon is obsessed about Communism. We can't restrain him when he's angry—and he has his hand on the nuclear button" and Ho Chi Minh himself will be in Paris in two days begging for peace.[388]
>
> ***Richard M. Nixon***

There are problems with using the madman approach to foreign policy. If you use it on a nuclear power such as the Soviet Union, that power may launch a preemptive nuclear strike. During the Easter Invasion, Nixon proved that he was capable of anything. He threatened to mine Haiphong Harbor. This was risky business, since if a Soviet supply ship delivering supplies to North Vietnam hit a mine and Soviet citizens were killed, there could be major consequences and possibly confrontation between the U.S. and the Soviet Union. Nixon actually did order the mining in May 1972, but no Soviet citizens were injured. There is very little evidence that Nixon's madman approach achieved any positive result.

While Nixon was playing the madman in the Oval Office, Henry Kissinger was negotiating with the Soviets over the Strategic Arms Limitation Treaty and also with China. Vietnam was in the background, but Kissinger tried to connect treaties with Soviet support for a Vietnam peace treaty. The problem was that the Soviets had less leverage on the North Vietnamese than the U.S. did on the South Vietnamese.[389]

At the same time, the U.S. was trying to negotiate a peace settlement with Hanoi with South Vietnam as a reluctant participant. These secret peace talks were going on in Paris, and Kissinger, Nixon's national security advisor, represented the U.S. At the same time, Nixon was under fire from Congress and the American people over the Vietnam War. Since Lam Son 719 failed to delay the Hanoi invasion of South Vietnam, the NVA went forward as planned in March 1972. This invasion was called the Easter Invasion (the label "Spring Invasion" was also used). By this time, many U.S. troops had been withdrawn from Vietnam or were in stand-down mode, with about 6,000 combat troops of the 70,000 remaining. The NVA invasion would be countered by ARVN units and U.S. air support.

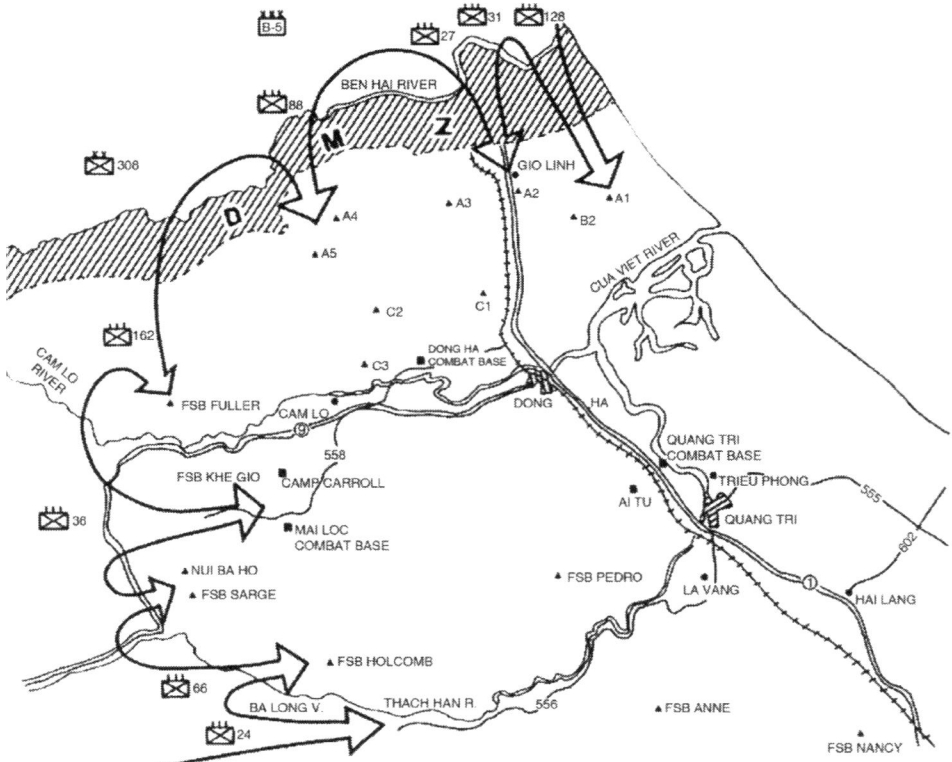

The NVA Easter Invasion, 1972 (Ngo Quang Troung).

Figuring that domestic American pressures would prevent Nixon from reintroducing American forces in Vietnam, they [Hanoi] were also out to cripple the Vietnamization effort. Pham Van Dong publicly stated that it was necessary to prove the failure of Vietnamization to prove to Nixon that "he has everything to lose except the honorable exit we are determined to enable him to make." Nixon was privately glum. With the U.S. forces virtually out of action in Vietnam, America's position and prestige hinged on the Saigon regime: "the weak link in our whole chain," as he noted in his diary. "The real problem," he wrote, "is that the enemy is willing to sacrifice in order to win, while the South Vietnamese simply aren't willing to pay that much of a price in order to avoid losing."[390]

Stanley Karnow

If the U.S. combat troops could not fight in this major NVA invasion, why were they not sent home in 1971? The answer was politics.

As the New Year approached, Nixon considered making 1971 the last year of America's involvement in Vietnam. Just before Christmas, he had shared his thinking with Kissinger and Haldeman. In April 1971, Nixon said, he could go to South Vietnam, tour the country and reassure Thieu about the consequences of the impending final withdrawal. Then he would come home and announce that America's role in Vietnam was over. Kissinger strenuously protested Nixon's timetable. If U.S. combat troops came out by the end of 1971, he argued, the Communists could start trouble the following year. That meant the Nixon administration would pay the political price in the 1972 presidential election. Nixon should promise instead only that he would get American troops out by the end of 1972. That schedule would get him safely past his reelection. Nixon saw the wisdom in Kissinger's argument that guaranteeing his second term would require American soldiers to go on dying.[391]

A. J. Langguth

The NVA had a good plan. It would strike across the DMZ in the north while other columns would attack east through the central highlands to the coast. In the south, the attack was launched above Saigon. Giap committed 120,000 NVA troops plus thousands of VC. This was not an attempt to conquer South Vietnam, but was intended to demonstrate to the U.S. that the ARVN would always lose. In this way Hanoi hoped to influence the peace talks going on at that time. The attacks were launched on 30 March 1972.

The ARVN numbers were impressive. South Vietnam had over one million men under arms and outnumbered the NVA by ten to one, but the ARVN was a hollow force. Nearly half of the force were local units tied to the ground. Thieu's maneuver battalions were spread across South Vietnam and had to counter three separate well-planned thrusts.

The NVA made good progress. In the MR 2, one ARVN division fled as the NVA approached Kontum, the province capital. The Montagnards who watched them flee called them "the rabbit soldiers."[392] The ARVN province regional commander, General Nguyen Van Toan, was a crony of Thieu. For years he had reaped profits from the cinnamon trade. He was very smooth, a good talker, but could not fight. Thieu reached this conclusion and fired him during the Easter invasion.[393] To the north, in MR 1, Thieu replaced the incompetent Lam, who had failed during Lam Son 719, with General Ngo Quang Truong. One of two of Troung's divisions was made up of recruits, and this division fled at the time the NVA approached.[394] The division that fled was the 3rd ARVN Division, two regiments of which were made up of convicts, deserters, and inept officers.[395]

It depended upon leadership. General Abrams was well aware of the ARVN leadership problem and issued the following order. "Effective immediately, no Vietnamese commander will be air lifted out of a unit defensive position by U.S. fixed wing aircraft or helicopter unless such evacuation is directed personally by the ARVN corps commander. Inform your counterpart."[396] Some examples of what occurred in the Easter Offensive of 1972 are provided, below.

Cowardice and Deceit

The NVA invasion of South Vietnam in 1972 was met with bravery and competence by ARVN soldiers and small unit leaders, but the campaign was nearly lost by the corruption and cowardice of the ARVN leadership. Author David Fulghum provides an example when he tells the story of Camp Carroll, an ARVN position in MR 1 that was under NVA attack.

> The sprawling firebase had endured three days of shelling, but as Easter Sunday dawned Camp Carroll, in Camper's [the U.S. Senior Advisor] opinion, remained strong enough to survive at least another week. At 2:30 P. M. on Easter Sunday, April 2, the ARVN officers held a meeting closed to the Americans, shortly after Dinh [the ARVN commander] came to Camper at his bunker and told him that a cabal of disaffected ARVN officers had forced him to negotiate a surrender of the camp complete with its artillery, ammunition, and American advisors. After being told by 3d Division headquarters that no reserves could be spared for Camp Carroll, Dinh said, in an interview aired on Communist radio after the fight, he believed "we would die if we remained in the base and we would also die in large numbers" if they tried to retreat. As a result, "The commanders of the various units reported to me that most of the soldiers did not want to resist the liberation forces anymore." The white flag was to go up in an hour. Col. Dinh offered to join Camper in a suicide pact to preserve their "honor." When the American declined, Dinh suggested that they mix in with the surrendering soldiers and escape into the high grass. Camper turned down that offer too.[397]
>
> **David Fulghum**

Camper organized a U.S. airlift out. There were a few ARVN soldiers who would refuse to surrender, and with his advisors, Camp got out while the ARVN surrendered. Also in MR 1, The NVA captured the province capital of Quang Tri on 1 May 1972.

At this point, Nixon stepped up the war and ordered the bombing of targets in North Vietnam. He increased B-52 bombing of the invading NVA forces. He threatened that he would mine the North Vietnamese port, Haiphong Harbor, to stop the flow of supplies to Hanoi. On 8 May 1972, Nixon addressed the nation.

> After describing the North Vietnamese invasion, I outlined our three options: an immediate withdrawal, a negotiated peace, or a decisive military action to end the war. I said that I had rejected the first option because it would be immoral to abandon our South Vietnamese allies to Communist tyranny and because it would encourage aggression throughout the world. I explained that while I preferred the second option, "it takes two to negotiate" and the North Vietnamese had proven to be unwilling partners. Therefore, I said, the United States really had no choice at all: "There is only one way to stop the killing. That is to keep the weapons of war out of the hands of the international outlaws of North Vietnam." In order to leave the door open for later negotiations, I concluded with a reiteration of our basic terms for a fair peace settlement.
>
> Antiwar critics and the news media competed with each other in denouncing our action. One senator remarked that the decision was "reckless and wrong." Another said that "the President must not have a free hand in Indochina any longer." One newspaper called the decision a "desperate gamble" and urged that Congress should cut off funds for the war to "save the President from himself and the nation from disaster." Another claimed that the President "has lost touch with the real world." One legislator topped them all when he breathlessly intoned that the President "has thrown down the gauntlet of nuclear war to a billion people in the Soviet Union and China....Armageddon may be only hours away." There was nearly unanimous agreement that, as one network reporter put it, our action "practically kills prospects of a summit" with the

Soviet leadership. Most of the members of Congress, my cabinet, and my staff shared the view that the summit would probably be off.[398]

Richard M. Nixon

After the invasion, Gerald C. Hickey recalled.

In mid-August 1972 I had a long discussion with Nay Luett about the situation. He reported that there were estimated to be around 150,000 highlanders in refugee camps, and he figured that since 1965, some 200,000 highland people (both civilians and military personnel) had died because of the war. At least 85 percent of highland villages had, for one reason or another, been displaced. Whole ethnic groups had been forced to abandon their traditional territories. The Bru well illustrated the effect of the war on one group; whereas in 1965 there were an estimated forty thousand Bru, only some seven thousand could now be accounted for. Not one Bru village remained in place.[399]

Gerald C. Hickey

The Invisible Army

"This invasion could not have been held at this point without U.S. air support; however, ten times the air power could not have done the job if the armed forces of South Vietnam had not stood and fought."[400]
General Creighton Abrams

While the ARVN soldiers were fighting for their lives to survive the NVA Easter Invasion, the remaining U.S. forces were in stand-down mode. U.S. Army forces would not be committed to counter the NVA invasion. Generally, the U.S. was out of Vietnam as a combat force after 1972. Historian Lewis Sorley explained General Abrams's dilemma.

Abrams noted the contribution of American support, and that it was only a contribution: "This invasion could not have been held at this point without U.S. air support; however, ten times the air power could not have done the job if the armed forces of South Vietnam had not stood and fought."

And he concluded: "The South Vietnamese government, its armed forces and its people are holding together in this crisis.

We can anticipate more heavy fighting and additional hardships for the people of South Vietnam in the coming weeks. The leaders of Hanoi are staking everything on military victory. The fabric of what the South Vietnamese have built here with our assistance has survived its severest test. The qualities demonstrated by the South Vietnamese people, in my judgment, assure that they will continue to hold."

Because the drawdown had essentially stripped him of ground combat units, Abrams was, observed a contemporary account, "in a position almost unique in military history. Though a soldier all his life, General Abrams now finds himself fighting a war using massive American air and naval forces rather than ground-combat units."[401]

Lewis Sorley

At the time of the Easter Invasion, John Paul Vann was the senior advisor to the ARVN general commanding MR 2. He had the equivalent rank of a U.S. major general. By the Easter offensive, nearly all U.S. troops were out of MR 2. He commanded no U.S. combat troops, but as senior advisor he controlled U.S. advisors that remained in MR 2. Vann had a good ability to cajole and intimidate the ARVN generals, motivating them to fight: a badly needed gift.

One of the three NVA strikes into South Vietnam had as its objective the small provincial capital, Kontum, some miles north of Pleiku, the headquarters of MR 2. If the NVA took Kontum, they could proceed south and seize Pleiku and then east to the sea, cutting South Vietnam in half. This was mountainous terrain near the tri-border area. In order to seize Kontum, the NVA took as its initial objective Tan Canh, near Dak To. If the NVA could seize Tan Canh or the nearby firebases along Rocket Ridge, they could overrun Kontum. Rocket Ridge was a string of fortified artillery positions that ran along Highway 14. These had been constructed by the U.S. Army and were passed on to the ARVN as a part of Vietnamization. They shielded the approaches to Kontum.

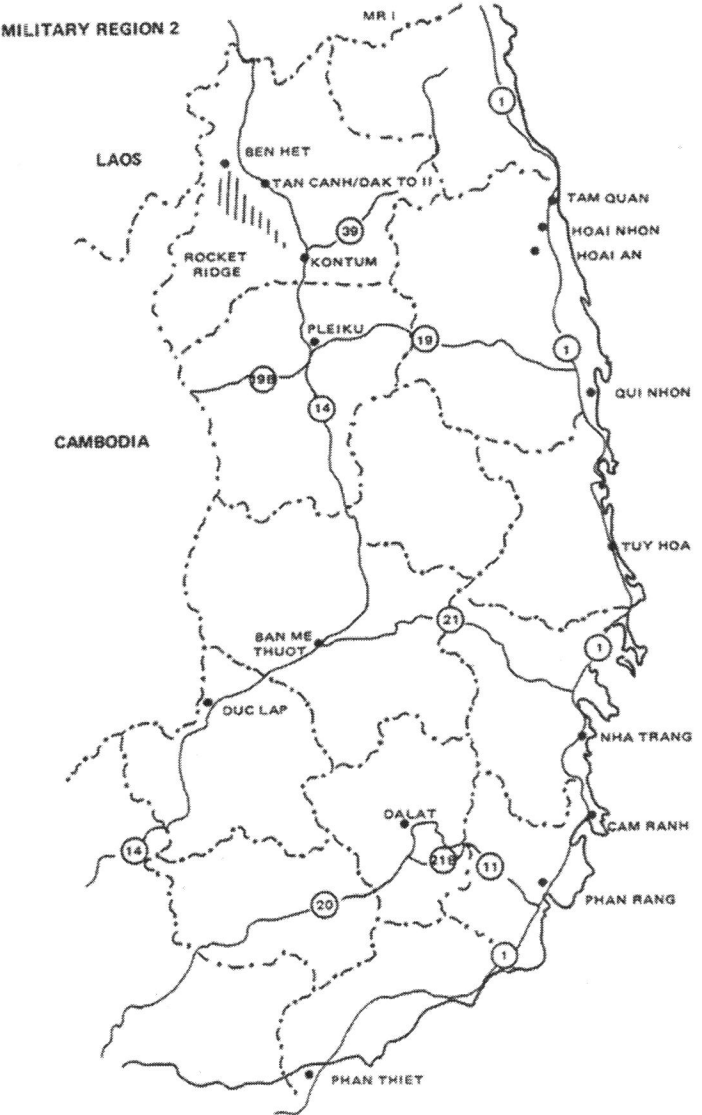

Attack on Kontum (Ngo Quang Truong).

Author Neil Sheehan summarized the situation.

. . .Dzu [the ARVN II Corps commander] with Vann's encouragement, invested the equivalent of an ARVN division, roughly 10,000 men, in the defense of Tan Canh. He and Vann had placed the headquarters of the 22nd Division with two of its infantry regiments there and reinforced them with separate infantry battalions, the 22nd's own armored cavalry regiment, and most of a second independent regiment of armor. Because Tan Canh was the most forward position, the alignment was a gamble of the highest order. If the Rocket Ridge line broke and Route 14 running south from Tan Canh to Kontum was cut, these forces around Tan Canh with their accompanying artillery, tanks, APCs, trucks, and other fighting gear would be enveloped and isolated. If the Tan Canh defenses themselves cracked, it would be impossible with troops as unsteady as the ARVN to conduct an orderly retreat down a single mountain road. The division would disintegrate. More was at risk than an ARVN division. If either eventuality occurred, the forces needed to hold Kontum would be lost.[402]

Neil Sheehan

John Paul Vann in his Saigon Headquarters (U.S. Government).

The NVA assembled 35,000 troops to attack Kontum under one its best generals, Hoang Minh Thao, one of General Giap's favorite commanders.[403] The NVA force was methodical in its advance. First came the engineers with earth-moving equipment to build roads at night. Sound carries great distances in the mountains, and the defenders could hear the sounds of construction. Next came the NVA tanks, and the defenders could see the headlamps of the tanks from a very far distance as they moved toward them. This was a conventional war not seen in South Vietnam since the French war. It was terrifying for the ARVN.

NVA lack of experience in conventional warfare showed here. The NVA tanks (T-54s—late 1950s vintage) came on without supporting infantry, which made them vulnerable to anti-tank fire and ARVN infantry, especially at night. John Paul Vann had made sure that the ARVN division and Dak To had M-72 LAWs (light antitank weapons) available. While the M-72s were used effectively in other regions, there were problems at Dak To: the ARVN and PF militia ran away. Other approaches were tried. A C-130 aircraft was loaded with a 105mm howitzer and flew over the battlefield firing at tanks. The problem was that it only had high explosive (HE) ammunition and no anti-tank rounds. It did score hits on NVA tanks, but the HE rounds produced only a bad headache for crew members. The T-54s survived the hits.[404]

There were limited effective ARVN units in MR 2 available to repel the NVA attack, but reinforcements were sent in. Vann coordinated air support and helped with resupply. He would fly through heavy fire to pinpoint targets, report results, adjust fire, and land in order to encourage ARVN commanders and provide supplies. His efforts were instrumental in stopping the NVA attack in western MR 2.

Tan Canh did not hold long. The ARVN rabbit soldiers ran away quickly.[405] After taking Tan Canh, the NVA stopped to resupply and reinforce before attacking Kontum city. This was a three-week delay because the NVA was focused on the other two fronts in MR 1 and MR 3, which failed. While the NVA delayed the attack on Kontum city, U.S. B-52s devastated NVA troops with concentrated carpet bombing. Vann coordinated most of this battle. The NVA retreated.

Another tactical emergency was declared at Polei Kleng at 0800 on 8 May. VNAF tactical air responded with A-1s and A-37s. USAF Spectres and F-4s also responded. The weather worsened, but the VNAF and USAF FACs continued to work over the area as much as possible. However, at 0500 the next morning the enemy attacked again. After a heavy bombardment, the 64th NVA Regiment assaulted, with 20 tanks leading the way. The Rangers knocked out five tanks with M-72s and again beat back the enemy assault. Heavy incoming fire forced the defenders into bunkers and trenches. The soldiers' families, 300 Montagnard women and children, were crowded in with them. Women carried ammo and cared for the wounded. Lightly wounded men returned to the firing line. Most of the radio antennas were knocked out by direct fire from the surrounding hills, and the enemy began to destroy the remaining bunkers systematically one by one. Early on 9 May, Major Chuyen and his deputy, Captain Phan Thai Binh, decided to abandon the camp rather than be captured. The hundreds of wives and children were going to make withdrawal slow and difficult, but they could not be left behind.

At 0400 on 9 May, the Rangers used a Bangalore torpedo to blow a gap in the defensive wire, and Lieutenant Kchong, a Montagnard, led the 1st Company out into the darkness. He was followed by Major Chuyen and his CP group. They went east. Captain Binh with the remaining Rangers and the women and children left last and headed north. A VNAF L-19 [aircraft] contacted them by radio when it arrived over the camp, and they informed the pilot they were outside the camp and enemy tanks were now inside. The pilot managed to call in jets to bomb the camp before he was shot down and forced to bail out.

As Captain Binh and his group neared the Dak Poko River, they were almost surrounded. Firing while they retreated, they managed to fight their way to the river. The Rangers held off the enemy while the wounded, the women, and the children crossed the river to safety. The NVA then started mortaring the crossing site. One mother was killed, but her baby, attached to her in the typical Montagnard sling, continued to suckle. A Ranger cut the sling and carried the baby across the river, which was now running red with blood. Only 97 people reached the safety of the far bank, from where they were taken into Kontum. The others were killed, captured, or lost in the jungle. Major Chuyen was captured and then killed."[406]

Gerald Hickey also described the NVA attack and the plight of the Montagnards.

The main thrust of the destructive 1972 offensive began on 31 March, when the Communists launched an offensive at the Demilitarized Zone. On 2 April Sedang, Jeh, and Halang farmers paused in their task of preparing fields for planting when they heard large explosions coming from the direction of fire bases Charlie, Yankee, and Delta that the Americans had established on the ridge dominating the Dak To Valley and Route 14. The withdrawing Americans had turned the fire bases over to the South Vietnamese, and the villagers knew that the explosions indicated a rocket attack by the Communists. This time, however, the explosions lasted for days, prompting Sedang farmers to leave their fields and retreat into their houses in anticipation of a battle.

On 17 April a North Vietnamese unit attacked what was now called "rocket ridge," overrunning fire base Charlie and scattering its five hundred defenders. Fire bases Yankee and Delta were immediately abandoned. The Communists had two divisions (the 2d and 320th), in addition to two independent regiments of infantrymen, an artillery regiment, and a sapper regiment. On Saturday, 24 April, North Vietnamese Russian tanks crashed into the compound of the forward headquarters of the South Vietnamese 22d Division at Tan Canh while other units attacked nearby Dak To. The South Vietnamese made no effort to defend the post and fled at the sight of the tanks. Not long after, American bombers began to swoop over the Dak To valley as helicopters attempted to evacuate the American advisers (one helicopter with six advisers was shot down). Soldiers of the 22d Division, mixed with Vietnamese civilians from Tan Canh, began pouring southward on Route 14 to seek refuge in Kontum. As they carried the bad news that Dak To and Tan Canh had fallen, highlanders in villages along Route 14 either fled into nearby forests or joined the exodus southward. . . .At the Ministry for Ethnic Minorities' Development in Saigon the staff worked feverishly on plans to remove the growing number (now estimated at around fifteen thousand) of highland refugees caught in Kontum. Minister Nay Luett on 14 May consulted in Pleiku with John Paul Vann concerning assistance in removing the refugees. Vann informed him that he already had taken twenty thousand Vietnamese out of Kontum and could do nothing for the highlanders because the American senior province adviser (a colonel) and the Vietnamese province chief claimed that the highlanders did not want to leave the city. The province chief planned to organize them to defend the city against an expected North Vietnamese assault. Furious at this news, Luett went to Kontum, where he was greeted by Sedang, Jeh, Halang, Rengao, Bahnar, and Jarai Arap refugees who told him that they were very anxious to leave because of the heavy fighting and shelling. Luett returned to Pleiku to confront Vann, who agreed to arrange for aircraft to take the highland refugees to Pleiku. Unlike the Vietnamese, who stormed the planes and helicopters, highlanders lined up in orderly fashion, putting the elderly and children on the aircraft first. By 17 May some eight thousand had been airlifted to Pleiku. Kek and his fellow Kon Horing villagers boarded an American chinook helicopter in Kontum and were flown to Pleiku, where they were housed in an abandoned supply dump. Fortunately, the highlanders remained in village groups where there was cohesion and leadership, both of which made it easier to organize refugee relief. But the panic that had seized Kontum now spread to Pleiku, sending an estimated 80 percent of the Vietnamese population down Route 19 to Qui Nhon or down Route 21 to Nha Trang. Regional Forces abandoned their weapons to flee with their families. Most of the civil servants left, and only one doctor was left at the province hospital. As in Kontum, Vietnamese soldiers looted the shuttered shops and houses. Although the refugees were removed from the chaos of downtown Pleiku, they faced an increasingly dire situation because of insufficient housing, lack of firewood, and shortage of water. Then, too, there was the possibility of a Communist attack on Pleiku. This situation prompted Minister Nay Luett to plead with the American officials that the refugees be moved southward to Ban Me Thuot. The Americans responded that there were no aircraft available because the Communists had blown up the large ammunition dump near the airstrip and all of the aircraft were needed to fly in new supplies. Vann agreed to allow refugees to board empty military trucks in a large convoy going down Route 14 to Ban Me Thuot. Because the refugees in the supply dump were living under the worst conditions, it was agreed that they would be the first to leave on the convoy. Most of them, however, were reluctant to go farther south away from their villages. Nay Luett came to reassure them that when the situation improved, his ministry would arrange transportation back to their villages. Looking very confused and anxious, the refugees climbed onto the trucks to begin the arduous and perilous trip down Route 14 through territory infested with Communist troops.[407]

Gerald Hickey

In eastern MR 2, Vann had a different problem. In Binh Dinh province on the coast, he was faced with ARVN leadership cowardice on an unimaginable scale, and Regional Forces-Popular Forces (RF/PF) troops were deserting by the thousands. The ARVN commander of the 40th Regiment, Colonel Tran Heiu Duc, refused to fight and did not fire a round. As the NVA approached, he withdrew his troops and fell back to higher ground; he kept falling back until he ran out of higher ground. Vann tried to intervene. On 19 April 1972, he arranged air support and a convoy of M-113s to allow Duc to withdraw in an orderly manner. At that point Duc fled, leaving all of his remaining troops and wounded behind. The Binh Dinh districts of Bong Son and Tam Quam easily fell before the NVA advance, and 200,000 people in Binh Dinh province were now under NVA control.[408]

There were worse examples of cowardice. ARVN medical helicopters landed to pick up the wounded. While the wounded lay ready for pickup, the ARVN Military Police (MPs) had concocted a scheme to extort money from the able-bodied ARVN troops for a place on the medevac helicopters. Half of the loot went to the ARVN helicopter crews. As the wounded were left dying at the medevac site, the ARVN MPs and helicopter crews counted their money.[409] The ARVN had lessons learned from Lam Son 719: allow the escape of able-bodied soldiers scrambling over the wounded, but also make a profit from it.

The distance between Pleiku, the ARVN MR 2 headquarters, and the province headquarters at Kontum is 42 KM. On 9 June 1972, John Paul Vann loaded into his chopper at Pleiku. Even though it was night, he needed to go to Kontum. By this time, he was the senior U.S. person in MR 2 and had a very busy schedule. He had always been a risk-taker and would rather take a helicopter and save time than go by road or air the next day. By his actions, he had secured a victory for the ARVN in MR 2. After a celebration at Pleiku, he lifted off at 9 p.m. He said at the time, "I've been in Kontum every day since this thing got started."[410] En route, Vann's helicopter crashed before it reached Kontum. It was dark, and the aircraft went into the trees. There is no evidence to suggest that the crash was the result of enemy action. All aboard were killed. They were flying low. The Montagnards cut trees and burn foliage to plant their crops. Vann did not know or had forgotten that there was a spot between Pleiku and Kontum where the Montagnards preserved a small grove of trees to bury their ancestors. All other terrain was devoid of any trees on this route. On that night, the pilot went in at maximum speed to the grove of trees, and his helicopter exploded. ARVN Rangers saw the crash and wanted payment for finding John Paul Vann's body, which was untouched by the crash because he was thrown free of the aircraft, but he was killed instantly. The Rangers robbed Vann's body of his wristwatch, wallet, and his Rutgers ring before returning Vann's body.[411] This might be one of the best summaries of why the South Vietnamese lost the war. There was no ARVN leadership; no one in charge; every man for himself. The Easter Invasion proved that some units fought bravely, but many others fled, and many were only concerned about piling up money. They knew that the war was lost, and they needed money to escape Vietnam and find a new life. The leadership of the corrupt Saigon regime was doing the same thing. It all came down to a lack of ARVN professional leadership.

Malcolm Browne was a journalist in 1972 when he worked with John Paul Vann.

While the Viet Cong got better and better at negating the American technological advantage, the Americans never really grasped that the war was not about who had the most firepower. To the very end Nixon believed the bombs could prevail or at least forestall defeat. Even John Paul Vann, who was celebrated as a maverick for his disavowal of U.S. military tactics in the early years of the war became a great believer in air power. Toward the end of his life in '72 he frequently called for B-52 strikes. He had once criticized the American approach to guerrilla war as comparable to trying to sink a cork with a sledgehammer. It was astonishing how he had changed. I was with him practically every day in the final weeks of his life. In an earlier phase of the war he condemned saturation bombing, but now he was calling almost daily for B-52 strikes known as "arclights."

B-52 attacks often consisted of three bombers each loaded with thirty five-hundred-pound bombs. They dropped them in a rectangle and this saturation bombing was designed to blast everything out of existence. One time I was a mile from a B-52 attack. Even from a mile away you could feel your clothing slapping against your skin from the concussions. It just seemed inconceivable to me that anything—even earthworms—could survive such a devastating attack. And yet about ten minutes after this raid the unit I was accompanying began to draw fairly heavy and effective fire from the people who had been underground during the attack. Of course maybe forty percent had been killed and many others had their eardrums shattered, but they were still an effective fighting force.[412]

Malcolm Browne

Neil Sheehan, Vann's biographer, was able to find the crash site several months after the crash. He found that there were few helicopter parts that could be identified except for a twisted tail boom. Sheehan provided this summary at the end of his book.

The wreckage was scattered around the grove for fifty to sixty yards. I saw a small, low square of hewn logs planted upright in the ground nearby and asked the Montagnard lieutenant what it was. "Dead men here," he said. "Dead men here," he repeated, sweeping his hand about. The grove was the hamlet graveyard. The tribal people had left the trees in their natural state to guard the graves and to provide shade for their burial rites. Now I also knew what had happened on that night. John Vann had come skylarking up the road, mocking death again, unaware that these figures of death were waiting for him in this grove.[413]

Neil Sheehan

By mid–September 1972, the NVA Easter Invasion had petered out, thanks to massive U.S. air support and determined ARVN resistance. The NVA had sustained as many as 100,000 casualties in this campaign, along with the loss of nearly half of its tanks, artillery, and other major implements of war.[414] In that year, 39,000 ARVN soldiers died.[415]

Hanoi had gained ground in the offensive and Saigon would make efforts to gain it back as peace approached.

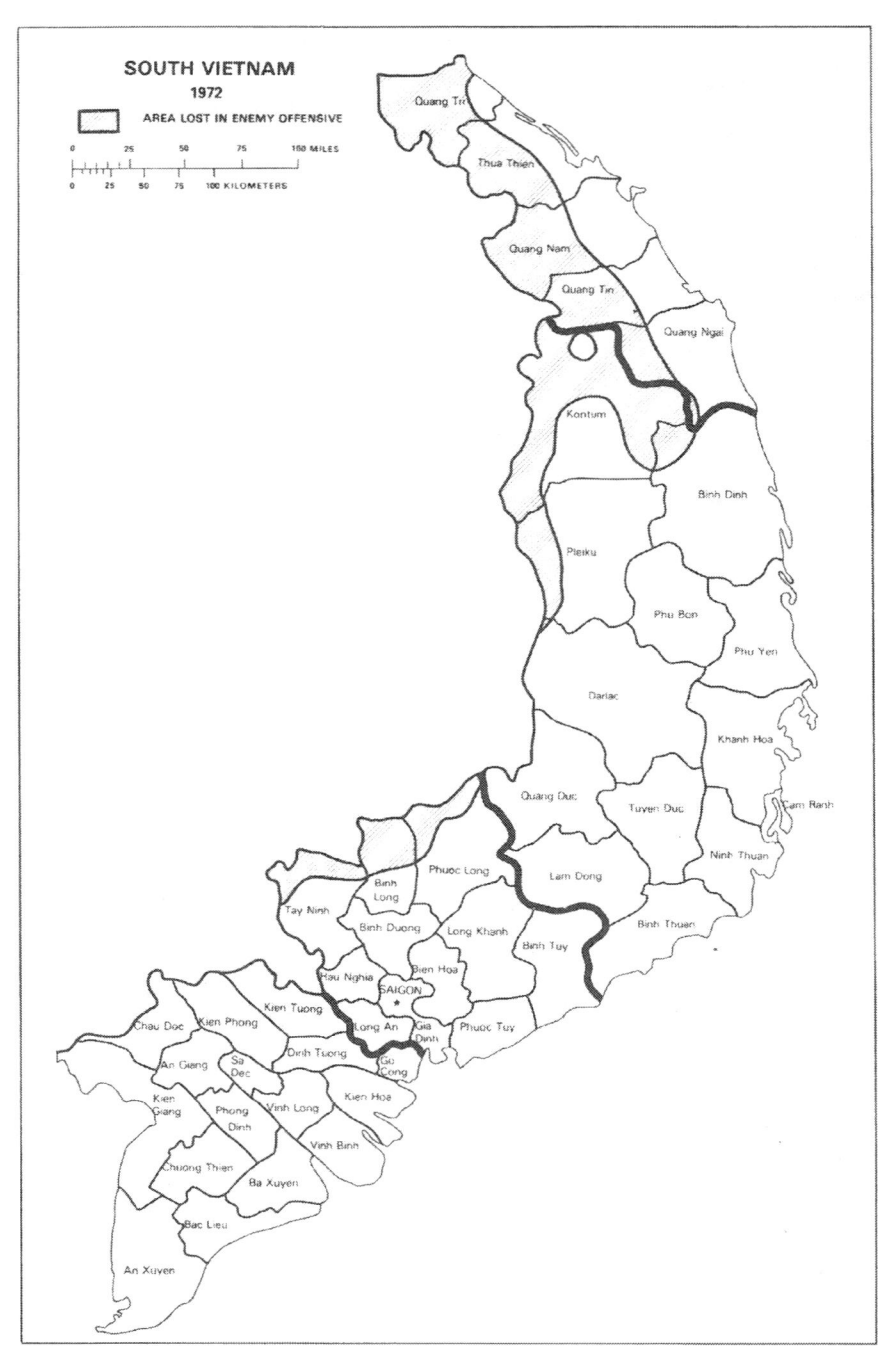

Area Lost During the Easter Offensive (Cao Van Vien)

The Home Front

Perhaps the greatest problem in the home front was that none of the administrations could adequately explain to the American people why we were in Vietnam and what was going on. It is very difficult for parents of a son just killed in action to understand how the domino theory explained why their son died. The American people watched the news every night, and it was fascinating getting daily video from the battlefield. When they saw the coverage of dead U.S. soldiers, could anyone blame them for asking "What in the hell are we doing there?" As their son's body was being shipped back to the states, they were told that we were fighting to defend our Cold War "credibility."[416] There is no evidence that Moscow or Beijing shared that view.[417] Media coverage of the war in Vietnam is the subject of many articles and books, but the point is that the U.S. government failed its people. Van Nguyen Duong, a South Vietnamese officer during the war, summarized the problem.

> On the first day Nixon arrived in the White House [20 January 1969] he heard the echoes of anti-war demonstrators from the Lincoln Memorial demanding peace. The president recognized the continued decline of American public support for the war in Vietnam rooted in the Johnson administration's deceitful war strategy for the intervention in South Vietnam by ground combat forces in the previous years. The anti-war movement was launched on college campuses by separate protest groups. At first it only expressed strong sentiment against the war and there was no structure or coordination among these groups. However, in March 1965, when President Johnson sent the first combat unit to Danang [Da Nang], some 25,000 people immediately demonstrated in Washington; the majority were students. Thereafter, anti-war sentiment congealed into a "movement" with the emergence of several anti-war organized groups on several campuses around the country. These groups were led by intellectuals, social and

political activists, including several congressmen. Some of them were: David Dellinger, a journalist and founder of a pacifist newspaper, who first came to Hanoi and met Ho Chi Minh in 1966; Senator Eugene McCarthy, a Democratic Party liberal and presidential candidate, who had given the mass of young Americans the faith of "New Politics"; and Jerry Rubin, a newspaper reporter and socialist activist who led the "teach-in" speeches at Berkeley University and founded the Yippies, or Youth International Party. The anti-war movement largely opposed U.S. government on several crucial issues: The war policy in Vietnam, attrition strategy, random air strikes and civilian massacre, U.S. troop casualties.

The draft of mostly poor black and white students for military services in Vietnam while favoring the sons of the rich and upper class by the so-called "deferment" system which allowed them to continue their studies in college.

Defense spending had cut into the domestic budget that pushed Congress to refuse to pass some civil right measures. The cuts gravely affected the "Great Society." [418]

Van Nguyen Duong

Students were protesting because they did not want to be cannon fodder for the war, and in 1967, thirty thousand marched on the Pentagon.[419] Students also identified with the Vietnamese people and their sacrifices.[420] Other extreme groups also protested and caused deaths. Bernardine Dohrn, a member of the Weathermen,[421] suggested that the protests would hasten the end of the war by raising its social cost.[422]

The college and university campuses were in turmoil. Prior to 1967 the sons of the white middle class had largely avoided the war through the escape of the college deferment. By 1967 the needs of the Green Machine were such that the draft had taken significant numbers of them as they graduated. The threat of being conscripted for a war that was the object of wide-spread moral revulsion made marchers and shouters out of young men who might have been less concerned over the victimization of an Asian people and the turning into cannon fodder of farm boys and the sons of the working class and the minorities. The appeal of the cause aroused women students in equal number and with equal passion.[423]

Neil Sheehan

Jim Long, recently returned from service in Vietnam, had a different view of the protests.

One of the worst days of my life, Monday, 24 Aug 70, early morning after four anti-war extremists/cowards fertilizer-fuel-oil-bombed Sterling Hall [University of Wisconsin], housing the Army Mathematics Research Center, their purported target. As I came upon the scene and sat down on a grassy knoll next to the hall, and the remains of Robert Fassnacht, a physics research assistant, were being removed—my eyes welled.

There was evil in my country, no different than the evil I experienced in South Vietnam. Anti-war groups stated he was a casualty of political necessity. Tell it to his widow and three orphaned children.[424]

Jim Long

President Nixon summarized the student protests. It was a statement of the unpopularity of the Vietnam War in the U.S. among students and others.

Today, many Americans remember the demonstrations against the war as flocks of flower children marching in orderly candlelight processions. But what we saw from the White House at the time was quite different. Until 1968, antiwar demonstrators were basically peaceful, seldom doing more than holding "teach-ins" and symbolically burning their draft cards. But that had changed by 1969. Students shot at firemen and policemen, held college administrators hostage at knifepoint, stormed university buildings with shotguns in hand, burned buildings, smashed windows, trashed offices, and bombed classrooms. In the academic year 1969–70, there were 1,800 demonstrations, 7,500 arrests, 247 arsons, 462 injuries—two-thirds of them to police—and 8 deaths. The violence was not limited to college campuses; it was a national epidemic. From January 1969 through February 1970, there were over 40,000 bombings, attempted bombings, or bomb threats, most of which were war related. These caused $21 million of property damage, hundreds of injuries, and 43 deaths. Violence was becoming the rule, not the exception, in campus protests. Following the announcement of the incursions into Cambodia, a new wave of violent protest swept the country. At the University of Maryland, fifty people were injured when students ransacked the ROTC building and skirmished with police. In Kent, Ohio, a crowd of hundreds of demonstrators watched as two young men threw lighted flares into the army ROTC building on the campus of Kent State University and burned it to the ground. Ohio's governor called in the National Guard. A few days later, a large crowd of students began throwing rocks and chunks of concrete at the guardsmen, forcing them up a small hill. At the top, the soldiers turned, and someone started shooting. Four people—two protesters and two bystanders—were killed.[425]

Richard M. Nixon

Some veterans were unhappy because they did not get a parade when they got home, but most only wanted to be treated decently and not be attacked by crazy anti-war demonstrators. Below are a few accounts of veterans returning. One veteran related that he left for Vietnam at age nineteen and returned a year later. He met with his girlfriend and her mother. Her mother objected and told her that this man looked to be in his mid-thirties and could not be the same man that she had said farewell to a year earlier. She assured her mother that he was the same man and they married.

Philip Caputo summarized in his book, *A Rumor of War*.

Beyond adding a few more corpses to the weekly body count, none of these encounters achieved anything; none will ever appear in military histories or be studied by cadets at West Point. Still, they changed us and taught us, the men who fought in them; in those obscure skirmishes we learned the old lessons about fear, cowardice, courage, suffering, cruelty, and comradeship. Most of all, we learned about death at an age when it is common to think of oneself as immortal. Everyone loses that illusion eventually, but in civilian life it is lost in installments over the years. We lost it all at once and, in the span of months, passed from boyhood through manhood to a premature middle age. The knowledge of death, of the implacable limits placed on a man's existence, severed us from our youth as irrevocably as a surgeon's scissors had once severed us from the womb. And yet, few of us were past twenty-five.[426]

Philip Caputo

Phillip Hoffman shares his homecoming story:

Brothers Steve and Tom picked me up at the St. Louis airport, and we headed straight for the nearest airport bar to celebrate my return. It was there I had my first encounter with a civilian who showed bias against veterans in uniform. A surly waitress carded me and then refused to accept my military I.D. She insisted on a driver's license, which I didn't have. The conversation heated after my brothers got involved, and only when the bar manager stepped in did things quiet down. He apologized to me and made things right.[427]

Phillip Hoffman

As 1972 closed, U.S. forces in numbered 24,000. The total of U.S. dead stood at 58,082.[428]

1973–The Year of the Buffalo

My greatest mistake was the failure to win that war in Vietnam and end it in the first six months of my presidency.[429]

Richard M. Nixon

Paris Peace Accords

Nixon took advantage of this Easter Invasion victory to push for a peace treaty. Kissinger negotiated a settlement with Hanoi, the VC, and with Thieu as a reluctant participant (he refused to recognize the VC as a legitimate government). On 27 January 1973, the Paris Peace Accords were signed. The agreement stipulated that all U.S. advisors and other troops (about 23,700 people) would withdraw within 60 days and our remaining bases would be dismantled. All U.S. prisoners of war would be released.

The agreement carried the following major provisions:
1. It called for a cease-fire in place.
2. It required the withdrawal of United States troops and an exchange of POW's within sixty days.
3. It prohibited both the United States and North Vietnam from sending more troops into South Vietnam.
4. Equipment could be replaced only on an item-for-item basis.
5. It created two Commissions—the Joint Military Commission (South Vietnam-NVA/VC) and the International Commission on Control and Supervision (Hungary, Poland, Indonesia, and Canada) to enforce the cease-fire and compliance with the agreement.
6. It set up a National Council of National Reconciliation and Concord to organize free elections in South Vietnam.
7. It established the integrity of the DMZ using the terms of the Geneva Accords of 1954.

There were, of course, other provisions, but the above established the fundamental structure of the agreement.[430]

Phillip B. Davidson

The U.S. embassy staff remained until the final defeat of South Vietnam in 1975. There were many other U.S. people, such as aid workers, inspectors, and staff that were to coordinate the U.S. withdrawal.

The first POWs were repatriated in February 1973. North Vietnam pledged that it would not to try to reunify the country by force. An international control commission was set up to supervise the agreement. A sticking point throughout the negotiations was the status of remaining NVA in South Vietnam. Hanoi refused to withdraw these troops. In the end, Kissinger acquiesced and the U.S. signed with no guarantee that the NVA troops would be withdrawn. There was a vague reference that Hanoi would not resupply them. Kissinger said "A North Vietnam withdrawal had been unobtainable for ten years...We could not make it a condition for a final settlement. We had long passed the threshold." In response to criticism, he said, "You don't understand. I want to meet their terms. I want to end this war before the election. What do you want us to do? Stay there forever?"[431] This left the South Vietnamese in a precarious position. With no U.S. forces to support them and a very dedicated force of NVA and VC within their border, it was only a matter of time before Hanoi would attack again. Nixon gave Thieu his personal assurances that if Hanoi attacked, the U.S. would come to South Vietnam's aid.[432]

Alexander Haig worked for Kissinger and later served as Nixon's Chief of Staff. After the war he recalled a discussion that he had had with Richard Nixon.

> It's absolutely untrue that the Christmas bombing was designed to just get Thieu to accept the agreement worked out between Washington and Hanoi. Precisely the opposite was the case. What really happened was the North Vietnamese put their finger in Kissinger's eye after he thought he had "peace at hand." Then when the negotiations resumed the president sent me over to sit in with Kissinger in the last sessions. It wasn't necessary, however, because

Henry was as angry at the North's duplicity as I was. The Vietnamese withdrew every single concession they had made so there was no agreement. The North Vietnamese broke off negotiations and we were forced to begin the so-called Christmas bombing, this time with most of the wraps taken off. The bombing began in order to get the negotiations started up again. There was no alternative other than surrender.

You know, President Thieu wouldn't pass the litmus test of a Wilsonian democrat, not by a long shot, but I think he was a realistic patriot who truly believed that the peace settlement that was imposed on him by Washington was flawed because it permitted a major North Vietnamese presence in the South was dependent on sanctions that he began to question knowing the body politic in Washington. But there wasn't anybody, from the president to Kissinger to anybody else, that intentionally double-crossed Saigon. Don't buy that line. I think Nixon and Kissinger both felt they got the best deal they could get. Had American Congress taken a responsible position, had we applied sanctions in the face of clearly apparent North Vietnamese violations of the Accords, and had we continued to support South Vietnam with supplies and equipment, it would have been sufficient to hold those accords together.

But that wasn't to be. Even Nixon's secretary of state and secretary of defense were vehemently opposed to the war. Years later President Nixon said, "Al you think Watergate was my greatest mistake." And I said, "Well, I might think that." [Laughs.] He said, "It wasn't. My greatest mistake was the failure to win that war in Vietnam and end it in the first six months of my presidency. You told me at the time I had the opportunity to do that when the EC-131 [U.S. intelligence plane] was shot down off North Korea." My recommendation then was to react very strongly with air strikes against North Korea then go to Moscow and tell them we're now going to bring the battle to Hanoi unless we have a settlement that returns South Vietnam to sovereign control of the southern people. But the president decided to turn the other cheek because the secretaries of defense and state and many of his advisers were vehemently opposed. Nixon told me that his failure to act then was his greatest mistake. Watergate drew most of its venom from that failure. The president had enough sense to know that both of these problems had merged. Some of the atrocities of Watergate were a direct product of the failures of Vietnam. The so-called plumbers were established by the president through John Ehrlichman without the knowledge of Henry Kissinger or myself. That was a product of presidential paranoia justified by a measure of disarray in the body politic. Watergate and Vietnam blended and one drew great strength from the other. Certain elements of Watergate—like the Pentagon Papers leakage—led Nixon to undertake protective measures which, when added to the break-in of the Democratic Campaign Headquarters in 1972, really proved to be fatal in the long run.[433]

Alexander Haig

Militarily, the agreement [Paris Peace Accords] was a failure. No attempt was made in the text to spell out who controlled what piece of real estate in the south or to pinpoint where the two sides were to pick up the replacement material both were permitted to receive on a one-for-one basis. These and other critical questions were left to be resolved by the two sides after the cease-fire. Two 'truce teams' were created for this purpose. One, the Joint Military Commission (JMC), was made up of representatives of the major combatants. The other, the International Commission of Control and Supervision (ICCS), was composed of Hungarians, Poles, Indonesians and Canadians. The ICCS was to arbitrate any disputes concerning enforcement of the cease-fire that the JMC could not. Yet neither of them was of much use at all, for under the terms of the agreement they, too, were to be governed by the unanimity principle. Neither could take any action without the consent of all its members. Under the circumstances this was a prescription for perpetual stalemate.

Realizing the defects of the draft accord, Kissinger had tried during the final stages of the Paris negotiations to incorporate some safety catches into it. Since he had not been able to persuade the North Vietnamese to withdraw their forces from the south, he attempted to erect obstacles to a further build-up. The Communists, as well as the Saigon authorities, were prohibited under the terms he forced on them from 'accepting' additional troops into South Vietnam after the cease-fire, and were obliged to withdraw their forces from Laos and Cambodia - a provision that was meant to shut down NVA supply lines and sanctuaries there.

In his haste to conclude the agreement, however, Kissinger allowed some imprecise language to slip into the text that defeated his purposes. According to the terms he agreed to, the restriction on the introduction of additional manpower and material into South Vietnam was to take effect only 'from enforcement of the cease-fire';

in other words, only at the moment the two sides stopped fighting. Up to then, Communist troops were legally quite free to go on 'accepting' reinforcements from Hanoi - which they did.

Kissinger also made a botch of the provision dealing with Laos and Cambodia. Inexplicably, he neglected to include in it a deadline for the withdrawal of NVA troops from either country. In later public testimony he insisted he had reached a secret 'unconditional understanding' with Le Due Tho that ensured a pullout. But the North Vietnamese denied this, and simply left their troops in place.

To sweeten the pill, Nixon assured Thieu that Saigon could count on continued military aid at the 'one-billion-dollar level' and economic aid at the 'eight-hundred-million range' for several years. Kissinger promised that if `Hanoi's lack of good faith in the agreement could be demonstrated, 'American retaliation would be massive and brutal.'

Thieu, quite understandably, was delighted by these reassurances. For the first time the United States was giving him an explicit pledge of economic and military aid at precise levels and a very nearly explicit promise to bomb Hanoi into submission if necessary. That Nixon and Kissinger were essentially talking out of turn, offering far more than they could deliver without Congressional approval, did not trouble him. Being an accomplished manipulator himself, he assumed they would find a way.

In Hanoi, meanwhile, the party leaders who had led the Democratic Republic of Vietnam through so many years of war had settled on a new strategy of conquest. As with Kissinger, their initial objective was 'equilibrium.' Yet equilibrium for them was not merely a means to a stalemate, as it was for Washington, but a stepping stone to something more. By achieving military equality with Saigon, they were hopeful of keeping Thieu so far off balance that he would succumb eventually to the 'internal contradictions' of his regime.[434]

Frank Snepp

Indochina (Center of Military History).

The Paris peace talks to end the Vietnam War had been going on since 1968. After the NVA Easter Offensive in South Vietnam they resumed on 29 June 1972. Hanoi announced a new proposal that gave rise to hope of a ceasefire in the immediate future contingent upon an agreed solution to end the war by 31 October. The U. S. agreed to try to reach an agreement. Hanoi anticipated an agreement and in mid-October a NVA drive was launched to gain territory in South Vietnam before the ceasefire. By the end of October ARVN counterattacks had nullified NVA gains. Negotiations continued and an outline of a peace agreement was reached on 26 October. Signature of the peace agreement would occur on 23 January and a ceasefire would go into effect on 27 January. Hanoi again planned an offensive to gain territory before the ceasefire went into effect and this effort became known as LANDGRAB 73.[435]

Both North and South Vietnam had suffered severe losses during the Easter Offensive. South Vietnam lost control of large areas of its northernmost provinces of Quang Tri, Thura Thien, Quang Nam and Quang Tin. Additionally, the western fringes of II and III CTZ were lost to the NVA. While the Paris Peace Talks were in progress, one of the sticking points in the negotiations was Hanoi's insistence that the agreement would be a ceasefire in place. NVA and VC would retain control over areas that they occupied. The agreement did not require the withdrawal of NVA forces from South Vietnam. U. S. air support that had been vital during the Easter Offensive would end on 27 January 1973.

> Perhaps most ominous for the future, Saigon's ground forces, with most of the infantry divisions still closely tied to particular localities, remained without adequate mobile reserves to counter concentrated attacks like those the North Vietnamese had launched in 1972. American airpower had filled the gap during that offensive, but the days of that support's availability were numbered.[436]
>
> *Graham A. Cosmos*

Equipment was allowed to be replaced under the agreement on a one-for-one basis. This led to a crash supply of material supplied by the U. S. called Enhance Plus to upgrade South Vietnam's capabilities before the agreement went into effect.

Liberation Front strategists warned that Saigon intended to flood the countryside with troops and espoused countervailing efforts. Hanoi initially sought to dampen their ardor. Its forces weakened by the 1972 campaign, with food shortages in some parts of the Mekong delta and the central coast plus wounds to lick in the North, Hanoi wished to establish a baseline of compliance with the Paris agreement. North Vietnamese planners envisioned an immediate political struggle, with military efforts more prominent later on. General Giap viewed the problem as one of disparities between local forces and regular troops and began an effort to rebuild the main forces. For the present Hanoi tried to implement a policy of the "Five Forbiddens"—it would be forbidden to attack the South Vietnamese, attempt to break up their land grabs, surround outposts, shell them, and build combat villages. The NLF saw a parallel with the abandonment of the resistance in the South after the 1954 Geneva agreements and wanted no part of that. Many of the early operations in the war of the flags were thus Liberation Front initiatives.[437]

John Prados

The time from the end of October to the beginning of the ceasefire divides into three distinct periods. The first lasted until mid-December during which time the Republic sought to solidify its position and the North Vietnamese and the NLF conducted a shrill campaign to convince the world that the US had reneged on a previous agreement. The second was the period of the intensive bombing of Hanoi and Haiphong from 18 to 29 December, after which the third period of resumed negotiations began and ended with the implementation of the ceasefire on 28 January 1973.

During November and the first half of December, President Thieu was busily preparing his people for the ceasefire. His hard-line stand on ceasefire terms gained wide support from rival political factions and the Saigon press. President Nixon's victory and MG Haig's subsequent visit to Saigon heartened the South Vietnamese. The Republic sent envoys throughout the Far East to explain the nation's position and solicit support. At home news bulletins and public meetings were used to gain popular support for national sovereignty and self-determination; opposition to a coalition government was also stressed. In addition, 5,000 military cadets and trainees were sent to the secure villages to explain to the people the Republic's position on the ceasefire, inform them of the RVNAF victories and Communist difficulties, expose Communist ceasefire schemes, and inspire vigilance in the villagers. In December, when it became apparent that the Paris talks were again stalled, Thieu continued to exhort the South Vietnamese despite his pessimism. Just prior to and during the December bombing Thieu publicly inaugurated his Democracy Party in an attempt to gain a national political following. He also promulgated 37 laws in the three-week period before his special powers expired on 27 December. Thieu did not seek an extension of special powers. During mid-January MG Haig came once more to Saigon for a final meeting with President Thieu. Technical discussions had resumed on 2 January in Paris, and many sensed that a ceasefire was near.[438]

Steve Sherman

A joint military commission was established under the terms of the accords that would determine areas controlled by each side. This commission called the International Commission of Control and Supervision (ICCS) was composed of representatives from Canada, Indonesia, Hungary and Poland. The ICCS was to supervise the ceasefire, the withdrawal of troops, the dismantlement of military bases, the activity at ports of entry and the return of captured military personnel and foreign civilians. It was to report on the implementation, or violation, of the Peace Agreement and Protocols. In practice, the ICCS was crippled by its own operating principles that required unanimity in agreements. Poland and Hungary would support the Communist side of an issue while Indonesia and Canada would take the opposite position.[439]

Lieutenant General Phillip B. Davidson who was the

MACV Chief of Intelligence for two years during the Vietnam War summarized the status of the two sides at the time of the Paris Agreement.

> Immediately after the signing of the Paris Agreement, the RVNAF were stronger in South Vietnam than their Communist foes. South Vietnam had almost one million men under arms (counting Regulars, Local Forces, Militia, and Home Guards), and in Operation ENHANCE PLUS the United States had dumped vast amounts of equipment on RVNAF. Much of this equipment, however, the RVNAF could neither use nor maintain. The North Vietnamese had about 219,000 troops in South Vietnam. Their combat efficiency and morale had been dealt a savage blow by the horrendous casualties of the Easter offensive and the long-term effects of the United States air strikes and mining operations in North Vietnam. Col. Gen. Tran Van Tra, the commander of the COSVN B-2 front (an area comprising all South Vietnam south of the Central Highlands) wrote that "in 1973 our cadres and men were fatigued, we had not had time to make up for our losses, all units were in disarray, there was a lack of manpower, and there were shortages of food and ammunition . . ."

> These statistics of relative strengths, however, are misleading. Only about 200,000 of the 450,000 ARVN regulars were in the infantry divisions and other combat units. The rest were absorbed by the huge administrative and logistical "tail," another legacy the United States Army left ARVN. The South Vietnamese Air Force and Navy totaled another 100,000, while some 525,000 were in the Regional and Popular Forces. The NVA had about 148,000 combat troops in South Vietnam and 71,000 in support.

> Again, the figures can be misleading if taken without reference to other Order of Battle factors, such as organization, training, leadership, weaponry, morale, and mission—the intangibles of military strength.

> Two of these intangibles were critical in any assessment of relative strength. First, North Vietnamese forces in South Vietnam, while battered and under strength, were sound and capable of restoration and expansion. In contrast, the foundation and structure of the RVNAF were rotten and askew and provided no scaffolding upon which to build an effective force. Furthermore, these fundamental RVNAF deficiencies could be cured only by tearing down the existing structure, an extremely

dangerous operation requiring years, perhaps decades, of effort in the face of an implacable foe. A second factor, mission, was also important. The NVA mission was strategically offensive, although on occasion the Communists might be forced onto the tactical defensive. The South Vietnamese were on the strategic defensive, forced to defend (largely from static positions) villages, bases, and LOC's. This difference in mission gave the strategic initiative ("the Big I") to the Communists and with it the eventual advantage of attacking when, and where, and in what strength they chose.[440]

Phillip B. Davidson

LANDGRAB 73 fighting in South Vietnam lasted until the Paris Peace Accords went into effect and beyond that date. Fighting after the ceasefire was classed as a violation investigated by the ICCS with determination made on which country controlled the contested area. Both North and South Vietnam sought to maximize areas in South Vietnam that were under their control.

Hanoi's plan would be conducted in three phases:

1) Phase I was the propaganda phase. It started by forming propaganda teams in the occupied areas. Next, all available sewing machines were confiscated together with blue and red sewing material to make thousands of National Liberation Front (NLF) flags. These would be displayed when the ICCS representatives were inspecting areas in order to establish that the areas were under NLF control on ceasefire day and thereafter. Local VC units would control roads and villages when ICCS representatives were in the area.

2) Phase II was the implementation phase. When the ceasefire was announced, the people would be encouraged to rise up against the Saigon government and local VC units would attack government bases and positions. Maximum effort would be made to

cause confusion and disrupt the government pacification program.

3) Phase III was the consolidation phase. Every effort would be made to frustrate Saigon countermeasures.[441]

Cao Van Vien

Additionally, the NVA mounted four division-sized attacks in violation of the ceasefire agreement. Three of these were aimed at NVA entry points into South Vietnam for supplies and equipment. On the eve of the signing of the agreement South Vietnam launched preemptive strikes.

The War of the Flags was waged throughout South Vietnam from 23 January 1973 to the ceasefire (27 January) and beyond that date into February. After the ceasefire hundreds of violations were recorded. The fighting went on in all four Corps Tactical Zones. The below map shows terrain identified by Hanoi's Military Regions.

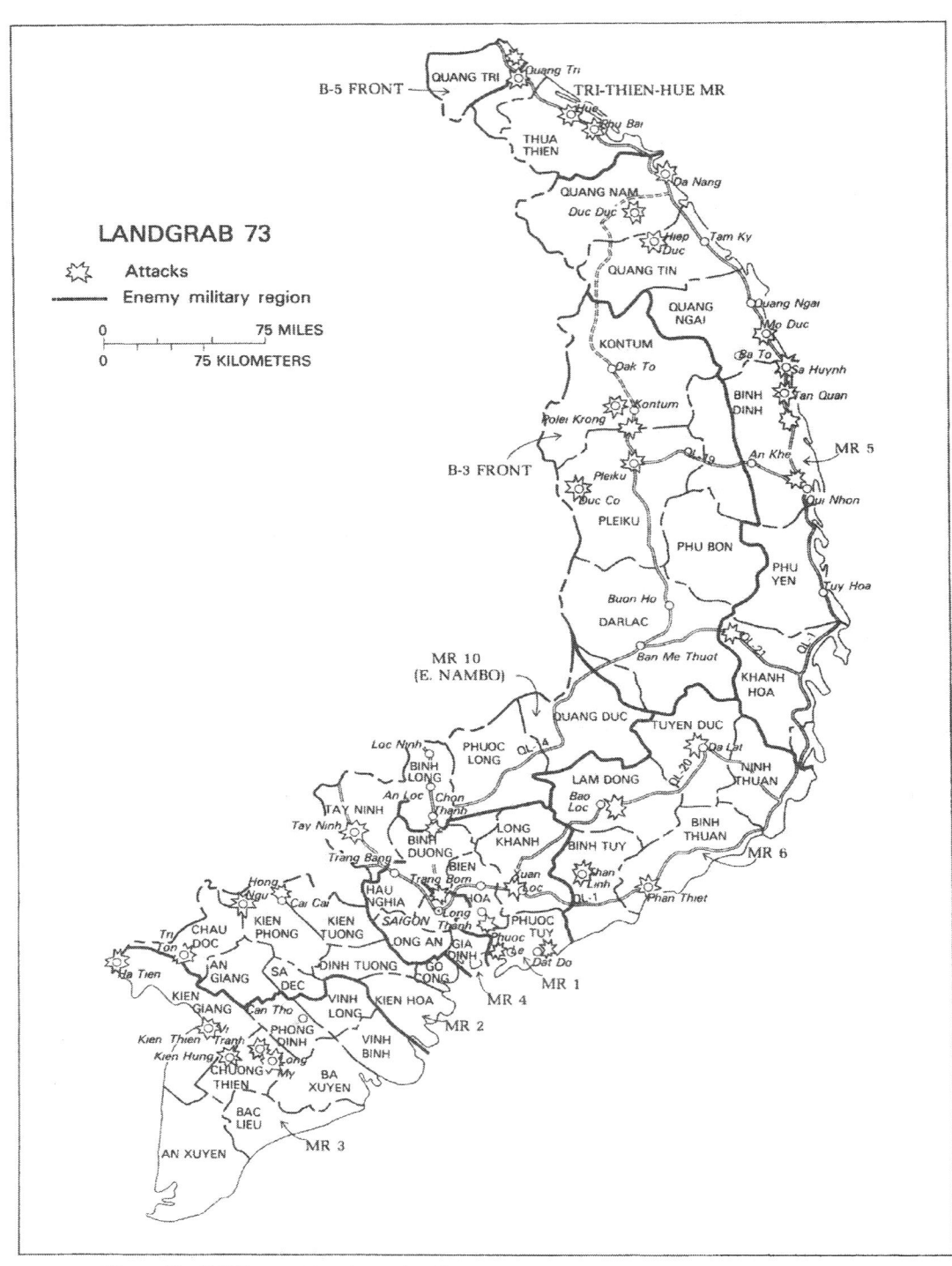

Hanoi's Military Regions in South Vietnam (William E. Le Gro)

First Corps Tactical Zone (I CTZ)

I CTZ was the northern most zone and saw heavy fighting. The Cua Viet Naval Base 10 KM south of the DMZ was attacked by South Vietnamese marines and was captured a few hours before the ceasefire with the help of U. S. air and naval gunfire. Following the ceasefire U. S. support was no longer available and the marines were forced to withdraw.[442]

> In the northern part of South Vietnam, Military Region 1, the NVA B5 Front was in no condition to launch anything but local attacks, as NVA leadership apparently recognized. On the other hand, the B5 Front had no intention of giving up any of the terrain in northern Quang Tri Province for which it had paid so dearly during 1972. . . . Likewise, south and west of Quang Tri City, the B5 Front forces prevented any expansion of the Airborne Division's positions into the hills south of the Thach Han River and against the Thach Han River line itself.[443]

The B-5 Front reinforced its defenses west of Quang Tri City and additional antiaircraft units were brought in bringing the total to 11 regiments. Also, an additional tank battalion arrived from North Vietnam. The NVA would contain ARVN units while local forces would infiltrate villages to get larger areas counted under their control. Soon NLF flags were seen flying in many of the hamlets but ARVN soon recovered most of these.

In Thua Thien Province the NVA attacked in the area surrounding Hue and captured several hamlets. The NVA also moved to cut Highway 1 (called the "Street without Joy"), before it was ejected.

In Quang Nam Province rocket attacks were staged against Da Nang and Duc Duc was attacked. Lines of communication, district headquarters and ARVN positions were also attacked. The NVA also supported the VC in infiltrating hamlets and villages. ARVN forces recovered some of these.

In Quang Tin Province an important NVA logistic base in the Que Son valley was at Hiep Duc. Two days after Christmas the ARVN 3rd Infantry Division launched an attack against the base that was initially successful and the 3rd Division was reinforced with the 51st Infantry Regiment to continue the attack and seize the enemy's FSB West that guarded the eastern approach to Hiep Duc. The attack against FSB West failed. The NVA contained ARVN in the Que Son Valley and prevented Saigon units from reaching the NVA logistical base in the Hiep Duc region. The 3rd Infantry Division then moved to clearing hamlets that had been seized. By the end of January only one hamlet remained under Hanoi's control in the Dai Loc District.[444]

> Significant activity in the northern part of Quang Ngai Province during January consisted of elements of the 1st Ranger Group and 6th Regiment capturing large amounts of enemy food supplies. On 22 January the 1st Ranger Group was relieved of the responsibility for the western portion of the Binh Son-Son Tinh Districts by elements of the 13th Regiment. The rangers moved south to assume the responsibility for operations to retake the Ba To District Town, part of the I Corps pre-ceasefire plan. The attack was to begin on 23 January, but poor weather conditions and enemy activity stalled the operation until the 27th. Ba To remained in enemy hands on 28 January.
>
> Farther south on the 25th of January a task force from the 4th Regiment initiated an operation to reopen Route 1 between Sa Huynh and the Military Regions 1 and 2 boundaries, where a link-up was planned with 22nd Division units. The operation progressed well until 27 January, when enemy units launched attacks in the area. By the end of the month the enemy controlled a strip extending from nine kilometers north of Sa Huynh to three kilometers south.[445]
>
> **_Steve Sherman_**

North of the II CTZ in Quang Ngai Province the VC attacked province and district capitals and the NVA assisted in the attack of Duc Tho district. The NVA attacked throughout the lowlands. On 27 January district and provincial capitals were attacked while Highway 1 was cut in several places. Several RF/PF outposts were overrun. In southern Quang Ngai Province the NVA successfully defended the district town of Ba To. This town had been controlled by the NVA since fall of 1972. At Mo Duc the NVA 2nd Division used a battalion to support the VC defense of Mo Duc. A second battalion defended the base area while a third was used to support the attack in Duc Tho District. On 27 January the NVA 141st Regiment attack reached Highway 1 south of Duc Tho and secured the area south to the II CTZ border. The port of Sa Huynh was captured. The NVA had blocked the north-south line of communications and the ARVN counterattacked and drove the NVA out of Sa Huynh on 16 February. Hanoi was outraged since Sa Huynh was seized the day before the ceasefire yet the area was awarded to Saigon.[446]

II CTZ

II CTZ included most of the Central Highlands the home of many of the Montagnard tribes. The NVA objectives in II CTZ were to cut Highway 1 along the coast (called the "Street without Joy"), hold the ARVN 22nd Division in its bases and grab as much of the population as possible that densely populated the coastal region of II CTZ.

> The southern part of Communist Military Region 5 included Binh Dinh, Phu Yen, and Khanh Hoa Provinces. Intelligence collected before the ceasefire provided an accurate preview of what could be expected there. The enemy's objectives were to isolate the northern districts of Binh Dinh, hold the ARVN 22nd Division in its bases, cut Highway 1 (the only north-south route of any importance under South Vietnamese control), and gather to the NLF as much land and as many people as possible. From the NVA point of view, the prospects for success seemed good, for large segments of the population

in the coastal areas of Binh Dinh and Phu Yen had long been sympathetic to the VC, and the ARVN 22nd Division had yet to establish any reputation for excellence in battle. Since the area along Highway 1 was fairly densely populated, it would provide a significant population base.[447]

William E. Le Gro

From the 23rd to the 28th of January attacks against the ARVN 41st Regiment kept it in its bases while the NVA 2nd Division attacked Sa Huynh and Tam Quan districts. From there the NVA moved south along the coast cutting Highway 1 just south of Bong Song pass. In these heavy attacks the NVA lost heavily and failed to achieve any significant gains. Further south along the coast of II Corps the area was more lightly populated and there were no ARVN units assigned but the RF/PF units successfully defended this area in Ninh Thuan, Binh Thuan and Binh Tay provinces. Further inland on the morning of 28 January an NVA battalion attacked the Tuyen Duc province capital, Da Lat but was quickly driven off.

Further west along the Cambodian border the NVA mounted attacks on the key cities of Pleiku, Kontum and Ban Me Thuot. The initial effort was to hold the ARVN 23rd Division in its base areas. When this was accomplished, attacks were mounted against the cities. The attacks were timed just before the ceasefire so that the key areas would be in NVA hands with no time for ARVN to counterattack before the ceasefire. Additional attacks were mounted against the Montagnard camps along the Cambodian border. The NVA 320th Division attacked Duc Co on 20 January and occupied the camp the next day. On 27 January the NVA 10th Division attacked Polei Krong and Trung Nghia. The ARVN 85th Ranger Battalion was forced to withdraw.

By the ceasefire all of the NVA areas had been recaptured except Duc Co. By mid-February the balance of land held in II CTZ was largely the same as it was at the end of December 1972. Highway 1 that runs along the coast was never successfully cut. The NVA had suffered devastating losses in their attacks and their combat effectiveness was seriously degraded.[448]

> As the ceasefire approached the enemy actions were characterized by hamlet infiltration, highway interdiction, stand-off attacks, and limited ground attacks generally focused on Territorial Forces. In the 23d Division area the forces north of Kontum City were subjected to standoff attacks and a bridge approximately nine kilometers north of the city was damaged and traffic disrupted. Pleiku was isolated from ground resupply as Route 19 was interdicted . . . .North of the city Route 14 was cut on the Kontum-Pleiku Province boundary. Pleiku City was subjected to repeated attacks of 122mm rockets, but the intensity of fire was low, and little damage was reported. To the south of city along Route 14 in northern Darlac Province several hamlets were entered by the enemy. Territorial Forces were unable to return the hamlets to government control prior to the ceasefire. Along the coast the pattern of activity was the same. Route 1 was interdicted between Hoai An and Tam Quan in Binh Dinh Province. Four bridges were damaged or destroyed, and six hamlets infiltrated in northern Phu Yen Province. In Lam Dong Province Route 20 was interdicted and a hamlet infiltrated at the Tuyen Duc Province boundary. ARVN and Territorial Forces reacted to all of the enemy activity, however, all highways remained interdicted and several hamlets remained contested at month's end. Enemy ceasefire violations were at a high level, but other than the limited hamlet infiltrations, no significant ground was lost to the enemy.[449]

Steve Sherman

III CTZ

III CTZ surrounds Saigon that has the greatest population in Vietnam. The NVA had insufficient resources to enter Saigon so the population was spared the horrors that occurred during Tet '68. In addition to seeking to increase areas under their control, the VC also sought to establish their capital for South Vietnam in III CTZ. Acts of terrorism by the VC were minimized since they wanted to avoid alienating the population.[450]

The enemy's Eastern Nam Bo Region was roughly the same as South Vietnam's Military Region 3 (Binh Tuy, Gia Dinh, Hau Nghia, and Long An Provinces were excluded). In addition to scheduling attacks close to the ceasefire date, the NVA in October 1972 had also learned that it lacked the strength to infiltrate the Saigon area with main forces. Thus LANDGRAB 73 in Eastern Nam Bo did not begin until a few days before the ceasefire was to become effective, and Saigon was not an objective.[451]

William E. Le Gro

In early January the ARVN III Corps mounted a clearing operation up the road from Saigon toward An Loc.[452] The NVA tried its own land grab in the Saigon River corridor. This was successful and reached Tri Tam in the Michelin rubber plantation. The ARVN disrupted NVA plans for pre-ceasefire operations with the help if B-52 bombing strikes. The NVA 7th Division was bottled up in the Michelin plantation and was not able to accomplish any increase in control of the area. The NVA 9th Division was forced into defensive positions around An Loc and Loc Ninh near the Cambodian border.

The NVA attempted to increase the intensity of attacks during the period of 23-25 January. The NVA and VC scored some success. A total of 144 hamlets were contested at one time or another but only 14 remained under NVA/VC control by 3 February. The NVA/VC sustained heavy casualties without achieving any significant goals in III CTZ.[453]

From 20 to 24 January enemy activities remained at a very low level throughout Military Region 3, as III Corps forces conducted operations in and around population centers. After the ceasefire announcement was made, enemy activities increased steadily up until the morning of 28 January. Most consisted of attacks-by-fire and small scale ground attacks. The Bien Hoa Air Base received 28 122mm rockets on 26 January, and Tan Son Nhut Air Base received 33 122mm rockets on 28 January. One American was killed at Bien Hoa, one civilian was killed and 20 injured at Tan

Son Nhut.

After the ceasefire became effective at 0800 hours, 28 January, enemy incidents continued in a definite pattern. Tay Ninh City and northern Hau Nghia Province were focal points of ceasefire violations until the end of the month. Violations were characterized by hamlet infiltration, attacks-by-fire, and lines of communication interdiction. Immediately following the ceasefire, violations occurred generally through the center of the corps area, from Tay Ninh City through northern Hau Nghia and southern Binh Duong Provinces, and along Route 1 to the east. For one day emphasis shifted to hamlet infiltration in provinces surrounding the Capital Military District. On the last day of the month violations had decreased and again shifted to hamlet infiltration along Routes 1 and 22. The northern provinces remained relatively quiet during the post ceasefire period. The only terrorist activity known to have occurred in the region after the ceasefire occurred during the night of 29-30 January. Both the hamlet chief and assistant hamlet chief of Trung Nhi Hamlet in Binh Duong Province were assassinated. During the last few hours of January, reports indicated that activity in Tay Ninh Province had stabilized; all Military Region 3 hamlets were under friendly control except for 13 hamlets along Route 1 northeast of Trang Bang in Hau Nghia Province.[454]

Steve Sherman

IV CTZ

IV CTZ encompassed the Mekong Delta, the richest rice producing region called the "Rice Bowl of Asia." The NVA planned to capture areas in the Delta that would offer the greatest possibility of expansion in the future. Areas along the Cambodia border in the northern Delta were attacked including Ha Tien, Hong Ngur and Cai Cai.

Just as the ARVN preempted enemy operations in Military Region 3 so it did also in the Mekong Delta. In a delta-wide operation known as DONS KHOI, the ARVN and territorials planned to attack for six days beginning on 15 January, but so spectacular were the early successes that the operation was extended for six more days. Losses of over 2,000 killed and disruptions in deployment and logistical activity, coming just before LANDGRAB 73, seriously affected the enemy's ability to launch a significant offensive.[455]

William E. Le Gro

On 23 January two NVA battalions crossed the Cambodian border into IV CTZ. They were targeted on seizure of Hong Ngur and destruction of government posts along the border. At the Cai Cai camp NVA casualties were heavy and the NVA failed to seize the camp. The NVA attacks tapered off in Kien Phong Province until the eve of the ceasefire.

At Kien Hung the NVA 18B Regiment surrounded the town but South Vietnamese troops held. Widespread attacks of towns and villages occurred in the southern part of IV CTZ but no more than 20 were contested at any one time and none were held by the NVA. Roads remained open in IV CTZ.[456]

During 21 to 24 January enemy activity was light and widely scattered with Chuong Thien Province, the Tri-Border area, and the Seven Mountains region having the most significant combat activity. After the ceasefire announcement on 28 January, enemy activity throughout the Delta increased significantly and was directed at villages, territorial outposts, and ARVN base areas and outposts. Friendly forces were actively patrolling and responding to enemy initiatives. Just prior to the ceasefire agreement signing, and for the remainder of the month, the preponderance of enemy activity occurred in Chuong Thien Province, and along the Khmer border in Chau Doc and Kien Phong Provinces. Other activity in the military region was widely scattered and of less intensity. By the last day of the month the situation had started to stabilize. Government officials reported an absence of enemy initiatives against primary lines of communication, and with the exception of a few short-term interdictions, all roads and canals remained open to traffic.[457]

Steve Sherman

The actions seen in all four Corps Tactical Zones

demonstrated NVA and VC weakness in offensive actions and defense of their terrain. The losses from the Easter Offensive had not been replaced and that was felt by the Communists throughout South Vietnam. The Communists lost over 5,000 troops between 28 January and 9 February with no measurable improvement in the areas that they controlled. Hanoi had delayed the start of its offensive operations until it was too close to the ceasefire. Hanoi had assumed that Saigon would not counterattack because of the presence of the ICCS teams. The limited capabilities of local VC forces were more than matched by South Vietnam's troops. The VC broke down their forces into small groups and attacked too many targets at once. These had no staying power. The ARVN was able to react to limited Communist successes and eliminate them one-by-one.[458]

William E. Le Gro

After LANDGRAB 73

Hanoi learned from LANDGRAB 73 that there was an urgent need to rebuild and reinforce NVA forces in South Vietnam. In the weeks following the ceasefire over 200 major violations were committed as they rebuilt their forces.

Included among these violations was the movement on 6 February of a 175-truck convoy through the DMZ and the march of 223 tanks from Laos and Cambodia into South Vietnam. By mid-April, some 7,000 NVA truck crossings of the DMZ were reported. Huge convoys rolled down the expanded and hardened Ho Chi Minh Trail system. During 1973, Hanoi infiltrated over 75,000 troops, increased its tank strength from 100 to 500, and almost doubled its heavy artillery strength. The NVA augmented its antiaircraft strength in South Vietnam drastically. By the end of April, thirteen *new* AA regiments had taken up positions in South Vietnam, and the 263rd Surface-to-Air Missile (SAM) Regiment established itself at Khe Sanh.

NVA construction kept pace with the influx of men and equipment. In 1973, thirteen new airfields were built in South

Vietnam. The Ho Chi Minh Trail was widened and modernized. A new all-weather road was pushed from Khe Sanh down the east side of the Annamite Chain to link up to Highway 14 down to An Loc. Altogether the NVA added 12,000 miles of roads. A fuel pipeline was built from North Vietnam deep into South Vietnam, and a modern radio network linked NVA forces throughout South Vietnam.

While the North Vietnamese made a major effort to rebuild and augment their military capability in South Vietnam, they decided that the main effort initially would be to overthrow the Thieu government by political means. Actually, the Politburo could do little else. The Communist forces in South Vietnam were incapable of a major offensive, and such an attack might bring the feared United States air arm back into the fray—a consequence to be avoided at all costs. Beyond the military aspects, the Paris Agreement had legitimatized the PRG and would give it a voice in South Vietnam, and the agreement might protect their territorial gains against the stronger and more aggressive RVNAF.[459]

Phillip B. Davidson

When Congress voted to halt the bombing of Cambodia in mid-summer, 1973, Thieu was incredulous. As master in his own domain he could not imagine Nixon might not be master in his. . . .

Thieu decided the wisest thing he could do was to demonstrate to the Americans once again that he was worthy of their support. As the summer came to an end, he therefore launched several ambitious military operations, ostensibly to clear NVA units out of base camps in the delta and along the Cambodian border north of Saigon, but in fact to eliminate any lingering American doubts about his capabilities.

With the pressure mounting, Hanoi's military leaders, General Giap and his Chief of Staff; General Van Tien Dung, began clamoring for a response in kind. But their arguments foundered on the reticence of Hanoi's chief patrons. Neither the Soviets nor the Chinese would guarantee massive new military aid in the summer and fall of 1973, and though both agreed to increase economic assistance, they insisted on attaching all sorts of strings to insure it was used wisely.

In view of these constraints, the Politburo decided in early October that it had little choice but to move cautiously and conservatively on the battlefield.

Quite coincidentally, the drive in Congress to limit the President's war-making authority had just come to a head: on the seventh the House and Senate overrode a presidential veto and passed the monumental War Powers Act, making it illegal for the President to introduce American forces into any 'hostile' situations for more than sixty days without Congressional approval. As confirmation of American intent and of Nixon's political impotence, it duly impressed the North Vietnamese.

Throughout all this, American intelligence kept Hanoi's policy-makers under close scrutiny. Within a week or so of the first strategic raid, the CIA station was inundated with agent reports about the direction of the campaign. One report, which we considered `pure gold,' indicated that NVA forces in the south would not be significantly expanded during the next half year - certainly not enough to fuel a countryside `general offensive.'

Though the strategic-raids campaign was to be a modest undertaking, its target was Saigon's Achilles' heel - the economy. In the months since the cease-fire prices in South Vietnam's marketplace had increased by a staggering sixty-five percent; unemployment had skyrocketed with the departure of the last American GIs; and the value of economic aid had continued to decline as a result of worldwide inflation. And the worst, of course, was still to come. Thanks to the Arab oil embargo arising out of the latest Middle East war, petroleum prices around the world would soon quadruple.

To make matters worse, American military aid to Saigon was slipping. In late December, the Pentagon advised General Murray, the Defense Attache, that Congress was likely to pare the Administration's new aid budget to roughly $1 billion, far less than expected.

Murray pleaded with Martin [Ambassador] to alert the South Vietnamese to this prospect, so they could begin conserving their resources. But Martin refused. Such a display of candor, he feared, might demoralize Thieu and his commanders and diminish his own political leverage with them.[460]

Frank Snepp

As the Year of the Buffalo ended there was much reason for optimism on both sides. A peace treaty had been signed, prisoners had been exchanged, parity existed between the two sides and it was thought at the time the United States was achieving an honorable exit from the war. The cumulative number of U.S. dead since the start of our involvement was 58,150.

1974–The Year of the Tiger

"Nguyen Van Thieu was then forced to fight a poor man's war. Enemy firepower had decreased by nearly 60 percent. . . Its mobility was also reduced by half . . ."[461]

Van Tien Dung, NVA

President Nixon started his second term as president after a landslide reelection victory in 1972. As the popularity of the Vietnam War waned in the United States, Congress was busy at work to reduce his authority in Vietnam by reducing funding to that region. Congress was eventually successful. General Cao Van Vien, the South Vietnamese Chairman of the Joint General Staff at that time summarized their problems.

> Ravaged by war for over a quarter-century, South Vietnam had very little to contribute to the war effort except manpower and blood. Financially and materially, South Vietnam had to depend on military aid provided by the United States, the factor that largely decided the outcome of the war. On 2 April 1973 President Thieu was received by President Nixon in the Western White House at San Clemente. Together the two leaders discussed problems related to economic and military aid to South Vietnam and examined the continuing cease-fire violations and the Communist buildup. The visit shored up our confidence in continuing U.S. aid during the postwar period.
>
> Fully aware of the difficulties the United States was facing in its own house, economically and politically, the Republic of Vietnam made every effort to enforce austerity and to maintain and preserve invaluable military assets as soon as the cease-fire was in force. It was hoped that reductions in military aid, if and when made, would be timed and graduated to reflect a true improvement in the military situation on the one hand and the development of the national economy of South Vietnam on the other.
>
> During the first few months of 1973, following this belt-tightening policy and assuming that the enemy would respect the Paris Agreement to some extent, JGS and USDAO [US

Defense Attache Office] came up with a fiscal year 1975 military aid budget recommendation of $1,600 million. President Nixon submitted a revised figure of $1,474 million to Congress, but, in addition, he asked for $474 million as a supplement to the fiscal year 1974 budget to cover increased operational expenses and the replacement of lost and damaged war material and another $266 million to make up for a deficit incurred in the previous fiscal year.

President Thieu sent me, as chairman of JGS, to the United States in April 1974 to seek support for our aid request. At the Pentagon, I made a presentation of the military situation in South Vietnam, substantiated by documents and photographic evidence of the enemy's escalating violations and his massive movement of men and arms into the country. Officials of the U.S. Department of Defense heartily assured me of their full support. Unfortunately, the U.S. Congress rejected all supplemental aid requests and merely authorized a fiscal year 1975 ceiling of $1 billion, of which only $700 million was finally appropriated. And this amount included operational expenses for USDAO ($46 million appropriated out of $100 million requested). The final appropriation came as a shock to the army and people of South Vietnam. It was certain that the huge gap between requirements and resources that had just been created could never be closed no matter how much self-restraint was imposed and how well the budget was managed.[462]

Cao Van Vien

Meanwhile, Nixon became involved in the Watergate scandal, and he ultimately resigned on 9 August 1974. Previously, Nixon's vice president, Spiro Agnew, had been convicted of crimes and stepped down. Gerald Ford had been appointed vice president and then succeeded Nixon. If President Thieu thought that he could count on Nixon's help in his coming conflict, that possibility was now gone. President Gerald Ford now had to shoulder the responsibility for funding South Vietnam's war.

The dispute between the administration and Congress over the FY 74 Vietnam program, clearly won by the latter, was only the preliminary to the main event: the fight for the FY 75 authorization and appropriation.

By imposing rigid controls, the RVNAF managed to survive through the summer. Many of its vehicles were on blocks, its aircraft grounded because of parts and fuel shortages, its radios silent for lack of batteries, and its far-flung outposts suffering from inadequate artillery support. The stream of supplies had dwindled to a trickle, and weeks would pass after the start of the new fiscal year before the pipeline would again be flowing.

Meanwhile, General Murray [Defense Attache Office, Saigon] arrived in Washington at the end of April 1974 to consult with the Defense Department and services on military assistance programs. He followed this visit with a brief, much needed vacation and returned to Vietnam toward the end of May. On 23 May, Admiral Bigley cabled General Murray that the House had passed the Defense Authorization Bill for FY 74 with the familiar ceiling of $1,126 million for MASF, while the Senate Committee was recommending $900 million. The best compromise in committee conference that Defense could expect was a $1 billion ceiling, but the likelihood that this would be trimmed on the Senate floor was great. The Admiral asked General Murray to furnish some impact statements describing the results in Vietnam if the authorized program for FY 75 were $1,126 million, or reduced respectively to $900 million, $750 million, or $600 million. . . .General Murray then reviewed the current situation and the impact FY 74 funding constraints had had on the RVNAF. "Cuts and economies have mortgaged the future," he told Washington. The entire program was in trouble. Because stock replenishment had been at a virtual standstill for over four months, the stockage of many common supplies was below safety levels. Included in this category were clothing, spare parts, tires, batteries, and M-16 rifle barrels. Despite intensive management of shortages to afford minimum combat support to engaged units, the deadline rate on vehicles, weapons, and communications equipment was bound to increase during the next quarter. In other words, even if the authority to requisition the supplies needed were provided at that moment, the lag in order-to-ship time would prevent immediate recuperation.[463]

It was against this backdrop that the war would continue.

As 1974 began, the South Vietnamese appeared to be holding their own, at least militarily. They held most of the territory they had occupied in January 1973, but they had lost isolated outposts and fire support bases, mostly in the Western Highlands of South Vietnam. Monstrous problems, only dimly perceived in 1973, began to surface in 1974. Some were of Saigon's making; some were made for them by the United States.

The first impact of the drastic cuts in military aid fell on the military capability of the RVNAF. The Americans had taught, trained, and organized the South Vietnamese to fight the war "American-style "—with high-tech devices, air mobility, and profuse expenditures of ammunition and other material. While in theory the South Vietnamese should have adapted their armed forces to the revised conditions brought on by the Paris Agreement, in reality such a reorganization and reorientation was impossible. The South Vietnamese lacked the military experience and expertise, the equipment and facilities, and the time to dismantle its armed forces and remold them. Beyond that, any such upheaval would have invited a determined attack by the NVA forces in South Vietnam.

The debilitation of the RVNAF's material capabilities was equaled, or exceeded, by the resulting blow to ARVN morale. The decreased use of ammunition meant more ARVN casualties, and under the shortages, the wounded, particularly, suffered. Evacuation of the injured was frequently delayed, and often had to be accomplished on Honda motorbikes or by a train of four or five gasless ambulances pulled by a truck. When the wounded arrived at a hospital, they found a shortage of medicines, antibiotics, bandages, intravenous fluids, and other life-saving devices. With the advent of the wet season and the onset of malaria, the supply of insect repellent was exhausted.

The shortages ravaged soldier morale in other ways. ARVN clothing allowances, always inadequate, were cut below subsistence level: boots were replaced every nine months instead of every six months; the issue of boot socks dropped from three to two pairs per year; the issue of uniforms was rigidly controlled. The cuts also impacted directly on the ARVN soldier's family life and on his military effectiveness. . . .The price of rice rose 143 percent between 1972 and 1974, but the farmers still lost money. The plight of the farmers in 1974 became as desperate as that of their urban counterparts. Underlying these economic woes was the old problem of corruption. In April 1974, the "fertilizer scandal" erupted, revealing a high-level plot to hoard and sell fertilizer at inflated prices on the black market. Implicated in it were Thieu, his family, his minister of trade, and ten province chiefs. USAID in one study of the South Vietnamese economy stated that corruption was "enough to have been a key factor in the 1973-1974 recession.[464]

Phillip B. Davidson

The View from Hanoi

As 1974 began, the Politburo failed to see clearly the signs of the approaching disintegration of the South Vietnamese government, its social fabric, and its armed forces. Hanoi simply couldn't believe that the RVN might well collapse from its own afflictions. One of the factors which blinded the North Vietnamese to the erosion of the Thieu government was the weakness of their own PRG, particularly in the cities. In fact, the PRG itself was laced with major problems of manpower and morale. Ironically, the Politburo—the self-appointed experts at combining military, political, and psychological *dau tranh*—nearsightedly pursued the path established by the 21st Plenum, a path posted by three landmark decisions: 1. to intensify the NVN political *dau tranh* against South Vietnam and the United States; 2. to complete NVA preparations for a major offensive scheduled tentatively for 1976; and 3. to conduct more aggressive military operations during 1974. In March 1974 the NVN Military Committee and NVA General Staff recommended to the Politburo (which approved) that in 1974 the NVA forces in South Vietnam intensify its attacks on isolated ARVN outposts, bases, and communication centers. The military committee called this tactic "strategic raids."[465]

Phillip B. Davidson

The Strategic Raids

In spite of NVA defeats in early 1974, Hanoi's planning

continued to focus on offensive action in South Vietnam.

> The NVA Military Committee and its subordinate headquarters intended these strategic raids to accomplish both general and specific goals. The general goals were: 1. To regain the initiative, which ARVN had generally held in 1973; 2. To gain control of additional territory and people; 3. To attrite ARVN forces; 4. To lower South Vietnamese morale by a combination of aggression and attrition; and 5. To sharpen the combat edge of their troops and staffs in preparation for the 1975 offensive.[466]
>
> ***Phillip B. Davidson***

The NVA Strategic Raids were conducted from March through October 1974 and were successful in achieving the goals of the NVA Military Committee.[467] General Cao Van Vien, the Chairman of the South Vietnamese Joint General Staff (JGS) at that time, explained South Vietnam's strategy and difficulties.

> Our strategy immediately after the cease-fire had four major objectives. First and foremost, we were determined to keep the national territory intact and to maintain full control over the population. If any area were seized by the enemy, the armed forces had to wrest it back at all costs. Second, the armed forces were to complete their reorganization with particular emphasis on replenishing and reequipping units which had suffered significant losses during the enemy offensive of 1972, restoring a sizable general reserve, and consolidating the territorial forces. Third, the armed forces would seek to improve and modernize all their aspects but especially their logistics, firepower, and mobility. Fourth, the armed forces would continue to assist in the national pacification and development program and take part in other national projects—such as the consolidation of the military territorial structure at the village level and the farmland reclamation and resettlement program—all geared to achieve the "three-self" goal of national policy (self-defense, self-management, self-sufficiency).[468]
>
> ***Cao Van Vien***

The South Vietnamese effort to hold all ground or win it back at all costs would become increasingly difficult due to decreasing ARVN mobility and reduced manpower. The target level of 1.1 million troops required at least 200,000 new recruits annually to replace losses. This could not be achieved. Up to one quarter of the strength was lost due to desertions each year and enormous draft dodging occurred in a nation that had been at war for over twenty years. Young people expected that peace was now at hand and evaded the draft. The ARVN countered the problem by deactivating old units no longer required (such as railroad battalions) and assigning the troops to combat units. To counter the static nature of most ARVN units the JGS created additional airborne, ranger and marine units into mobile regional groups. All of these actions were made more difficult by increasing U. S. military aid funding cuts. The fact that U. S. air support was no longer available following the ceasefire added to South Vietnam's problems. Against this background the NVA launched the Strategic Raids.[469]

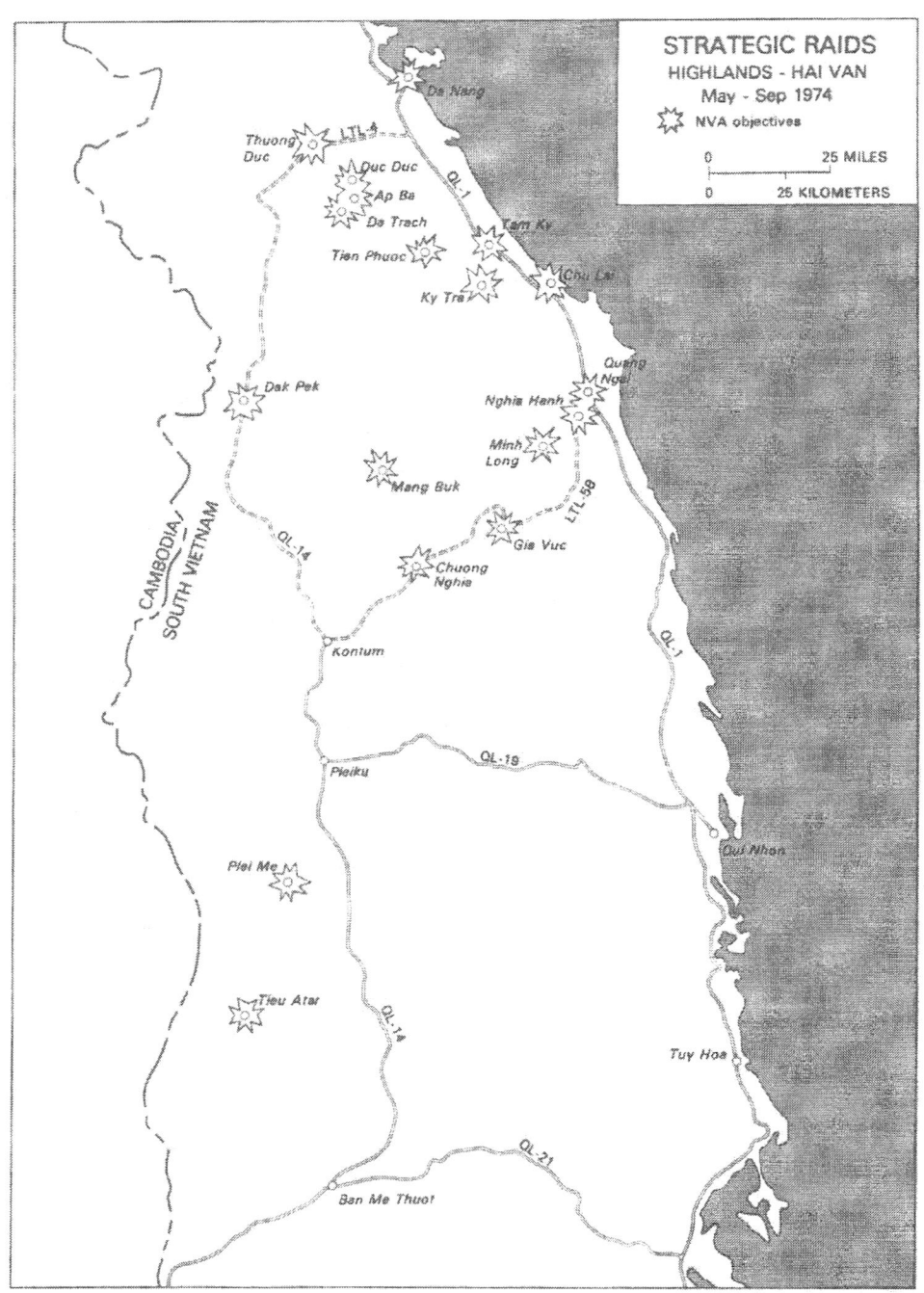

Highland Strategic Raids (William E. Le Gro).

Strategic Raids were being conducted by the NVA and VC throughout South Vietnam except in the Mekong Delta, Military Region (MR) 4.[470] "To the enemy MR 4 would be only a diversionary battlefield where supporting activities such as harassments and traffic interdiction would take place."[471] Heavy fighting occurred in both MR 1 and MR 2.

The Imperial capital of Hue was the former feudal and Imperial capital of Vietnam located in Thua Thien Province. It had seen heavy fighting and Communist atrocities during the Tet '68 campaign. From the start of 1974 the NVA maintained heavy pressure on the ARVN defending Hue. The national railroad and Highway 1 ran through Thua Thein Province and the railroad carried freight and passengers between Hue and Da Nang. In May the Communists increased efforts to disrupt the railroad using mines that destroyed track and caused civilian casualties. The enemy demonstrated that it had the capability to stop railroad service any time that it chose to do so. Hills overlooking the lines of communication were attacked by the NVA in the summer of 1974. The ARVN reinforced. The contest continued into December when the RVNAF resumed military traffic into Phu Bai.

In Quang Nam Province the NVA captured villages in western districts near the major port of Da Nang. The westernmost position in the province at Thuong Duc was attacked when shelling began on 29 July. Casualties mounted as the shelling continued. Increasing pressure triggered a request to Saigon for the release of the 1st Airborne Brigade general reserve for deployment to Quang Nam Province. While this deployment helped secure Da Nang it was too late for Thuong Duc which was overrun on 7 August. On the 29th of July when the NVA first attacked Thuong Duc, the 21st Ranger Battalion protecting Duc Duc came under heavy attack which continued through the summer months as casualties on both sides mounted. By fall ARVN had lost more than 4,700 troops in the fighting in and around Duc Duc and the ARVN defensive line south of Duc Duc remained unchanged.

The first contingent of the 1st Airborne Brigade arrived at Da Nang on 8 August. The 2nd and 3rd Airborne Brigades of the 1st Airborne Division were also deployed to MR 1. The NVA had occupied Hill 1062 and used it as an observation post to direct artillery fire on ARVN positions. The division was given the mission to take the hill and what followed was a contest that lasted for weeks and cost both sides thousands of casualties. By the end of 1974 ARVN controlled the hill, the rainy season had set in and both sides could prepare for the next dry season, but by then the war would be over.

In the spring of 1974, in Quang Tin Province the NVA sought to improve lines of communication to the coast from the sparsely populated mountain districts. An attack on the village of Ky Tra, a road junction near Chu Lai was followed by attacks on ARVN bases and outposts throughout both Quang Tin and Quang Nghia Provinces. Elements of the 2nd ARVN Division attempted to relieve Ky Tra and failed. The 12th and later the 11th and 14th Ranger Groups were also committed to forward positions in the hills before government control was reestablished.

In Quang Ngai Province the NVA initiated heavy attacks throughout the province on the night of 19 July 1974. Rockets were fired at Chu Lai, but the intensity of attacks declined after five days. There were few ARVN forces available to meet the attacks and small posts were seized without response. The district headquarters at Ming Long was overrun and by the end of the year the initiative in Quang Ngai Province was in the hands of the NVA. The NVA had an increasing flow of troops and supplies from North Vietnam while ARVN resources were on the decline.

Further south in MR 2 Dak Pek came under attack. The 88th Ranger Battalion defended the camp when it was attacked by the NVA. The rangers held out until 16th May when the camp was overrun. Survivors escaped to Kontum City.

Tieu Atar was a frontier post northwest of Ban Me Thuot manned by two companies of Montagnard RF troops. It interfered with the NVA line of communication. The camp was overrun on 27 May. It joined the lengthening list of outposts seized by the NVA.

Mang Buk was a camp 50KM north of Kontum City. It was near a Communist supply route connecting Kontum with Binh Dinh and Quang Ngai Provinces. Mang Buk was lightly defended by two RF companies when the siege started on 25 July. On 19 August two NVA battalions attacked and overran Mang Buk. The survivors fled to Ghuong Nghia, the last remaining outpost in Kontum Province.

Ghuong Nghia's turn came on 3 October when the 28th NVA Regiment overran the 254th RF Battalion. There were few survivors. The last outpost in Kontum Province had fallen.

In Pleiku Province the Plei Me camp was defended by the 82nd Ranger Battalion. The siege of Plei Me started in August 1974 shortly after Mang Buk had fallen. The 320th NVA Division committed four battalions to the attack on Plei Me. Unlike the Kontum Province camps, Plei Me had good supporting artillery to use against the NVA and the rangers held Plei Me. The 320th Division withdrew after suffering heavy losses.[472]

RVNAF had taken serious losses in the Highlands, but even more was at stake in the area surrounding Saigon.

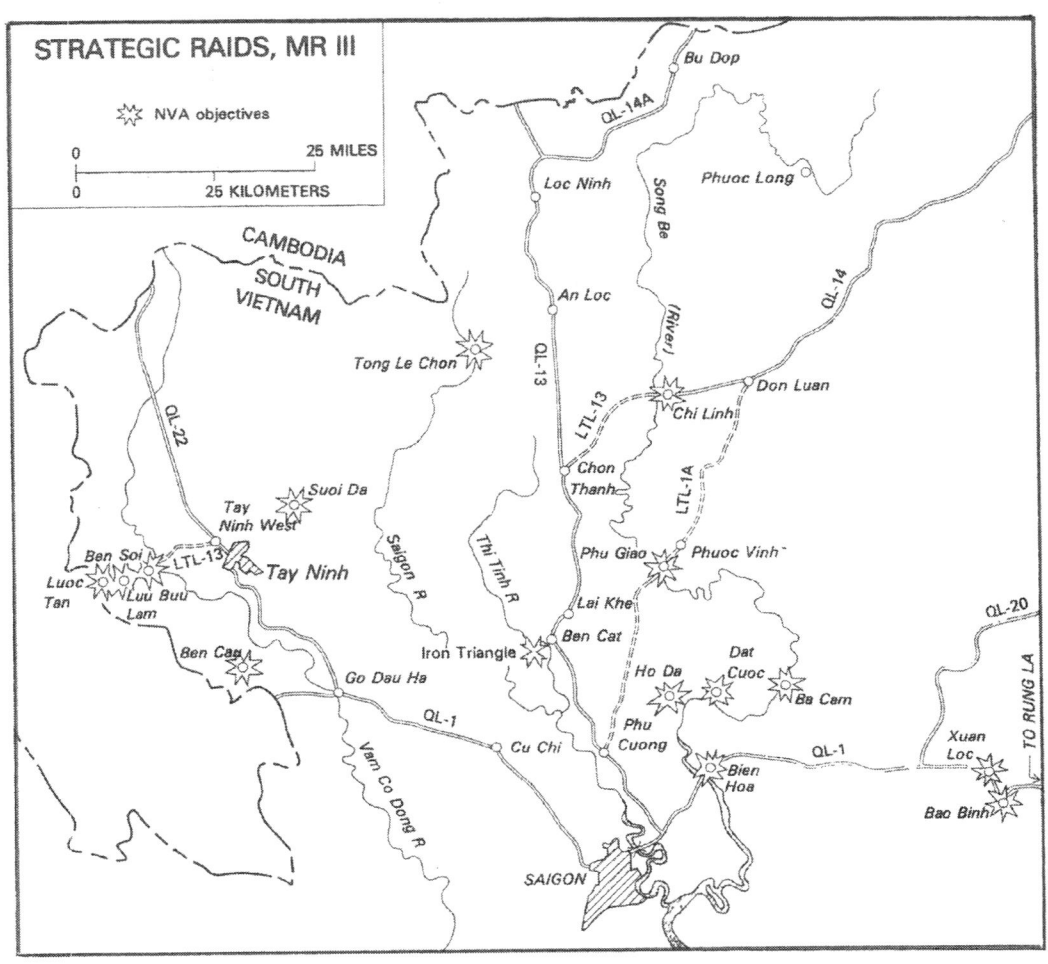

Strategic Raids-MR 3 (William E. Le Gro)

While Strategic Raids were being conducted by the NVA and VC in the Highlands, the raids were also underway in MR 3. The NVA chose to attack from Cambodia into South Vietnam in an area of MR 3 where the border juts out into Vietnam, an area called the Parrot's Beak, only 30 miles from Saigon, a high priority target for Hanoi. In January 1974 captured NVA soldiers revealed that the NVA was moving troops in Cambodia to attack into MR 3. The ARVN attacked the NVA after it entered South Vietnam in a battle called the Tri Phap Operation, 12-19 February 1974. The aggressive ARVN attack stopped the NVA advance causing heavy casualties especially among the NVA support units. This was followed by a similar operation called the Svay Rieng Operation that had the same outcome. This was the last ARVN offensive operation. Supply constraints on fuel, ammunition and flying hours forced the RVNAF into a static role able to support only local defense of major bases [473]

In spite of severe loses to the RVNAF in early 1974, Hanoi pressed ahead with its move against Saigon. Lai Khe was the last government position that had an uninterrupted connection to Saigon 25 miles away. In the first week of April the NVA overran Chi Linh north of Lai Khe and were now in position to move south, seize Lai Khe and move on to Saigon. To the west, Tong La Chon had been under siege since the ceasefire. Tong La Chon was cut off and the defending 92nd Ranger Battalion could not evacuate its wounded and was resupplied by air. It could not be reinforced and needed to be evacuated. After indecision in Saigon, the local commander, Colonel Ngon was ordered to hold at all costs but could not hold and withdrew ending one of the longest sieges of the war. The last ranger survivors entered An Loc on 15 April. The NVA now had unrestricted east-west access and control of the Saigon River corridor.

The next move by the NVA was in May with a coordinated attack toward Saigon. The NVA 9th Division main attack was into the Iron Triangle, the scene of many battles during the Second Indochina War. The NVA 7th Division conducted the supporting attack against ARVN positions near Phu Giao northeast of Lai Khe. The 9th Division attack started on 16 May and it seized An Dien near Ben Cat. The ARVN counterattack by the 18th Division and supporting armor finally succeeded after heavy fighting. The last An Dien NVA stronghold fell on 5 June but fighting continued in the region for weeks. The Iron Triangle campaign finally ended with South Vietnam's victory on 4 October.

The air and logistical base at Bien Hoa was less than 15 miles northeast of Saigon and beyond the reach of major NVA forces. This posed a different problem for the NVA. Saigon had adequate forces to counterattack against any NVA thrust so an attack by Hanoi risked the possibility of being cut off. A different approach was needed and in this case artillery, rocket, small unit and sapper attacks were employed to disrupt Bien Hoa operations and inflict damage. The first attack occurred on 3 June and continued throughout the summer. Supplies were destroyed but no aircraft were lost.

Xuan Loc east of Saigon was also a target of the Strategic Raids. Xuan Loc was the capital of Long Khanh Province and near the beginning of Route 20 where it joined Route 1. The terminus of the railroad that ran up the coast was also located there. A regiment of the ARVN 18th was usually located at Xuan Loc to operate against enemy base areas. NVA and VC efforts to interdict the highways began in May when ARVN troops left Xuan Loc to meet other threats in the region. Route 1 was cut but in late July the 7th Ranger Group was successful in clearing nearly all of the area.

Tay Ninh was located northwest of Saigon on Highway 22 near the Cambodian border. In August the NVA mounted attacks on outposts and rocket attacks on Tay Ninh City and the surrounding area. The NVA purpose was to increase control over areas close to the Cambodian border. Strong defense by RF units inflicted heavy casualties on the NVA and its units were withdrawn into Cambodia for refitting and replacements. The summer and fall Strategic Raids of 1974 in MR 3 caused heavy casualties among many of the NVA units but it increased NVA base areas and stockpiling of supplies around Saigon. Hanoi would be prepared for the next phase of its offensive against South Vietnam.[474]

The Great Spring Victory

In his serialized account of the "Great Spring Victory" Senior General Van Tien Dung of the North Vietnamese Army described deliberations of the Central Military Party Committee and the General Staff as they reviewed the events of the summer campaign. He wrote of how, between April and October, from Thua Thien to Saigon, NVA forces had stepped up the offensive actions and had won great victories. The facts were, of course, that the NVA was stalemated at the extremes of this long battlefield—in Thua Thien and around Saigon—but had overrun isolated bases in the Central Highlands and succeeded at great cost in penetrating to the edge of the Quang Nam lowlands. This latter success loomed large in significance to General Dung and NVA planners. . . .the numerous, more easily won objectives in the highlands demonstrated to the satisfaction of the North Vietnamese high command that the time had arrived for an even bolder strategy. General Dung went on to relate how the General Staff reported to the Central Military Party Committee that the combat capability of our mobile main force troops was now altogether superior to that of the enemy's mobile regular troops, that the war had reached its final stage and that the balance of forces had changed in our favor.

General Dung believed, and the Military Committee and the General Staff agreed, that the NVA's superiority should be exploited in a new strategy. The NVA would no longer attack only to destroy the RVNAF but would combine this objective with attacks to "liberate" populated areas. It would move out of the jungles and mountains into the lowlands. NVA planners observed that, "the reduction of U.S. aid made it impossible for the puppet troops to carry out their combat plan and build up their forces" and that the South Vietnamese were "forced to fight a poor man's war," their firepower having decreased "by nearly 60 percent because of bomb and ammunition shortages" and their mobility was reduced "by half due to lack of aircraft, vehicles and fuel."

According to General Dung, the conference of the Politburo and the Central Military Committee met in October, considered the General Staff's assessments and recommendation, and unanimously agreed on the following:

1. The puppet troops were militarily, politically and economically weakening every day and our forces were quite stronger than the enemy in the south.

2. The United States was facing mounting difficulties both at home and in the world, and its potential for aiding the puppets was rapidly declining.

3. We had created a chain of mutual support, had strengthened our reserve forces and materiel and were steadily improving our strategic and political systems.

4. The movement to demand peace, improvement of the people's livelihood, democracy, national independence and Thieu's overthrow in various cities was gaining momentum. . . .   Comrade Le Duan drew an important conclusion that became a resolution: Having already withdrawn from the south, the United States could hardly jump back in, and no matter how it might intervene, it would be unable to save the Saigon administration from collapse. Phuoc Long became the battleground for the first test of this assessment.[475]

William E. Le Gro

Phuoc Long Province was an attractive target for Hanoi.

Phuoc Long was the primary target in Phase One [Hanoi's offensive plan], and the district seat of Dong Xoai was the key to capturing the province. Dong Xoai had long been a Communist objective, as the town controls an important road junction where Route 14 ends. Northward, the highway connects Phuoc Long to Quang Duc and goes on to Ban Me Thuot, the capital of Darlac province in the southern portion of the Central Highlands. Taking Dong Xoai would isolate Phuoc Binh, the provincial capital of Phuoc Long, and open Route 14 for the requested additional divisions to reinforce the B-2 Front. Tra committed elements of two divisions and his remaining armor and heavy artillery to capture Dong Xoai.

Phuoc Long was an easy mark. It was lightly populated by Montagnards, and only four RF battalions and several dozen PF platoons defended the large, mountainous province. For the South Vietnamese, supplying the province was even harder than defending it. The roads into Phuoc Long had been cut by PAVN troops shortly after the ceasefire, and resupply depended on C-130 cargo planes. In

November, after repeated intelligence warnings by the JGS that Tra's B-2 Front planned to attack Phuoc Long, III Corps flew in the reconnaissance companies of the 5th, 18th, and 25th Divisions to provide reinforcements.[476]

George J. Veith

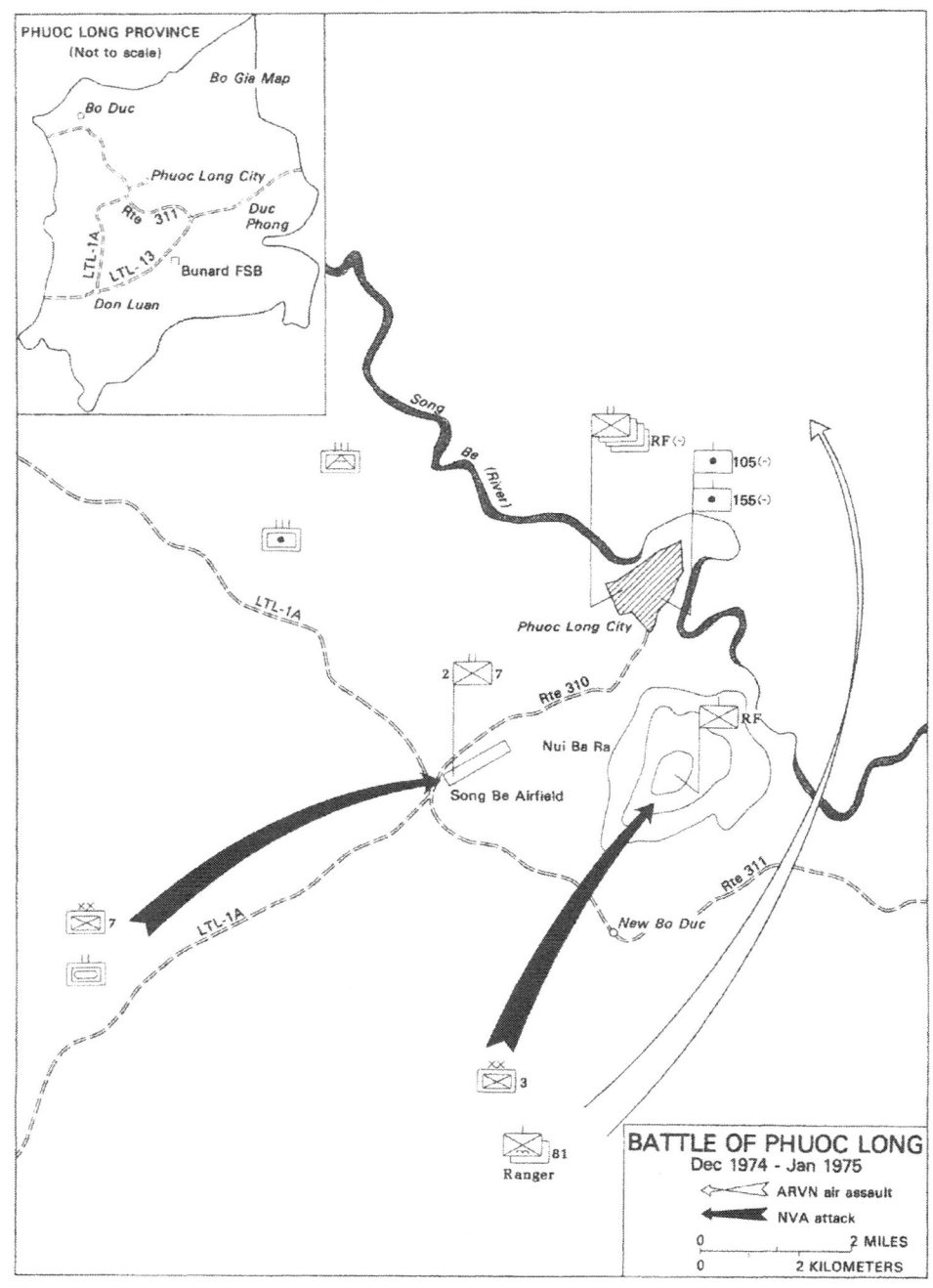

Battle of Phuoc Long (William E. Le Gro)

Phuoc Long city lies 75 miles northeast of Saigon adjacent to the Cambodian border. The city is close to the site of the Dak Son massacre of 1967 where the Communists murdered hundreds of unarmed men, women and children with flamethrowers. Phuoc Long Province is composed of four districts: Bo Duc, Don Luan, Duc Phong and Phuoc Binh. The province population of 30,000 is composed mostly of Montagnards from the Stieng (Ma) and Mnong tribes. The Montagnards work harvesting lumber and rubber from the plantations. The terrain of Phuoc Long Province is mountainous with heavy dense vegetation that denies aerial observation. The Communists used Phuoc Long Province as a base area. The city's airfield, Song Be, has an asphalt surface and can accommodate aircraft up to and including the C-130.

The supply of Phuoc Long was ordinarily done by truck via Interprovincial Route 1A and National Route 14. Local products went to Saigon by the same route. Only one week after the cease-fire, however, the Communists cut this main supply artery at many places. Airlift by helicopters and propeller-driven planes then became the main supply means for the city and the four district towns. The monthly requirement was 400 to 500 tons, mostly rice, salt, sugar, ammunition, and fuel. Beginning in August 1974, III Corps made a concerted effort with II Corps to open National Route 14. The operation somewhat relieved the burden on airlift resources which now were needed for the secure delivery of such critical items as ammunition, fuel, and medical supplies. However, on 14 December 1974, the district town of Duc Phong, which lay astride the supply route, was overrun by the Communists, and Phuoc Long again became dependent on airlift. And airlift became increasingly costly and unreliable due to the enemy's antiaircraft fire.

Phuoc Long was defended by five Regional Force battalions [Most sources indicate that there were only four] varying from 750 to 900 men; forty-eight Popular Force platoons, totaling approximately 1,000 men, mostly Montagnards; and four territorial artillery sections. This force was later augmented by the 2d Battalion of the 7th Infantry, two artillery sections from the 5th Division (six additional 105-mm. and four 155-mm. howitzers), and three reconnaissance companies of the 5th, 18th, and 25th Divisions.[477]

Cao Van Vien

The summer and fall of 1974 in South Vietnam's 3d Military Region had been difficult times. Unlike the losses in Military Regions 1 and 2, however, very little terrain of consequence had been given up to the NVA summer offensive. The divisional battles in Binh Duong, Tay Ninh, and Bien Hoa Provinces had produced thousands of casualties, but all positions—except those on the Tay Ninh-Cambodian frontier—were eventually retaken by ARVN troops. The mop-up of the Iron Triangle was not completed until 24 November, the eve of the next phase of the NVA offensive, the most significant step before the ultimate offensive of 1975.

Since Phuoc Long Province was far outside the defenses of Saigon, its importance to South Vietnam was essentially political in that the government could still claim possession of all province capitals. On the other hand, the presence of RVNAF bases deep inside otherwise NVA-controlled territory was an anathema to the enemy. Several important COSVN tactical and logistical units and activities were in the Bo Duc-Bu Dop complex of villages and plantations. The COSVN M-26 Armor Command, usually with three of its tank battalions, was based at the Bu Dop airfield only 25 kilometers from the ARVN base at Song Be. The COSVN Engineer Command had a headquarters at Bo Duc and kept three or more battalions working on roads between Loc Ninh and Bu Gia Map to the northeast. Anti-aircraft battalions, transportation battalions, training centers, and other rear service organizations contributed to a relatively dense NVA military population, nearly within medium artillery range of Phuoc Binh, the capital of Phuoc Long Province. Additionally, four major NVA infiltration-supply routes traversed Phuoc Long Province from north to south, past RVNAF bases and crossed sections of National Route 14 patrolled by South Vietnamese troops.[478]

William E. Le Gro

Summer in Phuoc Long Province had been relatively uneventful. In August an enemy soldier turned himself in at Phuoc Long Sector Headquarters. He revealed recent NVA activity. Two NVA patrols had conducted reconnaissance, one at Song Be and the other at Duc Phong District. Since the recons were not followed up by attacks, the province chief concluded that they were related to infiltration or logistical movements and posed no serious threat to Phuoc Long. He was wrong.

Phuoc Long required 500 tons of rice each month; half was locally produced so convoys were needed to move the rest as well as ammunition and other supplies. The enemy had cut Highway 14 east of Phuoc Binh-Song Be so road-clearing operations were needed before supplies could be moved. The alternative was resupply by air but restrictions on flying hours and fuel made this option available only for emergencies.

A resupply convoy was planned for early November so the Phuoc Long Sector Commander, Colonel Nguyen Tan Thanh started a road-clearing operation. The operation was successful and in the course of the operation, four NVA soldiers were killed near Duc Phong. These were found to be from the 201st NVA Regiment of the 3rd NVA Division. An NVA Regiment this close to Duc Phong was an ominous sign.

Colonel Thanh had several thousand troops at his disposal. Most were in four RF battalions. He also had several dozen PF platoons scattered around the sector defending hamlets. For artillery support he had four 155mm and 16 105mm howitzers. For the remainder of November and early December it was relatively quiet in Phuoc Long Province.[479]

Hanoi selected the 301st NVA Corps composed of the 3rd and 7th NVA Divisions to attack Phuoc Long Province. Additionally, the NVA had a tank battalion, an artillery and anti-aircraft regiment as well as local-force sapper and infantry units. This was several times the strength of the forces immediately available to the province. The corps would concentrate on the four widely dispersed RF battalions.

On 13 December 1974 the first attack fell on the district town of Don Luan while on 14 December both Duc Phong and New Bo Duc Subsectors were attacked and overrun. Don Luan held. A sector counterattack retook New Bo Duc on 16 December. The Phuoc Binh Subsector headquarters near the province headquarters also held out. The VNAF flew in six 105mm howitzers, ammunition and other supplies carrying out the wounded. On 21-22 December NVA artillery damaged one C-130 and destroyed another as the aerial resupply continued. Meanwhile, the NVA took New Bo Duc for the last time. By 17 December the only positions in ARVN hands were the Song Be airstrip, Phuoc Long City and the crest of Nui Ba Ra ridge overlooking the entire region (see above map).

At this time enemy advances toward Tay Ninh and Binh Tuy were in progress. Also, NVA attacks were underway in MR 1 and MR 2. Saigon had a dilemma. The attacks on Tay Ninh and Binh Tuy needed to be stopped but the political impact of losing the first South Vietnam province, Phuoc Long, to the NVA was significant. Resources were committed to Phuoc Long and the 2nd Battalion of the 7th ARVN Division was lifted from Lai Khe to Song Be Airstrip. The corps commander also requested that part of the airborne brigade be moved from MR 1 to Phuoc Long but the request was denied. The Airborne brigade was already engaged in fighting the NVA in MR 1.

On 26 December the 7th NVA Division finally overran Don Luan. Refugees poured into Song Be while the RVNAF desperately sought to resupply the beleaguered garrison by air. The NVA had established seven antiaircraft positions around the city denying the use of the airstrip for resupply aircraft. Ten attempts were made to drop supplies in early January 1975 but none could be retrieved by Song Be's defenders.

On 6 January 1975 NVA tanks were seen approaching Song Be. As a last gesture, two companies of ARVN's best troops from the 81st Airborne Rangers were sent into Song Be. As the tanks entered the city they were followed by sappers as they rolled through the streets. The sappers mopped up and established strong-points as the tanks rolled on. Most of the tanks that were destroyed were hit by 90mm recoilless rifles or M79 LAW missiles. Often the range was too close and the missiles bounced off before they could arm themselves. To make tank kills more difficult, NVA mechanics had welded steel plates on the sides of the tank hulls. Tank crews stayed buttoned up during the advance to prevent grenades from being tossed down the hatches. It was a bloody end for Song Be the last outpost in Phuoc Long Province.

General Cao Van Vien summarized the battle and its consequences.

At the time of his attack against Phuoc Long, the enemy also launched attacks at two other places in MR 3: in the north of Tay Ninh and at Hoai Duc-Tanh Linh (Binh Tuy Province). His aim was clearly to stretch our lines and prevent us from reinforcing Phuoc Long. The capture of Phuoc Long crowned the enemy's conscious and systematic efforts. Since December 1974 he had successively overrun the outlying districts, and by the time the battle began the city had been practically sealed off. The outcome of the battle could have been foreseen from the start. To confront the NVA main force of two divisions and its complements of armor and artillery, all the sector of Phuoc Long could put up was Regional Force troops, augmented at the last minute by one regular battalion. The organization for the defense was also incomplete. A sudden and last-minute change in the defense plan prevented the garrison from organizing and consolidating its positions. The province chief proved unable to control his forces, and as a result his reports to III Corps were mostly inaccurate.

The enemy in contrast enjoyed a tremendous numerical advantage. He also benefited from a few technical and tactical innovations. The armor of his tanks, for example, had been supplemented to provide an air space or cushion and protect the sides of the vehicles from antitank rockets. Enemy sappers made no attempt to penetrate in small groups by night as they usually did in advance of the main force. Instead, in this battle they were carried into the city by tanks with the main attacking force. The enemy's artillery was accurate, and the intensity of its fire was frightening. Because of his advantage in firepower, he attacked only during daytime. He was also able to monitor our radio communications, and he knew in advance our every tactical move.

To best sum up what contributed to the loss of Phuoc Long, let us hear the comment of an airborne trooper, a veteran of An Loc, who had fought in the battle:

> The enemy troops were not so good and so courageous as we might have thought. There were simply too many of them. The enemy's artillery fire was fierce and many times more accurate than it had been during the battle of An Loc. Enemy tanks had something new and strange. Our M-72 rockets were unable to knock them out. We hit them; they stopped for a while then moved on. Our air support was not very effective; the planes flew too high. If only we could have had B-52s like we did at An Loc!

Militarily, the capture of Phuoc Long gave the enemy extended control over a very large area. Three of his base areas were now linked together in a continuous arc from the Cambodian border across northern MR 3 with access routes toward Ham Tan on the coast. Psychologically and politically, the loss of Phuoc Long, the first provincial capital of South Vietnam permanently seized by the Communists, came as a shock to the population and the armed forces. The apparent total indifference with which the United States and other non-Communist countries regarded this tragic loss reinforced the doubt the Vietnamese people held concerning the viability of the Paris Agreement. Almost gone was the hope that the United States would forcibly punish the North Vietnamese for their brazen violations of the cease-fire agreement. The people's belief in the power of the armed forces and the government was also deeply shaken. To the Communists Phuoc Long was not merely a military victory. What they had gained psychologically and politically was more important. It was their first big step toward total military conquest, boldly taken yet apparently without fear of any reaction from the United States. What more encouragement could the Communists have asked for? And what a good chance for them to step up propaganda against our government and to appeal to our troops to quit their ranks and join the Communists.[480]

Cao Van Vien

William E. Le Gro was assigned to the U. S. Defense Attaché Office, Saigon during the Battle of Phuoc Long. He recorded the final hours of the defeat.

NVA artillery was devastating, particularly after 3 January when the rate of fire increased from about 200 rounds per day to nearly 3,000. Structures, bunkers, and trenches collapsed, and casualties mounted. ARVN artillery was out of action, its guns destroyed by fire from tanks, recoilless rifles, and 130-mm. guns. Finally, on 6 January, the province chief realized that he could no longer influence the battle. With no artillery and shattered communications, under direct fire from four approaching T54 tanks, and seriously wounded, he and what remained of his staff, withdrew from Song Be. The NVA had captured the first province capital since the cease-fire.

There were some military and civilian survivors from Song Be. Pitiful little bands of Montagnards trekked through the jungles to Quang Duc, and VNAF helicopters rescued about 200 men of the Rangers, 7th Infantry, and sector territorials in the days immediately following the collapse. The province chief never made it to safety. His wounds slowed him down and he was not seen again. A few members of the command group eventually reached the ARVN outpost of Bu Binh on

Highway 14 in Quang Duc. RVNAF losses were staggering. Over 5,400 officers and men of the 7th Infantry, Airborne Rangers, and territorials were committed; less than 850 survived. Especially costly were the high losses in the Airborne Ranger Battalion-85 troopers survived—and in the 2d Battalion, 7th Infantry, fewer than 200 returned from Phuoc Long. About 3,000 civilians, Montagnards and Vietnamese, out of 30,000 or more, escaped Communist control. The few province, village, and hamlet officials who were captured were summarily executed.

Although it was the time of the dry, northeast monsoon, unseasonably heavy torrents drenched Saigon. As this writer's Vietnamese driver dolefully remarked, even the gods were weeping for Phuoc Long.[481]

William E. Le Gro

1975–The Year of the Cat

They won't come back even if we offered them candy.[482]
Pham Van Dong

U. S. Response to Phuoc Long

The conquest of Phuoc Long Province was clearly the most blatant breach of the cease-fire agreement thus far. Anticipating its fall, the U.S. Department of State on 3 January 1975 asserted that the offensive "belies Hanoi's claims that it is the United States and South Vietnam who are violating the 1973 Paris truce agreements and standing in the way of peace." The PRG promptly rejected the accusation, and North Vietnam's Communist Party newspaper claimed that the offensive was "a legitimate right of riposte" in defense of the Paris agreements. On 13 January, the State Department released the text of an official protest, dated 11 January, delivered to the non-Vietnamese participants in the International Conference on Vietnam and to members of the International Commission of Control and Supervision:

The Department of State of the United States of America . . . has the honor to refer to the Agreement on Ending the War and Restoring Peace in Viet-Nam signed at Paris January 27, 1973, and to the Act of the International Conference on VietNam signed at Paris March 2, 1973.

When the Agreement was concluded nearly two years ago, our hope was that it would provide a framework under which the Vietnamese people could make their own political choices and resolve their own problems in an atmosphere of peace. Unfortunately this hope, which was clearly shared by the Republic of Viet-Nam and the South Vietnamese people, has been frustrated by the persistent refusal of the Democratic Republic of Viet-Nam to abide by the agreement's most fundamental provisions. Specifically, in flagrant violation of the Agreement, the North Vietnamese and "Provisional Revolutionary Government" authorities have:

—built up the North Vietnamese main-force army in the South through the illegal infiltration of over 160,000 troops;

—tripled the strength of their armor in the South by sending in over 400 new vehicles, as well as greatly increased their artillery and antiaircraft weaponry;

—improved their military logistics system running through Laos, Cambodia and the Demilitarized Zone as well as within South Viet-Nam, and expanded their armament stockpiles;

—refused to deploy the teams which under the Agreement were to oversee the cease-fire;

—refused to pay their prescribed share of the expenses of the International Commission of Control and Supervision;

—failed to honor their commitment to cooperate in resolving the status of American and other personnel missing in action even breaking off all discussions on the matter by refusing for the past several months to meet with U.S. and Republic of Viet-Nam representatives in the Four-Party Joint Military Team;

—broken off all negotiations with the Republic of Viet-Nam including the political negotiations in Paris and the Two Party Joint Military Commission talks in Saigon answering the Republic of Viet-Nam's repeated calls for unconditional resumption of the negotiations with demands for the over throw of the government as a pre-condition for any renewed talks; and

—gradually increased their military pressure, over-running several areas, including 11 district towns, which were clearly and unequivocally held by the Republic of Viet-Nam at the time of the cease-fire. The latest and most serious escalation of the fighting began in early December with offensives in the southern half of South Viet-Nam which have brought the level of casualties and destruction back up to what it was before the Agreement. These attacks—which included for the first time since the massive North Vietnamese 1972 offensive the over-running of a province capital (Song Be in Phuoc Long Province)—appear to reflect a decision by Hanoi to seek once again to impose a military solution in Viet-Nam. Coming just before the second anniversary of the Agreement, this dramatically belies Hanoi's claims that it is the United States and the Republic of Viet-Nam who are violating the Agreement and standing in the way of peace.

The United States deplores the Democratic Republic of Viet-Nam's turning from the path of negotiation to that of war, not only because it is a grave violation of a solemn international agreement, but also because of the cruel price it is imposing on the people of South Viet-Nam. The Democratic Republic of Viet-Nam must accept the full consequences of its actions. We are deeply concerned about the threat posed to international peace and security, to the political stability of Southeast Asia, to the progress which has been made in removing VietNam as a major issue of great-power contention, and to the hopes of mankind for the building of structures of peace and the strengthening of mechanisms to avert war. We therefore reiterate our strong support for the Republic of Viet-Nam's call to the Hanoi-"Provisional Revolutionary Government" side to reopen the talks in Paris and Saigon which are mandated by the Agreement. We also urge that the . . . [addressee] call upon the Democratic Republic of Viet-Nam to halt its military offensive and join the Republic of Viet-Nam in re-establishing stability and seeking a political solution.

While the staffers in the State Department were putting together this carefully worded note, the North Vietnamese were claiming that the U.S. was flying reconnaissance over South Vietnam to assist the "Saigon administration to intensify its bombing and landgrabbing operations against the PRG-controlled areas." Defense Department spokesmen defended the appropriateness of U.S. aerial reconnaissance in Indochina in view of the extreme provocation by the North Vietnamese. The photography was of some intelligence value to the South Vietnamese but it was rarely, if ever, useful for targeting. U.S. reconnaissance over Laos was stopped on 4 June 1974, and a good part of the timely, detailed evidence of the flow of men and equipment into the South from North Vietnam terminated at that time. Significantly, the President made no mention of Vietnam in his State of the Union message delivered to Congress on 15 January. In a press conference on 21 January, he said that he could foresee no circumstances in which the U.S. might actively re-enter the Vietnam War.

North Vietnamese leaders carefully analyzed the U.S. reaction to Phuoc Long, General Van Tien Dung reporting it this way: It was obvious that the United States was in this position: Having withdrawn from Vietnam, the United States could hardly return. All the conferees [at the Politburo Conference 18 December to 8 January] analyzed the enemy's weakness which in itself heralded a new opportunity for us. To fully exploit this great opportunity we had to conduct large-scale annihilating battles to destroy and disintegrate the enemy on a large scale.

The dramatic and conclusive victory in Phuoc Long, and the passivity with which the United States reacted to it, confirmed the earlier North Vietnamese estimates that the time for the decisive blow had arrived. The concepts for the spring offensive were discussed and sharpened during this midwinter conference in Hanoi. . . .[483]

William E. Le Gro

During 1973 and 1974, the most devastating impact on South Vietnam was the severe reduction in U. S. aid and other support caused by the U. S. Congressional action.

Hanoi's target was Saigon. If the north could seize Saigon, it would end the war. They knew that Thieu would ultimately try to concentrate his forces to defend Saigon, the Capital Military Region. The initial NVA attack was against Pruco Long province in the southeast. It was a key junction on Route 14. The troops at the province capital of Pruco Binh were no match for the NVA and surrendered on 6 January 1975. There was no reaction from the U.S. The Saigon regime was stunned. The U.S. Congress had done a good job of limiting the power of the president to re-enter the war. The possibility of the U.S. re-entering the war was not a concern for Hanoi. In the words of the Hanoi diplomat Pham Van Dong, "They won't come back even if we offered them candy."[484] The initial success of the NVA at Pruco Binh encouraged Hanoi to mount a full-scale invasion of South Vietnam. This was a year ahead of their plan to destroy the South Vietnam regime and reunite the country.

Kissinger tried to use diplomacy to prevent an NVA invasion. He met with the Soviet Union and the Chinese to obtain their intervention and offered better relations with the U.S. as an incentive, but he was not successful.[485]

Hanoi chose Ban Me Thuot in the central Highlands of South Vietnam as the target. Ban Me Thuot was the capital of Darlac province. It was originally the hunting lodge of Emperor

Bao Dai which had been turned into MACV's quarters. It is high in the mountains with a very pleasant climate. General Vien Tien Dung would command the invasion of South Vietnam. He would later succeed Giap as Hanoi's Minister of Defense. Ban Me Thuot was a strange target for the invasion, and it surprised the South Vietnamese.

> To summarize Hanoi's military analysis of the reasons for choosing Ban Me Thuot, the two main east-to-west roads from the coast to the Central Highlands are Routes 19 and 21. Only one road, Route 14, runs north to south through the Central Highlands. Route 1 runs along the coast. Ban Me Thuot straddles the vital road junction of Route 14 and Route 21, just as Pleiku does for Routes 14 and 19. The Politburo chose Ban Me Thuot because it was surrounded by coffee plantations that provided good cover for attacking forces; it was lightly defended; and Route 21 to Nha Trang was wide open. Pleiku, on the other hand, was heavily defended, and its avenues of approach offered little concealment. If PAVN forces had taken Pleiku, they would then have had to fight the ARVN 22nd Division down Route 19 to the sea. Moreover, grabbing the Ban Me Thuot section of Route 14 and the section near Duc Lap, combined with the section recently captured in Phuoc Long, would provide Hanoi's reserve forces a motorized artery straight to Saigon. Plus, Ban Me Thuot held the major but lightly guarded ammunition dump, the Mai Hac De supply depot, an enticing target for the Communist logisticians. In hindsight, it appears the logical choice, but as Thao notes, Hanoi had chosen the northern section of the Central Highlands (Kontum and Pleiku) six out of seven times. The main reason was logistics: Kontum and Pleiku were hundreds of miles closer to the main PAVN supply coffers. Only during Tet '68 had PAVN attacked Ban Me Thuot, and then only for a few days before retreating.[486]
>
> ***George J. Veith***

Dung was faced by the ARVN regional commander, Pham Van Phu, who could assemble forces equal to those of Dung. Dung feinted an attack at Pleiku but concentrated his divisions far to the southeast. It was a brilliant strategy, and it worked because it was unexpected. The NVA concentrated three divisions at Ban Me Thuot on 10 March 1975, and the South

Vietnamese defenders fled. A FULRO splinter group assisted the NVA in the capture of Ban Me Thuot.[487]

Thieu now believed the South Vietnamese government needed to redeploy its military forces to defend the most populous and economically significant parts of the country. Those areas were the heartland of South Vietnam, from the southern portion of II Corps—a line stretching across the country from Ban Me Thuot to Tuy Hoa on the coast—to the southernmost tip of the Mekong Delta. This was a larger version of the old Cochin China section of the country, that part considered truly "southern" by the people of Vietnam There was a longstanding and distinct cultural identity among the people of this region, and Thieu hoped to use it to rally them against the northern invaders. Most of South Vietnam's natural resources, including the all-important oil deposits and the majority of the agricultural base, lay within this area. Thieu would abandon much of I Corps, although he wanted to hold Da Nang as an enclave for a future counterattack to regain lost territory. He also wanted to defend Hue if possible, but he felt it would be difficult to hold against a determined thrust.

Accordingly, it was imperative to recapture Ban Me Thuot, which anchored the northwestern end of Thieu's bisected South Vietnam. If the Communists held the town, they could threaten Saigon from three directions: from Dalat in the north, Nha Trang in the east, and Tay Ninh in the west. Thieu had absorbed this lesson from the French, who had used the Montagnard capital as their main stronghold in the Highlands. Moreover, Thieu wanted to destroy the 320th Division, which he thought had taken the city. Lastly, he wanted to retrieve his troops from isolated and vulnerable positions in the Highlands. Otherwise, "they would be decimated because of a lack of reserves to support them and the inability of the air force to resupply them." After retaking the city, Thieu could then move against Pleiku or Kontum. Thieu named his new strategy "Light at the top, heavy at the bottom." Since he was fearful of leaks and spies, only a select few were informed of his decisions. That did not include the Americans.[488]

George J. Veith

Thieu consulted with Phu who was already safe with his family in Nha Trang.[489]

Thieu began by asking Phu for his analysis of the situation. Painting a dismal picture, Phu noted that Route 19, the most important road in the Highlands, was cut in two places. The other main roads were blocked as well. He also informed Thieu that his forces had just captured a soldier from the 316th Division near Ban Me Thuot. Thieu grimly absorbed the news. He was well aware that the addition of a strategic-reserve division to the PAVN forces in the Highlands had decisively tipped the balance of forces against ARVN.

After Phu finished speaking, Thieu asked him if he could retake Ban Me Thuot with the forces currently deployed around the town. Phu said no, and he asked for reinforcements from the Airborne Division to retake the city. Thieu denied his request. Turning to Vien, Thieu asked if there were any other reserves. Vien stated that Phu had already received the last unit, the 7th Rangers. With no reserves available, Thieu ordered Phu to redeploy his regular units from Pleiku and Kontum and retake Ban Me Thuot. Most important, no one was to know about the plan, including the Americans. The Montagnard regional and popular forces and the local administrations in Pleiku and Kontum would remain and defend their areas as best they could.[490]

George J. Veith

The best escape route for the ARVN appeared to be Highway 14 through Cheo Reo. Preparations started immediately.

Phu ordered Colonel Ly to plan a corps-sized road march from Kontum and Pleiku along Route 7B to Nha Trang. The movement would occur between 16 and 19 March. The bulk of the corps headquarters would relocate via helicopter to Nha Trang, while the 6th Air Division would transfer from Pleiku to the Nha Trang and Phan Rang airbases. The engineers would repair the road and bridges. Ly would move in the convoy with a light corps headquarters.[491]

George J. Veith

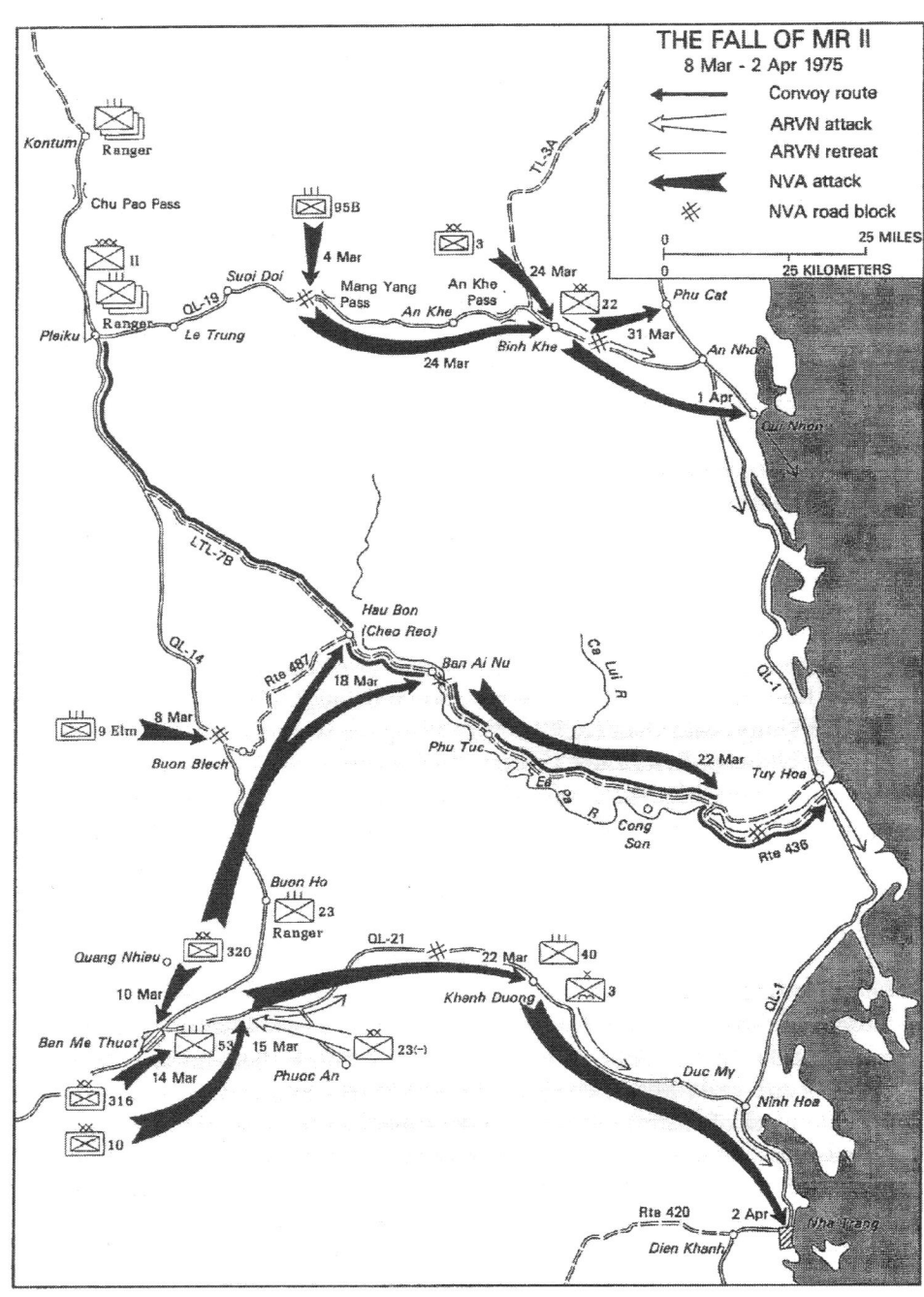

Fall of MR 2 (J. Edward Lee and H. C. Haynesworth).

All of the ARVN officers and soldiers who had roots down in MR 2 now had to pack quickly, load their families and belongings acquired over perhaps as long as thirty years, and get on the road east to escape.[492] Some senior ARVN officers abandoned their troops and ordered or bribed helicopter pilots to fly them, their families, and gold to the coast.[493] That left behind about 200,000 soldiers, Montagnards, and their families in MR 2 that had been abandoned by their leadership.[494] As the ARVN officers and soldiers with their families fled east and south in panic, throwing away their uniforms and weapons, the NVA cut Highway 19 and other roads east and south.

After two days on Highway 14 and then on Route 7-B, the part of the convoy out of Pleiku and Kontum that included the journalist Nguyen Tu reached Hau Bon [Cheo Reo], the capital of Phu Bon province. Tu wrote on the eighteenth:

On the heels of refugees evacuating Pleiku and Kontum, the people of Hau Bon are also leaving their city.

Refugees from Pleiku and Kontum who reached Hau Bon in small groups made the long journey in two days. The majority are still far behind, dragging their feet on the dirty road under a scorching sun by day and chilled by night in the forests.

It was not possible to say how many children fell during the walk, how many helpless old people were standing along the road unable to move, how many others were suffering from thirst and hunger during the walk to freedom and democracy.

A Ranger officer told me: 'This time, I can never look straight to my people again.'

A private said: `Damnit, we got away without any fighting. I prefer to fight and run away if we lose. I will accept that.'

An Air Force captain said: 'It is sad, very sad, especially when we look back at Pleiku, a deserted city now. We can see only fires and fires. I am very sad.'

`I am stunned. . . . Look at these people, the young ones. Isn't this miserable?' another soldier added. . . .

The people at Hau Bon today followed en masse the flow of refugees from Pleiku and Kontum. Women, children, youngsters, and the elderly — all in small groups with their belongings either on their backs or in their hands — rushed out of their houses as they saw the convoy approaching. The same scenes of plundering and ransacking of the homes by unidentified people reappeared. . . .

Many sections of the town were set afire. . . Phu Bon has capitulated not to the enemy but by its own. . . .

After Kontum and Pleiku on Sunday, Hau Bon became a lost town on Tuesday.

Nguyen Tu

There were at least 100,000 people in what Nguyen Tu had begun calling the 'Convoy of Tears' out of the Central Highlands. And before nightfall on Tuesday, the eighteenth, when lead elements in the column had pushed only a few miles east of Hau Bon, the convoy of tears became a convoy of death.

The head of the convoy was blocked at a downed bridge. And now elements from the division whose commander General Dung had set themselves up in high ground all around the convoy lashed out at it on Sunday night. They flailed it like a mongoose flailing a snake. Nguyen Tu wrote on Wednesday, the nineteenth:

> The leading part of our convoy got through the ambush point under a screen of supporting fire. But the tail end had to leave the road and pass through the jungle. I was in the tail end.
>
> Rebel mountain tribesmen armed with our (American) weapons and Communist B-41 rockets and AK-47 rifles shot into the convoy, while Communist artillery struck from all directions.
>
> Many trucks were hit by shells and burst into flames and exploded.
>
> The trucks were crammed with soldiers, children, old people. They fell everywhere.
>
> Those who walked fell to machine-gun bullets. Their blood flowed in tiny streams.
>
> The roaring artillery, crackling small arms, screams of the dying and crying of the children combined into a single voice from hell.
>
> The Rangers resisted all night, permitting the tail end of the convoy to flee into the jungle.
>
> At last, 200 of us succeeded in climbing up Chu Del hill, about six miles from Cheo Reo, 210 miles north of Saigon.

Helicopters contacted us and moved in for rescue. The operation was difficult, because Chu Del is a narrow and steep hill.

Finally, in an operation that evening and the next morning, 200 persons were lifted out and rescued.

That *Chinh Limn* felt free to publish that dispatch less than a week after Paul Leandri was killed as a consequence of writing a story that implicated the Montagnards in the attack on Ban Me Thuot was the first clear indication that Saigon had decided that Nguyen Van Thieu had lost the mandate of heaven.

On Wednesday afternoon, I got on the last Air Vietnam flight to Nha Trang. All scheduled flights out of Nha Trang were booked, so the office arranged a charter for Thursday morning.

From Mike Marriott, who had come back up the coast, I pieced together what turned out to be an accurate idea of the size and location of the convoy and what was happening to it. I was principally a courier on this trip, but wrote three spots I would phone to New York as soon as I got back to Saigon.

That night, I ate with the crew on the open deck of a restaurant on the beach. The lobsters and clams and squid were simpler and better and much cheaper than the same fare at the hotel, but for the first few minutes I wished I were back in the hotel garden, where waiters brought moist facecloths and used, knowing, conspiratorial girls did not try to sit on my lap.

The next morning, from nine thousand feet up and a mile or two off the coast, the land was a full smudge of green and brown. At that angle, most of the settlements were shielded by trees. 'New Hampshire,' I thought. 'Maine.' Here and there, inland, thin clouds of gray or white smoke twisted slowly in the sky. I realized that I did not know whether the smoke marked combat or burning farmers' fields.

As we came in north over the huge airfield at Bien Hoa, I could see Tan Son Nhut twelve miles ahead. When the bored, middle-aged Franco-Vietnamese pilot had learned that I had a hundred hours in the plane, he had let me fly it down the coast. Now I gave the controls back to the man and turned my full attention to Bien Hoa, and the divided highway that connected the air base to the capital, the American- and Japanese-built factories in industrial zones along the highway, asphalt and steel flung across rice paddies. I was untroubled by forebodings. The outskirts of

Bangkok would look much the same, only more industrialized, less militarized. I stared down in simply boyish fascination. There was nowhere else I would willingly be.[495]

David Butler

There is no accurate count of the Vietnamese who were killed in MR 2 due to Thieu's decisions. Meanwhile, Thieu sat in his palace in Saigon, waiting for word about his army in MR 2 and when it would arrive to help defend his Saigon regime. There was no longer an ARVN MR 2 army. The army in MR 2 was now NVA. By late March 1975, Da Nang, South Vietnam's second largest city, on the Northern coast in MR 1, was a South Vietnamese stronghold and nearly a million refugees were streaming into it for safety. It did not work. On 29 March 1975, the NVA entered the city as the ARVN threw away their uniforms and weapons and fled. There are some remarkable videos taken at that time. While thousands of women and children waited to be airlifted out of Da Nang or by boat to safety, Pan Am sent a jet to Da Nang to evacuate people. ARVN soldiers pushed aside women and children and rushed the aircraft and quickly over-loaded it. As the aircraft took off, the many ARVN soldiers outside the aircraft hung on to the cargo hatch and other parts of the aircraft. As the aircraft gained altitude, they fell to their deaths.

At the port of Da Nang, things were much worse. Thousands of women and children crowded the docks to escape on fishing boats or other craft. ARVN soldiers shot women and children in order to make room for themselves.[496]

By this time the Hanoi strategy had shifted. Based upon the collapse of the ARVN seen so far, Hanoi decided to accelerate and destroy the Saigon regime, now rather than later. Dung received orders to liberate the south quickly before the rains started in May. On 7 April 1975, Dung had planning under way. The offensive against Saigon would be launched no later than the last week in April.[497] At that time, there were six thousand Americans remaining in South

Vietnam. The U.S. ambassador, Graham Martin, delayed evacuation because he believed that Saigon could be held. It was a fatal error for many South Vietnamese who should have been evacuated but were not because time ran out.

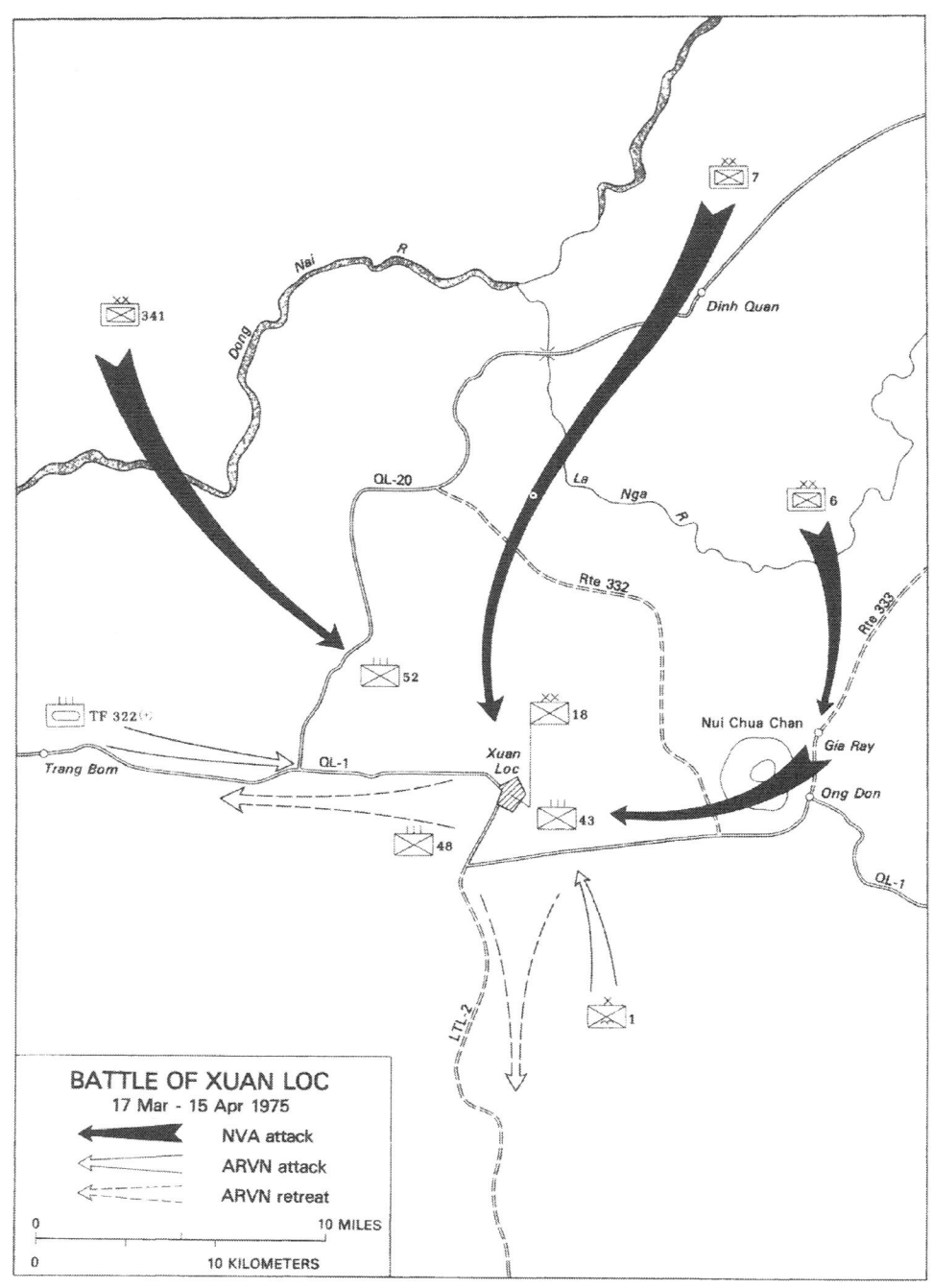

Xuan Loc (William E. Le Gro).

A small force of ARVN troops defended the Route 1 avenue of approach as the NVA moved toward Saigon. Xuan Loc was located thirty-five miles northeast of Saigon. On 9 April the entire IV NVA Corps attacked the ARVN 18th Division. The IV NVA Corps included three divisions (the 6th, 7th, and 341st) and supporting tanks and artillery. The ARVN 18th Division had supporting ranger battalions and was later reinforced by the 1st Airborne Brigade. The 82nd Ranger Battalion had just conducted an escape through enemy lines and was moved to the Xuan Loc airport. It would be under the control of the 43rd ARVN Regiment. The Montagnards of the ranger units and the ARVN troops held out until 22 April and were then forced to withdraw.[498] General Van Tien Dung commanded the NVA forces and summarized the battle from his prospective.

In the early days of April 1975, the town of Xuan Loc turned into a crucial enemy defense zone for III Corps, as it protected Saigon from the east; this was one strong point in the U.S.-Saigon distant defense line. The enemy tried to hold Xuan Loc to block two of the routes our troops could use to advance into Saigon—Route 1 and Route 20. At that time our troops on Route 1 had advanced nearly to Phan Rang, and on Route 20, after liberating Lam Dong, Da Lat, and Tuyen Duc, our troops had advanced down close to Kiem Tan. The enemy tried to hold Route 15 from Saigon to Vung Tau to bring in American aid coming to Saigon by sea, and that was one of the very routes they later used in flight.

If they could hold Xuan Loc and Long Khanh, then the Bien Hoa-Nhan Trach-Ba Ria-Vung Tau line would not come under direct pressure, and the airfields at Bien Hoa and Tan Son Nhut could still operate. So, they were trying to hold this zone at whatever cost. Their Third Army Corps, and in particular their 18th division, were still intact and had not yet been hit hard. . . .On April 9 our Fourth Army Corps, including the 7th division, the 341st division, the 6th division, and the Zone 7 forces, with Brigadier-General Hoang Cam as commander and Brigadier-General Hoang The Thien as political officer, opened fire on Xuan Loc. The units of the Fourth Army Corps, with all their experience in combat, were for the first time confronting an enemy who had reached the end of the road and were ready to risk their lives.

The enemy dispatched all the forces of their 18th division, reinforced by the 3rd cavalry brigade; one element of the 5th division, which was defending Route 13, and the artillery battalions directly attached to them; the ranger groups from III Corps; and the crippled ranger groups from I Corps and II Corps which had not yet had time to reorganize, and flung them pell-mell into Xuan Loc. It was a test of troops and a test of generals by the Americans and Saigon as they faced the danger of collapse.

That was not yet enough. The enemy also sent the 1st paratroop brigade to the Xuan Loc front, and mobilized their remaining air forces from Bien Hoa, Tan Son Nhut, and Can Tho at the highest possible level, in order to postpone their day of doom. But that was not enough, either. . . .The battle for Xuan Loc was fierce and cruel from the very first days. Our 7th, 6th, and 341st divisions had to organize many assaults into town, striking and striking again to destroy each target, and had to repel many enemy counterattacks. The enemy's 43rd regiment was seriously crippled. Our campaign artillery and the artillery units with our divisions had to use extra quantities of shells. A number of our tanks and armored cars were damaged, and others had to return to their staging areas for more fuel and ammunition. . . .

During the days that the Fourth Army Corps was assaulting Xuan Loc, we urgently had to develop plans for the attack on Saigon as well as direct the regional headquarters and the Fourth Army Corps command to change their fighting style. We also reinforced the Fourth Army Corps with the 95th regiment and sent them additional materiel.

Tran Van Tra went down to the Fourth Army Corps from Loc Ninh again to tell them about the new style of fighting and supervise its implementation. We advised that once the enemy had amassed troops to try to save Xuan Loc, we need not concentrate our forces and continue attacking them head on. We should shift our forces to strike counterattacking enemy units in the outer perimeter, where they had insufficient defense works and were not in close coordination with each other, before they could get their feet on the ground. We should use our long-range artillery to destroy the Bien Hoa airbase and keep it under control so enemy fighter planes could not take off.

After capturing Tuc Trung and Kiem Tan and wiping out the 52nd regiment of Saigon's 18th division, we continued along Route

20 to the Dau Giay intersection and set up a firm blockade of a section of Route 1, knocking out one tank and beating back the enemy's 3rd cavalry brigade coming up from Bien Hoa as reinforcements. Xuan Loc had been cut off from Saigon. The town and the headquarters of their 48th regiment were still under artillery fire, and at Bau Ca their 3rd cavalry brigade was still blocked and couldn't move a muscle. The Fourth Army Corps used artillery to choke off the enemy artillery positions gradually, and to wipe out each element of the 48th regiment and 1st paratroop brigade, which had just arrived as reinforcements. . . .Xuan Loc was liberated. The eastern gateway to Saigon was open, ready to welcome the forces of the Second and Fourth Army Corps and the 3rd division from Zone 5 to the final strategically decisive battle. The 3rd division prepared to advance toward Ba Ria and Vung Tau. Thus before the date for launching the general offensive on Saigon-Gia Dinh, the eastern wing of troops had established a most advantageous attack position.[499]

Van Tien Dung

Phillip Davidson summarized the battle of Xuan Loc.

The fighting featured mass NVA infantry attacks supported by extremely heavy artillery fire (the ARVN troops at Xuan Loc took over 20,000 rounds of artillery and rockets). ARVN held out until 22 April and then had to withdraw. The 18th ARVN Division lost about 30 percent of its strength (almost all its riflemen) while destroying 37 NVA tanks and killing over 5,000 Communist attackers. In this final epic stand ARVN demonstrated for the last time that, when properly led, it had the "right stuff."[500]

Phillip B. Davidson

As the NVA took over Saigon in 1975, President Thieu was seen running to an aircraft even though he had vowed to fight to the end.[501] Thieu deserted his country on 25 April and flew to Taiwan. He was eventually replaced by General Duong Van "Big" Minh, the man who had replaced Diem twelve years earlier.[502]

At this time, General Nguyen Cao Ky flew over the battlefield and concluded that the NVA would win. He then flew his helicopter to land on a U.S. carrier.[503]

As the NVA approached Saigon, the evacuation of U.S. citizens and some South Vietnamese was in full swing. It was a tight schedule to get people out to carriers and other ships standing by. Many strange things happened as the South Vietnamese regime collapsed. South Vietnamese IBM employees were told to stay at their jobs because they were needed to process payrolls for the ARVN. This was de ja vu. In the last days of Hitler in April 1945, as he prepared to commit suicide and the Soviet army was overwhelming Berlin, German army clerks were writing out requisitions for paper clips and other admin supplies that would be needed in 1946. On 30 April 1975, many South Vietnamese were evacuated by helicopters landing on U.S. carriers that were standing by.

Vu Hy Thieu was with the NVA forces advancing on Saigon. Years later he recalled the event.

> When the U.S. Army started their withdrawal we knew that victory was close. In 1974, I was sent to a liberated zone in Tay Ninh. For the first time eight years, I was given a small salary. The first thing I bought was ice cream. Those of us from Hanoi love ice cream.
>
> By March 1975 there was news of victory everywhere. Early in April knew we knew that we would win. I was ordered to prepare everything for the publication of a newspaper for Saigon. So we began to set up *Liberated Saigon (Sai Ge'e Giai Phong)*. I served as editor and also created the paper's design. Saigon people, unlike those of us from Hanoi, are very informal and easygoing, so I wanted to make the design of the newspaper simple, much like it had been before 1975. I put the word *Liberated (Giai Phong)* in small letters below a much bigger *Saigon* because my intention was to remove *Liberated* from the title a few months later. But people wanted to keep it and it's still there.
>
> On April 25 we were ordered to move toward Saigon. On April 29 we spent the night in a rubber plantation fifteen miles from Saigon but no one could sleep. We just kept looking at our watches. Early the next morning we started for Saigon. On the way we saw

lots of dead bodies beside the road and some trucks on fire with southern soldiers inside. In the city people crowded the streets to welcome us. They came close to touch our hands. At first, we had no idea where to go, so we pulled over in front of a movie theater and took a break. People brought us food and watched us while we ate. They even examined us to make sure we didn't have tails like monkeys. Mixing with the crowd were ARVN soldiers who had stripped off their uniforms and wore only shorts and T-shirts. I was deeply moved to see a patch of sun on a high wall. It had been nine years of jungle living since I had seen the sun rising over a city.[504]

Vu Hy Thieu

General Minh, the last Saigon head of state, prepared to meet the NVA representatives.

Colonel Bui Tin, deputy editor of Quan Doi Nhan Dan, the North Vietnamese army newspaper, was covering the campaign as a correspondent. But as the ranking officer with the unit, his first duty was to take the surrender. "I have been waiting since early this morning to transfer power to you," announced General Minh as Bui Tin entered the room. "There is no question of your transferring power," replied Bui Tin. "Your power has crumbled. You cannot give up what you do not have…The war for our country is over."[505]

Stanley Karnow

It was evident that the NVA did not want to interfere with the U.S. departure from Vietnam. A greater concern was renegade South Vietnam soldiers who would turn their guns on Americans trying to depart, but this did not occur. The final chapter captured by many cameras was U.S. helicopters landing and shuttling people out to the fleet. As far as is known, all U.S. personnel were evacuated, but many South Vietnamese key officials and intelligence people were left behind. By delaying the evacuation, Ambassador Martin caused the deaths of many South Vietnamese who were later executed by the NVA, but the total will never be known. Ambassador and Mrs. Martin were among the last to be taken out, clutching the U.S. flag. He looked like a corpse. Martin's stepson was among the 58,000 U.S. service men and women killed in Vietnam. This was a very sad ending to a tragic war.

Years after the war, Vo Nguyen Giap met with Robert McNamara in Hanoi.

In the mid-nineties Giap participated in discussions held in Hanoi between an American delegation led by wartime U.S. Secretary of Defense Robert McNamara and a group of Vietnamese historians, retired generals, and former diplomats. McNamara hoped to examine wartime "misunderstandings" between the two countries and identify possible "missed opportunities" for negotiating an earlier end to the war. An initial exchange between McNamara and Giap revealed a fundamental difference in their historical views of the war:

McNamara: "We need to draw lessons which will allow us to avoid such tragedies the future."

Giap: "Lessons are important. I agree. However, you are wrong to call the war a 'tragedy.' Maybe it was a tragedy for you, but for us the war was a noble sacrifice. We did not want to fight the United States, but you gave us no choice."[506]

Christian G. Appy

The Fall of Saigon—Refugee Evacuation (U.S. Department of Defense).

Summary

During the Vietnam War, the South Vietnamese and Americans conducted bombing raids, defoliated the countryside with herbicides, and forcibly relocated villagers. The Communists mounted ambushes and assaults on villages, and shelled and rocketed towns. Normally a people who lived in a slow-changing mode, the highlanders displayed resilience as refugees, devising adaptation strategies to preserve their man-nature-cosmos. Harmony. But the war eventually drove most ethnic groups from their native areas and into alien physical environments and refugee camps where they became totally dependent on outside agencies for their every need. When the Vietnam War ended in 1975, between 200,000 and 220,000 of the estimated one million highlanders had died. Around 85 percent of their villages either had been destroyed or abandoned. But a great many of those who died were not killed by bullets or bombs. They perished because their world was shattered. [507]

Gerald Hickey

The Second Indochina War demonstrated the value and valor of the Montagnards fighting against the NVA and VC. They were sacrificed in economy of force operations too often and if they had been properly supported by the Saigon government they could have had a greater impact on the war. They could have become the deciding factor.

John Loving the U. S. Army advisor to Regional Forces in III Corps summarized best why the war was lost by the South Vietnamese.

. . . . I would soon learn that the thing that we could never give our counterparts was the will to fight. They fought because they had to, while their enemies, the VC and the North Vietnamese regulars, fought with a burning desire, fueled by nationalism, to unite their country and rid it of foreign influence.[508]

John Loving

4. Third Indochina War
(1 May 1975-23 October 1991)

Like many others, I'm ashamed of how our government now treats the Montagnards left in Vietnam. Future insurgent movements that the United States may sponsor may look at how the U.S. government treated past insurgent movements.[509]

George E. Dooley

As the Saigon government of Nguyen Van Thieu teetered on defeat, the forces of the insurgent Khmer Rouge (KR) army under Pol Pot closed in on the capital of Cambodia, Phnom Penh. It fell on 17 April 1975 defeating the government of Lon Nol and ending the war in Cambodia. North Vietnam won its war with the south two short weeks later. The Communists seized power in Laos soon after that.

The Cambodia Conflict

Prince Norodom Sihanouk was Cambodia's Head of State (1960-1970) who attempted to steer a neutralist course for his country. Sihanouk was deposed by General Lon Nol who led the military coup of 1970 against him and became the self-proclaimed President of the U.S.-backed Khmer Republic, ruling until 1975. Lon Nol was opposed by revolutionaries called the Khmer Rouge led by Pol Pot. Grant Evans, the Australian anthropologist and historian summarized the rise to power of the Khmer Rouge.

> The Khmer Rouge came to power as a result of the social disintegration and political collapse that occurred when Sihanouk was overthrown and the country was abruptly propelled into the vortex of the Indochina War, rather than as a deep-seated movement of social protest and political change. By 1975 the CPK [Communist Party Kampuchea] had 14,000 members and an army of 58,000. Their ranks had grown enormously in a mere five years, but the Khmer Rouge had very few people through

which to rule a nation of 7 million people, especially civilian cadres. About 3 per cent of the Vietnamese population and 1 per cent of the Lao population are party members. Had the CPK recruited as successfully as the Vietnamese Communist Party, its membership would have been more than 200,000. Had it done as well as the Lao People's Revolutionary Party, it would still have had 70,000 members, rather than a mere 14,000. . . . .One Khmer Rouge recruit later described the situation as follows:

> Contacts between the upper levels and the lower levels were like contacts between heaven and earth. . . . A comrade only knew about himself and himself alone. There was no question of knowing anything about matters of the situation in which one found oneself. At the same time the party's 'security branch', working under the direction of the highest leaders, set about eliminating those regarded as untrustworthy. This was not a matter of open arrests of known opponents of the party 'centre'. Those who were suspected simply disappeared, before they had a chance to do any damage.[510]

Grant Evans

An uneasy peace settled in between the two Communist countries of Vietnam and Cambodia, but border incidents occurred.

The immediate catalyst of the Third Indochina War was not Hanoi's alleged expansionism, but the violent and provocative conduct of Pol Pot's regime. It is thus on the nature of the DK regime rather than on the alleged regional ambitions of Vietnam that we have to focus if we wish to understand the genesis of the Third Indochina War. In the chaos that followed the overthrow of Sihanouk, the Khmer Rouge rose from extreme isolation to state power in only five years. Its resort to terrorist methods of rule was a symptom of weakness and insecurity rather than a sign of strength. It resulted in a highly centralized military police state, headed by a family clique, which cultivated nationalist delirium in a desperate attempt to establish its legitimacy. As Anthony Barnett has pointed out, this is only one of a number of wars precipitated in the late 1970s and early 1980s by unstable dictatorships in an attempt to create internal unity, with similarly disastrous consequences, among them Somalia's invasion of Ethiopia,

Uganda's invasion of Tanzania, Iraq's invasion of Iran and Argentina's occupation of the Falklands.[511]

Grant Evans

The Cham

Journalist Elizabeth Becker described the plight of the Chams in Cambodia.

There were irregular but intensifying purges of hill people in the northeast, even in Ratanakiri, where the central committee had gone into hiding in the late sixties and Pol Pot discovered the natives' oppression.

The Khmer Rouge policy of eliminating ethnic differences and creating a new race had the greatest effect on the Muslim Chams. These exotic people were twice doomed, for their "foreign race" and their "reactionary" faith. For generations they had avoided being absorbed into the society of Buddhist Khmers.

The Cham had always lived apart in Cambodia. They are believed to be descendants of the people of Champa, which was overrun by the Vietnamese. They ran away from the invading Vietnamese army until they reached modern-day Cambodia. They built their own villages, centered around a mosque, and observed their own dietary laws, dressed and groomed according to their faith, and established professional specialties as fishermen and merchants of cloth.

There was a richness to Cham culture. The women coiffed their long, thick tresses in elaborate styles and covered their heads with long, bright scarves. The men wore skullcaps, and many grew beards. Their priests, or muftis, wore turbans. The Khmer, predictably, had an assortment of derogatory Cham stereotypes. Cham men who went about the countryside selling cloth to Khmer villagers and driving hard bargains were considered proficient liars and commercial thieves. The exotic look of Cham women inspired stories of their promiscuity. Their language and script were alien—Arabic—so Chams were believed to have a special way with magic, from telling fortunes to administering curses. And they were Muslims, a strident orthodox faith that believes in one God and is part of the Judeo-Christian tradition—in utter contrast to Buddhism. . . .The Chams had few avenues of escape from the Khmer Rouge and were too militant to accept the destruction of their culture and religion. In less than four years of Khmer Rouge rule as many as one-half of the Chams died. But they did fight back. It is remarkable that most reports of rebellion were among the ethnic minorities—the ethnic Thais in Koh Kong province, the Chams, even the Chinese who individually stood up and courted death by pleading for help in their own language to advisors from Beijing.

The majority of Cambodians, those who spoke the right language and were ethnically and culturally "proper" Khmers, also lost their culture, their families, their way of life during the revolution. But there were few reports of uprisings by them. Some escaped to Thailand or Vietnam, others committed suicide. Perhaps their centuries-long tradition of following absolute rulers prevented them from striking back at the Khmer Rouge.

They were not the only people in the twentieth century who became too dehumanized by tyranny to revolt. It happened in other countries of Asia, Europe, Africa, and Latin America, in countries with concentration camps, torture, and famine. People in these conditions do not react with "rage and violence, but their conspicuous absence is the clearest sign of dehumanization" that paralyzes a nation. The people of Cambodia increasingly acted like a nation of "deaf-mutes" as waves of terror swept across the country, just as was predicted in their prophecy of the end of the world.[512]

Elizabeth Becker

The Laos Sojourn

After 1975 Communist victories in Vietnam and Cambodia a key relationship developed between Laos and Vietnam.

The third country in Indochina convulsed by war between Communists and the more or less democratic governments backed by the United States was Laos. One of the key relationships that developed after the fall of dominoes in 1975 was that between Laos and Vietnam.

The cessation of American aid to Laos in mid-1975 effectively ended the Lao sojourn within the western sphere of influence, while the complete Pathet Lao takeover in December of that year registered Laos' decisive shift into the 'socialist camp'. It is common wisdom among most journalists and many academics writing about Indochina that from that point on Laos became a virtual Vietnamese 'colony'. Arthur J. Dommen, author of a major study on Laos before the Communist takeover, calls the country `a satellite of Vietnam' and the Vientiane government a 'puppet' of Hanoi.' Another specialist, Martin Stuart-Fox, has written of Laos: 'All major areas of decision-making from foreign policy to economic planning and military security are dependent on Vietnamese direction'. Indeed many have asserted that Laos was Vietnam's prototype for the formation of the 'Indochina Federation' — composed of Vietnam, Laos and Cambodia. No one has put this view more forcefully than Dommen:

> The stationing of Vietnamese troops in Laos today is obviously aimed at defending the independence, sovereignty, territorial integrity and cultural construction not of Laos, but of a Greater Vietnam, envisioned by Ho Chi Minh's successors and supported by the Soviet bloc. This Greater Vietnam will make Laos far more a part of Vietnam than the Indochinese Federation Ho envisioned when his preoccupation was with the expulsion of the French. . . .Vietnam has replaced France as the colonial power in Indochina.[513]

Grant Evans

The Hmong

One of the ethnic minorities effected by the alliance between Vietnam and Laos after 1975 was the Hmong. The Hmong people are an ethnic group that live mainly in Southern China, Vietnam and Laos. During the Second Indochina conflict the Hmong were loyal supporters of the U. S. effort to defeat the Communist Pathet Lao insurgents in Laos. Their efforts included rescuing downed American pilots and attempts to block the Ho Chi Minh Trail. Jane Hamilton-Merritt is a journalist who followed the plight of the Hmong for many years. She has testified in Congress concerning the plight of the Hmongs.

> After the defeat of the United States in Southeast Asia in 1975, the Communists came to power in South Vietnam, Cambodia, and Laos. The men in Hanoi took control, directly or indirectly, of Laos. While the Vietnam War was over for the Americans, the fighting continued for the indigenous people, as the new regimes

tried to eliminate opposition. The United States paid little attention to the plight of its former allies. Most Americans wanted to forget the conflict which had divided the nation. For many Americans, the only reminder of that war was the resettlement in the United States of tens of thousands of refugees from Laos, Cambodia, and Vietnam.

Soon after the Jimmy Carter administration came to power in 1977, it actively sought U.S. restoration of diplomatic recognition of Vietnam. Assistant Secretary of State Richard Holbrooke initiated talks with Vietnamese officials in March 1977. In June 1978, Vietnam joined Comecon, the East European economic community. On December 25, 1978, Vietnam invaded and occupied Pol Pot's Cambodia, installing a pro-Hanoi government and pushing the murderous Pol Pot regime into the countryside. In now unified Vietnam, repression against the large Chinese community created Chinese refugees, known as the "boat people," who had begun to flee Vietnam in late 1978. In February 1979, China invaded Vietnam, but the tough Vietnamese military mauled the Chinese forces. That same month, Carter's attention turned to Iran where anti-Shah forces threatened a revolution which endangered some 35,000 Americans who worked there. In the late summer of 1979, neither the White House nor most Americans were interested in Southeast Asia. Few knew anything about Laos, much less about the Hmong.[514]

Jane Hamilton-Merritt

1976–The Year of the Dragon

Vietnam. . . had no desire to drag those things out and rub salt in the American wounds.[515]

Hoang Tung

The end of U. S. involvement in Vietnam did not bring the demobilization of the Vietnamese armed forces. Instead they were funneled into reconstruction of a country devastated by years of war. As one writer put it.

> The Second Five Year Plan, which was principally a development plan, had discounted defence development. . . .Vietnam certainly expected a long period of peace after the liberation of Indochina in 1975, and it assumed that defence would no longer need the priority that it had during the previous three decades, and thus allow the unfettered pursuit of economic goals of reconstruction and development.[516]

Nayan Chanda was an Indochina correspondent for the *Far Eastern Economic Review*. He visited Indochina before the fall of Saigon and throughout the Third Indochina War.

Waiting for the Dollar Rain

> Not long after the spring of 1975, when American television had presented images of the frantic flight of refugees and American officials before the Communist advance on Saigon, Washington developed amnesia about Indochina. It froze $150 million of Vietnamese assets in the United States and slapped a trade embargo on Cambodia and Vietnam. After a short-lived flutter over the *Mayaguez* in May Indochina sank below the horizon of American consciousness.
>
> A few days after the Communist victory in Saigon I asked a soldier guarding the U.S. Embassy why there was not an NLF flag over the building, since they were raised over other "liberated" Western embassies. "We are not authorized to raise one," he replied. This was not simply a bureaucratic oversight. Hanoi was jubilant at having won the war, but it was more

concerned about winning the peace. In July 1975 in Hanoi I asked party daily *Nhan Dan* editor Hoang Tung when he was going to publish the "Saigon papers"—the enormous quantity of secret American documents seized in Saigon. Among the confidential documents were the computer tapes on the CIA operations in Vietnam that were left behind by the fleeing officials of its Vietnamese counterpart—the Central Intelligence Office (CIO) of South Vietnam. Tung was very firm in his response. Vietnam, he said, had no desire to drag those things out and rub salt in the American wounds.[517]

Nayan Chanda

1977–The Year of the Snake

Pol Pot tried to convince Souphanouvong that Laos should maintain independence vis-à-vis Vietnam. It was a dialogue of the deaf.[518]

Nayan Chanda

While Vietnam sought reproachment, normalization of relations and even aid from the United States, major problems continued to expand with its neighbor Cambodia. There had been border incursions by the Khmer Rouge into Vietnam before, but an attack in September 1977 was unparalleled in terms of brutality and the number of Vietnamese civilians murdered. Vietnam would respond.

The Tay Ninh Massacre

On the morning of September 26, Nam [Major Phuong Nam, a press official] was summoned by General. Tran Van Tra, the commander of the Seventh Military Region, which covers Ho Chi Minh City and several provinces to the west bordering Cambodia. The general, a legendary military hero in the South, who had personally commanded the assault on Saigon in April 1975, was beside himself with rage. Two nights before, Khmer Rouge attackers had struck inside Tay Ninh Province, killing hundreds of civilians. This was the second time that the Khmers had mounted murderous raids on a Saturday night, when the commanders were away from their posts, many spending time with their families in Ho Chi Minh City. . . .After months of planning, including Giap's personal assessment on the ground, the Vietnamese Army launched its first important, but unpublicized, military operation against Cambodia, in October 1977. After driving armored columns up to fifteen miles into the bordering Cambodian province of Svay Rieng, the Vietnamese feigned retreat. As a battalion of Khmer Rouge infantry entered Vietnamese territory in hot pursuit, another waiting Vietnamese column swung from the side and caught several hundred of them in a mousetrap. However, the losses suffered by the Khmer Rouge did not seem to stop them one bit.[519]

Nayan Chanda

While the burgeoning fight between Vietnam and Cambodia would be the proximate cause of alliance changes in Asia, the underlying cause was Cold War alliances. New alliances were forming in 1977. Moscow was supporting Vietnam against China and China was supporting Cambodia against Vietnam.

The Red Prince Tries for Peace[520]

On December 17 Prince Souphanouvong [President of Laos] arrived at Phnom Penh's Pochentong Airport to a solemn reception. His meeting with Pol Pot immediately made it clear that there was no chance of averting an open rupture. The Cambodians did not even want to publicize the fact that Pol Pot received the Lao president. During a tense meeting at the government guesthouse overlooking the Tonle Sap River, Souphanouvong urged Pol Pot not to disrupt the unity of the three Indochinese countries forged through years of struggle against common enemies. "But Pol Pot did not want to listen. To all that," a senior Lao official told me later, "and he just kept on saying all sorts of bad things about Vietnam." Pol Pot tried to convince Souphanouvong that Laos should maintain independence vis-à-vis Vietnam. It was a dialogue of the deaf.[521]

Nayan Chanda

The December Invasion

A sizable force of the Vietnamese infantry and artillery, including the elite Ninth Infantry Division, launched a massive attack on Cambodia from half a dozen points along the border, with two principal prongs heading toward the capital. Troops on T-54 tanks and M-113 armored personnel carriers spearheaded the drive along Route 1 and Route 7 leading toward Phnom Penh. The Vietnamese purpose was, as Hoang Tung later explained to me, "first to chase them [the Khmer Rouge] from our territory and then deal a heavy blow to their divisions, to make them realize that we are not passive as they have assumed and to tell them that they have to choose the other solution—negotiations. "

The first of the Vietnamese objectives was achieved almost

effortlessly. Vietnamese forces backed by artillery barrages had gone into Cambodia like a knife through soft butter. Hundreds of Khmer soldiers were killed and wounded in the Vietnamese search-and-destroy operation. The fortunate among the wounded were carried on stretchers to Phnom Penh. Although there were hospitals to shelter the injured, they had little else to comfort them. A campaign for donating blood was started among the small population of cadres and families who lived on the outskirts of the near-deserted capital. The sudden emergency brutally brought home the effects of the Khmer Rouge revolution. Hundreds of bourgeois doctors had been dispatched to the countryside for hard labor, and many had been executed. Hospitals were being run by paramedics—peasant boys turned "revolutionary doctors." Their attempts at blood transfusions wrought disaster. . . . Public revelation of the conflict would be accompanied by the announcement of suspension of diplomatic relations with Vietnam. Khmer Rouge cadres did not seem to mind the military setback as they gloated over the diplomatic coup. "We got 'em first. On hearing the news, the world is going to jump," was how Khmer Rouge cadres talked about their announcement. [522]

Nayan Chanda

1978–The Year of the Horse

Rust Bucket Tours Inc., might have been responsible for generating in two years close to a quarter million boat people, thirty to forty thousand of whom perished at sea.[523]

Nayan Chanda

While Vietnam continued to solicit aid from China and support for its actions against Cambodia, its cause was not helped by breaking news from Ho Chi Minh City in early 1978.

The Gold of Cholon

On 20 March 1978 Hanoi ordered a raid on Cholon in Ho Chi Minh City. Cholon was the business heart of Ho Chi Minh City and was largely a Chinese district home to thousands of merchants. Demonstrations followed the raid with Chinese crowds chanting and carrying a portrait of Mao Zedong. Inventories of goods were seized and it was said that thousands in hidden gold bars were hauled away. Inventoried goods were declared nationalized. This triggered a Chinese exodus from Vietnam.[524]

> In the summer of 1978 the Vietnamese Public Security Bureau set up offices in coastal towns in the South to build boats and dispatch the Chinese (or Vietnamese posing as Chinese) after collecting a hefty fee in gold and dollars.[30] The operation, dubbed by Western diplomats in Hanoi as "Rust Bucket Tours Inc.," might have been responsible for generating in two years close to a quarter million boat people, thirty to forty thousand of whom perished at sea.[525]
>
> *Nayan Chanda*

Eastern Zone Purge

While Vietnam was moving ahead with its purge of the Chinese, Cambodia was conducting its own purges of a decidedly more vicious nature.

Pol Pot explained his policies at his first 'press conference' (an interview with Yugoslav journalists) in 1978:

'We are building socialism without a model,' smiled the head of the Communist Party and Premier of Democratic Kampuchea, Pol Pot. 'We do not wish to copy anyone; we shall use the experience gained in the course of the liberation struggle. There are no schools, faculties or universities in the traditional sense, although they did exist in our country prior to liberation, because we wish to do away with all vestiges of the past. There is no money, no commerce, as the state takes care of provisioning all its citizens. We did not have money or commerce in the liberated territory either. The cities have been resettled, because this is the way things had to be. Some three million town dwellers and peasants were trying to find refuge in the cities from the depredations of war. We could not provide enough food for them, and there were imperialist plans to organize guerrilla movements and a counter-revolution in the populated cities. . . .We evacuated the cities; we resettled the inhabitants in the rural areas where the basic living conditions could be provided for this segment of the population of new Cambodia. The countryside should be the focus of attention for our revolution, and the people will decide the fate of the cities.'[526]

On June 25 Radio Phnom Penh startled the world by claiming that the regime had crushed a coup attempt fomented by Vietnam and the Central Intelligence Agency. While few believed claims of such an absurd partnership, simultaneous Vietnamese propaganda about uprisings in Cambodia confirmed that something very serious indeed was happening. It was not until two years after the event that details of killings and rebellion in the Eastern Zone emerged or that its full significance was understood. . . . Over sixty thousand Cham minority people—mostly in the Kompong Cham area—were massacred for their Islamic faith. Some of the most vicious killings of Vietnamese civilians were perpetrated by Eastern Zone units—of course with the Center's blessings. Nevertheless, the fact remains that, whether as a consequence of their dissent or because of Pol Pot's self-fulfilling paranoia about the Eastern Zone, this part of Cambodia produced the largest number of cadres who rose up against him or were crushed by the

Center before they could do anything.[527]

Nayan Chanda

A Time of Opportunity

The Soviet Union saw an opportunity to increase its influence in Asia while Vietnam and Cambodia were stepping up their purges and moving toward a confrontation. The United States also stepped into the fray.

> As the summer of 1978 drew to a close, both Vietnam and China secretly drew up their war plans. But before the guns boomed, it was a time for winning friends and isolating the enemy. One of the biggest prizes in the Hanoi-Peking race was the friendship and support of the very one they had so recently sought to expel from Asia entirely—Uncle Sam.[528]

Nayan Chanda

After extensive negotiations on 15 December 1978, the United States and The People's Republic of China (PRC) announced that the U. S. had transferred official diplomatic recognition from the Republic of China (ROC) to the PRC. Beijing acknowledged that the U. S. would continue to maintain commercial, cultural, and other unofficial ties with Taiwan, but it was recognized that there was one China and that was the PRC with the ROC a part of it. The impact of this was that China became a part of the U. S. anti-Soviet strategy with the U. S. siding with China in its disputes with Vietnam. The U. S. was now concerned with the Soviet strategy to encircle China through Moscow's ties with Vietnam.[529]

After normalizing relations with the U. S. China's Deng Xiaoping visited President Jimmy Carter and discussed a wide range of issues including Vietnam. Jimmy Carter recalled.

> As for other troubled areas, I spoke briefly of what we were doing in Iran, and told him we wanted a stable, peaceful government there, formed in accordance with the Iranian

constitution. I said we believed the best way to treat Vietnam as an aggressor was to isolate it from the rest of the world; for the first time the developing countries in the United Nations had recently condemned Vietnam along with the Soviet Union and Cuba. I tried to encourage the Chinese to use their influence in North Korea to help arrange direct talks between the government authorities of North and South Korea. I was not sure I was making much progress on that point, but at least Deng understood my position.

We agreed that it would be a serious mistake for us to unite against the Soviet Union, a move that would only further isolate the Soviets. I commented that it was best to have a policy of cooperation with them when they were constructive, and competition with them when they were not. Our preference was to avoid war permanently, not just to postpone it for twenty-two years!

Deng then responded to my request that he use China's influence with North Korea to keep the peace. He said that many people had raised the question of Korea with him; there was absolutely no danger of a North Korean attack. It was not yet possible for the People's Republic of China and South Korea to have trade relations or direct communication, but he hoped South Korea would accept North Korea's proposals for talks and elections leading to a merger. The Soviet Union's relationship with North Korea had never been very strong, he said. It had waned considerably in recent years because the Soviets had tried to influence the government's policies—and if China tried to pressure North Korea, it too would lose its influence.

It was almost time to prepare for the evening banquet, but Deng requested that we leave our large group of advisers so that he could discuss a more confidential matter with me. Fritz, Cy, Zbig, and I went with Deng and the interpreters from the Cabinet Room into the Oval Office, and listened carefully as the Chinese leader outlined his tentative plans for China to make a punitive strike across its border into Vietnam. When he asked for my advice, I tried to discourage him, pointing out that the Vietnamese were increasingly isolated in the world community and were being condemned because they were aggressors, having crossed the border into Kampuchea. It might arouse sympathy for them and cause some nations to brand China as a culprit if Chinese forces moved toward Hanoi. Furthermore, I said, his potential military move would help to refute one of our best arguments for the new Sino-American relationship: that it would contribute toward more peace and stability in Asia. The Vice Premier thanked me for my comments, and added that it was highly desirable for China that its arrogant neighbors know they could not disturb it and other countries in the area with impunity.[530]

Jimmy Carter

Laos – The Killing Continues

A seldom publicized war continued while alliances were forming among the Soviet Union, Vietnam, China, Cambodia, and the United States. While diplomats conversed and invasions were threatened among these principals, the killing continued in Laos. Jane Hamilton-Merritt recorded the accounts of Hmong survivors who escaped the Laotian government's attempts at genocide.

> Their increasingly successful attacks against Hmong villages and enclaves and the relentless search for former Vang Pao [Hmong leader] soldiers whipped the Communists into a frenzy for a "final solution." As the enemy net tightened in the interior mountains, more and more Hmong families, defenseless against the superior Communist forces and their poisons from the sky, sought sanctuary on Phou Bia, the highest mountain in Laos.
>
> During the American time, the skies around Phou Bia had been active with planes flying between the various Lima Sites [USAF navigational radar sites] around it. This mountain massif, reaching almost 10,000 feet, crested into clouds and fog south of the Plaine des Jarres [PDJ]. Only rarely were its top peaks free of these shrouds. Hmong had never lived high on Phou Bia because it was too cold and there was no water. They considered it inhospitable and generally avoided it, though some inhabited its lower reaches. Although they did not know this mountain well, they reasoned that the Vietnamese would not follow and they would be safe. . . .
>
> On November 22, 1978, enemy forces attacked Lo Cheng's area. In the heavy fighting, his family and others ran to hide in the jungle. There, many women and children were captured and taken away. Outnumbered and outgunned, Lo Cheng and several unit leaders fled, heading for Phou Bia and Chao Fa leader Yong Joua. By now, tens of thousands of Hmong were in hiding on the slopes

of Phou Bia. On the run for years, they had long ago exhausted food supplies. Now, they were eating leaves, bugs, lizards, mice, buds, and bark and desperately digging holes, hoping groundwater would seep in.

Vang Kai and his family came to the Phou Bia area to escape the wrath of the enemy. One of only about 500 men in his area who had a weapon, he carried an M-16, with the last of his ammunition strapped to his body. His group's meager arsenal consisted of several M-79 mortars, a few M-16s, and old carbines. Some men had only crossbows and clubs with which to protect their families. The Hmong were virtually defenseless against the well-supplied Vietnamese artillery, air force, ground troops, and poisons.

During the first week of December, Hmong scouts reported between 6,000 and 7,000 enemy in the area. With the enemy so close, fires for cooking grass or a snared bird or for warming the weary and cold during the near-freezing nights were forbidden. Such life-giving fires only betrayed. Weak and ill from lack of food and medicine, dirty and in tatters, these frightened people, exhausted from years of unrelenting pursuit by the enemy, dug holes and constructed branch and leaf lean-tos to hide-from the Goliathan forces.

In early December 1978, Communist artillery-85s, 105s, 155s, and 130s—slammed into the jungle, ripping up trees, knocking down jungle protection, exposing Hmong to Vietnamese and Lao gunners and to the sky. Enemy pilots, flying abandoned U.S. spotter planes, attacked with conventional weapons and with poison bombs, darts, and nails. In the ceaseless barrage, Hmong dug deeper for protection. Vang Kai, his, brother, and their families shared the same hole. "We were trapped like animals. We dared to come out of the holes only at night to search for leaves and wild plants to feed the children. If we went out in the daylight, the Vietnamese soldiers killed us. If we had a fire, they would see it and kill us. There was no water, no food, no fires."

Day after day, night after night the enemy with its massive artillery and air power bombed, strafed, and pounded the slopes of Phou Bia. Vang Kai knew they were doomed. "There was no way off Phou Bia. There was no way we could survive the Communist bombardment. The forest around us was broken and burned. No food. No water. Children dying from starvation. Dead bodies everywhere. Holes with dead Hmong and live Hmong. Still we fought back. There was no choice; we had no place to run."

Two days before Christmas and two days before Vietnam's invasion of Cambodia, the final push came. Vang Kai thought death was near. "December 23, 1978, the attack was so intense that every Hmong knew he would die this day if he did not get away from the attack. Men, women, and children crawled from their holes, trying to run away, to hide somewhere, anywhere, from the fighting. The Vietnamese soldiers chased them. Hmong fought back in hand-to-hand combat with knives, crossbows, and clubs.". . . .A Hmong who had fought with the French at Dien Bien Phu and later with the Americans took the 60 survivors to a cave near Muang Om at the base of Phou Bia. "We lived on three ears of corn a day and water that trickled through the walls of the cave. After five months, there was nothing to eat. At night, I went outside to dig the roots with my hoe, but roots give little life. Anyone who was pregnant must lose the baby. Little children cannot have life for mothers have no milk. . . .Even though they were emaciated and weak, they walked six nights and three days to reach the banks of the Mekong. When they arrived, he looked at those around him. "Of the 60 people I took with me to the cave, only 17 still had life."[531]

Jane Hamilton-Merritt

1979–The Year of the Goat

No one could know better than the people of Nanning how many thousands of coffins had returned from Vietnam.[532]

Nayan Chanda

Land of Liquid Bodies

Vietnam moved quickly to cross the Cambodian border in its invasion of the country. Pol Pot's regime was easily toppled and Phnom Penh was occupied on 7 January 1979. Hanoi established the People's Republic of Kampuchea (PRK) to rule Cambodia.

After the Vietnamese toppled Pol Pot's regime in 1979, outsiders had access to abundant evidence of the appalling brutalities that had taken place under his rule. A Polish journalist who visited Prey Veng in February 1979 described the discovery of thousands of putrefying corpses left behind by the fleeing Khmer Rouge. Survivors of the massacre told him that 22,000 people had been killed in the town market and their bodies thrown into the town sewers; the slaughter was brought to a halt only by the Vietnamese invasion. 'Have you heard of liquid bodies?' he later asked a journalist in Bangkok. 'What we saw were the remains, which were just liquefied flesh with millions of maggots and worms.' Western journalists were soon allowed in, and confirmed this picture. The Cambodia Pol Pot left behind was described in March by AAP reporter Harish Charandola as 'a land of skulls, gore and stench'. Taken to Prey Veng, he found the stink 'unbearable'. It was not just that the town sewers were choked with rotting corpses; in the surrounding countryside, 'shallow, unmarked graves are everywhere. Bones are everywhere just below the surface.'[533]

Grant Evans

The Thai Domino

Thailand was the non-Communist domino that did not fall.

The Thai government had played a central role in the USA's struggle to 'contain' Communism in Asia — when SEATO was formed in 1954, its headquarters had been established in Bangkok. After the fall of Indochina to Communism, and the visible retreat of American military power in the region, many of Thailand's political and military leaders believed that they faced a serious danger of invasion from Vietnam, and that support from Laos and Cambodia for the Communist-led insurgents operating in the north and northeast of Thailand would make it almost impossible for the government to defeat the insurgents. The smiles from Hanoi after 1975 were welcome, but the fear and the mistrust remained. The fall of Pol Pot's regime to Vietnamese troops in 1979 only intensified these feelings. The belief that Thailand would be the next 'domino' to fall was shared by many on the Left as well.*534*

Grant Evans

The Chinese Invasion

On 17 February 1979 the Chinese People's Liberation Army (PLA) crossed the Sino-Vietnamese border. Vietnam's alliance with the Soviet Union and mistreatment of Vietnam's Chinese minority were the major reasons. The PLA was able to seize a border town, Lang Son, the gateway to the Red River Delta. Within hours Peking announced that its objectives had been achieved and withdrawal from Vietnam started on 5 March 1979. This Chinese excursion cost Peking thousands of lives "No one could know better than the people of Nanning [in China] how many thousands of coffins had returned from Vietnam."[535]

1980–The Year of the Monkey

The Vietnamese soldiers built their own barracks, grew vegetables for themselves, and concentrated on their garrison duties, interfering as little as possible in the activities of the Khmer population.[536]

Grant Evans

A Casual Army of Occupation

Vietnam's occupation of Cambodia after its invasion continued for years.

By 1980 the number of Vietnamese troops in Cambodia had risen to 200,000 but Cambodia did not look like a country under military occupation. It was common enough to see individual soldiers or small groups of them wandering around unarmed, sitting by the side of the road chatting with Khmer peasants, or bargaining in town markets like anybody else. Nobody seemed to take any particular notice of them. The Vietnamese soldiers built their own barracks, grew vegetables for themselves, and concentrated on their garrison duties, interfering as little as possible in the activities of the Khmer population.

The Vietnamese concentrated their own efforts on the military objective of securing the country against Pol Pot's forces. Behind the shield they provided, their Cambodian allies set about creating a new government structure. The PRK administration was built up slowly, from the top down and from the centre outwards, which means that at the village level there was a period of anarchy between the overthrow of the Khmer Rouge and the establishment of local authorities integrated with the central government. In the eastern and central regions this phase lasted for only a few weeks, but in the west of the country it was not until May or June 1979 that the new administration was able to consolidate its control, and it remained fragile for some time after that.

The resources with which the PRK was built up were pitifully few. Pol Pot's terror had decimated the ranks of Cambodia's initially small class of educated and professionally skilled people, and many of those that survived took advantage of the chaos that followed the Vietnamese invasion to flee the country. But it was not just a shortage of suitable people — almost everything was lacking. Even in February 1980, when there was a clearly functioning administration, it had to do without almost all the usual paraphernalia of modern bureaucracy. There were pens and paper, but they were not easy to come by. There were no telephones, and hardly any typewriters.[537]

Grant Evans

Oscar Salemink, Professor of Anthropology at the University of Copenhagen summarized the situation in Cambodia.

The Khmer Rouge, holding Democratic Kampuchea [DK] in an iron grip, wished to restore its control over the Mekong Delta and portions of the Central Highlands. Historically, some of these areas had once belonged to the Khmer Empire. After numerous cruel Khmer Rouge attacks on towns and villages on Vietnamese soil, Vietnam's People's Army struck back in late 1978, and effectively occupied most of Cambodia by early 1979 while installing a `friendly' regime in Phnom Penh. China, as Cambodia's main ally and Vietnam's erstwhile benefactor, decided (in the words of Deng Xiaoping) 'to teach Vietnam a lesson' — a lesson that proved costly to both sides. . . .From 1979 the genocidal Khmer Rouge along with two other Khmer resistance groups were kept afloat with massive foreign aid from China, Thailand and Western countries, until the Vietnamese military withdrawal from Cambodia in 1989.

Other actors in the conflict included Thailand, the US and other nations, but also a number of smaller guerrilla groups operating in various countries. One guerrilla group that was active in Vietnam's Central Highlands after 1975 was the *Front Une de la Lutte des Races Opprimies,* or FULRO. . . .After the Communist takeover, FULRO ranks soon swelled because of Montagnard dissatisfaction over the issues of autonomy, sedentarization, New Economic Zones and re-education. Around 1980, FULRO forces counted some 7000 guerrillas, and a full-scale war was being fought out in the Highlands, which included aerial bombardments. From 1982 on, the Communist regime adopted a more conciliatory position, which bore fruit on the battlefield. That year, one group of around 200 FULRO warriors made it through Cambodia to the Thai border, where they were held prisoner in a Khmer Rouge guerrilla camp. Since 1975 FULRO had received support from the Khmer Rouge, just as it had received support from the successive Cambodian regimes before 1975. What they did not know was that in April 1975 when entering Pnomh Penh the Khmer Rouge had summarily executed FULRO's leadership, including Y Bham Enuol. In 1986, the FULRO prisoners managed to escape to Bangkok, and were admitted as refugees to the US. In August 1992, the last remnants of FULRO surrendered to the forces of the UN Transitional Authority in Cambodia, to be shipped to the US.[538]

Oscar Salemink

Third Indochina War: Final Years

Fate of the Montagnards

As the Republic of South Vietnam crumbled, on April 4, 1975, there was an emergency meeting at the Ministry for the Development of Ethnic Minorities (MDEM) between Minister Nay Luett, his senior staff and US Deputy Ambassador George Jacobson, Ed Sprague, and Mack Prosser. Jacobson promised Minister Nay Luett that if the Communists attacked Saigon, he and his entire staff and their families would be evacuated; they never were. Jacobson also told Minister Nay Luett that FULRO and other Montagnards should flee to the jungle and set up a resistance and continue a guerrilla action against the Vietnamese Communists and if not outright promised at that time, it was heavily implied that the U.S. would provide support to them; that too never happened.

After the communist takeover of South Vietnam in 1975, thousands of Montagnards were slaughtered by the communist regime while they fled their villages in the Central Highlands to the jungles of Cambodia; some survived this ordeal. Later others escaped from the concentration-reeducation camps to join them in Cambodia; among them were a few FULRO members who managed to survive the onslaught. Relentless pursuit by Communist forces, betrayal, inadequate supply of guns and ammunition and a paucity of medicines and food, thousands of Montagnards, men, women and children were either hunted down by the NVA and killed, or died from malnutrition and other diseases. Not knowing the fate of their leader Y-Bham, FULRO reemerged as a military force to fight a guerrilla war against the Communist Vietnamese for the next several years.

According to the Director of the Documentation Center of Cambodia when the Khmer Rouge took over Phnom Penh on April 17, 1975, they ordered a city-wide evacuation, hundreds of people fled to the French Embassy for refuge. Upon pressure from the Khmer Rouge under the direction of Comrade Nhem, the French Embassy expelled an estimated 150-300 Montagnards (of mostly Rhade and Jarai ethnicity), men, women, and children who had fled the Communist takeover of the Central Highlands of Vietnam. Among them was Y-Bham Enoul, the President of FULRO, who had been put under house arrest by a Captain Souleman on orders of his superior Col. Les Kosem after Y-Bham's exclusion of the Chams when changing FULRO to the FLHPM. Also at the French Embassy were others in the FULRO leadership, along with a number of FULRO "young Turks" (some had joined the Cambodian army) many were accompanied by their families. Reportedly, they were all trucked to the National Soccer Stadium and summarily executed during the Khmer Rouge's murderous rampage. Col. Les Kosem somehow escaped the carnage, fled to Malaysia and died years later.[539]

Michael D. Benge

In 1977 the Khmer Rouge (KR) executed an incredibly effective ruse that resulted in the capture and servitude of thousands of Montagnards.

In two Russian Hind helicopters left over from the Lon Nol Government, a KR delegation in USSF uniforms flew into Duc Co, Vietnam on the border. They told the Montagnards that USSF teams were in Cambodia and the Montagnard president, Y-Bham Enuol in Phnom Penh, had summoned them for training and supplies. For two years the Montagnards had been waiting on the promised US support. Their combat losses against the NVA were devastating and ammunition was extremely low. Many of their people had been slaughtered by the NVA and many more were in prisons and "reeducation." At risk of the same fate, they fell for the KR trick.

One KR helicopter sortie after another flew the Montagnard fighters from Duc Co, Vietnam deep into Cambodia. As they off-loaded and the two aircraft took off for another sortie, the Montagnards found themselves surrounded and compelled to give up their weapons. Unaware of the ruse, their fighters in Duc Co continued boarding the choppers and soon all were captives in KR territory. Their families escorted by the KR, began the long journey overland "to join their men."

Under threat of having their families killed, the Montagnard fighters were forced to serve in various KR units as pointmen and porters. Segregated from their men, the women were used as many are in war and their old people were forced to "clear" minefields and booby traps. As noise makers and extra mouths to feed, their infants and babies were killed. Tragically the ruse persisted via rumor, causing countless more Montagnards to follow their trails into the Killing Fields of Cambodia. Some reports have the eventual total at 40,000 people.[540]

But the story of FULRO and the Montagnards in the United States isn't finished. With the "normalization" of relations established by the Clinton administration, the Communist Vietnamese remain paranoid about the intentions of the US. Montagnards. They have even gone so far as to send at least two agents to the United States to find out what the Montagnard community is up to. The two agents were quickly caught and turned over to the FBI, and the agents confessed.

Perhaps it's the policy of the Clinton administration not to make waves with the Vietnamese (after all, Asian funds helped to reelect Clinton), or maybe there are other reasons. Nevertheless, the agents have not been prosecuted and have been allowed to remain in the United States. Another more troubling aspect is the administration's dismantling of the Orderly Departure Program [ODP].

After 1975, hordes of refugees (mostly Vietnamese) began to flee Vietnam to escape the Communists. Many fled by foot across Cambodia to Thailand, others went by boat to Thailand and to Hong Kong. Most of the people were refugees who had affiliations with the United States during the war and were being discriminated against by or had good reason to fear the Communist conquerors. Those who fled overland were met by Pol Pot's people in Cambodia and many were killed or starved during the trek. The ones who went by boat were often attacked by Thai pirates that preyed on the exodus from Vietnam. Embarrassed by the slaughter still going on, Congress passed the ODP.

The ODP was designed to identify Vietnamese (and ethnic minorities) who had assisted the United States during the Vietnam War and faced discrimination by the Communists. To keep their departure "orderly" and safe, an ODP office was established at the

American embassy in Bangkok, Thailand. Since there was no U.S. recognition of the Communist regime in Vietnam, international voluntary agencies (also known as nongovernmental agencies, NGOs) screened the applications and made recommendations to the State Department and the Immigration and Naturalization Service.

Individuals who should be granted political asylum in the United States were to be identified and given visas to enter. It all sounds wonderful, doesn't it? But the reality has not been.

First, the Vietnamese were not about to let Montagnards leave Vietnam. Their goal since 1975 has been to kill off the Montagnards or to force their assimilation.

Second, the venal Vietnamese Communists recognized an opportunity to make money with the ODP: They began selling exit permits and even false certificates of incarceration (required sometimes by ODP as proof of having undergone reeducation) to people having the money and wanting to leave. Unfortunately, that didn't apply to Montagnards as they are mostly poor and have no money.

Many Montagnards who had been approved by the U.S. government for entry into the United States have not been able to buy exit permits. The ODP has ended, and they are still in Vietnam. Less than a thousand Montagnards have made it to the United States.

For Montagnards without money, the Communist officials offered them a deal: leave your spouse and family in Vietnam and take a Vietnamese spouse and children on your passport to the United States. Then when the "family" arrives, the "spouse" says I don't know this person and want to be resettled on my own. So the United States had to accept the situation and then allow the spouse to move her/his real family to this country.

But the problem is not just one with the Communist Vietnamese. Fundamental U.S. government official policy is to deny the Montagnards exist as former allies.

For those Montagnards with FULRO connections, the State Department now says that FULRO is an insurrectionary organization, and no legitimate government has the right to deal with revolutionaries. By the same reasoning, the American colonists' revolt against the British was illegitimate, and their alliance with France was therefore illegal.

Even though Amnesty International still lists the Montagnards as an oppressed people, the State Department has taken the side of the

Communists. Why then was it official policy to help the Montagnards in the 1960s and 1970s?

To many former SF people, the United States has simply abandoned its friends, and that is shameful.

I was one of the first who reported the false "family" and "spouse" trick, but still have been unable to get some Montagnard friends out. Even after extensive letter-writing campaigns to Illinois and Wisconsin senators, the State Department refused to act. One Jarai friend of mind was designated an applicant of "special concern." He has been refused even an interview.

I can understand the antiwar movement crowd now in the White House does not like me or my kind. After all, we went and did what they didn't have the guts to do. But is Vietnam still so personally embarrassing that we have to compromise our integrity and leave our friends behind? I guess it is. No wonder some allies of the United States consider us not very dependable.

Like many others, I'm ashamed of how our government now treats the Montagnards left in Vietnam. Future insurgent movements that the United States may sponsor may look at how the U.S. government treated past insurgent movements. Is there any wonder that the Kurds of Iraq haven't sided with the United States? The United States has abandoned the Montagnards; the Kurds know that they'll be abandoned, too. There's no reason for me to be proud of being an American.[541]

George E. Dooley

"We must know how to use our military units correctly, so as to send them in large numbers to open land and create new economic zones. These units must consist of many soldiers and fighters who are unshakeable and enthusiastic in their revolutionary spirit and desire to succeed so as to move mountains and dig rivers that will transform these empty regions and deserts into land covered with fertile fields supporting a thriving population."[542]

Prime Minister Pham Van Dong, DRV, 1977

The "empty regions and deserts" which Pham Van Dong referred to in this 1977 address were the highlands of modern Vietnam. Rising from the Gulf of Tonkin in the northeast, this collection of cragged hills and deep valleys stretches westward, looping around the Red River lowlands as it drops southward down the central coastline before finally vanishing into the Mekong delta. This massif makes up almost half of Vietnam territorially today. It teems with rivers, forests, animals, and some of Vietnam's most important natural resources (zinc, ore, bauxite, and silver) and plantation crops (rubber, coffee, and tea). It also offers protection. During the First Indochina War, the northern highlands were home to the Democratic Republic of Vietnam and the site of its historic battle victory over the French in 1954. A few years later, the DRV pushed its supply lines further southward through the central highlands to feed and arm forces fighting the Americans. Without the highlands, there would have been no victory at Dien Bien Phu and no operational Ho Chi Minh Trail. Speaking in 1977, as Vietnamese Communists prepared to go to war again over Indochina, Pham Van Dong had good reason to dispatch soldiers into these areas. He erred, however, when he spoke of the highlands as empty places. They were not and the prime minister knew it. He had served there during the 1940s.[543]

Christopher Goscha

Montagnard Use of Elephants (Olen C. Phipps, Jr.).

A large number of FULRO followers, now calling themselves Dega-FULRO, most of them Rhadé, went into the forests to organize resistance to Communist rule. When large Communist forces moved against them, the Dega-FULRO insurgents' only support came from the Khmer Rouge. According to Y Yok Ayun, in 1984 some 307 Dega-FULRO insurgents, discouraged by lack of outside support, elected to move across Cambodia to reach

Thailand a year later. Two Rhadé in the group had since their youth participated in elephant hunts in Cambodia so they knew the trails. Foraging, fishing, and hunting sustained them, and in lean times they ate elephant meat, normally not in the Rhadé diet. Adjusting to the different environment, they ate leaves that ants were eating and in water containing a bullet cartridge they put leaves, which were thrown away if they turned dark. After a period in a Thailand refugee camp, 200 of these refugees, of whom 126 were Rhadé, were sent in November 1986 to North Carolina.[544]

Gerald Hickey

1982 CIA Meeting in Bangkok

[The essence of this meeting was provided by the USG employee who served as interpreter and coincides with that of the Montagnard leaders who were present.]

In the late seventies The Forgotten Army leadership with their families crossed Cambodia for Thailand in five successive groups of fifty people each. Their mission was to find Americans and supplies for their beleaguered Forgotten Army. Over the course of a year as each group reached the Thai border, Thai police denied their entry and interned them in Refugee Camp #8.

Each time they tried to infiltrate two or three men into Thailand to reach the US embassy in Bangkok, Thai police jailed them as illegal immigrants. Finally in 1982 a meeting was arranged with CIA representatives and the Montagnard leaders made their plea for weapons and supplies, pleas that were rejected. Instead, the CIA in concert with the Thai military, expelled them from Thailand into the hands of the KR.

From 1982 until 1985 they languished near Dangrek, Cambodia, trapped between the Thai military on the border and the surrounding KR stronghold. They did not fight for the KR. In the confusion of a 1985 NVA attack, they escaped into Thailand. Later discovered by the Thai military, this time they were interned in Refugee Camp #2. But word of their arrival reached American advocates and soon they were granted political asylum. The 212 were flown to the Philippines for six months of preparation prior to resettlement in North Carolina in November, 1986.

By 1992 only 400 of their fighters, by now mostly second-generation guerrillas, remained alive at their field headquarters in eastern Cambodia. Ammunition exhausted and starving, they were found by UN forces, granted US asylum and resettled in North Carolina. Since 1992 the US Montagnard community has grown from the 612 of The Forgotten Army to 3,000 through the US Orderly Departure Program (ODP).

The majority of The Forgotten Army troops suffer from battle wounds that never healed properly, intestinal parasites, and other maladies from their years in the jungle. The cancer rate for all 3,000 US Montagnards is very high, mostly the Agent Orange variety and those associated with the Yellow Rain the Communists dumped on them after 1975.

No other allies in US history sacrificed so much, for so long. They fought valiantly under conditions and against odds, that few, if any US servicemen have ever endured.[545]

Michael D. Benge

H'Yoanh Buonya's Journey

H'Yoanh Buonya was a Montagnard teenage girl residing near Cheo Reo when the NVA arrived. She recalled events after the Communist take-over in 1975.

> In early spring of 1975, the North Vietnamese soldiers came to the houses and gardens, and they talked to the older villagers. "Where are your young people? We know that you have some here. Tell them not to hide, not to be scared. The new government needs them. Come to our meetings! Everyone in the village must come to our meetings every afternoon and learn how our new government is going to help them. We expect to see the young ones here, along with their parents." . . . And so with great hesitation, we did as they told us. The village started filling up again, and the young people down by the river and in the fields came out to hear about the good news and the good government. Hammering could be heard throughout the villages as houses were repaired after so much neglect, and dogs again barked in the streets.[546]

H'Yoanh Buonya

It wasn't long before repression by the North Vietnamese caused Montagnards to leave their villages. H'Yoanh Buonya continued her narrative.

After 1975, countless numbers of Montagnards fled deep into the jungles of Cambodia to continue their fight against the Vietnamese. They were joined by those escaping from the concentration camps and a continuous stream of villagers in small bands fleeing the severe repression in Vietnam. Montagnards by the thousands died of starvation, disease, or were killed by the Vietnamese. Some of the Montagnards chose to cross Cambodia to the Thai border for survival, essentially one of the three known depleted battalions of FULRO, with a few women and children. This meant walking through unfamiliar jungles and crossing the Mekong River on homemade rafts. The Montagnards had to negotiate permission to pass through the territory of each independent band of the Khmer Rouge. They were under constant threat of being pressed into service by the Khmer Rouge, and many were. The men were used as porters or point men, and others were used to clear mine fields and booby traps. In 1986, 212 survivors at a refugee camp on the Thai border were evacuated to the Philippines, where they were provided several months of preparation for their arrival in Greensboro, North Carolina, in November of that year. A second group of 400 Montagnards, deemed by the press as the "Lost Battalion," were found by the United Nations in 1992 in Cambodia along the Vietnamese border and were soon flown to the United States to join the first group. A third battalion of Montagnards and their dependents attempted to cross Laos for the safety of Thailand but were met by a large Vietnamese army unit and annihilated.

The Vietnam War extracted its toll, and one of the most tragic and little-known consequences was the decimation and destruction it brought to the Highland People. By War's end in 1975, around 85 percent of their villages were either in ruins or abandoned. Of the estimated one million highlanders, between 200,000 and 220,000 had died or were killed.[547]

H'Yoanh Buonya

H'Yoanh Buonya with thousands of others fled Vietnam and made their way through Cambodia to reach Thailand where they hoped to be evacuated to the United States. They spent years travelling and in camps before finally reaching Thailand.

After we had been settled at Section 6-E, Lot Dega, Site II South for six months, a group meeting was called one evening. "We will be leaving Site II very soon," our leaders said. It was a surprise to most of us, but there had been rumors. The appointment for our group interviews was at the office of Emigration and Naturalization Service on April 7, 1986.

The night before, I felt joy mixed with nervousness and insecurity, and I slept little, but the next morning, we were all prepared and ready to be on time for the interviews. Most of us had happy faces and spoke in low anxious voices: "What will the questions be? Will all of us stay together?"

The officials greeted us at the office with smiles and handshakes and called us for interviews by families. They had officers who spoke Thai, Cambodian, Vietnamese, and English, but Anup Siu acted as our interpreter. We did not need to worry about questions, as they were general—about our ages, our nationality, where we had been in the last few years, and if we were willing to go to a different country. They took our photographs, and after our papers were completed, they informed us that the United States of America would accept us and that we would be moving to a place called Panot Nikham where we would receive medical examinations and applications for visas. They did not know how long that would take.

I looked at Y-Ji and smiled, but I could feel apprehension between us as well as excitement. We just did not know what it all meant. We had fought so hard, waited so long, and here it was right in front of us.

A few days later, we said good-bye to our Site II South friends. Through our happiness, I could see the sadness of some who still had no place to go. I tried to be encouraging, saying that they would probably be called next for an interview. I prayed that it was the truth.

The bus ride to Panot Nikham was not as long as the last one, and the camp was not as large. It was a place for processing emigrants who were leaving the country. Two-story houses, made of concrete floors and tin roofs, replaced the leaf houses of Site II South. Groups were not kept together, and families were assigned to houses with others who had already been processed. The officers just pointed to a house and said, "You go there!"

We walked in to find that we shared the limited space with three other families—Chinese, Thai, and Cambodian—and were relieved to hear that everyone spoke enough Vietnamese to communicate.

There was a water pump from a well near our house, but the lines were usually very long. Sometimes I compared the comfort of the leaf-covered forest floor with the ungiving concrete floor. I imagined that when we got to America, the floors would be softer.[548]

H'Yoanh Buonya

Today, H'Yoanh Buonya resides in North Carolina with her family. With the help of her friend, Harriet Hill, she recorded her experiences and her book was published in 2013.[549]

As their guerrilla war continued and U.S. support never materialized, FULRO in the jungles of Cambodia was down to three depleted battalions of freedom fighters. One battalion tried to make it across Laos to Thailand -- never to be heard from again -- evidently annihilated by the North Vietnamese Army who maintained a large base there and occupied the South Eastern part of Laos. A second battalion negotiated a right-of-passage with the Khmer Rouge through the northern part of Cambodia only to be held captive in the Western part of Cambodia and used to fight the Vietnamese invaders. During one big battle, the Khmer Rouge faded into the jungle leaving the Montagnards to fight alone.

When the Vietnamese retreated, the Montagnards fled with their families across the border to a refugee camp in Thailand. On November 24, 1986, 212 Montagnard FULRO resistance fighters and dependents arrived in North Carolina for resettlement. The third, dubbed by the press as "The Lost Battalion," comprised of 400 men women and children, was discovered by news reporter Nate Thayer, in the jungle in Northeastern Cambodia in 1992, and was flown to the US to rejoin the other group of survivors. After arriving in the U. S., the Montagnard freedom fighters, in a decision marked by language similar to that of Nez Perce Chief Joseph vowed that "FULRO would fight no more," and it was disbanded.[550]

Michael D. Benge

The Paris Peace Agreements of 1991, formally titled Comprehensive Cambodian Peace Agreements were signed on October 23, 1991, and marked the official end of the Cambodian–Vietnamese War. A peace keeping mission was established under which the UN took over as the government of a state.

Since 1975 the Vietnamese government has resettled over one million lowland Vietnamese in the highlands in order to bring Vietnamese culture and lowland adaptations to the highlanders. Highlanders are being moved into Vietnamese settlements to enable their "transition to socialism," a process of Vietnamization that threatens what remains of their shattered world.[551]

Gerald Hickey

Biographical Sketches

Events in the lives of individuals in this history are provided, below.

Creighton Williams Abrams, Jr., was born in Springfield, Massachusetts, on 15 September 1914. Abrams graduated from the U.S. Military Academy with the class of 1936. He was commissioned in the armor branch and served during World War II. He was an aggressive and successful armored commander, receiving two Distinguished Service Crosses for bravery. He served in the Korean War and was promoted to general in 1964. He was assigned as General Westmoreland's deputy in Vietnam and succeeded him on 10 June 1968. Abrams stressed pacification rather than Westmoreland's policy of search and destroy. Abrams returned to the U.S. and was appointed U.S. Army Chief of Staff in June 1972. He died of cancer in September 1974. He was the only Army Chief of Staff to die in office.

Dean Gooderham Acheson was born on 11 April 1893 in Middletown, Connecticut. He attended Yale and served in the National Guard during World War I. He served in the State Department during World War II. He was appointed secretary of state on 21 January 1949. He served four years in this position. He was accused of responsibility for the loss of China after Mao defeated the Nationalists in 1949. Acheson returned to private life in 1953 and died of a stroke in Sandy Spring, Maryland, on 12 October 1971.

Bao Dai was the last emperor of Vietnam. He was born in Hue, Vietnam, on 22 October 1913. His reign as emperor was from 8 January 1926 to 25 August 1945. He collaborated with the Japanese during World War II, but was retained by Ho Chi Minh as his "supreme advisor" to add legitimacy to Ho's regime. From 13 June 1949 to 25 August 1955, he was chief of state. He was ousted by Ngo Dinh Diem in 1955 and moved to France, where he died in Paris on 30 July 1997.

Charles Alvin Beckwith remained in the army after the

Vietnam War and achieved the rank of colonel. He was instrumental in the formation of Delta Force, a Special Operations Unit He led the effort to rescue the U. S. hostages held in Iran in 1980. The mission was aborted due to helicopter failures during a sandstorm and a subsequent crash which led to several deaths. After the 'debacle in the desert,' Beckwith retired from the army. He wrote a book about Delta Force and died on 13 June 1994.

William Laws Calley was a U.S. Army officer and was convicted as a war criminal for the murders that he committed at My Lai, South Vietnam. Calley was born in Miami, Florida, on 8 June 1943. He dropped out of college due to failing grades and then held jobs such as bellhop and dishwasher before entering the army, where he graduated from OCS and was commissioned a second lieutenant in the infantry in 1967. He was deployed to South Vietnam as a platoon leader. He was not well liked by his troops, who described him as lacking in common sense. At My Lai he murdered unarmed civilians and was convicted of the murders and sentenced to life in prison. President Nixon later issued Calley a conditional pardon, reducing the sentence to time served but upholding Calley's dishonorable discharge. After his release, he resided in Atlanta, Georgia.

Christian de Castries was the French commander at the Battle of Dien Bien Phu in 1954. de Castries was born in Paris on 11 August 1902. He served in World War II and was assigned as the French commander at Dien Bien Phu in December 1953. After the defeat of the French, he was repatriated and retired from the French army in 1959. de Castries died in Paris on 29 July 1991.

William Egan Colby became Director of Central Intelligence (DCI) after the Vietnam War. He served as DCI under Presidents Nixon, Ford and George H. W. Bush. Colby died on 27 April 1996.

Phillip Buford Davidson, Jr. was the Department of Army Assistant Chief of Staff for Intelligence following his service in Vietnam. He was also Assistant Professor of Military History at

West Point. Davidson died on 7 February 1996 in San Antonio, Texas. He is buried in Arlington National Cemetery.

Ngo Dinh Diem was born on 3 January 1901 in Quang Binh, Vietnam. Following the 1954 Geneva Accords and the departure of the French from Vietnam, Diem became president of the Republic of Vietnam (South Vietnam). Diem was a Catholic and adopted oppressive polices toward the Montagnard natives and the Buddhist majority. His lack of popular support and his losing policies in the war led the U.S. to support a coup to replace Diem. Diem was assassinated along with his brother Ngo Dinh Nhu on 2 November 1963 in Saigon.

Pham Van Dong was Prime Minister of Vietnam from 1976 until he retired in 1987. He died on 29 April 2000.

Roger H. Donlon received the Medal of Honor for his actions at the battle of Lam Dong. He was the first Medal of Honor recipient in the Vietnam War. He retired at the rank of colonel. Donlon later wrote two books about his experiences: *Outpost of Freedom* and *Beyond Nam Dong*.

George Edward Dooley served in the U. S. Army for 23 years and following his retirement he was employed as an accountant and business manager at St. John's Military Academy, Northwestern University and other institutions. He documented his experiences in his book entitled *Battle for the Central Highlands, A Special Forces Story*. Dooley died in Clarksville, Tennessee on 19 July 2018.

Le Duan became General Secretary of the Party when South Vietnam was defeated in 1975. He endorsed the Vietnamese invasion of Cambodia of December 1978. He died on 10 July 1986.

Van Nguyen Duong was taken prisoner by the Communisis during the fall of South Vietnam in 1975. He was imprisoned for 13 years for "re-education." He immigrated to the United States in 1991 and lives in Honolulu, Hawaii. Van Nguyen Duong wrote a book about his experiences in 2008 entitled *The Tragedy of Vietnam: A South Vietnamese Officer's Analysis*.

Y Bham Enuol was in Phnom Penh when it fell to the Khmer Rouge on 17 April 1975. He along with other FULRO leaders sought refuge in the French embassy. The French handed over Y Bham Enuol and the others to the Khmer Rouge who moved them to the Lambert Stadium where it is thought that all were executed.

Bernard B. Fall was a war correspondent and historian who covered the Vietnam War from its earliest days. Fall was born in Austria on 19 November 1926. He moved to France, and after the fall of France during World War II, he fought with the Resistance against the Nazis. After the war, he moved to the U.S. and studied at Syracuse and Johns Hopkins University. Fall visited Vietnam several times, writing several books, including *The Street Without Joy*, which may have been his best. He predicted the defeat of the French and the U.S. because of their failure to understand the Vietnamese society and adopt tactics such as pacification. On 21 February 1967 while accompanying a U.S. unit in Vietnam, Fall stepped on a land mine and was killed.

Vo Nguyen Giap was born in Quang Binh Province, Vietnam, on 25 August 1911. He commanded NVA forces during the French war and the Vietnam War that ended in 1975. Giap graduated from the University of Hanoi with bachelor's degrees in politics, economics, and law. He fought with the resistance against the Japanese during World War II. During the French war, he defeated the French in the battle of Dien Bien Phu in 1954. He continued in command of NVA forces in the war against the U.S. that ended with the surrender of the Saigon regime in 1975. Since his retirement after the war, he has written books and is active in political affairs in Vietnam. At this writing he is over one hundred years old.

Alexander Meigs Haig, Jr., was born in Philadelphia, Pennsylvania, on 2 December 1924. He studied for two years at the University of Notre Dame before entering the U.S. Military Academy, where he graduated in 1947. He served in the Korean War and commanded a battalion in Vietnam before returning to the U.S., where he was assigned to the U.S. Military Academy in 1967. In 1969 he was appointed an assistant to national security advisor Henry Kissinger. In that position, he helped negotiate the Vietnam ceasefire talks in 1972. When H.R. Haldeman resigned as Nixon's Chief of Staff due to the Watergate scandal, Haig was assigned to that position until 1974, when he became NATO supreme commander. He retired from the army in 1979. After retirement, he held various civilian positions in industry. When Ronald Reagan was elected president, he appointed Haig secretary of state. When Reagan was wounded in an assassination attempt on 30 March 1981, Haig committed what could be considered the most publicized gaffe in U.S. history. Haig implied that he was in charge of the government until the vice president arrived in Washington from a trip. To the press, he said, "Constitutionally, gentlemen, you have the president, the vice president, and the secretary of state in that order.... I am in control here, in the White House pending the return of the vice president." Apparently, Haig had forgotten about the 25th Amendment to the Constitution, which places two people between the secretary of state and the vice president. The media had a field day. After that, Haig continued as secretary of state, resigning on 5 July 1982. He died on 20 February 2010. He is respectfully remembered by all who served with him, including this author and Henry Kissinger, who gave Haig's eulogy at the Basilica of the National Shrine of the Immaculate Conception on 2 March 2010.

Paul D. Harkins was born in Boston, Massachusetts, on 15 May 1904. He graduated from the U.S. Military Academy with the class of 1929. He advanced in rank to command U.S. forces in Vietnam (1962–1964). He was known by his staff as "General Blimp" because he inflated the success of the RVNAF. He was removed from command in Vietnam and retired in 1964. Harkins died in Dallas, Texas, on 21 August 1984.

Colonel Oran Henderson was court-martialed for his effort to cover up the My Lai massacre. Henderson was born in Indianapolis, Indiana, on 25 August 1920. At the time of the massacre, Henderson had twenty-five years of service, including World War II and the Korean War, and commanded a brigade in the Americal Division that was responsible for the My Lai massacre. Henderson was found not guilty. He died of pancreatic cancer in 1998.

Gerald Canon Hickey continued his ethnographic research with the highlander people until leaving Vietnam in 1973. He has published many books about the Montagnards. He died on 10 November 2010.

Harold K. Johnson was born in Bowesmont, North Dakota, on 22 February 1912. He attended the U.S. Military Academy, graduating with the class of 1933. He was commissioned in the infantry, and his assignments included the 57th Infantry (Philippine Scouts). With the fall of Bataan, Johnson became a prisoner of war of the Japanese. After World War II, he served in the Korean War and in Vietnam. He was appointed the U.S. Army Chief of Staff in 1964. Johnson retired from the army in 1967 and died of cancer in Washington, D.C., on 24 September 1983.

Francis John Kelly after service in Vietnam undertook the task to completly reorganization the Special Forces Group, at the same time revising the doctrine. In September 1970 he was assigned as Senior Army Advisor to the State of Colorado in Denver. He died on 26 December 1997 in Aurora Colorado.

Henry Alfred Kissinger was born in Furth, Germany, on 27 May 1923. He and his family fled Germany in 1938 to escape persecution by the Nazis. They settled in New York City, where Kissinger attended high school and started community college. He was drafted into the army in 1943 and served in the 84th Division in Europe. Following the war, he earned his bachelor's degree, followed by his master's and Ph.D. at Harvard in 1954. He advanced in the academic community and was the director of the Harvard Defense Studies Program between 1958 and 1971. Nixon chose Kissinger to be his national security advisor in 1968, and Kissinger later served as secretary of state under Nixon and Gerald Ford. He helped achieve a settlement to the war in Vietnam and also worked to achieve detente with the Soviet Union and the opening of China. Since retiring, he has authored several books and resides today in Kent, Connecticut, and New York City.

Samuel W. Koster was the commander of the U.S. Army Americal Division, who tried to cover up the My Lai massacre of 1968. Koster was born in West Liberty, Iowa, on 29 December 1919 and graduated from the U.S. Military Academy with the class of 1942. Koster was investigated for his efforts to cover up the massacre, but charges were dropped due to lack of evidence. Subsequent investigations led to his demotion, and he retired in disgrace after he was stripped of his Distinguished Service Medal in 1973. Koster died in Annapolis, Maryland, on 23 January 1986.

Nguyen Cao Ky was born in Hanoi, Vietnam, on 8 September 1930. Ky started as an infantry officer but was sent for pilot training by the French before Vietnam was partitioned. Ky moved to South Vietnam and joined the air force. He rose through the ranks and eventually became the commander of South Vietnam's air force. In November 1963, Ky participated in the coup that resulted in the assassination of Ngo Dinh Diem. In the succession of generals who followed Diem's death, Ky eventually sided with Nguyen Van Thieu, and the two ran for office in 1967, Thieu for president and Ky as his running mate. In the 1971 election, Ky was sidelined, and Thieu won the presidency. When the NVA defeated the South in 1975, Ky fled to the U.S. and settled in Westminster, California, where he ran a liquor store. Ky died in Kuala Lumpur, Malaysia, on 23 July 2011.

Melvin R. Laird was born in Omaha, Nebraska, on 1 September 1922. Laird graduated from Carleton College in Minnesota and served in the navy during World War II. After the war, he succeeded his deceased father in the Wisconsin State Senate and became Secretary of Defense under President Nixon in 1969. Laird became the architect of Vietnamization, the policy that allowed the U.S. to exit the war in Vietnam. He left office in 1973 and has written many articles since then.

Curtis LeMay was born in Columbus, Ohio, on 15 November 1906. LeMay worked his way through college, graduating from Ohio State

University with a bachelor's degree in civil engineering. He received a reserve commission in the United States Air Force in 1929 and a regular commission in 1930. He served in World War II and directed a campaign of massive bombing of Japan that caused hundreds of thousands of Japanese casualties. He was appointed Chief of Staff of the U.S. Air Force in 1961. During the war in Vietnam, he continued to urge the use of massive air power to defeat Hanoi, and this may have caused Hanoi to return to the conference table in 1972. He retired in 1965 and died at March Air Force Base, California, on 1 March 1990.

Henry Cabot Lodge, Jr. led the U.S. delegation that signed the Paris Peace Accords with North Vietnam, leading to the end of the Vietnam War. He died in Beverly, Massachusetts on 27 February 1985.

John C. Loving left the service after he returned to the United States following his tour of duty in South Vietnam. He obtained a graduate degree from the University of Richmond and worked as a real estate developer in Raleigh, North Carolina. In 2006 he published a book describing his service in South Vietnam entitled *Combat Advisor: How America Won the War and Lost the Peace in Vietnam.*

Nay Luett was promised that he and his family would be evacuated by the U. S. as the Communists closed in on Saigon in April 1975. The promise was not kept and he was arrested by security forces and sent to a labor camp. Nay Luett spent eight years in the labor camp and is believed to have died there in 1983.

Theodore C. Mataxis served as the Commandant of Cadets at Valley Forge Military Academy following his retirement from the U.S. Army. BG Mataxis died on 8 March 2006. He is buried in Sandhills State Veterans Cemetery in North Carolina.

Robert S. McNamara was selected by President John F. Kennedy to be his secretary of defense shortly after Kennedy took office. McNamara was born on 9 June 1916. He remained in office, serving Lyndon B. Johnson, after Kennedy was assassinated. McNamara is the longest-serving secretary of defense, 1961–1968. He resigned to head the World Bank and departed his position as Secretary of Defense during the Tet Offensive of 1968. Toward the end of his life he admitted that the Vietnam War was wrong and regretted his involvement. He died on 6 July 2009.

Doung Van Minh "Big Minh" was born in My Tho province, Vietnam, on 16 February 1916. Minh joined the French army at the start of World War II. He became a South Vietnamese general and politician who helped Ngo Dinh Diem consolidate power after Vietnam was partitioned in 1955. Later he led the coup that resulted in the death of Diem, for which he was blamed. Minh lasted only three months as president after Diem's death. He was replaced by General Khanh in a bloodless coup that occurred in January 1964. Khanh allowed Minh to remain in South Vietnam, but Minh was ultimately exiled. In 1975, as South Vietnam collapsed during the North Vietnamese invasion, Minh took over as president and surrendered to the NVA on 30 April 1975. Minh was allowed to leave the country, and he died in Pasadena, California, on 6 August 2001.

Ho Chi Minh was born Nguyen Sinh Cung in Nghe An Province, Vietnam, on 19 May 1890. He used a number of aliases throughout his life in order to avoid arrest but is known today as Ho Chi Minh. Ho Chi Minh was educated in Hue and traveled extensively, visiting France, the U.S., Russia, China, and the United Kingdom. In 1941, he returned to Vietnam to lead the Viet Minh independence movement. He led the Viet Minh against the French and the Japanese, receiving support from the U.S. At the end of World War II, Ho declared the independence of Vietnam under the title of the Democratic Republic of Vietnam. A war with France ensued that ended with the 1954 Geneva Accords, which divided the country with Ho as leader in the North. The war with the South and the U.S. that followed ended in 1975. Ho Chi Minh died of a heart attack at his home in Hanoi on 2 September 1969.

Thomas Hinman Moorer was born in Mount Willing, Alabama, on 9 February 1912. He graduated from the U.S. Naval Academy with the class of 1933 and served as a pilot during World War II. Moorer served as chief of naval operations between 1967 and 1970. He became chairman of the Joint Chiefs in 1970 and retired in 1974. Moorer died in the U.S. Naval Hospital in Bethesda, Maryland, on 5 February 2004.

Madame Nhu was born of a wealthy family in Hanoi, Vietnam, on 22 August 1924. She married Ngo Dinh Nhu in 1943. He was the brother of Ngo Dinh Diem, who would become the president of South Vietnam. At the time of her marriage, she converted from Buddhism to her husband's religion, Catholicism. Since Diem was a lifelong bachelor, Madame Nhu became the First Lady of South Vietnam. She was considered by many to be a schemer like her husband and was prone to making candid public statements, sometimes critical of the United States. When Diem and Ngo Dinh Nhu were assassinated in a coup d'état on 2 November 1963, Madame Nhu was traveling in the U.S. She moved to Rome in exile and later moved to France. Her property in Vietnam was confiscated by the new government. In her last years she returned to Rome, where she died on 24 April 2011.

Ngo Dinh Nhu was born in Phu Cam, Vietnam, on 7 October 1910. He was the younger brother of the first president of South Vietnam, Ngo Dinh Diem. Nhu received his bachelor's degree in literature in Paris. He pursued academic interests until the end of World War II, when he became politically active and helped in mobilizing support for his brother Diem. In 1963, the Buddhist majority rose up against the pro–Catholic regime of Diem. Both Nhu and his brother were assassinated on 2 November 1963.

Marshal Lon Nol was born in Prey Veng, Cambodia, on 13 November 1913. He served as prime minister and defense minister of Cambodia. In 1970, he mounted a successful coup against Prince Norodom Sihanouk, the Cambodian head of state. Lon Nol proclaimed himself to be the president of the Khmer Republic. He then gave Hanoi and the VC twenty-four hours to leave Cambodia, and he closed the port Sihanoukville, a source of supply for them. Lon Nol suffered a stroke in 1971, and his effectiveness started to decline. He had relied on U.S. aid, but by 1975, he was only able to hold the capital, Phnom Penh, against the Khmer Rouge. On 1 April 1975, he resigned and fled the country to Indonesia and then to the U.S. while the Khmer Rouge took over. Lon Nol died in Fullerton, California, on 17 November 1985.

Bruce Palmer, Jr., was born in Austin, Texas, on 13 April 1913. He graduated from the U.S. Military Academy with the class of 1936. He served in World War II and commanded the XVIII Airborne Corps, 1965–1967. In Vietnam he commanded II Field Force and became acting Chief of Staff of the U.S. Army in 1972. Palmer retired from the army in 1974 and died on 10 October 2000.

William R. Peers was born in Stuart, Iowa, on 14 June 1914. He graduated from the University of California with a degree in education in 1937 and served during World War II, the Korean War, and Vietnam. In Vietnam he commanded the IFFV and the 4ID before being assigned to investigate the My Lai massacre in 1969. His report assigned blame and led to courts-martial. General Peers died in San Francisco, California, on 6 April 1984.

Pol Pot was opposed by the Vietnamese who installed a rival Marxist–Leninist faction opposed to Pol Pot and renamed the country the People's Republic of Kampuchea. Pol Pot and his Khmer Rouge retreated to a jungle base near the Thai border. Until 1993, they remained part of a coalition internationally recognized as Cambodia's legitimate government. Pol Pot was placed under house arrest, where he died on 15 April 1998, possibly from suicide.

H. Norman Schwarzkopf, Jr. remained in the army after his Vietnam Service and eventually achieved the rank of four-star general. He planned and led Operation Desert Storm—an extended air campaign followed by a highly successful 100-hour ground offensive—which defeated the Iraqi Army and liberated Kuwait in early 1991. He died on 27 December 2012.

Prince Norodom Sihanouk was born in Phnom Penh, Cambodia, on 31 October 1922. He attended cavalry school in France and was selected as King of Cambodia in 1941. During World War II, the Japanese took control of Cambodia. At the end the war, Sihanouk proclaimed Cambodia's independence and held a series of appointments as prime minister until 1960, when he was elected head of state. Sihanouk worked to maintain Cambodia's neutrality during the Vietnam War but allowed North Vietnam and China to maintain bases in eastern Cambodia. He was deposed by Lon Nol in 1970 and fled to Beijing, China. Lon Nol was deposed by the Khmer Rouge in April 1975, and Vietnam invaded Cambodia and ousted the Khmer Rouge in 1978. Sihanouk returned to Cambodia and in 1993 became the King of Cambodia. He departed on a self-imposed exile in January 2004, first to North Korea and then to China, where he died on 15 October 2012.

Prince Souphanouvong was the figurehead President of Laos from December 1975 to August 1991. He died on 9 January 1995.

Nguyen Van Thieu was born in Phan Rang, Vietnam, on 5 April 1923. Initially, Thieu joined the Viet Minh Communists but quit after a year and joined the South Vietnamese army, rising in rank to command a division by 1960. Thieu participated in the coup against Diem in November 1963 and became a member of the military junta after Diem's death. He became head of state in 1965 and then president until the fall of Saigon in 1975. His regime was noted for corruption and the appointment of commanders based upon their politics and loyalty to him rather than their competence. He fled the country shortly before the Communists overran South Vietnam in 1975. Thieu died in Boston, Massachusetts, on 29 September 2001.

John Paul Vann was born in Norfolk, Virginia, on 2 July 1924. Vann enlisted during World War II and remained in the service after the war. He also served in the Korean War and Vietnam. He was an outspoken critic of the RVNAF at the battle of Ap Bac and retired from the army in 1963. Vann returned to Vietnam as a U.S.

civilian employee in 1965 and became senior advisor in MR 2. His greatest contribution may have been during the NVA Easter Invasion of South Vietnam, when he coordinated air support and was instrumental in the defeat of the NVA. Vann was killed in a helicopter crash near Kontum on 9 June 1972. He was posthumously awarded the Presidential Medal of Freedom and the Distinguished Service Cross for his actions from 23– 24 April 1972.

Cao Van Vien escaped from Saigon just before the Communist victory in April 1975 and fled to the United States. He died on 22 January 2008.

William Childs Westmoreland was born in Saxon, South Carolina, on 26 March 1914. He attended the U.S. Military Academy, graduating with the class of 1936. He served in World War II and the Korean War and commanded U.S. forces in Vietnam. He has been criticized for his focus on search-and-destroy operations when most agree that pacification should have been our primary policy. The NVA Tet Offensive of 1968 was a military victory for the U.S. and its allies but was a political disaster in the U.S. and caused an increasing percentage of the population to turn against the war. Westmoreland was replaced by General Creighton Abrams in 1968 and then became U.S. Army Chief of Staff. Westmoreland retired from the army in 1972 and spent a good deal of the rest his life defending his reputation. Mike Wallace interviewed Westmoreland for a CBS special. Wallace implied that Westmoreland had lied about enemy strength prior to Tet '68 for political reasons. Westmoreland sued, and a lengthy trial ensued. Westmoreland settled for an apology from CBS. Westmoreland died in Charleston, South Carolina, on 18 July 2005.

Appendix A, Names, Acronyms and Terms

I Corps or I Corps Tactical Zone (CTZ) — RVNAF military command controlling forces in Military Region 1, which includes South Vietnam's five northernmost provinces.

II Corps or II Corps Tactical Zone (CTZ) — RVNAF military command controlling forces in Military Region 2, the central highlands and adjoining coastal lowlands.

III Corps or III Corps Tactical Zone (CTZ) — RVNAF military command controlling forces in Military Region 3, the area from the northern Mekong Delta to the southern highlands.

IV Corps or IV Corps Tactical Zone (CTZ) — RVNAF military command controlling forces in Military Region 4, the area of the Mekong Delta.

IFFV—I Field Force, Vietnam, located in Nha Trang, exercised control over U.S. forces located in II CTZ.

IIFFV—II Field Force, Vietnam, located in Bien Hoa province, exercised control over U.S. forces located in III and IV CTZ.

agent orange—A defoliant chemical used by the US in the Vietnam War.

4ID—U.S. 4th Infantry Division.

AA—antiaircraft.

ABN—airborne.

advisors—Term applied to U.S. service personnel who provided advice and assistance to South Vietnamese units.

AID—Agency for International Development.

AK-47—An assault rifle used by Soviet Bloc, Chinese, and North Vietnamese forces.

animism— The attribution of a soul to plants, inanimate objects, and natural phenomena.

An Quang—Militant arm of organized Buddhists in South Vietnam.

AO—Area of Operation.

APC—Armored personnel carrier.

ARCOM—Army Commendation Medal. When awarded for

valor, a "V" device is added.

ARVN—Army of the Republic of South Vietnam.

Attleboro—Special operation in fall 1966 in III Corps.

AW—automatic weapons.

AWOL—Absent without leave.

B-52—U.S. heavy bomber that composed the U.S. strategic response.

baby boomer—A person born in the U.S. between the end of World War II and 1964.

back-channel—Informal flag officer correspondence.

Bajaraka Movement—Montagnard autonomy movement, a precursor to the FULRO.

Barrel Roll—Code name for flights begun in December 1964 by American and South Vietnamese planes against North Vietnamese targets in Laos.

Base area—Communist base camp. Usually containing fortifications, supply depots, hospitals, and training facilities.

BC—body count.

berm—dike or ledge.

Black Jack 33—Special operation, 27 April-24 May 1967 in III Corps in conjunction with Project Sigma, Detachment B-56.

Black Jack 41—Special operation in spring 1967 in Seven Mountains region.

Black Panthers—A far left group founded in 1966 and active until 1982. Its doctrine called primarily for the protection of black neighborhoods from police brutality, but it also espoused Marxism-Leninism doctrine.

Bouncing Betty—A land mine that when triggered launches an anti-personnel mine about a meter into the air before it explodes.

BS—Bronze star medal. When awarded for valor, a "V" device is added.

C-130—Four-engine turboprop military cargo aircraft used extensively in Vietnam.

C-rations/C-rats—Individual canned rations used in the field.

CA—civil affairs or civic action.

Cambodian Liberation Army—also called Khmer Liberation Army. Communist armed forces of National United Front of Kampuchea (FUNK).

CARE— Cooperative for American Relief Everywhere.

Cedar Falls—Code name for large operation in 1967 by American troops in the Iron Triangle.

Central Highlands—The highland area in the western part of Vietnam.

Central Massif —Another name for the Central Highlands.

CGDK—Coalition Government of Democratic Kampuchea.

cherries—Newly assigned troops.

CHICOM—Chinese Communist.

Chieu Hoi—Open-arms or amnesty program promoted by the South Vietnamese Government to encourage insurgents to rally to the government.

Chinook—CH-47 cargo/troop carrying helicopter.

CIDG—Civilian Irregular Defense Group was a program established by the CIA in 1961 to counter Viet Cong influence in the rural areas. Local people were trained by U.S. Special Forces to defend their villages. Later, the CIDG unit activity was expanded to include conventional operations against the VC and NVA.

C&C—Command and control.

CIA—Central Intelligence Agency.

CINCPAC—Commander-In-Chief, Pacific: Commands all U.S. forces in the Pacific.

click or klick— Distance measurement in kilometers.

Cloverleaf Pattern—A patrolling pattern.

Cobra-Bell AH-IG Huey Cobra—Fast attack helicopter armed with machine guns, grenade launchers, and rockets.

Cofram—Special U. S. Army artillery shell with tremendous fragmentation effect.

COMUSMACV—Commander, United States Military Assistance Command, Vietnam.

Conex—A large steel storage container.

Cooper-Church Amendment—Enacted on 5 January 1971. It ended funding for U.S. ground troops and military advisors in Cambodia and Laos after 30 June 1970. It barred air operations in Cambodian airspace in direct support of Cambodian forces without congressional approval, and it ended American support for Republic of Vietnam forces outside territorial South Vietnam.

CORDS—The Civil Operations and Revolutionary Development Support was established under MACV in 1967. CORDS organized U.S. civilian agencies in Vietnam within the military chain of command.

corps—Two or more divisions, responsible for the defense of a Military Region.

Cosmoline—A rust preventative, brown- colored, grease- like paste applied to weapons after they are manufactured in order to protect them from weather while they are shipped to the users.

COSVN—Central Office for South Vietnam. Communist military and political headquarters for southern South Vietnam.

County Fair—A form of "cordon and search" in which American and South Vietnamese troops surrounded a village; while South Vietnamese police searched for arms, guerrillas, and political infrastructure, the villagers were provided entertainment and welfare services.

CP—Command post.

CPK—Communist Party Kampuchea.

CTZ—Corps Tactical Zone. Identifies the four military regions that composed South Vietnam. The CTZs are the same as Military Regions (MRs).

DCO—deputy commanding officer.

D–Day—A day set for launching a military operation.

dau tranh—or struggle, has two pincers, armed and political.

Dega—A name used by members of the Rhade tribe.

Delaware—Code name for American-South Vietnamese

operation in the spring of 1968 in the A Shau Valley.

DEROS—Date eligible for return from overseas. The date a soldier's tour of duty was to end.

Desoto—Code name for U. S. Navy patrols in the Gulf of Tonkin.

div.—division.

DK—Democratic Kampuchea.

dog tags—Metal tags that soldiers carried that identified their name and other information.

Domino Theory—President Eisenhower defined the Domino Theory that expressed the belief that if a country fell to the Communists, others would follow like dominos.

DMZ—Demilitarized zone. Established by the 1954 Geneva accords, provisionally dividing North Vietnam from South Vietnam along the seventeenth parallel.

DOW—died of wounds.

Draw-down—Reduction in force.

DRV—Democratic Republic of Vietnam (North Vietnam).

DSC—Distinguished Service Cross. The nation's second highest medal of valor. The equivalent for valor in flight is the DFC or Distinguished Flying Cross.

DZ—Drop zone. Preplanned landing area for parachutists and/or parachuted equipment.

economy of force—The principle of employing all available combat power in the most effective way possible, in an attempt to allocate a minimum of essential combat power to any secondary efforts.

elephant soldiers—Name used by the Montagnards to describe U.S. troops. It depicted the enormous amount of equipment carried by each soldier.

El Paso I & II—Code names for proposed American-South Vietnamese ground operations in Laos.

EM—enlisted men.

FAC—Forward air controller. Pilot or observer who directs strike aircraft and artillery.

Fairfax—Code name for joint American-South Vietnamese Army operations in 1967 to secure the environs of Saigon.

Farmgate—Code name for early U. S. Air Force support of the South Vietnamese Air Force.

fast mover—A military jet aircraft.

FFORCEV—Field Force, Vietnam.

fields of fire—area covered by weapons.

flak—anti-aircraft fire.

FLHP—Front for the Liberation of the High Plateau.

FNG—Fucking new guy.

FOB—forward operations base.

fragging—Killing or attempting to kill a fellow soldier or officer, usually with a fragmentation grenade.

free fire zone—Designated area in which any weapons or weapon systems might fire without having to coordinate with the main headquarters.

friendly fire—Fire impacting on friendly troops by mistake.

FSB—Fire support base. Semi-fixed artillery base established to increase indirect fire coverage of an area and to provide security for the firing unit.

FULRO—Front Unifie de Lutte de la Race Opprimee. The autonomous movement of Montagnards in Vietnam to separate themselves from the South Vietnamese regime.

freedom bird—Term applied to all aircraft that carried U.S. service members back to the U.S. after serving in Vietnam.

FWMAF—Free World Military Assistance Forces.

G2—Assistant Chief of Staff for military intelligence.

Game Warden—Code name for a long-running project of the U. S. Navy to keep South Vietnam's internal waterways open.

Great Society—The LBJ policy with a set of domestic programs whose aims were elimination of poverty and racial injustice. Anti-war Democrats complained that spending on the Vietnam War choked off the Great Society.

grunt—Slang word for an infantry soldier or marine.

GSW—gun shot wound.

guerilla warfare—Guerrilla warfare is a form of irregular warfare using military tactics including ambushes, sabotage, raids, hit-and-run tactics, and mobility to fight a larger traditional military force.

GVN—Government of the Republic of Vietnam.

Hamlet Program—The rural peasants would be provided security, being physically isolated from Communist insurgents, and support services in defended hamlets, thereby strengthening ties with the central South Vietnamese government. It was hoped this would lead to increased loyalty by the peasantry towards the government. In the end, the program led to a decrease in support for Diem's regime and an increase in sympathy for Communist efforts.

harbor site—A location used to set up camp for the night.

Hastings—Code name for U. S. Marine Corps operations in conjunction with ARVN troops and South Vietnamese marines in Quang Tri province in summer and fall of 1966.

HE—High Explosive.

HES—Hamlet evaluation system. Method of rating hamlets and villages to ascertain the level of pacification.

highlander—Another name for Montagnard.

hooch—A small living quarter or hut.

HopTac—Code name for program begun in late 1964 to expand security in the region around Saigon.

huey—Helicopters that were used to move troops and provide fire support and medevac.

hump or humping—A term meaning a foot soldier's march across terrain.

IG—Inspector General.

immersion foot—A skin condition of the feet that results after exposure to warm, wet conditions for long periods of time. Large watery blisters appear which are painful and begin to peel away from the foot itself. It is also called trench foot.

indirect fire—Bombardment by mortars or artillery in which shells travel on an indirect trajectory to an unseen target.

Indochina—A term used to describe the French colony in Southeast Asia that included Cambodia, Laos, and Vietnam.

J-2—Assistant Chief of Staff for military intelligence, MACV.

JCS—Joint Chiefs of Staff. Consisting of chairman, U.S. Army Chief of Staff, U.S. Navy Chief of Naval Operations, U.S. Air Force Chief of Staff, and the U.S. Marine Corps Commandant. Advises the President, the National Security Council, and the Secretary of Defense.

JGS—Joint General Staff, the South Vietnamese military organization that directed the activities of the RVNAF.

Junction City—Code name for large operation in 1967 by American and South Vietnamese troops in War Zone C.

JUSPAO—Joint United States Public Affairs Office.

KBA—Killed by Air.

KIA—Killed in action.

Kit Carson Scouts—Program involving the use of former Viet Cong combatants as intelligence scouts for American infantry units.

KKK—Khymer Kampuchea Krom (underground Cambodian faction).

klicks—Distance measurement in kilometers.

KPRP—Kampuchean People's Revolutionary Party.

KR—Khmer Rouge.

KSCB—Khe Sanh Combat Base.

laager—A fortified camp site.

LAW—M72 light anti-tank weapon. A shoulder-fired rocket with a one-time, disposable launcher.

Leaping Lena—Code name for small South Vietnamese patrols operating in Laos along the Ho Chi Minh Trail in 1964.

LLDB—Lac Luong Dac Biet (South Vietnamese Special Forces).

LN—liaison.

LPRP—Lao People's Revolutionary Party.

LRRP—Long-range reconnaissance platoon.

LZ—Landing zone (for helicopters).

Market Time—Code name for a long-running project of

American and South Vietnamese navies to prevent North Vietnamese infiltration into South Vietnam by sea.

Masher—Code name for an operation begun in early 1966 by American troops in Binh Dinh province; later renamed WHITE WING.

Matrilineal descent—The tracing **of** descent through the female line.

M16—American rifle used by U. S. and allies in Vietnam.

M72—Light anti-tank weapon (LAW) is a shoulder-fired, 66mm, unguided missile used by U.S. troops and Allies against tanks, bunkers, and other targets.

M79—A U.S. single-shot, shoulder-fired grenade launcher that fires a 40x60mm grenade.

M113—Armored personnel carriers used by both ARVN and U.S. forces.

Maggie's drawers—A red flag waved across the face of a target, indicating a miss.

mad minute—Concentrated fire by all weapons at maximum rate. Usually used to demonstrate fire power.

MACV—Military Assistance Command, Vietnam: U.S. command for all U.S. military activities in Vietnam.

MAF—Marine Amphibious Force.

MARS—Military Auxiliary Radio System. Sponsored by the Department of Defense, this system, manned by volunteers, allowed service members to contact their families in the U.S. via radio from Vietnam.

massif—Another name for the Central Highlands.

matriarchal—A social system in which females hold the primary power positions.

medevac–Medical evacuation by helicopter.

Me Generation–Also called America's "worst generation;" who were totally self-focused and did not wish to provide any service to their country.

Mermite can—A food container.

MF—Mike Force.

MGF—Mobile guerrilla force.

mg—machine gun.

MIA—Missing in Action.

Mike or MSF—Mobile Strike Force.

Minigun—A weapons system composed of a series of Gatling-style rotating barrels that rotate and fire at a high rate, powered by an electric motor.

moi—savages.

Montagnard/Yards—minority mountain people who live in simple societies in the Central Highlands.

monsoon—A seasonal reversing wind, accompanied by corresponding changes in precipitation: heavy rain for weeks that blocks roads.

MP—Military Police.

MPC—Military payment certificate. A form of currency used to pay U.S. military personnel in Vietnam and other overseas countries. This prevented the circulation of U.S. greenbacks that could be used for illegal purposes.

MR—Morning Report.

MR—Military Region. Term that replaced Corps Tactical Zone. One of four geographic zones (MR 1, MR 2, MR 3, and MR 4) into which South Vietnam was divided for purposes of military and civil administration.

MSR—Main supply route.

napalm—Jellied gasoline that explodes when dropped and produces intense heat.

NCO—Noncommissioned officer (noncom): enlisted ranks including corporal and sergeant, up to and including command sergeant major.

NDP—Night defensive position.

NLF—National Liberation Front, officially the National Front for the Liberation of the South. Formed on December 20, 1960, its aim was to overthrow South Vietnam's government and reunite the North and the South. NLF included Communists and non–Communists.

Nungs—Tribal group of non-Indonesian stock originally from the highlands of North Vietnam who provided special units for South Vietnam's Army.

NVA—North Vietnamese Army.

OB—operations base.

OCO— Office of Civil Operations; an agency for coordinating the American pacification effort.

OCS—Officer Candidate School; provided a way for enlisted soldiers to obtain commissions after they entered active duty.

ODP—Orderly Departure Program; a program to permit immigration of Vietnamese to the United States of America and to other countries. It was created in 1979 under the auspices of the United Nations High Commissioner for Refugees. The objective of the ODP was to provide a mechanism for Vietnamese to leave their homeland safely and in an orderly manner to be resettled abroad.

OER—Officer Efficiency Report, an officer evaluation used to determine career, promotions and assignments.

ONTOS—U. S. Marine Corps tank-killer vehicles armed with a 106-mm recoilless rifle.

OP—Observation Post.

OPCON—Operational Control.

Operation Castor—French airborne operation to establish an airhead at Dien Bien Phu during the First Indochina War.

Operation Niagara—U.S. Seventh Air Force close air support campaign carried out from January through March 1968. Its purpose was to serve as an aerial umbrella for the defense of the U.S. Marine Corps Combat Base at Khe Sanh.

Oplan 34A—Covert operations begun in 1961 by the South Vietnamese against North Vietnam.

OPlan 3—7 Proposal prepared in the spring of 1964 for American air operations in three phases involving attacks against enemy forces retiring into Laos and Cambodia.

OPORD—Operations Order.

pacification—A process of countering a counterinsurgency by controlling the terrain to provide security for the population.

PAVN—People's Army of Vietnam (the NVA).

palace guard—In Vietnam, these were units that could be called in to protect the South Vietnamese president against coup attempts.

Parasol-Switchback—1963 program supplying funds for use with the CIDG in Vietnam.

PCS—Permanent Change of Station.

pearls—During the French war in Vietnam, captured French soldiers were held for ransom by the Viet Minh until cash was paid for their release. For this reason, they were called pearls.

Pegasus—Code name for operation to re-establish ground contact with the Khe Sanh Combat Base in April 1968.

percs—Benefits available to service members.

PF—Popular Forces. South Vietnamese village defense units.

Phoenix program *(Phung Hoang)*—An intelligence-gathering program designed to neutralize the Vietcong infrastructure through identification and arrest of key party cadres. It was also perverted by locals to settle old scores.

point—Lead soldier/marine on a patrol.

Politburo—Policy-making and executive committee of the Communist party.

POW or PW—Prisoner of war.

Prairie Fire—Code name for small American-South Vietnamese patrols operating in Laos along the Ho Chi Minh Trail.

prov—provisional.

PSYOPS—psychological operations.

punji stake—A sharpened bamboo stake placed in the bottom of a pit.

quad—Four heavy machine guns that traverse from a single pedestal and which are fired simultaneously by a single gunner.

rabbit soldiers—Name used by Montagnards to describe South Vietnamese soldiers because they ran away fast.

RC–292—Combat net radio antenna.

RF/PF—Regional Forces/Popular Forces. South Vietnamese

provincial-level and village-level defense forces.

Recondo—A school to train U. S. Army troops for long-range reconnaissance patrols. A similar school was organized later for ARVN troops.

REMF—Rear-echelon mothefr----er. An expression to describe soldiers in rear areas who performed administrative duties and were not assigned to combat units. The term overlooks the fact that in a guerrilla war, those in rear areas frequently find themselves in the front lines of combat.

Rolling Thunder—Code name for a long-running program of American and South Vietnamese air operations against North Vietnam.

ROTC—Reserve Officer Training Corps: a college-based program for training commissioned officers of the United States armed forces.

RPD—Ruchnoy Pulemyot Degtyaryova (RPD) is a light machine gun developed by the Soviet Union and used by NVA, VC, and other countries.

RPG—Rocket-propelled grenade used by enemy forces.

RR—recoiless rifle.

RZ—reconnaissance zone.

RVN—Republic of Vietnam.

RVNAF—Republic of Vietnam Armed Forces, including ARVN, PFs, RFs, VNAF, VNMC, and VNN.

S-1—A unit personnel/admin officer.

S-2—A unit military intelligence officer.

S-3—A unit operations officer.

S-4—A unit supply officer.

S-5—A unit civil affairs officer.

SA—small arms.

SAM—surface-to-air missile.

sapper—NVA/VC sappers were commando raiders adept at penetrating allied defenses.

satchel charges—Explosive packs small enough to be easily carried and placed on targets.

seabees—naval construction engineers.

SEAL—Sea, air, land teams. American and South Vietnamese Navy commandos.

SEATO—Southeast Asia Treaty Organization.

SF—special forces.

SFG—special forces group.

SFGA—special forces group (airborne).

shaman— A person regarded as having access to, and influence in, the world of good and evil spirits.

SLAM—Seeking, locating, annihilating, and monitoring operations (U.S.) to coordinate reconnaissance and firepower resources in concentrated attacks by fire.

slash-and-burn—An agricultural technique that involves the cutting and burning of plants in forests or woodlands to create fields for planting crops.

slicks—Helicopters used to lift troops or cargo with only protective armaments systems.

spider hole—Is typically a shoulder-deep, protective round hole, not as deep as a foxhole, and often covered by a camouflaged lid. In a spider hole, a soldier can stand and fire a weapon.

SOG—Studies and Operations Group; conducted covert unconventional warfare operations.

SOP—standard operating procedure.

Snake Eye—A low-level bomb with pop out fins.

SPARS—significant problem area reports.

SRV or SRVN—Socialist Republic of Vietnam.

SS—Silver star: a valor award.

stand-down—A relaxation of status of a military unit or force from an alert or operational posture.

Starlight scope—An optical instrument that allows images to be produced in levels of light approaching total darkness.

Strategic Hamlet Program—A plan by the governments of South Vietnam and the United States during the Vietnam War to combat the Communist insurgency by pacifying the countryside and reducing the influence of the Communists among the rural population.

Strela—A series of Russian-manufactured antiaircraft missiles.

striker— infantry soldier.

swidden—An area of land cleared for cultivation by slashing and burning vegetation.

Switchback—Operation in which the Army began assuming responsibility for U. S. participation in the CIDG program, 1962-July 1963.

tac—tactical.

Tally Ho—Code name for air reconnaissance and attack immediately north of and within the DMZ.

TAOR—Tactical area of responsibility.

Task Force Oregon—U. S. Army force organized in April 1966 to provide reinforcements in the I Corps Zone, predecessor of the Americal Division.

TDY—temporary duty.

Tiger-Hound—Code name for air reconnaissance and attack in the Laotian panhandle, begun in 1966.

TOC—tactical operations center.

TOE—table of organization and equipment.

tracers—An ammunition round that has a small pyrotechnic charge in its base. When fired, it makes the trajectory of the round visible and allows the firer to track the flight of the bullet and adjust his aim.

Tet—Vietnamese lunar New Year holiday period.

TOW—Tube-launched optically-tracked wire-guided anti-tank missile.

Tropospheric scatter or tropo—A method of transmitting and receiving microwave communications signals over long distances.

Truong Son Force—A quick reaction force of Montagnards employed in the Central Highlands.

USAF—U. S. Air Force.

USAID—U.S. Agency for International Development.

USARV—United States Army, Vietnam.

USASF—United States Army Special Forces.

USDAO—United States Defense Attache Office.

USIA—U. S. Information Agency.

USMA—United States Military Academy, located at West Point, New York.

USMC—United States Marine Corps.

USOM—United States Operation Mission.

USSF—United States Special Forces.

Vandergraft—Artillery fire support base built in 1968 by U. S. Army troops on the approaches to Khe Sanh and later manned by U.S. marines.

VCP—Vietnamese Communist Party.

Viet Cong or VC—Guerilla soldiers in South Vietnam.

Viet Minh—Term used in the French war to describe the Communist army under Ho Chi Minh.

ville—A small village.

VN—Vietnamese.

VNAF—South Vietnamese Air Force.

VNMC—South Vietnamese Marine Corps.

VNN—South Vietnamese Navy.

VNSF—Vietnamese Special Forces.

VPA—Vietnam Peoples' Army (see also PAVN).

White Wing—Code name for an operation begun in early 1966 by American troops in Binh Dinh province; originally called *Masher.*

WIA—wounded in action.

Yankee Team—Code name for U. S. Air Force and Navy reconnaissance flights beginning in May 1964 over Laos.

York—Code name for a proposed series of American-South Vietnamese operations to sweep the A Shau Valley and nearby border regions in preparation for possible operations in Laos.

Appendix B, Chronology

1930

Ho Chi Minh organizes the Indochinese Communist Party to oppose French colonial rule.

1932

March 9: Bao Dai, a puppet leader of the French, proclaims himself emperor of Vietnam.

1941

May: Ho Chi Minh forms the Viet Minh Forces to fight the French and Japanese.

1945

July: At the Potsdam Conference, Vietnam is divided in two along the seventeenth parallel by a demilitarized zone.

September 2: Ho Chi Minh declares Vietnam's independence from the French by establishing the Democratic Republic of Vietnam in Hanoi.

September 26: The first American advisor is killed in Vietnam. Lieutenant Colonel A. Peter Dewey, of the Office of Strategic Security (the precursor to the Central Intelligence Agency), is mistaken for a French officer and shot by Communist Viet Minh soldiers.

1946

December 19: The First Vietnam War begins when Ho's Viet Minh forces attack French forces in Hanoi.

1949

July: Bao Dai proclaims the establishment of the State of Vietnam.

1950

January 18: China recognizes the Democratic Republic of Vietnam.

February 7: The United States recognizes Bao Dai's government.

June 27: President Harry S Truman sends military aid to French forces in Vietnam.

December 30: The United States, France, Vietnam, Cambodia, and Laos sign a Mutual Defense Assistance Agreement.

1954

May 7: The Viet Minh defeat the French at Dien Bien Phu.

June 24: Defeat of French Groupement Mobile 100 at Mang Yang Pass.

July 20–21: The French sign a ceasefire agreement. Vietnam is divided along the seventeenth parallel. Ho Chi Minh controls North Vietnam; Bao Dai rules South Vietnam.

1955

February 12: U.S. military advisors start to train South Vietnamese army officers.

October 26: Ngo Dinh Diem defeats Bao Dai in a referendum and declares himself president of South Vietnam.

1959

July 8: Two Americans are killed during an attack at Bien Hoa. Major Dale Buis and Master Sergeant Chester Ovnard are the first Americans to die in combat in Vietnam.

1960

December 20: The National Liberation Front (NLF) — the Viet Cong—is formed to overthrow the government in South Vietnam.

1961

April 17: Bay of Pigs invasion of Cuba fails.

May: President John F. Kennedy announces that the United States may have to send troops to Vietnam.

December 10: A "white paper" published by the U.S. State Department claims that South Vietnam is threatened by Communist aggression from North Vietnam.

1962

April: President Diem approves the Strategic Hamlet Program.

December 31: The number of military advisors in Vietnam reaches 11,300.

1963

January 2: Battle of Ap Bac.

January 3: Plei Mrong Attack.

May 1: Buddhists gather in Hue to protest against the Diem government. Riots ensue for several months.

August 24: The U.S. embassy in Saigon receives a cable from Washington that recommends removing Diem from office.

November 1: A military coup overthrows President Diem, who is later executed. Diem is replaced by Vice President Nguyen Ngoc Tho and General Duong Van Minh. Strategic Hamlet Program ends shortly after Diem's death.

November 22: President Kennedy is assassinated. Lyndon B. Johnson is sworn in as new president.

1964

January 30: General Minh is overthrown in another military coup.

July 5: Battle of Nam Dong.

August 2: The U.S. destroyer *Maddox* is attacked by Vietnamese torpedo boats in the Gulf of Tonkin. The details about the attack remain under dispute. A second attack occurs

August 4, also subject to controversy.

August 5: Everett Alvarez, Jr., is shot down near the North Vietnamese coast and becomes the first American prisoner of war in Vietnam.

August 7: Congress approves the Gulf of Tonkin Resolution, that gives President Lyndon B. Johnson the authority to use "all necessary steps, including the use of armed force," to protect any member of the Southeast Asia Treaty Organization (the United States, France, Britain, Australia, New Zealand, Pakistan, Thailand, and the Philippines).

September 19: First FULRO uprising.

November 3: President Johnson is reelected.

1965

February 15: Ambush at Mang Yang Pass.

March 8: The first American combat troops–3,500 Marines—land at Da Nang.

April 17: The Students for a Democratic Society hold the first major antiwar rally in Washington, D.C.

June 30: Siege of Duc Co begins.

July 28: President Johnson announces that U. S. Forces in Vietnam will be increased to 125,000.

October 19: Siege of Plei Me.

November 14: Ia Drang Valley Campaign begins.

December 17: Second FULRO uprising.

December 31: United States military strength in Vietnam reaches 184,300. The number of U.S. dead this year is 1,928. The cumulative number of U.S. dead since the start of our involvement is 2,344.

1966

March 8: A Shau Valley Special Forces Camp attacked.

April 12: American B-52s bomb North Vietnam for the first time in retaliation for a Viet Cong attack on U.S. troops.

July 6: American POWs are marched through the streets of

Hanoi and attacked by an angry mob.

September 14: Operation Attleboro.

December 31: The official number of U.S. military personnel in Vietnam reaches 385,300. The number of U.S. dead this year is 6,350. The cumulative number of U.S. dead since the start of our involvement is 8,694.

1967

January 1: 4th Infantry Division launches *Operation Sam Houston* in the Central Highlands.

April 6: 4th Infantry Division *Operation Francis Marion* starts in the Central Highlands.

April 24: The First Battle of Khe Sanh (The Hill Fights) starts.

June 17: Operation Greeley (4th Infantry Division and 173rd Airborne Brigade) launched at Dak To followed by *Operation MacArthur* on 3 November.

August 26: The Battle of Con Thien starts.

September 3: General Nguyen Van Thieu is elected president of South Vietnam with General Ky as Vice President.

October 27: The Battle of Song Be starts.

October 29: The Border Battle of Loc Ninh starts.

December 1: The Border Battle of Dak To ends.

December 31: The number of American military personnel in Vietnam is now 485,000. The number of U.S. dead this year is 11,363. The cumulative number of U.S. dead since the start of our involvement is 20,057.

1968

January 21: The siege of Khe Sanh by the North Vietnamese begins.

January 23: North Koreans seize U. S. ship, the Pueblo off of the Korean coast.

January 31: The North Vietnamese begin the Tet Offensive, a massive surprise attack against South Vietnam.

February 6-7: Battle of Lang Vei.

March 16: Lieutenant William L. Calley and men in his platoon massacre between 400 and 600 Vietnamese civilians in the small village of My Lai.

March 28: Tet Offensive Phase 1 ends.

March 31: President Johnson announces he will not run for reelection.

April 4: Martin Luther King, Jr. is assassinated.

May 5: Tet Offensive Phase 2 begins.

May 10: Peace talks between U.S. and Vietnamese officials begin in Paris.

August 9: Tet Offensive Phase 3 begins.

August 24: Battle of Duc Lap.

October 31: President Johnson halts the bombing of North Vietnam.

December 31: U.S. military personnel in Vietnam officially number 536,600. The number of U.S. dead this year is 16,899. The cumulative number of U.S. dead since the start of our involvement is 36,956.

1969

March 18: President Richard M. Nixon approves the secret bombing of Viet Cong bases in Cambodia. The bombings continue through April 1970.

June: U.S. troop strength peaks at 543,400. President Nixon announces that 25,000 U.S. troops will be withdrawn from Vietnam, the beginning of "Vietnamization."

September 2: Ho Chi Minh dies.

December 31: The number of U.S. troops in Vietnam declines to 475,000. The number of U.S. dead this year is 11,780. The cumulative number of U.S. dead since the start of our involvement is 48,736.

1970

February 20: Henry Kissinger, President Nixon's advisor on national security, meets secretly with North Vietnamese officials in Paris to negotiate a peace treaty.

April 29: The U.S. and South Vietnamese armies invade Cambodia to attack North Vietnamese and Viet Cong bases.

May 4: National Guardsmen kill four students at Kent State University during campus riot.

June 24: The U.S. Senate repeals the Gulf of Tonkin Resolution.

December 31: U.S. forces in Vietnam fall to 334,600. The number of U.S. dead this year is 6,173. The cumulative number of U.S. dead since the start of our involvement is 54,909.

1971

January 30: Lam Son 719 begins.

February: South Vietnamese troops, in a test of Vietnamization policy, invade Laos. They are decisively beaten.

March 29: Lieutenant Calley is the only U.S. service member convicted of the My Lai massacre.

June 13: The *New York Times* begins publishing excerpts from the Pentagon Papers, a massive study by the Pentagon on the military policy in Vietnam.

October 3: President Thieu is unopposed and reelected as president of South Vietnam.

December 31: Almost 200,000 troops have been withdrawn from Vietnam. The official figures of U.S. troops still in Vietnam fall to 156,800. The number of U.S. dead this year is 2,414. The cumulative number of U.S. dead since the start of our involvement is 57,323.

1972

March 30: The North Vietnamese launch a massive attack on three fronts in South Vietnam called the Spring (or Easter) Offensive.

April: U.S. troops left in Vietnam number 69,000.

May 8: U.S. forces begin mining Haiphong and other ports in North Vietnam.

June 17: Five men arrested for Watergate complex break in.

October 21: The United States and North Vietnam reach a ceasefire agreement.

November 7: President Nixon is reelected in a landslide victory.

December 18: The "Christmas Bombing Raids" on Hanoi and North Vietnam begin; they go on for eleven days.

December 31: U.S. forces in Vietnam number 24,000. The number of U.S. dead this year is 759. The cumulative number of U.S. dead since the start of our involvement is 58,082.

1973

January 23: Start of LANDGRAB 73.

January 27: The United States, South Vietnam, and North Vietnam sign the Paris Peace Accords, ending the U.S. war in Vietnam.

February–March: North Vietnam returns 591 American prisoners of war.

March 29: The last remaining U.S. combat troops leave Vietnam.

August 14: American military operations in Vietnam end.

December 31: Only 50 U.S. troops are left in Vietnam. The number of U.S. dead this year is 68. The cumulative number of U.S. dead since the start of our involvement is 58,150.

1974

April: NVA Strategic Raids in South Vietnam begin.

May 9: Congress begins Nixon impeachment hearings.

August 9: Nixon resigns and is replaced by Gerald Ford.

December 12: Battle of Phuoc Long begins.

1975

January 6: Battle of Phuoc Long ends with a South Vietnamese defeat.

Spring: The North Vietnamese Army launches its final offensive against South Vietnam.

April 2: South Vietnam's Military Region 2 falls to the NVA.

April 15: NVA defeats the ARVN at the battle of Xuan Loc.

April 17: Fall of Phnom Penh. Cambodian war ends

April 21: President Thieu resigns.

April 30: The North Vietnamese Army enters Saigon, the capital of South Vietnam. The remaining Americans and some South Vietnamese in Saigon are evacuated by helicopter. The war in Vietnam ends. The cumulative number of U.S. dead since the start of our involvement is 58,220 including those who died of wounds after 1975.

May 4: Khmer Rouge attack Vietnamese islands.

May 12: Khmer Rouge capture U. S. freighter *Mayaguez*.

August 18: China pledges economic aid to Cambodia.

October 30: Moscow pledges economic aid to Vietnam.

1976

February 6: China signs military aid agreement with Cambodia.

April 2: Prince Sihanouk resigns as Cambodia's head of state.

April 14: New Cambodian government, Democratic Kampuchea headed by Pol Pot is announced.

September 9: Chairman Mao Zedong dies.

1977

January 21: President Jimmy Carter pardons most Vietnam War draft dodgers.

February 24: China announces that it cannot provide new aid to Vietnam.

April 30: Khmer Rouge attack villages in Vietnam.

July 17: Vietnam signs friendship treaty with Laos.

September 24: Khmer Rouge attack a Vietnamese village, hundreds killed.

December 25: Vietnam attacks Cambodia.

1978

March 24: Vietnam clamps down on ethnic Chinese.

May 24: Pol Pot attacks his own troops in Eastern Zone.

November 3: Vietnam signs friendship treaty with Moscow.

December 15: U. S./China normalization announced.

December 25: Vietnam invades Cambodia.

1979

January 7: Vietnam occupies Phnom Penh.

February 17: China invades Vietnam.

March 6: China withdraws from Vietnam.

March 27: Soviet Navy arrives at Cam Ranh Bay, Vietnam.

1989

September 26: Vietnam withdraws from Cambodia.

1991

October 23: Paris Peace Agreement ends the Third Indochina War.

1995

July 11: U. S. normalizes relations with Vietnam.

Appendix C, Special Forces Detachments[552]
(Courtesy of Steve Sherman)

I Corps Tactical Zone

Detachment & Dates[555]	Location	Province	CSF[553]	Notes[554]
A1/132, A1/131 A1/124, A-727, A-731, A1/323, 08/xx/62-11/30/64	Khe Sanh	Quang Tri	Bru	TDY
A5/122, A-101 11/30/64-12/19/66				PCS
A-101 12/19/66-12/27/67	Lang Vei (old)	Quang Tri	Bru	PCS
A-101 12/17/67-02/07/68	Lang Vei (new)	Quang Tri	Bru	PCS
A-101 04/01/68-08/27/70	Mai Loc	Quang Tri	Bru	PCS
A1/433, A1/434 05/30/63-03/11/64	Ta Bat	Thua Thien	VN	TDY[556]
A1/434B, A1/421 A1/113 01/01/64-02/24/65	A Shau	Thua Thien	VN	TDY
A5/334, A-102 02/24/65-03/12/66	A Shau	Thua Thien	VN	PCS Overrun
A-102 (FOB) 05/25/65-12/08/65	A Luoi AKA Ta Bat (new)			PCS FOB
A1-324 01/28/66-05/02/66	Tien Phuoc	Quang Tin	VN	TDY
A-102 05/02/66-10/31/70	Tien Phuoc	Quang Tin	VN	PCS
77th BRDB 11/01/70-12/03/72				to 14 RG

A5/1 09/09/62-02/15/63	Ba To (old)	Quang Ngai	Hre	TDY
A5/1, A-729, A-726, A1/112 02/04/63-04/18/65		Quang Ngai	Hre	TDY
A5/113, A-103 04/18/65-01/31/69	Gia Vuc	Quang Ngai	Hre	PCS
A-107 02/01/69-				VNSF
70th BRDB xx/xx/70-10/30/72				With-drawn to 11 RG
A1/114, A1/234, A1/223 01/28/63-02/xx/64	Son Ha	Quang Ngai	VN	TDY
A1/412B 06/06/64-08/07/64	A Ro	Quang Nam	VN	TDY
A5/331, A-104 08/07/64-04/24/65	A Ro	Quang Nam	VN	PCS
A-104 04/28/65-08/31/70	Ha Thanh	Quang Ngai	VN	PCS
85th BRDB 9/1/1970				
A-727, A1/431, A1/412A 09/xx/63-6/11/64	Kham Duc	Quang Duc	VN	TDY[557]
A5/4, A-732, A-728 02/15/63-02/02/64	Tra My	Quang Tin	VN	TDY
A-732, A-728, A1-322 01/01/64-11/06/65	Kham Duc	Quang Duc	VN	PCS
B5/330, B-13 01/10/65-06/25/66				PCS[558]

408

A5/12x, A-105 11/06/65-05/12/68				
A-105 06/24/68-10/31/70	Nong Son	Quang Nam	VN	PCS
78th BRDB 11/1/1970	Nong Son	Quang Nam	VN	
A-730, A-726, 02/15/63-09/04/64	Ruong Ruong/ Nam Duc/ Ta Ro/ Ta Rau/ Nam Dong	Quang Nam	VN	TDY
A-726, A1-224	Thua Thien	VN		TDY
A1/324 10/27/64-02/05/65	Ta Ko	Quang Nam	VN	TDY
A5/114, A-106 03/29/65-09/30/70	Ba To (New)	Quang Ngai	VN	PCS
69th BRDB 10/1/1970				
A1/323, A1/123, 10/22/62-08/23/63	Tra Bong (old)	Quang Ngai	VN/ Cua	TDY[559]
A-107 08/28/65-08/31/70	Tra Bong	Quang Ngai	VN	PCS
81st BRDB 9/1/1970				to 15RG
A1/423, A1/431 04/21/63-12/14/63	Phuoc Son	Quang Nam	VN/ MTD	TDY from Hoa Cam
A-110, A-108 02/15/66-09/30/70	Minh Long	Quang Ngai	VN	PCS
68th BRDB 10/1/1970				to 11RG
A1/35, A1/313 11/30/61-3/xx/63	Hoa Cam, Danang	Quang Nam		TDY

Detachment & Dates	Location	Province	CSF	Notes
A1/132, A1/214, A1/213, A1/224 03/11/63-07/11/64	An Diem	Quang Nam	VN/ MTD	TDY to Nam Dong
A-109 02/13/66-11/15/70	Thuong Duc	Quang Nam	VN/ Koho	PCS
79th BRDB 11/16/70-08/07/74				Overrun
B-16 03/xx/65-11/14/70	Gio Lin, Con Thien/ MSG/ MGF	Quang Tri	Nung/ VN/Hre	PCS

II Corps Tactical Zone

Detachment & Dates[562]	Location	Province	CSF[560]	Notes[561]
B-20	MSG/ MGF	Pleiku	VN/ Rhade/ Jarai	
A1/114A, A1/123A A1/422, A1-221 12/xx/63-05/28/65	Plei Ta Nangle	Binh Dinh		TDY
A5/332, A5/223 10/xx/64-06/30/69	An Khe	Binh Dinh		PCS to Chu Lai
B5/22, B-20, A-220	Qui Nhon	Binh Dinh		
A1/223, A1/112, A1/231 02/xx/64-04/19/65	Kannack	Binh Dinh	VN/ Hre	TDY (from San Ha)
A5/112, A-221 04/xx/65-01/22/66	Kannack	Binh Dinh		PCS to Cung Son (New)
A-221 01/xx/66-03/31/69	Cung Son (new)	Phu Yen	VN/ MTD	PCS to RF/PF

A1/311, A1/224A A1/313A 05/28/62-08/01/63	Cung Son (old)	Phu Yen	VN/ MTD	TDY
A1/313, A1/114, A1/123, A1/232, A1/233 04/21/63-04/19/65	Dong Tre	Phu Yen	VN/ MTD	TDY
A5/231 A-231, A-222 04/xx/65-01/22/66	Dong Tre	Phu Yen	VN/ MTD	PCS to RF/PF
A5/3, A-731 09/09/62-08/02/63	Van Canh (old)	Binh Dinh	Jarai/ VN	TDY
A1321B, A1/213 xx/xx/65-01/01/66	Van Canh (new)	Binh Dinh	Jarai/ VN	TDY
A5/223, A-223 01/01/66-06/xx/69	Van Canh (new)	Binh Dinh	Jarai/ VN	PCS to 4th BN MSF
A1/213, A1/412 A1/432, A1/424, A1/433, A1/432 10/12/62-05/03/65	Buon Beng	Phu Bon	VN/ Jarai/ Bahnar	TDY
A5/224, A-224 05/21/65-8/2/68	Phu Tuc	Phu Bon	VN/ Jarai/ Bahnar	PCS (to RF/PF)
A5/501 1964-1965	Hoai An	Binh Dinh	VN/ MTD	PCS
A1/121B, A1/223 1965	Hoai An	Binh Dinh	VN/ MTD	TDY
A-222A, A225, A-225A 01/xx/66-06/24/67	Le Hai	Phu Yen	VN/ MTD	PCS
A1-123 04/27/65-10/20/65	Binh Khe	Binh Dinh	VN/ Jarai	TDY
A1/112 09/17/65-02/23/66	Mai Linh	Phu Bon	VN/Jarai /Rhade	TDY

411

A5/226, A-226 02/01/66-12/02/67	Mai Linh			PCS
A1/321, A1/114 04/27/65-04/15/66	Bong Son	Binh Dinh	VN	TDY
A5-227, A-227 03/07/66-06/12/67	Bong Son			PCS
A-227 06/12/67-03/31/69	Ha Tay	Binh Dinh	VN/ MTD	PCS
A1/122, A1/211 06/01/65-11/25/65	Tuy Phuoc	Binh Dinh	VN	TDY to ROKs
A5/228, A-228 11/25/65-12/15/67	Vinh Thanh	Binh Dinh	VN	PCS
A-120 12/15/67-xx/xx/xx	Vinh Thanh	Binh Thanh	VN	VNSF to RF/PF
A1/35, A1/113A 11/xx/61-09/15/63	Buon Enao	Darlac	Rhade	TDY
A1/334 A1/214A, A1/113	(Buon Ho and Buon Dan Bak),			TDY
A5/2, A1/223 07/21/62-12/05/64	Buon Dan Bak	Darlac	Rhade/ Jarai	TDY
A1/113, A1/232	Buon Ea Ana, Ban Don			
A1/223, A736,	Ban Don and Buon Uing			
A5/214 11/20/64-01/17/65	Ban Don	Darlac	Rhade /Jarai	PCS
A5/214 01/01/65-03/24/65	Suoi Doi	Darlac		PCS
A-231 12/11/67-09/30/70	Tieu Atar	Darlac	VN/ Rhade/ Jarai	PCS

71st BRDB 10/01/70-xx/xx/xx	Tieu Atar	Darlac		to Ben Het
A1/223B, A5/2A 08/xx/62-01/27/64	Buon Tan Mo	Darlac	Rhade/ /Jarai	TDY
A1/221, A1/212, A1/231B	Mewal Plantation/ Buon Uing/ Buno Yum/ Buno Ea Soup	Darlac		TDY
A1/231, A1/312 01/06/64-12/21/64	Buon Brieng	Darlac	Rhade	TDY
A5/232, A-232 11/xx/64-09/10/65				PCS
A-232 09/30/65-01/01/66	Bao Loc (new)	Darlac		PCS
A-232 01/01/66-03/31/69	Tan Rai	Darlac	Rhade	PCS to RF/PF
A1/334B, A1/111A 08/03/62-07/19/63	Buon Ho	Darlac	Mnong/ Rhade	TDY
A1/214, A1/133, A1/132, A1/1xx 08/20/63-11/09/64	Buon Mi Ga	Darlac	Mnong/ Rhade	TDY TDY[563]
A5/212 11/xx/64-04/28/65	Buon Mi Ga			PCS
A-233 04/28/65-08/08/66	Buon Ea Yang	Darlac	Mnong/ Rhade	PCS
A-233 08/08/66-09/20/70	Trang Phuc	Darlac	Jarai/ Rhade	PCS
72nd BRDB 9/21/1970	Trang, Phuc AKA Ban Don	Darlac		

A1/311, A1/411 A1/414 08/01/62-01/17/64	Dam Pau	Tuyen Duc	Koho	TDY
A1/423, A1/431 01/17/64-05/03/65	Phey Srunh	Tuyen Duc	Koho	TDY
A5/1xx, A-234 04/xx/65-05/13/65	Phey Srunh	Tuyen Duc	Koho	PCS
A-234 05/13/65-03/31/70	An Lac	Darlac	VN/ MTD	PCS to RF/PF
A5/17, A5/33, A5/412 02/03/63-05/05/64	Djirai	Lam Dong	Koho/ Bulach	TDY to Go Dau Ha
A-235 03/xx/66-03/31/70	Nhon Co	Quang Duc	VN/ MTD	PCS to RF/PF
A1/113B, A1/221 09/09/62-04/xx/63	Lac Thien	Darlac	VN/ MTD	TDY[564]
A1/312B, A1/323B A1/334B, A1/311B 05/xx/63-01/15/65	Bu Prang (old)	Quang Duc	VN/ MTD	TDY
A5/223 01/15/65-xx/xx/65	Bu Prang (old)	Quang Duc	VN/ Rhade	PCS
A236 05/20/65-09/30/67	Lac Thien	Darlac	VN/ Mnong	PCS to RF/PF
A-236 10/05/67-11/30/70	Bu Prang	Quang Duc	VN/ Rhade	PCS
89th BRDB 12/01/70-09/xx/73	Bu Prang	Quang Duc		Overrun to 21 RG
B1/xx, B1/50, A1/233, A1/122, A1/113 02/02/62-02/28/66	Song Mao	Binh Thuan		TDY
A5/212 11/08/65-02/28/66	Song Mao	Binh Thuan	VN/ MTD	PCS
A-237 01/08/66-08/03/68	Luong Son	Binh Thuan	VN/ Cham	PCS to RF/PF

A1/113A, A1-321, A1/133, A1-433, A1/112A 03/xx/62-02/20/64	Phuoc Thien	Binh Thuan	VN/ Cham	TDY
A-238 07/xx/66-06/30/69	Buon Blech	Darlac	Rhade	PCS to RF/PF
A1/134, A1/312 12/26/62-6/11/63	Krong Kno	Darlac	VN/ MTD	TDY
A1-312A, A1-323A 04/21/63-11/01/64	Buon Sar Pa	Darlac	Rhade	TDY to Eagle Flight
A1-334A, A1/311A	Plei Buk	Darlac	Jarai	TDY
A-239 11/14/66-12/30/70	Duc Lap	Darlac	Mnong/ Rhade	PCS
96th BRDB 01/01/71-10/06/73				to 21 RG
A1/112A, A1/131 A1/134, A1/122, A1/133 01/15/63-01/22/65	Polei Krong	Kontum	VN/ Sedang	TDY
A7/8, A-241 03/25/66-08/31/70	Polei Kleng	Kontum	VN/ Rhade/ Jeh	PCS
62nd BRDB 9/01/70-05/09?/72	Le Thanh			Overrun to 22 RG
A5/13, A-733, A-749, A-733DP, A-749A, A5/231, A-211, A-242 10/01/64-11/30/70	Dak Pek	Kontum	Sedang/ VN	TDY
88th BRDB 11/30/70-05/16/74				Overrun by NVA to 22 RG
A1/334B 01/16/65-05/xx/65	Plateau Gi	Kontum	VN/ Bahnar	TDY

A-214, A-243 05/xx/65-01/15/69				PCS from Suoi Doi
A-111 01/15/69-				VNSF to PF
B1-50(-) 04/30/62-01/14/65	Dak To (old)	Kontum	Sedang/ VN	TDY[565]
A1/332, A1/112B, A/733A, A1-224 A-749A, A-733DT,				to Eagle Flight & A-243
A-218 05/26/65-08/18/65	Dak Sut	Kontum	Sedang/ VN	PCS[566]
A1/322 08/26/65-02/14/66	Dak To (New)	Kontum	Sedang/ VN	TDY
A7/1, A-244 01/20/66-05/15/68	Dak To	Kontum	Sedang/ VN	PCS
01/01/68-12/31/70	Ben Het	Kontum	Sedang/ VN	PCS
95th BRDB 01/01/71-10/12/72	Ben Het	Kontum	Sedang/ VN	Overrun to 22 RG
A-7/12 xx/xx66-11/30/70 A-245	Dak Seang	Kontum	Sedang/ KKK	PCS
90th BRDB 12/01/70-				
A1/222 04/30/62-08/29/63	Mang Buk	Kontum	Katang/	TDY
A5/15, A-735[567] 07/xx/64-03/xx/66			VN	PCS
A-246 03/xx/66-03/31/70	Mang Buk	Kontum	Katang/ VN	PCS to RF/PF
A1/334A, A1/214A 03/10/64-11/xx/64	Plei Djereng	Pleiku	Jarai/ Rhade	TDY

A5/232,A-213, A-251 11/xx/64-10/31/70				PCS
80th BRDB 11/01/70-1/27/73	Le Minh			to 21 RG
A1/314, A1/422 A1/322, A1/321, A1/333 11/01/62-12/xx/64	Plei Mrong	Pleiku	Jarai/ VN	TDY
A5/233, A-212, A-252 12/xx/64-05/01/67				PCS
A-113 05/01/67-10/31/70				VNSF
83rd BRDB 11/01/70-xx/xx/xx				to Gia Nghia 24 RG
A5/16, A-736 09/24/62-08/22/63	Plei Yt	Pleiku	Bahnar/ Jarai	TDY
A-752, A-736 A1/214A, A-752, A1/224 08/03/63-05/xx/65	Chu Dron	Pleiku	Bahnar/ Jarai	TDY
A5/12x, A-215, A-253 05/xx/65-10/31/70	Duc Co	Pleiku	Bahnar/ Jarai	PCS
81st BRDB 11/01/70-2/28/73				to 24 RG
A1/123A, A1/321 A1/334, A-751A 4/10/63-11/xx/64	Plei Do Lim	Pleiku	Jarai/ VN	TDY
A5/224, A-216, A-254 11/xx/64-08/02/66				PCS
08/02/66-				VNSF

Detachment & Dates	Location	Province	CSF	Notes
A-751, A-735, A-751, A1/313 08/01/63-12/05/64	Plei Me	Pleiku	Jarai/ VN	TDY
A5/1xx, A-217, A-255 12/05/64-10/31/70				PCS
82nd BRDB 11/01/70-09/02/74				to 24 RG

III Corps Tactical Zone

Detachment & Dates[570]	Location	Province	CSF[568]	Notes[569]
A5/29, A5/30 01/20/63-12/28/63	Nuoc Vang	Phuoc Thanh	VN/ Camb Stieng	TDY to Bu Ghia Map
A-324, A-321 03/05/67-xx/xx/68	Ben Soi	Tay Ninh	VN/ Camb	PCS
A-136/A-120 xx/xx/68-08/31/70				VNSF
65th BRDB 09/01/70-				to 33 RG
B1/220/A1/124A A1/112 07/20/64-04/xx/65	Suoi Da	Tay Ninh	VN/ Camb	TDY
A-322 04/xx/65-02/28/67	Suoi Da			PCS to Prek Loc
A-322 03/30/67-12/19/67	Prek Loc			PCS to Katum
A-322 01/09/68-10/31/70	Katum	Tay Ninh	VN/ Camb/ Cham	PCS
84th BRDB 11/1/1970-				

A-323 03/xx/66-12/22/67	Trai Bi	Tay Ninh	VN	PCS to Thien Ngon
A-323 12/08/67-09/30/70	Thien Ngon	Tay Ninh	VN	PCS
73rd BRDP 10/01/70-				
B-33 05/xx/65-11/30/70	Hon Quan	Binh Long	VN/Camb/ Stieng	PCS Closed
A5/7, A5/35 01/20/63-11/30/63	Tuc Trung	Binh Khanh	VN	TDY to Minh Thanh
A5/35/ A5/xx/ A5/132 09/xx/63-10/xx/64	Minh Thanh	Binh Long	VN/ Camb/ Stieng	TDY
A5/222, A-331, A-325, A-332 10/xx/64-04/30/70				PCS to RF/PF
A-331	Loc Ninh			
74th BRDB 05/01/70-04/06/72				Overrun
A-332B, A-325, A-333 05/xx/65-01/04/67	Chon Thon	Binh Long	VN/ Camb/ Stieng	PCS to Chi Linh
A-333 01/04/67-12/15/69	Chi Linh	Binh Long	VN/ Camb/ Stieng	PCS to 1st Cav
A-334 03/11/67-11/30/70	Tong Le Chon	Tay Ninh	VN/ Camb/ Cham	PCS
92nd BRDB 12/01/70-04/11/74				to 32 RG
B5/320, B-34 05/xx/65-05/31/70	Song Be	Phuoc Long	VN/ Camb/ Stieng	PCS

A5/8, A5/30 12/27/62-10/03/63	Bu Ghia	Phuoc Long	VN/ Camb/ Stieng	TDY to Bu Dop
A5/9, A5/133, A1/124A, A5/113A, A1/234A 11/20/63-03/15/65	Bu Ghia Map	Phuoc Long	VN/ Stieng/ Camb	TDY
A5/341B 03/xx/65-07/22/65	Bu Ghia Map	Phuoc Long	VN/ Camb/ Stieng	PCS to Bu Dop
A5/30, A5/4, A5/113 09/15/63-03/xx/65	Bu Dop	Phuoc Long	VN/ Camb/ Stieng	TDY
A5/133B, A1/124B A5/341A, A-341 03/xx/65-12/31/70				TDY PCS
97th BRDB 1/10/1971-				
A-342 05/26/65-01/31/70	Dong Xoai	Phuoc Long	VN/ Camb/ Stieng	PCS to RF/PF
A-343 04/26/66-05/31/70	Duc Phong	Phuoc Long	VN/ Rhade/ Camb	PCS to RF/PF
A-344 04/02/67-04/30/70	Bunard	Phuoc Long	VN/ Camb/ Rhade	PCS
??BRDB 05/01/70-				
A-353, A-326 11/15/67-10/31/70	Duc Hue	Long An	VN/ Camb/ Chinese	PCS
83rd BRDB 11/01/70-				to 33 RG

Detachment & Dates[573]	Location	Province	CSF[571]	Notes[572]
B-36 06/01/67-11/19/70	III MSF	Phuoc Tuy	VN/ Camb/ MTD?	PCS to UITG/ FANK
A-362 xx/xx/xx-11/30/70	Trang Sup	Tay Ninh	VN/ Nung	PCS
12/01/70-06/30/71				vated

IV Corps Tactical Zone

Detachment & Dates[573]	Location	Province	CSF[571]	Notes[572]
A-412 10/xx/65-11/15/68	Kinh Quan II	Kien Tuong	VN/ Camb/ Nung	PCS
A-144				VNSF
A-431, A-413 5/xx/65-10/31/70	Binh Thanh Thon	Kien Tuong	Camb/ Nung Hoa Hao	PCS
86th BRDB 11/01/70-	Moc Hoa			
A-414 3/xx/68-08/11/70	Thanh Tri	Kien Phuong	VN/ Camb	PCS
67th BRDB 8/12/70-	Moc Hoa			to 25 RG
A-415 04/xx/65-10/02/70	Tuyen Ngon	Kien Tuong	VN/ Camb/ Nung	PCS
75th BRDB 10/2/70-	Moc Hoa			Deacti-vated
A-429, A-421 05/xx/66-11/30/70	Ba Xoai	Chao Duc	VN/ Camb/	PCS
94th BRDB	Phu Bai			to 15RG
A-422 07/xx/64-06/27/67	Vinh Gia	Chao Doc	VN/ Camb/	PCS

A-149 6/27/77-11/30/70				VNSF
93rd BRDB 12/01/70-	Chi Lang			to 15 RG
A-425, A-431 04/xx/65-09/30/70	Cai Cai	Kien Tuong	VN/ Camb/	PCS
76th BRDB 10/01/70-	Moc Hoa			to 25 RG
A-432 09/xx/70-11/30/70	Chi Lang	Chao Duc	VN/ Camb/	PCS
85th BRDB 12/01/70-	Chi Lang			to 7RG
A-442 06/15/68-08/31/70	To Chau (new)	Kien Giang	VN/ Camb/ Nung	PCS
66th BRDB 09/01/70-	Chi Lang			

Appendix D, Montagnard Tribes

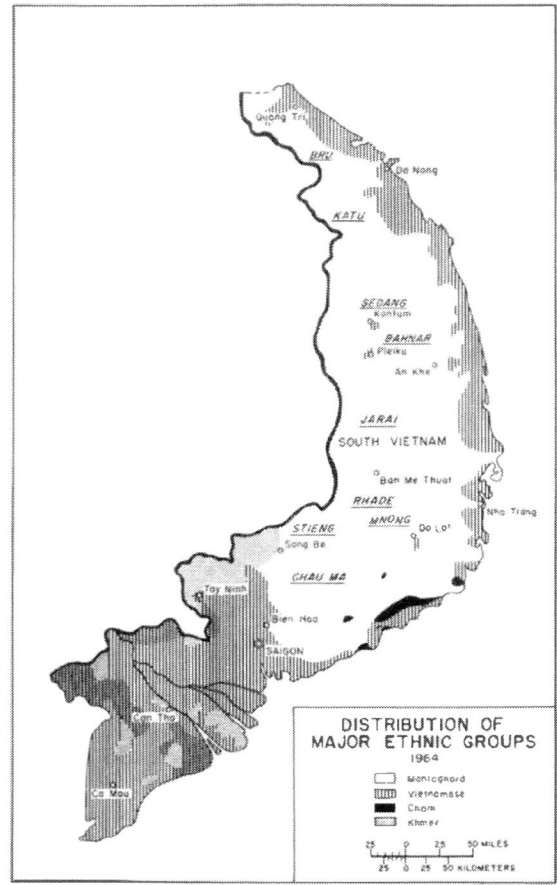

Ethnic Groups (Francis J. Kelly)

The information in this appendix was extracted from a U. S. Army pamphlet published in 1966. As such, the information was current during the 2nd Indochina War, but much has changed since then. Population and geographic area numbers are no longer accurate but much of the ethnic information about the tribes remains valid. All the highland groups in Vietnam are part of two large ethnic groups: the Malayo-Polynesian and the Mon-Khmer.

The Bahnar

The Bahnar tribes, numbering between 80,000 and 200,000, occupy a strategic area of approximately 4,000 square kilometers in the Central Highlands of the Republic of Vietnam. The Bahnar dialects are Mon-Khmer in origin and are related to those of the Stieng, M'nong, and Sedang, three other important tribal groups. Family structure is based on a bilateral kinship system, with neither male nor female dominant. The family and the village are the basic units of political organization. Villages are grouped into a regional association or *toring* for purposes of administering intervillage matters such as hunting, fishing, and farming rights. Clan structure or organization appears to be lacking. Extremely religious, the Bahnar interact continually with the animistic spirits surrounding them. The meaning and origin of the name Bahnar is unknown. Although the precise number and breakdown of Bahnar tribal subgroups is in dispute, most authorities agree that the following are subgroups: Alakong, Bonam, Golar, Ho Drong, Jo Long, Kon Ko De, Kontum, Krem, Roh, Tolo (Tolotenir), and To Sung. Despite the fact that there is insufficient evidence to substantiate their claims, other sources include the Cham-Hrui, Rolo, Boutes, and Rengao among the Bahnar. The various Bahnar subgroups can be roughly divided as follows: Eastern Bahnar subgroups — Alakong, Bonam, Kon Ko De, Krem, Roh, and Tolo, Western Bahnar subgroups — Ho Drong, Golar, Jo Long, Kontum, and To Sung. The general patterns of customs and traditions differ between the Eastern and Western subgroups. The Hroi are also usually classified as a Bahnar subgroup. However, since the Hroi have been greatly influenced by the Rhade and the Cham, two important Malayo-Polynesian groups, this subgroup is the subject of a separate chapter in this volume. The Hroi would also be considered an Eastern Bahnar subgroup. Although the differences are largely due to varying degrees of contact with other peoples, the dialects of the Eastern Bahnar are more closely related to one another than they are to the dialects of the Western Bahnar. Although no accurate records exist, the Bahnar population was estimated at 80,000 in 1952, but estimates for 1960 indicated that they may number as many as 200,000. They live north of the Darlac Plateau in the area comprising the western portion of Binh Dinh Province, northwestern Phu Yen Province, northeastern Phu Bon and Pleiku Provinces, southeastern Kontum, and southwestern

Quang Ngai Province. As closely as can be determined, the groups neighboring the Bahnar include: the Jarai to the west and southwest; the Rengao to the northwest; the Sedang, Monom, and Hre to the north; the ethnic Vietnamese to the east; and the Cham to the east and southeast. The area inhabited by the Bahnar is centered in the Binh Dinh Mountains and consists mainly of rounded hills of crystalline rock, many of which are over 3,000 feet in elevation. Main drainage is into the Song Ba River and its tributaries. The climate of this mountainous area is influenced by both the summer (May — October) and winter (mid-September — March) monsoon winds, which provide a regular seasonal alternation of wind. In the summer these winds come mainly from the southwest; in the winter, from the northeast. Agriculture is greatly dependent upon the rain brought by the summer monsoon. The winter monsoon also provides some precipitation, although this is quite undependable. In contrast to the monsoon, during July and August excessively arid local winds are dominant. Called the "Winds of Laos," these hot, dry winds, sometimes blowing with extreme violence and provoking intense evaporation, descend the eastern edges of the Bahnar land, which slopes to the coastal area. Inland temperatures are lower than those along the coastal lowland areas, differing by more than 15 degrees during the winter months. Much of the Bahnar area is covered by rain forest, though some savanna is evident to the south. The tropical rain forest has a three-story canopy, the topmost layer consisting of large trees whose crowns form an almost continuous canopy 75 to 90 feet high. Below this is a second canopy of smaller trees, reaching a height of 45 to 60 feet. Next is a fair abundance of seedlings and saplings of various sizes. Humidity is high, and many herbaceous plants, such as orchids, woody climbing plants, and liana, are common. The rain forest area can usually be penetrated with little difficulty. Savanna areas consist principally of tranh (Imperata cylindrica) grass — a tall, coarse grass used for thatching roofs of houses; when young and tender, tranh is used for grazing. Probably repeated cultivation, fire, and poor soil conditions have created these savanna areas. Various wild animals are found in the forests: bears, buffaloes, elephants, boars, deer, tigers, and monkeys. The forest abounds with leeches and other bloodsuckers, especially during and after heavy rains. Transportation is very difficult in this region, particularly during the rainy season. The Song Ba River, a broad stream in its lower reaches, is seldom used for navigation due to shifting channels and variable depths. Large boats can utilize short stretches during the high-water season caused by the rain-bearing monsoon, whereas only small native craft can use the waterways at other times of the year. The Song Ba tributaries are generally navigable by only the smallest craft. A number of roads cross the Bahnar area: National Route 14 connects Kontum with Pleiku and Ban Me Thuot to the south and runs north and east to Hoi An on the coast. An Khe is located on National Route 19, which links An Khe with Pleiku.

Bahnar Paramilitary Capabilities

The Bahnar have a reputation as skilled and capable fighters, both offensively and defensively. They pride themselves on their skill as hunters. The Bahnar are capable scouts, trackers, and guides, and if given intensive modern training, support, and leadership, they could become exceptionally effective in jungle combat.

The territory inhabited by the Bahnar is one of the most strategic in the Republic of Vietnam. Viet Cong supply lines run through the Bahnar area and the presence of the Viet Cong in comparatively large numbers is a constant factor in the day-to-day lives of the tribesmen. The Bahnar have been forced, under threat of terror and reprisals, to give the Viet Cong support in the form of food, finances, and labor. When the tactics of subversion, propaganda, and simple cajolery fail to subdue the Bahnar, the Viet Cong resort to murder and other brutalities.

Although the Bahnar have a reputation for being aggressive and canny fighters and reportedly display initiative and sophistication in defending themselves, they are often coerced into cooperating with the Viet Cong. Unless given Government training and support, the isolated Bahnar do not have the means and backing to withstand Viet Cong hostility.

The Bahnar village has a traditional organization for defense against surprise attack. The communal house, normally used as the sleeping place for the bachelors of the village, is in addition a stronghold for defense in terms of warfare conducted with lances, knives, and crossbows. From the communal house, the Bahnar warriors can effectively defend the village. Formerly, Bahnar villages were surrounded by a stockade, but in recent years these have been replaced by fences. Due to increased military activity within the area, more secure perimeter defenses are probably now employed.

The Bahnar determination to defend themselves is strongly influenced by their estimates of probable success. If faced with superiority in numbers or weapons, the Bahnar may capitulate rather than fight. This characteristic is not unique to the Bahnar; rather, it is common among people inadequately armed, trained, and led.

427

Although the Bahnar prefer defensive to offensive warfare, they have a reputation for engaging in aggressive warfare if provoked. They have reportedly been capable of mounting well-organized attacks on distant villages.

The Bahnar have traditionally relied upon spears, swords, crossbows, and poisoned arrows as weapons. They are also well acquainted with the use of traps, pits, and spiked foot traps (concealed sharpened sticks). Some Bahnar have been trained in the use of modern weapons and have had military instruction from the French, Vietnamese, and Americans.

Because of their relatively small physical size, the tribesmen are more comfortable and adept with small light weapons than with heavier ones. The tribesmen can handle large weapons that are easily disassembled and quickly reassembled. Traditionally, the Bahnar take good care of their weapons; if they can carry and handle a weapon conveniently, they will generally use it well.

The Bahnar are less proficient in the use of more sophisticated devices, such as mortars, explosives, and mines, because of their difficulty in understanding the more theoretical and technical aspects of timing and trajectory.

Like other tribal groups, the Bahnar learn more readily from actual demonstrations of techniques and procedures than they do from standard classroom methods. Tribesmen with military service under the French are an asset in the training and instruction of younger tribesmen.

The Bru

The Bru, the most northern of the Montagnard tribal peoples in the Republic of Vietnam, inhabit an area on the borders of the Republic of Vietnam, Laos, and North Vietnam. Bru tribesmen live in isolated, autonomous villages in Quang Tri and Thua Thien Provinces, in Laos, and in North Vietnam. They have no central tribal political organization. The Bru language belongs to the Mon-Khmer language family and is related to the languages of the Her, Cue, Bahnar, and Sedang, Bru society is patriarchal and lineage and inheritance follow the male line. Also called the Broun, Ca-Lo, Gallery, Leo, Leung, Van Kiel, and Mnong Kong, the Bru are estimated to number between 40,000 and 50,000 persons. Approximately 26,000 to 38,000 Bru tribes people live in the Republic of Vietnam: 8,000 to 20,000 in the Hong Hoa District of Quang Tri Province, 8,000 in the vicinity of Lao Bao on the Laotian border, and about 10,000 in the area of Cam Phu. Some Bru are also found in North Vietnam and Laos, but population estimates were not available for the tribespeople in these two countries. The Bru in the Republic of Vietnam inhabit the Annamite Mountains west of Quang Tri in the area near the 17th parallel. They may also inhabit a plateau region, Kha Leung, located to the west of the Annamite Mountains in Laos. Other Bru are found north of the 17th parallel in North Vietnam. The Annamite Mountains are of folded limestone, with steep declivities on the eastern or coastal side and a more gentle slope on the western or Laotian side. The rugged terrain makes travel through these mountains very difficult; generally, travel routes through the mountains follow the rivers. Several high mountain peaks dominate the rough terrain of the Bru area: north of National Route 9 are Dong Sa Mui (about 5,240 feet) and Dong Voi Mep, also called Dent du Tigre (about 5,820 feet). In the southern Bru area, Quang Ngai (about 5,750 feet) dominates National Route 9. The mountains south of the Bru region, below Hue, are overshadowed by the gigantic Massif de l'Ataouat which rises to about 6,980 feet. Two major rivers, the Bo Dien and the Han Giang, flow east from the mountains into the China Sea. In its upper reaches, the Han Giang is also known as Song Quang Tri and Da Krong. The Se Pone River flows west out of the Bru area into Laos. National Route 9, the major road crossing the Bru area, extends inland from Dong Ha, following the Bo Dien River. At Mai Lanh, the highway turns south to follow the upper reaches of the Han Giang River, then it winds through a mountain pass just south of Dong Voi Mep; finally at Lao Bao the highway enters Laos, paralleling the course of the Se Pone River. For centuries the course of Route 9, determined by the nature of the terrain, has been the principal egress from these mountains to the coast. Part of this journey, from just west of Huong Hoa, is commonly made by water down the Han Giang River to the coast at Quang Tri. In crudely made dugout canoes, the Bru navigate the many mountain streams and small rivers. The climate of the Bru region is affected by both the summer (May-October) and winter (November-January) monsoons, which provide a regular seasonal alternation of wind. In summer, these winds blow mainly from the southwest; in the winter, from the northeast. Agriculture is greatly dependent upon the rain brought by the summer monsoon. Precipitation is high, averaging over 60 inches in the lower elevations to more than 150 inches in the higher elevations and on some slopes. Normally the weather is warm and humid, but the temperatures in the mountains are generally lower than those along the coast. The high and relatively evenly distributed precipitation gives this area rain forest vegetation of two distinct belts. At the higher elevations is the primary rain forest, where the trees, with an average height of 75 to 90 feet, form a continuous canopy. Below this canopy are smaller trees of 45 to 60 feet in height, and below this second layer is a fair abundance of seedlings and saplings. Orchids, other herbaceous plants, epiphytes, and woody climbing plants known as lianas are profuse. Little light penetrates this type of forest and there is not much ground growth. During the dry season, the forest can usually be penetrated on foot with little difficulty. The second belt or secondary rain forest, which develops after land in the primary rain forest has been cleared and then left uncultivated, is more extensive in this area. In this forest the trees are small and close together, and there is an abundance of ground growth, lianas, and herbaceous climbers. Penetration is difficult without the constant use of the machete.

Bru Paramilitary Capabilities

Given the incentive and motivation and provided with the necessary training, leadership, and support, the Bru can become an effective force against the Viet Cong. The tribesmen can serve as informers, trackers and guides, intelligence agents, interpreters, and translators. With intensive training and support, the Bru can be organized to defend their villages against the Viet Cong; with good leadership, they can be organized into an effective counterguerrilla combat unit. U.S. personnel who worked with the Bru reported that the tribesmen were effective and loyal soldiers.

In the past, the Bru were considered capable fighters, whether fighting offensively in raids against other groups or defensively within their villages. Recently some Bru have been trained by U.S. personnel and are familiar with U.S. operational techniques as well as modern equipment.

When psychological pressures to win Bru support fail, the Viet Cong have resorted to outright brutality and terror. Frequently, the Bru yield to and cooperate with the Viet Cong; without Government training and support, they do not have the wherewithal to oppose the Viet Cong. Except for the resettled communities, Bru villages have no able organization for defense. Bru villagers with adequate training and support have shown their willingness to defend themselves and will occasionally initiate aggressive action against the Viet Cong.

The inclination of the Bru to fight aggressively is one that must be developed and supported with modern weapons and training. They defend themselves vigorously when they, their families, or their villages are threatened and when they have adequate resources and chances for success.

In the past, the Bru relied upon crossbows and spears. The Bru also are familiar with the use of traps, pits, and concealed sharpened sticks used as foot traps. Some Bru have received military training from U.S. personnel and are familiar with modern weapons. Their relatively small stature limits the type of weapons the Bru can use, but they are proficient in handling light weapons such as the AR15 rifle, the Thompson submachine gun, and the carbine. The tribesmen are less proficient in the use of the M-1 or the Browning automatic rifle, although they can handle larger weapons which can be disassembled, carried by two or more men, and then quickly reassembled.

The Bru pride themselves upon their hunting skill and their mastery of traditional weapons; they are equally as proud of their skill and marksmanship with modern weapons. If a Bru can carry and handle a weapon conveniently, he will use it well.

The Bru have difficulty handling sophisticated devices—such as mortars, explosives, and mines—as proficiently as hand weapons. They find the more abstract and technical aspects of such weapons—such as timing trajectories—difficult to absorb.

The Bru can absorb basic military training and concepts. Their natural habitat gives them an excellent background for tracking and ambush activities; they are resourceful and adaptable in the jungle.

The Bru learn techniques and procedures readily from actual demonstration using the weapon itself as a teaching aid. They do not learn as well from blackboard demonstrations, an approach which is too abstract for them.

The Cua

The Cua, one of the least known Montagnard tribal groups of the Republic of Vietnam, inhabit the rough mountainous terrain of northern Quang Ngai Province and the south-central portion of Quang Tin Province. They have no central tribal political system nor governing force. Autonomous Cua villages form an identifiable tribal grouping through intermarriage and shared language, customs, and traditions. The Cua language belongs to the

Mon-Khmer language family and is closely related to the language of the Hre, the neighboring tribal group to the south. Cua society is patriarchal, the lineage and inheritance follow the male line. The Cua number between 15,000 and 20,000 persons. The Cua should not be confused with the Cao, a subgroup of the Katu. The Katu are not contiguous with the Cua but are separated from them by the Jeh tribal group. The Cua inhabit the eastern portion of the area of the Annam Cordillera known as the Massif du Ngoc Ang. This massif is a series of rounded hills, primarily of shale, slate, and schist, with occasional isolated granite peaks, some of which are 8,000 feet high. The eastern part of the massif is flanked by a series of eroded plateaus. East of the massif, the Cua inhabit the Tra Bong area of Quang Ngai Province and the Bong Mieu area of Quang Tin Province. These areas rise sharply from the narrow coastal plain and are cut by many narrow, steep river valleys with short and swift-flowing streams. The Cua territory overlooks the lowland coastal regions and valleys inhabited by the Vietnamese, who are settled as far west as the market town of Tra Bong. On the western edge of the Cua area is the Jeh tribe, and to the south are the Sedang and Hre. The climate of the region is affected both by the summer (May — October) and winter (November — January) monsoons. In the summer, the warm, moist, and unstable winds come mainly from the southwest and cause heavy local showers and thunderstorms. In the winter, a northeasterly airflow up the eastern slopes of the Annam Cordillera causes cloudy, rainy weather. Precipitation is high — averaging 120 inches in the lower elevations and more than 150 inches in the higher areas and on certain slopes. Normally, the weather is warm and humid, with the wettest season occurring during the summer. Clouds are frequent, especially during the winter months, and thick fog is common but is dispersed by the morning sun. Temperatures vary over 15 degrees between the summer and the winter seasons. Actual surface temperatures average 60 to 65 degrees Fahrenheit in winter (January) and over 80 degrees in summer (July). Severe typhoons rarely reach the Cua territory, although they have an important influence on the climate of the area. Mild typhoons occur between July and November and are usually preceded by high winds and cool, dry weather. When they do strike, they bring heavy rainfall that may last throughout the night and into the morning, causing floods and heavy damage, including the uprooting of forests. Two types of rain forest, with vegetation of tropical broadleaf trees and bamboo, appear in two distinct belts. In the higher, more inaccessible regions is the primary rain forest, with tall trees that occasionally reach heights of 135 feet and form a continuous canopy. Below this canopy is a middle level of smaller trees and a third layer of seedlings and saplings. Orchids and other epiphytes, and woody climbing plants known as lianas, are also common. Little sunlight penetrates to the ground. Bamboo and rattan are particularly luxuriant along watercourses. Although from the air the primary rain forest appears impenetrable, it can be traversed on foot with little difficulty. The lower areas and slopes to the east are covered with secondary rain forest, which develops where a primary rain forest has been cleared and then abandoned. The trees are small and close together, with heavy ground growth and abundance of lianas and other climbers. Only a few isolated high trees appear. This forest is difficult to travel, being impenetrable without constant use of the machete. On the highest slopes of the area inhabited by the Cua, the only vegetation may be waist-high grass. Few roads exist in the Cua area. One secondary road connects 92 with National Route 1 at Tarn Ky and runs through the Bong Mieu region, ending at the village of Tra My, where it becomes a track eventually reaching Kontum. Another secondary road starts at National Route 1 just north of Quang Ngai and goes west into Cua country for a short distance until it too turns into a track. Both of these roads were so damaged during the Indochina War that they are little more than trails. They are full of potholes and, during rains, provides channels for rushing torrents of water. Trails are few in number and difficult, if not impossible, to sight from the air. Rivers are short and often run through narrow, high valleys. They are, for the most part, unnavigable, although during high water small boats and canoes can be used on some stretches. During periods of high water, however, the occasional typhoons make water transportation even more hazardous.

Cua Paramilitary Capabilities

The Cua are not particularly noted as warriors, although one source credits them with being aggressive in the field when they are well trained and well led. The Cua do pride themselves on their skill as hunters; with intensive training, support, and leadership, they might become effective in jungle warfare. At present, the Cua are capable scouts, trackers, and guides.

When the psychological pressures or conversion to subversive activities fail, the Viet Cong have resorted to outright brutality and terror. Frequently, the Cua yield and cooperate with the Viet Cong. The isolated Cua do not have the wherewithal to oppose the Viet Cong and need Government training and support. Cua villages have no able organizations for defense except those equipped, trained, and organized by the Government.

The Cua have traditionally used spears and crossbows with poisoned arrows. They are well acquainted with the use of traps, pits, and concealed sharpened sticks (used as foot-traps). Presumably, some of the Cua have been trained in the use of modern weapons by both the Government and the Viet Cong.

Their relatively small stature limits the modern weapons the Cua can use; but they are proficient in handling light weapons such as the AR.15 rifle, the Thompson submachine gun, and the carbine. The tribesmen are less proficient in the use of the M-1 or the Browning Automatic Rifle, although they can handle larger weapons which can be disassembled and quickly reassembled. If a Cua can carry and handle a weapon conveniently, he will use it well.

The Cua cannot handle sophisticated devices, such as mortars, explosives, and mines, as proficiently as hand weapons. They find it difficult to understand the more abstract and technical aspects—such as timing trajectories—of such weapons.

Photographs show Cua villages have no outside defenses against surprise attack. However, houses and villages are usually built in relatively inaccessible and easily defensible locations. Formerly, the villages were surrounded by stockades, but these were replaced with fences during the French colonial period. As military action in Cua areas intensifies, perimeter defense may again be employed.

The Cua inclination to defend themselves is strongly influenced by their estimated probable success. If faced with an enemy with vast numerical and weapons superiority, the Cua will capitulate rather than fight.

The Cua can absorb basic military training and concepts. Their natural habitat gives them an excellent background for tracking and ambush activities; they are resourceful and adaptable in the jungle.

The Cua learn techniques and procedures most readily from actual demonstration, using the weapon itself as a teaching aid. They do not learn as well from blackboard demonstrations; such an approach is too abstract for them.

The Cua who have received some modern military training are

invaluable in training the younger tribesmen.

The Halang

The Halang inhabit the rough, mountainous terrain near the intersection of the borders of Laos, Cambodia, and the Republic of Vietnam. It is estimated that the Halang population in all three countries exceeds 40,000. Of Mon-Khmer ethnic origin, the Halang speak a language closely related to that of their north-eastern neighbors, the Sedang. Halang society is patriarchal and the autonomous village constitutes the highest level of political organization. Their agrarian economy depends on slash-and-burn agriculture for the primary crop of rice and the secondary crop of corn. Believing in a host of animistic spirits, the Halang spend their lives appeasing evil spirits, yet they consider the veneration of good spirits unnecessary. The Halang, also known as the Selang, are called Saleng by the Laotians. The word halang reportedly means "mixed blood." The only reported subgroup of the Halang are the Halang-Doan, most of whom live in Laos. However, the classification of the Halang-Doan is confusing, for they are sometimes treated as a separate group, or even as a subgroup of the Sedang. The exact number of Halang is unknown. In 1962 it was estimated there were 30,000 Halang in the Republic of Vietnam, 10,000 in Laos, and "some" in Cambodia. During the past 10 years the Halang have evidently been moving continually westward into Laos and Cambodia, so that only a minority may now reside in the Republic of Vietnam.

In the Republic of Vietnam, the Halang live in the western and southwestern portions of Kontum Province, contiguous to the Laotian and Cambodian borders. The Dak Hodrai, a tributary of the Se San River, traverses this region from north to south. There are no major roads in this area. On the north and northeast the Halang are surrounded by the Sedang; on the east, by the Rengao; and on the southeast and south, by the Jarai. The Bahnar are located a bit further south and east, around the city of Kontum. The Halang area consists of heavily forested rolling hills and steep mountains cut by many narrow river valleys. The paucity of roads, trails, and navigable waterways precludes passage through the region, especially during the rainy season from April to mid-September. The summer monsoon (April-mid-September) and the winter monsoon (mid-September-March) provide a regular seasonal alternation of wind. In the summer, these winds come mainly from the southwest; in the winter, from the northeast. Agriculture is greatly dependent upon the monsoon-borne rain. Precipitation is high — averaging more than 80 inches in the lower elevation and more than 150 inches in the higher areas. Normally the weather is warm and humid, with frequent cloudiness. The high and relatively evenly distributed precipitation gives this area rain forest vegetation of two distinct belts. At the higher elevations is the primary rain forest, where the trees, with an average height of 75 to 90 feet, form a continuous canopy. Below this canopy are smaller trees of 45 to 60 feet in height, and below this second layer is a fair abundance of seedlings and saplings. Orchids, other herbaceous plants, epiphytes, and woody climbing plants known as lianas are profuse. Little light penetrates this type of forest and there is not much ground growth. During the dry season, this forest can usually be penetrated on foot with little difficulty. The second belt or secondary rain forest, which develops after land in the primary rain forest has been cleared and then left uncultivated, is more extensive in this area. In this forest the trees are small and close together, and there is an abundance of ground growth, lianas, and herbaceous climbers. Penetration is difficult without the constant use of the machete. The Dak Hodrai, the principal river of the region, flows in a north-south direction through the center of the Halang territory. Farther to the west, in Cambodia and Laos, the Halang area gradually becomes a plateau near the Se Kong River. The rugged terrain of the Halang territory and the large forested areas are unfavorable for helicopter and other air operations.

Halang Paramilitary Capabilities

Given the incentive and motivation and provided with the necessary training, leadership, and support, the Halang could possibly become an effective force against the Viet Cong. The tribesmen could serve as informers, trackers and guides, intelligence agents, interpreters, and translators. With intensive training and support, the Halang could be organized to defend their villages against the Viet Cong.

Consideration should be given, however, to the Halang tendency to avoid the conflict between the Vietnamese Government and the Viet Cong. The westward migration of the Halang into Laos and

Cambodia should also be examined before making plans for the military use of the tribesmen.

The Halang military experience appears to be limited to the traditional tribal raiding, involving weapons such as the crossbow, lance, and knife. There are no reports in the available literature that Halang tribesmen have received modern military training from the French, Vietnamese, or Americans.

The Hre

The Hre are one of the largest Mon-Khmer-speaking Montagnard tribal groups in the Republic of Vietnam. Estimated to number at least 27,000 and perhaps as many as 210,000 persons, the Hre live in both the river valleys and highlands of Quang Ngai Province. The highest order of political organization among the Hre is the village unit, although in the past they have combined into larger groups against Annamese (ethnic Vietnamese) aggression. Shared language, customs, and traditions are the major factors uniting these autonomous villages into an identifiable tribal grouping. Hre families are patriarchal, and kinship is reckoned along the male line. Their religion is animistic and involves belief in good and evil spirits which dwell in both persons and the natural environment. When traditional customs have been violated or ill luck strikes, animals are sacrificed to placate these spirits. Many Hre are sedentary and practice irrigated wet-rice agriculture; the remainder are seminomadic and practice slash-and-burn agriculture. The name Hre is used to describe the large tribal group which inhabits the river valleys and mountainous areas to the west of Quang Ngai. Although the Hre use the term to mean only those members of the group who live along the Song Re or Hre River, the term Hre is used by outsiders as the generic name for the entire group. Hre subgroups are named after rivers in the tribal area: the Dvak, Kare (Kha-Re, Kre), Tava, and Ba Vach or Ba Voch. Although these names are used by the tribesmen, the only division of the tribe commonly used by outsiders is that of highland and lowland groups. The highland Hre inhabit the isolated mountain areas and the upper reaches of the numerous rivers of the area while the lowland group inhabits the remaining areas of the Hre territory. Although the exact population figures are not available, the Hre are one of the largest Montagnard groups: estimates vary from 27,000 to as high as 210,000, with the most probable estimates ranging from 90,000 to 120,000. The Hre are concentrated in the river valleys of the eastern part of the Annam Cordillera in Quang Ngai and northern Binh Dinh Provinces. To the east, they overlook the lowland coastal delta regions; while to the west, the Hre live in sparse settlements in the mountains almost as far as the Massif du Ngoc Ang and the Plateau of Kontum. The coastal lowlands to the east and northeast of the Hre are inhabited by ethnic Vietnamese. To the north are the Cua; to the west, the Sedang; and to the south, various Bahnar groups. These three tribal groups have languages, customs, and economic conditions which differ from the Hre, especially the lowland Hre. The Hre area is a remnant of a series of eroded plateaus dominated by high isolated peaks, some as high as 5,400 feet. The area consists mainly of slate, shale, schist, and other friable rocks. The plateau rises quite sharply from the narrow coastal plain and has many river valleys, some broad and meandering. The rivers, however, are short and swift, with varying currents and depths — a consequence of rain-bearing monsoons and typhoons. The summer monsoon (May-October) and the winter monsoon (November- January) provide a regular seasonal alternation of wind. In the summer, these winds come mainly from the southwest; in the winter, from the northeast. The eastern portion of the region has the most rain from September to January, while in the western portion the rainy season occurs during the summer months. Agriculture is greatly dependent upon the monsoon-borne rain. Precipitation is high — averaging more than 80 inches in the lower elevations and more than 160 inches in the higher areas. Normally the weather is warm and humid, with frequent cloudiness, especially from January to April, in the eastern foothills. Temperatures vary by roughly 15 degrees between summer and winter. Actual surface temperatures average 60 to 65 degrees Fahrenheit in winter (January) and above 80 degrees Fahrenheit in summer (July). Typhoons, occurring between July and November, also influence the climate. Preceded by high winds and cool, dry weather, the typhoons bring heavy rainfall, sometimes lasting 24 hours, that often floods and uproots the forests. However, intensive typhoons rarely reach the western part of the Hre area. The high and relatively evenly distributed precipitation gives this area rain forest vegetation of two distinct belts. At the higher elevations is the first belt, primary rain forest, where the trees of an average height of 75 to 90 feet form a continuous canopy. Below 162 this canopy are smaller trees of 45 to 60 feet in height, and below this second layer is a fair abundance of seedlings and saplings. Orchids, other herbaceous plants, epiphytes, and woody climbing plants known as lianas are profuse. Little light penetrates this type of forest, and there is not much ground growth. During the dry season, this forest can usually be penetrated on foot with little difficulty. The second belt, or secondary rain forest, which develops after land in the primary rain forest has been cleared and then left uncultivated, is more extensive in this area. In this forest the trees are small and close together, and there is an abundance of ground growth, lianas, and herbaceous climbers. Penetration is difficult without the constant use of the machete. The secondary rain forest is an especially unhealthy malaria area. Malaria, rather than the dense forest or the warlike tribes, has inhibited deeper Vietnamese penetration from the east. Despite proximity to one of the most densely populated Vietnamese areas, there has been little migration or settlement of the foothills and mountains of the Hre area — except for former military colonies. Few roads exist in the Hre area. A main road extends from Mo Due, on National Route 1, to Kontum through Ba To and Gia Vuc. Formerly a bumpy path, this road was paved in the middle 1950's. A narrow and tortuous road, this highway is not dependable, as the Viet Cong frequently damage it. Other roads or trails (which will accommodate jeeps) extend from Quang Ngai to Ba To and from Quang Ngai to Gia Vuc, along the Song Tra Khuc River. Trails are few, difficult to traverse, and are almost invisible from the air. Horses are used to transport goods; bicycles are a popular means of travel in the lowlands. Rivers are, for the most part, impassable. Even during high water, only very small boats and canoes can navigate the rivers. During low water seasons, the riverbed reveals many impeding rocks. Additional hazards to water transportation are typhoons and monsoons.

Hre Paramilitary Capabilities

Given the incentive and motivation and provided with the necessary training, leadership, and support, the Hre can become an effective force against the Viet Cong. Like the Sedang, the Hre are rated among the best and most tenacious Montagnard fighters. The tribesmen can serve as informers, trackers and guides, intelligence agents, interpreters, and translators. With intensive training and support, the Hre can be organized to defend their villages against the

Viet Cong; with good leadership they can be organized into an effective counterguerrilla combat force.

When psychological pressures to win Hre support fail, the Viet Cong have resorted to outright brutality and terror. Frequently, the Hre yield and cooperate with the Viet Cong; without Government training and support, they do not have the wherewithal to oppose the Viet Cong. Hre villages with adequate training and support will defend themselves and will occasionally initiate aggressive action against the Viet Cong.

Lowland Hre villages are not organized for defense against surprise attack. In the highland areas, however, houses and villages are purposely built in easily defensible locations. In the past, highland Hre villages were surrounded by stockades, but these fortifications were gradually replaced with fences. More secure perimeter defenses may again be employed due to current military action in the Hre area.

The traditional Hre weapons are spears, swords, buffalo hide shields, and crossbows with poisoned arrows. The Hre have long used traps, pits, and concealed sharpened sticks or foot traps. Some Hre had military training with the French and the Viet Minh and know how to use modern weapons. Their relatively small stature limits the weapons the Hre can use, but they are proficient in handling light weapons such as the AR.15 rifle, the Thompson submachine gun, and the carbine. The tribesmen are less proficient in the use of the M-1 or the Browning automatic rifle, although they can handle larger weapons which can be disassembled and quickly reassembled.

The Hre pride themselves upon their hunting skill and their mastery of traditional weapons; they are equally as proud of their skill and marksmanship with modern weapons. If a Hre can carry and handle a weapon conveniently, he will use it well.

The Hre have more difficulty handling sophisticated devices, such as mortars, explosives, and mines, than hand weapons. They find it difficult to absorb the more abstract and technical aspects—such as timing trajectories—of such weapons.

The Hre can absorb basic military training and concepts. Their natural habitat gives them an excellent background for tracking and ambush activities; they are resourceful and adaptable in the jungle.

The Hre learn techniques and procedures readily from actual demonstration, using the weapon itself as a teaching aid. They do not learn as well from blackboard demonstrations, an approach which is too abstract for them.

Those Hre who have served with the French are invaluable in training the younger tribesmen.

The Hroi

The Hroi are located in the inland mountains west of the coastal cities of Qui Nhon and Tuy Hoa in the central region of the Republic of Vietnam. Numbering between 5,000 and 10,000, the Hroi, usually classified as a Bahnar subgroup, comprise two groupings: one influenced by the Malayo-Polynesian Chams and the Rhade tribe, the other influenced by the Mon-Khmer culture of the Bahnar. The dialect of the former is related to the languages of the Rhade and Cham, and the dialect of the latter resembles those of other Bahnar subgroups. The Hroi live in autonomous villages and, although they have a matrilineal kinship system, village political authority is held by a male village chief. The Hroi economy is based on the cultivation of dry rice by the slash-and-burn technique. Their religion is animistic, involving beliefs in spirits inhabiting all their surroundings. The Hroi, sometimes called Hroy or Bahnar-Cham, are considered a subgroup of the eastern division of the Bahnar tribe. The Tuy Hoa-Qui Nhon railroad divides the Hroi territory into two areas. The eastern Hroi, who inhabit the area between the railroad and the coast, have close cultural ties to the Rhade and Cham; the western Hroi, located between the railroad and Cheo Reo, are more closely related to the other Bahnar subgroups. There are no reports of any specific subgroups among the Hroi. The Hroi are a small Montagnard group. According to one source, they number about 10,000; according to another source, 5,045; and a third source estimates that there are 6,176 Hroi. The Hroi are located generally east of Cheo Reo and south of An Khe in an area bordered on the north by Route 19, on the east by the coastal plain, and on the south and west by the Song Ba River. At Tuy An, the coastal railroad curves inland and northwest, following the Song Cai River into the mountainous region where the Hroi live ; it emerges from the Hroi area at Qui Nhon, a large coastal town. The Hroi region is drained by many small rivers and streams. The terrain is rugged, with the mountains ranging in elevation from 1,500 to 3,000 feet. Although many mountains in the Hroi area are covered with secondary forest growth, there may also be sections of the area that are essentially grassland, with few trees, while in isolated parts of the Hroi region, on higher peaks and ridges, is found the primary rain forest. The secondary rain forest, the predominant type of forest in the Hroi area, develops after land in the primary rain forest has been cleared and then left for a time uncultivated. In this forest the trees are small and close together and there is an abundance of ground growth, woody climbing plants known as lianas, and herbaceous climbers. Penetration is difficult without constant use of the machete. The primary rain forest, at higher elevations, has three levels. Very old and large trees, with an average height of from 75 to 90 feet, form a continuous canopy. Below this canopy are smaller trees, varying from 45 to 60 feet in height, and below this second level is a fair abundance of seedlings and saplings. Orchids, other herbaceous plants, epiphytes, and lianas are profuse. Little light penetrates this type of forest and there is not much ground growth. During the dry season, this forest can usually be penetrated on foot with little difficulty. The climate in the Hroi area is influenced by two monsoon winds — one from the southwest in the summer (May to October), the other from the northeast in the winter (mid-September to March). Agriculture is greatly dependent on the rainfall (up to 150 inches) brought by the summer monsoon. Temperatures in the mountains are lower than those in the coastal regions.

Hroi *Paramilitary Capabilities*

Given the incentive and motivation and provided with the necessary training, leadership, and support, the Hroi could become an effective force against the Viet Cong. The tribesmen could serve as informers, trackers, and guides, intelligence agents, interpreters, and translators. With intensive training and support, the Hroi could be organized to defend their villages against the Viet Cong; with good leadership they could, particularly the western group, be organized into an effective counterguerrilla combat unit.

In the past, the western Hroi were considered capable fighters, whether fighting offensively in raids against other groups or defensively within their villages. These tribesmen reportedly take great pride in their hunting and fighting abilities. The eastern Hroi, on the other hand, are a very peaceful people with no reported experience in warfare.

When psychological pressures to win Hroi support fail, the Viet Cong have resorted to outright brutality and terror. Frequently, the Hroi yield and cooperate with the Viet Cong; without Government training and support, they do not have the wherewithal to oppose the Viet Cong. Hroi villages have no able organization for defense except those equipped, trained, and organized by the Government.

In the past, the Hroi relied upon crossbows, spears, swords, knives, and wooden shields. Hroi knives have a straight blade with a slightly curved hilt almost as long as the blade. Hroi crossbows are larger and stronger than those of most other Montagnard tribes. Arrows are bamboo with one end sharply pointed; the other end has a leaf tied to it. Circular wooden shields, about 3 feet in diameter, have two inside straps for the arm. The Hroi are also familiar with the use of traps, pits, and concealed sharpened sticks used as foot traps. Some Hroi may have received modern military training from the French, but there was no documented information on this question.

Their relatively small stature limits the type of weapons the Hroi can use, but they are proficient in handling light weapons such as the AR.15 rifle, the Thompson submachine gun, and the carbine The tribesmen are less proficient in the use of the M-1 or the Browning automatic rifle, although they can handle larger weapons which can be disassembled, carried by two or more men, and then quickly reassembled.

The Hroi learn techniques and procedures readily from actual demonstration, using the weapon itself as a teaching aid. They do not learn as well from blackboard demonstrations, an approach which is too abstract for them.

The Jarai

Numbering approximately 150,000 persons, the Jarai form one of the largest tribal groups in the Republic of Vietnam. The Jarai tribe consists of seven distinct subgroups and is spread throughout a large section of the Central Highlands. Of Malayo-Polynesian ethnic stock, the Jarai speak a language related to that of the Rhade, another large and important tribe which lives south of the Jarai. The Jarai are a matrilineal group and live in villages which, individually, form the highest political structure attained by the Jarai. They have a subsistence economy based primarily on the slash-and-burn cultivation of dry rice. The Jarai also engage in hunting, fishing, and a limited amount of trade. The Jarai are an intensely religious people who believe they live in constant interrelation with animistic spirits. In the past, the Jarai had a reputation for being fierce, aggressive warriors, and until recently the Jarai have remained relatively isolated from outside influences. In their own tribal language, the tribe's name is Nak-drai. They are called Charai by the Vietnamese, Djarai by the French, and Chalai by the Laotians. Jarai is the spelling used by American observers. Anthropologists generally agree upon the following Jarai subgroups: Ho'drung, Habau, Arap, Sesan, Chu Ty, Plei Kly, and Cheo Reo. The entire Jarai tribe numbers approximately 150,000. The Jarai tribe inhabits an extensive area including most of the provinces of Pleiku and Phu Bon, the southwestern corner of Kontum Province, and the eastern portion of the Cambodian province of Ratanakiri. Scattered Jarai settlements are also found in the northern areas of Darlac Province and the western part of Phu Yen Province. There are three major areas of Jarai concentration — around the towns of Pleiku and Plei Kly in Pleiku Province and Cheo Reo in Phu Bon Province. The Jarai Ho'drung are found in the region around the town of Pleiku; the Habau in the Lake To'nueng area; the Arap in the Plei Tell area, in northern Pleiku Province, and in the eastern part of Ratanakiri Province in Cambodia; the Plei Kly in southern Pleiku Province and northern Darlac Province; and the Cheo Reo in the region of Cheo Reo in Phu Bon Province. Neighboring groups include the Halang to the northwest, the Rengao and Sedang to the north, the Bahnar to the northeast and east, the Hroi to the east, and the Rhade to the south. The Jarai in the eastern portion of the tribal area also have contact with the Cham and Vietnamese. The western portion of Jarai territory is bordered by various tribal peoples of Cambodia. The Jarai tribe is located on the northern part of the Darlac Plateau, which is separated from the coast by the Annamite Mountains. Ranging from 1,000 to 2,500 feet in altitude, the Darlac Plateau has a foundation of basalt covered by reddish soil in some areas and a granite and rhyolite rock base (volcanic rock) covered with a thin mantle of soil in others. Above the generally rolling land of the plateau north of Pleiku, rise a number of extinct volcanoes, some of which contain crater lakes. In the east, the Jarai area is drained by the Song Ba River and its tributaries. The Song Ba flows eastward through the Annamite Mountains and empties into the South China Sea. In the west, the Jarai area is drained by the

Srepok River and some of its tributaries. The Srepok flows westward into Cambodia and joins the Mekong River. Two important highways cross the Jarai area. National Route 14, a major north-south highway, runs from Ban Me Thuot through Pleiku and on to Kontum. National Route 19 runs east from the Cambodian border through Pleiku to the coast at Qui Nhon. At this writing, travel on these two highways is often hazardous due to Viet Cong activities. The climate of the plateau area inhabited by the Jarai is influenced by both the summer (April — October) and winter (mid- September — March) monsoon winds which provide a regular seasonal alternation of wind. In the summer these winds come mainly from the southwest; in the winter, from the northeast. Agriculture is greatly dependent upon the rain brought by the summer monsoon. The winter monsoon also provides precipitation, though this rainfall varies greatly. On the whole, the Darlac Plateau receives from 50 to 150 inches of precipitation with most rain falling 258 in the higher areas in the north. The greatest rainfall occurs in July and August. There are local elevational variations in rainfall and wind patterns. Temperatures in the highland area are lower than along the coastal lowland areas, differing by more than 15 degrees during the winter months. Much of the Jarai area is covered by monsoon forest which is fairly open and relatively easy to traverse, as it is without dense undergrowth. The monsoon forest turns brown during the dry winter season, and many of the trees lose their leaves. During the summer or rainy season, travel becomes very difficult because of flooding and quagmires — elephants are then the best means of travel. Some of the forest undergrowth is tranh (Imperata cylindrica), a coarse, tall grass used as thatch for the roofs of Jarai houses. Tranh, when young, provides fair herbage. Bamboo growth is frequently found in low, wet areas where the monsoon forest has been cultivated and then abandoned by the tribesmen. In a few years these areas are again covered by forests, for the bamboo protects the seedling trees.

Jarai Paramilitary Capabilities

Given the incentive and motivation and provided with the necessary training, leadership, and support, the Jarai can become an effective force against the Viet Cong. The tribesmen may be used as informers, trackers and guides, intelligence agents, interpreters, and translators.

445

With intensive training and support, the Jarai can be organized to defend their villages against the Viet Cong; with good leadership, they can be organized into an effective counterguerrilla combat unit.

When the psychological pressures or conversion to subversive activities fail, the Viet Cong have resorted to outright brutality and terror. The tribesmen have been openly murdered, whole villages intimidated, food and money exacted as tribute, tribesmen forced to labor in the jungle to build roads and traps, tribesmen used as beasts of burden to carry supplies, and occasionally villages have been attacked and destroyed completely.

Frequently, the Jarai yield and cooperate with the Viet Cong. The isolated Jarai do not have the wherewithal to oppose the Viet Cong, and need Government training and support. Jarai villages have no able organization for defense except those equipped, trained and organized by the Government. Jarai villages with adequate training and support will defend themselves and will occasionally initiate aggressive action against the Viet Cong.

The inclination of the Jarai to fight aggressively is one that must be developed and supported with modern weapons and training. The Jarai defend themselves vigorously when they, their families, or their villages are threatened and when they have adequate resources and a chance for success.

In the past, the Jarai relied upon crossbows, spears, lances, swords, and knives and were very skillful in their use. Recently, they have received training in the use of modern weapons. Their relatively small stature limits the weapons the Jarai can use; but they are proficient in handling light weapons such as the AR.15 rifle, the Thompson submachine gun, and the carbine. The tribesmen are less proficient in the use of the M-1 or the Browning Automatic Rifle, although they can handle larger weapons which can be disassembled and quickly reassembled.

The Jarai pride themselves upon their hunting skill and their mastery of traditional weapons; they are equally as proud of their skill and marksmanship with modern weapons. If a Jarai can carry and handle a weapon conveniently, he will use it well.

The Jarai are less proficient with sophisticated devices, such as mortars, explosives, and mines, than with hand weapons. They find it difficult to absorb the more abstract and technical aspects, such as timing trajectories, of such weapons.

The Jarai can absorb basic military training and concepts. Their natural habitat gives them an excellent background for tracking and ambush activities; they are resourceful and adaptable in the jungle.

The Jarai learn techniques and procedures most readily from actual demonstration, using the weapon itself as a teaching aid. They do not learn as well from blackboard demonstrations; such an approach is too abstract for them.

Some Jarai are veterans of service with the French and are invaluable in training the younger tribesmen.

The Jeh

Regarded as one of the most isolated and primitive of the Montagnard tribal groups of the Republic of Vietnam, the Jeh live in the rugged, mountainous Laos-Vietnam border region. The Jeh are of Mon-Khmer ethnic and linguistic stock, as are the nearby Katu and Sedang. Jeh society is patriarchal and their autonomous villages constitute the group's highest level of social and political organization. The Jeh economy is based on the slash-and-burn cultivation of dry rice. The exact number of the Jeh (or Die, as they are often called) is not recorded. Recent estimates vary from 7,000 to 18,000. In 1964 an American missionary estimated that the Jeh numbered approximately 15,000 persons. The Jeh live in the mountainous region along the Se Kemane, Poko, and Dak Mi Rivers in southern Quang Nam, western Quang Tin, and northwestern Kontum Provinces. Some Jeh also live across the border in Laos. Roughly, the Jeh may be placed within the region bounded on the north by Dak Nhe; on the east by Phuoc Son; on the south by Dak Sut; and on the west in Laos by the eastern edge of the Bolovens Plateau. The Sedang inhabit the area to the south of the Jeh, the Katu are located to the north, and the Cua are found to the east. The region is covered with monsoon and primary rain forests. The monsoon forest, along the lower elevations near watercourses, is relatively easy to penetrate. During the dry winter season, the monsoon forest turns brown and many of the trees lose their leaves. During the summer rainy season travel is difficult because of the quagmires produced by flooding. Primary rain forest covers the more inaccessible regions (usually the highest elevations). Here the trees, with an average height 309 of 75 to 90 feet, form a continuous canopy. Below this canopy are smaller trees 45 to 60 feet in height, and below this second layer is a fair abundance of seedlings and saplings. Orchids, other herbaceous plants, epiphytes, and woody climbing plants known as lianas are profuse. Little light penetrates this forest; hence, there is little ground growth. During the dry season, this forest can usually be penetrated on foot with little difficulty. Areas of secondary rain forest develop after land in the primary rain forest has been cleared and then left uncultivated. Here the trees are small and close together, and there is an abundance of ground growth, lianas, and herbaceous climbers. Penetration is difficult without the constant use of the machete. There are few roads, trails, or navigable waterways in the Jeh area, and travel is difficult. Travel is especially inhibited during the rainy season from April to mid-September. The climate of the Jeh area is influenced by two monsoon winds, one from the southwest in the summer (April to mid-September) and the other from the northeast in the winter (mid-September to March). Agriculture is greatly dependent upon the summer monsoons, which bring up to 150 inches of rain yearly and create local floods. Temperatures in the Jeh region are as much as 15 degrees lower than in the coastal lowland regions. The Jeh area is crossed by Vietnam's National Route 14, a hard-surfaced, militarily important communication route running north from Kontum through Dak To, Dak Sut, Dak Gle, turning east at Thuong Due to reach the coast at Hoi An.

Jeh Paramilitary Capabilities

Given the incentive and motivation and provided with the necessary training, leadership, and support, the Jeh can become an effective force against the Viet Cong. The tribesmen can serve as informers, trackers and guides, intelligence agents, interpreters, and translators. With intensive training and support, the Jeh can be organized to defend their villages against the Viet Cong; with good leadership, they can be organized into an effective counterguerrilla combat unit. The Jeh have a reputation for engaging in aggressive warfare if they are provoked or if they have a justifiable reason.

In the past the Jeh were considered capable fighters, whether fighting offensively in raids against other groups or defensively within their villages. Some Jeh had military training with the French and are capable of sophisticated combat operations. Recently some Jeh have been trained by U.S. personnel and are familiar with U.S operational techniques as well as modern equipment.

When psychological pressures to win Jeh support fail, the Viet Cong have resorted to outright brutality and terror. Frequently, the Jeh yield and cooperate with the Viet Cong; without Government training and support, they do not have the wherewithal to oppose the Viet Cong. Jeh villages have no able organization for defense except those equipped, trained, and organized by the Government. Jeh villages with adequate training and support will defend themselves and will initiate aggressive action against the Viet Cong.

In the past the Jeh relied upon crossbows, spears, swords, and knives. The Jeh also are familiar with the use of traps, pits, and concealed sharpened sticks used as foot traps. Some Jeh received military training from the French and are familiar with modern weapons. Their relatively small stature limits the weapons the Jeh can use, but they are proficient in handling light weapons such as the AR.15 rifle, the Thompson submachine gun, and the carbine.

The tribesmen are less proficient in the use of the M-1 or the Browning Automatic Rifle, although they can handle larger weapons which can be disassembled, carried by two or more men, and then quickly reassembled.

The Jeh pride themselves upon their hunting skill and their mastery of traditional weapons; they are equally as proud of their skill and marksmanship with modern weapons. If a Jeh can carry and handle a weapon conveniently, he will use it well.

The Jeh cannot handle sophisticated devices—such as mortars, explosives, and mines—as proficiently as hand weapons. They find more abstract and technical aspects of such weapons—such as timing trajectories—difficult to absorb.

The Jeh can absorb basic military training and concepts. Their natural habitat gives them an excellent background for tracking and ambush activities; they are resourceful and adaptable in the jungle.

The Jeh learn techniques and procedures readily from actual demonstration, using the weapon itself as a teaching aid. They do not learn as well from blackboard demonstrations, an approach which is too abstract for them.

Some Jeh are veterans of service with the French and are invaluable in training the younger tribesmen.

The Katu

The Katu, a Mon-Khmer Montagnard group, inhabit the territory inland from the coastal cities of Da Nang and Hoi An and across the border into Laos. The tribe is divided into the "highland" and the "lowland" Katu: the "highland" Katu inhabit the higher mountains near the Laotian border, while the "lowland" Katu live in lower mountains nearer the coastal regions. The Katu have a patriarchal social organization and live in widely dispersed villages. The household consists of the extended family. The head of the extended family is the household head and owns all the family property. Leadership in Katu villages is provided by a chief and a council of elders. In some villages the chief is elected; in other villages the position is hereditary. All aspects of the social, political, and economic life of the Katu are influenced by their religious beliefs. In addition to offering animal sacrifices, the Katu engage in blood hunts or ritual murders to appease the spirits. The name Katu, meaning savage, is applied to this group by neighboring tribes. The Katu are also known as the Kato, Ka-Tu, or Kantu. The Katu refer to themselves as "Monui" or "people" followed by the name of their specific village. Recent estimates of the Katu population range from 20,000 to 30,000. A source dated 1938 estimated the number of Katu at 25,000. The Katu inhabit the northern plateau and mountain regions of the Republic of Vietnam, west of the cities of Da Nang (Tourane) and Hoi An (Faifo). Katu villages are concentrated along the slopes and valleys of the Song Giang, Song Cai, and Song Boung Rivers in the Provinces of Quang Nam and Thua Thien. Scattered 347 Katu villages are also found in Quang Tin Province, and an undetermined number of Katu live in Laos. As noted, the Katu are commonly divided into "lowland" and "highland" groups. There are at least four Katu subgroups. The Ngung Bo and the Thap are both eastern lowland groups, the former living along the tributaries of the upper Se Khong River, the latter living east of the Cao in the An Diem hinterland. The Ataouat, or Ka-Taouat, and the Cao, western highland groups, live in the Ataouat Massif, where the Se Khong and the Song Boung Rivers originate. The neighbors of the Katu include the ethnic Vietnamese to the east and northeast, the Jeh tribe to the south, the Phuong tribe to the northwest, and various Laotian tribal peoples to the west. The Katu territory in the Annam Cordillera is bordered on the south and west by the Massif du Ngoc Ang and on the west and north by the Massif du Pouak. This area, a plateau rising sharply from the narrow coastal plains, is cut by gorges and is dominated by isolated peaks, including one rising to a height of 8,200 feet. In general the rivers are short, flowing swiftly through steep rocky valleys. Rain-bearing monsoons and typhoons frequently and rapidly alter the currents and depth of these rivers. The summer monsoon (May-October) and the winter monsoon (November-January) provide a regular seasonal alternation of wind. In the summer, these winds come mainly from the southwest; in the winter, from the northeast. The eastern portion of the region has the most rain from September to January, while in the western portion the rainy season occurs during the summer months. Agriculture is greatly dependent upon the monsoon- borne rain. Precipitation is high — averaging more than 80 inches in the lower elevation and more than 150 inches in the higher areas. Normally the weather is warm and humid, with frequent cloudiness, especially from January to April. Temperatures vary by roughly 20 degrees between summer and winter. Actual surface temperatures average 60 to 65 degrees Fahrenheit in winter (January) and above 85 degrees Fahrenheit in summer (July). Typhoons influence the climate of this area and are especially dangerous from July to September, when heavy rainfall often causes extensive material damage by flooding and the uprooting of forests. During the rainy season the area is virtually inaccessible. The high and relatively evenly distributed precipitation gives this area rain forest vegetation of two distinct belts. At the higher elevations is the primary rain forest, where the trees, with an average height of 75 to 90 feet, form a continuous canopy. Below this canopy are smaller trees of 45 to 60 feet in height, and below this second layer is a fair abundance of seedlings and saplings. Orchids, other herbaceous plants, epiphytes, and woody climbing plants known as lianas are profuse. Little light penetrates this type of forest and there is not much ground growth. During the dry season, this forest can usually be penetrated on foot with little difficulty. The second belt or secondary rain forest, which develops after land in the primary rain forest has been cleared and then left uncultivated, is more extensive in this area. In this forest the trees are small and close together, and there is an abundance of ground growth, lianas, and herbaceous climbers. Penetration is difficult without the constant use of the machete. There are no roads in the Katu area. The jungle has reclaimed the French-built, dry-weather, unsurfaced road running from Da Nang to Kontum and extending through the southeastern section of the area along the Son Thu Bon River. In any case, it would be difficult to keep any road in year-round usable condition. There are very few trails in the area, and they are difficult, if not impossible, to see from the air. The rivers, often embedded in valleys with steep longitudinal profiles, are for the most part unnavigable. During high water, very small boats and canoes can pass through the rivers; however, typhoons increase the danger of water transportation.

Katu Paramilitary Capabilities

Given the incentive and motivation and provided with the necessary training, leadership, and support, the Katu can become an effective force against the Viet Cong. The tribesmen may be used as informers, trackers and guides, intelligence agents, interpreters, and translators. With intensive training and support, the Katu can be organized to defend their villages against the Viet Cong; with good leadership, they can be organized into effective counterguerrilla combat units.

Under threat of terror and reprisals, the Katu have been forced to give the Viet Cong support in the form of food, taxes, and labor. When tactics of subversion, propaganda, and simple cajolery fail to subdue the Katu, the Viet Cong resort to murder and brutality.

Frequently, the Katu yield to and cooperate with the Viet Cong. The isolated Katu do not have the wherewithal to oppose the Viet Cong; they need Government training and support. Most Katu villages have no organization for defense that is effective against modern weapons, except for the few villages equipped, trained, and organized by the Government. Katu villages with adequate training and support will defend themselves and will occasionally initiate aggressive action against the Viet Cong.

Traditionally, the Katu village has been organized for defense against surprise attack: the village site was chosen for inaccessibility, and the villages were formerly surrounded by a stockade, with sharpened bamboo stakes and traps placed along access trails. Furthermore, bamboo tubes filled with poisoned water were left near their fields to be drunk by the intruder.

Traditional weapons of the Katu are spears, swords, crossbows, and poisoned arrows. The poison used on the arrows is a form of curare poison made from plants of the genus *strychnos*. The Katu are familiar with the use of traps, pits, and concealed sharpened sticks used as spiked foot traps.

Their relatively small stature limits the weapons the Katu can use, but they are proficient in handling light weapons such as the AR.15 rifle, the Thompson submachine gun, and the carbine. The tribesmen are less proficient in the use of the M-1 or the Browning Automatic

Rifle, although they can handle large weapons which can be disassembled and quickly reassembled.

The Katu pride themselves upon their hunting skill and their mastery of traditional weapons; they are equally as proud of their skill and marksmanship with modern weapons. If a Katu can carry and handle a weapon conveniently, he will use it well.

The Katu seem unable to handle sophisticated devices, such as mortars, explosives, and mines, as proficiently as they handle hand weapons. They have difficulty absorbing the more abstract and technical aspects—such as timing trajectories—of such weapons.

In warfare on their own terms, the Katu are quite willing, often even anxious, to initiate offensive action. Their traditional blood hunts, during which warriors often traveled considerable distances to attack neighboring villages, may contribute to their willingness to fight offensively. However, the Katu are reluctant to fight unless they enjoy a clear superiority either in numbers or weaponry. They favor night attacks and fighting from ambush. The Katu defend their villages unless attacked by a vastly superior force; in that event they will take refuge in the forest.

The Katu can absorb basic military training and concepts. Their natural habitat gives them an excellent background for tracking and ambush activities : they are resourceful and adaptable in the jungle.

The Katu learn techniques and procedures more readily from actual demonstrations using the weapon itself as a teaching aid. They do not learn as well from blackboard demonstrations: such an approach is too abstract for them.

The Koho

The Koho-speaking peoples, composed of several distinct groups — the Chrau, Kil, Lat, Laya, Ma, Nop, Pru, Rien, Sre, and Tring — are one of the larger Montagnard groups of the Republic of Vietnam, The Koho inhabit an extensive mountainous area extending from Saigon in the south to Da Lat in the north. Despite their proximity to two major cities of the Republic of Vietnam, and despite the size of the area they inhabit, information concerning all of the Koho groups is meager. The Koho language, spoken by all the groups with only minor variations, is Mon-Khmer in origin and is related to the languages of the Bahnar, Stieng, M'nong, and other important tribal groups. With the exception of the Ma, the Koho

453

groups are matrilineal and live in village units of varying size. The village forms the highest permanent political organization attained by these groups. The Koho groups, also called Coho, Kohov, and Cohov, number approximately 90,000 persons. The Kil, also known as the Gil or Chil, call themselves Kou N'Ho (Children of the Pines). The Laya are sometimes identified as Rion or Riong, but the Laya and the Rion or Rien are usually considered two separate groups. The Sre are also called Cau Sre, which means "People of the Rice." A North Vietnamese source reported a total of 10,000 for the Lat, Nop, Laya, Co Don (unknown affiliation) and To-La (unknown affiliation) combined. Population figures are not available for the Chrau, Kil, Pru, and Rien groupings. The Ma number between 20,000 and 30,000 persons; the Sre, about 30,000. One Koho group, the Chrau, is believed to have several subgroups: Ro, Bajieng, Mru, Jre, Buham, Bu-Preng, and Bla. Because the Ma is the one group which substantially diverges from the general Koho cultural pattern, a separate chapter in this volume treats the Ma group. The Koho territory extends from just north of Saigon to the area of Da Lat. In the northern part of the Koho area the Lang Bian Mountains rise to about 6,000 feet and overlook the Da Lat Plateau. Made up of rolling hills, the Da Lat Plateau is separated from the Bao Loc or Djiring Plateau by the wide alluvial valley of the Da Dung River. Northwest of the Bao Loc Plateau, near the great bend in the Da Dung River, there are sharp mountains rising as high as 4,500 feet. On both sides of the Da Dung River is dang terrain, consisting of steep ridges reaching a height of approximately 2,000 feet. A chain of mountain peaks 3,000 feet high lies south of the Djiring Plateau, reaching as far south as Saigon, and continuing to the area between the coast and the lower Da Dung River. Much of the Koho land is covered with secondary forest growth, the result of reforestation of cleared land. This type of forest is abundant with vines and brush interlaced with a new growth of closely spaced trees. Such tangled thicket makes travel through these areas very difficult. The Sre, for example, live in U-shaped river valleys and are surrounded by secondary forest growth. In some areas of the Koho territory, the higher mountain ridges and peaks still retain a growth of primary rain forest, which has three levels. The highest level is a canopy formed by trees 75 to 90 feet high; some very old trees are 125-150 feet high and are especially venerated by tribesmen as, the abode of spirits. The middle level has shorter trees and vines, while the lowest level consists of seedlings and saplings. Northeast of Da Lat, in the area inhabited by the Kil, are pine forests. The climate of the Koho area is affected by two monsoon winds, one coming from the southwest in the summer, May to mid-September, and the other from the northeast in the winter, November to March. Agriculture is greatly dependent on the summer monsoons, which brings up to 150 inches of annual rainfall. Temperatures in the Koho regions are at least 15 degrees lower at all times of the year than in the coastal regions. Da Lat, in the Koho area, was a French summer resort because of its cool mountain climate. National Route 14 passes slightly to the west of the Koho area, while Route 20 runs through the area across the Bao Loc Plateau from Saigon to Da Lat. Other roads link Di Linh with Gia Nghia, Phan Thiet with Di Linh, Phan Rang with Da Lat, and Due Trong with Ban Me Thuot.

Koho Paramilitary Capabilities

Given the incentive and motivation and provided with the necessary training, leadership, and support, the Koho can become an effective force against the Viet Cong. The tribesmen are potential trackers, guides, interpreters, and intelligence agents. With intensive training and support, the Koho can be organized to defend their villages against the Viet Cong; with good leadership they can be organized into an effective counterguerrilla combat force.

In the past, the Koho were considered capable fighters, whether fighting offensively in raids against other groups or defensively within fortified villages. Some Koho had military training with the French and are capable of sophisticated combat operations. Recently some Koho have been trained by U.S. personnel and are familiar with U.S. operational techniques as well as modern American equipment.

In the past, the Koho relied upon crossbows, spears, lances, swords, and knives and were very skillful in their use. Their relatively small stature limits the weapons the Koho can use, but they are proficient in handling light weapons such as the AR.15 rifle, the Thompson submachine gun and the carbine. The tribesmen are less proficient in the use of the M-1 or the Browning Automatic Rifle, although they can handle larger weapons which can be disassembled and quickly reassembled.

The Koho pride themselves upon their hunting skill and their mastery of traditional weapons; they are equally as proud of their skill and marksmanship with modern weapons. If a Koho can carry and handle a weapon conveniently, he will use it well.

The Koho cannot handle sophisticated devices, such as mortars, explosives, and mines, as proficiently as hand weapons. They cannot absorb the more abstract and technical aspects—such as timing trajectories—of such weapons.

The Koho can absorb basic military training and concepts. Their natural habitat gives them an excellent background, for tracking and ambush activities; they are resourceful and adaptable in the jungle.

The Koho learn techniques and procedures readily from actual demonstration, using the weapon itself as a teaching aid. They do not learn as well from blackboard demonstrations, an approach which is too abstract for them.

Some Koho are veterans of service with the French and are invaluable in training the younger tribesmen.

The Ma

The Ma are one of several distinct groups which comprise the Koho-speaking peoples — an important grouping of Montagnards speaking mutually intelligible languages in the Republic of Vietnam. The Ma speak one of the several closely related Koho dialects. These dialects all stem from the Bahnaric subgroup of the Mon-Khmer language stock. Although linguistically related, the Ma and the other Koho groups do not share the same type of social structure. Ma society is based upon patriarchal, patrilineal, and patrilocal organization. However, like the other Koho groups, the Ma extended family and village form the most important social and political units. The Ma inhabit the rough, mountainous terrain and alluvial plains of the Da Dung River region. Due to the variation in terrain the principal crop, rice, is cultivated by both dry and wet methods. Sometimes referred to as the Cau Ma, the Ma consist of several subgroups: To (Cho To), Ro (Cho Ro), J Sop (Cho Sop), Borse, Tou, Da Dong, Wang, Daa Guy, and the Krung. According to a North Vietnamese source the Ma group numbers approximately 30,000; a South Vietnamese source estimates the population at 21,500. The Ma tribesmen inhabit a sparsely populated strip of land bordering both banks of the upper Da Dung River. Their territory includes the northeastern portion of Phuoc Thanh Province, the northern tip of Long Khanh Province, a southeastern portion of Phuoc Long Province, the western half of Lam Dong Province, the southern portion of Quang Due Province, and extends into the eastern portion of Tuyen Due Province. Scattered villages are also found in a northern border area of Binh Tuy Province. In addition to the Ma, the Koho-speaking peoples are composed of the following groups: Chrau, Kil, Lat, Laya, Nop, Pru, Rien, Sre, and Tring. The general Koho social structure pattern is matrilineal and matrilocal. The geographic location of the Ro subgroup has not been determined as of this writing. The tribespeople neighboring the Ma are the M'nony to the north, various Koho groups to the east and south, and the Stieng to the West. The left bank of the Da Dung River includes Bao Loc Plateau, which has moderate relief rising to approximately 3,000 feet, sharp mountains with an elevation of about 4,500 feet, the typical terrain of the area — the dang — which consists of sharp mountain ridges rising to about 2,000 feet; and the alluvial plains along the Da Dung River and other watercourses of the area. The right bank of the Da Dung River is also dang terrain. The high and relatively evenly distributed precipitation gives this area rain forest vegetation of two distinct belts. At the higher elevations is the primary rain forest where the trees average 75 to 90 feet in height, forming a continuous canopy. Below this canopy are smaller trees of 45 to 60 feet in height, and below this second layer is a fair abundance of seedlings and saplings. Orchids, other herbaceous plants, epiphytes, and woody climbing plants known as lianas are profuse. Little light penetrates this type of forest, and there is not much ground growth. During the dry season, this forest can usually be penetrated on foot with little difficulty. The second belt or secondary rain forest which develops after land in the primary rain forest has been cleared and then left uncultivated, is more extensive in this area. In this forest the trees are small and close together, and there is an abundance of ground growth, lianas, and herbaceous climbers. Penetration is difficult without the constant use of the machete. The summer monsoon (April to mid-September) and the winter monsoon (November to March) provide a regular seasonal alternation of wind. In the summer these winds come mainly from the southwest, in the winter from the northeast. Agriculture is greatly dependent upon the monsoon-borne rain. Precipitation is high — averaging more than 80 inches in the lower elevation and more than 150 inches in the higher areas. Temperatures in the Ma region are as much as 15 degrees lower than those of the coastal regions. National Route 14 passes slightly to the west of the Ma area, Route 20 passes through the area across the Bao Loc Plateau, and a secondary road runs through the northeastern part of the area from Di Linh to Gia Nghia.

Ma Paramilitary Capabilities

Given the incentive and motivation and provided with the necessary training, leadership, and support, the Ma can become an effective force against the Viet Cong. The tribesmen can serve as informers, trackers and guides, intelligence agents, interpreters, and translators. With intensive training and support, the Ma can be organized to defend their villages against the Viet Cong; with good leadership, they can be organized into effective counterguerrilla combat units.

In the past, the Ma were considered capable fighters, whether fighting offensively in raids against other groups or defensively within their villages.

When psychological pressures to win Ma support fail, the Viet Cong have resorted to outright brutality and terror. Frequently, the Ma yield and cooperate with the Viet Cong; without Government training and support, they do not have the wherewithal to oppose the Viet Cong. Ma villages have no organization for defense except those equipped, trained, and organized by the Government. Ma villages with adequate training and support will defend themselves and will occasionally initiate aggressive action against the Viet Cong.

The inclination of the Ma to fight aggressively is one that must be developed and supported with modern weapons and training. They defend themselves vigorously when they, their families, or their villages are threatened and when they have adequate resources and chance for success.

In the past, the Ma relied upon crossbows, spears, and long knives. Nearly every Ma tribesman is equipped with a machete, a long, iron-bladed weapon with a curved handle that fits over his shoulder so that it may be easily carried. They often carry round wooden shields or *khel.* Fashioned from a tree trunk, these shields are decorated with circles and triangles symbolizing tiger teeth, fish, and the kapok flower. The Ma also are familiar with the use of traps, pits, and concealed sharpened sticks used as foot traps. The tribesmen who received military training from the French are familiar with modern weapons.

Their relatively small stature limits the weapons the Ma can use, but they are proficient in handling light weapons such as the AR.15

rifle, the Thompson submachine gun, and the carbine. The tribesmen are less proficient in the use of the M-1 or the Browning Automatic Rifle, although they can handle larger weapons which can be disassembled, carried by two or more men, and then quickly reassembled.

The Ma pride themselves upon their hunting skill and their mastery of traditional weapons; they are equally as proud of their skill and marksmanship with modern weapons. If a Ma can carry and handle a weapon conveniently, he will use it well.

The Ma cannot handle sophisticated devices—such as mortars, explosives, and mines—as proficiently as hand weapons. They find the more abstract and technical aspects of such weapons—such as timing trajectories—difficult to absorb.

The Ma can absorb basic military training and concepts. Their natural habitat gives them an excellent background for tracking and ambush activities; they are resourceful and adaptable in the jungle.

The Ma learn techniques and procedures readily from actual demonstration, using the weapon itself as a teaching aid. They do not learn as well from blackboard demonstrations, an approach which is too abstract for them.

Some Ma, veterans of service with the French, are invaluable in training the younger tribesmen.

The M'nong

The M'nong are one of the smaller Montagnard groups of the Republic of Vietnam. Divided into five distinct subgroups, the M'nong inhabit the militarily important western sector of the mountainous Darlac Plateau adjacent to the Republic of Vietnam-Cambodia border. Of Mon-Khmer ethnic stock, the M'nong speak a language related to that of the Ma and the Stieng, other highland groups that border on the M'nong area. The M'nong are a matrilineal group and live in villages which, individually, form the highest level of political organization they have attained. The M'nong have a subsistence economy based primarily on the slash-and-burn cultivation of rice, although some of the M'nong subgroups engage in wet-rice agriculture. The M'nong also engage in hunting, fishing, and a limited amount of trade. The M'nong are an intensely religious people who believe they live in constant interaction with animistic spirits. The M'nong have a reputation for

459

belligerence and until recently have remained comparatively isolated from outside influence. The M'nong population has been estimated at between 15,000 and 40,000: South Vietnamese estimates tend toward the lower figure; North Vietnamese estimates, toward the higher. The discrepancy can perhaps be accounted for by the considerable number of M'nong who live in Cambodia, believed by a recent source to be about 15,000. Although clear distinctions among M'nong subgroups are difficult to establish, certain locales and tribal subdivisions have been fairly well identified. Anthropologists generally agree on five major subgroups of the M'nong: the Nong or Dih, the Preh, the Gar or Phii Bree, the Cil or Kil, and the Kuenh. Several of these major subgroups have further divisions within them. The Bu Nor are related to the Nong. There are three related. The M'nong Cil (Kil) are not to be confused with the Koho group called Kil. The Koho, groups within the Preh subgroup: the Preh Rlam, the Prong, or R'but, and the Bu Dong. The Preh Rlam, in turn, comprise the Bu Rung and Dih Brih groups. The Gar contain two related groups: The Gar Cu and the Rlam. No subdivisions have been reported within the Gil and Kuenh. The M'nong live south and west of Ban Me Thuot and inhabit parts of the provinces of Darlac, Quang Due, and Tuyen Due. A large number of M'nong live across the border in southern Cambodia. There are also a few scattered M'nong villages in the provinces of Phuoc Long and Khanh Hoa. The villages of the Gar dot the banks of the Krong River, which flows westward from the Annamite Mountains through rugged mountain terrain and then into rolling hills. The Gar also inhabit the higher lands to the north and south of this area. The Gar Cu inhabit the higher mountains near Lang Bian Mountain, north of Dalat. The Rlam group of the Gar occupy the swampy lowlands around Lake Daak Lak. The Preh and Preh Rlam inhabit the area west of Lake Daak Lak. The Dih Brih and Bu Rung groups of the Preh Rlam are located west and southwest of the lake. The Bu Dong group of the Preh live in several villages in the Ban Don area near the Srepok River, northwest of Ban Me Thuot. The Prong live in the region of the High Donnai, east of Gia Nghia. The name High Donnai designates the upper reaches of the Dongnai River, which flows west from its source near Dalat, through Quang Due Province, and then turns south toward Saigon. The Nong and Bu Nor inhabit the area southwest of Lake Daak Lak near the Cambodian border. The Kuenh subgroup is found in the Lang Bian area, southeast of the

Rlam and east of the Gar.The Cil inhabit an area northeast of Dalat, between the Lat subgroup of the Koho tribe and the northern Raglai. The M'nong groups have as neighbors the Kpa, Ktul, K'drao, and Bio subgroups of the Rhade to the north, the Raglai to the east; various Koho groups to the south (the Ma, Tring, Lat and Rien) and the Stieng in the southwest. In the west, numerous Cambodian tribal peoples are the neighbors of the M'nong. The numerous M'nong groups are thinly dispersed over an area of high mountains, low-lying marshes and bogs, and verdant forests. South of the town of Ban Me Thuot is Lake Daak Lak, lying in a broad depression covered with marshes. Into this area flows the Srepok or Krong River from the Annamite Mountains in the east. The ample water supply to this flatland makes it suitable for irrigation and wet-rice cultivation. South of Lake Daak Lak, the high granite and volcanic rock mountains of the Lang Bian area rise to an altitude of roughly 6,000 feet. South of the Srepok River, between Lake Daak Lak and the Cambodian border, is an area consisting mostly of tropical forest which extends south to the High Donnai. Averaging 1.6 persons per square kilometer, this forest area has few sections where the population density reaches seven persons per square kilometer. The more populated sections are southward, near the edge of the High Donnai, where the fertility of the land improves somewhat, especially in the valleys. The High Donnai itself is virtually uninhabited. The monsoon forest of the M'nong area is open and generally easily traversed during the dry season. Usually from November through March — the dry season — the vegetation turns brown, and the trees lose their leaves. Then, from about April through mid-September, the rainfall gradually increases, reaching a maximum during July and August. The southwest monsoon of the wet summer season then slowly gives way to the northeast monsoon of the dry winter months. Even during the summer, however, strong, dry summer winds may result in excessive evaporation. The soil in the M'nong area is generally poor. As a result, except in the lowland marshes, the M'nong practice the swidden, or slash- and-burn, method of cultivation. The term mir is used both for this type of cultivation and for the plots of land which are cleared by this method. After forest land has been cultivated and then abandoned by the M'nong, small plants appear first, then bamboo. Protected by the bamboo, seedling trees thrive in the dense undergrowth, and, within a few years, a new forest begins to develop. During the dry season, however, fires are frequent and both the number and kinds of trees are reduced; only trees most resistant to fire survive, and seedlings and saplings become increasingly sparse. In the mature forest, much of the undergrowth is made up of a tall, coarse grass (imperata cylindrica). Animals graze on the grass when it is young; when it turns dry and yellow, the M'nong use it to thatch their huts. Although sparsely inhabited by human beings, these forests abound in animals — monkeys, rabbits, deer, tigers, and elephants. In the mountains of Lang Bian, tigers are especially numerous. There are few good roads in the territory of the M'nong. Travel is easier during the dry season, but four-wheel-drive vehicles are almost a necessity. Even with a Jeep or Land Rover, secondary roads become impassible during the wet season. Two national highways. Route 14 and Route 20, pass through the M'nong area, but travel on these roads is often hazardous due to Viet Cong activities.

M'nong Paramilitary Capabilities

A tradition of both aggressive and defensive warfare points to the likelihood that the M'nong will take up arms readily. Until recently, their raiding activities were common, showing they had no reservations about fighting. The M'nong will fight both aggressively and defensively. The Bu Dong subgroup has been particularly feared in battle; these tribesmen live on the Srepok River near the Cambodian border, and their main occupations have traditionally been hunting and fighting.

The traditional weapons of the M'nong include sabers, knives, lances, and crossbows. The M'nong learn to use these ancient weapons at an early age. Some tribesmen received military training in the use of modern weapons from the French and are now receiving some training from the Vietnamese Government.

The M'nong are accustomed to armed conflict but not for extended periods of time. Traditionally they have engaged in attacks and raids, but these were of short duration.

The Muong

The Muong, one of the largest tribal groups in the Indochinese region, are located primarily in North Vietnam on the southwestern fringe of the Red River Delta. There are, however, a few Muong groups in Laos and some resettled refugee Muong in the Darlac Plateau area of the Republic of Vietnam. Although the tribe numbers between 250,000 and 360,000, only about 10,000 tribesmen live in the Republic of Vietnam. Despite a few common features, the Muong are distinct from the other Montagnard peoples of the Republic of Vietnam in language, culture, and social structure. While the exact historical relationship between the Muong and the lowland Vietnamese has never been established, the Muong language is more closely related to that of the Vietnamese than to the Mon-Khmer or Malayo-Polynesian languages of the Montagnard tribes. The patrilineal culture of the Muong, in many ways more sophisticated than that of the other tribes, has been more responsive to outside influences. Their economy is mainly agrarian. They cultivate dry rice and a variety of other crops, raise animals, and engage in numerous crafts. In many ways their religion is similar to that of the lowland Vietnamese, including ancestor worship and belief in village guardian spirits. Their religion also involves, however, many animistic practices similar to those of the Montagnard tribal groups. Politically, the tribe retains remnants of a hierarchic political structure of hereditary elite families and dependent nonland-owning peasants. Since 1954, many Muong have emigrated from North Vietnam to Laos and the Republic of Vietnam. Because the name Muong has been loosely used and has a variety of current connotations, classification of the Muong is especially difficult. The word Muong derives from the Thai word meaning a territorial division. In the vicinity of Vinh, Muong is used to identify a Thai-speaking group, while a completely different term Nha Lang — is used for the tribe referred to in this study as Muong. The Muong themselves use a variety of names, including Mwal, Mwan, Mon, and corruptions of the Vietnamese word nguoi (people) , such as Nguoe and Ngue. These terms are all synonyms, not names of subgroups. However, other names are used to designate the Muong of specific localities. These areas, with the Muong name used in that area, are: Area Name Nghe An Nha Lang Quang Binh Nguon or Sach Mai Da AoTa Fourth Zone Tho. The largest Muong group inhabits the area south of the Red River in the Province of Ho Binh and comprises the majority of the provincial population. This group also extends into Thanh Hoa, Quang Binh, and Phu Tho Provinces. There are also smaller separate groups located around Quang Binh, Phu Qui, Yen Bay,

463

Son La, and Moc Chau. Two groups of Muong refugees have been resettled in the Republic of Vietnam: one group of about 5,000, near Ban Me Thuot; and a second group of about 3,000, near the Pleiku airport. Because all available information refers to the Muong in North Vietnam, the degree to which the Muong refugees retain their traditional culture is unknown. At the very least, however, their relocation to the Rhade and Jarai area is likely to have modified some of their traditional customs. It is possible that additional Muong refugees have fled to the south, or that the two groups originally resettled near Ban Me Thuot and Pleiku have expanded into other areas; but no further information is available. A 1961 study estimated the Muong population in the Republic of Vietnam to be 10,000 at that time. The Muong are unevenly distributed, and the shifting locations of their settlements are imprecisely known. On the whole, they are concentrated in the Ho Binh region. Farther away from this central area, their number grows fewer as they mingle with other tribes. There is a slow but constant westward migration, particularly in the Quang Binh region. Although there now are two small known groups in Laos, more may well have drifted across the border. The area inhabited by the refugee Muong groups in the Republic of Vietnam is the eastern part of the Darlac Plateau, about 1,500 feet above sea level and separated from the coastal plains by the mountains of Binh Dinh. The Ayounh River, a tributary of the Song Ba, drains the extreme eastern part of the plateau; the remainder is drained westward into Cambodia by numerous tributaries of the Srepok River. The climate of the Darlac Plateau is influenced by both the summer (April through October) and winter (mid-September to March) monsoon winds. In summer these winds come from the southwest, and in winter from the northeast. Successful agriculture in the area depends upon the rains from the summer monsoons. The winter monsoons also provide rainfall, but only at unreliable intervals. Most of the 50 to 150 inches of annual precipitation in the plateau region occurs during July and August. Temperatures on the plateau are lower than those in the coastal regions, differing by as much as 15 degrees during the winter months. The soft, powdery, basalt-based red earth of the Darlac Plateau once supported forests. Now, as a result of slash-and-burn agriculture, only small wooded areas remain on granite pegs (like Dhu Ebung near Ban Me Thuot) and along the peripheral chain of hills. With these exceptions, most of the region is a savanna-like plain of grass and bamboo. Here a large part of the undergrowth is tranh (Imperata cylindrica), a tall, coarse grass used for grazing when green and as house thatch when yellow and dry. The northern part of the plateau around Pleiku shows considerable evidence of earlier volcanic activity. Monsoon forest covers much of this area, which is generally free of dense undergrowth and easy to traverse. During the summer rains, however, travel is complicated by flooding. National Route 14 connects Ban Me Thuot with Pleiku to the north and Due Lap (Quang Due Province) to the south. Ban Me Thuot is linked with the coast — with Ninh Hoa in Khanh Hoa Province — by Route 21 and with Dalat by Route 20. Two airfields near Ban Me Thuot — an all-weather field north of the village and a seasonal field to the southeast — provide air accessibility. Pleiku is also the site of a major airfield. Route 19 extends from the Cambodian border and connects Pleiku with the coast at Qui Nhon.

Muong Paramilitary Capabilities

Unless given Government training and support, the Muong cannot effectively resist the Viet Cong. Villagers who are given adequate training and support would presumably defend themselves.

In the past, the Muong relied upon crossbows, spears, and knives. Some Muong received military training from the French and are familiar with modern weapons; before the Indochina War, the Muong reportedly produced some of their own firearms.

The Muong can absorb basic military training and concepts. They learn techniques and procedures readily from actual demonstration, using the weapon itself as a teaching aid. They do not learn as well from blackboard demonstrations, an approach which is too abstract for them.

Muong who are veterans of service with the French are invaluable in training the younger tribesmen.

The Raglai

The Raglai live inland from the coastal cities of Nha Trang and Phan Rang in the Republic of Vietnam to the north and south of Cham settlements. They speak a Malayo-Polynesian language related to that of the Rhade and Jarai. The Raglai have a matriarchal social organization and live in widely dispersed villages in mountainous terrain. All aspects of their social, political, and economic life are influenced by their strong animistic religious beliefs. The village unit is autonomous and represents the highest level of political organization among the Raglai. The Raglai, sometimes called "Orang Glai," or "Men of the Forest," are a tribal group numbering approximately 40,000 people; half are a northern group located in the mountains west of Nha Trang, and half a southern group who live to the west of Phan Rang. On ethnographic maps the Raglai are usually divided into these two geographic groups. The Raglai inhabit two separate areas near the coast of the Republic of Vietnam. The Northern Raglai area is in the mountains west of Nha Trang in Khanh Hoa Province. Some Northern Raglai villages are also found in eastern Tuyen Duc Province and northern Ninh Thuan Province. The Southern Raglai live in a long strip of mountainous land roughly paralleling the coast from Phan Rang in the north to Phan Thiet in the south. The Northern Raglai region is bordered on the west and south by the Koho groups, including the Kil and Tring. The Rhade live to the north, and the M'nong to the west, to the east are the settled, lowland peoples, including the Cham and the ethnic Vietnamese. The Raglai, like the Rhade and Jaria, have been influenced culturally and linguistically by the Cham. The Southern Raglai area is bordered by the Koho groups on the west and the Cham and the ethnic Vietnamese on the east. The areas inhabited by both Raglai groups are very rough and mountainous. The high mountains in the western portions of the Raglai areas (some peaks rise to 6,000 feet) isolate the Raglai from the neighboring Koho groups. Some Raglai villages are on the floors of deep valleys, while others are perched on the sides of steep mountains. The villages are small and are linked by narrow trails cut through underbrush. The summer monsoon (May to mid-September) and the winter monsoon (November-March) provide a regular seasonal alternation of wind. These winds come mainly from the southwest in the summer and from the northeast in the winter. Agriculture is greatly dependent upon the monsoon-borne rain. Precipitation is high — averaging more than 80 inches in the lower elevation and more than 150 inches in the higher areas. Temperatures vary by roughly 20 degrees between summer and winter. Actual surface temperatures average 60 to 65 degrees Fahrenheit in winter

(January) and above 85 degrees Fahrenheit in summer (July). These temperatures are lower than those of the coastal regions and the Raglai complain about the warmer climate in the lowlands. The high and relatively evenly distributed precipitation gives this area two distinct belts of rain forest vegetation. At the higher elevations is the first belt, the primary rain forest, where the trees, with an average height of 75 to 90 feet, form a continuous canopy, with occasional breaks by trees 125 to 150 feet high. Below this canopy are smaller trees of 45 to 60 feet in height, and below this second layer is a fair abundance of seedlings and saplings. Orchids, other herbaceous plants, epiphytes, and woody climbing plants known as lianas are profuse. Little light penetrates this type of forest, and there is not much ground growth. During the dry season, this forest usually can be penetrated on foot with little difficulty. The second belt or secondary rain forest, which develops after land in the primary rain forest has been cleared and then left uncultivated, is more extensive in this area. In this forest the trees are small and close together, and there is an abundance of ground growth, lianas, and herbaceous climbers. Penetration is difficult without the constant use of the machete. Before the present Vietnamese conflict, the Raglai traveled by raft down the numerous rivers to the coastal cities of Nha Trang, Phan Rang, and Phan Thiet. The road from Phan Rang to Da Lat passes through Raglai territory, following the general route of the inland railroad which links these two cities. The north-south coastal highway, Route 1, skirts the edge of the Raglai regions and also parallels the main north-south railroad.

Raglai Paramilitary Capabilities

Given the incentive and motivation and provided with the necessary training, leadership, and support, the Raglai can become an effective force against the Viet Cong. The tribesmen can serve as informers, trackers and guides, intelligence agents, interpreters, and translators. With intensive training and support, the Raglai can be organized to defend their villages against the Viet Cong; with good leadership, they can be organized into an effective counterguerrilla combat unit.

In the past the Raglai were considered capable fighters, whether fighting offensively in raids against other groups or defensively within their villages. The Raglai were recently reported to be ferocious fighters, but no specific details are available to substantiate this assertion.

No information was available at this writing which described the participation of Raglai tribesmen in modern military operations. Nor was there any information stating whether the Raglai have been trained by the French, Vietnamese, or United States military forces.

Very little information was available about the weapons used by the Raglai. Their traditional weapons were crossbows, spears, and knives. An early account reported that the Raglai tipped their arrows and spears with virulent poison obtained from the upas *(antiaris)* tree. A strong preparation of this poison apparently caused death within minutes.

The Rengao

The Rengao, one of the smaller Montagnard tribes of the Republic of Vietnam, inhabit a mountainous region west of the city of Kontum. They have long been known as one of the more belligerent highland tribes. The Rengao are of Mon-Khmer ethnic and linguistic stock and speak a language related to that of the neighboring Bahnar. The village units of the Rengao form the highest political organization of the tribe. Religion plays an important role in the lives of the tribesmen: they believe that spirits and ghosts constantly intervene in human affairs. The name Rengao, variously spelled Reungao, Rongao, Ro-ngao, and Rangao, is a Bahnar word meaning "frontier" or "border." This name was applied to the group when they were considered the westernmost subgroup of the Bahnar tribe. Although there are no accurate records of the exact number of Rengao, it has been estimated that they number approximately 10,000 persons. The Rengao live in autonomous villages scattered over a strip of land extending from the border of Pleiku Province in the south, through the center of Kontum Province, to the north near Dak Sut, The rugged Massif du Ngoc Ang, a compact group of mountains, dominates the terrain to the northwest. Bordering the Rengao are the Halang on the west, the Sedang on the north and east, the Bahnar on the southeast, and the Jarai on the south. In general, the region inhabited by the Rengao consists of rounded hills, some of which rise as high as 6,000 feet. Towards the north, the terrain is quite rugged, with granite outcroppings reaching 7,000 feet in height. The Bla and the Po Ko Rivers join in the Rengao area and flow south to form the Se San River, a tributary of the Mekong. The Rengao region is covered with a moderately heavy forest, which is generally easy to traverse, except during the summer rainy season. During the winter the forest turns brown, and many of the trees lose their leaves. Part of the undergrowth is tranh (Imperata cylindrica), a coarse, tall grass with which the Rengao thatch the roofs of their houses. When young, this grass provides grazing land for domestic animals. Bamboo growth is found in low, wet areas and in recently abandoned fields. The bamboo protects seedling trees, and eventually the forest again covers these areas. The climate of the Rengao area is influenced by two monsoon winds, one coming from the southwest in the summer (April to mid-September) and the other from the northeast in the winter (mid-September to March), Agriculture is greatly dependent on the summer monsoons, which bring as much as 150 inches of rain yearly and create local floods. Temperatures in the region are approximately 15 degrees lower than those along the coastal low-land regions. National Route 14, running northwest from Kontum, skirts the eastern portion of the Rengao area. Another route running west from Dak To to the Laotian border crosses the Rengao territory. An airfield at Kontum provides seasonal air accessibility to the region.

Rengao Paramilitary Capabilities

Reportedly, the Rengao are skilled and effective fighters both in offensive and defensive combat. The Rengao are capable scouts, trackers, and guides; if given intensive modern training, support, and leadership, they could become exceptionally effective in jungle warfare.

Proximity to the city of Kontum, an important highland population center, makes the Rengao territory militarily significant. In the early 1960's, the region was crossed by Viet Cong supply routes and served as a refuge area for Viet Cong military units.

Under threat of terror and reprisals, the Rengao have been forced to give the Viet Cong support in the form of food, finances, and labor. When the tactics of subversion and propaganda do not result in gaining the support of the tribes people, the Viet Cong resort to murder and other brutalities.

By tradition, a Rengao village is organized against surprise attack. The communal house in the center of the village, normally used as the sleeping quarters for bachelors, serves as a stronghold for defense in terms of warfare conducted with lances, knives, and crossbows. Formerly villages were surrounded by stockades, but in recent years these have been replaced by fences. Due to increased military activity within the area, more secure perimeter defenses may now be employed.

The traditional Rengao weapons are spears, swords, and crossbows, with poisoned arrows. The Rengao are familiar with the use of traps, pits, and spiked foot traps (concealed sharpened sticks). Some Rengao who have had military training from the French, Vietnamese, and Americans know how to use modern weapons.

Their relatively small physical size makes Rengao tribesmen more comfortable and adept with small, light weapons. They can handle larger weapons that are quickly assembled and disassembled. Traditionally the Rengao take good care of their weapons: if they can carry and handle a weapon conveniently, they will generally use it well.

The Rengao are less proficient in the use of the more sophisticated weapons such as mortars, explosives, and mines, because of difficulty in understanding the theoretical and technical aspects of timing and trajectory.

The Rengao learn more readily from actual demonstration of techniques and procedures than they do from standard classroom methods. Tribesmen with military service under the French are an asset in training the younger tribesmen.

The Rhade

For decades the Rhade tribe has been considered the most important and most strategically located of the Montagnard tribes in the Republic of Vietnam. The Rhade is one of the largest tribes, numbering between 100,000 and 120,000 and inhabiting an extensive strip of the Darlac Plateau. The Rhade language is of Malayo-Polynesian origin and is related to the languages of the Jarai and the Raglai. The tribe is a matrilineal group, living in village units that form the political organization of the tribe. The Rhade are a very religious people, living in constant interaction with the animistic spirits that surround them. The name Rhade is the French variation of the Montagnard name, Ete. Some authorities believe that ete (or ede) designates a type of bamboo and that the name of the Rhade would therefore be those who live in the bamboo. The Vietnamese use this Montagnard term, while Rhade is the name commonly used by the French and Americans. Rhade is the usual spelling, though some investigators spell it Raday. Some claim the word rhade is a corruption of the expression anak Ae Adie, which means "Children of the Master of the Sky," or "Children of God." Anthropologists generally agree on the following Rhade sub-groups: Rhade Kpa, Rhade M'dhur, Rhade A'dham, Ktul, Epan, Bio, K'drao, and H'wing. Although some sources consider the Bih a Rhade subgroup, most state that the Bih may originally have been a Rhade group, but they diverged and joined the M'nong tribe. Although no accurate records are available indicating the exact number of Rhade, estimates range from 100,000 to 120,000 with roughly 68,000 of this total registered in Ban Me Thuot. Precise figures are difficult to obtain because many of the Rhade do not bother to declare births and deaths in their families and a few, mostly those in the army, have legally become Vietnamese. The Rhade tribe is centered around the village of Ban Me Thuot and can be found throughout Darlac Province. Rhade groups also inhabit the northwestern quarter of Khanh Hoa Province, the southwestern corner of Phu Yen, and the southern border areas of Phu Bon and Pleiku Provinces. There are also scattered groups of Rhade in Cambodia near the Darlac border. The Rhade Kpa, around the Ban Me Thuot area, have more contact with the Vietnamese than most of the other subgroups because Ban Me Thuot is the center of plantations operated by the Vietnamese. To the south and southwest are several M'nong sub-groups. North of the Kpa are the Rhade A'dham subgroups. The A'dham are located on the southern edge of Jarai territory. East of the A'dham and the Kpa are the M'dhur and Ktul (or Klul) sub-groups. These people inhabit a north-south strip from the edge of Jarai territory to the southern portion of Darlac Province where their neighbors are various M'nong groups, primarily the M'nong Cil. East of the Ktul area is another north-south strip inhabited by Rhade subgroups; from north to south, the Bio, Epan, H'wing, K'drao, and another group of the Bio. The Jarai, the Hroi, and a few Cham border the northernmost Bio and the Epan. The southernmost Bio border on the M'nong Cil area to the southwest and Raglai territory to the south. The Vietnamese touch the eastern edge of all these areas. The eastern part of the Darlac Plateau is about 1,500 feet above sea level. The Ayounh River, a tributary of the Song Ba, drains its extreme eastern part. The rest of the plateau is drained by numerous tributaries of the Srepok River, flowing westward into Cambodia. The plateau is separated from the coastal plains by the mountains of Binh Dinh. The climate of the Darlac Plateau is influenced by both the summer (April through October) and winter (mid-September to March) monsoon winds. In the summer, these winds come from the southwest and in the winter, from the northeast. Agriculture in the area is greatly dependent upon the rain brought by the summer monsoons. The winter monsoons also provide precipitation, though this is quite unreliable. The plateau region receives from 50 to 150 inches of precipitation annually, the heaviest rains falling in July and August. Temperatures in the plateau are lower than in the coastal regions, differing by as much as 15° during the winter months. The soft, powdery, basalt-based, red earth of the Darlac Plateau once supported forests. Now, as a result of the slash-and-burn agricultural processes, only small wooded areas remain on granitic pegs (Dhu-Ebung near Ban Me Thuot) and along the peripheral chains of hills. Otherwise, the whole region is a savanna-type area of grassy plains and bamboo. Tranh (Imperata cylindrica), known as lalang or alang-alang in Malaya, makes up a large part of the undergrowth. It is a tall, coarse grass that turns yellow when dry. When young, it is good for grazing, but it is principally used as thatches for houses. Ban Me Thuot, located in the main area of Rhade concentration, is on Route 14 which connects it with Pleiku to the north and Due Lap (Quang Due Province) to the south. Ban Me Thuot is connected with the coast (Ninh Hoa in Khanh Hoa Province) by Route 21 and with Dalat by Route 20. Two airfields near Ban Me Thuot — an all-weather field north of the village and a seasonal field to the southeast — provide air accessibility to the region.

Rhade Paramilitary Capabilities

The Rhade may be used as informers, intelligence agents, propaganda agents, labor and service forces, trackers and guides, interpreters and translators, and as self defense forces in addition to use in organized counterguerrilla combat units. Given good leadership, the paramilitary potential of the Rhade is excellent.

In addition to their familiarity with the local terrain and environment, the Rhade have considerable stamina and are capable of sustained, long-range, cross-country marches in this difficult terrain. They are skilled in the use of various hunting weapons, such as crossbows, knives, spears, traps, and snares; they are now trained to use modern weapons and equipment.

Rhade trained by colonial French forces are reportedly excellent soldiers. Those with French Army training are likely to be capable of sophisticated combat operations. Many Rhade have also been trained by U. S. personnel and are familiar with U. S. operation techniques as well as modern equipment.

The ability of the Rhade to accept and absorb military instruction is limited to some extent by the generally low level of education. However, the factors mentioned above seem sufficiently significant to warrant attempts to develop greater receptivity to instruction.

The Sedang

Numbering between 40,000 and 80,000, the Sedang, a Mon-Khmer tribal group in the Republic of Vietnam, speak a language related to those of the Bahnar, M'nong, Halang, Hre, Stieng, and Koho tribes. The village is the basic political unit; the household, consisting of an extended family living in a longhouse, is the basic economic unit. The father is the head of the household, but kinship is reckoned on both the male and female sides of the family. The Sedang have a subsistence economy based on slash-and-burn agriculture. Their religion is animistic, involving the belief that spirits inhabit the lands, vegetation, animals, and objects around them. The Sedang live in the area northwest of Kontum, the capital of Kontum Province and one of the larger and more important cities of the Republic of Vietnam. The first highland tribe to receive U.S. military training and equipment, the Sedang were also the first tribe to actively resist the Viet Cong. The Sedang have referred to themselves collectively as Ha(rh)ne-dea(ng). Within the framework of this overall name, the tribesmen employed two additional names to indicate a geographical distinction among their tribal members; they referred to members in the eastern portion of their territory as Se-Dang, and to those in the western portions as He-Dang. A North Vietnamese source gives the size of the Sedang population as 80,000; South Vietnamese source as 57,376. A missionary in 1962 reported the number as 40,000. The Sedang are concentrated in the Province of Kontum, with scattered villages across the border in Laos. The Sedang tribe is composed of a number of subgroups, each with a distinct dialect. The subgroups include the Danja, the To-drah, the Kmrang, the Duong, and the Cor or Ta-Cor. The word to-drah means "brush" and the To-drah subgroup is known as the "people of the sparse forest (brush)." The To-drah subgroup is located northeast of the Rengao in the mountainous region between the Psi and Bla Rivers. The word kmrang means "great forest," and the Kmrang subgroup is designated as the "people of the great forest." They live between the Poko and the Psi Rivers in the craggy mountains as far north as Ngoc Linh, the highest mountain in the Republic of Vietnam. The Jeh live to the north of the Sedang. To the northeast and east the Sedang are surrounded by the Kayong and Monom who separate them from the Cua and Hre. The Bahnar live to the southeast of the Sedang. The Rengao, whose name means "borders" and who are believed to be a mixed Bahnar-Sedang tribal group inhabit the area to the south and southeast of the Sedang, separating the Sedang from the Jarai. Southwest of the Sedang are the Halang. The region inhabited by the Sedang is quite rugged with granite outcroppings, some of which reach 2,598 meters in height, such as the summit of Ngoc Linh. The Poko, Kan Ta, and Psi Rivers join one another in the Sedang area and flow southward to form the Sesan River, which flows south and then west into Cambodia to become a tributary of the Mekong River. The Sedang area is covered with monsoon and tropical rain forests. The monsoon forest is fairly open and easy to travel through, since there is little dense undergrowth. The monsoon forest turns brown during the dry winter season, and many of the trees lose their leaves. During the summer rainy season, when travel becomes difficult because of flooding, the elephant is a useful means of transportation. The dense tropical rain forest has three levels. The highest level is a canopy created by ancient trees from 125 to 150 feet high; the middle level has shorter trees and vines; and the lowest level is underbrush. Little grass or herbaceous vegetation grows on the forest floor. A secondary rain forest, also in the Sedang area, develops when a cleared forest area has been left uncultivated for a number of years. Here the trees are small and very close together; an abundance of vines and brush entwined around trees forms tangled thickets, making travel difficult. The climate of the Sedang area is influenced by two monsoon winds, one coming from the southwest in the summer (April to mid-September) and the other from the northeast in the winter (mid-September to March). Agriculture is greatly dependent on the summer monsoons, which bring heavy rains — up to 150 inches 722 annually — creating local floods. Temperatures in the region are as much as 15 degrees lower than along the coastal lowland regions. National Route 14 extends northwest from Kontum, through the Sedang area to Dak To and north to beyond Dak Sut, where it turns east to the coast at Hoi An, south of Da Nang.

Sedang Paramilitary Capabilities

The Sedang have a reputation as skilled and capable fighters in both offensive and defensive warfare. They have a long history of warfare and are proud of their skill as warriors and hunters. The Sedang have natural abilities and instincts which are useful in modern jungle warfare. Given support and leadership, Sedang may become effective forces in modern military operations.

The Sedang were the first Montagnard tribe to receive U.S. military training and equipment, as well as the first tribe to actively resist the Viet Cong. Early in 1962 the Sedang began receiving U.S. assistance; by the middle of that year, they had been formed into a Montagnard Self-Defense Corps comprising two battalions of armed tribesmen. The platoons of this military force were distributed among 57 armed villages, with about one platoon of 10 men in each village. Approximately 650 hand weapons were distributed among the villages. With these arms and training, the villagers aggressively resisted the Viet Cong.

In June 1962, a Sedang village was attacked by a Viet Cong force. Armed with only traditional weapons, the villagers drove off the Viet Cong attackers. Two days later, the Viet Cong returned; after an hour's fighting, they penetrated the village and took away all the young men. This and similar incidents have turned the Sedang against the Viet Cong.

Americans working with the Sedang evaluate them highly as fighters. It has been reported that every man, woman, and child in the Sedang area is an effective soldier.

The traditional Sedang weapons are spears, swords, crossbows, and poisoned arrows. The Sedang are familiar with the use of traps, pits, and concealed, sharpened bamboo sticks—spiked foot traps.

As noted, some Sedang have received training in the use of modern weapons from U.S. military personnel. Their relatively small physical size makes the Sedang more comfortable and adept with small, light weapons. Traditionally the Sedang have taken good care of their weapons.

Like many mountain tribes, the Sedang are skilled and proud hunters—their skill and pride are transferred to their use and care of modern weapons. If a Sedang tribesman can conveniently carry and handle a weapon, he can be expected to use it well.

In warfare on their own terms, the Sedang are willing, often even anxious, to use offensive tactics. However, they are reluctant to fight offensively without superiority in numbers or in weaponry; nevertheless, the Sedang defend their villages even if attacked by a clearly superior force. Night attacks and fighting from ambush are their favorite methods.

The Stieng

The Stieng are a large tribal group living on both sides of the Republic of Vietnam-Cambodia border some 75 miles north-north-west of Saigon. Of Mon-Khmer ethnic stock, the Stieng speak a language similar to that of the Bahnar, M'nong, Sedang, and other important Montagnard groups. The Stieng have a patriarchal society and live in villages which individually form the highest level of political organization they have attained. The Stieng have a subsistence economy based primarily on the slash-and-burn cultivation of dry rice and supplemented by hunting and fishing. An intensely religious people, the Stieng believe they live in constant interaction with animistic spirits. Among the last of the highland groups to be subdued by the French, the Stieng have a reputation for belligerence and, until recently, have remained isolated from outside influences. The Stieng, sometimes called the Budip, number about 60,000 people. Approximately 23,000 live in South Vietnam in the region northwest of Saigon, while the remainder live in the neighboring provinces of Binh Long and Phuoc Long; some Stieng are also in the provinces of Tay Ninh, Binh Duong, Phuoc Thanh, Quang Due, and, possibly, Bien Hoa. Although specific information on the subgroups of the Stieng was not available, there appeared to be four subgroups — the Budip, the Budeh, the Bulach, and the Bulo. The specific location of these groups is unavailable. The Stieng inhabit an area bordered on the northeast by the M'nong tribe, on the east by the Ma group, and on the south by the Vietnamese. The Khmer, who are to the west and southwest, share a large portion of territory with the Stieng in the provinces of Binh Long and Phuoc Long. The Stieng area rarely exceeds 500 feet in elevation. The landscape varies from low, undulating foothills, strewn with rocks and lava blocks, to flat terrain. The gray, red, or brown soils are generally the compact basaltic type. The red soils are deep because of the decomposition of the easily crumbled basalt or the volcanic ash. The brown soils, less rich in clay than the red soils, are lighter, less cohesive, and easier to work. All the soils in the area are rich in chemicals and, when cleared, are excellent for the cultivation of rubber trees. The area receives a great deal of rain, generally more than 78 inches per year. The unusually heavy rainfall, during the period from April to mid-September, comes from masses of humid equatorial air moving from west to east. The air masses lose their moisture as they rise on their approach to the high plateau areas. Most of the Stieng area is covered with a dense rain forest of three levels. The highest level is a canopy created by very old trees, 125 to 150 feet high; the middle level has shorter trees and vines; and the lowest level is underbrush. Little grass grows on the forest floor. Occasional glades are covered with tranh (Imperata cylindrica) grass, while rocky areas of lava blocks and conglomerate masses are covered with light forests, consisting mainly of thorny bamboo. Areas along water-courses have particularly luxuriant growths of rattan and bamboo. Although the area has an annual dry season in the winter (November to March), the forest is almost always extremely humid, either because of the heavy rainfall during the spring and summer seasons or because of the seepage of water through the soil during the dry season. However, the vegetation along the riverbeds and in the occasional glades or rocky patches suffers severely from drought during the relatively dry winter months. The Stieng area has few large animals, with the exception of roving herds of elephants and boars. Hunting in the Stieng area is difficult because of the scarcity of large game. An inexperienced hunter might easily starve. However, many small mammals — porcupines, scaly anteaters, squirrels, civets, and monkeys — as well as reptiles, birds, and insects are found in this region. During the wet season, numerous leeches and other bloodsuckers appear in the forests. Many springs in the forest area are breeding places for malaria- bearing mosquitoes. Cambodian and Vietnamese peasants in bordering locations are aware of the health hazards and are reluctant to go into the Stieng forest or to spend any extended period of time there. The lowlands in the southwest portion of the Stieng territory are comparatively open and are under cultivation. Rubber plantations are scattered throughout the southern and western portions of this area. Many rivers and streams flow through the western Stieng low-land area; mountain streams are prevalent in the eastern part near the Annamite Mountains. The Song Bo is the principal river. National Route 13 runs north to south in the western area near the Cambodian border; Route 14 runs southwest to northeast through the Annamite Mountains in the eastern section. Secondary roads and trails are few in the Stieng area. All roads in this region are difficult to maintain.

Stieng Paramilitary Capabilities

The Stieng are reportedly skilled and capable fighters, both offensively and defensively. They are skilled hunters, trackers, scouts, and guides with experience which, if coupled with intensive modern training, support, and leadership, could result in the development of exceptionally effective units for jungle combat.

In the past, organized under the leadership of the village chief, the Stieng tribesmen fought well. Prior to any military action, plans were considered fully, being discussed by every villager. Women played an active supporting role by outfitting and supplying the men with weapons and food before a raid and by assisting in preparation of the almost impenetrable barricades around the village. The barricade was a formidable, circular wall of felled trees with leaves and branches facing away from the village. Many branches and pieces of bamboo were placed on top of one another and interlaced, concealing thousands of razor-sharp pointed sticks, traps, and snares to confront the enemy. The Stieng simply waited behind the barricade and picked off their enemies as they attempted to fight their way through the barricade. The density of the obstruction would render the enemy momentarily defenseless, unable to use his weapons.

At present, there is no formal, adequate organization for the preparation of offensive or defensive action under modern conditions. To establish such organization, capable hunters and village chiefs who are recognized and respected among the Stieng would appear to be the persons to initiate action.

Despite a reputation for vigorous defense the Stieng determination to defend themselves is strongly influenced by estimates of probable success. If faced with an enemy of numerical and weapon superiority, the Stieng will capitulate rather than fight, a characteristic not unique to the Stieng but common among people inadequately armed, trained, and led.

Given suitable weapons, training, and leadership, it is believed that the traditional Stieng desire to defend themselves, their families, and villages would express itself effectively.

Although the Stieng prefer defensive warfare, reportedly, they are aggressive if provoked; in the past they have mounted well-organized attacks on distant villages. However, the tribesmen have a history of raiding other tribes, sometimes traveling long distances by foot. In the past, Stieng raiding parties of between 100 and 200 men would set out on an expedition without any real order. Proceeding surreptitiously through the jungle, avoiding rice fields and main roads, and camping overnight near water sources, the Stieng would time their arrival for a sudden surprise attack just before sunrise.

Traditionally, the Stieng have relied upon spears, swords, billhooks, crossbows, and poisoned arrows and were familiar with the use of traps, pits, and concealed sharpened sticks used as spiked foot traps. Some Stieng are trained in the use of modern weapons, and some have military knowledge gained from service with the French.

Because of their relatively small physical size—an average height of about 5 feet 5 inches—the tribesmen are more comfortable and adept with small light weapons, such as the AR.15 and carbines, rather than the heavier M-1 rifle or BAR. The tribesmen can use weapons easily disassembled and quickly assembled. The Stieng have a tradition of taking good care of their weapons.

The Stieng are skilled hunters and excellent marksmen. They take great pride in their careful and skilled handling of weapons. When the Stieng can carry and handle a weapon conveniently, they will generally use it well.

The Stieng can handle devices such as mortars, explosives, and mines; however, their proficiency with these weapons is limited by their lack of understanding of the more theoretical and technical aspects of timing and trajectory. Nevertheless, the Stieng are capable of being trained in the use of some sophisticated devices.

The Stieng may be capable of absorbing the more basic military training and concepts better than many of the neighboring tribes, for their history shows an aptitude for such training. They are accomplished in their use of terrain, tracking, and ambush, and they are resourceful and adaptable in the jungle. The Stieng learn readily by actual demonstration of techniques and procedures. The tribesmen who have seen service with the French are an asset in the training and instruction of their fellow Stieng.

The Cham

Among the minorities of the Republic of Vietnam, one of the smallest and least known is the Cham group. A people of Malayo-Polynesian stock, the Cham developed under both Hindu and Moslem influence in their early history. The imprint of these two civilizations, although altered by local tradition and superstition, is still evident in the customs, mores, and religious practices of the Cham. Cham adherents of Brahmanism and of Islam call themselves Cham Kaphir and Cham Bani respectively. For centuries a race of warriors and pirates, the Cham defended their vast and prosperous Kingdom of Champa from numerous invasions. However, in 1471, the empire finally collapsed before Annamese (ethnic Vietnamese) invaders. Only the grandiose temples and sanctuaries, irrigation systems, sculpture, woven cloth, and jewelry remain as evidence of this once great civilization. The descendants of the once powerful Cham, numbering between 16,000 and 45,000, are scattered along the eastern coast of the Republic of Vietnam and near the Cambodian border. These people now eke out a living as artisans, farmers, and fishermen. The Cham live in small village settlements, grouped according to matrilineal kinship ties. Their language belongs to the Malayo-Polynesian family and is related to the Rhade, Jarai, and Raglai tongues. The Cham are extremely religious and perform daily rituals to appease animistic spirits. In Sanskrit, Champa is the name of a bush and of a flower. The descendants of the peoples of the Kingdom of Champa are still known as the Cham, though the Vietnamese refer to this group as the Nguoi Champa. The Cham have also been called, together with the Montagnard tribes, the "People of Thuan Thanh," a name derived from the second character of Binh Thuan and the second character of Chien Thanh (the capital of the Kingdom of Champa). The French and Americans refer to these people as Cham, Tchame, and Tiame. Other spellings of the name are: Kiam, Thiame, Tjame, and Tsiam. In the mountainous areas of Khanh Hoa, Ninh Thuan, and Binh

Thuan, the Cham are also referred to as the Ha. Some uncertainty surrounds the present-day clan system of the Cham. One source claims that the Cham are divided into several clans: the Ca-Giong, the Da-Vach, and the true (orthodox) Cham. The Ca-Giong Cham are said to inhabit the northern part of Quang Ngai Province and the area of Dakley in Kontum. The Da-Vach Cham occupy a region farther south near Ba To, Minh Long, and the southern part of the district of Son Ha. The orthodox Cham live in the region between the Da-Vach and the Ca-Giong. Estimates of the number of Cham in the Republic of Vietnam range from 16,000 to 130,000. Recent calculations vary between 16,000 and 45,000. In the districts of Phan Rang (Ninh Thuan Province) and Phan Ri (Binh Thuan Province), the Cham population is estimated at 20,000, and in the districts of Xuan Loc (Long Khanh Province) and Tanh Linh (Binh Tuy Province), 3,000. The Cham are believed to be slowly increasing in number, but under the influence of the Montagnards and the Vietnamese, they are gradually losing their distinct cultural identity. Many have been assimilated into the general Vietnamese culture and do not represent a true ethnic minority. Cham villages are scattered throughout two principal areas in the Republic of Vietnam along the Cambodian border in Tay Ninh and Chau Doc Provinces and in the central lowlands along the eastern slope of the Annamite mountain chain in the provinces extending from Quang Ngai to Binh Tuy. The greatest number seem to be situated around Phan Thiet and Phan Ri in Binh Thuan Province and near Phan Rang in Ninh Thuan Province. The Cham live in proximity to a number of ethnic groups in addition to the Vietnamese. In Quang Ngai Province, the Cham have the Hre tribe to the west, the Cua to the northwest, and the M'nong to the southwest. The Cham in Binh Dinh Province live primarily in the south, adjacent to the Bahnar in the west and the Hroi in the south. In Khanh Hoa Province, the Cham have settled along the northeast border near the Rhade to the west and northwest and the Hroi to the north. In Phu Yen Province, the Cham inhabit the southern districts of Son Hoa and Dong Xuan with the Jarai to the southwest and the Rhade to the west. The Cham in Ninh Thuan reside in the eastern portion of the province, near Phan Rang, and have the Churu and Raglai as neighbors to the northwest. In Binh Thuan Province, the Cham are located near Phan Ri, Hoa Da, and Phan Thiet with the Koho to the south and the west, the Churu to the northwest, and the Raglai to the north and northwest. The Cham in

Long Khanh live in the south central area of the province around Xuan Loc, with the Koho to the north. In Binh Tuy Province the Cham inhabit the region around the town of Tanh Linh and along the coast above Ham Tan in proximity to the Koho and the Chrau in the west. The Cham in Tay Ninh and Chau Doc Provinces are located near the provincial capitals and are surrounded by Malays and Khmers. The territory of the Cham can most conveniently be discussed by covering the two major areas — the central coastal area and the delta area — of Cham habitation separately. The Cham inhabit a strip along the coast of the Republic of Vietnam from Quang Ngai Province in the north to Binh Tuy Province in the south. They are also found in the delta provinces of Chau Doc and Tay Ninh on the Cambodian border. The coastal regions of Quang Ngai, Binh Dinh, and Phu Yen are characterized by low sand dunes, alluvial deposits, and lagoons. In general, the relief does not exceed 600 feet, but in some areas the coast almost disappears, where mountain spurs reach shoreward and separate the lowlands. The fertile lowland plains produce two crops of rice annually (in April and September). Several fast- moving rivers — the Thu Bon, the Kim Son, and the Ba — drain eastward into the South China Sea. The provinces of Khanh Hoa and Ninh Thuan are characterized by the most jagged and irregular section of the Vietnamese coastline. High wooded mountains rise precipitously from narrow, marshy, and relatively infertile plains lying at the heads of deep-water inlets enclosed by peninsulas bounded by cliffs. The Song Cai River, which enters the Bay of Nha Trang at the town of Nha Trang carves a broad valley inland through mountains exceeding 1,800 feet in height. A few miles south of Nha Trang the rugged terrain gives way to low-lying sand dunes surrounding the Lagoon of Thui Trieu. This lagoon, with the marshlands behind it, empties into the Bay of Cam Ranh. The narrow coastal plain of this region is drained by several small streams and is overgrown in some places by mangroves. The coast becomes irregular again just south of Mui Da Vach with mountains rising steeply inland to a height of over 2,500 feet. The Song Kinh Dinh River enters the Bay of Phan Rang 2 miles below the port of Phan Rang on the coastal plain. From Phan Rang south, the coast follows a northeast-southwest course. Between Phan Rang and Phan Thiet, both the summer and winter monsoons blow parallel to the shore, causing this region to receive the lowest rainfall in the entire country. Cliffs rise abruptly from the sea at Mui Dihn limiting the coastal plains to a narrow strip of sand and mud fringing the Bay of Mui Dinh. The Bay of Phan Ri is bounded by a forest on the east and a barren region to the west The latter is formed by an isolated upland zone separated from the Annamite Mountains by the Song Luy valley bordering the coast. Three inlets backed by woods divide the Bay of Phan Ri from the Bay of Phan Thiet. The wooded coastal plain, extending inland for some distance, is marked by thousands of acres of sand dunes which reach a height of 26 to 50 feet. The mountains rise behind the dunes about 20 miles to the west. The sterility of the soil, the irregularity of the rainfall, and the damage from tropical storms limit the rice yields in this area, which is the least populated part of the lowland coastal region. The Cham in the Long Khanh and Binh Tuy Provinces occupy the lowland plantation, or the southern plantation area in the vicinity of Saigon. The soil of this region is composed of ancient alluvial, or gray, lands and in some regions red basaltic lands. Despite heavy rainfall, the area is well drained. The delta area inhabited by the Cham — Chau Doc and Tay Ninh Provinces — is to the west of Saigon along the Cambodian border. Extensive drainage projects have converted the marshy ground into intensively cultivated land. During the dry season early maturing or floating varieties of rice are grown. The eastern portions of the area are marked by small farms, whereas the outlying newly drained lands are characterized by larger farms. Several rivers dissect the delta regions settled by the Cham, principally the Hau Giang (Bassac) River, which flows through Chau Doc and the Vam Co Dong River, which traverses Tay Ninh. Canals provide irrigation and transportation for small craft. The coastal regions inhabited by the Cham are well served by transport facilities. The Trans-Vietnam Railroad follows the coast from the inner side of the sand dunes in Quang Ngai Province down to the Song Luy valley, where it turns inland and continues to Saigon. Branch railway lines connect the cities of Qui Nhon and Phan Thiet to the Trans-Vietnam Railroad. National Route 1 roughly follows the path of the railroad along the coast. Route 1 connects, with secondary links in some cases, Route 14 at Quang Ngai and Tuy Hoa ; Route 19, at Binh Dinh ; Route 21 at Ninh Hoa ; and Route 11 at Phan Rang. Several secondary roads lead inland from Phan Ri, Phan Thiet, and Ham Tan. There are all-weather airfields at Quang Ngai, Qui Nhon, Song Cau, Tuy Hoa, Nha Trang, Cam Ranh, Ninh Thuan, Long Xuyen, Bien Hoi, and Phan Thiet.

Seasonal fields are located at Due My, Ninh Hoa, Trai Ca, Phan Rang, Ca Na, Song Mao, Phan Ri, and Song Luy. The Chau Doc and Tay Ninh regions are linked with Saigon by Routes 20 and 22 respectively.

Cham Paramilitary Capabilities

There is very little information pertinent to the paramilitary capabilities of the Cham. During the French Indochina War, the Cham did fight with the French against the Viet Minh. Experience during that war indicated that only a few Cham officials, guided by French and Vietnamese administrative authorities, were necessary to rally the rest of the Cham population to fight the Viet Minh. It is not known at this writing whether the Cham would actually respond in this way in the current struggle with the Viet Cong.

The Khmer

The Khmer, a people of Cambodian descent, form the second largest ethnic group in the area formerly known as Indochina. In the Republic of Vietnam, these remnants of a vast, ancient empire now number between 400,000 and 600,000 and are scattered throughout the Mekong Delta area. The Khmer language belongs to the Mon-Khmer language family and is related to the M'nong and Bahnar tongues. Khmer social organization is patriarchal, but the women wield considerable influence in the household and in divorce and inheritance proceedings. Like the Cham minority group, the Khmer were influenced by Indian civilization in their early history and have retained cultural elements which reflect this tradition. Whereas the Vietnamese practice Mahayana Buddhism, the majority of the Khmer adhere to Theravada Buddhism. Principal economic activities consist of irrigated rice cultivation, fishing, fruit and vegetable farming, and weaving. According to legend, the Khmer kings were descended from the great hermit and seer, Kambu Svayambhuva; "Kambuja," translated by the French to "Cambodge" and by the British to "Cambodia," is a derivative of his name. Early Chinese inscriptions contain the word "Kambudjadesa" or "sons of Kambu." The name Khmer refers to the dominant population of Cambodia and differs from the term "Cambodian," which encompasses other groups in addition to the ethnic Khmer and also designates any national of the country of that name. In the Republic of Vietnam, the names Khmer, Khmer Krom, and Cambodian are used interchangeably when speaking of the people descended from the ancient Khmer of the Empire of Funan. Size of Group Population figures for the Khmer in the Republic of Vietnam, which are little more than informed estimates, range between 400,000 and 600,000. In 1957, the largest concentrations of Khmer were located in the following provinces: Chau Doc (then called An Giang), 40,978; Ba Xuyen, 118,328; and Kien Giang, 42,022. The majority of the ethnic Khmer, the total group numbering about 2,600,000, inhabit Cambodia in the Tonle Sap region; smaller groups have settled in Thailand and Laos. The Khmer are located in settlements throughout the Mekong Delta, particularly around Khanh Hung (formerly Soc Trang) and Vinh Loi (Bac Lieu) in Ba Xuyen Province; Rach Gia and Ha Tien in Kien Giang Province; Phu Vinh (formerly Tra Vinh Province); Can Tho in Phong Dinh Province; and in the Provinces of Tay Ninh and Chau Doc. Scattered Khmer settlements are also found near the towns of Long Xuyen, Cholon, Vinh Long, Tan An, and Bien Hoa. The Vietnamese are the principal neighbors of the Khmer. In Tay Ninh and Chau Doc, the Cham and Malays live in small settlements adjacent to the Khmer and maintain a harmonious relationship with them despite religious differences. The Stieng tribe, the closest Montagnard group, inhabits Binh Long Province near the Khmer of Tay Ninh Province.

Khmer Paramilitary Capabilities

The Khmer soldier is reportedly loyal, good natured, robust, and, with good leadership, brave. Although he is generally not aggressive, experience has shown that when his way of life is threatened, he will answer the threat aggressively. Since most Khmer are of peasant origin and are accustomed to hard work and a minimum of comfort, the Khmer soldier can endure considerable privation. Many have great manual dexterity and can be trained as technicians.

Since the founding of the Khmer Empire, the Khmer have waged both offensive and defensive wars against the neighboring Cham, Vietnamese, and Thai. In 1945, when the Viet Minh began to operate openly, the French recruited many

485

Khmer soldiers to fill their regiments. Organized in homogeneous units and led by subaltern officers of their own group, the Khmer were excellent soldiers. They did not yield to fatigue and were courageous in combat.

The Cao Dai, with its headquarters located in an area heavily populated by Khmer (Tay Ninh), also recruited the Khmer for its armies.

Along the Cambodian border is a group of Khmer, who, after years of fighting and bloodshed, have turned more and more to banditry, pillage, and terrorism. Prince Sihanouk of Cambodia has charged that the Communists, as early as the 1930's, organized a small number of these Khmer into fighting units. According to Sihanouk, this small contingent of Khmer auxiliaries was directed to infiltrate Cambodia to pillage and terrorize the populace.

The Khmer are doubtless familiar with modern methods of warfare as a result of experience acquired through their association with the French, as well as through the military operations of the Viet Cong and Vietnamese Government forces in the delta region. Indeed, a sizeable number of Khmer are currently serving in the Vietnamese Army.

Notes

[1] Now called Ho Chi Minh City.

[2] Francis J. Kelly, *U. S. Army Special Forces, 1961-1971, Vietnam Studies* (Washington: Department of Army, 1973), 20-24.

[3] In the 1960s, estimates of the number of Montagnards in Indochina were well over a million.

[4] Kelly, 20-24.

[5] Stanley Karnow, *Vietnam, A History, The First Complete Account of Vietnam at War* (New York: The Viking Press, 1983), 169.

[6] *Ibid.*, 85.

[7] Ho was known by several names over the years, but in this history I refer to him by the last name that he used: Ho Chi Minh.

[8] Karnow, 121.

[9] Alan Axelrod, *The Real History of the Vietnam War, A New Look at the Past* (New York: Sterling Publishing, 2013), 55.

[10] *Ibid.*, 140.

[11] *Ibid.*, 144.

[12] *Ibid.*, 140.

[13] *Ibid.*, 135.

[14] Christopher Goscha, *Vietnam: A New History* (New York: Basic Books, 2016), 427-428.

[15] The Japanese were allowed to retain their emperor; Hirohito who was not tried as a war criminal.

[16] *Ibid.*, 147.

[17] *Ibid.*, 135.

[18] *Ibid.*, 149–150.

[19] Philippe Devillers, *Historia du Vietnam de 1940 a 1952* (Paris: Editions du Seuil, 1953).

[20] Goscha, 428-431.

[21] Goscha, 428.

[22] *Ibid.*, 178.

[23] *Ibid.*, 188.

[24] Dean Acheson, *Present at the Creation, My Years in the State Department* (New York: W. W. Norton, 1969), 677.

[25] *Ibid.*, 691.

[26] McCarthy was called "Tail-Gunner Joe" because he claimed that he was a tail-gunner in a U.S. aircraft in the Pacific during World War II: he flew one mission. He started a witch hunt looking for communists in the U.S. that at times violated the rights of citizens.

[27] Karnow, 169.

[28] *Ibid.*, 189. In some ways this battle was similar to Lam Son 719, fought nearly twenty years later.

[29] Douglas Porch, *The French Secret Services, A History of French Intelligence from the Dreyfus Affair to the Gulf War* (New York: Farrar, Straus and Giroux, 1995), 118-119.

[30] Goscha, 431-432.

[31] Karnow, 196.

[32] *Ibid.*, 191.

[33] The U.S. had decided to shore up its ally, France, by providing a small amount of air support, but it did not come close to what was needed at Dien Bien Phu.

[34] Karnow, 195.

[35] *Ibid.*

[36] *Ibid.*, 196.

[37] McGovern and Buford are not listed on the Vietnam Veterans Memorial wall, nor are several other people killed before the earliest casualties on the wall. Criteria needed to be established when the people who invented the wall got started, and Jan Scruggs, who founded the memorial, and others chose 1959 as the start of casualties on the wall. On the other end were the criteria established for those who died after the war. Suicides and those who died of Agent Orange and other diseases were not added. A famous example is Lewis Burwell Puller, Jr. Puller was a marine like his father, the famous "Chesty" Puller, and was badly wounded in Vietnam. He survived but lost both legs and was the subject of at least one book. He finally killed himself years later. Puller's name is not on the wall.

[38] Bernard B. Fall, *Street Without Joy: The French Debacle in Indochina.* (Mechanicsburg: Stackpole Books, 1994), 190.

[39] *Ibid.*, 211

[40] Shelby L. Stanton, *The Rise and Fall of an American Army: U. S. Ground Forces in Vietnam, 1965-1973* (New York: Balantine Books, 1985), 3-4.

[41] Karnow, 204.

[42] *Ibid.*, 214.

[43] Phillip B. Davidson, *Vietnam at War, The History 1946-1975* (New York: Oxford University Press, 1988), 288.

[44] Karnow, 214.

[45] *Ibid.*, 238.

[46] Michael Lind, *Vietnam, The Necessary War* (New York: Simon and Schuster, 1999), 35.

[47] Michael D. Benge, "The Montagnard Revolt," in *Indochina in the Year of the Dragon-1964, ed.* Steve Sherman, (Houston: RADIX Press, 2014), 199.

[48] *Ibid.*, 195-196.

[49] J. P. Harris, *Vietnam's High Ground, Armed Struggle for the Central Highlands, 1954-1965* (Lawrence: University Press of Kansas, 2016), 43-46.

[50] Goscha, 432-439.

[51] These were most likely kidnapped and did not go voluntarily.

[52] Harris, 38-42.

[53] *Ibid.*, 33-38.

[54] *Ibid.*, 46-48.

[55] Christian G. Appy, *Working Class War, American Combat Soldiers in Vietnam* (Chapel Hill: University of North Carolina Press, 1993),104.

[56] *Ibid.*

[57] Harris, 76.

[58] Goscha, 299.

[59] Axelrod, 96–97.

[60] Kelly, 5-10.

[61] Shelby L. Stanton, *The Green Berets at War, U. S. Army Special Forces in Southeast Asia 1956-1975* (Novato: Presideo Press, 1985), 87.

[62] *Ibid.*, 89.

[63] *Ibid.*, 90.

[64] Gordon M. Patric, *The Vietnams of the Green Berets* (Chesterton: Self-Published, 1969), 23-25.

[65] Harris, 69-74.

[66] The LLDB were frequently ineffective. These individuals were often corrupt and shared the Vietnamese view that the Montagnards were savages: not qualities that would help them lead. See Dooley, 122-123.

[67] Stanton, *Green Berets at War*, 41-43.

[68] Harris, 76.

[69] Kelly, 24-25.

[70] John C. Loving, *Combat Advisor: How America Won the War and Lost the Peace* (New York: Universe, Inc., 2006), 28.

[71] Martin J. Dockery, *Lost in Translation: Vietnam, A Combat Advisor's Story* (New York: Ballantine Books, 2003), 25.

[72] Jeffrey J. Clark, *Advice and Support: The Final Years, The U. S. Army in Vietnam* (Washington: Center for Military History, U. S. Army, 1988), 49-66.

[73] Thomas P. McKenna, *Kontum The Battle to Save South Vietnam*

(Lexington: The University Press of Kentucky, 2011), 8-9.

[74] Loving, 28.

[75] Harris, 79-80.

[76] *Ibid.*, 68-69.

[77] Daniel Ellsberg, *Secrets: A Memoir of Vietnam and the Pentagon Papers* (New York: Penguin Group, 2002), 151.

[78] Karnow, 255-258.

[79] Harris, 84.

[80] *Ibid.*, 109-110.

[81] Stanton, *Green Berets at War*, 44.

[82] *Ibid.*, 51-52.

[83] Michael A. Eggleston, *Exiting Vietnam: The Era of Vietnamization and American Withdrawal Revealed in First-Person Accounts* (Jefferson: McFarland & Company, Inc., Publishers), 199.

[84] Harris, 131.

[85] Patric, 80.

[86] Deborah Shapley, *Promise and Power: The Life and Times of Robert McNamara* (Boston: Little, Brown, and Company, 1993), 250.

[87] Maurice Isserman and Michael Kazan, *American Divided: The Civil War in the 1960s* (Oxford: Oxford University Press, 2008), 88.

[88] A.J. Langguth, *Our Vietnam: The War 1954– 1975* (*New* York: Simon & Schuster, 2000), 202. Ap Bac was considered to be the first major victory of the Viet Cong since Dien Bien Phu.

[89] Isserman, 87.

[90] Langguth, 204–205; Neil Sheehan, 263–265.

[91] George C. Herring, *America's Longest War: The United States and Vietnam, 1950–1975* (Boston: McGraw-Hill, 2002), 113.

[92] Langguth, 208; Arthur M. Schlesinger, Jr., *A Thousand Days: John F. Kennedy in the White House* (New York: Houghton Mifflin Company, 2002), 985.

[93] Shapley, 250. Diem would be killed later in 1963. The point is that Diem's views and actions in 1963 were precisely the same as South Vietnamese President Thieu's in 1971 during and after Lam Son 719. It seems that the South Vietnamese would never change their way of doing business.

[94] Karnow, x.

[95] This conclusion by Karnow is hard to support. It would appear that most historians provide evidence to prove that Ho was a Communist and not a nationalist, but it all depends upon the time frame. When as a young man he appeared in Geneva in 1919, where World War I peace

accords were being discussed, he was apparently a nationalist.

[96] Karnow, 11.

[97] *Ibid.*, 262.

[98] *Ibid.*

[99] Neil Sheehan, *A Bright Shining Lie, John Paul Vann and America in Vietnam* (New York: Random House, 1988), 313.

[100] Karnow, 323–324.

[101] Sheehan, 316. Vann shared the same dry sense of humor as Sheehan. It made life livable.

[102] Sully would return after Diem's death. He was later killed when his aircraft crashed.

[103] Harkins was not relieved of his command, he was simply replaced by Westmoreland. Sheehan maintained that the reason was that the army leadership was as guilty as Harkins in misleading the public. See *Bright Shining Lie*, 376.

[104] Sheehan, 283.

[105] Mark Moyar, *Triumph Forsaken, The Vietnam War, 1954-1965.* (Cambridge: Cambridge University Press, 2006), 165-166.

[106] *Ibid.*, 194-205.

[107] Sheehan, 270–272.

[108] Langguth, 204.

[109] Harris, 138.

[110] Kelly, 38-42.

[111] Michael D. Benge, "The Montagnard Revolt," in *Indochina in the Year of the Dragon-1964, ed.* Steve Sherman, (Houston: RADIX Press, 2014), 196-197.
Sherman, *Indochina in the Year of the Dragon*, 196-197.

[112] Y-Thinh wasn't the only one imprisoned, some were killed. The Diem regime crushed the BAJARAKA Movement that resulted in the death of several Montagnard leaders and the imprisonment of Y-Bham Enuol, Paul Nur, Nay Luett, Y-Thih Eban, Siu Sip, Touneh Yoh and Y-Ju Eban -- sentenced to six years in prison in Hue City.

[113] Michael D. Benge, "The Montagnard Revolt," in *Indochina in the Year of the Dragon-1964, ed.* Steve Sherman, (Houston: RADIX Press, 2014), 196-197.

[114] Kelly, 43-54.

[115] Langguth, 216.

[116] Harris, 138-172.

[117] Karnow, 265.

[118] *Ibid.*, 277.

[119] *Ibid.*, 310–311.

[120] Appy, 75.

[121] Harris, 173-175.

[122] Robert Pisor, *The End of the Line, The Siege of Khe Sanh* (New York: W. W. Norton, 1982), 44.

[123] Karnow, 324.

[124] *Ibid.*, 325.

[125] *Ibid.*, 326.

[126] *Ibid.*, 367–374.

[127] Pisor, 43-44.

[128] Harris, 183-184.

[129] *Ibid.*, 194-195.

[130] Stanton, *Green Berets at War*, 74-76.

[131] Roger H. C. Donlon, *Outpost of Freedom* (New York: Avon Books, 1965), 138-140.

[132] Gerald C. Hickey, *Window on a War, An Anthropologist in the Vietnam Conflict* (Lubbock: Texas Tech University Press, 2002), 138-140.

[133] *Ibid.*

[134] Shelby L. Stanton, *The Green Berets at War, U. S. Army Special Forces in Southeast Asia 1956-1975* (Novato: Presideo Press, 1985), 85.

[135] Michael A. Eggleston. *The 10th Minnesota Volunteers, 1862-1865* (Jefferson: McFarland & Company Publishers, 2012), 16-19. Little Crow was killed during this Indian War and his body was tossed into a garbage pit. His remains were recovered and reburied a century later by Native American leaders.

[136] Gillespie's story was told in the January 1965 issue of National Geographic Magazine.

[137] John Prados, *Vietnam, The History of an Unwinnable War, 1945-1975.* (Lawrence: University Press of Kansas, 2009), 119-120

[138] Barry Petersen, *Tiger Men.* (London: Sidgwick & Jackson, 1988), 81.

[139] It is believed that Y-Bham Enuol was executed by Khmer Rouge after the fall of Cambodia in 1975.

[140] Petersen, 72-86.

[141] Ted Mataxis, Jr., "The War in II Corps Tactical Zone," in *Indochina in the Year of the Snake-1965, ed.* Steve Sherman, (Houston: RADIX Press, 2015), 175.

[142] David Sigler, *Vietnam Battle Chronology, US Army and Marine Corps Combat Operations, 1965-1973* (Jefferson: McFarland & Company, Inc., Publishers, 1992), 1.

[143] H. Norman Schwarzkopf, *The Autobiography, It Doesn't Take a Hero*

(New York: Bantam Books, 1992), 139.

[144] Harris, 220.

[145] Charles M. Simpson, *Inside the Green Berets, The First Thirty Years, A History of the U.S. Army Special Forces* (Novato: Presideo Press, 1983), 167-168.

[146] Shelby L. Stanton, *The Green Berets at War, U. S. Army Special Forces in Southeast Asia 1956-1975* (Novato: Presideo Press, 1985), 93-96.

[147] Simpson, 120-121.

[148] Stanton, *Green Berets at War*, 234.

[149] Karnow, 395

[150] William C. Westmoreland, *A Soldier Reports.* (New York: Doubleday & Company, 1976), 178.

[151] Stanton, *Green Berets at War*, 110.

[152] Schwarzkopf, 126-139.

[153] Edward F. Murphy, *Dak To, America's Sky Soldiers in South Vietnam's Central Highlands* (New York: Ballantine Books, 2007), 172.

[154] Chickering, William, "After the Montagnard Revolt." *VVFH Magazine, Volume 1, Issue, 2018.* 17-18.

[155] Beckwith would later gain fame for his role in the aborted attempt to rescue the Iranian embassy hostages in 1980.

[156] Charles A. Beckwith, *Delta Force: A Memoir by the Founder of the U. S. Military's Most Secretive Special Operations Unit* (New York: William Morrow, 1983) 76-78.

[157] John Prados, *The Blood Road, the Ho Chi Minh Trail and the Vietnam War.* New York: John Wiley & Sons, Inc., 1999), 143.

[158] Harold G. Moore and Joseph L. Galloway, *We Were Soldiers Once. . . . and Young, Ia Drang-the Battle that Changed the War in Vietnam* (New York: Harper Collins Publishers, 1992), 250.

[159] *Ibid.*, 199.

[160] Appy, 134-135.

[161] Hickey, *Window on a War*, 179-182.

[162] Stanton, *Green Berets at War*, 111.

[163] It was also used to ferry Vietnamese recruits and in this role was called the "Vomit Comet."

[164] John Prados, *The Hidden History of the Vietnam War* (Chicago: Ivan R. Dee, 1995), 81. The FULRO also used flares to signal the uprising.

[165] American Embassy, Saigon. *Montagnard Dissidence: FULRO.* 23 December 1965. 1-2.

[166] Petersen, 219-220.

[167] Michael A. Eggleston, *Unpublished memoir.*

[168] Patric, *The Vietnams of the Green Berets,* 89-91.

[169] *Ibid.,* 90-91.

[170] Westmoreland, 205.

[171] Stanton, *The Rise and Fall of an American Army*, 21–22.

[172] Harris, 431-434.

[173] Sigler, 10.

[174] Simpson, 168.

[175] Langguth, 427.

[176] Axelrod, 167. Infiltration increased to 6,000 per month in 1967.

[177] Shelby L. Stanton, *The Green Berets at War, U. S. Army Special Forces in Southeast Asia 1956-1975* (Novato: Presideo Press, 1985, 123.

[178] Simpson, 146-150.

[179] Stanton, *Green Berets at War*, 125-126.

[180] Stanton, *Green Berets at War,* 117-122. In May 1969 the U. S. ventured into the A Shau valley to attack Ap Bia Mountain in what became known as the Battle of Hamburger Hill. The attack achieved nothing and the U. S. promptly withdrew after the battle never to return to the A Shau Valley.

[181] Simpson, 167-168.

[182] Sigler, 31.

[183] Michael A. Eggleston, *Dak To and the Border Battles of Vietnam, 1967-1968.* (Jefferson: McFarland & Company, Inc., Publishers, 2017), 38.

[184] The Europeans viewed the war as a dangerous conflict that could explode into wider conflict, involving China and perhaps even the Soviet Union. Further, the war was eroding U.S. support to the Allies.

[185] Davidson, *Vietnam at War*, 441.

[186] *Ibid.*

[187] James P. Coan, *Con Thien: The Hill of Angels* (Tuscaloosa: The University of Alabama Press, 2004), 24.

[188] Davidson, *Vietnam at War*, 466.

[189] *Ibid.,* 442.

[190] This was unlikely to succeed, because in addition to dog tags, the dead soldier had to be identified by someone who knew him. If it did succeed, it would have a devastating effect on next of kin and would get media attention; another nasty reminder of the war.

[191] Stanton, *Green Berets at War,* 132.

[192] Hickey, *Window on a War*, 211-213.

[193] Eggleston, *Dak To and the Border Battles of Vietnam, 1967-1968,* 36.

[194] *Ibid.*

[195] *Ibid.*

[196] *Ibid.,* 38.

[197] *Ibid.*

[198] *Ibid.,* 38-39.

[199] *Ibid.,* 75.

[200] *Ibid.,* 75-91.

[201] Stanton, *Green Berets at War,* 145.

[202] *Ibid.,* 140.

[203] Davidson, *Vietnam at War,* 468.

[204] Prados, *Vietnam, The History of the Unwinnable War, 1945–1975,* 224–225.

[205] Gordon L. Rottman, *Special Forces Camps in Vietnam, 1961–1970* (New York: Osprey Publishing, 2005), 52–53.

[206] John McCoy, *Unpublished Memoir.*

[207] Stanton, *Green Berets at War,* 141.

[208] Prados, *Vietnam, The History of the Unwinnable War* 226.

[209] Davidson, *Vietnam at War,* 468–469.

[210] "The War: The Massacre at Dak Son," *Time Magazine,* 15 December 1967.

[211] Eggleston, *Unpublished Memoir.*

[212] Sigler, 64.

[213] General Westmoreland used similar words in late 1957, but later denied that he had used them.

[214] Prados, *Vietnam, The History of the Unwinnable War,* 224.

[215] Sheehan, 708.

[216] *Ibid.,* 712–713.

[217] Davidson, *Vietnam at War,* 478.

[218] Prados, *Vietnam, The History of the Unwinnable War,* 232.

[219] *Ibid.*

[220] Edward Doyle and Samuel Lipsman, *The Vietnam Experience: America Takes Over 1965–1967* (Boston: Boston Publishing Company, 1982), 183.

[221] Davidson, *Vietnam at War,* 446.

[222] Prados, *Vietnam, The History of the Unwinnable War,* 231.

[223] *Ibid.*

[224] *Ibid.,* 239.

[225] Steven C. Vorthmann, "Hill 875, Dak To, Vietnam," 2016.

[226] Prados, *Vietnam, The History of the Unwinnable War,* 235.

[227] *Ibid.,* 241.

[228] Oscar Salemink, *Ethnography of Vietnam's Central Highlands.* (Honolulu: University Press of Hawaii, 2003), 313.

[229] Kelly, 119-120.

[230] Charles Hartley and Bruno Rizzato, "Kontum (II CTZ)," in *Indochina in the Year of the Monkey-1968, ed.* Steve Sherman, (Houston: RADIX Press, 2017), 196-197.

Steve Sherman, *Indochina in the Year of the Monkey-1968.* (Houston: RADIX Press, 2017), 96-99.

[231] Greg Jones, *Last Stand at Khe Sanh, The U. S. Marines Finest Hour in Vietnam.* (Boston: De Capo Press, 2014), 34.

[232] Prados, *The Hidden History*, 166.

[233] Moyers S. Shore, II, *The Battle of Khe Sanh.* (Washington, D. C. History and Museums Division, Headquarters, U. S. Marine Corps, 1969), 1-2.

[234] Murphy, *The Hill Fights*, 17.

[235] *Ibid.*, 23.

[236] Davidson, *Vietnam at War*, 443.

[237] Numbers of troops on both sides at Khe Sanh fluctuated at different times. Most sources indicate that two NVA divisions or about 20,000 people were in place at the time the siege started on 20 January 1968. They were opposed by two Marine battalions with supporting units or about 2000 people. Both sides could quickly reinforce, if required, and did.

[238] Westmoreland, 244-245.

[239] Aside from many political reasons why this would never happen, the simple fact was that nuclear weapons delivered in that area would be largely ineffective because of the terrain.

[240] Murphy, *The Hill Fights*, 4.

[241] *Ibid.*, 4-6.

[242] *Ibid.*, 5-6.

[243] Shore, 10.

[244] *Ibid.*, 11.

[245] *Ibid.*, 13.

[246] Steven A. Johnson, *Cammie Up! Memoir of a Recon Marine in Vietnam 1967-1968.* (Jefferson: McFarland & Company, Inc., Publishers, 2012), 49.

[247] Murphy, *The Hill Fights*, 279-281.

[248] Clark Dougan and Stephen Weiss. *The American Experience in Vietnam.* (Boston: Boston Publishing Company, 1988), 42.

[249] Murphy, *The Hill Fights*, 281.

[250] Jones, 9.

[251] *Ibid*, 20.

[252] Murphy, *The Hill Fights*, 283.

[253] John Prados, *In Country, Remembering the Vietnam War* (New York: Ivan R. Dee, Publisher, 2011), 215-216.

[254] Jones, 33.

[255] *Ibid.*, 25-27.

[256] *Ibid.*, 34.

[257] *Ibid.*, 1.

[258] *Ibid.*, 61.

[259] *Ibid.*

[260] *Ibid.*, 62.

[261] *Ibid.*, 68-69.

[262] *Ibid.*, 76.

[263] John Morocco, *Thunder from Above: Air War, 1941–1968* (Boston: Boston Publishing Company, 1984), 52.

[264] Pisor, 250-261,

[265] William R. Phillips, *Night of the Silver Stars, The Battle of Lang Vei* (New York: St. Martin's Paperbacks, 1997), 132.

[266] *Ibid.*, 3.

[267] Stanton, *Green Berets at War*, 148.

[268] Phillips, 20.

[269] *Ibid.*, 68-69.

[270] *Ibid.*, 95.

[271] Stanton, *Green Berets at War*, 157.

[272] *Ibid.*, 159.

[273] *Ibid.*, 152-153.

[274] *Ibid.*, 131-132.

[275] *Ibid.*, 163-164.

[276] Stanton, *Green Berets at War*, 157-161.

[277] John Albright, John H. Cash and Allan W. Sandstrum, *Seven Firefights in Vietnam.* (Washington: Office of the Chief of Military History, United States Army, 1970), 137.

[278] *Ibid.*, 137-138.

[279] Pisor, 250-261.

[280] Davidson, *Vietnam at War*, 477.

[281] Westmoreland later claimed that he gave the appearance of being unaware because he did not want Hanoi to know that he knew of their impending attack.

[282] Prados, *Vietnam, The History of the Unwinnable War*, 233.

[283] *Ibid.*, 242.

[284] James H. Willbanks, *The Tet Offensive: A Concise History* (New York: Columbia University Press, 2007), 81.

[285] Prados, *Vietnam, The History of the Unwinnable War*, 243.

[286] *Ibid.*, 233.

[287] Karnow, 534.

[288] Sheehan, 720.

[289] The Wise Men were a group of prestigious leaders such as Dean Acheson and Averell Harriman that LBJ convened to offer him advice.

[290] Prados, *Vietnam, The History of the Unwinnable War*, 249.

[291] Langguth, 474.

[292] *Ibid.*

[293] Eggleston, *Exiting Vietnam,* 72.

[294] Davidson, *Vietnam at War*, 450.

[295] Prados, *Vietnam, The History of the Unwinnable War*, 242.

[296] *Ibid.*, 249.

[297] *Ibid.*

[298] Shapley, 600–601.

[299] CBS was sued by General Westmoreland because a CBS broadcast alleged that General Westmoreland deliberately underestimated enemy strength before the Tet offense in order to show progress in Vietnam. The case was settled out of court.

[300] Shapley, 600–601.

[301] *Ibid.*, 606.

[302] Shapley, 442–444. Years later, when McNamara participated in the documentary *"Fog of War,"* he was asked if he had been fired or just resigned. His immediate answer was he didn't know. Then, in a rare moment of honesty, he said that he had asked his long-time friend from the *Washington Post*, Kathrine Graham. Her reply: "Bob, you were fired. Everyone knows that." McNamara lived on to die at age ninety-three.

[303] Stanton, *Green Berets at War*, 176.

[304] Herring, 257-258.

[305] The one-war concept focused on protecting the population so that the civil government could establish its authority.

[306] Stanton, *Green Berets at War*, 173-174.

[307] *Ibid.*, 176.

[308] *Ibid.*, 177.

[309] *Ibid.*, 176.

[310] Prados, *The Blood Road*, 281.

[311] Stanton, *Green Berets at War*, 182.

[312] *Ibid.*, 182-183.

[313] *Ibid.*, 177-178.

[314] *Ibid.*, 178.

[315] *Ibid.*, 180-181.

[316] Sigler, 85.

[317] Stanton, *Green Berets at War*, 269.

[318] *Ibid.*, 186-191.

[319] The Great Society was a set of domestic programs such as the Job Corps and Head Start launched by President Johnson in 1964–1965. Many of the programs were choked off by a lack of funding due to the Vietnam War.

[320] Alexander M. Haig, Jr., *Inner Circles: How America Changed the World, A Memoir* (New York: Warner Books, 1992), 226.

[321] Nguyen Duy Hinh, *Lam Son 719.* (Fort McNair: U. S. Army Center of Military History, 1979), 96.

[322] Prados, *Vietnam, The History of the Unwinnable War,* 390.

[323] Kelly, 143-145

[324] Sigler, 111.

[325] Eggleston, *Unpublished Memoir.*

[326] Kelly, 150.

[327] *Ibid.*, 147-152.

[328] Hickey, *Window on a War*, 288-289.

[329] Eggleston, *Unpublished Memoir.*

[330] *Ibid.*

[331] Sheehan, 739.

[332] David Fulghum and Terrence Maitland, *The Vietnam Experience: South Vietnam on Trial, Mid- 1970 to 1972* (Boston: Boston Publishing Company, 1984), 61–64.

[333] General Thomas Matthew Rienzi, *Communications-Electronics, 1962–1970 (Vietnam Studies)* (Washington: U.S. Government Printing Office, 1972), 144.

[334] *Ibid.*, 145–146.

[335] Eggleston, *Unpublished Memoir.*

[336] When the equipment arrived in the States it was determined that it was unusable, something we all knew. Six years in the tropics is not kind to electronics.

[337] Eggleston, *Unpublished Memoir.*

[338] *Ibid.*

[339] Lewis Sorley, *Thunderbolt: General Creighton Abrams and the Army*

of His Times (Bloomington: Indiana University Press, 2008), 305.

340 Sigler, 123.

341 Tom Marshall, *The Price of Exit*. (New York: Ballantine Books, 1998), 230-231.

342 Henry Kissinger, *Ending the Vietnam War* (New York: Simon and Schuster, 2003), 198.

343 David Fulghum and Terrence Maitland, 64– 65.

344 Historical Division Joint Secretariat, *History of the Joint Chiefs of Staff and the War in Vietnam 1971–1973* (Washington: Department of Defense, 1970), 7.

345 Andrew Wiest, *Vietnam's Forgotten Army Heroism and Betrayal in the ARVN*. (New York: New York University Press, 2008), 203.

346 Lewis Sorley, *A Better War: The Unexamined Victories and Final Tragedy of America's Last Years in Vietnam* (New York: Harcourt, 1999), 255.

347 Sorley, *Thunderbolt*, 307.

348 Van Atta, 345.

349 *Ibid.*

350 Sorley, *A Better War*, 270–271.

351 David Fulghum and Terrence Maitland, 88.

352 *Ibid.*, 70.

353 *Ibid.*, 75.

354 Dale Van Atta and President Gerald R. Ford, *With Honor: Melvin Laird in War, Peace, and Politics* (Madison: The University of Wisconsin Press, 2008), 348.

355 David Fulghum and Terrence Maitland, 85– 86.

356 Hinh, 90.

357 David Fulghum and Terrence Maitland, 87.

358 Richard Nixon, *No More Vietnams* (New York: Arbor House, 1985), 137.

359 Jeffrey Kimball, *Nixon's Vietnam War* (Lawrence: The University Press of Kansas, 1998), 246; Langguth, 579.

360 Historical Division Joint Secretariat, *History of the Joint Chiefs of Staff and the War in Vietnam 1971-1973* (Washington: Department of Defense, 1970), 15.

361 Kissinger, *Ending the Vietnam War*, 188.

362 Eggleston, *Exiting Vietnam,* 154.

363 Kissinger, *Ending the Vietnam War*, 204.

364 Van Atta, 350.

365 Davidson, *Vietnam at War*, 660.

[366] Kimball, 247.

[367] Karnow, 632.

[368] *Ibid.*

[369] Van Atta, 351.

[370] Bui Diem, *In the Jaws of History* (Bloomington: Indiana University Press, 1999), 287.

[371] Keith William Nolan, *Into Laos: The Story of Dewey Canyon II/Lam Son 719, 1971* (Novato: Presidio Press, 1986), 23.

[372] Fulghum and Maitland, 23.

[373] *Ibid.*, 25.

[374] General Bruce Palmer, Jr., *The 25 Year War: America's Military Role In Vietnam* (Lexington: The University Press of Kentucky, 1984), 155.

[375] Nolan, 23.

[376] Fulghum and Maitland, 9.

[377] *Ibid.*, 8.

[378] *Ibid.*, 9.

[379] Sorley, *A Better War*, 129.

[380] Sheehan, 650-651.

[381] Ronald L. Beckett, *Jack of All Trades: An American Advisor's War in Vietnam, 1969–70* (Mechanicsburg: Stackpole Books, 2016). 228–229.

[382] A U. S. Marine was asked how he could do a body count of dismembered pieces. His reply "Count the arms and legs and divide by four".

[383] Stanton, *The Rise and Fall of an American Army*, 270.

[384] Fulghum and Maitland, 37.

[385] *Ibid.*, 16.

[386] *Ibid.*, 20.

[387] *Ibid.*, 22.

[388] H. R. Haldeman, *The Ends of Power* (New York: Time Books, 1978), 122.

[389] Karnow, 644.

[390] *Ibid.*, 642.

[391] Langguth, 576.

[392] Sheehan, 775.

[393] Karnow, 641.

[394] *Ibid.*, 639–641.

[395] Langguth, 598.

[396] Sorley, *Thunderbolt*, 322–323.

[397] Fulghum and Maitland, 140.

[398] Nixon, *No More Vietnams*, 146.

[399] Hickey, *Window on a War*, 335.

[400] Sorley, *Thunderbolt*, 320.

[401] *Ibid.*

[402] Sheehan, 764.

[403] *Ibid.*, 755.

[404] *Ibid.*, 770.

[405] *Ibid.*, 775.

[406] Thomas P McKenna, *Kontum The Battle to Save South Vietnam* (Lexington: The University Press of Kentucky, 2011), 157.

[407] Hickey, *Shattered Worlds*, 459-472.

[408] Sheehan, 760–763.

[409] *Ibid.*, 763.

[410] *Ibid.*, 785.

[411] *Ibid.*, 786.

[412] Appy, 71-72.

[413] Sheehan, 789.

[414] Sorley, *Thunderbolt*, 328.

[415] Sheehan, 785.

[416] Isserman, 67–68.

[417] *Ibid.*, 78.

[418] Van Nguyen Duong, 126.

[419] David Reynolds, *One World Divisible: A Global History Since 1945* (New York: W. W. Norton & Company, 2000), 283.

[420] Jeremy Varon, *Bringing the War Home: The Weather Underground, the Red Army Faction, and Revolutionary Violence in the Sixties and Seventies* (Berkeley: University of California Press, 2004), 123.

[421] An American radical left-wing organization.

[422] Varon, 157.

[423] Sheehan, 717.

[424] Eggleston, *Exiting Vietnam,* 87. Three of the murderers were apprehended, tried and convicted. The fourth fled to Canada and as of 2014 was still at large.

[425] Nixon, *No More Vietnams*, 126.

[426] Philip Caputo, *A Rumor of War* (New York: Henry Holt and Company, 1977), xv.

[427] Philip Duncan Hoffman, *Humping Heavy: A Vietnam Memoir,* 2011, 195.

[428] Sigler, 132.

[429] Appy, 401-402.

[430] Davidson, *Vietnam at War*, 730.

[431] Karnow, 648.

[432] Kissinger, *Ending the Vietnam War*, 462.

[433] Appy, 401-402.

[434] Frank Snepp, *Decent Interval, The American Debacle in Vietnam and the Fall of Saigon* (New York: Penguin Books, 1977), 53-54.

[435] William E. Le Gro, *Vietnam from Ceasefire to Capitulation* (Washington: U. S. Army Center of Military History, 1985), 21.

[436] Graham A. Cosmos, *MACV, The Joint Command in the Years of Withdrawal, 1968-1973* (Washington: Center for Military History, U. S. Army, 2006), 392.

[437] Prados, *Vietnam, The History of an Unwinnable War, 1945-1975*, 518.

[438] Steve Sherman, Editor, *MACV Command History, 1972-1973 (Part I)* (Houston: RADIX Press, 2019), 146.

[439] General Cao Van Vien, *The Final Collapse* (Washington: Center of Military History, United States Army, 1983), 28.

[440] Davidson, *Vietnam at War,* 735-737.

[441] Vien, 29-31.

[442] *Ibid.*, 31-32.

[443] Le Gro, 21.

[444] *Ibid.*, 21-23.

[445] Sherman, 168.

[446] Le Gro, 23-24.

[447] *Ibid.*, 24.

[448] *Ibid.*, 24-25.

[449] Sherman, 180.

[450] Le Gro, 25.

[451] *Ibid.*, 23-24.

[452] Prados, 518.

[453] Le Gro, 25-26.

[454] Sherman, 186.

[455] Le Gro, 26.

[456] *Ibid.*, 26-27.

[457] Sherman, 193.

[458] Le Gro, 32.

[459] Davidson, *Vietnam at War,* 737-738.

[460] Snepp, 86-87.

[461] Davidson, *Vietnam at War,* 747.

[462] Vien, 46-47.

[463] Le Gro, 84.

[464] Davidson, *Vietnam at War,* 747-750.

[465] *Ibid.*, 752.

[466] *Ibid.*, 753.

[467] *Ibid.*, 757.

[468] Vien, 42.

[469] *Ibid.*, 42-48.

[470] MR 4 was also called IV Corps Tactical Zone-IV CTZ.

[471] Vien, 56.

[472] Le Gro, 110-131.

[473] *Ibid.*, 89-95.

[474] *Ibid.*, 96-109.

[475] *Ibid.*, 132.

[476] George J. Veith, *Black April, the Fall of South Vietnam 1973-1975* (New York: Encounter Books, 2012), 101.

[477] Vien, 58-60.

[478] Le Gro, 132-133.

[479] *Ibid.*, 132-133.

[480] Vien, 60-68.

[481] Le Gro, 133-137.

[482] Karnow, 664.

[483] Le Gro, 138-139.

[484] Karnow, 664.

[485] *Ibid.*

[486] Veith, 129.

[487] Hickey, *Shattered World*, 128.

[488] Veith,174.

[489] Langguth, 647.

[490] Veith, 177.

[491] *Ibid.*, 186.

[492] In Saigon one could visit what could today be called a mall. There were many vendors selling gold in all forms at the prevailing rates. The convenient thing was that aside from gold bars (bulky and heavy), one could purchase gold-leaf sheets. These were small and light, the sort of thing that you could split up among your family members if you were fleeing for your lives.

[493] Phu killed himself as the NVA entered Saigon.

[494] Karnow, 665.

[495] David Butler, *The Fall of Saigon* (London: Sphere Books, Ltd., 1986), 102-105.

[496] Karnow, 666.

[497] *Ibid.*

[498] Veith, 437-449.

[499] Van Tien Dung, *Our Great Spring Victory* (New York: Monthly Review Press, 1977), 165-169.

[500] Davidson, *Vietnam at War*, 789-790.

[501] Morley Safer, *Flashbacks: On Returning to Vietnam* (New York: Random House, 1990), 203.

[502] Langguth, 658.

[503] *Ibid.*

[504] Appy, 194.

[505] Karnow, 669.

[506] Appy, 43.

[507] Hickey, *Shattered World,* 1-2.

[508] Loving, 28.

[509] Dooley, 258.

[510] Grant Evans and Kevin Rowley, *Red Brotherhood at War, Vietnam, Cambodia, and Laos since 1975* (New York: Verson, 1984), 92-93.

[511] *Ibid.*, 301.

[512] Elizabeth Becker, *When the War Was Over* (New York: Public Affairs, 1998), 251-253.

[513] Evans, 59-60.

[514] Jane Hamilton-Merritt, *Tragic Mountains: The Hmong, The Americans and the Secret Wars of Laos, 1942-1992* (Bloomington: Indiana University Press, 1993), 10-11.

[515] Nayan Chanda, *Brother Enemy, The War After The War.* (New York: Collier Books, 1986), 142-145.

[516] Evans, 38.

[517] Chanda, 142-145.

[518] Chanda, 204-205.

[519] *Ibid.*, 193-198.

[520] The Red Prince Souphanouvong was, along with his half-brother Prince Souvanna Phouma and Prince Boun Oum of Champasak, one of the "Three Princes" who represented respectively the communist (pro-Vietnam), neutralist and royalist political factions in Laos.

[521] Chanda, 204-205.

[522] *Ibid.*, 205-207.

[523] *Ibid.*, 247.

[524] *Ibid.*, 232-235.

[525] *Ibid.*, 247.

[526] Evans, 94-95.

[527] Chanda, 248-250.

[528] *Ibid.*, 262.

[529] *Ibid.*, 278.

[530] Jimmy Carter, *Keeping the Faith, Memoirs of a President.* (New York: Bantam Books, 1982), 205-206.

[531] Hamilton-Merritt, 400-404.

[532] Chanda, 356-362.

[533] Evans, 153-158.

[534] *Ibid.*, 181-193.

[535] Chanda, 356-362.

[536] Evans, 160-161.

[537] *Ibid.,* 160-161.

[538] Salemink, 261-262.

[539] Michael D. Benge, "The Montagnard Revolt," in *Indochina in the Year of the Dragon-1964, ed.* Steve Sherman, (Houston: RADIX Press, 2014), 200-205.

[540] Steve Sherman, Ed., *Broken Promise, Betrayal as Usual, and Other Readings about the U. S. Army Forces and the Montagnards of Vietnam.* Houston: RADIX Press, 1999), 100.

[541] Dooley, 256-258.

[542] Goscha, 404.

[543] *Ibid.*, 404-406.

[544] Hickey, *Shattered World*, 128-129.

[545] Sherman, *Broken Promise,* 101.

[546] Harriet Hill and H'Yoanh Buonya, *Escaping Viet Nam, H'Yoanh's Story* (Mustang: Tate Publishing, 2013), 119-120.

[547] *Ibid.*, 15-16.

[548] *Ibid.*, 376-377.

[549] Hill, Harriet and H'Yoanh Buonya, *Escaping Viet Nam, H'Yoanh's Story*. Mustang: Tate Publishing, 2013.

[550] Michael D. Benge, "The Montagnard Revolt," in *Indochina in the Year of the Dragon-1964, ed.* Steve Sherman, (Houston: RADIX Press, 2014), 205.

[551] Hickey, *Shattered World,* 2.

[552] Lists are compiled from Who's Who from 1st SFG(A) in RVN, Who's Who from 7th SFG(A) in RVN, Who's Who from 5th SFGA in RVN and SF Order of Battle Vietnam Theater 1957-1975.

[553] CSF is an acronym for Combat Strike Force. Abbreviations: VN is Vietnamese; MTD is Montagyard; Camb is Cambodian.

[554] TDY is acronym for temporary duty meaning that the detachment was assigned to the location on a temporary basis. PCS is acronym for

Permanent Change of Station meaning that the detachment was assigned to the location on a permanent basis.

555 Dates indicate when the location was opened and closed.

556 Katu Population, not CIDG.

557 Old French Fort

558 to Hon Quan (B-33).

559 to Plei Do Lim.

560 CSF is an acronym for Combat Strike Force. Abbreviations: VN is Vietnamese; MTD is Montagyard; Camb is Cambodian..

561 TDY is acronym for temporary duty meaning that the detachment was assigned to the location on a temporary basis. PCS is acronym for Permanent Change of Station meaning that the detachment was assigned to the location on a permanent basis.

562 Dates indicate when the location was opened and closed.

563 to Nha Trang Security Force.

564 to Buon Tan Mo/Buon Uing/Buon Yom.

565 FOBs at Tan Canh & Ban Liet.

566 from Plei Ta Nangle to NSF overrun.

567 Reopened as an FOB of Plateau Gi.

568 CSF is an acronym for Combat Strike Force. VN is Vietnamese; MTD is Montagyard; Camb is Cambodian..

569 TDY is acronym for temporary duty meaning that the detachment was assigned to the location on a temporary basis. PCS is acronym for Permanent Change of Station meaning that the detachment was assigned to the location on a permanent basis.

570 Dates indicate when the location was opened and closed.

571 CSF is an acronym for Combat Strike Force. VN is Vietnamese; MTD is Montagyard; Camb is Cambodian..

572 TDY is acronym for temporary duty meaning that the detachment was assigned to the location on a temporary basis. PCS is acronym for Permanent Change of Station meaning that the detachment was assigned to the location on a permanent basis.

573 Dates indicate when the location was opened and closed.

Bibliography

Books

Abu-Lughod, Janet L. Race, *Space, and Riots in Chicago, New York, and Los Angeles*. Oxford: Oxford University Press, 2007.

Adler, Bill. *Letters From Vietnam*. New York: Ballantine Books, 2003.

Acheson, Dean. *Present at the Creation, My Years in the State Department*. New York: W. W. Norton, 1969.

Albright, John, John H. Cash and Allan W. Sandstrum. *Seven Firefights in Vietnam*. Washington: Office of the Chief of Military History, United States Army, 1970.

Allen, Michael J. *Until the Last Man Comes Home, POWs, MIAs and the Unending Vietnam War*. Chapel Hill: The University of North Carolina Press, 2009.

Anderson, Charles R. *The Grunts*. New York: Berkley Books, 1985.

Anderson, Louis E. *John F. Kennedy*. Stamford: Brompton Books Corporation, 1992.

Andreas, Peter and Kelly M. Greenhill. *Sex, Drugs and Body Counts. The Politics of Numbers in Global Crime and Conflict*. Ithaca: Cornell University Press, 2010.

Appy, Christian G. *Working Class War, American Combat Soldiers in Vietnam*. Chapel Hill: University of North Carolina Press, 1993.

_____ *Patriots, The Vietnam War Remembered from All Studies*. New York: Penguin Books, 2003.

Archer, Michael. *A Patch of Ground, Khe Sanh Remembered.* Ashland: Hellgate Press, 2004.

Army, Department of the. *Minority Groups in the Republic of Vietnam, Ethnographic Study Series, DA Pamphlet 550-105.* Washington, DC.: Headquarters, Department of the Army, 1966.

Arnett, Peter. *Live from the Battlefield.* New York: Simon & Schuster, 1994.

Arthurs, Ted G. *Land with No Sun, A Year in Vietnam with the 173rd Airborne.* Mechanicsburg: Stackpole Books, 2006.

Asselin, Pierre. *A Bitter Peace, Washington, Hanoi, and the Making of the Paris Agreement.* Chapel Hill: The University of North Carolina Press, 2002.

Association of Graduates, United States Military Academy. *The Register of Graduates and Former Cadets of the United States Military, 2010.* West Point Association of Graduates, 2010.

Atkinson, Rick. *The Long Gray Line, The American Journey of West Point's Class of 1966.* New York: Henry Holt and Company, 1989.

Axelrod, Alan. *The Real History of the Vietnam War, A New Look at the Past.* New York: Sterling Publishing, 2013.

Bacn Research. *Vietnam War Photography.*

Baker, Mark. *Nam.* New York: William Morrow and Company, 1982.

Ball, Phil. *Ghosts and Shadows, A Marine in Vietnam 1968-1969*. Jefferson: McFarland & Company, Inc., Publishers, 1998.

Beckett, Ronald L. *Jack of All Trades, An American Advisor's War in Vietnam, 1969-70*. Mechanicsburg: Stackpole Books, 2016.

Becker, Elizabeth. *When the War Was Over*. New York: Public Affairs, 1998.

Beckwith, Charlie A. *Delta Force: A Memoir by the Founder of the U. S. Military's Most Secretive Special Operations Unit*. New York: William Morrow, 1983.

Bendell, Don. *Crossbow*. Naples: Speaking Volumes, LLC., 2013.

Benge, Michael D. "The Montagnard Revolt," in *Indochina in the Year of the Dragon-1964,* edited by Steve Sherman, 192-205. Houston: RADIX Press, 2014.

Berman, Larry. *No Peace, No Honor, Nixon, Kissinger, and Betrayal in Vietnam*. New York: The Free Press, 2001.

Berman, Paul. *A Tale of Two Utopias, The Political Journey of the Generation of 1986*. New York: W. W. Norton & Company, 1996.

Bernstein, Jonathan. *U. S. Army AH-1 Cobra Units in Vietnam*. Oxford: Osprey Publishing, 2003.

Berry, F. Clifton, Jr. *The Illustrated History of Sky Soldiers - The Vietnam War*. New York: Bantam Books, 1987.

Blakeley, H. W. *Famous Fourth, The Story of the 4th Infantry*

Division. Whitefish: Kessinger Publishing, 2013.

Blehm, Eric. *Legend*. New York: Crown Publishers, 2015.

Bradley, Mark Phillip. *Imagining Vietnam and America, The Making of Postcolonial Vietnam, 1919-1950*. Chapel Hill: The University of North Carolina Press, 2000.

Braestrup, Peter. *The Big Story*. Novato: Presidio Press, 1994.

Burns, Richard R. *Pathfinder, First In, Last Out*. New York: Ballantine Books, 2002.

Burruss, Lewis. *Mike Force*. Lincoln: iUniversal.com, Inc., 1989.

Butler, David. *The Fall of Saigon*. London: Sphere Books, Ltd., 1986.

Califano, Joseph A. *The Triumph & Tragedy of Lyndon Johnson, The White House Years*. New York: Touchstone, 1991.

Canfield, Roger. *Indochina in the Year of the Snake*. Houston: RADIX Press, 2015.

Caputo, Philip. *A Rumor of War*. New York: Henry Holt and Company, 1977.
_____ *10,000 Days of Thunder, A History of the Vietnam War*. New York: Byrun Press Visual Publications, Inc., 2005.

Carnes, Mark C. and John A. Garraty. *American Destiny, Narrative of a Nation, Volume II, Since 1865*. New York: Penguin Academics, 2006.

Carter, James M. *Inventing Vietnam: The United States and State Building 1954-1968*. New York: Cambridge University Press, 2008.

Carter, Jimmy. *Keeping the Faith, Memoirs of a President*. New York: Bantam Books, 1982.

Carey, Elaine. *Plaza of Sacrifices, Gender, Power, and Terror in 1968 Mexico*. Albuquerque: University of New Mexico Press, 2005.

Casey, Michael, Clark Dougan, Denis Kennedy, and Shelby Stanton. *The Vietnam Experience, The Army at War*. Boston: Boston Publishing Company, 1987.

Central Intelligence Agency, Office of Current Intelligence. *Lam Son Summary*. 1973.

Chafe, William H. *The Unfinished Journey, America Since World War II.* New York: Oxford University Press, 2007.
_____. *Civilities and Civil Rights, Greensboro, North Carolina and the Black Struggle for Freedom*. Oxford: Oxford University Press, 1980.

Chanda, Nayan. *Brother Enemy, The War After The War*. New York: Collier Books, 1986.

Chandler, David. *A History of Cambodia*. Boulder: Westview, 1996.

Chapla, John D. *The Men of Alpha Company, Combat with the 173rd Airborne Brigade, Vietnam 1969-1970*, 2012.

Childs, Leo, Major. *The First Infantry Division in Vietnam*. Vietnam: 121st Signal Battalion, 1969.

Clancy, Tom and General Carl Stiner. *Shadow Warriors, Inside the Special Forces*. New York: P. G. Putnam's Sons, 2002

Clark, Jeffrey J. *Advice and Support: The Final Years, The U. S. Army in Vietnam*. Washington: Center for Military History, U. S. Army, 1988.

Clodfelter, Michael. *Mad Minutes and Vietnam Months: A Soldier's Memoir*. Jefferson: McFarland & Company, Inc., Publishers, 1988.

Coan, James P. *Con Thien, The Hill of Angels*. Tuscaloosa: The University of Alabama Press, 2004.

Colby, William. *Lost Victory: A First Hand Account of America's Sixteen-Year Involvement in Vietnam*. Chicago: Contemporary Books, 1989.

Coleman, J. D. *Pleiku, The Dawn of Helicopter Warfare in Vietnam*. New York: St. Martin's Press, 1988.
_____. *Incursion*. New York: St. Martin's Paperbacks, 1991.
_____. *Air Cav, History of the 1st Air Cavalry Division in Vietnam 1965-1969*. New York: Turner Publishing Company, 2011.

Collier, Peter. *Medal of Honor Portraits of Valor Beyond the Call of Duty*. New York: Artisan, 2003.

Colodny, Len. *Silent Coup*. New York: St. Martin's Press, 1991.

Condominas, Georges. *We Have Eaten the Forest, The Story of a Montagnard Village in the Central Highlands of Vietnam*.

New York: Kodansha International, 1994.

Conover, Gregory B. *The Impact of an Operational Void: The Strategic Hamlet Program, 1961-1963.* Plano: Normby Press, 2015.

Cosmos, Graham A. *MACV, The Joint Command in the Years of Escalation, 1962-1967.* Washington: Center for Military History, U. S. Army, 2006.
_____ *MACV, The Joint Command in the Years of Withdrawal, 1968-1973.* Washington: Center for Military History, U. S. Army, 2006.

Cunningham, Michael H. *Lost in Vietnam, Found in America: A Saga of Vietnamese Boat People.* Self-Published, 2017.

Daddis, Gregory A. *Westmoreland's War, Reassessing American Strategy in Vietnam.* New York: Oxford University Press, 2014.

Daugherty, Kevin and Jason Stewart. *The Timeline of the Vietnam War.* San Diego: Thunder Bay Press, 2008.

Daugherty, Leo and Gregory Louis Mattson. Nam *A Photographic History.* Singapore: Michael Friedman Publishing Group, 2001.

Davidson, Phillip B. *Vietnam at War, The History 1946-1975.* New York: Oxford University Press, 1988.
_____. *Secrets of the Vietnam War.* Novato: Presidio Press, 1990.

Deac, Wilfred P. *Road to the Killing Fields, The Cambodian War of 1970-1975.* College Station: Texas A&M University Press, 1997.

Denny, Warren M. *The Long Journey Home from Dak To: The Story of an American Infantry Officer Fighting in the Central Highlands Republic of Vietnam 1967-1968*. New York: iUniverse, Inc., 2003.

Devillers, Philippe. *Historia du Vietnam de 1940 a 1952*. Paris: Editions du Seuil, 1953.

Diem, Bui. *In the Jaws of History*. Bloomington: Indiana University Press, 1999.

Dockery, Martin J. *Lost in Translation, Vietnam, A Combat Advisor's Story*. New York: The Random House Publishing Group, 2003.

Donlon, Roger H. C. *Outpost of Freedom*. New York: Avon Books, 1965.

Dooley, George E. *Battle for the Central Highlands, A Special Forces Story*. New York: Ballantine Books, 2003.

Doubek, Robert W. *Creating the Vietnam Veterans Memorial, The Inside Story*. Jefferson: McFarland & Company, Inc., Publishers, 2015.

Dougan, Clark and Stephen Weiss. *The American Experience in Vietnam*. Boston: Boston Publishing Company, 1988.
_____ . *Nineteen Sixty-Eight*. Boston: Boston Publishing Company, 1983.

Doyle, Edward and Samuel Lipsman. *The Vietnam Experience, America Takes Over 1965-1967*. Boston: Boston Publishing Company, 1982.

Dudziak, Mary L. *Cold War Civil Rights, Race and the Image of American Democracy*. Princeton: Princeton University Press, 2000.

Dung, Van Tien. *Our Great Spring Victory*. New York: Monthly Review Press, 1977.

Dunstan, Simon. *1st Air Cavalry in Vietnam, "The First Team"*. Hersham: Allan Publishing Limited, 2004.

Duong, Van Nguyen. *Tragedy of the Vietnam War: A South Vietnamese Officer's Analysis*. Jefferson: McFarland & Company Publishers, 2008.

Edelman, Bernard. *Dear American, Letters Home from Vietnam*. New York: W. W. Norton & Company, 1985.

Eggleston, Michael A. *Exiting Vietnam, The Era of Vietnamization and American Withdrawal Revealed in First-Person Accounts*. Jefferson: McFarland & Company, Inc., Publishers, 2014.
_____ *The 5th Marine Regiment Devil Dogs in World War I*. Jefferson: McFarland & Company, Inc., Publishers, 2016.
_____ *Dak To and the Border Battles of Vietnam, 1967-1968*. Jefferson: McFarland & Company, Inc., Publishers, 2017.
_____ *The 10th Minnesota Volunteers, 1862-1865*. Jefferson: McFarland & Company Publishers, 2012.

Eigen, Daryl J. *A Hellish Place of Angels, Con Thien: One Man's Journey*. Bloomington: iUniverse, 2012.

Elliott, David W. P. *The Third Indochina Conflict*. Boulder: Westview Press, Inc., 1981.

Ellsberg, Daniel. *Secrets: A Memoir of Vietnam and the Pentagon Papers*. New York: Penguin Group, 2002.

Epp, Karen Ross. *A Soldier's Letters from Vietnam to the World*. Bloomington: Author House, 2007.

Fall, Bernard B. *Street Without Joy: The French Debacle in Indochina*. Mechanicsburg: Stackpole Books, 1994.

Evans, Grant and Kevin Rowley. *Red Brotherhood at War, Vietnam, Cambodia, and Laos since 1975*. New York: Verson, 1984.

Fitzgerald, Frances. *Fire in the Lake, The Vietnamese and the Americans in Vietnam*. New York: Back Bay Books, 1972.

Flamm, Michael W. *Law and Order: Civil Unrest, and the Crisis of Liberalism in the 1960s*. New York: Columbia University Press, 2005.

Fletcher, Johnnie. *Duc Lap*.

Flood, Charles Bracelen. *The War of the Innocents*. New York: Bantam Books, 1970.

Foley, Michael S. *Confronting the War Machine: Draft Resistance During the Vietnam War*. Chapel Hill: University of North Carolina Press, 2003.

Ford, Daniel. *The Only War We've Got*. New York: IUniverse, 2001.

Foster, Randy E. M. *Vietnam Firebases 1965-1973, American and Australian Forces*. Long Island City: Osprey Publishing,

1987.

Frost, David. *Frost/Nixon, Behind the Scenes of the Nixon Interviews*. New York: Harper Perennial, 2007.

Fulghum, David, Terrance Maitland, and the editors of Boston Publishing Company, *The Vietnam Experience: South Vietnam on Trial: The Test of Vietnamization, 1970-1972*. Boston: Boston Publishing Company, 1984.

Gettleman, Marvin E., Jane Franklin, Marilyn B. Young, and H. Bruce Franklin. *Vietnam and America, The Most Documented History of the Vietnam War*. New York: Grove Press, 1995.

Giap, Vo Nguyen. *How We Won the War*. Philadelphia: Recon Publications, 1976.

Goldman, Peter, and Tony Fuller. *Charlie Company, What Vietnam Did to Us*. New York: William Morrow and Company, 1983.

Goldstein, Joseph, Burke Marshall, and Jack Schwartz. *The My Lai Massacre and Its Cover-up. Beyond the Reach of the Law? The Peers Report with a Supplement and Introductory Essay on the Limits of Law*. New York: The Free Press, 1976.

Goodwin, Doris Kearns. *The Most Revealing Portrait of a President and Presidential Power Ever Written, Lyndon Johnson and the American Dream*. New York: St. Martin's Griffin, 1976.

Goscha, Christopher. *Vietnam: A New History*. New York: Basic Books, 2016.

Green, Anna and Kathleen Troup. *The House of History, A*

Critical Reader in Twentieth-Century History and Theory. New York: New York University Press, 1999.

Gross, Chuck. *Rattler One - Seven, A Vietnam Helicopter Pilot's War Story*. Denton: University of North Texas Press, 2004.

Haig, Alexander M., Jr. *Inner Circles, How America Changed the World, A Memoir*. New York: Warner Books, 1992.

Hair, Joseph E. *Contact Charlie Company & "The Headhunter Platoon"*. Middletown: Self-Published, 2015.

Halberstam, David. *The Fifties*. New York: Random House Publishing Group, 1993.
_____. *The Making of a Quagmire*. New York: Ballantine Books, 1964.

Haldeman, H. R. *The Ends of Power*. New York: Time Books, 1978.

Hallin, Daniel C. *The Uncensored War, The Media and Vietnam*. Berkeley: University of California Press, 1986.

Ham, Paul. *Vietnam, The Australian War*. Australia: Harper Collins Publishers, 2008.

Hamilton-Merritt, Jane. *Tragic Mountains: The Hmong, The Americans and the Secret Wars of Laos, 1942-1992*. Bloomington: Indiana University Press, 1993.

Hammond, William M. *Reporting Vietnam, Media & Military at War*. Lawrence: University of Kansas Press, 1998.

Harris, J. P. *Vietnam's High Ground, Armed Struggle for the*

Central Highlands, 1954-1965. Lawrence: University Press of Kansas, 2016.

Harrison, James P. *The Endless War, Vietnam's Struggle for Independence.* New York: Colimbia University Press, 1989.

Hartzel, Jack T. *Reflections of My Past!* Middletown: Great Published, 2015.

Hay, John J., Jr. LTG. *Vietnam Studies Tactical and Material Innovations.* Washington, DC: U. S. Printing Office, 1989.

Herman, Edward S. and Noam Chomsky. *Manufacturing Consent, The Political Economy of the Mass Media.* New York: Pantheon Books, 1988.

Herring, George C. *America's Longest War, The United States and Vietnam, 1950-1975.* Boston: McGraw Hill, 2002.
_____. *The Pentagon Papers.* New York: McGraw-Hill, Inc., 1993.
_____. *LBJ and Vietnam (Administrative History of the Johnson Presidency).* Austin: University of Texas Press, 1994.

Hickey, Gerald C. *Shattered World, Adaptation and Survival Among Vietnam's Highland Peoples during the Vietnam War.* Philadelphia: University of Pennsylvania Press, 1993.
_____ *Village in Vietnam.* New Haven: Yale University Press, 1964.
_____ *Ethnic Groups of Mainland Southeast Asia.* New Haven: Human Relations Area Files Press, 1964.
_____ *Sons of the Mountains, Ethnohistory of the Vietnamese Central Highlands to 1954.* New Haven: Yale University Press, 1982.

_____*Free in the Forest, Ethnohistory of the Vietnamese Central Highlands, 1954-1976.* New Haven: Yale University Press, 2003.

_____*Kingdom in the Morning Mist, Mayrena in the Highlands of Vietnam.* Philadelphia: University of Pennsylvania Press, 1988.

_____*Window on a War, An Anthropologist in the Vietnam Conflict.* Lubbock: Texas Tech University Press, 2002.

Hill, Harriet and H'Yoanh Buonya. *Escaping Viet Nam, H'Yoanh's Story.* Mustang: Tate Publishing, 2013.

Hinh, Nguyen Duy. *Lam Son 719.* Fort McNair: U. S. Army Center of Military History, 1979.

Historical Division Joint Secretariat. *History of the Joint Chiefs of Staff and the War in Vietnam 1971-1973.* Washington: Department of Defense, 1970.

Hoang, Ngoc Lung. *The General Offensives of 1968-1969.* Washington, D. C.: U. S. Center of Military History, 1981.

Hoffman, Philip Duncan. *Humping Heavy: A Vietnam Memoir,* 2011.

Hudson, Christopher. *The Killing Fields.* London: Pan, 1984.

Hughes, George W. *Always a Soldier.* Denver: Outskirts Press, 2009.

HQ PACAF, Project *CHECO Report, Operation Attleboro.* S. E. Asia Team: HQ PACAF, 1967.

Isserman, Maurice and Michael Kazan. *American Divided, The Civil War in the 1960s.* Oxford: Oxford University Press, 2008.

Jackson, Jerome J. and Constance Emerson Crooker. *Doc Jackson's Letters Home, A Combat Medic's 1968 Letters from Vietnam.* Beaverton: JayCee Publishing, 2015.

Jacobs, Rodger. *Stained with the Mud of Khe Sanh, A Marine's Letters from Vietnam, 1966-1967.* Jefferson: McFarland & Company, Inc., Publishers, 2013.

Jackson, Karl, editor. *Cambodia; 1975-1978.* Princeton: Princeton University Press, 1989.

Johnson, Steven A. *Cammie Up! Memoir of a Recon Marine in Vietnam 1967-1968.* Jefferson: McFarland & Company, Inc., Publishers, 2012.

Johnson, Haynes. *The Best of Times, The Boom and Bust Years of America Before and After Everything Changed.* New York: Harcourt, Inc., 2002.

Johnson, Lt. Col. Richard M. *Lam Son 719: Perils of Strategy.* Carlisle: United States Army War College, 1996.

Jones, Greg. *Last Stand at Khe Sanh, The U. S. Marines Finest Hour in Vietnam.* Boston: De Capo Press, 2014.

Joyce, James. *Pucker Factor 10: Memoir of a U. S. Helicopter in Vietnam.* Jefferson: McFarland & Company, Inc., Publishers, 2003.

Just, Ward, ed. *Reporting Vietnam.* New York: The Library of America, 1998.

_____. *Reporting Vietnam, American Journalism 1959-1975.* New York: Literary Classics of the United States, 2000.

Kamps, Charles T., Jr. *The History of the Vietnam War, An Illustrated History of the War in South East Asia.* New York: The Military Press, 1988.

Kaplan, Fred. *The Insurgents: David Petraeus and the Plot to Change the American Way of War.* New York: Simon and Schuster, 2013.

Karnow, Stanley. *Vietnam, A History, The First Complete Account of Vietnam at War.* New York: The Viking Press, 1983.

Kelley, Michael P. *Where We Were in Vietnam, A Comprehensive Guide to the Firebases, Military Installations and Naval Vessels of the Vietnam War.* Ashland: Hellgate Press, 2002.

Kelly, Francis J. *U. S. Army Special Forces, 1961-1971, Vietnam Studies.* Washington: Department of Army, 1973.

Kerry, Bob. *When I Was a Young Man, A Memoir.* New York: Harcourt, Inc., 2002.

Ketwig, John. *…And A Hard Rain Fell, A GI's True Story of the War in Vietnam.* Naperville: Sourcebooks, Inc., 2002.

Kissinger, Henry. *Ending the Vietnam War. A History of American's Involvement in and Extraction from the Vietnam War.* New York: Simon & Schuster, 2003.
_____. *White House Years.* Boston: Little, Brown and Company, 1979.

Kitchin, Dennis. *War in Aquarius: Memoir of an American Infantryman in Action Along the Cambodian Border During the*

Vietnam War. Jefferson: McFarland & Company, Inc., Publishers, 1994.

Kimball, Jeffrey. *Nixon's Vietnam War*. Lawrence: The University Press of Kansas, 1998.

Krepinevich, Andrew F., Jr. *The Army and Vietnam*. Baltimore: The Johns Hopkins University Press, 1986
.

Kurlansky, Mark. *1968, The Year That Rocked the World*. New York: Random House, 2005.

Kuzmarov, Jeremy. *The Myth of the Addicted Army. Vietnam and the Modern War on Drugs*. Boston: University of Massachusetts Press, 2009.

Langguth, A. J. *Our Vietnam, The War 1954-1975*. New York: Simon & Schuster, 2000.

Lanning, Michael Lee. *The Only War We Had, A Platoon Leader's Journal of Vietnam*. New York: Ballantine Books, 1987.

Larson, Mike. *Heroes, A Year in Vietnam with the First Air Cavalry Division*. New York: iUniverse, 2008.

Lawrence, A. T. *Crucible Vietnam: Memoir of an Infantry Lieutenant*. Jefferson: McFarland & Company, Inc., Publishers, 2009.

Lawrence, John. *The Cat from Hue. A Vietnam War Story*. New York: Perseus Books Group, 2002.

Lawrence, Mark Atwood. *The Vietnam War, An International History in Documents*. New York: The Oxford Press, 2014.

_____ *The Vietnam War, A Concise International History*. New York: The Oxford University Press, 2008.

Lee, J. Edward and H. C. "Toby" Haynsworth. *Nixon, Ford and the Abandonment of South Vietnam*. Jefferson: McFarland & Company, Inc., Publishers, 2002.

Le Gro, William E. *Vietnam from Ceasefire to Capitulation*. Washington: U. S. Army Center of Military History, 1985.

Leppelman, John. *Blood on the Risers: An Airborne Soldier's Thirty-Five Months in Vietnam*. New York: Ballantine Books, 1991.

Lind, Michael. *Vietnam, The Necessary War*. New York: Simon and Schuster, 1999.

Logevall, Fredrik. *Embers of War, The Fall of an Empire and the Making of America's Vietnam*. New York: Random House Trade Paperbacks, 2013.

Loving, John C. *Combat Advisor: How America Won the War and Lost the Peace*. New York: Universe, Inc., 2006.

Loyte, Colonel J. F., Jr. *Project CHECO, Southeast Asia Report, Lam Son 719, 30 January-24 March 1971, The South Vietnamese Incursion into Laos*. 7th Air Force: HQ PACAF, 1971.

Luan, Nguyen Cong. *Nationalist in the Vietnam Wars, Memoirs of a Victim Turned Soldier*. Bloomington: Indiana University Press, 2012.

Luce, Don and John Sommer. *Vietnam: The Unheard Voices*.

Ithaca: Cornell University Press, 1969.

MacDonald, Peter. *The Victor in Vietnam. Giap.* New York: W.W. Norton & Company, 1993.

Maitland, Terrence and Peter McInerney. *The Vietnam Experience, A Contagion of War.* Boston: Boston Publishing Company, 1983.

Manchester, William. *Remembering Kennedy, One Brief Shining Moment.* Boston: Little, Brown and Company, 1983.

Maraniss, David. *They Marched into Sunlight, War and Peace Vietnam and America, October 1967.* New York: Simon & Schuster Paperbacks, 2003.

Mark, Roy. *Fixin' to Die Rag, Gooood Morning Vietnam. . . We've Just Had a Mid-Air Collision.* Charleston: CreateSpace, 2014.

Marshall, Tom. *The Price of Exit.* New York: Ballantine Books, 1998.

Mauldin, Bill. *Bill Mauldin's Army, Bill Mauldin's Greatest World War II Cartoons.* New York: Random House Publishing Group, 1944.

Mataxis, Ted Jr., "The War in II Corps Tactical Zone." in *Indochina in the Year of the Snake-1965,* edited by Steve Sherman, 175. Houston: RADIX Press, 2015.

McCullough, David. *Truman.* New York: Simon & Schuster, 1992.

McKenna, Thomas P. *Kontum The Battle to Save South*

Vietnam. Lexington: The University Press of Kentucky, 2011.

McMasters, H. R. *Dereliction of Duty: Johnson, McNamara, the Joint Chiefs of Staff, and the Lies That led to Vietnam*. New York: Harper Perennial, 1997.

McNamara, Robert S. *In Retrospect: The Tragedy and Lessons of Vietnam*. New York: Vintage Book, 1995.

Mertel, Kenneth D. *Year of the Horse: Vietnam, 1st Air Cavalry in the Highlands 1965-1967*. Atglen: Schiffer Publishing, Ltd., 1997.

Meyers, John S. *On the Ground, Secret War in Vietnam*. Oceanside: Levin Publishing Group, LLC, 2007.

Moore, Harold G. and Joseph L. Galloway. *We Were Soldiers Once. . . . and Young, Ia Drang-the Battle that Changed the War in Vietnam*. New York: Harper Collins Publishers, 1992.
_____. *We are Soldiers, Still, A Journey Back to the Battlefields of Vietnam*. New York: Harper Perennial, 2008.

Moore, Robin. *The Green Berets*. New York: Crown Publishers, Inc., 1965.

Morocco, John. *Thunder from Above: Air War, 1941–1968*. Boston: Boston Publishing Company, 1984.

Moyar, Mark. *Triumph Forsaken, The Vietnam War, 1954-1965*. Cambridge: Cambridge University Press, 2006.

Morris, Jim. *Devil's Secret Name*. Canton: Daring Books, 1989.
_____*War Story*. Boulder: Paladin Press, 1979.

Murphy, Edward F. *Dak To, America's Sky Soldiers in South Vietnam's Central Highlands*. New York: Ballantine Books, 2007.

_____. *The Hill Fights, The First Battle of Khe Sanh*. New York: Ballantine Books, 2003.

Murry, Gregory H. *Content with my Wages, A Sergeant's Story, Book I, Vietnam*. Austin: No End to Publishing Company, 2013.

Nelson, Deborah. *The War Behind Me, Vietnam Veterans Confront the Truth About U.S. War Crimes*. New York: Basic Books, 2008.

Nguyen, Lien-Hang T. *Hanoi's War, An International History of the War for Peace in Vietnam*. Chapel Hill: University of North Carolina Press, 2012.

Nguyen, Tin. *General Hieu, ARVN, A Hidden Military Gem*. Lincoln: iUniverse, Inc., 2003.

Nhu Tang, Truong. *A Viet Cong Memoir*. New York: Vintage Books, 1986.

Nesser, John A. *Ghosts of Thua Thien: An American Soldier's Memoir of Vietnam*. Jefferson: McFarland & Company, Inc., Publishers, 2008.

Nixon, Richard. *No More Vietnams*. New York: Arbor House, 1985.

Nolan, Keith William. *Into Laos, The Story of Dewey Canyon II/Lam Son 719, 1971*. Novato: Presidio Press, 1986.

North, Oliver L. *Under Fire, An American Story*. New York: Harper Collins, Inc., 1991.

Novick, Peter. *That Noble Dream, The "Objectivity Question" and the American Historical Profession.* Cambridge: Cambridge University Press, 1998.

Oates, Stephen B. and Charles J. Errico. *Portrait of America, Volume 2.* Boston: Houghton Miffilin Company, 2007.

Oberdorfer, Don. *Tet! The Turning Point in the Vietnam War.* Baltimore: The Johns Hopkins University Press, 1971.

Okendo, Lawrence D. *Sky Soldier, 173rd Airborne Infantry Brigade Separate, Battles of Dak To Vietnam.* Lawrence D. Okendo, 1988.

Olson, Rocky. *Sgt. Rock*: *Last Man Standing.* Zeroed-In Press, 2010.

Osborne, Milton E. *Strategic Hamlets in South Vietnam: A Survey and Comparison.* Ithaca: Cornell University, 1965.

Palmer, General Bruce, Jr. *The 25 Year War. America's Military Role In Vietnam.* Lexington: The University Press of Kentucky, 1984.

Park, Stephen L. *Boots: An Unvarnished Memoir of Vietnam.* Boston: Writers Amuse Me Publishing, 2012.

Patric, Gordon M. *The Vietnams of the Green Berets.* Chesterton: Self-Published, 1969.

Petersen, Barry. *Tiger Men.* London: Sidgwick & Jackson, 1988.

Pezzoli, Rar, Jr. *A Year in Hell: Memoir of an American Foot*

Soldier Turned Reporter in Vietnam 1965-1966. Jefferson: McFarland & Company, Inc., 2006.

Phillips, William R. *Night of the Silver Stars, The Battle of Lang Vei.* New York: St. Martin's Paperbacks, 1997.

Pimlott, John. *Vietnam, The Decisive Battles.* New York: Chartwell Books, 1997.

Pisor, Robert. *The End of the Line, The Siege of Khe Sanh.* New York: W. W. Norton, 1982.

Porch, Douglas. *The French Secret Services, A History of French Intelligence from the Dreyfus Affair to the Gulf War.* New York: Farrar, Straus and Giroux, 1995.

Prados, John. *In Country, Remembering the Vietnam War.* New York: Ivan R. Dee, Publisher, 2011.
_____. *Vietnam, The History of an Unwinnable War, 1945-1975.* Lawrence: University Press of Kansas, 2009.
_____. *The Hidden History of the Vietnam War.* Chicago: Ivan R. Dee, 1995.
_____. *Lost Crusader, The Secret Wars of CIA Director William Colby.* Oxford: University Press, 2003.
_____. *The Blood Road, the Ho Chi Minh Trail and the Vietnam War.* New York: John Wiley & Sons, Inc., 1999.

Prochnau, William. *Once Upon a Distant War, Young Correspondents and the Early Vietnam Battles.* New York: Random House, 1995.

Project CHECO Southeast Asia Report. *Lam Son 719, The South Vietnamese Incursion into Laos, 30 January - 24 March 1971.* HQ, PACAF, 1971.

Rawson, Andrew W. *Tet Offensive 1968, Battle Story*. Gloucestershire: The History Press, 2013.

Reynolds, David. *One World Divisible, A Global History Since 1945*. New York: W. W. Norton & Company, 2000.

Ricks, Thomas E. *The Generals American Military Command from World War II to Today*. New York: The Penquin Press, 2012.

Rienzi, General Thomas Matthew. *Communications-Electronics, 1962-1970 (Vietnam Studies)*. Washington: U. S. Government Printing Office, 1972.

Rogers, LtGen Bernard William. *Cedar Falls Junction City, A Turning Point*. Washington: Ross & Perry, Inc, 2001.

Roleff, Tamara. *The Vietnam War*. San Diego: Greenhaven Press, 2002.

Ronnau, Christopher. *Blood Trails, The Combat Diary of a Foot Soldier in Vietnam*. New York: Ballantine Books, 2006.

Rottman, Gordon L. *North Vietnamese Army Soldier 1958-75*. New York: Osprey Publishing, 2009.
_____. *Special Forces Camps in Vietnam, 1961-1970*. New York: Osprey Publishing, 2005.

Safer, Morley. *Flashbacks: On returning to Vietnam*. New York: Random House, 1990.

Salemink, Oscar. *Ethnography of Vietnam's Central Highlands*. Honolulu: University Press of Hawaii, 2003.

Santoli, Al. *Everything We Had, An Oral History of the*

Vietnam War. New York: Ballantine Books. 1981.

Schlesinger, Arthur M., Jr. *A Thousand Days: John F. Kennedy in the White House*. New York: Houghton Miffilin Company, 2002.

Schulman, Bruce J. *The Seventies*. New York: Da Capo Press, 2001.

Schmitz, David F. *The Tet Offensive, Politics, War, and Public Opinion*. Lanham: Rowland and Littlefield Publishers, Inc., 2005.

Schwarzkopf, General H. Norman. *The Autobiography, It Doesn't Take a Hero*. New York: Bantam Books, 1992.

Scott, Leonard B., LTC. *The Battle for Hill 875, Dak To, Vietnam, 1967*. Carlisle Barracks: U. S. Army War College, 1988.

Scruggs, Jan C. and Joel L. Swerdlow. *The Vietnam Memorial To Heal a Nation*. New York: Harper & Row, Publishers, 1985.
_____. *Dreams Unfulfilled: Stories of the Men and Women on the Vietnam Veterans Memorial*. Washington: Vietnam Veterans Memorial Fund, 2010.

Shapley, Deborah. *Promise and Power, The Life and Times of Robert McNamara*. Boston: Little, Brown, and Company, 1993.

Sheehan, Neil. *A Bright Shining Lie, John Paul Vann and America in Vietnam*. New York: Random House, 1988.

Sherman, Steve, Edr. *Broken Promise, Betrayal as Usual, and Other Readings about the U. S. Army Forces and the*

Montagnards of Vietnam. Houston: RADIX Press, 1999.
_____ *Indochina in the Year of the Dragon-1964.* Houston: RADIX Press, 2014.
_____*Indochina in the Year of the Monkey-1968.* Houston: RADIX Press, 2017.
_____ *MACV Command History, 1972-1973 (Part I).* Houston: RADIX Press, 2019.
_____ *MACV Command History, 1972-1973 (Part II).* Houston: RADIX Press, 2019.

Shore, Moyers S. II. *The Battle of Khe Sanh.* Washington, D. C. History and Museums Division, Headquarters, U. S. Marine Corps, 1969.

Shulimson, Jack. *U. S. Marines, The Defining Year, 1968.* Washington, D. C.: History and Museums Division, Headquarters, U. S. Marine Corps, 1997.

Sigler, David. *Vietnam Battle Chronology, US Army and Marine Corps Combat Operations, 1965-1973.* Jefferson: McFarland & Company, Inc., Publishers, 1992.

Simmons, David B. *Our Turn to Serve: An Army Veteran's Memoir of the Vietnam War.* Lexington: Xlibris Corporation, 2011.

Simpson, Charles M. *Inside the Green Berets, The First Thirty Years, A History of the U.S. Army Special Forces.* Novato: Presido Press, 1983.

Singer, Daniel. *Prelude to Revolution, France in May 1968.* New York: Hill and Wang, 1970.

Snepp, Frank. *Decent Interval, The American Debacle in Vietnam and the Fall of Saigon.* New York: Penguin Books,

1977.

Sorenson, Theodore C. *Kennedy*. New York: Harper & Row, Publishers, 1988.

Sorley, Lewis. *Thunderbolt: General Creighton Abrams and the Army of His Times*. Bloomington: Indiana University Press, 2008.

_____. *Honorable Warrior General Harold K. Johnson and the Ethics of Command*. Lawrence: University Press of Kansas, 1998.

_____. *A Better War: The Unexamined Victories and Final Tragedy of America's Last Years in Vietnam*. New York: Harcourt, 1999.

_____. *Westmoreland: The General Who Lost Vietnam*. Boston: Houghton Mifflin Harcourt, 2011.

Spector, Ronald H. *Advice and Support: The Early Years, The U. S. Army in Vietnam*. Washington: Center for Military History, U. S. Army, 1985.

Stanton, Shelby L. *Anatomy of a Division, 1st Cav in Vietnam*. Novato: Presideo Press, 1987.

_____. *The Green Berets at War, U. S. Army Special Forces in Southeast Asia 1956-1975*. Novato: Presideo Press, 1985.

_____. *The Rise and Fall of an American Army: U. S. Ground Forces in Vietnam, 1965-1973*. New York: Balantine Books, 1985.

_____. *Vietnam Order of Battle, A Complete Illustrated Reference to U. S. Combat and Support Forces in Vietnam, 1961-1973*. Mechanicsburg: Stackpole Books, 2003.

Summers, Harry G. *On Strategy, A Critical Analysis of the Vietnam War*. New York: The Random House Publishing

Group, 1982.

Suri, Jermi. *Power and Protest, Global Revolution and the Rise of Detente*. Cambridge: Harvard University Press, 2003.

Tang, Truong Nhu. *A Viet Cong Memoir, An Inside Account of the Vietnam War and Its Aftermath*. New York: Vintage Books, 1986.

Taylor, Maxwell D. *Swords and Plowshares, A Memoir*. New York: Da Capo Press, 1972.

Taylor, K. W. *Voices from the Second Republic of South Vietnam (1967-1975)*. Ithaca: Cornell University, 2014.

Telfer, Gary L., Major. *U. S. Marines in Vietnam, Fighting the North Vietnamese, 1967*. Washington D. C.: History and Museums Division, Headquarters, U. S. Marine Corps, 1984.

Terry, Wallace. *Bloods: An Oral History of the Vietnam War*. New York: Ballantine Books, 1985.

Thao, Hoang Minh. *The Vietnamese Military During the Resistance War Against the U. S. for National Salvation and Defense*. Vietnam: The Gioi Publishers, 2014.

Thayer, Thomas C. *War Without Fronts, The American Experience in Vietnam*. Annapolis: Naval Institute Press, 1986.

Thi, Lam Quang. *The Twenty-Five Year Century - A South Vietnamese General Remembers the Indochina War to the Fall of Saigon*. Denton: University of North Texas Press, 2001.

Tho, Brig. Gen. Tran Dinh. *Indochina Monographs, The Cambodian Incursion*. Fort McNair: U. S. Army Center of

Military History, 1979.

Thomas, Evan. *Robert Kennedy, His Life*. New York: Simon and Schuster, 2000.

Tolson, John J., Lieutenant General. *Vietnam Studies Airmobility - 1961-1971*. Washington: Department of the Army, 1999.

Tram, Dang Thuy. *Last Night I Dreamed of Peace, The Diary of Dang Thuy Tram*. New York: Three Rivers Press, 2007.

Troung, Ngo Quang. *The Easter Offensive of 1972. Indochina Monographs*. Fort McNair, Washington, D.C.: U. S. Army Center of Military History, 1980.

Tucker, Spencer C. *The Encyclopedia of the Vietnam War, A Political Social, & Military History*. New York: The Oxford University Press, 1998.

Uhl, Michael. *Vietnam Awakening: My Journey from Combat to the Citizens' Commission of Inquiry on U. S. War Crimes*. Jefferson: McFarland & Company, Inc., Publishers, 2007.

US Congress. Senate. The Plight of the Montagnards. 150th Congress., 2nd Sess., 1998. S. HRG. 105-465.

Van Atta, Dale and President Gerald R. Ford. *With Honor: Melvin Laird in War, Peace, and Politics*. Madison: The University of Wisconsin Press, 2008.

Varon, Jeremy. *Bringing the War Home, The Weather Underground, the Red Army Faction, and Revolutionary Violence in the Sixties and Seventies*. Berkeley: University of California Press, 2004.

Vien, General Cao Van. *The Final Collapse.* Washington: Center of Military History, United States Army, 1983.

Veith, George J. *Black April, the Fallof South Vietnam 1973-1975.* New York: Encounter Books, 2012.

Vuic, Kara Dixon. *Officer, Nurse, Woman, The Army Nurse Corps in the Vietnam War.* Baltimore: Johns Hopkins University Press, 2010.

Westmoreland, William C. *A Soldier Reports.* New York: Doubleday & Company, 1976.

Whalon, Pete. *The Saigon Zoo, Vietnam's Other War: Sex, Drugs Rock 'N' Roll.* Conshohocken: Infinity Publishing Company, 2009.

Wheeler, James Scott. *The Big Red One, America's Legendary 1st Infantry Division from World War I to Desert Storm.* Lawrence: University Press of Kansas, 2007.

Widmer, Ted. *Listening In. The Secret White House Recordings of John F. Kennedy.* New York: Hypereion, 2012.

Wiest, Andrew. *Vietnam's Forgotten Army Heroism and Betrayal in the ARVN.* New York: New York University Press, 2008.
_____. *The Boys of '67, Charlie Company's War in Vietnam.* New York: Osprey Publishing, 2012.

Wilensky, Robert. *Military Medicine to Win Hearts and Minds: Aid to Civilians in the Vietnam War.* Lubbock: Texas Tech University Press, 2004.

Willbanks, James H. *The Tet Offensive, A Concise History*. New York: Columbia University Press, 2007.

Williams, Kieran. *The Prague Spring and Its Aftermath, Czechoslovak Politics, 1968-1970*. Cambridge: Cambridge University Press, 1997.

Articles

Benge, Michael D. *The History of the Involvement of the Montagnards of the Central Highlands in the Vietnam War.* in "The Fall of Saigon". SACEI. Forum #8. March 2001. Outskirts Press.com.

Chickering, William. "After the Montagnard Revolt." *VVFH Magazine, Volume 1, Issue, 2018*. 17-18.

Eggleston, Michael A. "The Border Battles." *Indochina in the Year of the Goat – 1967,* 2016. 119-174.

Sochurek, Howard. "American Special Forces." *National Geographic Magazine,* January 1965. 38-64.
_____ "Vietnam's Montagnards." *National Geographic Magazine,* April 1968. 443-487.

"The Battle of the Slopes." *2/503d Newsletter, Issue 29,* 22 June 2011.

"Inside the Cone of Fire at Con Thien." *Life Magazine*, 27 October 1967.

"U.S. Troops Take Top of Hill 875 Defy Fierce Fire." *New York Times*, 22 November 1967.

"Excerpts From Talk by Westmoreland." *New York Times*, 22

November 1967.

"Battle of the Slopes." *Sky Soldier Magazine,* Autumn 2015, Volume31, Number 4, 11.

"A Look Down the Road." *Time Magazine*, 19 February 1965.

"The Massacre of Dak Son." *Time Magazine*, 15 December 1967.

"The Invasion Ends." *Time Magazine,* 5 April 1971.

"Dak To." *Vietnam Magazine,* April 2015.

"Ten Great Battles of Vietnam."*Vietnam Magazine*, 2012.

Prados, John. "Dak To: One Hell of a Fight." *VVA Veteran*, January-February 2012.

"Win Bitter Viet Battle." *Washington Evening Journal, Washington, Iowa*, Nov 23, 1967.

"33 Days of Violent Sustained Combat." *Veterans of Foreign Wars Magazine*, March 2006.

Web Sites

2/503rd Vietnam Newsletter. www.corregidor.org/VN2-503/fbp/issue_29/index.html (last accessed on 12 March 2016).

4th Infantry Division. www.ivydragoons.org/afteractionreports.htm (last accessed on 28 March 2016).

American War Library. americanwarlibrary.com/vietnam/vwc24.htm (last accessed on

28 March 2016).

Army Publications. "Presidential Unit Citations." armypubs.army.mil/epubs/pdf/go6942.pdf (last accessed on 12 March 2016).

Center of Military History. www.history.army.mil/art/A&I/vietnam/vn-inf.htm (last accessed on 28 March 2016).

Congressional Medal of Honor Society. "Archive." www.cmohs.org/recipient-archive.php (last accessed on 12 March 2016).

Con Thien "The Hill Of The Angels." www.vietvet.org/jhconthn.htm (last accessed on 28 March 2016).

Dak To. www.history.army.mil/books/vietnam/tactical/chapter7.htm (last accessed on 28 March 2016).

National Archives. http://www.archives.gov/research/military/vietnam-war/casualty-statistics.html (last accessed on 28 March 2016).

Sony Pictures Classics. www.sonyclassics.com/fogofwar (last accessed on 18 March 2016).

The Battle of Kontum. www.thebattleofkontum.com (last accessed on 28 March 2016).

The Official Home Page of the United States Army. www.army.mil/ (last accessed on 28 March 2016).

U. S. Army Center of Military History. www.history.army.mil/index.html (last accessed on 28 March 2016).

U. S. Defense Department. "Medal of Honor Recipients." valor.defense.gov/Recipients (last accessed on 12 March 2016). Vietnam Veterans' Memorial. thewall-usa.com (last accessed on 28 March 2016).

Vietnam Veterans' Memorial. www.virtualwall.org/ (last accessed on 12 March 2016).

Wikipedia. en.wikipedia.org/wiki/Battle_of_Khe_Sanh (last accessed on 28 March 2016).

Television

Cronkite, Walter, *Vietnam War*, DVD, 2003.

National Geographic, *Inside the Vietnam War,* DVD, 2008.

PBS, *Vietnam: A Television History*, DVD, 1983.

The Battle of Dak To – The Lost Film, DVD, March 2014.

Films

The Green Berets, directed by John Wayne (Batjac Productions, 1968).

Go Tell the Spartans, directed by Ted Post (Mar Vista Films, 1978).

The Killing Fields, directed by Roland Joffe (Goldcrest Films, 1984).

Vestige of Honor, directed by Jerry London (Universal

Television, 1990).

Unpublished Materials

Chang, Sa Won. *Unpublished memoir*.
Donahue, Paul. Papers. *Unpublished memoir*.
Eggleston, Michael A. *Unpublished memoir*.
Walls, Gary. *Unpublished memoir*.

Public Documents

American Embassy, Saigon. *Montagnard Dissidence: FULRO*. 23 December 1965. 1-2.
Department of the Army. *After Action Report - Operation Sam Houston Conducted by the 4th Infantry Division*. Office of the Adjutant General: 28 June 1967.
Headquarters, 4th Infantry Division. *Combat Operations After Action Report - Operation Francis Marion*. Office of the Commanding General: 25 November 1967.
Headquarters, 4th Infantry Division. *Combat Operations After Action Report - Battle of Dak To*. Office of the Commanding General: 3 January 1968.

Index

*Page numbers in **bold** provide photo of subject.*

-A-

Buddhist, 43, 47, 57, 90, 95, 101, 167, 335, 370, 377, 381, 399
Buon Brieng, 101, 125
Buon Enao, 62, 63, 64, 65, 74, 84, 85, 86, 87, 89, 412

-C-

Calley, William, 12, 233, 234, 369, 402, 403
Cam Ranh Bay, 127, 128, 406
Cambodia, 10, 14, 18, 20, 22, 45, 47, 55, 71, 102, 109, 111,
    112, 134, 138, 161, 204, 207, 211, 212, 216, 223, 258, 263,
    264, 279, 281, 283, 296, 298, 312, 333, 334, 335, 336, 337,
    338, 339, 341, 342, 343, 344, 345, 346, 348, 350, 351, 352,
    353, 354, 355, 356, 357, 361, 362, 364, 366, 370, 377, 378,
    379, 384, 388, 391, 398, 402, 403, 405, 406, 435, 436, 437,
    444, 459, 464, 471, 474, 476, 484, 486, 492, 505, 512, 517,
    522
Cambodian border, 62, 71, 111, 113, 115, 138, 148, 201, 276,
    278, 280, 283, 298, 303, 308, 351, 445, 460, 462, 465, 478,
    480, 486
Cambodian Incursion, 5, 211, 213, 227, 535
Cambodian Liberation Army, 383
Camp Carroll, 173, 183, 239
Cao Dai, 25
Capital Military District, 279
Capital Military Region, 314
Caputo, Philip, 258, 259, 502, 511
Carter, Jimmy, 338, 346, 348, 405, 506, 512
Catecka, 138
Catholic, 43, 57, 91, 370, 377
Central Highlands, 5, 10, 13, 20, 29, 32, 33, 41, 48, 50, 51, 58,
    63, 76, 86, 100, 101, 118, 124, 125, 134, 136, 155, 269, 275,
    282, 299, 300, 315, 320, 354, 355, 356, 370, 383, 389, 390,
    395, 401, 425, 443, 489, 493, 496, 513, 515, 520, 521, 528,
    531, 538
Central Intelligence Agency (CIA), 13, 40, 49, 50, 51, 59, 62,

-D-

Dak Sut, 416, 447, 468, 475

Dak To, 3, 41, 42, **110**, 114, 137, 138, 139, 140, 145, 154, 242, 246, 248, 401, 415, 416, 448, 469, 475, 493, 494, 495, 515, 516, 528, 529, 532, 539, 540, 541, 542

Darlac, 49, 59, 62, 63, 65, 72, 86, 87, 88, 96, 100, 105, 125, 277, 300, 314, 412, 413, 414, 415, 425, 444, 459, 463, 470

Davidson, Phillip, 13, 135, 155, 156, 158, 194, 224, 260, 268, 270, 282, 289, 290, 327, 369, 370, 488, 494, 495, 496, 497, 498, 500, 502, 503, 504, 505, 514

de Castries, Christian, 12, 39, 369

Defense Department, 59, 62, 75, 286, 287, 313, 389, 541

Diem, Ngo Dinh, 13, 16, 17, 18, 19, **34**, 35, 43, 45, 46, 47, 48, 49, 50, 51, 53, 57, 72, 73, 74, 77, 78, 79, 80, 81, 82, 83, 84, 86, 87, 88, 89, 90, 91, 92, 93, 94, 101, 106, 137, 192, 226, 327, 368, 370, 374, 376, 377, 379, 387, 398, 399, 490, 491, 501, 515

Dien Bien Phu, 12, 14, **37**, 38, 39, 40, 43, 48, 118, 120, 135, 185, 350, 360, 369, 371, 391, 398, 488, 490

DK (Democratic Kampuchea), 385

DMZ, 44, 135, 157, 170, 177, 216, 226, 234, 238, 260, 273, 281, 385, 395

Do Cao Tri, 213

Dockery, Martin, 66, 489, 515

Domino Theory, 47, 48, 195, 255, 351, 352, 385

Don Luan, 303, 306

Dong Xoai, 300, 420

Donlon, Roger, 13, 96, 98, 99, 370, 492, 515

Dooley, George, 13, 333, 359, 370, 489, 505, 506, 515

Doung Van Minh, 17, 376

draft, (U. S. Selective Service), 101, 200, 233, 256, 257, 263, 291, 405

Duc Co, **111**, 112, 276, 356, 400, 417

Duc Duc, 273, 293

Duc Lap, 111, 201, 315, 402, 415, 517

Duc Phong, 303, 305, 306, 420

Duc Tho, 274

Dung, Van Tien, 217, 283, 285,299, 313, 315, 320, 322, 325, 327, 454, 456, 457, 505, 516

Duong Van "Big" Minh, 17, 91, 327, 376, 399

Dzu, Ngo, 210, 244

-E-

Eagle Flight, 103

Easter Offensive, 5, 235, **236**, 239, 241, 242, 251, 253, 254, 260, 266, 269, 281, 282, 380, 536

Eggleston, Michael, 1, 2, 3, 11, 125, 149, 154, 209, 211, 212, 215, 490, 492, 494, 495, 498, 499, 500, 502, 516, 538, 542, **563**

Eisenhower, Dwight, 47, 94, 385

elephant, 109, 188, 191, 170, **361**, 362, 385, 426, 445, 462, 474, 477

Enhance Plus, 267, 269

-F-

Fall, Bernard, 14, 41, 42, 43, 371, 517

France, 14, 17, 18, 27, 32, 33, 35, 36, 41, 50, 68, 337, 358, 368, 371, 376, 377, 379, 398, 400, 488, 533

French Groupment Mobile 100 (G. M. 100), 41, 42, 43, 104, 106

FULRO, 10, 11, 14, 100, 101, 102, 104, 122, 123, 124, 125, 126, 161, 201, 207, 211, 316, 354, 355, 356, 357, 358, 361, 364, 366, 371, 382, 386, 400, 493, 542

-G-

General Offensive, General Uprising (GO-GU), 95, 104, 134

Ghuong Nghia, 295

Gia Nghia, 125, 455, 458, 460

Giap, Vo Nguyen, 14, 37, 38, 39, 40, 43, 48, 135, 167, 170,

171, 184, 238, 245, 267, 283, 315, 330, 341, 371, 518, 526

Great Society, 93, 108, 205, 256, 386, 499

Great Spring Victory, 6, 299, 505, 516

Greensboro, 165, 364, 512

Gulf of Tonkin, 94, 359, 385, 399

Gulf of Tonkin Resolution, 94, 195, 212, 359, 385, 399, 400, 403

-H-

H'Yoanh Buonya, 7, 363, 364, 366

Ha Thanh, 203, 408

Haig, Alexander, 14, 205, 261, 263, 268, 371, 372, 499, 519

Haiphong, 235, 240, 267, 403

Halang, 248, 249, 435, 436, 437, 444, 468, 473

Hanoi, 10, 14, 16, 17, 28, 32, 37, 43, 47, 50, 51, 53, 84, 92, 94, 95, 96, 118, 120, 129, 134, 135, 136, 137, 152, 154, 155, 156, 157, 158, 161, 170, 192, 193, 194, 196, 198, 200, 206, 217, 218, 223, 236, 237, 238, 240, 242, 253, 256, 260, 261, 262, 264, 266, 267, 270, 271, 272, 274, 275, 281, 283, 289, 296, 297, 298, 300, 305, 311, 312, 313, 314, 315, 322, 328, 330, 334, 337, 338, 339, 344, 346, 347, 351, 352, 371, 374, 375, 376, 377, 397, 401, 404, 497, 509, 528

Harkins, Paul, 15, 78, 81, 84, 93, 94, 194, 372, 491

Hau Bon (Cheo Reo), 17, 41, 123, 125, 211, 317, 319, 320, 321, 363, 441, 444

Hau Nghia, 278, 279

Healy, Michael, 204, 205

Henderson, Oran, 15, 372, 373

Hickey, Gerald, 10, 15, 98, 99, 122, 123, 137, 210, 241, 248, 250, 332, 362, 367, 373, 492, 493, 494, 499, 502, 504, 505, 506, 520

Hiep Duc., 274

Highway 1, 273, 275, 276, 293

Highway 9, 216

Highway 14, 201, 242, 282, 305, 310, 317, 319

-I-

IV CTZ, 279, 280, 381, 504
III Marine Amphibious Force (MAF), 167, 171
Ia Drang Valley, 118, 119, 124, 400
Indochina, 1, 4, 6, 7, 10, 20, 22, **26**, 28, 30, 31, 33, 46, 50, 51, 54, 62, 104, 223, 240, **265**, 297, 313, 332, 333, 334, 336, 337, 339, 352, 355, 360, 388, 391, 406, 424, 433, 465, 484, 487, 488, 489, 491, 492, 496, 506, 510, 511, 516, 517, 526, 533, 535, 536, 538
International Commission of Control and Supervision (ICCS), 260, 263, 268, 270, 281, 311, 312
Iron Triangle, 297, 304, 383

-J-

Jarai, 17, 49, 63, 77, 115, 137, 210, 249, 356, 359, 410, 411, 412, 413, 415, 416, 417, 426, 435, 443, 445, 446, 447, 464, 466, 468, 470, 474, 480
Jeh, 248, 249, 415, 432, 447, 448, 449, 450, 474
Johnson, Harold, 15, 373, 518
Johnson, Lyndon (LBJ), 17, 91, 93, 108, 111, 127, 129, 153, 186, 193, 194, 195, 205, 212, 255, 375, 386, 399, 400, 402, 495, 498, 502, 504, 511, 520
Joint Chiefs of Staff (JCS), 59, 93, 388, 500, 521, 527
Joint General Staff (JGS), 19, 67, 209, 285, 286, 290, 291, 301, 388
Joint Military Commission, 260, 263, 312
Joint United States Public Affairs Office, 388

-K-

Karnow, Stanley, 40, 80, 193, 237, 329, 487, 488, 490, 491, 492, 493, 498, 501, 503, 504, 505, 523
Katu, 432, 447, 449, 452, 453, 507
Kaufman, Harold, 146
Kelly, Francis, 15, 22, 25, 60, 65, 85, 89, 162, 208, 209, 210, 373, 424, 504

Kennedy, John (JFK), 17, 57, 58, 59, 62, 78, 79, 80, 81, 90, 91, 93, 375, 399, 490, 508, 512, 526, 532, 534, 537

Kent State, 258, 403

Khanh Hoa, 275, 460, 465, 466, 471, 472, 480, 481, 482

Khanh, Nguyen, 88, 101, 376

Khe Sanh (KSCB), 5, 39, 44, 135, 136, 154, 157, 162, **165**, 166, 167, **168**, 169, 170, 171, 172, 173, 174, 175, 178, 179, 180, 181, 183, 184, 185, 186, 187, 190, 191, 216, 220, 223, 281, 282, 388, 391, 392, 396, 401, 407, 492, 496, 509, 522, 528, 530, 533

Khmer, 18, 280, 333, 335, 336, 341, 342, 343, 351, 353, 354, 356, 361, 364, 366, 371, 377, 378, 379, 383, 388, 405, 424, 425, 428, 432, 435, 437, 441, 447, 449, 453, 456, 459, 463, 468, 473, 476, 484, 485, 486, 492

Khmer Rouge, 333, 334, 335, 341, 343, 354, 356, 364, 366, 371, 378, 379, 405

Kissinger, Henry, 15, 16, 205, 216, 224, 235, 236, 237, 260, 261, 262, 263, 264, 314, 372, 373, 402, 500, 503, 510, 523

Koho, 49, 410, 413, 414, 453, 455, 456, 460, 466, 473, 481

Kontum, 41, 42, 86, 88, 118, 125, 162, 163, 203, 238, 242, **243**, 244, 245, 246, 247, 248, 250, 276, 277, 295, 315, 316, 317, 319, 320, 380, 415, 416, 425, 433, 435, 438, 444, 447, 451, 468, 469, 473, 481, 489, 496, 502, 526, 540

Koster, Samuel, 16, 374

Ky, Nguyen Cao, 16, 126, 327, 374, 401, 433

-L-

Lac Thien, 87, 123, 125, 414

Lai Khe, 297, 306

Laird, Melvin, 16, 205, 218, 220, 225, 226, 374, 500, 536

Lam Dong, 277, 325, 370, 414, 457

Lam Son 719, 5, 39, 216, 217, 218, 220, 221, 223, 224, 226, 227, 236, 238, 250, 403, 488, 490, 499, 501, 521, 522, 525, 528, 530

LANDGRAB 73, 6, 265, 266, 270, **272,** 278, 280, 281, 404

Lang Vei, 5, 161, 162, 165, 167, 173, 178, 187, 188, 190, 191, 401, 407, 497, 530

Laos, 18, 20, 22, 37, 45, 47, 55, 71, 109, 134, 138, 161, 166, 177, 178, 187, 188, 191, 212, 216, 217, 218, 219, 221, 222, 223, 224, 263, 264, 281, 312, 313, 333, 336, 337, 338, 341, 342, 348, 352, 364, 366, 379, 382, 384, 385, 388, 391, 392, 396, 398, 403, 405, 426, 428, 435, 436, 447, 449, 463, 474, 485, 501, 505, 517, 519, 525, 528, 530

Laotians, 188, 190, 191, 435, 444

Layton, Gilbert, 62, 88, 89

Le Duan, 13, 300, 370

Le Due Tho, 264

Le Gro, William, 272, 276, 278, 280, 281, 287, 292, 296, 300, 302, 304, 309, 310, 314, 324, 503, 504, 525

LeMay, Curtis, 93, 374

LLDB, 63, 96, 123, 130, 152, 162,189, 198, 199, 200, 388, 489

Loc Ninh, 5, 148, **149**, 150, 151, 152, 153, 278, 304, 326, 401, 419

Lodge, Henry Cabot, 16, 90, 155, 375

Lon Nol, 18, 211, 333, 356, 377, 379

Long Khanh, 298

Loving, John, 16, 65, 71, 72, 332, 375, 489, 490, 505, 525

-M-

M16, 389

M-16, 163, 172, 173, 287, 349

Ma, 303, 453, 456, 458, 459, 477

MAAG, 57

MACV, 60, **66**, 67, 68, 69, 75, 78, 79, 103, 105, 123, 147, 152, 156, 158, 193, 199, 204, 233, 269, 315, 384, 388, 389, 503, 514, 533

Madame Nhu, 17, 377

Mai Linh, 123, 125, 411

malaria, 115, 288, 439, 478

Mang Yang Pass, 104, 105, 106, 398, 400

Mao Zedong, 344, 405

Martin Luther King, 233, 402

Martin, Graham, 66, 233, 284, 323, 329, 330, 337, 402, 489, 497, 513, 515, 518, 530

Mary Ann, Fire Support Base, 230

Mataxis, Theodore, 17, 102, 103, 228, 375, 492, 526

May Offensive, 198, 200

Mayaguez, 339, 405

McNamara, Robert, 17, 78, 93, 94, 194, 195, 196, 197, 330, 375, 490, 498, 527, 532

Mekong Delta, 279, 293, 316, 354, 381, 484

Mekong River, 15, 44, 364, 445, 474

Mike Forces, 106, 132, 108, 187, 188

Minh, 4, 17, 27, 32, 36, 37, 38, 39, 41, 45, 55, 91, 150, 187, 218, 245, 329, 341, 376, 399, 409, 416, 419, 481, 484, 535

Mnong, 303, 413, 414, 415, 428

M'nong, 425, 453, 459, 462, 466, 471, 473, 476, 481, 484

Mobile Strike Company, 188

Mobile Strike Force, 106, **107**

Moi, 100, 130

Montagnard Dwelling, **24**

Moore, Harold, 116, 119, 120, 493, 527

Moorer, Thomas, 17, 376, 377

Moscow, 27, 255, 262, 342, 346, 405, 406

MR 1, 48, 135, 148, 150, 201, 203, 218, 238, 239, 240, 246, 273, 274, 293, 294, 304, 306, 322, 381, 390

MR 2, 4, 5, 14, 19, 29, 41, 42, 48, 59, 60, 74, 76, 77, 91, 99, 109, 119, 128, 138, 139, 140, 142, 143, 144, 146, 147, 148, 150,153, 158, 175, 176, 177, 187, 188, 197, 198, 199, 200, 201, 203, 228, 234, 238, 239, 242, 246, 248, 250, 251, 268, 269, 274, 280, 282, 285, 289, 290, 293, 294, 300, 301, 304, 306, **317**, 318, 319, 322, 370, 371, 372, 376, 377, 379, 380, 381, 388, 390, 393, 397, 399, 400, 402, 403, 405, 411, 412, 417, 421, 444, 454, 457, 474, 482, 485, 493, 496, 505, 506, 529, 538, 539, 542, 543

393, 404, 405, 415, 496, 504

-O-

-P-

Phuoc Binh, 300, 303, 304, 305, 306
Phuoc Long, 6, 148, 153, 300, **302**, 303, 304, 305, 306, 307,
308, 309, 310, 311, 312, 313, 314, 315, 404, 419, 420, 457,
460, 476
Plei Djereng, 111, 123, 125, 126
Plei Kanong, 123
Plei Me, 12, 115, 117, 118, 119, 295, 400, 417
Plei Mrong, 399, 416
Pleiku, 42, 43, 52, 60, 61, 88, 103, 104, 105, 106, 111, 112,
113, 115, 123, 124, 125, 126, 128, 131, 137, 138, 154, 162,
210, 214, 215, 242, 248, 250, 276, 277, 295, 315, 316, 317,
319, 320, 410, 416, 417, 425, 444, 464, 468, 471, 513
Pol Pot, 18, 333, 334, 335, 338, 341, 342, 345, 351, 352, 353,
357, 378, 405, 406
Polei Kleng, 247
Polei Krong, 276
Project GAMMA, 204
Pruco Binh, 314
Pruco Long, 314

-Q-

Quang Nam, 266, 273, 293, 299, 408, 409, 410, 447, 450
Quang Ngai, 203, 274, 294, 295, 407, 408, 409, 426, 429, 431,
437, 481
Quang Tin, 230, 266, 274, 294, 407, 408, 431, 447, 450
Quang Tri, 166, 167, 170, 188, 240, 266, 273, 387, 407, 410,
428
Qui Nhon, 104, 105, 127, 162, 215, 249, 410, 441, 445, 465,
483

-R-

Radcliff, Camp, 104, 115, 211, 214, 215
Raglai, 461, 465, 467, 468, 470, 480
Ranger, 70, 117, 180, 183, 207, 209, 247, 274, 276, 293, 294,

-S-

201, 204, 207, 209, 212, 214, 215, 222, 234, 237, 238, 245, 248, 251, 253, 262, 263, 264, 266, 267, 270, 271, 274, 275, 277, 278, 281, 283, 284, 287, 288, 293, 295, 296, 297, 298, 299, 300, 303, 304, 306, 309, 310, 312, 313, 314, 315, 316, 321, 322, 325, 326, 327, 328, 329, 331, 332, 333, 339, 341, 355, 370, 371, 375, 379, 380, 386, 387, 399, 405, 453, 460, 476, 483, 493, 503, 504, 511, 533, 535, 537, 538, 542

Saigon River, 278, 297

Saleng, 435

Schwarzkopf, H. Norman, 18, 112, 113, 114, 378, 492, 493, 532

Sedang, 248, 249, 415, 416, 425, 428, 432, 435, 438, 439, 444, 447, 468, 473, 475, 476

Sheehan, Neil, 78, 80, 81, 82, 212, 231, 232, 244, 252, 253, 257, 490, 491, 495, 498, 499, 501, 502, 532

Sihanouk, Norodom, 18, 211, 333, 334, 377, 378, 379, 405, 486

Song Be, 148, 303, 304, 305, 306, 307, 309, 312, 401, 419

Souphanouvong, Prince, 18, 341, 342, 379, 505

Special Forces, 10, 11, 12, 13, 15, 20, 22, 25, 57, 58, 59, 60, 61, 63, 66, 67, 74, 75, 85, 96, 99, 100, 103, 105, 106, 107, 109, 111, 115, 123, 124, 126, 130, 131, 132, 137, 138, 139, 142, 146, 150, 152, 161, 167, 169, 173, 178, 187, 188, 189, 190, 198, 199, 200, 202, 203, 204, 205, 207, 208, 209, 220, 370, 373, 383, 388, 396, 400, 407, 487, 489, 492, 493, 494, 495, 513, 515, 523, 531, 533, 534, 538

Spring Invasion, 236

State Department, 170, 193, 311, 313, 358, 359, 368, 399, 487, 508

Stieng, 303, 418, 419, 420, 425, 453, 457, 459, 473, 476, 478, 479, 485

Strategic Hamlet Program, 63, 73, 74, 81, 93, 104, 394, 399, 514

Strategic Raids, 6, 283, 289, 290, 291, **292**, 293, **296**, 298, 404

Street Without Joy, 14, 41, 167, 273, 275, 371, 517

Strike Force, 89, 99, 103, 199, 203, 390, 506, 507

Sully, Francois, 81, 213, 491

-T-

Tan Canh, 165, 242, 244, 246, 248, 507
Tan Son Nhut., 279
Tay Ninh, 16, 71, 201, 279, 298, 304, 306, 307, 316, 328, 341, 418, 419, 420, 476, 481, 485, 486
Tchepone, 217, **219**, 220, 221, 222
TCK-TKN, 134 (see also General Offensive, General Uprising (GO-GU)
Tet, 5, 154, 155, 156, 157, 158, **160**, 161, 162, 165, 171, 180, 186, 187, 192, 193, 194, 197, 198, 200, 203, 220, 277, 293, 315, 376, 380, 395, 401, 402, 498, 529, 531, 532, 538
Thai, 7, 50, 51, 204, 247, 351, 352, 354, 357, 362, 364, 365, 378, 463, 485
Thailand, 47, 336, 351, 352, 354, 357, 358, 362, 364, 366, 400, 485
Thao, Hoang Minh, 74, 245, 315, 535
Thieu, Nguyen Van, 16, 18, 19, 126, 150, 157, 215, 217, 218, 221, 222, 223, 224, 226, 234, 237, 238, 260, 261, 262, 264, 267, 268, 282, 283, 284, 285, 286, 289, 300, 314, 316, 317, 321, 322, 327, 328, 333, 374, 379, 401, 403, 405
Thua Thien, 167, 273, 293, 299, 407, 409, 428, 450, 528
Thuong Duc, 203, 209, 293
Thura Thien, 266
Tien Phuoc, 209
Tong La Chon, 297
Tonkin Gulf Resolution, see Gulf of Tonkin Resolution
Trung Nghia, 276
Tuy Hoa, 157, 158, 165, 316, 441, 483
Tuyen Duc, 86, 276, 277, 325, 413, 466

-U-

U. S. Congress, 314

U.S. Agency for International Development (USAID), 59, 69, 381, 289, 395

U.S. Marines, 114, 169

USARV, 395

USDAO, 285, 286, 396

USMACV, 94

-V-

Van Nguyen Duong, 14, 54, 255, 256, 370, 502

Vann, John Paul, 19, 77, 78, 80, 81, 82, 83, 211, 232, 242, 244, **245**, 246, 247, 248, 249, 250, 251, 252, 253, 379, 380, 491, 532

Vien, Cao Van, 19, 254, 271, 285, 286, 290, 304, 307, 309, 315, 317, 380, 503, 504, 537

Viet Cong (VC), 10, 13, 49, 54, 57, 58, 59, 60, 61, 63, 65, 71, 73, 75, 76, 77, 78, 79, 81, 82, 83, 84, 90, 92, 93, 95, 96, 98, 99, 100, 102, 104, 105, 106, 108, 109, 111, 112, 113, 124, 128, 130, 131, 133, 134, 135, 136, 137, 140, 148, 150, 151, 152, 153, 154, 156, 157, 158, 161, 162, 164, 165, 167, 171, 172, 182, 191, 192, 193, 198, 200, 209, 210, 211, 214, 226, 230, 233, 238, 252, 260, 261, 266, 270, 273, 274, 276, 277, 278, 281, 293, 296, 298, 332, 377, 383, 388, 392, 393, 396, 398, 400, 402, 403, 427, 430, 434, 436, 439, 440, 442, 443, 445, 446, 448, 452, 455, 458, 462, 465, 467, 469, 473, 475, 484, 486, 490, 528, 535

Viet Minh, 17, 19, 22, 30, 32, 35, 36, 37, 38, 39, 40. 41, 42, 43, 44, 45, 47, 51, 104, 118, 376, 379, 392, 396, 397, 398, 440, 484, 485

Vietnamization, 3, 195, 198, 205, 206, 207, 209, 210, 211, 216, 217, 223, 224, 228, 237, 242, 367, 374, 402, 403, 490, 516, 518

Vinh Loc, Nguyen Phuoc, 19, 112, 122, 125, 137

-W-

561

-X-

-Y-

About the Author

Michael A. Eggleston is an author who has published books and articles about America's wars including several about the war in Vietnam where he served two tours of duty in the 1960s and seventies. He was born and raised in Minnesota and is a 1961 graduate of the U. S. Military Academy (USMA) at West Point. Eggleston has thirty year's service in the U.S. Army and twenty years' experience in industry retiring as a Senior Director. He is a member of the Sons of the American Revolution, the Association of Graduates, USMA, and the Minnesota Historical Society. Mr. Eggleston and his wife of 47 years, the former Margaret Rogers reside in Nokesville, Virginia. The Egglestons have four children and eight grandchildren who also reside in Virginia.

Eggleston can be contacted at maeggles61@gmail.com His website can be viewed at www.egglestonshistory.com. (August 2019).

Made in the USA
Columbia, SC
05 April 2025